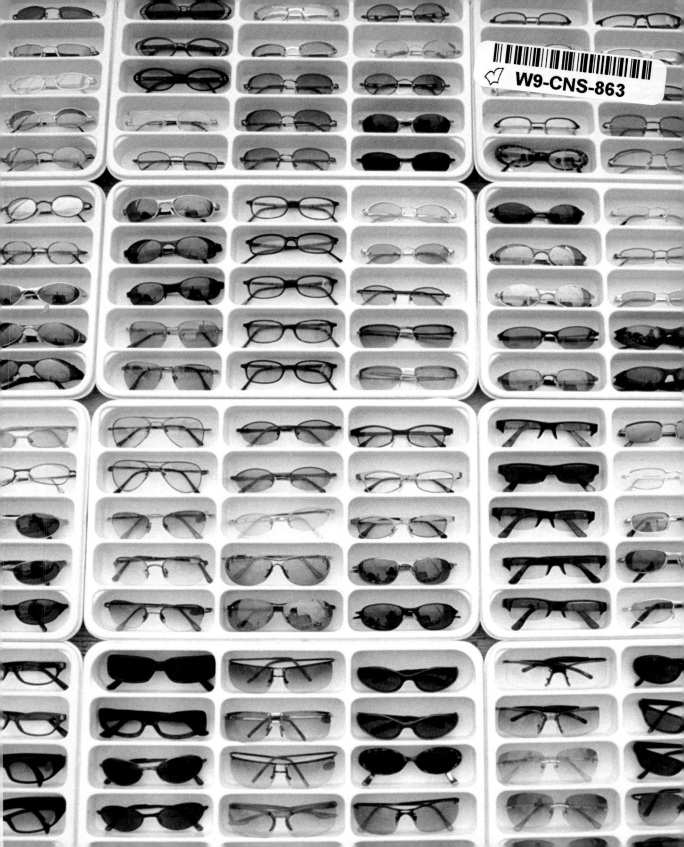

Seeing the Pattern

Readings for Successful Writing

Seeing the Pattern

Readings for Successful Writing

KATHLEEN T. McWHORTER
Niagara County Community College

Bedford/St. Martin's
Boston ▪ New York

For Bedford/St. Martin's

Developmental Editors: Laura Arcari, Beth Ammerman
Senior Production Editor: Harold Chester
Production Supervisor: Jennifer Wetzel
Marketing Managers: Karita dos Santos, Rachel Falk
Art Director: Lucy Krikorian
Text Design: Lisa Delgado
Copy Editor: Alice Vigliani
Indexer: Kirsten Kite
Photo Research: Linda Finigan
Cover Design: Donna Lee Dennison
Cover Photo: Carl Schneider, Workbook.com
Composition: Pine Tree Composition, Inc.
Printing and Binding: R.R. Donnelley & Sons Company

President: Joan E. Feinberg
Editorial Director: Denise B. Wydra
Editor in Chief: Nancy Perry
Director of Marketing: Karen Melton Soeltz
Director of Editing, Design, and Production: Marcia Cohen
Managing Editor: Erica T. Appel

Library of Congress Control Number: 2005921114

Manufactured in the United States of America.

1 0 9 8 7 6
f e d c b a

For information, write: Bedford/St. Martin's, 75 Arlington Street, Boston, MA 02116   (617-399-4000)

ISBN: 0-312-41905-8 (paperback)
      0-312-45461-9 (hardcover)

EAN: 978-0-312-41905-9 (paperback)
     978-0-312-45461-6 (hardcover)

Preface

My goal in writing *Seeing the Pattern* was to create a rhetorically arranged reader for the first-year composition course that addresses the learning challenges that students face while covering the skills that other college-level readers assume students already possess. Many students find reading essays challenging and interpretation and critical analysis difficult. They may also lack the basic writing skills expected of incoming first-year students. Moreover, today's students are visual learners; they respond to graphics and color. To accommodate these learning characteristics, I have developed innovative techniques to strengthen students' reading and writing skills and help them understand the various rhetorical patterns and then use them in their own writing. Visuals, annotated essays, graphic organizers, and revision flowcharts in *Seeing the Pattern* enable students to conceptualize, or "see," rhetorical patterns and apply them effectively in their own writing. Through this unique, highly visual, student-centered approach, the book offers direct instruction in writing skills, a diverse collection of compelling readings that demonstrate effective writing, and an apparatus that guides students in successfully comprehending, analyzing, and critically responding to the readings. The result is a visually oriented rhetorical reader that offers underprepared students the extra help they need to achieve success in their college-level writing.

Features to Help Students Learn

Seeing the Pattern provides abundant help and support for inexperienced readers and writers through the application of tools and techniques that I developed over more than thirty years of teaching. I have found that students need to be taught how to approach writing as a process instead of as a linear task. They also need to understand why readings are assigned in a writing class. In *Seeing the Pattern*, I have made explicit both the process of writing and the reasons for reading. Because students need to know how to learn to write by using the key elements presented in a reader — writing process instruction, sample student essays, professional essays, and apparatus — I have found it helpful to show how to make connections between these textual elements and students' own writing. For example, students need to be told directly and specifically *how* to read and *how* to learn from a sample student essay. Similarly, they need to be told *what to look for* as they read a professional essay and *how to apply what they find* to their own writing. I have tried to make these connections and processes specific throughout *Seeing the Pattern*.

I have also observed that many students are overwhelmed by writing assignments, particularly by the vast and seemingly endless range of choices available for both content and organization of an essay. Students are also confused by the lack of structure and specific guidelines for their writing assignments. In my experience, the rhetorical modes are helpful in overcoming both of these problems. Rhetorical modes both limit and focus, enabling students to work comfortably and more confidently. For these reasons, I have arranged *Seeing the Pattern* rhetorically. Specific features of the book that I have designed to help students improve their writing include the following.

A Visual Approach to Writing

Because beginning college students often are more comfortable with and learn more effectively using visual images rather than words, *Seeing the Pattern* employs a visual approach to writing instruction.

- *Graphic Organizers provide students with a tool for both analyzing readings and planning and revising their own essays.* These visual representations of content and structure help students see at a glance how essays are structured and offer students a useful tool for their own writing.

- *Revision Flowcharts help students read their own essays, as well as those of their peers, with a critical eye.* These diagrams prompt students to locate and annotate key elements — such as thesis, topic sentences, and transitions — in their own writing and to consider the effectiveness of each element as they revise.

- *Illustrations serve as prompts for writing and tools for understanding.* Throughout the book, visuals serve as writing prompts and as tools for analysis. Among the visuals are Writing Quick Start activities at the start of each chapter, which ask students to respond to a photograph, and unique Visualizing the Reading questions following each reading, which use illustrations as a means of understanding and analyzing the essay.

- *A full-color design makes material accessible and easy to use,* with annotated essays, figures, boxes, and lists that summarize key information.

Engaging and Accessible Readings

Because students who enjoy what they are reading will approach assignments with interest and enthusiasm, the sixty-five professional readings and twelve student essays were carefully chosen to engage students as well as to function as strong rhetorical models. The readings in each chapter vary in length and difficulty; many are shorter and more accessible than in other readers, allowing students to be successful in their reading before working with longer, more difficult texts. The readings include reliable and class-tested essays by well-known writers like Amy Tan, Langston Hughes, and Scott Russell Sanders; contemporary readings on compelling topics that today's students will respond to, including media violence, terrorism, and makeover television shows; and two short stories and a poem. The readings come from a wide range of sources, including newspapers, popular magazines, Web sites, and scholarly texts, representing the diverse texts students encounter in both their personal and their academic lives.

- **Seeing the Pattern** *offers more coverage of reading than other rhetorical readers,* helping students to understand the reading/writing connection and approach their reading with confidence.

- *A Guide to Active Reading* opens the book and introduces the skills students need to actively read and analyze a text.
- *Two annotated essays, one professional and one student, in each rhetorical chapter* guide students in identifying the key features of the essays.
- *A unique section in each rhetorical chapter on how to read essays using that pattern* gives students tips for what to look for, highlight, and annotate.

Apparatus That Encourages Active Participation

Seeing the Pattern encourages active participation by students before, during, and after they read. The comprehensive apparatus comprises headnotes, prereading activities, marginal glosses, comprehension questions, vocabulary questions, discussion and journal prompts, and a wide variety of writing assignments, including paragraph-length and Internet research assignments. Additional apparatus that is unique to this book includes the following two features for each reading.

- *Visualizing the Reading* activities present graphic organizers, images, and other visual devices to help students understand the reading and writing strategies used by the author.
- *Building Your Critical Thinking Skills* questions introduce students to important critical thinking concepts — such as bias, tone, and connotation — and ask them to explore how one such concept is used in the reading.

The Most Help with Writing of Any Rhetorical Reader

Seeing the Pattern offers more thorough writing coverage than other readers and at a level more appropriate to the needs of today's students.

- *Three full chapters introduce students to the writing process,* with plenty of skill-building exercises, a running student example, and Essay in Progress activities that lead students through each step in writing an essay. Helpful lists and boxes — such as Guidelines for Writing a Thesis Statement, and Questions to Ask as You Revise — provide easy-to-consult reference tools that students can return to as they work on their own writing.
- *Comprehensive introductions to each rhetorical chapter* demonstrate how the pattern offers a useful tool for writing. Students learn the characteristics of the pattern, view a graphic organizer that presents these characteristics visually, and read annotated professional and student essays that are representative of the pattern. A chapter on combining patterns gives students helpful tips for effectively using the modes in combination in their own writing.
- *Practical help for everyday grammatical problems* enables students to work on mechanical issues within the context of their own writing. Editing tips in each chapter alert students to common grammatical problems associated with each rhetorical pattern. In addition, Chapter 4, "Revising and Editing Your Essay," offers a concise guide to common errors to avoid.

- ***A comprehensive chapter on finding and using sources*** addresses locating sources, evaluating sources, incorporating quotations, avoiding plagiarism, and documenting sources using MLA style.

Practical Survival Strategies for Success in College

A unique chapter titled "Keys to Academic Success" focuses on the study, reading, and work habits that underprepared students need special help with. Sections on managing time, juggling commitments, and managing stress provide advice that students will find helpful in both college and the workplace.

Useful Ancillaries for Students and Instructors

The print and electronic resources that accompany *Seeing the Pattern* offer support for both students and instructors.

Electronic Ancillaries

- ***Book companion site: bedfordstmartins.com/seeingthepattern.*** The Web site includes information on conducting online research and downloadable versions of all of the Graphic Organizers and Visualizing the Reading charts in the book.
- ***Exercise Central.*** This extensive collection of interactive online grammar exercises is easy to use and convenient for students and instructors alike. Multiple exercises on different grammar topics, at two levels, ensure that students get as much practice as they need. Customized feedback turns skills practice into a learning experience, and the reporting feature allows both students and instructors to monitor and assess student progress. Exercise Central can be accessed through the Book Companion Site for *Seeing the Pattern*.

Print Ancillaries

- ***Instructor's Resource Manual.*** This resource is valuable for all types of instructors, but especially for adjunct instructors, who often don't receive their teaching assignments until the last minute. Part One includes sample syllabi along with chapters on teaching with *Seeing the Pattern* and helping underprepared students in the first-year writing classroom. Part Two includes teaching tips for each chapter in *Seeing the Pattern*, including brief overviews of each of the readings in the book with sample answers to questions posed in the text. It also provides a bibliography of books and articles in rhetoric and composition.

Acknowledgments

A number of instructors and students from across the country have helped me develop *Seeing the Pattern*. I would like to express my gratitude to the following instructors who provided detailed, valuable comments and suggestions about the manuscript and choice of reading selections: Renee Bangerter, Fullerton College; Gary Bennett, Santa Ana College; Bryan Berry, Wheeling Jesuit University; Rita Kahn, California State University, Pomona; Richard J. Johnson, Kirkwood

Community College; Christine Kraisler, North Idaho College; Ronald W. Link, Miami-Dade College; Gwen Macallister, Covenant College; Donna Rigby, Weber State University; Cary D. Ser, Miami-Dade College; and James Wallace, King's College.

I am grateful to the following students whose essays appear in this text: Julie Bohet, Rudy De La Torre, Nicholas Destino, Robin Ferguson, Heather Gianakos, Geneva Lamberth, Kyle Mares, Nathan Nguyen, Melissa Parker, Ryan Porter, Danielle Cruz, and Aphonetip Vasavong.

Judy Voss deserves much credit and recognition for her thoughtful editing of the manuscript, as does Alice Vigliani for her careful and judicious copyediting of my final draft. Thanks also to Linda Finigan for her work finding images for the text and to Carolyn Lengel and Elizabeth Gruchala Gilbert for their research assistance.

Many people at Bedford/St. Martin's contributed to the creation and development of *Seeing the Pattern*. Each person with whom I worked demonstrates high standards and expertise in the field of college writing. Joan Feinberg, president of Bedford/St. Martin's, is a trusted and creative advisor who helped me conceive of this book and guided me in identifying the features of my teaching that translate to more help in this book for students. I appreciate her ongoing support and encouragement.

I also must thank Nancy Perry, editor in chief, for her forthright advice and valuable assistance in making many of the important decisions about this book's approach and content. She is a true professional whose high standards I admire. I also appreciate the advice and guidance of Denise Wydra, editorial director. Denise has always demonstrated remarkable knowledge of how students think and write, and I am grateful for her contributions to the development of this text. I value the contributions of Beth Ammerman, editor, in the final revision of the manuscript, for offering important and fresh perspectives on the project.

I also appreciate the advice and guidance that Karen Melton Soeltz, marketing director, and Rachel Falk, marketing manager, have provided at various junctions in the writing of this text. Thanks also to Nathan Odell, associate editor, for overseeing the development of the Web site for the book. To Harold Chester, senior project editor, I extend my thanks for conscientiously and carefully guiding the book through production. Kristy Bredin and Laura King, editorial assistants, helped prepare the manuscript in innumerable ways. I thank them both.

I owe the largest debt of gratitude to Laura Arcari, editor, for helping me plan and carry out the writing of this book. Her creative energy and enthusiasm are endless; her perseverance and persistence are admirable; her attention to detail is limitless; her knowledge of the field of college writing exceptional. She deserves my whole-hearted thanks.

Finally, I would like to thank the many students who have inspired me to create a book that directly addresses their needs and learning characteristics. They have shown me how they think and learn, and as a result I have discovered effective teaching strategies that can help all students learn to write. My students, then, have made the most significant contribution to this book; they are the reason I enjoy both teaching and writing.

Contents

"On Friday, June 16, 1999, when I was wrongfully arrested at my Harlem apartment building, my perception of everything I had learned as a young man was forever changed — not only because I wasn't given even a second to use the manners my parents taught me, but mostly because the police, whom I'd always naively thought were supposed to serve and protect me, were actually hunting me."

Chapter 11 ▸ Definition: Explaining What You Mean 392

Thematic Contents

Using *Seeing the Pattern* to Improve Your Writing

One of the easiest and best ways to learn something is to study or observe other people performing the same task. You might, for example, learn how to cast a fishing line by watching other people fishing. Or you might learn how to roll out pie crust or frost a cake by watching other cooks. Even though writing is more complex than casting a fishing line or frosting a cake, it still can be learned by observing and studying other writers.

This book is a collection of readings that is intended to help you improve your writing by studying the work of other writers. The readings offer models of good writing by both professional writers and students. As you work with the essays in this book, you will discover that both professional writers and student writers follow the same principles in organizing and presenting their ideas. By analyzing the choices that the writers in this book have made, you can develop and improve your own writing.

In addition to offering models of good writing, the readings in this book address interesting topics and current issues important to many students. You will read about a suicide hot line, Internet hoaxes, and television makeover shows, for example. Because the readings are stimulating and thought-provoking, you will find them easy to write about. Some of the readings offer new ways of looking at familiar ideas. For example, Dave Barry's essay "We've Got the Dirt on Guy Brains" offers a humorous view of the differences between men's and women's views of cleanliness. Other readings introduce topics of a more serious nature. The reading "Profile of a Terrorist," for instance, discusses types of terrorists, their motives, and their styles of operation.

The readings also serve as good examples of different methods of organization. This reader is organized by rhetorical modes — that is, writing strategies commonly used by writers. Rhetorical modes, also known as patterns of development, provide a structure with which to develop a piece of writing. Each of the chapters in Part Two introduces a new rhetorical mode and offers concrete suggestions for how to organize and present ideas in an essay using this type of writing strategy. By reading essays developed in particular ways, you can learn to use these methods of development in your own writing.

How to Use This Book

This book has three main parts. They are described below, along with suggestions for how each part can help you become a skilled, successful writer.

PART ONE: SKILLS FOR SUCCESS IN READING AND WRITING. This part prepares you to read and to write effectively about your reading. The first chapter offers strategies for remembering what you read, understanding difficult text, and expanding your vocabulary through reading. Chapters 2 to 4 guide you, step-by-step, through the process of writing an essay and give specific advice in planning, drafting, writing, and revising your essay. If you follow the guidelines in these chapters, you can be confident that you have written a well-developed and well-organized essay. The four chapters in Part One are intended to make your life easier as you continue to work through the book, completing assigned readings and writing about them.

PART TWO: READINGS FOR WRITERS. The seventy-three readings in this section are organized to help you learn the most about writing. Each chapter contains essays that follow a particular pattern of development. For example, all the essays that are narratives (essays that make a point by telling a story) appear in one chapter, all the essays that compare and contrast two or more things or ideas appear in another chapter, all the essays that build an argument are grouped in another chapter, and so forth.

There are ten chapters in Part Two that teach ten different ways of developing an essay. Each chapter begins with a "how-to" section that explains the pattern of development, guides you through a sample reading, and offers suggestions for writing an essay using that pattern of development. Each chapter also gives you the opportunity to study a sample student essay written according to that pattern of development.

PART THREE: STUDENT RESOURCE GUIDE. The final two chapters contain general information about research and being a successful student. Chapter 15 deals with research and includes topics such as locating and using sources, avoiding plagiarism, and evaluating and documenting sources. Chapter 16, Keys to Academic Success, is designed to help you become a successful student. You will learn how to manage your time, work with classmates, take effective class notes, and manage stress, for example. You may find it helpful to read this section right away, so as to get your semester off to the right start; or you can refer to specific sections as needed throughout the semester. Take a moment now to discover what topics are covered in Part Three.

How to Learn about Writing by Reading

You can dramatically improve your skills as a writer by reading the writing of others. Writing improvement through reading, however, does not just happen; you have to make it happen. As you read, it is easy to get caught up in the message — the ideas, the issues, and the new information you are acquiring — and neglect to notice *how* the writer is presenting his or her message. To improve your writing skills, you have to focus on the writer's technique. Use the following tools included in this text to enhance your understanding of the readings.

Graphic Organizers. Graphic organizers — diagrams that show the organizational structure of an essay — are introduced in Part One and are featured in the chapter introductions in Part Two. By studying the graphic organizer for a particular pattern of development before you read the essays in the chapter, you will know what parts to look for while you read. You can also use the graphic organizers as you draft and revise your own writing.

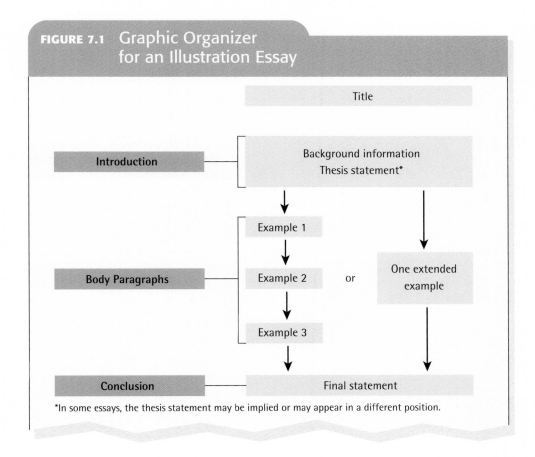

FIGURE 7.1 Graphic Organizer for an Illustration Essay

Title

Introduction — Background information / Thesis statement*

Example 1 → Example 2 → Example 3

Body Paragraphs

or

One extended example

Conclusion — Final statement

*In some essays, the thesis statement may be implied or may appear in a different position.

Annotated Essays. In the introductions to the chapters in Part Two, you will find one annotated professional essay and one annotated student essay. Pay attention to the annotations as you read. They call attention to specific parts of the essay or emphasize particular techniques used by the writer.

Annotations point out writing features and essay characteristics

Thesis statement and key points are highlighted or underlined

As the youngest of five girls and two boys growing up in Cincinnati, I was raised to believe that if I worked hard, was a good person, and always told the truth, the world would be my oyster. I was raised to be a gentleman and learned that these qualities would bring me respect.

While one has to earn respect, consideration is something owed to every human being. On Friday, June 16, 1999, when I was wrongfully arrested at my Harlem apartment building, my perception of everything I had learned as a young man was forever changed — not only because I wasn't given even a second to use the manners my parents taught me, but mostly because the police, whom I'd always naively thought were supposed to serve and protect me, were actually hunting me.

Introduction: background about White's upbringing

Thesis statement that also summarizes the action

In addition to using these tools, plan on reading each assigned essay at least two times. During the first reading you should concentrate on the writer's message. Then you should reread the essay at least once more to analyze its writing features. For example, you might read it to determine how the thesis statement is supported. You might read it yet again to examine its overall method of organization or to consider the language the writer used to create a particular impression. Taking the time to closely read and understand the essay and the writing strategies used by the author will help improve your own writing.

How to Use the Questions and Activities That Accompany the Professional Readings

Each reading comes with numerous questions and activities to help you understand it and be able to write about it. Here's how to use these features to get the most out of the readings.

Headnotes and Prereading Activities. The headnote is the brief introduction that appears after the title and author and before the reading itself. It was written by the author of this book, not by the person who wrote the reading. It gives some background about the author of the reading, lists other major works he or she has written, identifies when and where the reading was first published, and focuses your attention on one or more writing techniques used in the reading. After the headnote you will find two prereading activities: Focus on Understanding, and Focus on the Topic.

Be sure to read the headnote and the prereading activities before you start the reading itself. Knowing something about the author will make the essay seem more personal, and you may understand the author's ideas and viewpoints more clearly. Also, knowing the source can give you an idea of what to expect in the reading and may suggest the audience for whom it was written. The writing techniques mentioned in the headnote and the prereading activities will help you focus on the author's writing strategies and better understand the topic.

Piedra

Gary Soto

Gary Soto (b. 1952) decided while in college that he wanted to be a poet. Born and raised in Fresno, California, he has published not only poetry but also essays, plays, short stories, and novels for children and adults, including *Taking Sides* (1991), *Too Many Tamales* (1992), *Snapshots from the Wedding* (1997), and *Amnesia in a Republican County* (2003). In much of his writing Soto draws on his experiences in the Mexican American neighborhood where he grew up, but he emphasizes that most of the details and characters in his work come from his imagination rather than from his past.

> *Background information about the author*

This selection appears in *The Effects of Knut Hamsun on a Fresno Boy*, a collection of essays published in 2000. In this essay Soto describes the place where his family went on picnics when he was young. Notice how he uses visual details, especially color, to create an image in the reader's mind.

> *Source of the reading*
>
> *Writing techniques used by the author*

Focus on Understanding   Read to discover what Piedra is and why it is significant.

> *Key information to look for as you read*

Focus on the Topic   In class or in your journal, write a description of a special place that you visited as a child.

> *Connections between the reading and your knowledge about the topic*

The river was gray-blue when you sat on the bank, and gray when you stood on the bank, and swift and cold no matter how you looked at it in autumn. River rock splayed the water, so that it leaped white like fish; leaped up and fell back to join the gray-cold current, southward, to feed Avocado Lake.   1

Piedra. River of rock, place where our family went for a Saturday picnic. It was a fifteen-mile drive past plum and almond orchards, dairies, the town with its green sign, Minkler — Population 35. *Mexicanos* pruning orange trees on ladders, and our mother's talk that if our grades didn't improve we would be like *those* people. Past cows with grassy jaws, past fallen fences, groceries, tractors   2

Avocado Lake: A small lake located east of Fresno, California

Minkler: A small town along Route 180, east of Fresno, California

> *Marginal glosses explain or identify unfamiliar terms, people, events, and places. You might find it helpful to read these before starting the essay itself so you don't interrupt your reading*

Questions and Activities That Follow the Reading. It is helpful to look at the questions that follow the reading before you actually begin reading the essay. This is not cheating or skipping ahead. Rather, it is a way to focus your attention on what to look for as you read. Each type of question builds specific skills to improve your ability to write about what you have read. After you have read the essay once, you will need to reread certain passages in order to answer the questions; each question is answerable based on information contained in the reading. Look for evidence in the essay that supports your answers. Also use the following tips as you work through each section.

- ***Understanding the Reading.*** Use these questions to test your understanding before you go to class. If you cannot answer these, you have not fully understood the reading and should reread it, using the suggestions in the box, Difficult Readings: Specific Problems and Strategies for Solving Them (p. 12).
- ***Visualizing the Reading.***

Visualizing the Reading

Study the photo taken at a contemporary revival meeting. What do you learn about revival meetings from this photo that you have not already learned from "Salvation"? Write a list of details gathered from your analysis of the picture that would add meaning to Hughes's essay.

Here a photo of a contemporary revival meeting is used as a comparison and contrast to Langston Hughes's description of a revival in his essay "Salvation."

The question about the image prompts you to think critically about the author's use of description

The activities in this section enable you to visualize the content, structure, or features of the essay by completing a graphic organizer, filling in a chart, or — as shown here — responding to a photograph that relates to the reading.

- ***Examining the Characteristics of the Writing Pattern.*** To answer these questions about specific characteristics of the reading, you may need to reread parts of the essay or, at times, even the entire essay.
- ***Building Your Word Power.*** These questions expand your vocabulary and build your awareness of the interesting ways writers use language. To answer these, be sure to reread the sentence or paragraph in which each word or phrase is used, since a word's meaning often depends on the context in which it appears.
- ***Building Your Critical Thinking Skills.*** Each reading includes a critical thinking activity that focuses on a specific skill, such as identifying tone, determining point

of view, or evaluating sources. The skill is briefly explained, and then questions ask you to apply the skill to the reading.

- ***Reacting to the Reading: Discussion and Journal Writing.*** Think about these questions before you go to class so that you will feel confident and ready for class participation. Record your thoughts before class in the margin next to the question or in your journal.

- ***Applying Your Skills: Writing Assignments.*** This section contains a variety of writing assignments that require you to respond to the reading or a related topic. The first question generally gives a short assignment that involves writing a paragraph according to the pattern of development featured in the chapter. Use this assignment as a warm-up activity to get started thinking and writing before you tackle the longer essay-length assignments that follow. Even if an assignment is not given in the first question, read through all of them; they will stimulate your thinking and help you see possible connections and applications of the reading.

How to Learn from Student Essays

Most of the chapters in this book include one essay by a college student. You are probably wondering why they are included and how you should use them. Many students find they can learn more about writing by looking at sample essays than simply by reading "how-to" tips, suggestions, and guidelines. Other students find that they can learn different things about writing by studying the work of other students than by reading professional essays. When approaching a student essay, consider the following suggestions.

- **Don't get discouraged.** You may say, "I'll never be able to write like that"; but remember that each writer has a unique style and unique ideas to pass along. Don't try to sound exactly like the student writer whose work you are reading. Instead, try to use the some of the same techniques. For example, if writer begins with a striking statistic, consider whether you could begin your own essay with a striking statistic.

- **Think of student essays as trial balloons.** The student essays enable you to observe how other students used the advice given in the chapter before you are asked to apply it in your own writing. You will see things that work that you may want to try, and you may see things that you are fairly sure would not work for you. For example, one writer may use transitions in a way that makes ideas easier to follow, but another may follow an organizational method that would be difficult to apply to your topic.

- **Focus on characteristics**. Each chapter in Part Two presents the characteristics of the particular method of organization being discussed. Chapter 6, Description, for example, has a section titled Characteristics of Descriptive Essays. For each characteristic, look to see how the student essay demonstrates some or all of the characteristics. As you discover the various characteristics of writing that the student essay emphasizes, mark or annotate them.

- **Focus on techniques.** Each chapter in Part Two contains a section that offers techniques and suggestions for writing a particular type of essay. Review these techniques, and observe how the student writer applied them.
- **Focus on what is new and different.** As you read, you will see writers taking approaches that are different from those you have taken in the past. Consider whether these techniques might work in your own writing. The box below offers suggestions of what to look for as you read.

What to Look for in Student Essays

Look for <u>Different</u>	What is different from other writing you have read?
Look for <u>Striking</u>	What captures your attention?
Look for <u>Effective</u>	What works particularly well?
Look for <u>Creative</u>	What is unique and nontraditional?
Look for <u>Fun</u>	What techniques might be fun to try?
Look for <u>Challenges</u>	What techniques would be challenging to try?

- **Use student essays to train your critical eye.** While the student essays in this book are reasonably good models, they are not perfect. Look for ways they can be improved. Use the questions following each student essay to evaluate its features. Once you can see ways to improve someone else's essay, you will be better equipped to analyze and improve your own.
- **Use graphic organizers to grasp the essay's structure.** In Part Two, a graphic organizer is presented for each pattern of organization. Compare the essay to the graphic organizer, noticing how the essay contains each element identified in the graphic organizer.

How to Use the Tools for Planning, Drafting, and Revising

Because much of the work you will be doing in your composition class will be centered on writing, I've included a number of features that my own students have found especially helpful in planning, drafting, and revising their writing. The following features are included to help you develop your skills as a writer.

Revision Flowcharts. Many chapters include flowcharts that will help you identify what needs to be revised in a first draft. Each flowchart lists key questions to ask and offers suggestions for how to correct any weaknesses you uncover. You can also use the questions to guide classmates who are reviewing your essay.

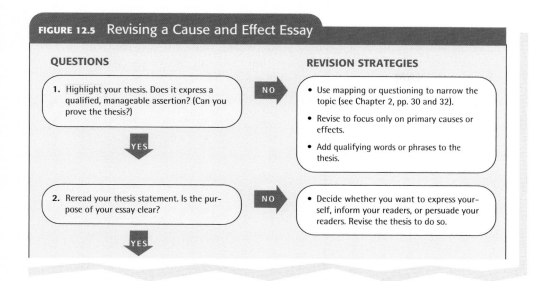

FIGURE 12.5 Revising a Cause and Effect Essay

QUESTIONS

1. Highlight your thesis. Does it express a qualified, manageable assertion? (Can you prove the thesis?)

YES

2. Reread your thesis statement. Is the purpose of your essay clear?

YES

REVISION STRATEGIES

NO

- Use mapping or questioning to narrow the topic (see Chapter 2, pp. 30 and 32).
- Revise to focus only on primary causes or effects.
- Add qualifying words or phrases to the thesis.

NO

- Decide whether you want to express yourself, inform your readers, or persuade your readers. Revise the thesis to do so.

Go through the numbered questions one-by-one to identify weaknesses or areas for improvement in your writing.

If the answer to any of the questions is "no," use the revision suggestions as a guide to improving that aspect of your essay.

Editing Tips and Troublespots. In each chapter in Part Two, you will find a section devoted to editing suggestions specific to the pattern of development being discussed in that chapter. This section alerts you to common grammatical errors students often make and shows you how to avoid or correct them. In addition, you should refer to the Common Errors to Avoid section in Chapter 4 (p. 81) for a concise guide to the errors that student writers make most frequently.

Lists of Tips and Guidelines for Writing. Throughout the book are numerous tips and guidelines for planning, drafting, and revising your writing; these suggestions are presented in lists that are easy to identify and understand. On the inside back cover of the book is a reference directory to all this material. Refer to the directory when you need help with a specific writing task, such as developing a thesis statement. Consider highlighting the items on the directory that you refer to most often in your writing.

A Final Word

When I began college I was a good reader, but not an especially talented writer. I didn't make the connection between reading and writing until a friend, who was helping me revise a paper on which I had received a low grade, explained that the features you look for when you read are the ones you want to be sure to include when you write. After that point, writing became easier because I understood how the processes of reading and writing are connected and that readings actually offer a kind of "mirror image" of strategies and techniques to include in your own writing. As you work through this book, see if my friend's advice works for you. The effort you expend in developing your writing skills will pay off in all that you do. Never stop trying to improve. I know that I will not, because writers can always learn new skills and techniques. I wish you success.

Seeing the Pattern

Readings for Successful Writing

Part◆One

Skills for Success in Reading and Writing

A Guide to Active Reading

WRITING QUICK START

Study the photo below. In particular, pay attention to different individuals' level of involvement with the basketball game they are watching. On a sheet of paper or in a new computer file, jot down some words that describe the two male fans standing in the center of the picture. Then do the same for the two female fans seated in front. Write a paragraph that compares how these two sets of fans differ in their level of participation while watching the sporting event.

How you read directly affects how you write. This book is a collection of model readings and student essays that you will use to improve your writing skills. To get the most out of this book, you must become an *active and critical reader*. This type of reader becomes engaged and involved with a reading assignment by responding to ideas the reading contains — by analyzing, challenging, and evaluating them.

Changing Some Misconceptions about Reading

Much misinformation exists about how to read effectively and efficiently. Here is some advice to guide your reading.

- **Not everything on a page is equally important.** Whether you are reading an article in a magazine, a biography of a president, or an essay in this book, each text contains a mixture of important and not-so-important ideas and information. Your task as a reader is to sort through the material and evaluate what you need to know.

- **You should not read everything the same way.** What you read, how rapidly and carefully you read, what you pay attention to, and what — if anything — you skip are all affected by your intent. For instance, if your psychology instructor assigns an article from *Psychology Today* as a basis for class discussion, you would read it differently than if you were preparing for a quiz based on the article. Your familiarity with a topic also affects how you read. If you are not familiar with a topic, you would read an essay about it much more slowly than someone with considerable knowledge of the subject. Effective readers vary their reading techniques to suit what they are reading and their reason for reading it.

- **Reading material once is usually not sufficient.** In most academic situations you will need to read chapters, articles, or essays more than once to discover the author's viewpoint, to summarize the author's key ideas, and to analyze the reliability and sufficiency of the supporting evidence.

- **Not everything in print is true.** Just as you don't believe everything you hear, neither should you believe everything you read. Be sure to read with a critical, questioning eye. As you read, try to distinguish facts from opinions, value judgments, generalizations, and the author's purpose for writing.

Reading Actively

When you attend a ball game or watch a soap opera, do you get actively involved? If you are a baseball fan, at ball games you probably cheer some players and criticize others while evaluating plays and calls. Similarly, if you are a soap-opera fan, you get actively involved in your favorite program, reacting to sudden turns of events and sympathizing with certain characters while despising others. By contrast, if you are not a fan of a baseball team or soap opera, you might watch the game or show passively, letting it take its course with little personal involvement

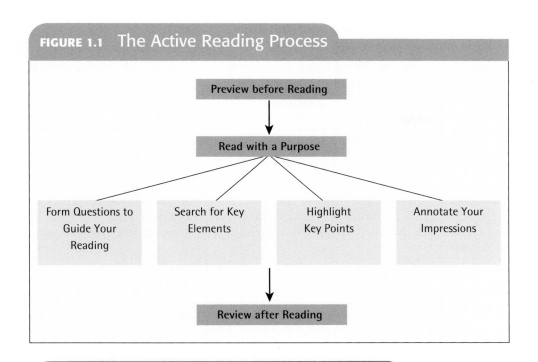

FIGURE 1.1 The Active Reading Process

Preview before Reading

Read with a Purpose

Form Questions to Guide Your Reading

Search for Key Elements

Highlight Key Points

Annotate Your Impressions

Review after Reading

Approaches to Reading: Active versus Passive

Passive Reading	Active Reading
Passive readers begin reading.	Active readers begin by reading the title, evaluating information provided about the author, and considering what they already know about the subject. Then they decide what they need to know before they begin reading.
Passive readers read the essay only because it is assigned.	Active readers read the essay while looking for answers to questions and key elements.
Passive readers read but do not write.	Active readers read with a highlighter or pen in hand. They highlight or underline, annotate, and write notes as they read.
Passive readers close the book when finished.	Active readers review, analyze, and evaluate the essay.

on your part. Like fans of a sports team or soap opera, active readers get involved with the material they read. They question, think about, and react to ideas using the process outlined in Figure 1.1.

Strategies for Reading

The box above shows how active and passive readers approach a reading assignment in different ways. As you can see, active readers get involved by using a step-by-step approach. This section explains some active reading strategies that will help you get the most out of your reading.

Preview before Reading

You probably wouldn't pay to see a movie unless you knew something about it. Similarly, you should not start reading an essay without getting a sense of its content. **Previewing** is a quick way to familiarize yourself with an essay's content and organization. In addition to helping you get interested, previewing provides you with a mental outline of the material so you know what to expect in the reading. This is useful because it enables you to decide what you need to know from the material. To preview a reading assignment, use the following guidelines.

Guidelines for Previewing

1. **Read the title, subtitle, and the author.** The title and subtitle may indicate what the reading is about. Check the author's name to see if it is one you recognize; if any introductory information about the author is included, be sure to read that too.

2. **Read the introduction and the first paragraph.** These sections often provide an overview of the essay.

3. **Read any headings and the first sentence following each one.** Headings, taken together, often form a mini-outline of the essay. The first sentence following a heading usually explains the heading further.

4. **For a reading with few or no headings, read the first sentence in a few of the paragraphs on each page.**

5. **Look at any photographs, tables, charts, and drawings.**

6. **Read the conclusion or summary.** The conclusion draws the reading to a close. If the reading concludes with a summary, it gives a condensed view of the reading.

7. **Read any prereading or end-of-assignment questions.** These questions will focus your attention on what is important in the reading and on what you might be expected to know after reading it.

The following essay has been highlighted to illustrate the parts you should read while previewing. Preview the essay now.

No More Pep Rallies!

Etta Kralovec

Etta Kralovec has spent her professional life as a teacher and educator. She taught high school for twelve years and then earned a doctorate in education from Columbia University. She later earned a Fulbright Fellowship to Zimbabwe to establish a program for future teachers there. Her interest in finding better ways to teach led her to write *The End of Homework* (2000).

Kralovec's most recent work is *Schools That Do Too Much* (2004), which expands on the idea presented in "No More Pep Rallies!" (which first appeared in *Forbes* magazine in 2003). As you read, pay attention to the evidence she provides to demonstrate that schools spend too much of their limited money on extracurricular activities. Think about whether or not Kralovec's evidence convinces you that her argument is sound.

Everyone agrees that we've got to improve academic achievement in America's public schools. So why is it that school districts distract students from core academics with a barrage of activities — everything from field hockey to music, drama, debating and chess teams? And there's more: Drug education and fundraising eat away at classroom time. All manner of holidays, including Valentine's Day, get celebrated during the school day, as well as children's birthdays. These diversions are costly. They consume money and time.   1

Here's a bold proposition: Privatize school sports and other extracurricular activities, and remove all but basic academic studies from the classroom. Sound like sacrilege? Look at what these extras really cost.   2

School budgets include a section that appears to cover the costs of all   3
extracurricular activities. But when a school board member and I did a
full analysis of the $4.8 million budget of our public high school on Mount
Desert Island, Me., we found that the listed costs were the tip of the ice-
berg.

Embedded in other line items were the maintenance of the field and   4
gym, insurance for sports teams, transportation to away games, the school
doctor's salary, the standby ambulance mandated for home games and
compensation for teachers who double as sports coaches. (Not to mention
that teachers who coach often hold only morning classes and spend the
rest of their days on sports.) Our study revealed that while 5% of the
school budget officially falls in the nonacademic section, when we fac-
tored in all of the real costs, the number was closer to 10%, or $480,000.

At a recent school board meeting in Searsport, Me., parents were as-   5
tonished to learn that the school spent $50,000 fixing the ball field be-
cause game officials said they wouldn't officiate there if the field wasn't
repaired. Parents reminded the board that the previous year the school
had sent seven members of the golf team in a 72-passenger bus to a golf
tournament 100 miles away. Last year 70% of the students at that school
barely met standards in math and reading.

The culture of sports that exists in many American high schools has a   6
cost that can't be measured in budget numbers. Time off for pep rallies,
homecoming week and travel to away games are all supported, if not encouraged, by teachers, principals and peers. There's no question that this
focus on sports saps the time, attention and energy that students should
put into academics.

The U.S. is the only industrialized country where competitive athlet-   7
ics and extensive extracurricular offerings are sponsored and paid for by
the public school system. What would happen if we held all school programs to a simple standard — that they must contribute to reading, writing, mathematics, science and history, as defined by state learning
standards?

The extracurricular activities, now deemed central to the mission of   8
public schools, would have to be sponsored by other institutions and organizations. Get businesses, religious organizations, the YMCA and the
Scouts to take responsibility for competitive sports and other extracurricular activities.

Moving these programs out of public schools and into the community   9
would not reduce their positive impact. Rather, extracurricular activities
could play a larger role in the life of our towns and neighborhoods.

Schools are asked to do too much and end up doing too little. We have   10
all heard about how difficult it is to find leaders to run the nation's

schools. It's not surprising. We ask principals to raise standards in mathematics, literacy and science, even while they must manage an elaborate physical plant that serves as a community theater, sports arena and orchestra hall. Learning the basics is often only a by-product of our public education system.

Read with a Purpose

If you tried to draw the face side of a one-dollar bill from memory, you would probably remember very little about its details. In much the same way, if you read an essay thinking, "Well, it was assigned, so I had better read it," you probably won't remember much of it. Why does this happen? According to a psychological principle known as *intent to remember,* you remember what you decide to remember. So, if you begin reading an essay without first deciding what you need to know and remember, you won't be able to recall any more about the essay than you could about the dollar bill.

Form Questions to Guide Your Reading. Before you begin reading, you should improve your intent to remember. Look again at the Guidelines for Previewing on page 6. You can use these parts of a reading to form questions. Then, as you read, you can answer those questions and thereby strengthen your comprehension and memory of the material. Here are some suggestions to help you get started with devising your own questions to guide your reading.

- **Use the title of a reading to devise questions.**

ESSAY TITLE	QUESTION
"Wounds That Can't Be Stitched Up "	What kind of wounds cannot be repaired?

- **Use headings to devise questions.** This heading from the essay "How the Oscars Work" can easily be turned into a question to guide your reading.

HEADING	QUESTION
"Picking the Winners"	How are the winners chosen?

Not all readings, of course, lend themselves to these particular techniques. For some readings without headings, you may need to dig deeper into the introductory and final paragraphs to form questions. Or you may discover that the subtitle is more useful than the title. As you ask questions about a reading, you should also be on the lookout for several essential key elements.

Search for Key Elements in the Essay. When you know what to look for as you read, you will read more easily and faster and do less rereading. In reading assigned articles, essays, or chapters, search for the following key elements.

- **The title and subtitle.** In some essays, the title announces the topic and reveals the author's point of view. In others, the meaning or significance of the title becomes clear only after you have read the entire essay.
- **The introduction.** The opening paragraph should provide background information, announce the subject, and capture the reader's attention.

For more about thesis statements, see Chapter 2, p. 36.

- **The thesis statement.** The **thesis** states the one main idea that the whole piece of writing explains, explores, or supports. The thesis is often placed in the first or second paragraph of an essay, but it may at times appear at the end instead. Occasionally, an essay's thesis is implied or suggested rather than stated directly.
- **The support and explanation.** The body of the essay should support or give reasons for the author's thesis. Each body paragraph has a topic sentence, which should in some way explain or support the essay's thesis statement.
- **The conclusion.** The concluding paragraph or paragraphs of an essay may restate the author's thesis, offer ideas for further thought, or suggest new directions.

You'll learn much more about each part of an essay in Chapters 2 and 3.

Now read the entire reading "No More Pep Rallies!" on page 7. Be sure to look out for key elements as you read.

Highlight Key Points. As you write about what you have read, you will want to return to the main points of the reading to refresh your memory. To locate and remember these points easily, it is a good idea to read with a highlighter or pen in hand. Highlighting is an active reading strategy because it forces you to sort important from less important ideas. Use the following guidelines to make your highlighting as useful as possible.

Guidelines for Highlighting

1. **Decide what kinds of information to highlight before you begin.** What types of tasks will you be doing as a result of your reading? Will you write a paper, participate in a class discussion, or take an exam? Think about what you need to know, and tailor your highlighting to the task at hand.
2. **Read first; then highlight.** First read a paragraph or section; then go back and mark what is important. This approach will help you control the tendency to highlight too much.
3. **Be selective.** If you highlight every idea, none will stand out.
4. **Highlight key elements, words, and phrases.** Mark the thesis statement, the topic sentence in each paragraph, important terms and definitions, and key words and phrases that relate to the thesis.

Annotate Your Impressions. Annotating is a way to keep track of your impressions, reactions, and questions as you read. When you annotate, you jot down your ideas directly in the margins. Later on, when you are ready to write about or discuss the reading, your annotations will help you focus on major issues and questions. Here is a list of what you might annotate.

- The thesis and other important points
- Sections about which you need further information
- Sections in which the author reveals his or her reasons for writing
- Ideas you disagree or agree with
- Inconsistencies

Sample annotations for a portion of "No More Pep Rallies!" are shown below.

Everyone agrees that we've got to improve academic achievement in America's public schools. So why is it that school districts distract students from core academics with a barrage of activities — everything from field hockey to music, drama, debating and chess teams? And there's more: Drug education and fundraising eat away at classroom time. All manner of holidays, including Valentine's Day, get celebrated during the school day, as well as children's birthdays. These diversions are costly. They consume money and time.

> My school didn't celebrate these!

Here's a bold proposition: Privatize school sports and other extracurricular activities, and remove all but (basic) academic studies from the classroom. Sound like sacrilege? Look at what these extras really cost.

> Thesis
> What is considered

School budgets include a section that appears to cover the costs of all extracurricular activities. But when a school board member and I did a full analysis of the $4.8 million budget of our public high school on Mount Desert Island, Me., we found that the listed costs were the tip of the iceberg.

> to be "basic"?
> Is this true of most school budgets?

Review after Reading

If you are willing to spend a few minutes reviewing and evaluating what you read, you can increase dramatically the amount of information you remember. To review material after reading, you can use the same steps that are involved in previewing (p. 6). Do your review immediately after you have finished reading. Reviewing does not take much time. Your goal is to touch on each main point one more time, not to embark on a long and thorough study. Pay particular attention to the headings, any highlighting and annotating that you did, and the conclusion of the reading.

As you already know, active reading involves much more than moving your eyes across lines of print. It is a process of actively searching for ideas and sorting important ideas from less important ones. You may need to read an essay more than once because comprehension is often gradual. On the first reading, you may grasp some ideas but not others. On the second reading, other ideas may become clear. Do not hesitate to reread.

As part of your review, it is also helpful to write a brief summary of the essay. See the section on summarizing later in this chapter for detailed suggestions on how to write a summary (p. 13).

Difficult Readings: Specific Problems and Strategies for Solving Them

Problems	Strategies
You cannot concentrate.	1. Take limited breaks. 2. Tackle the assignment at peak periods of attention. 3. Divide the material into sections. Make it your goal to complete one section at a time. 4. Give yourself a reasonable deadline for completing the assignment.
The sentences are long and confusing.	1. Read aloud. 2. Divide each sentence into parts and analyze the function of each part. 3. Express each sentence in your own words.
The ideas are complicated and hard to understand.	1. Reread the material several times. 2. Rephrase or explain each idea in your own words. 3. Make outline notes. 4. Study with a classmate; discuss difficult ideas. 5. Look up the meanings of unfamiliar words in a dictionary.
The material seems disorganized or poorly organized.	1. Study the introduction for clues to organization. 2. Pay more attention to headings. 3. Read the summary or conclusion. 4. Try to discover the organization by writing an outline or drawing a graphic organizer (see pp. 51 and 52).
You cannot get interested in the material.	1. Think about something you've experienced that is related to the topic. 2. Work with a classmate, discussing each section as you go.
You cannot relate to the writer's ideas or experiences.	1. Find out some background information about the author. 2. Put yourself in the writer's position. How would you react?
The subject is unfamiliar; you lack background information on the subject.	1. Obtain a more basic text or other source that moves more slowly, offers more explanation, and reviews fundamental principles and concepts. 2. For unfamiliar terminology, consult a specialized dictionary within the field of study. 3. Ask your instructor to recommend useful references.

Understanding Difficult Text and Visuals

All students experience difficulty with a reading assignment at one time or another. Perhaps this will happen because you just can't "connect" with the author, or because you find the topic uninteresting or the writing style confusing. Regardless of the problem, however, you know you must complete the assignment. The box on page 12 lists some problems that students experience with difficult reading material and identifies strategies for solving them.

Using a Graphic Organizer

If you are having difficulty following a long or complicated essay, try drawing a graphic organizer. Just as a road map shows the relationship of streets and highways to one another, a graphic organizer — a diagram or map of ideas — shows how a reading is structured and how its main points are related. Think of a graphic organizer as a means of tracking the author's flow of ideas. By drawing an organizer, you can follow the author's development of ideas.

Drawing a graphic organizer is an active way to review and connect major ideas. The standard format for a graphic organizer format is shown in Figure 1.2. When you draw a graphic organizer, be sure it includes all the key elements in the reading. An example of a graphic organizer for "No More Pep Rallies!" is shown in Figure 1.3. Work through the organizer and reread the essay, paragraph by paragraph, at the same time. (To draw detailed graphic organizers using a computer, visit bedfordstmartins.com.)

Using a Summary to Check Your Understanding

Another strategy for understanding difficult text involves writing a **summary,** a brief statement of major points. We all practice summarizing every day. When a friend asks, "What was the movie about?" we reply with a summary of the plot. A summary presents only the main ideas, not details. Your summary of a movie would not include specific scenes or dialogue, for example. When summarizing a text, your summary should be much shorter than the original, depending on the amount of detail needed. Summarizing is an excellent way to check whether you have understood the reading. There is no sense in trying to respond and write about something you do not understand clearly. If you have difficulty writing a summary, this is a sign that you do not fully know what is important in the reading.

Many students keep a journal in which they write summaries of essays, stories, and books they have read. Journal writing is a good way to generate and record ideas about a reading, and the journal entries can serve as useful sources

For more on journals, see Chapter 2, p. 26.

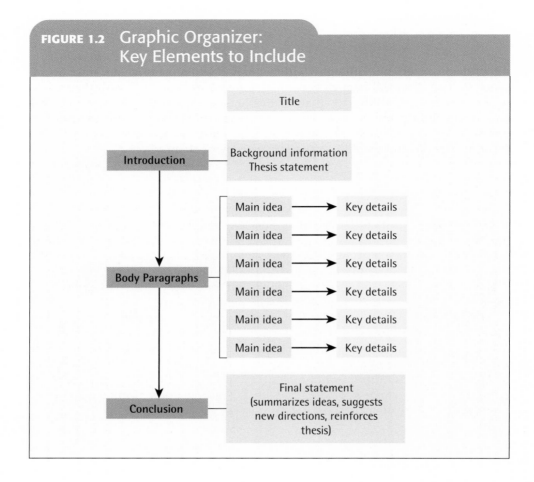

FIGURE 1.2 Graphic Organizer: Key Elements to Include

of ideas for writing papers. To write an effective and useful summary, use the guidelines on page 16.

One good way to identify what to include in a summary is to write a *summary note* for most or all paragraphs. Summary notes are marginal annotations that briefly state the key issue presented in each paragraph. You can easily convert these notes into sentences for your summary. The box on page 17 shows some of one student's summary notes for "No More Pep Rallies!" along with summary sentences that have been generated from her notes. The student then used these sentences in her summary, also shown on page 17.

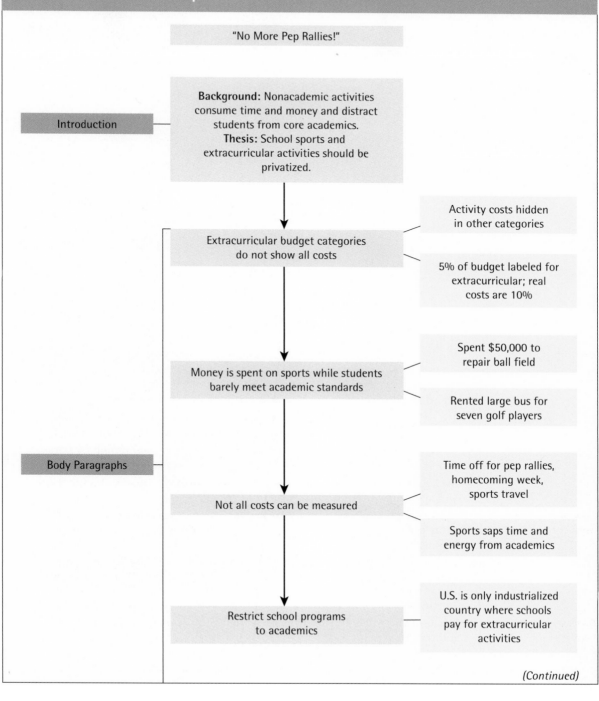

FIGURE 1.3 Graphic Organizer for "No More Pep Rallies!"

"No More Pep Rallies!"

Introduction

Background: Nonacademic activities consume time and money and distract students from core academics.
Thesis: School sports and extracurricular activities should be privatized.

Extracurricular budget categories do not show all costs

- Activity costs hidden in other categories
- 5% of budget labeled for extracurricular; real costs are 10%

Money is spent on sports while students barely meet academic standards

- Spent $50,000 to repair ball field
- Rented large bus for seven golf players

Body Paragraphs

Not all costs can be measured

- Time off for pep rallies, homecoming week, sports travel
- Sports saps time and energy from academics

Restrict school programs to academics

- U.S. is only industrialized country where schools pay for extracurricular activities

(Continued)

FIGURE 1.3   *(Continued)*

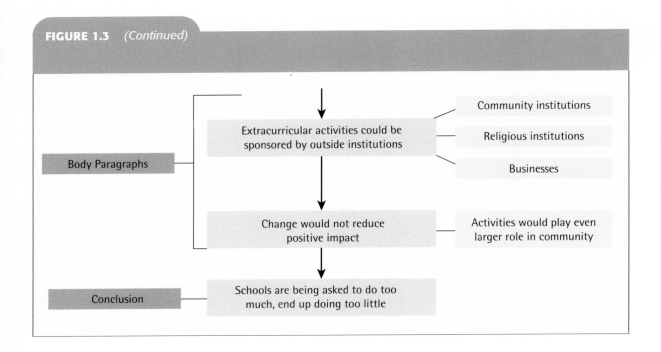

Guidelines for Writing a Summary

1. **Read the entire essay before attempting to write anything.**
2. **Use your annotations.** Any highlighting or marginal notes that you made while reading will help you pick out what is important to include in your summary.
3. **Write your summary as you reread the essay.** Work paragraph by paragraph as you write your summary.
4. **Write an opening sentence that states the author's thesis, the most important idea the entire essay explains.**
5. **To avoid plagiarism, be sure to express the author's ideas and thesis in your own words.** If you want to include something in the author's own words, be sure to use quotation marks.
6. **Include the author's most important supporting ideas.** Your summary should include each key idea in brief, concise form. Do not include your own impressions, reactions, or responses; your summary should be a factual reporting of just the key ideas.
7. **Present the ideas in the order in which they appear in the original source.** Be sure to use transitions (connecting words) as you move from one supporting idea to another.

For more on plagiarism, see Part 3, p. 632.

For more on transitions, see Chapter 3, p. 59.

(Continued)

8. **Reread your summary to determine if it contains sufficient information.** Would your summary be understandable and meaningful to someone who had not read the essay? If not, revise your summary to include additional information.

Converting Summary Notes to Summary Sentences

Marginal Summary Note	Summary Sentence
(para. 1) Activities detract from academics.	Academic achievement needs to be improved in public schools, but school districts are allowing extracurricular activities and sports to detract from academics.
(para. 4) Discusses hidden costs.	School budgets have categories for extracurricular activities, but some costs are hidden in other categories, making the true cost higher than it appears.
(para. 8) Business, religious, and community organizations could pay for activities.	These activities could be paid for by community institutions and businesses.

Academic achievement needs to be improved in public school, but school districts are allowing extracurricular activities and sports to detract from academics. For this reason, Etta Kralovec in "No More Pep Rallies!" argues that extracurricular activities and sports should be privatized and removed from the classroom. School budgets have official categories for extracurricular activities, but some costs are hidden in other categories, making the true cost higher than it appears. This high cost is illustrated by the example of one school district paying for improvements to its ball field while students barely met academic standards. However, not all costs can be measured. Sports also affect students' academic performance because they take time and energy away from studying. Public schools pay for extracurricular activities, making the United States the only industrialized country in the world that does so. Instead, the author proposes that these activities could be paid for by community institutions and businesses. Under the current system, schools are given too much responsibility and, as a result, can accomplish little.

Notice that the summary covers the main point of each of the paragraphs in the essay. Notice, too, that the summary is written in the student's own words; the phrases were not copied from the essay. Finally, notice that the order of ideas in the summary parallels the order of ideas presented in the reading and that transitions link the supporting ideas.

Reading Visuals

A writer may use a visual to clarify or emphasize an idea, reveal trends, condense information, or illustrate a point of view. For example, an article espousing the value of a college education may contain a graph comparing lifetime average salaries to emphasize the value of higher education. Writers sometimes include photographs to provoke an emotional response or further their theses. For example, an argument for increased U.S. aid to developing countries may use a photograph of an emaciated child to emphasize the effects of a recent famine while drawing out feelings of shock or pity to make the reader sympathetic. Writers also use visuals to help readers visualize a place or setting, understand a complicated process, or remember important information.

Because writers use visuals deliberately and creatively to shape the message they are sending, it is important to spend time studying and analyzing visuals that accompany text. To analyze a visual, ask yourself the following questions.

Questions to Ask about Visuals

1. **What does the visual show?** Examine the image closely to determine what is being shown. Do any particular elements in the image stand out? Consider whether action is taking place or has already happened. If the image is more informative, determine what type of information is being presented.

2. **What is the purpose of the visual?** Identify why an image has been included and what it contributes to the reading. Has it been included for illustration or to emphasize a particular point?

3. **What does the visual mean?** Interpret the meaning of the image, both alone and within the context of the reading. What is the intended message? If words are used within the image, consider how they shape the overall meaning of the visual.

4. **Is the visual accompanied by verbal text?** Is there a caption or other corresponding text? If so, determine how the visual and verbal text relate. Does one explain the other? What is stated and what is left unstated?

5. **What does the visual suggest?** How a visual makes you feel is an important part of its effect within the text. Consider also what questions or issues the image raises.

In "No More Pep Rallies!" a photo of two cheerleaders is included (p. 7). This photo helps readers visualize the issue suggested in the title, while emphasizing the popularity of and enthusiasm for school sporting events.

Expanding Your Vocabulary through Reading

Your vocabulary is one of your most valuable assets and an important factor in academic success. The words you use determine how you present yourself to others and how others perceive you. One of the best ways to improve your vocabulary is by reading — textbooks, newspapers, magazines, and most important, the essays in this book.

Improving Your Vocabulary

As you read the selections in this book, you will encounter both unfamiliar and familiar words used in unfamiliar ways. Use the following four suggestions to improve your vocabulary as you read.

Use Words You Already Recognize

One of the easiest ways to expand your vocabulary is to concentrate on words that you have seen before but cannot define precisely — and therefore do not use. Practically speaking, your vocabulary is made up of words that you know and *use*. Most college students understand more words than they actually use in their own speech or writing. For example, you probably know the meaning of the words *criteria, implication, legitimate,* and *rationed,* but have you used any of them lately?

To expand your vocabulary, start using the words you already recognize in conversation. Be sure, however, that you are certain of the meanings of the words you decide to use. Writing is ideally suited for expanding your vocabulary because it involves revision. As you draft papers, use whatever language comes to mind to express your ideas. Then, after you have revised the ideas in your writing, take a few minutes to study and evaluate your choice of words.

Pay Attention to Unfamiliar Words

When you find an interesting or unfamiliar word in a reading, mark it in the text. Look up its meaning and record it in a vocabulary log — a notebook or computer file for keeping track of words you want to learn. To help expand your vocabulary, the activities following each reading in this book contain a section titled "Building Your Word Power." Questions in this section ask about features of language and require you to define several words as they are used in the reading. If they are unfamiliar to you, add these words to your vocabulary log. In addition, many of the readings in this book include marginal notes that give the meaning of unfamiliar words.

Figure Out Unfamiliar Words without a Dictionary

If you were to look up every unfamiliar word that you ever came across in a dictionary, you would likely not have enough time to complete all your assignments. Often, you can figure out the meaning of a word by using one of the following strategies.

- **Look for clues in surrounding text.** You can often figure out a word from the way it is used in its sentence or in surrounding sentences. Sometimes the author may provide a brief definition or synonym. Other times, a less obvious context clue reveals meaning.

BRIEF DEFINITION:	**Janice *prefaced*, or introduced, her poetry reading with a personal story. [*Prefaced* means "introduced."]**
CONTEXT CLUE:	**In certain societies young children are always on the *periphery*, and never in the center, of family life. [*Periphery* means "the edges or the fringe," which is far away from the center.]**

- **Try pronouncing the word aloud.** Hearing the word will sometimes help you grasp its meaning. By pronouncing the word *magnific*, you may hear part of the word *magnify* and know that it has something to do with enlargement. *Magnific* means "large or imposing in size" and "impressive in appearance."

- **Look at parts of the word.** If you break down the parts of a word, you may be able to figure out its meaning. For example, in the word *nonresponsive* you can see the verb *respond*, which means "act or react." *Non* means "not," so you can figure out that *nonresponsive* means "not acting or reacting."

Use a Dictionary When Necessary

There will be times when you must look up a word in a dictionary. Be sure you have a collegiate dictionary readily available where you read and study, or access to an online dictionary. Do not rely solely on a pocket dictionary because it will not have enough definitions to suit your needs. Here are the names of a few commonly used collegiate dictionaries: *Merriam-Webster's Collegiate Dictionary*, 11th edition; *The American Heritage College Dictionary*, 4th edition; and *Microsoft Encarta College Dictionary*. There are also numerous dictionaries available online, including a version of the Merriam-Webster dictionary at www.m-w.com.

Commonly Used Language Features

As you read the selections in this book, you will encounter interesting and unusual features of language that authors use to express their meaning forcefully and uniquely. Many of these techniques involve **figures of speech,** or language used

Language Feature	Explanation	Example
Allusion	A reference to a person, place, thing, or literary work.*	Jackson displayed Herculean strength. (Hercules is a Greek hero known for might and courage.)
Euphemism	Words that hide or downplay the importance or seriousness of something.	The newspaper advertised *previously owned vehicles.* (used cars)
Doublespeak	Deliberately unclear or evasive language, usually a misleading euphemism.	The company is *downsizing its staff.* (firing employees)
Jargon	Specialized language used by particular academic fields or special groups that is not readily understood by the general public.	Computer language: GTG. (shorthand for "got to go")
Cliché	An overused expression that seldom carries specific meaning.	Don't count your chickens until they are hatched.
Foreign words and phrases	Words that are taken directly, without translation, from another language, often French or Latin.	The visiting dignitary committed a *faux pas.* (social blunder or mistake)
Idiom	Phrase that has a meaning other than what the words literally mean.	He decided to *bite the bullet.* (to face a painful situation bravely)
Imagery	Language that creates an impression by appealing to the reader's physical senses, most often sight.	The rich carpet of green grass glinted and rippled in the gentle breeze.
Simile (see also p. 149)	An explicit comparison between two things, typically introduced by the word *like* or *as.*	The surface of the wooden table shone *like a mirror.*
Metaphor (see also p. 149)	An implied comparison between two things without using the words *like* or *as.*	The woman politely accepted the criticism, but *icicles were hanging on her every word.* (she spoke in a cold, unfriendly manner)
Personification (see also p. 150)	Attributing human traits to nonhuman beings or inanimate objects.	As we walked through the jungle, the vines grabbed at our ankles with their wiry fingers.
Hyperbole	A deliberate and obvious exaggeration.	I could eat *40 pounds of that chocolate!*
Connotative meaning	The feelings and associations that accompany a word.	Both *untidy* and *grubby* mean "messy," but *grubby* suggests something dirty as well.
Restrictive word meaning	The meaning of a commonly used word that is unique to a particular field or discipline.	The word *run* in baseball has a specific meaning.

*If you are not familiar with an allusion an author makes, some good sources are dictionaries, encyclopedias, and specialized reference books. Online sources include www.bulfinch.org (*Bulfinch's Mythology*), www.bartleby.com, and www.britannica.com.

in nonliteral ways to create a striking impression. Paying attention to these features will expand your vocabulary as well as contribute to your understanding of the reading in which they appear. The accompanying table explains many of these language features. You will also find questions about these features in the "Building Your Word Power" section that follows each reading selection.

Planning Your Essay

WRITING QUICK START

Study the photo on this page. What do you think is happening in it? When or where is it taking place? On a sheet of paper or in a new computer file, write whatever comes to mind about the scene the photo depicts. You might write about times when you've felt the same emotions you think the soldier is expressing or times when you've seen people express strong emotions in a public place. Try to write nonstop for at least five minutes. Don't slow down to evaluate your writing or to phrase your ideas in complete sentences or correct grammatical form. Just record your thoughts.

You have just used *freewriting*, a method of discovering ideas about a topic. Read over what you wrote. Suppose you were asked to write an essay about joy or exuberance. Do you see some usable ideas in your freewriting? In this chapter you will learn more about freewriting as well as other methods that will help you generate ideas to write about. You will also learn how to focus an essay by considering why you are writing (your purpose), who you are writing for (your audience), and what

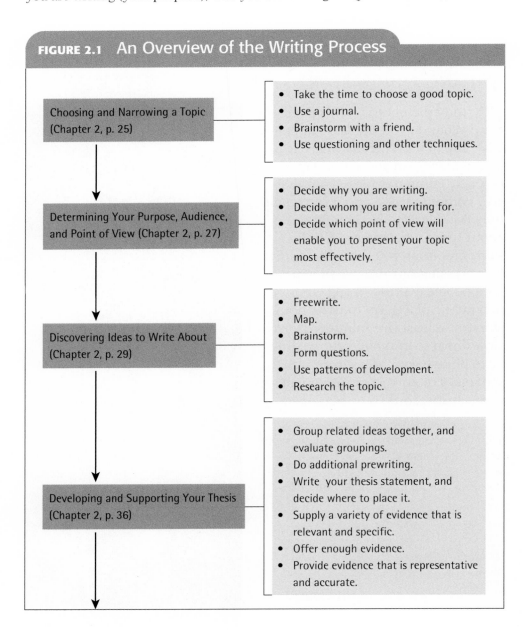

FIGURE 2.1   An Overview of the Writing Process

Choosing and Narrowing a Topic (Chapter 2, p. 25)

- Take the time to choose a good topic.
- Use a journal.
- Brainstorm with a friend.
- Use questioning and other techniques.

Determining Your Purpose, Audience, and Point of View (Chapter 2, p. 27)

- Decide why you are writing.
- Decide whom you are writing for.
- Decide which point of view will enable you to present your topic most effectively.

Discovering Ideas to Write About (Chapter 2, p. 29)

- Freewrite.
- Map.
- Brainstorm.
- Form questions.
- Use patterns of development.
- Research the topic.

Developing and Supporting Your Thesis (Chapter 2, p. 36)

- Group related ideas together, and evaluate groupings.
- Do additional prewriting.
- Write your thesis statement, and decide where to place it.
- Supply a variety of evidence that is relevant and specific.
- Offer enough evidence.
- Provide evidence that is representative and accurate.

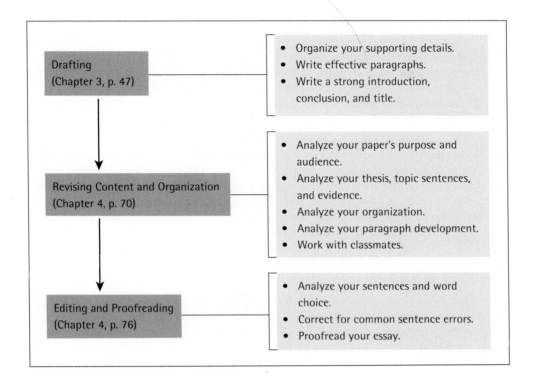

perspective you take toward the topic (point of view). Finally, you'll learn about writing a thesis and finding evidence to support it. These steps are all part of beginning the process of writing an essay, as illustrated in the overview in Figure 2.1.

Prewriting to Start the Assignment

Your first step is to read the assignment carefully. Are you being asked, for example, to *compare* two items or to *argue* for or against something? Has your instructor specified the length of the essay? When is the assignment due? If you have questions about any part of the assignment, be sure to check with the instructor.

Choosing and Narrowing a Topic

In some writing situations, the instructor will assign the topic or give you a number of choices. In other situations, the instructor will allow you to write on a topic of your choice. In the latter cases, use the following suggestions to choose a successful topic.

- **Invest time in making your choice.** It may be tempting to choose the first topic that comes to mind, but you will produce a better essay if you work with a topic that interests you and that you already know something about.
- **Use your journal as a source of ideas**. If you do not already keep a journal, start one now; try writing in it for a few weeks to see if it is helpful.
- **Discuss possible topics with a friend**. Conversations with a friend may help you discover worthwhile topics and provide feedback on topics you have already considered.

Once you have a topic, the next step is to narrow it so that it is manageable within the required length. If you are assigned to write a two- to four-page essay, for example, a broad topic such as divorce is too large. You might, however, write about infidelity as a cause of divorce or the emotional effects of divorce on children. To narrow a topic, limit it to a specific part or aspect. Techniques such as mapping and questioning, discussed later in this chapter (pp. 30, 32), will help you do so.

Keeping a Journal

A writing journal can be a useful tool for choosing a topic and developing writing skills. You can use a journal to record daily experiences and observations, explore relationships among people or ideas, ask questions, and test ideas. Whether you keep your journal in a notebook or on a computer file, use it frequently — every day if possible — to record your thoughts. You can use these ideas later in your writing, and working through them will help your writing skills develop. Here are some benefits of using a journal.

- **Use your journal to practice writing.** Record conversations, summarize or react to meaningful experiences, or release pent-up frustrations. Remember, regardless of what you write about, you are writing and thereby improving your skills.
- **Use your journal to experiment.** Try out new ideas and experiment with different voices, different topics, and different approaches to a topic.
- **Use your journal to warm up.** Like an athlete, a writer benefits from warming up. Use a journal to activate your thought processes, loosen up, and stretch your mind before tackling the writing assignment.
- **Use your journal as a source of ideas for papers.** If you are asked to choose your own topic for an essay, leaf through your journal for ideas to write about.
- **Use your journal to respond to readings.** Use it to collect your thoughts about and respond to a reading before writing an assigned essay.

The first journal entry is often the most difficult one to write. Once you've written a few entries, you'll begin to feel more comfortable. When writing in your journal, concentrate on capturing ideas — not on being grammatically correct. Try to write correct sentences, but do not focus on grammar and punctuation. Be sure to reread your journal entries on a regular basis. By doing so, you will discover that rereading is similar to looking at old photographs: They will bring back vivid snippets of the past for reflection and appreciation.

ESSAY IN PROGRESS 〔1〕

Using the suggestions on pages 25–26, write down at least three broad topics. Then narrow one of the topics so it is manageable for a two- to four-page essay.

Addressing Purpose, Audience, and Point of View

Once you have decided on a manageable topic, you are ready to determine your purpose and consider your audience.

Determining Your Purpose

A well-written essay should have a specific purpose or goal. There are three main purposes for writing: to *express* yourself, to *inform* the reader, and to *persuade* the reader. For example, an essay might express the writer's feelings about an incident of road rage, inform readers about the primary causes of road rage, or attempt to persuade readers to overcome their own road rage.

As you plan your essay, ask yourself two critical questions.

- Why am I writing this essay?
- What do I want this essay to accomplish?

Some essays can have more than one purpose. An essay on snowboarding, for instance, could inform readers about the benefits of snowboarding and then urge them to take up the sport.

Considering Your Audience

Considering your audience — the people who read your essay — is an important part of the writing process. After all, many aspects of writing depend on the audience; these include how you express yourself (the type of sentence structure you use, for example), which words you choose, what details and examples you include, and what attitude you take toward the topic. Your tone — how you sound to the audience — is especially important. Consider the following descriptions of a student orientation session.

TELLING A FRIEND

Remember I told you how nervous I am about attending college in the fall? Well, guess what? I went to my student orientation over the weekend, and it was much better than I had expected! I even met one of my psych teachers — they call them "instructors" here — and he was so nice and down-to-earth that now I'm starting to get excited about going to college.

WRITING FOR THE STUDENT NEWSPAPER

College student orientations are often thought to be stuffy affairs where prospective students attempt to mix with aloof professors. For this reason, I am pleased to report that the college orientation held last weekend was a major success and not a pointless endeavor after all. Along with my fellow incoming first-year students, I was impressed with the friendliness of instructors and the camaraderie that developed between students and faculty.

Notice how the two examples differ in terms of word choice, sentence structure, and type of information provided. The tone varies as well: The paragraph spoken to a friend has a casual tone, whereas the article written for the student newspaper is more formal. As you consider your audience, ask yourself the following questions.

- What does the audience know or not know about this topic? What do they need to know?
- What is the education, background, and experience of this audience?
- What attitudes, beliefs, opinions, or biases is this audience likely to hold?
- What tone do these readers expect me to take?

For many of the essays you write, your instructor will be the audience. In these situations, many students mistakenly think that they do not need to supply introductory or background information. In most cases, however, it is best to write as if the instructor were unfamiliar with your topic. Include background information, definitions of technical terms, and relevant details.

Choosing a Point of View

Point of view is the perspective from which you write an essay. There are three types: *first*, *second*, and *third person*. Think of point of view as the "person" you become as you write. For some essays, you may find first-person pronouns (*I, me, mine, we, ours*) effective, such as in an essay narrating an event in which you participated. For other types of essays, second-person pronouns (*you, your, yours*) are appropriate, such as in an essay that tells readers what to do: "First, you should measure . . ." Many textbooks, including this one, use the second person to address student readers.

In academic writing, the third-person point of view is often used. It is less personal and more formal than both the first and second person. When writing in the third person, an author uses people's names and third-person pronouns (*he, she, they*) to report what he or she sees.

EXERCISE 2.1

1. Write a one-paragraph description of a current television commercial for a particular product. Your audience is another college student. Now rewrite your paragraph for a different audience: a marketing instructor. In your new paragraph, analyze the factors that make the commercial interesting and appealing.

2. Working with a classmate, discuss which point of view (first, second, or third person) would be most appropriate in each of the following writing situations.

   a. an essay urging students on your campus to participate in a march against hunger to support a local food drive

   b. a description of a car accident on a form that the insurance company requires you to submit in order to collect benefits

   c. a paper for an ecology course on the effects of air pollution caused by a local industry

Finding Ideas to Write About

Many students report that one of the most difficult parts of writing an essay is finding enough to say about a narrowed topic. This is such a common problem that writers have developed many techniques for generating ideas. The most common methods are described here.

Freewriting

In freewriting, you write nonstop for a specific period of time, usually five to ten minutes. As you learned in the "Writing Quick Start" activity that opens this chapter, freewriting involves writing whatever comes to mind, regardless of its relevance to the topic. If nothing comes to mind, just write the topic, your name, or "I can't think of anything to write." Then let your mind run free: Explore ideas, make associations, jump from one idea to another. The following tips will help you.

- Be sure to write nonstop. Writing often forces thought.
- Write fast! Try to keep up with your thinking.
- Record ideas as they come to you and in whatever form they appear — words, phrases, questions, or sentences. Don't be concerned with grammar, punctuation, or spelling.

Next, reread your freewriting, and highlight or underline ideas that seem useful. Look for patterns and connections. Here is an annotated excerpt from one student's freewriting on the broad topic of violence in the media.

There seems to be a lot of <u>violence</u> in the media these days, particularly on TV. For example, last night when I watched the news, the cameraman showed people <u>getting shot in the street.</u> What kind of people watch this stuff? I'd rather watch a movie. It really bothered me because people get so turned off by such an ugly, <u>gruesome scene</u> that they won't want to watch the news anymore. But then we'd have a lot of <u>uninformed citizens.</u> There are too many already. Some people don't even know who the vice president of the U.S. is. A negative thing -- that is, the media <u>has a negative impact</u> on anyone or group who wants to do something about violence in the

Graphic portrayal of violence

Negative impact on viewers

Portrayal of minority and ethnic groups

inner city. And they create <u>negative impressions of minority and ethnic groups,</u> too. If the media shows one Latino man committing a crime, viewers falsely assume <u>all Latinos</u> are criminals. It's difficult to think of something positive that can be done when you're surrounded by so much violence. It's all so overwhelming.

A number of different subtopics surfaced from this student's freewriting: the media's graphic portrayal of violence, the media's negative impact on viewers, and the media's portrayal of minority and ethnic groups. In developing ideas for your own essay, freewriting may appeal to you because it lets you give your imagination free rein.

EXERCISE 2.2

Set a clock or timer for five minutes, and freewrite on one of the following broad topics. Then review and highlight your freewriting, identifying usable ideas with a common theme that might serve as an essay topic. Starting with this potential topic, freewrite for another five minutes to narrow your topic further and develop your ideas.

1. Rock 'n' roll
2. World Wide Web sites
3. How to be self-sufficient
4. Urban problems
5. Job interviews
6. Health care

Mapping

Mapping, or clustering, is a visual way to discover ideas and relationships. To create a map, follow these steps.

- Begin by writing your topic in the middle of a blank sheet of paper, and draw a box or circle around it.
- Think of ideas that are related to or suggested by your topic. Write down the ideas in clusters around the topic, connecting them to the topic with lines (see sample map on the next page).
- Draw arrows and lines, or use highlighting, to connect related ideas.
- Think of still more ideas, clustering them around the ideas already on your map.
- If possible, experiment with mapping on a computer, using a graphics program such as the draw function available in Microsoft Word. You can then cut and paste items from your map into an outline or draft of your essay.

The sample map shown in Figure 2.2 was done by a student working on the topic of the costs of higher education. In this map, the student compared attending a local community college and attending an out-of-town four-year college. A number of subtopics evolved, including transportation costs, social life, the avail-

FIGURE 2.2 Sample Map

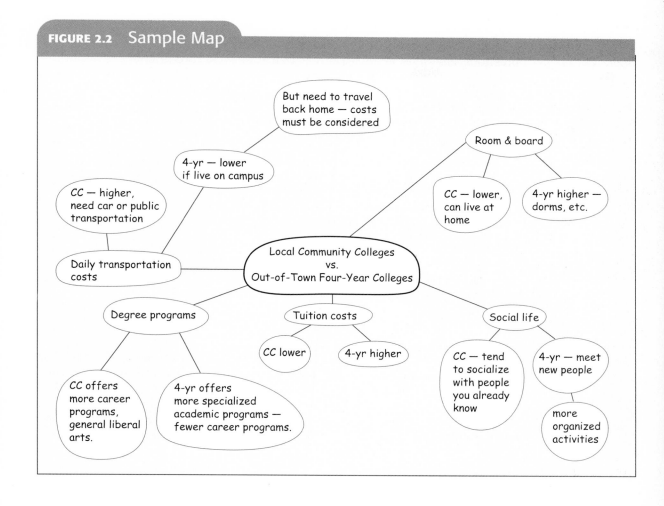

ability of degree programs, and room and board costs. Mapping may appeal to you if you like to deal with information and ideas in a visual way.

EXERCISE 2.3

Narrow one of the following topics. Then select one of your narrowed topics, and draw a map of related ideas as they come to mind.

1. Presidential politics
2. Purebred animals
3. Jewelry
4. Radio stations
5. Year-round schooling
6. Professional sports

Brainstorming

When you brainstorm, you list everything you can think of about a topic — impressions, emotions, and reactions as well as facts. Record brief words or phrases rather than complete sentences, and give yourself a time limit; it will force ideas to come faster. If you use a computer, you might use bullets or the indent function to brainstorm.

The following example shows a part of a student's brainstorming on the narrowed topic of the disadvantages of home schooling.

TOPIC: DISADVANTAGES OF HOME SCHOOLING

-Parents may not be expert in each subject

-Child does not learn to interact with other children

-Child does not learn to compete against others

-Parents may not be objective about child's progress

-Special programs (art, music, sports) may be omitted

-Child may feel strong pressure to achieve

-Services of school nurse, counselors, reading specialists not available

Three clusters of topics are evident — unavailable services and programs, limits of parents, and problems of social development. The student selected the cluster about social development, which is highlighted in yellow. He then did further brainstorming to generate ideas about his narrowed topic. As you can see, brainstorming is somewhat more structured than freewriting because the writer focuses only on the topic at hand.

EXERCISE 2.4

Choose one of the following subjects, and narrow it to a manageable topic for a two- to four-page paper. Then brainstorm, either alone or with one or two classmates, to generate ideas to write about.

1. Value of music
2. National parks
3. Misuse of credit cards
4. Fashions for teenagers
5. Telemarketing
6. Immigration

Questioning

Questioning is another way to discover ideas about a narrowed topic. Working either alone or with a classmate, write down every question you can think of about your topic. As with other prewriting strategies, focus on ideas, not correctness. It may help to imagine that you are interviewing an expert on the topic. Here is a partial list of questions one student generated on the narrow topic of the financial problems faced by single parents.

Why do many female single parents earn less than male single parents?

Is there a support group for single parents that offers financial advice and planning?

How do single parents find time to attend college to improve their employability?

How can single female parents who don't work outside the home still establish credit?

Is it more difficult for a working single parent to get a mortgage than for a couple in which only one spouse works?

These questions yielded several ideas for further development: income disparity, financial planning, and the establishment of credit. When you generate ideas for your own essay, questioning is a technique that you might enjoy using with other classmates.

EXERCISE 2.5

Working alone or with a classmate, choose one of the following topics, narrow it, and write a series of questions to generate ideas about it.

1. The campus newspaper
2. Learning a foreign language
3. Financial aid regulations
4. Late-night talk radio shows
5. Government aid to developing countries
6. Reality TV

Using the Patterns of Development

In Part 2 of this book you will learn nine different ways to develop an essay: narration, description, illustration, process, comparison and contrast, classification and division, definition, cause and effect, and argument. These methods are often called *patterns of development*. In addition to providing ways to develop an essay, the patterns of development may be used to generate ideas about a topic. Think of the patterns as doors through which you can gain access to your topic.

The list of questions in the box on page 34 will help you approach your topic through these different doors. For any given topic, some questions will work better than others. If your topic is voter registration, for example, the questions for definition and process would be more helpful than those for description.

As you write answers to the questions, also record any related ideas that come to mind. If you are working on a computer, create a table listing the patterns in one column and your questions in another. This way, you can brainstorm ideas about the various patterns.

Using the Patterns of Development to Explore a Topic

Pattern of Development	Questions to Ask
Narration (Chapter 5)	• What stories or events does this topic remind you of?
Description (Chapter 6)	• What does the topic look, smell, taste, feel, or sound like?
Illustration (Chapter 7)	• What examples of this topic are particularly helpful in explaining it?
Process Analysis (Chapter 8)	• How does this topic work?
	• How do you do this topic?
Comparison and contrast (Chapter 9)	• To what is the topic similar? In what ways?
	• Is the topic more or less desirable than those things to which it is similar?
Classification and division (Chapter 10)	• Of what larger group is this topic a member? What are its parts?
	• How can the topic be subdivided?
	• Are there certain types or kinds of the topic?
Definition (Chapter 11)	• How do you define the topic? How does the dictionary define it?
	• What is the history of the term?
	• Does everyone agree on its definition? Why or why not? If not, what points are in dispute?
Cause and effect (Chapter 12)	• What causes the topic?
	• How often does it happen? What might prevent it from happening?
	• What are its effects?
	• What may happen because of it in the short term? What may happen as a result of it over time?
Argumentation (Chapter 13)	• What issues surround this topic?

One student who was investigating the topic of extrasensory perception (ESP) decided to use the questions for definition and cause and effect. Here are the answers she wrote.

Definition (How can my topic be defined?)

- ESP, or extrasensory perception, is the ability to perceive information not through the ordinary senses but as a result of a "sixth sense" (as yet undeveloped in most people).
- Scientists disagree on whether ESP exists and how it should be tested.

Cause and Effect (Why does my topic happen? What are its effects?)

- Scientists do not know the cause of ESP and have not confirmed its existence, just the possibility of its existence.
- The effects of ESP are that some people know information that they would (seemingly) have no other way of knowing.
- Some people with ESP claim to have avoided disasters such as airplane crashes.

As you can see from this student's answers, using the patterns of development helps to focus on specific issues related to a topic.

EXERCISE 2.6

Use the patterns of development to generate ideas on one of the following topics. Refer to the box on page 34 to form questions.

1. Buying only American-made products
2. The increase in incidents of carjacking
3. Community policing in urban areas
4. Effects of labor union strikes on workers
5. Internet romance
6. Global warming

Researching Your Topic

Do some preliminary research on your topic in the library or on the Internet. Reading what others have written about the topic may suggest new approaches, reveal issues or controversies, and help clarify what you do and do not already know about the topic. This method is especially useful for an assigned essay with an unfamiliar topic or for a topic you want to learn more about.

Take notes while reading sources. In addition, be sure to record the publication data you will need to cite each source (author, title, publisher, page numbers, and so on). If you use ideas or information from sources in your essay, you must give credit to the sources of the borrowed material. It is a good idea to become familiar with the research process because you will probably need to use it at one

For more on conducting research, see Part 3.

time or another — in your writing class, in another class, in an internship, or on a job.

EXERCISE 2.7

Do library or Internet research to generate ideas on one of the narrowed topics listed here.

1. Shopping for clothes on the Internet or on television
2. Preventing terrorist actions in public buildings
3. Controlling children's access to television programs

ESSAY IN PROGRESS 2

Keeping your audience and purpose in mind, use one of the prewriting strategies discussed in this chapter to generate details about the topic you narrowed in Essay in Progress 1.

Developing and Supporting Your Thesis Statement

Once you have a narrowed topic and enough ideas to write about, it is time to make an assertion about the topic. Such an assertion is called a *thesis statement*. In the following sections you will learn how to write effective thesis statements and how to support them with evidence.

What Is a Thesis Statement?

A thesis statement is the main point of an essay. It explains what the essay will be about and expresses the writer's position on the subject. It may also give clues about how the essay will develop or how it will be organized. Usually a thesis statement is expressed in a single sentence. When you write, think of a thesis statement as a promise to the reader. The rest of your essay delivers on that promise.

Here is a sample thesis statement.

> Playing team sports, especially football and baseball, develops skills and qualities that can make you successful in life because these sports demand communication, teamwork, and responsibility.

In this thesis, the writer identifies the topic — team sports — and states the position that team sports, especially football and baseball, equip players with important skills and qualities. After reading this thesis, the reader expects to discover what skills and qualities football and baseball players learn and how these contribute to success in life.

Developing Your Thesis Statement

A thesis statement usually evolves as you explore a topic during prewriting; do not expect to be able to sit down and simply write one. As you prewrite, you may discover a new focus or a more interesting way to approach the topic. Expect to write several versions of a thesis statement before finding one that works. For certain topics you may need to do some reading or research to get more information about the tentative thesis. Your thesis may change, too, as you write and revise your paper.

Coming Up with a Working Thesis Statement

To come up with a preliminary thesis, or *working thesis*, for your paper, first reread your prewriting; look for and highlight the details that seem to fit together. Put similar details in groups, and write a word or phrase that describes each group.

One student, for example, was working on the topic of animal intelligence, especially in regard to dogs. When she reviewed her brainstorming, she saw that some of her details could be grouped into two general categories: details about learning and details about instinct. Here is how she arranged her ideas.

> Learning
>
> learn to take commands
>
> learn new tricks
>
> learn to read master's emotions
>
> learn housebreaking
>
> serve as guide dogs for blind people
>
> Instinct
>
> females deliver and care for puppies
>
> avoid danger and predators
>
> seek shelter
>
> automatically raise hair on back in response to aggression

Once you've grouped similar details together, the next step is to decide which group or groups of ideas best represent the focus your paper should take. In some instances, one group of details will be enough to develop a working thesis; but at other times, you will need to use the details in two or three groups. The student working on a thesis for the topic of animal intelligence among dogs evaluated her two groups of details and decided that instinct was unrelated to her topic. Consequently, she decided to write about learning.

If you are not satisfied with how you have grouped or arranged your details, you probably don't have enough details to come up with a good working thesis. If you need more details, use prewriting to generate additional ideas. Be sure to try a different prewriting strategy from the one you used previously. A new strategy may help you see the narrowed topic from a different perspective.

ESSAY IN PROGRESS 3

Review the prewriting you did about your narrowed topic in Essay in Progress 2. Highlight useful ideas, and identify sets of related details among those you have highlighted.

Writing an Effective Thesis Statement

A thesis statement should introduce your narrowed topic, revealing what your essay is about, and state the point you will make about that topic. Your thesis statement, or a sentence following it, may also preview the organization of your essay. Use the guidelines in the following list to write an effective thesis statement or to evaluate and revise your working thesis.

Guidelines for Writing a Thesis Statement

1. **Make an assertion.** An assertion, unlike a fact, takes a position, expresses a viewpoint, or suggests the approach you will take toward the topic.

   LACKS AN ASSERTION: Hollywood movies, like *Pearl Harbor* and *A Beautiful Mind*, are frequently based on true stories.

   REVISED: Hollywood movies, like *Pearl Harbor* and *A Beautiful Mind*, manipulate true stories to cater to the tastes of the audience.

2. **Be specific and provide enough detail.** Try to provide as much information as possible about your main point.

   TOO GENERAL: I learned a great deal from my experiences as a teenage parent.

   REVISED: From my experiences as a teenage parent, I learned to accept responsibility for my own life and for that of my son.

3. **Focus on one central point.** Limit your thesis to one major idea.

   FOCUSES ON SEVERAL POINTS: This college should improve its tutoring services, sponsor more activities of interest to Latino students, and speed up the registration process for students.

   REVISED: To better represent the student population it serves, this college should sponsor more activities of interest to Latino students.

(Continued)

4. Avoid announcing your main point. Don't use phrases such as "This essay will discuss . . ." or "The subject of my paper is . . ." Instead, state your main point directly.

> ANNOUNCES THE
> MAIN POINT: **The point I am trying to make is that people should not be allowed to smoke on campus.**
>
> REVISED: **The college should prohibit smoking on campus.**

EXERCISE 2.8

Working in a group of two or three students, discuss what is wrong with each of the following thesis statements. Then revise each one to make it more effective.

1. In this paper I will discuss the causes of asthma, which include exposure to smoke, chemicals, and allergic reactions.

2. Jogging is an enjoyable aerobic sport.

3. The crime rate is decreasing in American cities.

4. Living in an apartment has many advantages.

5. Children's toys can be dangerous, instructional, or creative.

ESSAY IN PROGRESS 4

Keeping your audience in mind, select one or more of the groups of ideas you identified in Essay in Progress 3, and write a working thesis statement based on these ideas.

The thesis statement can appear anywhere in your essay, but it is usually best to place it in the first or second paragraph as part of the introduction. When the thesis appears at the beginning of the essay, readers will know what to pay attention to and what to expect in the rest of the essay. When the thesis occurs later in the essay, you can build up to it gradually in order to prepare readers for it.

In some professional writing, especially in narrative or descriptive essays, the writer may not state the thesis directly. Instead, the thesis may be strongly implied by the details and the way they are organized. Although professional writers may use an **implied thesis**, academic writers — including professors and students — generally state their thesis. You should always include a clear statement of your thesis for your college papers.

Supporting Your Thesis Statement with Evidence

Once you have written a working thesis statement, the next step is to develop evidence that supports the thesis. **Evidence** is any type of information — such as examples, statistics, or expert opinion — that will convince the reader that your thesis is reasonable or correct. This evidence, organized into well-developed paragraphs, makes up the body of the essay. For more on visualizing the structure of an essay, see Chapter 3, p. 48.

For many topics, you will need to research library or Internet sources or interview an expert in order to collect enough supporting evidence for your thesis.

Choosing Types of Evidence

Although there are many types of evidence, it is usually best not to try to use them all. Analyze your purpose, audience, and thesis to determine which types of evidence will be most effective. The box below lists various types of evidence and shows how each type could be used to support a working thesis on acupuncture. Note that many of the types of evidence correspond to the patterns of development discussed in Part 2 of this text.

Types of Evidence Used to Support a Thesis

WORKING THESIS: Acupuncture, a form of alternative medicine, is becoming more widely accepted in the United States.

Type of Evidence	Example
Definition	Explain that, in acupuncture, needles are inserted into specific points of the body to control pain or relieve symptoms.
Historical background	Explain that acupuncture is a medical treatment that originated in ancient China.
Explanation of the process	Explain the principles on which acupuncture is based and how scientists think it works.
Factual details	Explain who uses acupuncture, on what parts of the body it is used, and under what circumstances it is applied.
Descriptive details	Explain what acupuncture needles look and feel like.
Narrative story	Relate a personal experience that illustrates the use of acupuncture.
Causes or effects	Discuss one or two theories that explain why acupuncture works. Offer reasons for its increasing popularity.
Classification	Explain types of acupuncture treatments.
Comparison and contrast	Compare acupuncture to other forms of alternative medicine, such as massage and herbal medicines. Explain how acupuncture differs from these other treatments.

(Continued)	
Advantages and disadvantages	Describe the pros (nonsurgical, relatively painless) and cons (fear of needles) of acupuncture.
Examples	Describe situations in which acupuncture has been used successfully: for example, by dentists, in treating alcoholism, for pain control.
Problems	Explain that acupuncture is not always practiced by medical doctors; licensing and oversight of acupuncturists may thus be lax.
Statistics	Indicate how many acupuncturists practice in the United States.
Quotations	Quote medical experts who attest to the effectiveness of acupuncture as well as those who question its value.

EXERCISE 2.9

Working in a group of two to three students, discuss and list the types of evidence that could be used to support the following thesis statement for an informative essay.

▸ **The pressure to become financially independent is a challenge for many young adults and often causes them to develop social and emotional problems.**

How might your evidence change for different audiences — young adults, parents of young adults, or counselors of young adults?

Collecting Evidence to Support Your Thesis

Use one or more of the following suggestions to help generate evidence for your thesis.

- Complete the worksheet for collecting evidence (Figure 2.3). For one or more types of evidence listed in the left column of the worksheet, give examples that support your thesis in the right column. Collect evidence only for those types that are appropriate for your thesis.
- Visualize yourself speaking to your audience. What would you say to convince the audience of your thesis? Jot down ideas as they come to you.
- On a sheet of paper or in a computer file, develop an outline of major headings. Leave plenty of blank space under each heading. Fill in ideas about each heading as they come to you.

FIGURE 2.3 Worksheet For Collecting Evidence

Purpose:_____

Audience:_____

Point of View:_____

Thesis Statement:_____

_____

Type of Evidence	Actual Evidence
Definition	
Historical background	
Explanation of a process	
Factual details	
Descriptive details	
Narrative story	
Causes or effects	
Classification	
Comparison and contrast	
Advantages and disadvantages	
Examples	
Problems	
Statistics	
Quotations	

- Draw a graphic organizer of your essay (see pp. 13–16 of Chapter 1), filling in supporting evidence as you think of it.
- Discuss your thesis statement with a classmate; try to explain why he or she should accept your thesis as valid.

ESSAY IN PROGRESS 5

Using the preceding list of suggestions for collecting evidence to support a thesis, generate at least three different types of evidence to support the working thesis statement you wrote in Essay in Progress 4. As you collect your evidence, locate and consult at least two sources.

Choosing the Best Evidence

In collecting evidence in support of a thesis, you will probably generate more than you need. Consequently, you will need to identify the evidence that best supports your thesis and that suits your purpose and audience. The following six questions will help you do so.

Questions to Ask about Your Evidence

1. **Is my evidence relevant?** All your evidence must clearly and directly support your thesis. Irrelevant evidence will distract your readers and cause them to question the validity of the thesis.

2. **Is my evidence specific?** Avoid general statements that will neither engage your readers nor help you make a convincing case for your thesis. To locate detailed, specific evidence, return to your prewriting or use a different prewriting strategy. You may also need to conduct research (see Part 3).

3. **Do I have a variety of evidence?** Using several kinds of evidence increases the likelihood that your evidence will be convincing. Using different types of evidence also shows readers that you are knowledgeable and informed about the topic, thus enhancing your own credibility.

4. **Do I have enough evidence?** The amount of evidence needed will vary according to your audience and your topic. To discover whether you have provided enough evidence, ask a classmate to read your essay and tell you whether he or she is convinced. If your reader is not convinced, ask what additional evidence is needed.

5. **Is my evidence representative?** Be sure the evidence you supply is typical and usual. Do not choose rare or exceptional situations as evidence because they will mislead the reader.

6. **Is my evidence accurate?** Gather information from reliable sources. Do not guess at statistics or make estimates. If you are not certain of the accuracy of a fact or statistic, verify it through research. For more on choosing reliable sources, see Part 3.

ESSAY IN PROGRESS **6**

Evaluate the evidence you generated in Essay in Progress 5. Select from it the evidence that you could use to support your thesis in a two- to four-page essay.

Students Write

In this and the remaining two chapters of Part 1, we will follow the work of Julie Bohet, a student in a first-year writing course who was assigned to choose a special interest or hobby and explain its value and importance. Julie decided to use questioning to narrow her topic and freewriting to generate ideas about the topic. Here is an example of her questioning.

What are some special interests or hobbies that are important to me?

music

soccer

movies

shopping

Julie decided to explore two of these experiences further: soccer and music. She did so by asking herself another question.

Why are each of these important in my life?

1. Soccer

I began playing as a young girl and enjoyed the competition and camaraderie of the sport.

Helped me learn cooperation and teamwork at an early age.

I often played on teams in which I was the only girl, which helped me to not be intimidated by boys and to be more assertive.

My favorite position was fullback (defense), but sometimes I played halfback, which helped me develop physical strength.

2. Music

I like listening to all different kinds of music — classical, rock, pop.

Playing music gives me an outlet for expression.

Listening to music makes me feel different emotions.

The life and music of composers — such as Beethoven — inspire me.

Playing music is challenging.

Music is something that's important in most people's lives.

Performing for an audience has taught me to trust in my ability.

After looking over the answers to her questions, Julie chose music as her topic, and she decided to focus on the importance of piano playing in her life. The following excerpt from her freewriting shows how she started to develop her topic.

I have to write for five minutes. I'm not sure what to say. My family and friends love music. Music is everywhere. In the car. on TV in stores. It's a big part of my life. I play piano, guitar, and a little clarinet. Now I play mostly classical music on piano but I used to play rock music on guitar. My favorite band is Radiohead. I think they are the most innovative rock band around today. But I think classical music takes more skill to write and play. Beethoven is one of my favorite composers because there is so much truth to his music and he is one of the most revolutionary composers that ever lived. One of my professors said Beethoven invented jazz. I read an article where Billy Joel said that all musicians owe their careers to him. I thought my first piano teacher was Billy Joel in disguise. This seems pretty funny now, but I was only 9 at the time! I wasn't too much into playing piano when I was younger, but now I like to practice and play. Performing in front of other people is hard, though. I get very nervous before I go on stage. I performed in talent shows at my high school in front of over 1,000 students. I also won the merit competition where I took lessons 2 years in a row. Even though I played for less people, it was more nerve-racking because there were judges. I have a long way to go to be a great pianist. Playing is about learning to play the notes and making it musical so that the audience can enjoy it.

After reviewing her responses to the questions about her topic and her freewriting, Julie decided that she would focus on how important listening to and playing music were to her life. She then wrote the following working thesis statement.

Both listening to and playing music has given me valuable experiences and created a focus in my life.

As you work through the remaining chapters of Part 1, you will see how Julie develops her first draft in Chapter 3 and her final draft in Chapter 4.

Drafting Your Essay

WRITING QUICK START

Study the cartoon on this page; it humorously depicts a familiar situation. Then, working alone or with one or two classmates, write a statement that expresses the main point of the cartoon. Your statement should not just describe what is happening; it should also express the idea that the cartoonist is trying to communicate to the audience.

"Go ask your search engine."

The statement you have just written is an assertion around which you could build an essay. Such an assertion is called a *thesis statement*. To write an essay, you would begin with prewriting and research and then write a thesis statement. At that point you would be ready to write a draft of your essay, including an effective introduction, conclusion, and title. This chapter will guide you through the process of developing an essay in support of a thesis statement.

The Structure of an Essay

Think of an essay as a complete piece of writing, much like a textbook chapter. For example, a textbook chapter might be titled "Human Rights: A Critical Issue." The first few paragraphs would probably introduce and define the concept of human rights. The text might then assert that human rights is a controversial global issue of growing importance. The rest of the chapter would discuss the issue in more detail and conclude with a summary.

Similarly, as you can see in Figure 3.1, an essay has a title and an introduction. It also makes an assertion, or thesis statement, which is explained and supported throughout the body of the essay. The essay ends with a conclusion.

Organizing Your Supporting Details

Before you begin writing the body paragraphs of your essay, decide on the evidence you will use to support your thesis and the order in which you will present the evidence.

Selecting a Method of Organization

There are three common ways to organize ideas: most-to-least or least-to-most order, chronological order, and spatial order.

Most-to-Least or Least-to-Most Order

If you choose this method, arrange your supporting details from most-to-least or least-to-most important, familiar, interesting (or some other key characteristic). You might begin with the most convincing evidence, or you could save the most compelling evidence for last.

A student, Robin Ferguson, was working on the thesis statement "Working as a literacy volunteer taught me more about learning and friendship than I ever expected." After she identified four primary benefits related to her thesis, she chose to arrange the benefits from least-to-most important. She decided that the friend-

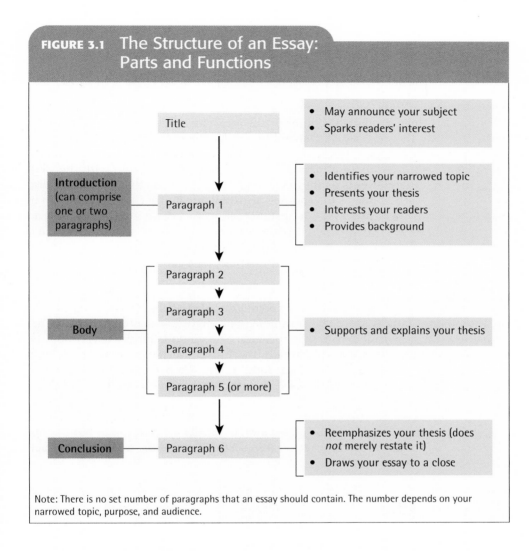

FIGURE 3.1   The Structure of an Essay: Parts and Functions

Title
- May announce your subject
- Sparks readers' interest

Introduction (can comprise one or two paragraphs)

Paragraph 1
- Identifies your narrowed topic
- Presents your thesis
- Interests your readers
- Provides background

Body

Paragraph 2
Paragraph 3
Paragraph 4
Paragraph 5 (or more)
- Supports and explains your thesis

Conclusion

Paragraph 6
- Reemphasizes your thesis (does *not* merely restate it)
- Draws your essay to a close

Note: There is no set number of paragraphs that an essay should contain. The number depends on your narrowed topic, purpose, and audience.

ship with her student, Marie, was the most important benefit. Here is how she organized her supporting evidence.

WORKING THESIS

Working as a literacy volunteer taught me more about learning and friendship than I ever expected.

LEAST IMPORTANT BENEFIT:	Learned about the learning process
MORE IMPORTANT BENEFIT:	Discovered the importance of reading for Marie
STILL MORE IMPORTANT BENEFIT:	Marie increased her self-confidence
MOST IMPORTANT BENEFIT:	Developed a permanent friendship with Marie

If Ferguson had decided to use a most-to-least order instead, she would have started her essay with the most important benefit — her permanent friendship with Marie.

Chronological Order

When you arrange supporting details in chronological order, you put them in the order in which they happened. Depending on the subject of the essay, the events could be minutes, days, or years apart. Chronological order is often used in narrative essays. A story about a marriage, for example, might begin with the wedding; include several events as they occurred, such as the births of children; and end with the death of one of the spouses. Chronological order is also common in essays that explain a process. For instance, if you were writing about how to assemble a bicycle, you would tell readers what to do first, second, third, and so on.

Spatial Order

When using spatial order, you organize details about the subject according to their location or position in space. For example, you might use spatial order in a descriptive essay about modern movie theaters. You could begin by describing the ticket booth, then the lobby, and finally the individual theaters. Similarly, you might describe a basketball court from right to left or a person from head to toe. Spatial organization is commonly used in descriptive essays as well as in classification and division essays.

When using spatial organization, try to picture the subject in your mind or sketch it on paper. "Look" at the subject systematically — from top to bottom, inside to outside, front to back. Imagine it in sections or pieces, and describe each piece.

EXERCISE 3.1

Working alone or with a classmate, choose one of the following thesis statements, and decide how you would organize its supporting evidence. Would you use most-to-least (or least-to-most), chronological, or spatial order? Write a few sentences explaining how you would organize the evidence according to the order you chose.

1. Despite the many pitfalls that await those who shop at auctions, people can find bargains if they prepare in advance.

2. My first day of kindergarten was the most traumatic experience of my childhood, one that permanently shaped my view of education.

3. Learning how to drive a car increases a teenager's sense of freedom and responsibility.

ESSAY IN PROGRESS ▉

Using the thesis statement and evidence you gathered for the Essay in Progress activities in Chapter 2, choose a method for organizing your essay. Then explain briefly how you will use that method of organization.

Preparing an Outline

Once you have written a thesis statement and chosen a method of organization for your essay, take a few minutes to write an outline or draw a graphic organizer of the main points in the order you plan to discuss them.

There are two types of outlines: informal and formal.

An informal outline, also called a *scratch* or *working outline*, is prepared early on in the writing process and doesn't adhere to a standard format. Typically it consists of a list of main points and subpoints, written in key words and phrases. Here is an informal outline of Robin Ferguson's essay.

THESIS:	Working as a literacy volunteer taught me about learning, teaching, and friendship, and perhaps most important, opened my eyes to the good that comes from reaching out to help others.
PARAGRAPH 1:	Learned about the learning process
	• Went through staff training program
	• Learned about words "in context"
PARAGRAPH 2:	Discovered the importance of reading for Marie
	• Couldn't take bus; walked to grocery store
	• Couldn't buy certain products
	• Couldn't write out grocery list
PARAGRAPH 3:	Marie increased her self-confidence
	• Made rapid progress
	• Began taking bus
	• Helped son with reading
PARAGRAPH 4:	Developed a permanent friendship
	• Saw each other often
	• Both single parents
	• Helped each other babysit
CONCLUSION:	I benefited more than Marie did.

Formal outlines use a standard outline format and are generally written later in the writing process after the essay has begun to take a more formal shape. There are two types of formal outlines: *topic outlines* that use only key words and phrases, and *sentence outlines* that use complete sentences. The following tips will help you prepare either a topic or a sentence outline.

Guidelines for Preparing an Outline

---

1. Always begins with a thesis statement.
2. Use Roman numerals (I, II), capital letters (A, B), Arabic numbers (1, 2), and lowercase letters (a, b) to designate levels of importance. Indent less important entries.
3. Begin every entry with a capital letter.
4. Put entries of roughly equal importance at the same level (all capital letters, for example).
5. Make sure that each entry explains or supports the topic or subtopic under which it is placed.
6. Make items at the same level grammatically parallel.

For more on parallelism, see Chapter 4, p. 78.

Here is part of a formal topic outline that a student wrote for an essay for her communication class.

<u>Thesis</u>: Speakers may have difficulty communicating if they don't know how to listen.

    I. Types of listening

        A. Participatory

            1. Involves the listener responding to the speaker

            2. Has expressive quality

                a. Maintain eye contact

                b. Express feelings using facial expressions

        B. Nonparticipatory

            1. Involves listener listening without talking or responding

            2. Allows speaker to develop his or her thoughts without interruption

Preparing a Graphic Organizer

Instead of preparing an outline, you may prefer to draw a graphic organizer. Whichever method you find most appealing, always begin by putting your working thesis statement at the top of your document. Then list the main points, leaving plenty of space between them. As details or examples occur to you, jot them down in the appropriate place.

For more on graphic organizers, see Chapter 1, p. 13.

The graphic organizer in Figure 3.2 was done for Robin Ferguson's essay, "The Value of Volunteering." As you read her organizer, notice that it follows the organization of her informal outline on p. 51.

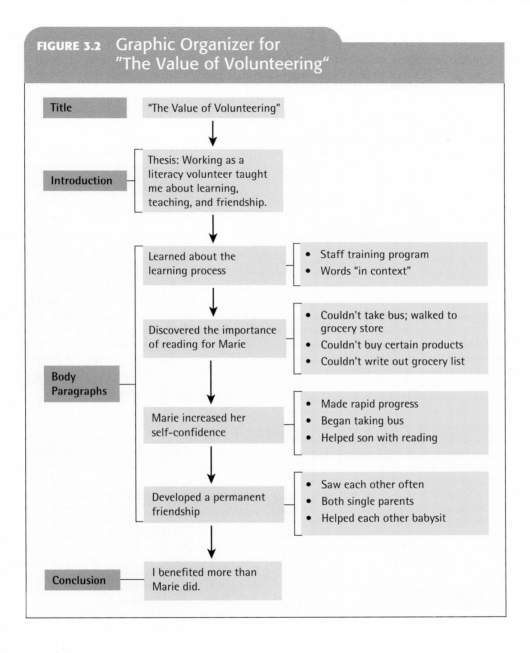

FIGURE 3.2 Graphic Organizer for "The Value of Volunteering"

Title
"The Value of Volunteering"

Introduction
Thesis: Working as a literacy volunteer taught me about learning, teaching, and friendship.

Body Paragraphs

Learned about the learning process
- Staff training program
- Words "in context"

Discovered the importance of reading for Marie
- Couldn't take bus; walked to grocery store
- Couldn't buy certain products
- Couldn't write out grocery list

Marie increased her self-confidence
- Made rapid progress
- Began taking bus
- Helped son with reading

Developed a permanent friendship
- Saw each other often
- Both single parents
- Helped each other babysit

Conclusion
I benefited more than Marie did.

ESSAY IN PROGRESS 2

For the topic you chose in Essay in Progress 1, write a brief outline or draw a graphic organizer to show the organizational plan of your essay.

Writing Effective Paragraphs

Your essay can be only as good as its supporting paragraphs. A well-developed supporting paragraph has a focused topic sentence and includes definitions, explanations, examples, or other evidence that supports the thesis. It must also use transitions and repetition to show how ideas are related. To visualize the structure of a well-developed paragraph, see Figure 3.3.

What Well-Focused Topic Sentences Must Do

Just as a thesis announces the main point of an essay, a topic sentence states the main point of a paragraph. In addition, each paragraph's topic sentence must support the thesis. In the second and third paragraphs of Robin Ferguson's essay on volunteering in a literacy program shown on page 55, the topic sentences are highlighted. As you read the paragraphs, note how each topic sentence states the main point of the paragraph and supports the essay's thesis: "Working as a literacy volunteer taught me more about learning and friendship than I ever expected."

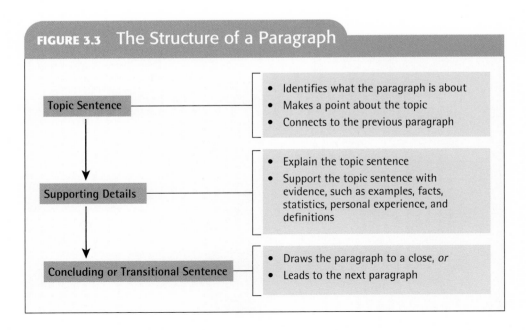

FIGURE 3.3   The Structure of a Paragraph

Topic Sentence
- Identifies what the paragraph is about
- Makes a point about the topic
- Connects to the previous paragraph

Supporting Details
- Explain the topic sentence
- Support the topic sentence with evidence, such as examples, facts, statistics, personal experience, and definitions

Concluding or Transitional Sentence
- Draws the paragraph to a close, *or*
- Leads to the next paragraph

When I first went through the training program to become a literacy volunteer, I learned about the process of learning -- that is, the way in which people learn new words most effectively. To illustrate this concept, the person who trained us wrote a brief list of simple words on the left side of a chalkboard and wrote phrases using the same words on the right side of the chalkboard. She instructed us to read the words and then asked which list of words we would be most likely to remember. We all said the words on the right because they made more sense in context.

The training I received, though excellent, was no substitute for working with a real student, however. When I began to discover what other people's lives are like because they cannot read, I realized the true importance of reading. For example, when I had my first tutoring session with my client, Marie, a 44-year-old single mother of three, I found out she walked two miles to the nearest grocery store twice a week because she didn't know which bus to take. When I told her I would get her a bus schedule, she confided to me that it would not help because she could not read it, and therefore she wouldn't know which bus to take. She also had difficulty once she got to the grocery store because she couldn't always remember what she needed. Since she did not know words, she could not write out a grocery list. Also, she could only identify items by sight, so if the manufacturer changed a label, she would not recognize it as the product she wanted.

Topic sentence: first benefit is that she learned about learning process

— *Example*

Topic sentence

Second benefit: importance of reading

— *Example*

To read Robin Ferguson's complete essay, see Chapter 14, p. 583.

When you write topic sentences for your own essay, keep the following tips in mind.

Guidelines for Writing Topic Sentences

1. **A topic sentence must support the thesis.** Each topic sentence must in some way explain the thesis or show why it is believable or correct.
2. **A topic sentence should state exactly what the paragraph is about.** Instead of writing general statements, tell the reader precisely what to expect. Often, your topic sentence will also preview the organization of the paragraph. In paragraph 2 of her essay, Ferguson might have written a vague topic sentence. Instead, she wrote a specific one.

VAGUE: **Literacy volunteers must undergo training.**

SPECIFIC: **When I first went through the training program to become a literacy volunteer, I learned about the process of learning -- that is, the way in which people learn new words most effectively.**

(Continued)

(Continued)

3. **A topic sentence can appear in any position within a paragraph.** Unless you have a good reason for placing a topic sentence elsewhere in the paragraph, it is usually best to place it first. This approach enables you to state your main point and then explain it. Occasionally, though, you will need one or two transitional sentences at the beginning of a paragraph. In these instances, your topic sentence would follow the transitional sentence(s), an approach Ferguson takes in paragraph 3. Keep in mind that a topic sentence can also appear last in a paragraph. This arrangement is common in argumentative writing because it enables the writer to present convincing evidence before stating his or her point.

EXERCISE 3.2

1. Read the following thesis statement. Then identify the one topic sentence in the list that does *not* support the thesis.

   To make a marriage work, a couple must build trust, communication, and understanding.

   a. Knowing why a spouse behaves as he or she does can improve a relationship.

   b. People get married for reasons other than love.

   c. The ability to talk about feelings, problems, likes, and dislikes should grow as a marriage develops.

   d. Marital partners must rely on each other to make sensible decisions that benefit both of them.

2. Revise each topic sentence to make it focused and specific. At least one of the revised topic sentences should also preview the organization of the paragraph.

   a. In society today, there is always a new fad or fashion in clothing.

   b. People watch TV reality shows because they find them irresistible.

   c. Procrastinating can have a negative effect on your success in college.

Achieving Unity and Providing Specific Details

In addition to including well-focused topic sentences, effective paragraphs are unified and provide concrete details that work together to support the main point.

Achieving Unity

In a unified paragraph, all the sentences directly support the topic sentence. The following sample paragraph lacks unity. As you read it, try to pick out the sentences that do not support the topic sentence (shown highlighted).

PARAGRAPH LACKING UNITY

(1) Much of the violence we see in the world today may be caused by the emphasis on violence in the media. (2) More often than not, the front page of the local newspaper contains stories involving violence. (3) In fact, one recent issue of my local newspaper contained seven references to violent acts. (4) There is also violence in public school systems. (5) Television reporters frequently hasten to crime and accident scenes and film every grim, violent detail. (6) The other day, there was a drive-by shooting downtown. (7) If the media were a little more careful about the ways in which they glamorize violence, there might be less violence in the world today and children would be less influenced by it.

Although sentences 4 and 6 relate to the broad topic of violence, neither one is *directly* related to the main point about the media promoting violence that is stated in the topic sentence. Both should be deleted.

EXERCISE 3.3

Working alone or in a group of two or three students, read each paragraph and identify the sentences that do not support the topic sentence. In each paragraph, the topic sentence is highlighted.

1.   (a) Today many options and services for the elderly are available that did not exist years ago. (b) My grandmother is eighty-five years old now. (c) Adult care for the elderly is now provided in many parts of the country. (d) Similar to day care, adult care provides places where the elderly can go for meals and social activities. (e) Retirement homes for the elderly, where they can live fairly independently with minimal supervision, are another option. (f) My grandfather is also among the elderly at age eighty-two. (g) Even many nursing homes have changed so that residents are afforded some level of privacy and independence while their needs are being met.

2.   (a) Just as history repeats itself, fashions have a tendency to do the same. (b) In the late 1960s, for example, women wore long peasant dresses with beads; some thirty years later, the fashion magazines are featuring this same type of dress. (c) This peasant style has always seemed feminine and flattering. (d) I wonder if the fashion industry deliberately recycles fashions. (e) Men wore their hair long in the 1960s. (f) Today, some men are again letting their hair grow. (g) Goatees, considered "in" during the beatnik period of the 1950s, have once again made an appearance in the 1990s.

Providing Enough Specific Supporting Details

The evidence you provide to support your topic sentences should be *concrete* and *specific*. It is also important to provide *enough* evidence so that your meaning is clear to the readers. To make your paragraphs concrete and specific, use these guidelines.

Guidelines for Writing Specific Paragraphs

1. **Provide exact details.** Include the names of people, places, brands, and other specific details.

   VAGUE: A friend of mine has a new car. It's yellow and low to the ground. It looks like the kind of car you see on racetracks.

   SPECIFIC: Peter's 2004 canary yellow Corvette has a black pinstripe down each side. Its mag wheels are shiny with new chrome, and the headlights pop up at the push of a button.

2. **Focus on *who, what, when, where, how*, and *why* questions.** Ask yourself these questions about your supporting details, and use the answers to revise your paragraph.

   VAGUE: Some animals hibernate for part of the year.

   What animals? *When* do they hibernate?

   SPECIFIC: Some bears hibernate for three to four months each winter.

3. **Use strong verbs to help readers visualize the action.**

   VAGUE: When Kasia came on stage, the audience became excited.

   SPECIFIC: When Kasia burst onto the stage, the audience screamed, cheered, and chanted, "Kasia, Kasia!"

4. **Use descriptive language that appeals to the senses (smell, touch, taste, sound, sight).**

   VAGUE: It's relaxing to walk on the beach.

   SPECIFIC: I walked barefoot on the warm sandy beach, breathing in the briny smell of the salt water and listening to the pounding of the waves.

5. **Use adjectives and adverbs to make your writing more concrete.**

   VAGUE: Working in the garden can be enjoyable.

   SPECIFIC: As I slowly weeded my perennial garden, I let my eyes wander over the pink meadow sweets and blue hydrangeas, all the while listening attentively to the chirping of a bright red cardinal.

EXERCISE 3.4

Working alone or in a group of two or three students, revise and expand the following paragraphs to make them specific and concrete. Feel free to add new information and new sentences.

1. I saw a great concert the other night in Dallas. Two groups were performing. The music was great, and there was a large crowd. In fact, the crowd was so enthusiastic that the second group performed one hour longer than scheduled.

2. Although it is convenient, online shopping is a different experience from shopping in an actual store. You don't get the same opportunity to see and feel objects. There is much that you miss. If you enjoy shopping, turn off your computer and support your local merchants.

Connecting Supporting Details with Transitions and Repetition

All the details in a paragraph must fit together and function as a connected unit of information. When a paragraph has coherence, its ideas flow smoothly, allowing readers to follow their progression with ease. Transitions (used both within and between paragraphs) and repeated words are useful devices for linking details and achieving coherence in writing.

Using Transitions

Transitions are words or phrases that lead the reader from one idea to another. Consider the two paragraphs from the student essay, "The Value of Volunteering," you read earlier (see p. 55); notice that transitions such as *however, that is,* and *for example* are used to link ideas. Some commonly used transitions are shown in the accompanying box.

In the two examples that follow, the first paragraph is disjointed and choppy because it lacks transitions, whereas the revised version is easier to follow.

WITHOUT TRANSITIONS

Most films are structured much like a short story. The film begins with an opening scene that captures the audience's attention. The writers build up tension, preparing for the climax of the story. They complicate the situation by revealing other elements of the plot, perhaps by introducing a surprise or additional characters. They introduce a problem. It will be solved either for the betterment or to the detriment of the characters and the situation. A resolution brings the film to a close.

WITH TRANSITIONS

Most films are structured much like a short story. The film begins with an opening scene that captures the audience's attention. Gradually, the writers build up tension, preparing for the climax of the story. Soon after the first scene, they complicate the situation by revealing other elements of the plot, perhaps by introducing a surprise or additional characters. Next, they introduce a problem. Eventually, the problem will be solved either for the betterment or to the detriment of the characters and the situation. Finally, a resolution brings the film to a close.

Commonly Used Transitional Expressions

Transitions That Show Space

Direction	inside/outside, along, above/below, up/down, across, to the right/left, in front of/behind
Nearness	next to, near, nearby, facing, adjacent to
Distance	beyond, in the distance, away, over there

Transitions That Show Time

Frequency	often, frequently, now and then, gradually, week by week, occasionally, daily, rarely
Duration	during, briefly, hour by hour
Reference to a particular time	at two o'clock, on April 27, in 2000, last Thanksgiving, three days ago
Beginning	before then, at the beginning, at first
Middle	meanwhile, simultaneously, next, then, at that time
End	finally, at last, eventually, later, at the end, subsequently, afterward

Transitions That Show Other Relationships

Items in a series	then, first, second, next, another, furthermore, finally, as well as
Illustration	for instance, for example, namely, that is
Result or cause	consequently, therefore, so, hence, thus, because, then, as a result
Restatement	in other words, that is, in simpler terms
Summary or conclusion	finally, in conclusion, to sum up, all in all, evidently, actually
Opposing viewpoint	but, however, on the contrary, nevertheless, neither, nor, on the one/other hand, still, yet

Transitions show connections not just between sentences but also from paragraph to paragraph. In "The Value of Volunteering," for example, the entire first sentence of the second paragraph on page 55 is a transition to a new subtopic: Ferguson tells the reader that she is done talking about training and will now discuss her actual experience as a tutor.

Using Repeated Words

Repeating key words or their *synonyms* (words that have similar meanings) or using pronouns that refer to key words in the essay also helps readers follow your ideas. In the following paragraph, notice how the highlighted words help to keep the reader's attention on the issue — the legal drinking age.

> Many years ago the drinking age in New York State was 18; now it is 21. Some young adults continue to argue that it should be 18 again. Whether a young adult is 20 or 21 does not make a big difference when he or she is consuming alcoholic beverages, young people say. However, statistics indicate that 20-year-olds who drink alcohol are at a greater risk for having an automobile accident than 21-year-olds. That difference is the reason the drinking age was changed.

Writing Your Introduction, Conclusion, and Title

It is not necessary to start writing an essay at the beginning and proceed straight through to the end. Some students, for example, prefer to start by writing a tentative conclusion. However, regardless of when you write your introduction, conclusion, and title, remember that these are important components of a well-written essay.

Writing a Strong Introduction

Your introduction creates a first, and often lasting, impression. It also establishes the tone of the essay — how you "sound" about the topic and what attitude you take toward your readers. In addition, the introduction should announce the narrowed topic of your essay, present the thesis statement, interest the readers, and provide any background information the readers may need.

For more on narrowing a topic, see Chapter 2, p. 25.

Because the introduction is crucial, take the time to get it right. The following suggestions will help you capture your readers' interest.

Guidelines for Writing a Strong Introduction

1. **Ask a provocative or disturbing question.**

   Should health insurance companies continue to pay for rehab services when patients consistently put themselves back into danger by using drugs again?

   (Continued)

(Continued)

2. Begin with a story or anecdote that is relevant to your thesis.

I used to believe that it was possible to stop smoking by simply quitting cold turkey. When I tried this approach, however, I became so uncomfortable that I started again just to alleviate the discomfort. I realized then that in order to quit smoking, I would need a practical solution that would overcome my cravings.

3. Offer a quotation that illustrates your thesis.

As Indira Gandhi once said, "You cannot shake hands with a clenched fist." This truism is important to remember whenever people communicate, but particularly when they try to resolve a conflict. Both parties need to agree that there is a problem and then agree to listen to each other with an open mind.

4. Cite a little-known or shocking fact or statistic.

Between 1963 and 1993, there was a 26 percent increase in the number of college students who admitted copying academic work from another student. This increase suggests that students' attitude toward cheating changed dramatically during that thirty-year period.

5. Move from general to specific.

The First Amendment is the basis for several cherished rights in the United States, and free speech is among them. Therefore, it seems unlawful — even anti-American — for a disc jockey to be fired for expressing unpopular views on the radio.

6. State a commonly held misconception and then correct it.

Many people have the mistaken notion that only homosexuals and drug users are in danger of contracting AIDS. In fact, many heterosexuals also suffer from this disease, and the number of heterosexuals who test HIV-positive is increasing every year. It is time the American public became better informed about the prevention and treatment of AIDS.

7. Describe a hypothetical situation that illustrates your thesis.

Suppose you were in a serious car accident and then slipped into a coma, with little hope for recovery. Unless you had a prewritten health care proxy that designated someone to act on your behalf, your fate would be left to medical doctors who knew nothing about you or your preferences for treatment.

8. Begin with an intriguing statement.

Recent research has shown that the color pink has a calming effect on people. In fact, a prison detention center in western New York was recently painted pink to make prisoners more controllable in the days following their arrest.

(Continued)

9. **Begin with a striking example.**

   The penal system is sometimes too concerned with protecting the rights of the criminal instead of the victim. For example, during a rape trial the victim is often questioned about his or her sexual history by the defense attorney. However, the prosecuting attorney is forbidden by law to raise the question of whether the defendant has been charged with rape in a previous trial.

10. **Make a comparison.**

   The process a researcher uses to locate a specific piece of information in the library is similar to the process an investigator follows in tracking a criminal; both use a series of questions and follow clues to accomplish their task.

Even if you use one of the preceding tips for your introduction, be careful to avoid these common mistakes.

- **Do not make an announcement.** Avoid opening comments such as "I am writing to explain . . ." or "This essay will discuss . . ."
- **Keep your introduction short.** One or two paragraphs is usually sufficient.
- **Avoid statements that may seem negative.** Saying "This process may seem complicated, but . . ." may make your readers apprehensive.
- **Avoid an overly familiar or chatty tone.** Opening with "Man, did it surprise me when . . ." is not appropriate.
- **Be sure your topic is explained adequately.** Do not begin an essay by stating, for example, "I oppose Proposition 413 and urge you to vote against it." Before stating your position on the topic, you need to explain the topic adequately.

Writing an Effective Conclusion

Your essay should end with a conclusion — a separate paragraph that reiterates (without directly restating) the importance of your thesis and that brings the essay to a satisfying close. The following tips will help you conclude effectively.

Guidelines for Writing a Solid Conclusion

1. **Look ahead — go beyond the scope of your essay.**

   For now, the present system for policing the Internet appears to be working. In the future, though, a more formal, structured procedure may be necessary.

   (Continued)

(Continued)

2. Remind readers of the importance of the issue.

As noted earlier, research shows that the seat-belt law has saved thousands of lives. These lives would almost certainly have been lost had this law not been enacted.

3. Offer a recommendation or make a call to action.

To convince the local cable company to eliminate pornographic material, subscribers should organize, contact their cable station, and threaten to cancel their service.

4. Mention broader implications of the issue.

When people consider whether the FBI should be allowed to tap private phone lines, the issue often leads them to the larger issue of First Amendment rights.

5. Conclude with a fact, a quotation, an anecdote, or an example that emphasizes your thesis.

The next time you want to send an angry email message, consider this fact: Your friends and enemies can forward those messages, with unforeseen consequences.

Just as with introductions, there are common pitfalls in writing conclusions. Here are some ways to avoid such mistakes.

- **Avoid a direct restatement of your thesis.** It will make your essay seem dull.
- **Avoid standard phrases,** such as "To sum up" or "In conclusion."
- **Avoid introducing major new points.** They belong in the body of your essay.
- **Avoid apologizing for yourself, your work, or your ideas.** Do not say, for example, "Although I am only twenty-one, it seems to me . . ."
- **Avoid softening or reversing your stance.** If, for instance, your essay criticizes someone's behavior, do not back down by saying, "After all, she's only human . . ."

Writing a Good Title

The title of your essay should suggest your topic and spark the readers' interest. The following suggestions will help you write effective titles.

Guidelines for Writing Effective Titles

---

1. Write straightforward, descriptive titles for most academic essays.

Lotteries: A Game Players Can Little Afford

(Continued)

2. **Ask a question that your essay answers.**

    Who Plays the Lottery?

3. **Use alliteration.** Repeating initial sounds (called *alliteration*) often produces a catchy title.

    Lotteries: Dreaming about Dollars

4. **Consider using a play on words or a catchy or humorous expression.** This technique may work well for less formal, nonacademic essays.

    If You Win, You Lose

5. **Avoid broad, vague titles that sound like labels.** Titles such as "Baseball Fans" or "Gun Control" give the reader too little information.

EXERCISE 3.5

For each of the following essays, suggest one or more titles. Try to use several of the preceding suggestions.

1. An essay opposing human cloning

2. An essay on causes and effects of road rage

3. An essay comparing fitness routines

ESSAY IN PROGRESS 3

Using the outline or graphic organizer you created in Essay in Progress 2, write a first draft of your essay. Be sure to write clear and effective topic sentences that support your thesis and unified paragraphs that support each topic sentence.

Students Write

The first draft of Julie Bohet's essay follows. Julie used her freewriting and her working thesis (see Chapter 2) as the basis for her draft, adding details by doing additional brainstorming. Because she was writing a first draft, Julie did not worry about correcting the errors in grammar, punctuation, and mechanics you will notice. (You will see her revised draft in Chapter 4.)

The Language of Music

Julie Bohet

Today we can access music in seconds, whether on the Internet, CDs, or the radio, music has become a vital element of everyone's lives. No matter popular music, hip-hop, rap, techno, house, rock, jazz, or classical, it would be hard to find a person who does not have strong opinions about music and listens to the music they like on a regular basis. For me, music is even more important since I experience it not by just listening to it, but on a deeper level than most listeners--by playing it. Both listening to and playing music has given me many valuable experiences and created a focus in my life.

My formal studies started when I was nine years old and living on Long Island when I started taking piano lessons with Billy Joel. Ok, so maybe my piano teacher wasn't really Billy Joel, but he looked so much like him and we lived so close to where Billy Joel actually lived that I used to think that maybe he was. After my family moved, I started lessons with Dianne, who would be my teacher through middle and high school. Under her instruction I started learning more complex and interesting pieces including my all-time favorite, Beethoven. This is when I started practicing for hours everyday because I couldn't get enough of playing this wonderful music.

Once I started really getting into my playing, I started gaining valuable experiences performing. I remember one time when I was still new at performing in front of people and I was playing music at a museum. I was playing "What Child Is This" and "Memory" from *Cats*. I was more nervous than usual since this was my first performance. "What Child Is This" was fine, but when I played "Memory," I got lost in the music and my nervousness and panicked because I didn't know what to do. I just stopped playing and everyone knew I had messed up. I was really upset when I left and I remember crying the whole car ride home. It was through experiences like this that I learned that I needed to not worry so much about messing up but always move on in the music no matter what happens.

I was constantly challenged to play things beyond my technical and musical capabilities, and I developed the skills of both playing technical works and putting my emotions into the music, making it interesting for the listener through the style of playing the notes or simply the way I would play the phrase.

Music provided me with an advanced way to develop my senses and skills. My sense of sight, sound, and touch, my ability to process the language of musical notation and develop it so that it is almost like speaking English. Also, I could express my emotions. Not necessarily that it became an outlet for my emotions in that I played an angry piece if I was angry or a happy piece when I was happy but that as a performer I become an actor, interpreting the music based on the few directions that the composer gives in sound, rhythm, volume, and other musical elements. I strive to give the pieces a human quality, taking the notes off the sheet music and making them a reality to myself and the listener. My role is to convey the composers thoughts and emotions as I feel them for myself at that very moment.

Listening to music is vastly different from playing it, though the musician, keeping the audience in mind must always listen to herself. Classical instrumental music provides me with a more emotional experience than music with words does because words give you something to think about, whereas the instrumental music just gives you something to feel. After I saw the movie *Immortal Beloved,* I was really drawn to the music of Beethoven in this sense -- the human struggle evident in his music was something that appealed to me because it was so honest and real and human. As I learn more about his life and music in my lessons, I am drawn to his music even more. Further, Beethoven's character has become one that I look to in admiration -- how he overcame his deafness and failing health to continue to do what was important to him. It's like the smaller-scale struggle that I take on every time I learn a new piece of music.

Listening to music is vital to everyone's life, but to perform it for others is a larger calling that helps me to share something that is so personal to me with others, and if not to expose them to classical music that they have probably never heard before to hopefully share a moment or two with them where they feel the same thing I am feeling. After a performance of Debussy's *Clair de Lune,* a member of the audience approached me and said that she had felt so emotionally overwhelmed by my performance of it that it brought tears to her eyes, and to make someone connect with what I am playing in such a way has made my playing satisfying and worthwhile.

Revising and Editing Your Essay

WRITING QUICK START

Study the photograph on this page, and write a brief paragraph describing it for someone who cannot see the picture. Then read what you wrote, revising and adding details to describe the image more fully. After you make these changes, will it be easier for a reader who cannot see the image to visualize the room?

When you rewrote your paragraph, did you include more details from the photo while leaving out unimportant details? The changes you made improved the content of your writing. In other words, you *revised* the description of the photo.

Revising an essay works in much the same way — revision helps you improve both what your essay says and how it says it. This chapter offers several different approaches to revising an essay. It also provides advice for editing and proofreading, the final steps in the writing process. Although revision may seem like a chore, it's definitely worthwhile because a thoughtful revision and careful edit can change a C paper to an A paper!

Revising Content and Organization

Revision is a process of looking again at your *ideas* to make them clearer and easier to understand. It is not merely a process of correcting surface errors and changing a word or two here and there. Even though revision may be time consuming, it is better to discover the problems in an essay while you still have time to correct them.

Making Revision Easier

The following tips will help you revise your essays efficiently.

Guidelines for Revision

1. **Allow time between drafting and revision.** After finishing your draft, set it aside for a while — overnight if possible. When you return to the draft, you will be able to approach it from a fresh perspective.

2. **Read your draft aloud.** Hearing what you have written will help you discover main points that are unclear, paragraphs that are confusing, and wording that needs improvement.

3. **Ask a friend to read your draft aloud to you.** Keep a copy of the draft in front of you as you listen, and mark places where your reader falters or seems baffled. These may be places where your message is not clear enough.

4. **Seek the opinions of classmates.** Ask a classmate to read and comment on your paper. This process, called *peer review*, is discussed on page 75.

5. **Look for consistent problem areas.** Be sure to look for problems — such as poor organization or a lack of details — that have shown up repeatedly in your earlier essays.

(Continued)

6. **Mark your typed or printed copy.** Even if you prefer to handwrite your draft, be sure to type it and print it out before you revise. A typed version will enable you to analyze the draft more impartially, to see a full page at a time, and to make annotations or corrections more easily. Leave wide margins so you have plenty of room to jot down new ideas.

ESSAY IN PROGRESS 1

Revise the graphic organizer or outline that you used to create the first-draft essay for Essay in Progress 3 in Chapter 3. The updated version should match up with the thesis and supporting points in your first draft.

Determining What to Revise

After reading your draft or after discussing it with a classmate, pinpoint areas that need improvement by answering the seven questions that follow. Then refer to the self-help flowcharts on pages 73–75 for suggestions on how to improve your writing.

Questions to Ask as You Revise

1. **Does your draft have a clear purpose and a specific audience?** A first draft is often unfocused; it may go off in several directions rather than having a clear purpose. For instance, one section of an essay on divorce may explain causes, and another section may argue that it harms children. A first draft may also contain sections that appeal to different audiences. For instance, one section of an essay about drug abuse might be written for parents, and other sections might be directed to teenagers.
   - *To check for clear purpose:* Write a sentence stating what the paper is supposed to accomplish. If you cannot write such a sentence, do some additional brainstorming and try again.
   - *To check for specific audience:* Write a sentence or two describing the intended readers — their knowledge, beliefs, and experience with the topic. If you are unable to do so, try to zero in on a particular audience and revise your essay with them in mind.

2. **Does your thesis, topic sentences, or evidence need improvement?** Once your paper is focused on a specific purpose and audience, the next step is to

(Continued)

For more on organizing your essay, see Chapter 3.

(Continued)

evaluate your thesis statement and your support for it. Use the flowchart in Figure 4.1 to evaluate your thesis statement, topic sentences, and evidence.

3. **Is your organization clear and effective?** Readers will not be able to follow your ideas if the essay does not hold together as a unified piece of writing. To be sure that it does, use the graphic organizer or outline of your draft to examine its organization. You can also ask a classmate to read your draft and explain to you how the essay is organized. If your classmate cannot do so, the organization probably needs further work.

4. **Does your introduction interest your reader and provide needed background information?** If not, use the suggestions on pages 61–63 to create interest.

5. **Does your conclusion draw the essay to a satisfactory close and reinforce the thesis statement?** If the conclusion does not follow logically from the introduction, use the suggestions for writing conclusions on pages 63–64.

6. **Does your title accurately reflect the content of the essay?** To improve the title, write a few words that "label" your essay, or look for key words in the thesis statement that might serve as part of a title. Also use the suggestions on page 64.

7. **Are your paragraphs well developed?** In a typical first draft, paragraphs may contain irrelevant information or lack a focused topic sentence. To evaluate your paragraph development, study each paragraph separately in conjunction with the thesis statement. Use the flowchart in Figure 4.2 to help you.

ESSAY IN PROGRESS 2

Evaluate the purpose, audience, and organization of the draft essay you wrote in Essay in Progress 3 in Chapter 3. Make notes on your graphic organizer or outline and directly on your paper.

ESSAY IN PROGRESS 3

Using the flowchart in Figure 4.1, evaluate the thesis statement, topic sentences, and evidence of your essay in progress. Make notes on your graphic organizer or outline and directly on your paper.

ESSAY IN PROGRESS 4

Using the flowchart in Figure 4.2, examine each paragraph of your essay in progress. Make notes on the draft copy of your essay.

QUESTIONS

REVISION STRATEGIES

1. **Does your essay have a thesis statement that identifies the topic and states your position or suggests your slant on the topic?** (To find out, state your thesis aloud without looking at the essay; then highlight the sentence in your draft essay that matches or is close to what you have just said. If you cannot find such a sentence, you have probably not written a well-focused thesis statement.)

 NO

- Reread your essay and answer this question: What one main point is most of this essay concerned with?
- Write a thesis statement that expresses that main point.
- Revise your paper to focus on that main point.
- Delete parts of the essay that do not support the thesis statement.

 YES

2. **Have you given your readers all the background information they need to understand your thesis?** (To find out, ask someone unfamiliar with your topic to read the essay, asking questions as he or she reads.)

 NO

- Answer *who, what, when, where, why*, and *how* questions to generate more background information.

 YES

3. **Have you presented enough convincing evidence to support your thesis?** (To find out, place checkmarks beside the evidence in the essay, and compare the evidence against the thesis.)

 NO

- Use prewriting strategies or do additional research to discover more supporting evidence.
- Evaluate this new evidence and add the most convincing evidence to your essay.

 YES

4. **Does each topic sentence logically connect to and support the thesis?** (To find out, underline each topic sentence. Read the thesis, and then read each underlined topic sentence. When the connection is not obvious, revision is needed.)

NO

- Rewrite the topic sentence so that it clearly supports the thesis.
- If necessary, broaden your thesis so that it encompasses all the supporting points.

 YES

(Continued)

FIGURE 4.1 *(Continued)*

QUESTIONS

5. **Is your evidence specific and detailed?** (To find out, go through your draft and reread where you placed checkmarks. Does each checkmarked item answer one of these questions: *Who? What? When? Where? Why? How?* If you have not placed a checkmark in a particular paragraph or have placed a checkmark by only one sentence or part of a sentence, you need to add more detailed evidence to that paragraph.)

NO →

REVISION STRATEGIES

- Name names, give dates, specify places.
- Use action verbs and descriptive language, including carefully chosen adjectives and adverbs.
- Answer *who, what, when, where, why,* and *how* questions to generate more detailed evidence.

FIGURE 4.2 Evaluating Your Paragraphs

QUESTIONS

1. **Does each paragraph have a clearly focused topic sentence that expresses the main point of the paragraph?** (To find out, underline the topic sentence in each paragraph of your draft. Then evaluate whether the topic sentence makes a statement that the rest of the paragraph supports.)

NO →

REVISION STRATEGIES

- Revise a sentence that is currently within the paragraph so that it clearly states the main point.
- Write a new sentence that states the one main point of the paragraph.

 YES

2. **Do all sentences in each paragraph support the topic sentence?** (To find out, read the topic sentence and then read each supporting sentence in turn. The topic sentence and each supporting sentence should fit together.)

NO →

- Revise supporting sentences to make their connection to the topic sentence clear.
- Delete any sentences that do not support the topic sentence.

 YES

QUESTIONS		REVISION STRATEGIES
3. Does the paragraph offer adequate explanation and supporting details? (To find out, place checkmarks beside supporting details. Is there other information the readers will want or need to know?)	NO →	• Add additional details if your paragraph seems skimpy. • Use the *who, what, when, where, why,* and *how* questions to generate the details you need. • Use the prewriting strategies in Chapter 2 to generate additional details.

YES ↓

| 4. Have you used transitional words and phrases to connect your sentences? (To find out, place brackets [ ] around transitional words and phrases. Be sure they separate main ideas. Read your paper aloud to see if it flows smoothly or sounds choppy.) | NO → | • Add transitional words and phrases where they are needed.

• Refer to the list of commonly used transitional expressions on page 60. |

YES ↓

| 5. Will it be clear to the readers how each paragraph connects to those that precede and follow it? (To find out, draw brackets [ ] around transitional sentences.) | NO → | • Add transitional sentences where they are needed. |

Working with Classmates as You Revise

Peer review is a process in which two or more students read and comment on each other's papers. Students might work together in class or outside of class or communicate via email or a computer network that links class members. Working with classmates is an excellent way to get ideas for improving your essays — and to discover how other students approach the writing process.

When other students review your essays, try to be open to criticism and new ideas. Don't feel obligated, however, to accept all the advice you are given. When you are the reviewer, use the Peer Review Questions on page 76 as the basis of your review. Be honest but tactful in your comments.

Peer Review Questions

1. What is the purpose of the paper?

2. Who is the intended audience?

3. Is the introduction fully developed?

4. What is the main point or thesis statement of the draft? Is it easy to identify?

5. Does the essay offer evidence to support each important point? Where is more evidence needed? Indicate specific paragraphs.

6. Is each paragraph clear and well organized?

7. Are transitions used to connect ideas within and between paragraphs?

8. Is the organization easy to follow? Point out places where the organization needs to be improved, and suggest ways to do so.

9. Does the conclusion draw the essay to a satisfying close?

10. What do you like about the draft?

11. What are its weaknesses, and how could they be eliminated? Underline or highlight sentences that are unclear or confusing.

ESSAY IN PROGRESS 5

Give your essay in progress to a classmate to read and review. Ask your reviewer to respond to the Peer Review Questions. Then revise your essay using the notes you took in response to Essay in Progress activities 2–4 and your reviewer's suggestions.

Editing and Proofreading

After revising your essay for content and organization, you are ready to edit and proofread it. Try to make the essay as effective and as error-free as possible. After all, careless sentences and grammatical errors detract from your credibility as a writer. They also suggest that you have not approached the task seriously, and that is not the impression you want to give to your writing instructor or to your audience.

Improving Your Sentences and Word Choice

Up to this point, you have focused on developing your ideas. Now, as you move to the editing stage, you will evaluate the effectiveness of the sentences and words you chose to express those ideas. An essay with good ideas will be ineffective if its sentences are vague and imprecise or if its words suggest an inappropriate tone or meaning. The two sections below offer suggestions for strenghtening and improving sentences and word choice.

Improving Your Sentences

To improve your sentences and make them more interesting, use the following questions.

1. **Are your sentences concise?**
   - Look for places where you can use fewer words without changing the meaning.

     ► ~~In light of the fact that~~ *Since* computer technology changes ~~every month or so,~~ *monthly* software upgrades are ~~what everybody has to do.~~ *necessary*

   - Avoid saying the same thing twice (redundancy).

     ► ~~My decision to choose the field of~~ *Choosing* accounting as my major will lead to steady employment.

   - Cut unnecessary phrases and clauses.

     ► ~~It is my opinion that~~ *F*ast food restaurants should post nutritional information for each menu item.

2. **Are your sentences varied?**
   - Use short **simple sentences** — comprising one **independent clause** and no **dependent clauses** — for emphasis and clarity. Don't use too many of these, or your writing will sound choppy.

     ► **Credit card fraud is rampant. Many people worry about it. Some don't buy items online.**

   - Use **compound sentences** — two or more independent clauses joined together — to connect equally important ideas.

     ► **Leon asked a question, <u>and</u> the entire class was surprised.**

     ► **Graffiti was scrawled on the subway walls<u>;</u> passersby ignored it.**

   - Use **complex sentences** — one independent clause and at least one dependent clause joined together — to show how one idea depends on the other. When the dependent clause comes first, it is followed by a comma.

     ► **Because the dam broke, the village flooded.**

   - Vary your placement of **modifiers**, words that describe or limit another part of the sentence.

MODIFIERS FIRST:	<u>Tired and depressed</u>, the divers left the scene of the accident.

An **independent clause** contains both a subject and a verb and expresses a complete thought. It can stand alone as a sentence. A **dependent clause** contains both a subject and a verb but does not express a complete thought. It cannot stand alone as a sentence.

MODIFIERS
IN THE MIDDLE: The divers, <u>tired and depressed</u>, left the scene of the
accident.

MODIFIERS
LAST: After leaving the scene of the accident, the divers looked
<u>tired and depressed</u>.

3. **Do your sentences have strong, active verbs?**

- Replace *to be* verbs (*is, was, were, has been*, and so on) with verbs that are more descriptive.
    - ▸ The puppy <u>was</u> afraid of the thunder.
    - ▸ The puppy <u>whimpered</u> and <u>quivered</u> during the thunderstorm.

- Replace other general verbs (*feels, became, seems, appears*, and so on) with verbs that are more specific.
    - ▸ The child <u>looked</u> frightened as she boarded the bus.
    - ▸ The child <u>trembled</u> and <u>clung</u> to her sister as she boarded the bus.

- Avoid sentences in which the subject does not perform the action.
    - ▸ <u>It was claimed</u> that the motorist failed to yield the right of way. (Who made the claim is not stated.)
    - ▸ <u>The cyclist claimed</u> that the motorist failed to yield the right of way.

4. **Are your sentences parallel in structure?** In other words, are similar ideas expressed in similar grammatical form?

- Keep nouns in a series parallel.
    - ▸ A thesis statement, ~~that is clear,~~ *clear* strong supporting paragraphs, and ~~a~~ *an interesting* conclusion ~~that should be interesting~~ are all elements of a well-written essay.

- Keep adjectives in a series parallel.
    - ▸ The youngsters were rowdy and ~~making a great deal of noise~~ *noisy*.

- Keep verbs in a series parallel.
    - ▸ The sports fans jumped and ~~were applauding~~ *applauded*.

- Keep other similar ideas within a sentence parallel.
    - ▸ The parents were pleased ~~about~~ *that* their children ~~playing~~ *played* congenially and that everyone enjoyed the sandbox.
    - ▸ It is usually better to study for an exam over a period of time than ~~cramming~~ *to cram* the night before.

EXERCISE 4.1

Using the editing suggestions in the preceding section, improve the following sentences.

Make these sentences concise.

1. In many cases, workers are forced to use old equipment that needs replacing due to the fact that there is a policy that does not permit replacement.

2. The president of Warehouse Industries has the ability and the power to decide who should and who should not be hired and who should and who should not be fired.

Combine each sentence pair into one compound or complex sentence.

3. A day-care center may look respectable.

   Parents assume a day-care center is safe and run well.

4. Restaurants are often fined or shut down for minor hygiene violations.

   Day-care centers are rarely fined or closed down for hygiene violations.

Add modifiers to these sentences.

5. The divers jumped into the chilly water.

6. The exam was more challenging than we expected.

Make the subject the performer of the action; add a subject if necessary.

7. Songs about peace were composed by folk singers in the 1960s.

8. The exam was thought to be difficult because it covered thirteen chapters.

Eliminate problems with parallelism.

9. The career counselor advised Althea to take several math courses and that she should also register for at least one computer course.

10. Driving to Boston is as expensive as it is to take the train.

Improving Your Word Choice

Each word in your essay contributes to or detracts from the meaning. Be sure to check your choice of words to see if they are the best ones for your purpose and audience. Use the following tips as a guide.

1. Replace any words that convey the wrong tone — that are too formal or too casual.

   TOO CASUAL: **This guy in my history class is a psycho; he never shuts up and he drives us nuts.**

   REVISED: **A man in my history class is always talking and interrupting; he annoys many students.**

2. Replace any words that don't convey the connotation — the feeling or attitude—you intend.

Connotation is different from **denotation** — a word's dictionary definition.

> *firmly*
> ► Sara ~~stubbornly~~ denied her daughter's request.
>   ∧

3. Replace general words with specific words.

> *crimson and white petunias*
> ► The ~~red flowers~~ were blooming in our yard.

Similes and metaphors are **figures of speech** — comparisons that make sense imaginatively but not literally.

4. Use fresh, appropriate comparisons. A **simile** is a direct comparison of two things that uses the word *like* or *as*. A **metaphor** is an implied comparison that does not use *like* or *as*.

  SIMILE: The child acts like a tiger.

  METAPHOR: The child is a tiger.

5. Avoid clichés, which are overused or trite expressions.

> *developed an acute case of food poisoning*
> ► After eating the raw oysters, I ~~felt sick as a dog.~~
>   ∧

6. Replace any weak verb-noun combinations that make a sentence wordy.

> *evaluated*
> ► The professor ~~made an evaluation of~~ her students' progress.
>   ∧

EXERCISE 4.2

Using the suggestions in the preceding section, complete the following exercises.

Revise the following informal sentences to make them more formal.

  1. The get-together starts this afternoon, so we need to start cleaning up this disaster now.

  2. I don't know why he isn't going, but I think Pedro is crazy to miss it.

Describe the different connotations of the words in each group.

  3. crowd/mob/gathering

  4. display/show/expose

Revise by adding concrete, specific details.

  5. The book I took on vacation was exciting reading.

  6. At the crime scene, the reporter questioned the witnesses.

Invent fresh figures of speech for the following.

  7. a man and woman obviously in love

  8. a lengthy supermarket line

ESSAY IN PROGRESS 6

For your essay in progress, evaluate and edit your sentences and word choice.

Common Errors to Avoid

This section describes seven common errors and provides tips on how to correct them. Be on the lookout for these errors as you revise and edit your essays.

For exercises on these errors, visit Exercise Central at bedford stmartins.com.

Error 1: Sentence Fragments

A **sentence fragment** looks like a sentence, but it is not. A fragment lacks one or more essential parts (such as a subject or a complete verb) or does not express a complete thought. To revise a sentence fragment, try these two general approaches.

1. **Attach the fragment to a nearby sentence, or**
2. **Rewrite the fragment as a complete sentence.**

Some fragments can be corrected either way:

► Jenny speaks Italian fluently. ~~And~~ *and* reads French well.

► Jenny speaks Italian fluently. ~~And~~ *She also* reads French well.

The following examples show several kinds of corrected fragments:

► The college *is* installing a furnace to heat the library.

► I plan to transfer next semester, ~~To~~ *to* live closer to home.

► Annie has always wanted to become an orthopedist. ~~That~~ *— that* is, a bone specialist.

► Until Dr. Jonas Salk invented a vaccine, ~~Polio~~ *, polio* was a serious threat to public health.

► The dodo is an extinct bird. ~~That~~ *It* disappeared in the seventeenth century.

Error 2: Run-on Sentences and Comma Splices

A **run-on sentence** (also known as a **fused sentence**) occurs when two or more independent clauses "run into" each other with no punctuation mark or connecting word. A **comma splice** occurs when two or more independent clauses (see p. 77) are joined only with a comma.

There are four easy ways to correct a run-on sentence or comma splice. Choose the method that best fits your sentence or intended meaning.

1. **Create two separate sentences.**

RUN-ON
SENTENCE: A résumé should be directed to a specific audience. ~~it~~ *It* should emphasize the applicant's potential value to the company.

COMMA SPLICE: To evaluate a charity, you should start by examining its

goals, *then* you should investigate its management practices.

2. **Join the clauses with a semicolon (;).**

COMMA SPLICE: Studies have shown that male and female managers

have different leadership styles, as a result, workers may respond differently to each.

3. **Join the clauses with a comma and a coordinating conjunction.**

Coordinating conjunctions (and, but, or, nor, for, so, yet) connect sentence elements that are of equal importance.

COMMA SPLICE: Some educators support home schooling, *but* others oppose it vehemently.

4. **Make one clause dependent.**

RUN-ON
SENTENCE: *Because* Facial expressions are very revealing, they are an important communication tool.

Error 3: Subject-Verb Agreement

Subjects and verbs must agree in person and number: *I drive, you drive, she drives*. **Person** refers to the forms *I* or *we* (first person), *you* (second person), and *he, she, it,* and *they* (third person). **Number** shows whether a word refers to one thing (singular) or more than one thing (plural). Here are three ways to revise common errors in subject-verb agreement.

1. **Make sure the verb agrees with the subject, not with words that come between the subject and verb.**

   ▶ The *number* of farmworkers *has* remained constant over several decades.

2. **Use a plural verb when two or more subjects are joined by *and*.**

   ▶ A dot and a dash represents the letter *A* in Morse code.

Indefinite pronouns refer to people, places, or things in general.

3. **Use a singular verb with most indefinite pronouns, such as *anyone, everyone, each, every, neither, no one,* and *something*.**

   ▶ Neither of the candidates *has* ~~have~~ run for office before.

   Other indefinite pronouns, such as *several, both, many,* and *few,* take a plural verb.

▶ Several of you jogs at least three miles a day.

Some indefinite pronouns, such as *all, any, more, most, some,* and *none,* take either a singular or a plural verb, depending on the noun they refer to.

goes
▶ Most of the water ~~go~~ into this kettle.
        ∧

▶ Some of the children in the study chooses immediate rather than delayed rewards.

Error 4: Pronoun Reference

A **pronoun** — a word that takes the place of a noun — should refer clearly to its **antecedent**, the noun or pronoun it substitutes for. Here are three ways to check your pronoun references.

1. **Make sure each pronoun refers clearly to one antecedent.**

   ▶ The hip-hop radio station battled the alternative rock station for the

   the alternative station
   highest ratings. Eventually, ~~it~~ won.
                                ∧

2. **Be sure to check for vague uses of *they, it,* and *you.***

   a Web page
   ▶ On the Internet, ~~they~~ claimed that an asteroid would collide with the earth.
                       ∧

   people often talk
   ▶ In Florida, ~~you often hear~~ about hurricane threats of previous years.
                 ∧

3. **Make sure the pronouns *who, whom, which,* and *that* refer to clear, specific nouns.**

   These storms make
   ▶ Lake-effect storms hit cities along the Great Lakes. ~~That makes~~ winter travel treacherous.
                                                           ∧

Error 5: Pronoun-Antecedent Agreement

Pronouns and antecedents must agree in **person**, **number**, and **gender**. Here are a few guidelines to follow when you are unsure of which pronoun or antecedent to use.

1. **Use singular pronouns to refer to singular indefinite pronouns, such as *anybody, each, either, everyone, none,* and *someone.***

   ▶ *Each* of the experiments produced *its* desired result.

If the pronoun and antecedent do not agree, change either the pronoun or the indefinite pronoun to which it refers.

People
▶ ~~Everyone~~ should check *their* credit card statements monthly.
  ∧

> *Everyone* should check ~~*their*~~ credit card statement monthly.
  ^his or her^

An alternative is to eliminate the pronouns entirely.

> *No one* should lose ~~*their*~~ job because of family responsibilities.
  ^a^

2. **Use a plural pronoun to refer to most compound antecedents joined by *and*.**

> *The walrus <u>and</u> the carpenter* ate *their* oysters greedily.

Exception: When the singular antecedents joined by *and* refer to the same person, place, or thing, use a singular pronoun.

> As a *father <u>and</u> a husband, <u>he</u>* is a success.

Exception: When *each* or *every* comes before the antecedent, use a singular pronoun.

> <u>*Every*</u> *nut and bolt* was in <u>*its*</u> place for the inspection.

Error 6: Confusing Shifts

A **shift** is a sudden, unexpected change in point of view, verb tense, voice, or mood that may confuse your readers. The four tips that follow will help you identify and correct confusing shifts.

1. **Refer to yourself, your audience, and the people you are writing about in a consistent way.**

> I discovered that ~~you~~ could touch some of the museum exhibits.
  ^I^

> When people study a foreign language, ~~you~~ also learn about another culture.
  ^they^

2. **Maintain a consistent verb tense, unless the meaning requires you to change tenses.**

> The virus *mutates* so quickly that it *develops* a resistance to most vaccines.

> Even though I have a good memory, yesterday I ~~forget~~ my mother's birthday.
  ^forgot^

3. **Use a consistent voice.**

Needless shifts between the active voice (the subject *performs* the action) and passive voice (the subject *receives* the action) can disorient readers and create wordy sentences.

> ~~One~~ group of volunteers ~~was given~~ a placebo, and ~~the researchers~~ treated another group with the new drug.
  ^The researchers gave one^ ^they^

To change a sentence from the passive voice to the active voice (see p. 78), make the performer of the action the subject of the sentence.

PASSIVE: The restraining order was signed by the judge.

ACTIVE: The judge signed the restraining order.

4. Use a consistent mood throughout a paragraph or an essay. Mood indicates whether the sentence states a fact or asks a question (**indicative mood**), gives a command or direction (**imperative mood**), or expresses a condition contrary to fact, a wish, or a suggestion (**subjunctive mood**). In the following paragraph, the original version contains shifts between the indicative and imperative moods.

> You shouldn't expect to learn ballroom dancing immediately, and remember that even Fred Astaire had to start somewhere. First, find a qualified instructor. Then, you should not be embarrassed even if everyone else seems more graceful than you are. Finally, keep your goal in mind, and you need to practice, practice, practice.

Error 7: Misplaced and Dangling Modifiers

A **modifier** is a word or group of words that describes or limits another part of a sentence. The tips that follow will help you correct misplaced or dangling modifiers, both of which can be confusing.

1. Place modifiers close to the words they describe. A **misplaced modifier** is in the wrong place in the sentence.

> ▸ The mayor ^angrily^ chided the pedestrians for jaywalking ~~angrily~~.

> ▸ The press reacted ^with horror^ to the story leaked from the Pentagon ~~with horror~~.

2. Revise a dangling modifier by rewriting the sentence. A **dangling modifier** is a word or phrase that does not modify anything in a sentence. Instead, it *seems* to modify something inappropriate in the sentence. Most dangling modifiers appear at the beginning or end of sentences.

> ▸ After ~~singing~~ ^Pavarotti sang^ a thrilling aria, the crowd surged toward the stage.

The original sentence suggests that the crowd sang the aria.

> ▸ Laying an average of ten eggs a day, the neighboring farmer ^his prize chickens give^ ~~is~~ proud of his ^reason to be^ henhouse.

The original sentence suggests that the farmer lays eggs.

Proofreading Your Essay

Once you are satisfied with your edited essay as a whole, you are ready for the final step of the writing process: *proofreading*. At this point your goals are to catch and correct surface errors — in grammar, punctuation, spelling, and mechanics — as well as keyboarding or typographical errors. Eliminating such errors will help create a favorable impression in readers — both of the essay and of you as its writer.

Print out a clean double-spaced copy of your essay specifically for proofreading. Do not attempt to work with a previously marked-up copy or on a computer screen. Then use the following suggestions to produce an error-free essay.

Guidelines for Proofreading

1. **Read your essay several times.** Each time focus on *one* error type — spelling, punctuation, grammar, mechanics, and so on.
2. **Read your essay backward.** Reading from the last sentence to the first will help you concentrate on spotting errors.
3. **Use the spell-check and grammar-check functions cautiously.** These functions can help you spot some kinds of errors, but they are not a reliable substitute for careful proofreading. A spell-check program, for example, cannot detect the difference in meaning between *there* and *their* or *to* and *too*.
4. **Read your essay aloud.** Reading aloud slowly will help you catch missing words, errors in verb tense, and errors in the singular or plural forms of nouns.
5. **Ask a classmate to proofread your paper.** Another reader may spot errors you have overlooked.

ESSAY IN PROGRESS 7

Proofread the essay you edited in Essay in Progress 6. Use the preceding guidelines to catch and correct errors in spelling, punctuation, grammar, and mechanics.

Students Write

After writing her first draft, which appears in Chapter 3 (pp. 66–68), Julie Bohet used the guidelines and revision flowcharts in this chapter to help her decide what to revise. For example, she realized that her essay actually focused on two topics — playing music and listening to music. She decided to focus more on her piano playing and to delete the material on the value of listening to music. You will see in her revised essay that in the introduction Julie briefly recognizes the value of listening to music but then she moves on to the importance of playing music. Julie also asked a classmate to review her essay. Using her own analysis and her classmate's suggestions, Julie revised her first draft. A portion of her revised draft, with her revisions marked, follows.

Revised Draft

Today we can access music in seconds. Whether on the Internet, CDs, or the radio,

We can listen to

music has become a vital element of everyone's lives. ~~No matter~~ popular music,

at any time, switching from Billy Joel to Beethoven with the turn of a dial.

hip-hop, rap, techno, house, rock, jazz, or classical , ~~it would be hard to find a person~~

In addition to entertaining us, listening to music helps us relax and remember

~~who does not have strong opinions about music and listens to the music they like on a~~

important events in our lives -- our first love, graduation, or a vacation with good friends.

~~regular basis.~~ For me, music is even more important since I experience it not by just

on the piano   *Being a musician*

listening to it, but on a deeper level ~~than most listeners~~ by playing it. ~~Both listening to~~

has affected my life because it has challenged me to develop my musical

~~and playing music has given me many valuable experiences and created a~~

abilities and to communicate my emotions with an audience through performance.

~~focus in my life.~~

Before Julie submitted her final draft, she read the essay several more times, editing it for sentence structure and word choice. She also proofread it once to catch errors in grammar and punctuation as well as typographical errors. The final version of Julie's essay follows.

Final Draft

The Language of Music

Julie Bohet

Today we can access music in seconds. Whether on the Internet, CDs, or the radio, music has become a vital element of most people's lives. We can listen to hip-hop, rap, techno, house, rock, jazz, or classical at any time, switching from Billy Joel to Beethoven with the turn of a dial. In addition to entertaining us, listening to music helps us relax and remember important events in our lives -- our first love, graduation, or a vacation with good friends. For me, music is even more important since I experience it not by just listening to it, but on a deeper level by playing it on the piano. In fact, being a musician has affected my life because it has challenged me to develop my musical abilities and to communicate my emotions with an audience through performance.

Although I started taking piano lessons at the age of nine, it was during high school that I became seriously interested in playing classical music. I began to challenge myself to play things beyond my technical and musical capabilities. Each time I mastered a difficult piece, I felt encouraged to learn other challenging pieces. In fact, part of the fun was proving to my teacher that I could learn pieces by Chopin and Rachmaninoff that she deemed too difficult for me. While these accomplishments gave me confidence in approaching different types of music, performing taught me how to communicate with an audience.

During a concert at a local museum, I began to recognize the importance of communicating with the audience. I was playing "What Child Is This" and "Memory" from the musical *Cats*. Because this was my first performance for the general public, I was very nervous. The first piece went well, but when I played "Memory," I began making a lot of mistakes. Panicked and embarrassed, I suddenly stopped playing. But my stopping only made the situation worse, as the audience looked at me in silence. I was very upset when I left the concert, and I remember crying during the whole car ride home. This experience taught me that while performing I shouldn't concentrate on my mistakes but should keep playing the music no matter what happens. Since then, I have had some equally embarrassing performances, but by playing through the piece I have been able to shield my feelings of panic, thereby making the mistakes less noticeable to the audience. In time, these experiences -- both good and bad -- have helped me to become a better and more confident performer.

Performing live has also taught me the importance of conveying emotion through my playing. Learning to play music is like learning to speak another language: I developed the muscles in my tongue (or fingers) to form the syllables and words; then I learned the basic letters (notes) and vocabulary (chords/harmonics) and sentences (phrases) until I became adept at reading and speaking this new language. However, despite my mastery of these technical skills, I still needed to learn the nuances of expression. That's why, even now, having mastered the basic skills of playing, I work very hard to interpret what the composer is expressing so that the music becomes real for the audience and makes a lasting emotional impact. Because on a certain level musicians must remain loyal to what the composer has written, interpreting the music is the most challenging part of performing. It is also the most rewarding, though, as I am able to infuse the piece with my own sense of meaning. This is what gives music its human quality and what makes it real and valuable to the listener.

I've learned how to give my performances this human quality by drawing upon my own emotions. This is not to say that I play a dark piece when I am angry or a cheerful piece when I am happy, but rather that through performance I have learned to become an actor. Composers give musicians some direction in terms of sound, rhythm, volume, and other musical elements, but it is up to me to interpret the music, much as an actor interprets a script. This interpretation gives the music its human quality, moving beyond the musical score to connect emotionally with the audience. My job as a musician is to convey the composer's thoughts and emotions as I feel them for myself at that very moment.

Listening to music is vital to many people, but to perform it for others is a larger calling. Performing for an audience allows me to share my personal connection to the composer and the music with others; hopefully, for at least a moment or two, the audience will feel the same thing that I am feeling. Such a moment occurred after a performance I did of Debussy's *Clair de Lune*. A member of the audience approached me and said that she had felt so emotionally overwhelmed by my performance that it brought tears to her eyes. Having someone connect with what I am playing in such a powerful way makes all the challenges of mastering the piano worthwhile.

Part ◆ Two

Readings for Writers

Narration: Recounting Events

WRITING QUICK START

Homelessness is a serious national problem with many causes. The photograph below shows a homeless man. Imagine the events that might have caused him to become homeless.

Did he lose his job? If so, why? Does he suffer from alcoholism, drug addiction, or mental illness? Does he have any family who might help him? Working by yourself or with a classmate, construct a series of events that may have led up to this situation. Then write a summary of the events you imagined.

What Is Narration?

A **narrative** relates a series of events, real or imaginary, in an organized sequence. It is a story, but *a story that makes a point*. Today you probably exchange family stories, tell jokes, read biographies or novels, and watch television sitcoms or dramas — all of which are examples of the narrative form. In addition, narratives are an important part of the writing you will do in college and in your career, as these examples illustrate.

- In a *sociology* class, as part of a discussion of authority figures, your instructor asks the class to describe situations in which they found themselves in conflict with an authority figure.
- Your job in *sales* involves frequent business travel, and your company requires you to submit a report for each trip describing the meetings you attended, your contacts with current clients, and new sales leads.

Narratives provide human interest, spark our curiosity, and draw us close to the storyteller. The following narrative relates the author's experience with racial profiling.

Right Place, Wrong Face

Alton Fitzgerald White

Alton Fitzgerald White (b. 1964) majored in musical theatre at Cincinnati's College Conservatory of Music. His Broadway career took off when he was cast in *Miss Saigon* in 1991, followed by parts in *The Who's Tommy* and *The Lion King*. From 1998 to 2000 he played the role of Coalhouse Walker Jr. in the Broadway musical *Ragtime*; the character is a black New Yorker in the early twentieth century who snaps under the strain of racist mistreatment, with tragic results. While appearing as Coalhouse Walker, the actor himself underwent a traumatic experience in New York City.

White wrote the following essay about his ordeal. As you read his narrative, which was published in 1999 in *The Nation* and in 2000 in the *Utne Reader*, pay attention to the way he makes his point by presenting a series of events that build to a climax.

Introduction:
background about
White's upbringing

As the youngest of five girls and two boys growing up in Cincinnati, I was   1
raised to believe that if I worked hard, was a good person, and always told the truth, the world would be my oyster. I was raised to be a gentleman and learned that these qualities would bring me respect.

While one has to earn respect, consideration is something owed to every human being. On Friday, June 16, 1999, when I was wrongfully arrested at my Harlem apartment building, my perception of everything I had learned as a young man was forever changed — not only because I wasn't given even a second to use the manners my parents taught me, but mostly because the police, whom I'd always naively thought were supposed to serve and protect me, were actually hunting me.

I had planned a pleasant day. The night before was a payday, plus I had received a standing ovation after portraying the starring role of Coalhouse Walker Jr. in the Broadway musical *Ragtime*. It is a role that requires not only talent but also an honest emotional investment of the morals and lessons I learned as a child.

Coalhouse Walker Jr. is a victim (an often misused word, but in this case true) of overt racism. His story is every black man's nightmare. He is hardworking, successful, talented, charismatic, friendly, and polite. Perfect prey for someone with authority and not even a fraction of those qualities. On that Friday afternoon, I became a real-life Coalhouse Walker. Nothing could have prepared me for it. Not even stories told to me by other black men who had suffered similar injustices.

Friday for me usually means a trip to the bank, errands, the gym, dinner, and then off to the theater. On this particular day, I decided to break my pattern of getting up and running right out of the house. Instead, I took my time, slowed my pace, and splurged by making strawberry pancakes. Before I knew it, it was 2:45; my bank closes at 3:30, leaving me less than 45 minutes to get to midtown Manhattan on the train. I was pressed for time but in a relaxed, blessed state of mind. When I walked through the lobby of my building, I noticed two light-skinned Hispanic men I'd never seen before. Not thinking much of it, I continued on to the vestibule, which is separated from the lobby by a locked door.

As I approached the exit, I saw people in uniforms rushing toward the door. I sped up to open it for them. I thought they might be paramedics, since many of the building's occupants are elderly. It wasn't until I had opened the door and greeted them that I recognized that they were police officers. Within seconds, I was told to "hold it"; they had received a call about young Hispanics with guns. I was told to get against the wall. I was searched, stripped of my backpack, put on my knees, handcuffed, and told to be quiet when I tried to ask questions.

With me were three other innocent black men who had been on their way to their U-Haul. They were moving into the apartment beneath mine, and I had just bragged to them about how safe the building was. One of these gentlemen got off his knees, still hand-cuffed, and unlocked the door for the officers to get into the lobby where the two strangers were standing.

2 — Thesis statement that also summarizes the action

3 — Background Information about White

4 — Comparison between what happens to him and what the character he plays experiences

5 — Sets the scene for action to begin

State of mind prior to action is established

6 — Action begins

7

Instead of thanking or even acknowledging us, they led us out the door past our neighbors, who were all but begging the police in our defense.

Tension builds

The four of us were put into cars with the two strangers and taken to the precinct station at 165th and Amsterdam. The police automatically linked us, with no questions and no regard for our character or our lives. No consideration was given to where we were going or why. Suppose an ailing relative was waiting upstairs, while I ran out for her medication? Or young children, who'd been told that Daddy was running to the corner store for milk and would be right back? My new neighbors weren't even allowed to lock their apartment or check on the U-Haul. 8

Tension continues

Realizes how naive he was

After we were lined up in the station, the younger of the two Hispanic men was identified as an experienced criminal, and drug residue was found in a pocket of the other. I now realize how naive I was to think that the police would then uncuff me, apologize for their mistake, and let me go. Instead, they continued to search my backpack, questioned me, and put me in jail with the criminals. 9

The rest of the nearly five-hour ordeal was like a horrible dream. I was handcuffed, strip-searched, taken in and out for questioning. The officers told me that they knew exactly who I was, knew I was in *Ragtime*, and that in fact they already had the men they wanted. 10

How then could they keep me there, or have brought me there in the first place? I was told it was standard procedure. As if the average law-abiding citizen knows what that is and can dispute it. From what I now know, "standard procedure" is something that every citizen, black and white, needs to learn, and fast. 11

Expresses outrage

I felt completely powerless. Why, do you think? Here I was, young, pleasant, and successful, in good physical shape, dressed in clean athletic attire. I was carrying a backpack containing a substantial paycheck and a deposit slip, on my way to the bank. Yet after hours and hours I was sitting at a desk with two officers who not only couldn't tell me why I was there but seemed determined to find something on me, to the point of making me miss my performance. 12

Identifies himself as victim of racial profiling

It was because I am a black man! 13

White analyzes the experience

I sat in that cell crying silent tears of disappointment and injustice with the realization of how many innocent black men are convicted for no reason. When I was handcuffed, my first instinct had been to pull away out of pure insult and violation as a human being. Thank God I was calm enough to do what they said. When I was thrown in jail with the criminals and strip-searched, I somehow knew to put my pride aside, be quiet, and do exactly what I was told, hating it but coming to terms with the fact that in this situation I was a victim. They had guns! 14

Climax

Before I was finally let go, exhausted, humiliated, embarrassed, and still in shock, I was led to a room and given a pseudo-apology. I was told 15 that I was at the wrong place at the wrong time. My reply? "I was where I live."

Everything I learned growing up in Cincinnati has been shattered. 16 Life will never be the same.

Conclusion: reference to thesis statement

Characteristics of Narrative Essays

As you can see from "Right Place, Wrong Face," a narrative does not merely report events; a narrative is not a transcript of a conversation or a news report. Although it does include events, conversations, and vivid descriptions, a narrative is more than a list; it is a story that conveys a particular meaning. It presents actions and details that build toward a climax, the point at which the conflict of the narrative is resolved. Most narratives use dialogue to present selected portions of conversations that move the story along.

Narratives Make a Point

A narrative makes a point or supports a thesis by telling readers about an event or a series of events. The point may be to describe the significance of the events, make an observation, or present new information. Often the writer will state the point directly, using an explicit thesis statement, but at other times he or she may leave the main point unstated, using an implied thesis. In "Right Place, Wrong Face," White states his main point clearly in paragraph 2: "when I was wrongfully arrested at my Harlem apartment building, my perception of everything I had learned as a young man was forever changed."

The following excerpt is from a brief narrative, written by a student, based on the photo at the start of this chapter. After imagining the series of events that might have brought the woman to homelessness, the student wrote this concluding paragraph.

Karen is a kind, older woman in an unfortunate circumstance who wants nothing more than to live in a house or an apartment instead of on the street. Unfortunately, thousands of Americans, through no fault of their own, share her hopeless plight. The homeless can be found on street corners, in parks, and under bridges -- even in the coldest months of winter. Too often, passersby shun them and their need for a helping hand. They either look away, repulsed by the conditions in which the homeless live, or gaze at them with disapproving looks and walk away, wrongly assuming that such people live this way out of choice rather than necessity.

Notice that the writer makes an explicit point about the homeless and about people's attitudes toward them. Note, too, how the details support the writer's point — that people wrongly assume that the homeless choose to live this way.

Narratives Convey Action and Detail

A narrative presents a detailed account of an event or a series of events. In other words, it is like a camera lens that zooms in and makes readers feel like they can see the details and experience the action. Writers of narratives can involve readers in several ways: through *dialogue*, with *physical description*, and by *recounting action*. In "Right Place, Wrong Face," both physical description and the recounting of events build suspense and make the story come alive. Readers can easily visualize the scene at White's apartment building and the situation at the police station.

Narratives Present a Conflict and Create Tension

An effective narrative presents a **conflict** — such as a struggle, question, or problem — and works toward its resolution. The conflict can be between participants or between a participant and some external force, such as a law, value, moral, or act of nature. In "Right Place, Wrong Face," there is a conflict between the way White was raised and the way he is treated by the police officers. **Tension** is the suspense created as the story unfolds and as the reader wonders how the conflict will be resolved. White first suggests tension in the third paragraph: "I had planned a pleasant day" implies that what was planned did not materialize. The tension builds in paragraphs 7–14, and the conflict is resolved in paragraph 15 when White is released. The point just before the conflict is resolved is called the **climax**. The main point of the story — how White's life is changed by the incident of racial profiling — is restated at the conclusion of the narrative.

Narratives Sequence Events

The events in a narrative must be arranged in an order that is easy for readers to follow. Often, but not always, a narrative presents events in chronological order. "Right Place, Wrong Face" uses this straightforward sequence. At other times, writers may use the techniques of flashback and foreshadowing to make their point. A **flashback** returns the reader to events that took place in the past, while **foreshadowing** hints at events that will happen in the future. Both techniques are used frequently in drama, fiction, and film. A soap opera, for instance, might open with a scene in which a woman is lying in a hospital bed, flash back to a scene showing the accident that put her there, and then return to the scene in the hospital. A television show might begin with a wedding reception that foreshadows problems the bride and groom will have in the future. When used sparingly, these techniques can build interest and add variety to a narrative, especially a lengthy chronological account.

Narratives Use Dialogue

Just as people reveal much about themselves by what they say and how they say it, dialogue can reveal a great deal about the characters in a narrative. In fact, dialogue is often used to dramatize the action, emphasize the conflict, and reveal the personalities or motives of the key participants in a narrative. Keep in mind that dialogue should resemble everyday speech; it should sound natural, not forced or formal. Consider these examples.

TOO FORMAL: Eva said to her grandfather, "I enjoy talking with you. The stories you tell of your early life in Mexico are very interesting. I wish I could visit there with you."

NATURAL: Eva said to her grandfather, "Your stories about Mexico when you were a kid are great. I'd love to go there with you."

Narratives Are Told from a Particular Point of View

Many narratives use the first-person point of view, in which the key participant speaks directly to the reader ("*I* first realized the problem when . . ."). Other narratives use the third-person point of view, in which an unknown storyteller describes what happens to the key participants ("The problem began when Saul Overtone . . .").

Both the first and third person offer distinct advantages. The first person allows the narrator to assume a personal tone and to speak directly to the audience, easily expressing his or her attitudes, feelings, interpretation, and commentary. When you narrate an event that occurred in your own life, as White does in "Right Place, Wrong Face," the first person is probably your best choice.

The third-person point of view gives the narrator more distance from the action and generally provides a more objective perspective than the first-person point of view. It also allows the narrator to reveal insights about a character's actions or personality, as can be seen in the following third-person narrative taken from a Hispanic folktale titled "La Llorona" (The Crying Woman).

People said Maria was certainly the prettiest girl in New Mexico. She might even be the most beautiful girl in the world. But because Maria was so beautiful, she thought she was better than everyone else.

Maria came from a hard-working family, and they had one of the finest homes in Santa Fe. They provided her with pretty clothes to wear. But she was never satisfied. She thought she deserved far better things.

JOE HAYES, *The Day It Snowed Tortillas*

Visualizing a Narrative Essay

It is often helpful to see the content and organization of an essay in simplified, visual form. The graphic organizer in Figure 5.1 is a visual diagram of the basic structure of a narrative. A graphic organizer can help you structure your

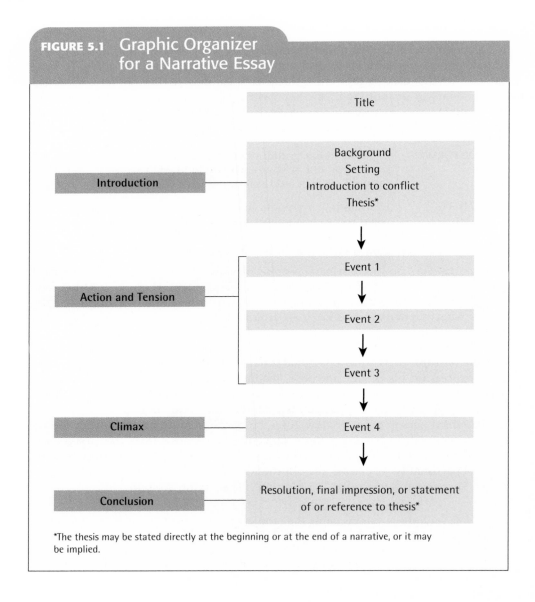

FIGURE 5.1 Graphic Organizer for a Narrative Essay

Title

Introduction —— Background / Setting / Introduction to conflict / Thesis*

Action and Tension —— Event 1 → Event 2 → Event 3

Climax —— Event 4

Conclusion —— Resolution, final impression, or statement of or reference to thesis*

*The thesis may be stated directly at the beginning or at the end of a narrative, or it may be implied.

writing, analyze a reading, and recall key events as you generate ideas for an essay.

Use this graphic organizer as a basic model, but keep in mind that narrative essays vary in organization and may lack one or more of the elements included in the model. Figure 5.2 is a graphic organizer based on the reading "Right Place, Wrong Face."

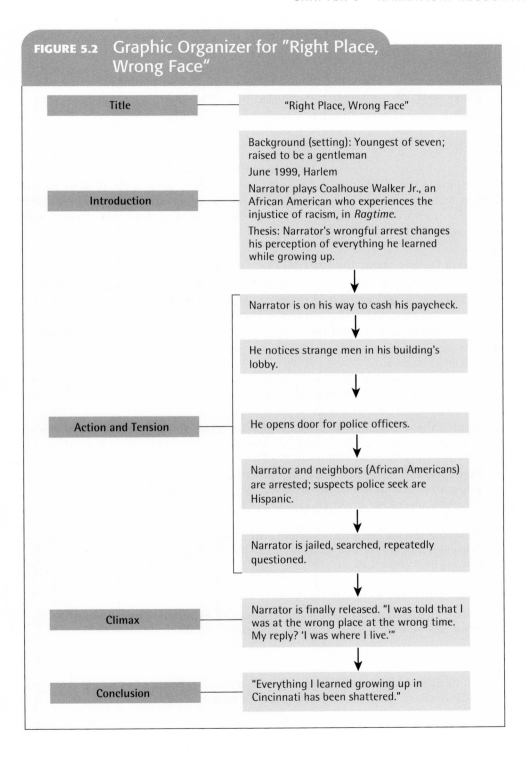

FIGURE 5.2 Graphic Organizer for "Right Place, Wrong Face"

| Title | "Right Place, Wrong Face" |

Introduction

Background (setting): Youngest of seven; raised to be a gentleman

June 1999, Harlem

Narrator plays Coalhouse Walker Jr., an African American who experiences the injustice of racism, in *Ragtime*.

Thesis: Narrator's wrongful arrest changes his perception of everything he learned while growing up.

Action and Tension

Narrator is on his way to cash his paycheck.

He notices strange men in his building's lobby.

He opens door for police officers.

Narrator and neighbors (African Americans) are arrested; suspects police seek are Hispanic.

Narrator is jailed, searched, repeatedly questioned.

Climax

Narrator is finally released. "I was told that I was at the wrong place at the wrong time. My reply? 'I was where I live.'"

Conclusion

"Everything I learned growing up in Cincinnati has been shattered."

Writing a Narrative Essay

To write a narrative essay, use the following steps. Pay particular attention to developing clear, vivid details that support your point.

Planning a Narrative Essay

For more on choosing a topic, see Chapter 2, p. 25.

The first step is to choose an experience or incident to write about. Be sure that it is memorable and vivid and that you are comfortable writing about it. After all, no student wants to discover, when a draft is nearly completed, that he or she cannot remember important details about an experience. At this stage, you should also decide whether to tell your story in the first or third person.

Gathering Details about the Experience or Incident

This step involves recollecting as many details about the experience or incident as possible and recording them on paper or in a computer file. Reenact the story, sketching each scene in your mind. Identify key actions, describe the main participants, and express your feelings. Here are a few ways to gather details.

Gathering Details for a Narrative Essay

1. **Replay the experience or incident in your mind.** Jot down exactly what you see, hear, smell, and feel — colors, dialogue, sounds, odors, and sensations. Also note how these details make you feel.
2. **Write the following headings on a piece of paper, or type them on your computer screen:** *Scene, Key Actions, Key Participants, Key Lines of Dialogue,* **and** *Your Feelings.* List your ideas under each heading systematically.
3. **Describe the incident or experience to a friend.** Have your friend ask questions as you retell the story. Jot down the details that the retelling and questioning help you recall.
4. **Describe the incident or experience aloud while tape-recording it.** Then listen to the tape and make notes.
5. **Consider different aspects of the incident or experience by asking** *who, what, when, where, how,* **and** *why* **questions.** Record your answers.

In addition, as you gather details for the narrative, be sure to include the types of details that are essential to an effective narrative.

- **Scene: Choose relevant sensory details.** Include enough detail about the place where the experience occurred to allow your readers to feel as if they are there. Details that appeal to the senses work best. Focus on important details that direct your readers' attention to the main points of the narrative, and avoid irrelevant details that distract from the main point.

- **Key actions: Choose actions that create tension, build it to a climax, and resolve it.** Be sure to gather details about the conflict. Answer the following questions.

  Why did the experience or incident occur?

  What events led up to it?

  How was it resolved?

  What were its short- and long-term outcomes?

  What is its significance now?

- **Key participants: Concentrate only on the appearance and action of people who were directly involved.** People who were present but not part of the incident or experience need not be described in detail or even included.

- **Key lines of dialogue: Include dialogue that is interesting, revealing, and related to the main point of the story.** To make sure the dialogue sounds natural, read the lines aloud, or ask a friend to do so.

- **Your feelings: Record your feelings before, during, and after the experience or incident.** Did you reveal your feelings then? If so, how? How did others react to you? How do you feel about the experience or incident now? What have you learned from it?

Developing Your Thesis

Once you have enough details, it is time to focus your thesis — the main point of your narrative. You probably have a working thesis in mind. Now is the time to improve it. In the following example, a student who decided to write about a burglary in her family's home wrote the following focused thesis statement for her narrative.

> After the break-in to our home, everyone in the family felt violated, as if none of our belongings was private or personal anymore.

Notice that the writer mentions the burglary and where it occurred before she expresses the main point of the narrative — that family members felt violated.

A thesis statement may be placed at the beginning of a narrative essay. In "Right Place, Wrong Face," for example, the thesis appears in the second paragraph. A thesis may also be placed at the end of a narrative, or it may be implied. Once you have a thesis, you may need to do some additional prewriting to develop supporting details.

For more on developing your thesis statement, see Chapter 2, p. 36.

Drafting a Narrative Essay

When you are satisfied with your thesis and your support for it, you are ready to organize your ideas and write the first draft. Decide whether you will put all events in chronological order, or whether you will use flashbacks or foreshadowing for dramatic effect. As you write, use the following guidelines to help keep the narrative on track.

Guidelines for Writing a Narrative Essay

1. **The introduction should capture the reader's attention, provide useful background information, and set up the conflict.** The introduction should also contain your thesis, if you have decided to place it at the beginning of the essay.

2. **The narrative should build tension as it leads up to the final resolution or climax.** Devote a separate paragraph to each major action or distinct part of the story, using transitional words and phrases such as *during, after*, and *finally* to connect events and guide readers along.

3. **The conclusion should end the essay in a satisfying manner.** A summary is usually unnecessary and may detract from the impact of the narrative. Instead, try ending in one of the following ways.

   - **Make a final observation about the experience or incident.** For an essay on part-time jobs in fast-food restaurants, a writer could conclude by saying: "Overall, I learned a more about getting along with people than I did about operating a franchise."

   - **Ask a probing question.** For an essay on adventure travel, a writer could conclude by asking: "Although the visit to rural Mexico was enlightening, the question remains: Do the native people really want or need us there?"

   - **Suggest a new but related direction of thought.** For an essay on racial profiling, a writer could conclude by suggesting that police sensitivity training might have changed the outcome of the situation.

   - **Reveal a surprising piece of information.** For an essay on the effects of serious phobias, a writer could conclude by stating that less serious phobias also exist — such as arachibutyrobphobia, which is the fear of peanut butter sticking to the roof of one's mouth.

   - **Refer back to the beginning.** For the essay about the home burglary, the writer might return to the beginning of the story, when family members still felt safe and unviolated.

   - **Restate the thesis in different words.** White does this in the final paragraph of "Right Place, Wrong Face."

Analyzing and Revising

If possible, set your draft aside for a day or two before rereading and revising it. As you reread, don't worry about errors in spelling, grammar, and mechanics; focus instead on improving the overall effectiveness of the narrative. Will it interest readers and make them want to know what happens next? Does it make your point clearly? To discover weaknesses in your draft, use the revision flowchart in Figure 5.3.

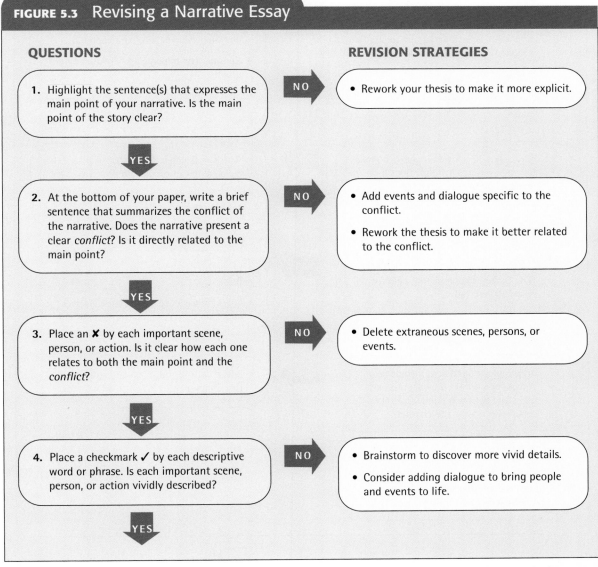

FIGURE 5.3 Revising a Narrative Essay

QUESTIONS

1. Highlight the sentence(s) that expresses the main point of your narrative. Is the main point of the story clear?

2. At the bottom of your paper, write a brief sentence that summarizes the conflict of the narrative. Does the narrative present a clear *conflict*? Is it directly related to the main point?

3. Place an ✘ by each important scene, person, or action. Is it clear how each one relates to both the main point and the *conflict*?

4. Place a checkmark ✓ by each descriptive word or phrase. Is each important scene, person, or action vividly described?

REVISION STRATEGIES

NO → • Rework your thesis to make it more explicit.

NO → • Add events and dialogue specific to the conflict.
• Rework the thesis to make it better related to the conflict.

NO → • Delete extraneous scenes, persons, or events.

NO → • Brainstorm to discover more vivid details.
• Consider adding dialogue to bring people and events to life.

(Continued)

QUESTIONS		REVISION STRATEGIES

5. In the margins of your paper, number the sequence of major events in chronological order. Is the sequence clear? If you use foreshadowing or flashbacks, is it clear where you do so?

NO →
- Look for gaps in the narrative, and add any missing events.
- Consider rearranging the events.
- Use transitions to clarify the sequence of events.

↓ **YES**

6. Underline the topic sentence of each paragraph. Is each paragraph focused on a separate part of the action?

NO →
- Be sure each paragraph has a topic sentence and supporting details (see Chapter 3).
- Consider combining closely related paragraphs.
- Split paragraphs that cover more than one event.

↓ **YES**

7. Wavy underline the dialogue. Is it realistic when you say it aloud? Does it directly relate to the *conflict*?

NO →
- Revise by telling a friend what you want the dialogue to express. Record what you say.
- Eliminate dialogue that does not add anything to the story.

↓ **YES**

8. Circle each personal pronoun and each verb. Do you use consistent point of view and verb tense?

NO →
- Reconsider your point of view and verb tense.
- Check for places where the tense changes for no reason, and revise to make it consistent.

↓ **YES**

9. Draw a box around your introduction and conclusion. Do they address each other and the main point? Does the conclusion resolve the *conflict*?

NO →
- Revise your introduction and conclusion (see Chapter 3).

↓ **YES**

10. Print out another draft to edit and proofread before turning the essay in.

Editing and Proofreading

The last step is to check your revised narrative essay for errors in grammar, spelling, punctuation, and mechanics. In addition, be sure to look for the types of errors that you tend to make in any writing assignments, whether for this class or any other situation. For narrative essays, pay particular attention to the following kinds of sentence problems.

Editing Tips and Troublespots: Narration

1. **Be certain that your sentences vary in structure.** A string of sentences that are similar in length and structure is tedious to read.

   ▸ We went to the Ding Darling National Wildlife Preserve located on

      Sanibel Island, Florida. ~~It was~~ *E*established in 1945 as the Sanibel Refuge*,*
      its
      ~~Its~~ name was changed in 1967 to honor the man who helped found it.

2. **Be sure to punctuate dialogue correctly.** Use commas to separate the quotation from the phrase that introduces it, unless the quotation is integrated into the sentence. If the sentence ends with a quotation, the period stays inside the quotation marks.

   ▸ As the wildlife refuge guide noted, "American crocodiles are an endangered species and must be protected."

   ▸ The wildlife refuge guide noted that "American crocodiles are an endangered species and must be protected."

3. **Use strong active verbs to make the narrative lively and interesting.**

   WEAK: The puppy was afraid of the fireworks.

   STRONG: The puppy whimpered and quivered as the fireworks exploded.

   Use verbs in the **active voice** (the subject performs the action). Avoid verbs in the **passive voice** (the subject is acted upon).

   PASSIVE: It was claimed by the cyclist that the motorist failed to yield the right of way.

   ACTIVE: The cyclist claimed that the motorist failed to yield the right of way.

   (Continued)

For more on improving your sentences, see Chapter 4, p. 77.

(Continued)

4. **Use consistent verb tense.** Most narratives are told in the past tense ("Yolanda discovered the glass in the front door was shattered . . ."). Fast-paced, short narratives, however, are sometimes related in the present tense ("Yolanda discovers the glass . . ."). Whichever tense you choose, be sure to use it consistently. Avoid switching between past and present tenses unless the context of the narrative clearly requires it.

(Students Write)

Aphonetip Vasavong is a native of Laos who was a nursing student at Niagara University when she wrote this essay. She wrote it in response to an assignment given by her first-year writing instructor to describe an event that changed her life. As you read the essay, notice how Vasavong's narrative creates conflict and tension and builds to a climax and resolution.

You Can Count on Miracles

Aphonetip Vasavong

Introduction: background on coincidences

Thesis

     Most of us have experienced unusual coincidences at least once in our lives -- coin-   1
cidences that are so unusual and meaningful that they could not have happened by
chance alone. Many events that seem coincidental often have simple explanations; however, some of these incidents have no simple explanations. I had such an experience
when I was eight years old and lost in the woods. Strange as it may seem, a rabbit led
me to safety; I would not be here today if it were not for that rabbit.

Vasavong's family background; why escape was necessary

     Until I was eight, my family lived in Laos. In 1986, however, my family and I left   2
Laos to prevent the Communists from capturing my father. He is an educated man, and
at that time the Communist government wanted to imprison educated people. The government was placing such people in concentration camps, similar to those used in
Germany and Eastern Europe during World War II, to prevent them from forming a party
that might overthrow the Communists. To protect my father from being captured and imprisoned in Laos, my family decided to immigrate to America.

Action begins

     We had to leave Laos quickly and secretively. In order to prevent suspicion, we told   3
our neighbors that we were taking a two-week family vacation to see our grandfather.

Instead, we stayed with our grandmother for two days, until we were able to find someone willing to escort us across the river to Thailand. On the second night, we planned to
board a boat that would take us to a small town where we could spend the night. I remember it was around 2 a.m. when my father woke us up. He divided the ten of us into
two groups of five because it was too risky to walk to the river as a large group; people
would be more likely to notice us and report us to the Communist soldiers. We were not
allowed to speak or make any noise at all because we might have awakened people or
disturbed their dogs. My father instructed us carefully: "Hold on to each other's jackets
and stay in line. Move carefully and quietly, and we'll all be safe soon."

Chronological sequence creates easy-to-follow narrative

Dialogue creates realism

    In a group with my brothers, my sister, and an escort lady, I was the last person in
line. On the way to the river, everyone else was walking fast through a dark, wooded
area, and I could not keep up with them. Somehow I accidentally let go of my sister's
jacket and got left behind in the woods. I was alone in the middle of what seemed like
nowhere. It was so dark I could not see anything or anyone. As I waited in terror for the
escort lady to come back to look for me, I started to cry. I waited a while longer, and
still no one came back for me.

4

Tension builds: Vasavong gets lost

    Suddenly, something ran out of the bushes onto a nearby path. I could see that it
was a rabbit. It was beautiful and bright, like a light. It came back toward me and stood
in front of me. I reached out to pet it, but it ran toward the same path that it had come
from a moment ago. I decided to follow the rabbit along the path. As I did, I was able
to see my way through the woods because the rabbit and the path were bright, while
the trees and the dense groundcover remained dark. I continued to follow the rabbit
along the path until it disappeared into the darkness. I looked around for the rabbit,
and what I saw instead was my family getting into the canoes. I turned back once more
to look for the rabbit, but it was gone. When I got on the canoe, I was relieved and
overjoyed to see my family again. My father pulled me close to him and whispered, "We
thought you were lost forever. How did you find us?"

5

Simile

Action continues: Vasavong follows the rabbit

Climax

    Unusual experiences such as mine occur to people everywhere, but most people do
not take the time to think about their meaning. Some critics argue that these occur-
rences are merely coincidental. My experience leads me to believe otherwise. Being lost
in the woods and having a brightly lit rabbit lead me safely to my family cannot be attributed to chance alone.

6

Conclusion: reaffirms the thesis that coincidences are not always due to chance alone

Responding to "Students Write"

1. Evaluate the effectiveness of Vasavong's thesis.
2. What ideas do you think should be expanded? That is, where did you want or need more detail?
3. How effectively does Vasavong establish conflict and create tension?
4. Where does Vasavong use foreshadowing? Explain its effectiveness.
5. Evaluate the title, introduction, and conclusion of the essay.

Reading a Narrative Essay

For more on previewing and other reading strategies, see Chapter 1.

It is usually a good idea to read a narrative essay several times before attempting to discuss or write about it. Preview the reading to get an overview of its content and organization. Then read it through to familiarize yourself with the events and action, noting who did what, when, where, and how. Finally, reread the narrative, this time concentrating on its meaning.

What to Look for, Highlight, and Annotate

When reading a narrative, it is easy to become immersed in the story and to overlook its importance or significance. Therefore, as you read, look for the answers to the following questions.

Understanding the Reading
- What is the role of each participant?
- What is the conflict?
- What is the climax?
- How is the conflict resolved?

Examining the Characteristics of Narrative Essays
- What main point does the writer make in the narrative?
- What is the writer's thesis? Is it stated directly or implied?
- What does the dialogue contribute to the main point?
- How does the writer create tension?
- What is the sequence of events? (For lengthy or complex narratives, it may be helpful to draw a graphic organizer or to number the sequence of events in the margins.)
- What is the author's purpose in writing this narrative?
- For what audience is it intended?

- What is the lasting value or merit of this essay? What does it tell about life, people, jobs, or friendships, for example?
- What techniques does the writer use to achieve his or her purpose? Is the writer successful?

How to Find Ideas to Write About

Because at times you may be asked to write a response to a narrative, keep an eye out for ideas to write about *as you read*. Pay particular attention to the issue, struggle, or dilemma at hand. Try to discover what broader issue the essay is concerned with. For example, a narrative about a worker's conflict with a supervisor is also concerned with the larger issue of authority. Once you've identified the larger issue, you can begin to develop ideas about it by relating it to your own experience.

Talking a Stranger through the Night

Sherry Amatenstein

Sherry Amatenstein is an author, journalist, and noted relationship expert who has appeared on radio and television talk shows such as *Live with Regis and Kelly* and *Geraldo*. She gives dating advice in an online column for ivillage.com, and her books on the subject include *The Q & A Dating Book* (2000) and *Love Lessons from Bad Breakups* (2002). This article, from the November 18, 2002, issue of *Newsweek*, describes her experience volunteering at Help Line, New York City's oldest crisis and suicide hotline.

As you read, notice how Amatenstein captures your interest by thrusting you immediately into the situation and creating suspense about the crisis. Pay attention to the way her use of dialogue reveals both the caller's and the author's state of mind.

Focus on Understanding   Read to discover what the author learned from manning a crisis hotline.

Focus on the Topic   In class or in your journal, write about a volunteer experience that you had. If you have never volunteered, write about a volunteer organization you admire.

Holocaust: Persecution of Jews and other minorities by the Nazis from 1933 to 1945

empathetic: Understanding of others' emotions and feelings

idealism: The act or practice of envisioning things in the best possible form

The call came 60 minutes into my third shift as a volunteer at the crisis hot line. 1
As the child of Holocaust° survivors, I grew up wanting to ease other people's pain. But it wasn't until after September 11 that I contacted Help Line, the nonprofit telephone service headquartered in New York. The instructor of the nine-week training course taught us how to handle a variety of callers, from depressed seniors to "repeats" (those who checked in numerous times a day).

We spent two sessions on suicide calls, but I prayed I wouldn't get one un-2 til I felt comfortable on the line. Drummed over and over into the 30 trainees' heads was that our role wasn't to give advice. Rather, we were to act as empathetic° sounding boards and encourage callers to figure out how to take action.

My idealism° about the hot line's value faded that first night, as in quick suc-3 cession I heard from men who wanted to masturbate while I listened, repeats who told me again and again about their horrific childhoods, know-nothing shrinks and luckless lives, and three separate callers who railed about the low intellect of everyone living in Queens (my borough!). Sprinkled into the mix were people who turned abusive when I refused to tell them how to solve their problems.

I tried to remain sympathetic. If I, who had it together (an exciting career, 4
great friends and family) found New York isolating, I could imagine how fright-

112

ening it was for people so untethered they needed a hot line for company. That rationale didn't help. After only 10 hours, I no longer cringed each time the phone rang, terrified it signified a problem I wasn't equipped to handle. Instead I wondered what fresh torture this caller had up his unstable sleeve.

Then Sandy's (not her real name) quavering voice nipped into my ear: "I 5 want to kill myself." I snapped to attention, remembering my training. Did she have an imminent plan to do herself in? Luckily, no. Sandy knew a man who'd attempted suicide via pills, threw them up, and lived. She was afraid of botching a similar attempt. Since she was handicapped, she couldn't even walk to her window to jump out.

Sandy's life was certainly Help Line material. Her parents had disowned 6 her 40 years before. She'd worked as a secretary until a bone-crushing fall put her out of commission. Years later she was working again and had a boyfriend who stuck with her even after a cab struck Sandy and put her back on the disabled list. They became engaged, and then, soap-opera like, tragedy struck again. Sandy's boyfriend was diagnosed with cancer and passed away last year. Now she was in constant pain, confined to a dark apartment, her only companion a nurse's aide. "There's nothing left," she cried. "Give me a reason to live."

Her plea drove home the wisdom of the "no advice" dictum. How could I 7 summon the words to give someone else's life meaning? The best I could do was to help Sandy fan the spark that had led her to reach out. I tossed life-affirming statements at her like paint on a canvas, hoping some would stick. I ended with "Sandy, I won't whitewash° your problems. You've had more than your share of sorrow. But surely there are some things that have given you pleasure."

whitewash: Hide the truth.

She thought hard and remembered an interest in books on spirituality. The downside followed immediately. Sandy's limited eyesight made it difficult for her to read. She rasped, "My throat hurts from crying, but I'm afraid if I get off the phone I'll want to kill myself again." 8

I said, "I'm here as long as you need me." 9

We spoke another two hours. She recalled long-ago incidents — most depressing, a few semi-joyful. There were some things she still enjoyed: peanuts, "Oprah," the smell of autumn. I again broached the topic of spirituality. My supervisor, whom I'd long ago motioned to listen in on another phone, handed me a prayer book. I read, and Sandy listened. After "amen," she said, "I think I'll be all right for the night." 10

Naturally, she couldn't promise to feel better tomorrow. For all of us, life is one day, sometimes even one minute, at a time. She asked, "When are you on again?" 11

I said, "My schedule is irregular, but we're all here for you, anytime you want. Thanks so much for calling." 12

As I hung up, I realized the call had meant as much to me as to Sandy, if not more. Despite having people in my life, lately I'd felt achingly lonely. I hadn't called a hot line, but I'd manned one, and this night had been my best in a long time. Instead of having dinner at an overpriced restaurant or watching HBO, I'd connected with another troubled soul in New York City. 13

Understanding the Reading

1. What information does Amatenstein reveal about herself and her reasons for volunteering at a crisis hotline?

2. What types of callers does Amatenstein encounter on her first night at Help Line? What effect do these early conversations have on her?

3. Cite several examples from the reading that suggest the author was helpful to Sandy.

4. What did the author learn about herself and others by manning the crisis hot line?

Examining the Characteristics of Narrative Essays

1. Evaluate Amatenstein's use of dialogue. What does it contribute to her essay?

2. Amatenstein includes the information that Sandy enjoyed "peanuts, 'Oprah,' the smell of autumn" (para. 10)? Why do you think the author included these details? How do they contribute to the narrative as a whole?

3. What narrative techniques does Amatenstein use to make you care about Sandy? How does the author use these techniques to build, create, and sustain tension?

4. Amatenstein makes her point about her experience at the end of the essay. Evaluate the effectiveness of using an implied thesis in the concluding paragraph.

5. Did you find the conclusion satisfying? Why or why not?

Visualizing the Reading

Review the reading and complete the empty boxes in the following graphic organizer. The first box has been done for you.

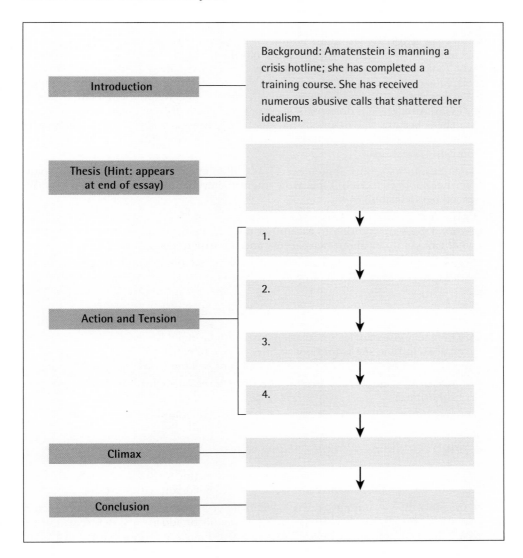

Introduction

Background: Amatenstein is manning a crisis hotline; she has completed a training course. She has received numerous abusive calls that shattered her idealism.

Thesis (Hint: appears at end of essay)

Action and Tension

1.

2.

3.

4.

Climax

Conclusion

Building Your Word Power

1. "Fan the spark" (para. 7) is an idiomatic expression. Explain its meaning.
2. Evaluate the simile "I tossed life-affirming statements at her like paint on a canvas" (para. 7). What picture does the expression create in your mind?

For a definition of simile and idiom, see the chart of commonly used language features on p. 21.

3. Explain the meaning of each of the following words as it is used in the reading: *horrific* (para. 3), *rationale* (4), *signified* (4), *imminent* (5), *botching* (5), and *dictum* (7). Refer to your dictionary as needed.

Building Your Critical Thinking Skills: Inferences

An **inference** is a reasoned guess about what is not known based on what is known. People make inferences many times every day. For example, you can infer that someone who looks at his or her watch frequently is concerned about getting somewhere on time. Because writers do not always directly state everything they want to communicate, you often have to read between the lines to get their full and complete meaning. In her essay, Amatenstein does not state that she is well off financially, but you can infer that she is because she mentions having "an exciting career" (para. 4) and choosing not to dine in "an overpriced restaurant" (para. 13). Use your inference skills to answer the following questions.

1. Amatenstein mentions September 11 as a date after which she decided to volunteer her services to Help Line. How might the events of September 11 have influenced her decision?

2. In the first paragraph, Amatenstein mentions that "[a]s a child of Holocaust survivors, I grew up wanting to ease other people's pain." Reading between the lines, what can you infer about her parents and her experience growing up with them?

3. From the information contained in the reading, what can you infer about the author's attitude toward living in New York City?

Reacting to the Topic: Discussion and Journal Writing

1. Amatenstein gives advice on relationships and dating in her professional life; however, at Help Line she is told not to offer advice to callers. Why might a crisis hotline differ from other settings where people are seeking help from outside sources?

2. In class or in your journal, explore the various reasons why someone might call a crisis hotline.

3. Discuss some of the reasons why people choose to volunteer.

Applying Your Skills: Writing Assignments

1. **Paragraph Assignment.** Write a paragraph narrating a situation in which talking to someone helped you solve a problem or provided you with a fresh perspective.

2. Using narrative techniques, rewrite Amatenstein's essay using the first person from Sandy's point of view. Feel free to make up details or add events. Before you begin, you will need to devise a new thesis statement Plan your essay before your write. For example, will you begin with Sandy's call to Amatenstein, or will you begin with the events of Sandy's life that lead up to her decision to call Help Line?

3. Brainstorm a list of situations in which you helped another person and found that it benefited you as well. Then select the best example and organize a sequence of events relating to that situation. After planning your paper, write a narrative essay describing the situation, making sure to include a thesis statement about the value of helping others.

4. **Combining Patterns.** Many high schools and colleges have community service requirements under which students volunteer their time and skills. Write an essay describing your view on whether mandatory community service is a good or bad idea. As part of your argument, include your own experiences to support your views.

5. **Internet Research.** Visit Help Line's Web site at www.helpline.org or the Web site of another crisis hotline on your campus or in your community to learn more about the services they offer. Then write an essay for your student newspaper explaining what the crisis hotline is and how it could be useful to students at your school.

Fish Cheeks

Amy Tan

Amy Tan (b. 1952) learned firsthand the difficulty of bridging two very different cultures while growing up in California with Chinese immigrant parents. She has explored problems with assimilation, culture clashes, and generation gaps in novels that include *The Joy Luck Club* (1989) and *The Bonesetter's Daughter* (2000); children's books, including *Sagwa, The Chinese Siamese Cat* (1994), on which PBS based an animated series; and essays, including her most recent collection, *The Opposite of Fate* (2003). The essay that follows was originally published in *Seventeen*.

As you read this narrative, notice how quickly Tan introduces the sources of conflict between characters. Also observe how little dialogue she uses — and pay attention to the significance of what the characters *do* say.

Focus on Understanding   Identify what the "fish cheeks" mentioned in the title are, and figure out why they are important.

Focus on the Topic   In class or in your journal, write about a time when you felt either proud of or embarrassed/ashamed of your family or your background.

1   I fell in love with the minister's son the winter I turned fourteen. He was not Chinese, but as white as Mary in the manger. For Christmas I prayed for this blond-haired boy, Robert, and a slim new American nose.

2   When I found out that my parents had invited the minister's family over for Christmas Eve dinner, I cried. What would Robert think of our shabby Chinese Christmas? What would he think of our noisy Chinese relatives who lacked proper American manners? What terrible disappointment would he feel upon seeing not a roasted turkey and sweet potatoes but Chinese food?

3   On Christmas Eve I saw that my mother had outdone herself in creating a strange menu. She was pulling black veins out of the backs of fleshy prawns.° The kitchen was littered with appalling mounds of raw food: A slimy rock cod with bulging eyes that pleaded not to be thrown into a pan of hot oil. Tofu,° which looked like stacked wedges of rubbery white sponges. A bowl soaking dried fungus back to life. A plate of squid, their backs crisscrossed with knife markings so they resembled bicycle tires.

4   And then they arrived — the minister's family and all my relatives in a clamor of doorbells and rumpled Christmas packages. Robert grunted hello, and I pretended he was not worthy of existence.

5   Dinner threw me deeper into despair. My relatives licked the ends of their chopsticks and reached across the table, dipping them into the dozen or so

prawns: Seafood similar to shrimp

tofu: Soybean cake

plates of food. Robert and his family waited patiently for platters to be passed to them. My relatives murmured with pleasure when my mother brought out the whole steamed fish. Robert grimaced. Then my father poked his chopsticks just below the fish eye and plucked out the soft meat. "Amy, your favorite," he said, offering me the tender fish cheek. I wanted to disappear.

At the end of the meal my father leaned back and belched loudly, thanking my mother for her fine cooking. "It's a polite Chinese custom to show you are satisfied," explained my father to our astonished guests. Robert was looking down at his plate with a reddened face. The minister managed to muster up a quiet burp. I was stunned into silence for the rest of the night. 6

After everyone had gone, my mother said to me, "You want to be the same as American girls on the outside." She handed me an early gift. It was a miniskirt in beige tweed. "But inside you must always be Chinese. You must be proud you are different. Your only shame is to have shame." 7

And even though I didn't agree with her then, I knew that she understood how much I had suffered during the evening's dinner. It wasn't until many years later — long after I had gotten over my crush on Robert — that I was able to fully appreciate her lesson and the true purpose behind our particular menu. For Christmas Eve that year, she had chosen all my favorite foods. 8

Understanding the Reading

1. Why is Tan so upset about Robert coming to dinner? How do the actions of her family members contribute to her despair?

2. What are some of the reasons — both stated and unstated — for Tan's mother choosing a traditional Chinese menu?

3. In what ways do the minister and his family react to the dinner?

4. What does Tan eventually realize about that evening and herself?

Examining the Characteristics of Narrative Essays

1. What might be Tan's purpose in addressing her conflicts with her own ethnic and cultural traditions in this essay?

2. Consider the questions posed by Tan in paragraph 2. Why do you think she includes the questions about what Robert might be thinking at the start of the essay?

3. Dialogue is used sparingly in Tan's essay. What did you learn from the dialogue that the physical and sensory details alone could not convey?

4. Consider the mother's words of advice in paragraph 7. Does Tan use an implied or explicit thesis? Is the use of actual dialogue more or less effective here than a more traditional thesis statement would be?

Visualizing the Reading

Using this chart or a similar one, record several examples of each of the characteristics of narrative essays used by Tan in "Fish Cheeks." One example, including the paragraph number, is shown for the "Uses Dialogue" category.

Narrative Characteristic	Examples
Makes a point or thesis	
Uses dialogue	1. "Amy, your favorite" (5)
Includes sensory details	
Recounts action	
Builds tension	
Presents a sequence of events	

Building Your Word Power

For a definition of al-lusion and hyperbole, see the chart of commonly used language features on p. 21.

1. The comparison "white as Mary in the manager" (para. 1) is a biblical allusion. Explain its meaning.

2. What effect does Tan achieve by using hyperbole in paragraph 3 to describe her mother's dinner menu?

3. Explain the meaning of each of the following words as it is used in the reading: *littered* (para. 3), *appalling* (3), *clamor* (4), *grimaced* (5), and *muster up* (6). Refer to your dictionary as needed.

Building Your Critical Thinking Skills: Point of View

For more on point of view, see Chapter 2, p. 28.

Point of view is the perspective from which an author tells a story. There are three types: first, second, and third person. Some authors use first person (*I*, *me*, *mine*, *ours*, *we*) as if they are participating in the story. In the second person, the author addresses the readers directly (*you*, *your*, *yours*). In the third person, the author does not participate in the story and reports events that involve others (*he, she, they*). When writing narratives, authors usually use the first or third person. Use your knowledge of point of view to answer the following questions.

1. What point of view does Tan use, and why is it effective?

2. How might this essay be different if Tan had used another point of view? What additional information might she have included?

3. According to the first sentence, the narrator of this essay is fourteen years old. Does the essay sound as if it were written by a girl of fourteen? Cite examples to support your answer.

Reacting to the Topic: Discussion and Journal Writing

1. Discuss the importance of family gatherings. Recalling one or two family events that you participate in, explain both the positive and — if applicable — negative outcomes of such gatherings. What functions might such family get-togethers serve?

2. Most people navigate at some time or another between different groups or cultures. For example, in high school you might have had good friends on the soccer team and in the drama club. In your journal or in class, explore the difficulties and benefits of being part of two cultures or groups.

Applying Your Skills: Writing Assignments

1. Paragraph Assignment. Write a paragraph narrating your experience in trying a new or unusual food. Be sure to explain your expectations, your experience tasting it, and your reactions afterward.

2. Keeping in mind characteristics of narrative essays, write an essay that uses dialogue to narrate a gathering with your own family or friends that involved a meal. Be sure to include a thesis and sensory details to support your main point.

3. Tan states that it was not until "years later" that she understood the real meaning of that night. Write an essay narrating a situation or experience that took you a long time to figure out.

4. Combining Patterns. Immigrants must live within a culture and traditions very different from those of their country of origin. To what extent should immigrants integrate themselves into the culture of their adopted country? To what extent should they preserve their traditional values and culture? Write an essay expressing your position on this issue.

5. Internet Research. Visit the Web site for the Chinese Historical Society of America at www.chsa.org or any other site that preserves and promotes Chinese American history. Then write an essay describing the resources, collections, and types of events offered. Discuss why these would be important to Chinese Americans as well as to people of other backgrounds.

Salvation

Langston Hughes

Langston Hughes (1902–1967) was born in Joplin, Missouri; attended Columbia University; and graduated from Lincoln University in 1929. In addition to working as a journalist for various periodicals, he was a prolific writer of poetry, drama, nonfiction, and short stories. He became a major part of the so-called Harlem Renaissance, a movement in 1920s New York City that celebrated the African American experience and, in particular, literary and artistic expression. Hughes is perhaps best known for his poems — collected in *Weary Blues* (1926), *Ask Your Mama* (1961), and *The Negro Mother* (1971), among others — which explore themes of race and protest and often borrow their rhythms from jazz music. The following essay was originally published in his autobiography, *The Big Sea* (1940).

As you read, notice that Hughes begins the essay by giving away the ending: He was saved, but "not really saved." Notice how this technique sparks your interest, making you want to hear the whole story behind this unusual statement. Pay attention also to the author's descriptions of the revival atmosphere. These details help to establish the author's dilemma.

Focus on Understanding   Read to discover what the author learns from attending the revival meeting.

Focus on the Topic   In class or in your journal, explore a situation in which you deceived someone or you were deceived.

I was saved from sin when I was going on thirteen. But not really saved. It happened like this. There was a big revival° at my Auntie Reed's church. Every night for weeks there had been much preaching, singing, praying, and shouting, and some very hardened sinners had been brought to Christ, and the membership of the church had grown by leaps and bounds. Then just before the revival ended, they held a special meeting for children, "to bring the young lambs to the fold." My aunt spoke of it for days ahead. That night I was escorted to the front row and placed on the mourners' bench° with all the other young sinners, who had not yet been brought to Jesus.

My aunt told me that when you were saved you saw a light, and something happened to you inside! And Jesus came into your life! And God was with you from then on! She said you could see and hear and feel Jesus in your soul. I believed her. I have heard a great many old people say the same thing and it seemed to me they ought to know. So I sat there calmly in the hot, crowded church, waiting for Jesus to come to me.

revival: meeting held to recruit people to Christianity or reaffirm their beliefs

mourners' bench: A designated pew in a church for sinners looking to be saved by the power of prayer

1

2

The preacher preached a wonderful rhythmical sermon, all moans and 3
shouts and lonely cries and dire pictures of hell, and then he sang a song about
the ninety and nine safe in the fold, but one little lamb was left out in the cold.
Then he said: "Won't you come? Won't you come to Jesus? Young lambs, won't
you come?" And he held out his arms to all us young sinners there on the
mourners' bench. And the little girls cried. And some of them jumped up and
went to Jesus right away. But most of us just sat there.

A great many old people came and knelt around us and prayed, old women 4
with jet-black faces and braided hair, old men with work-gnarled hands. And
the church sang a song about the lower lights are burning, some poor sinners
to be saved. And the whole building rocked with prayer and song.

Still I kept waiting to *see* Jesus.   5

Finally all the young people had gone to the altar and were saved, but one 6
boy and me. He was a rounder's° son named Westley. Westley and I were surrounded by sisters and deacons praying. It was very hot in the church, and getting late now. Finally Westley said to me in a whisper: "God damn! I'm tired o'
sitting here. Let's get up and be saved." So he got up and was saved.

rounder: An immoral and unrespectable person

Then I was left all alone on the mourners' bench. My aunt came and knelt 7
at my knees and cried, while prayers and songs swirled all around me in the
little church. The whole congregation prayed for me alone, in a mighty wail of
moans and voices. And I kept waiting serenely for Jesus, waiting, waiting — but
he didn't come. I wanted to see him, but nothing happened to me. Nothing! I
wanted something to happen to me, but nothing happened.

I heard the songs and the minister saying: "Why don't you come? My dear 8
child, why don't you come to Jesus? Jesus is waiting for you. He wants you. Why
don't you come? Sister Reed, what is this child's name?"

"Langston," my aunt sobbed.   9

"Langston, why don't you come? Why don't you come and be saved? Oh, 10
Lamb of God! Why don't you come?"

Now it was really getting late. I began to be ashamed of myself, holding 11
everything up so long. I began to wonder what God thought about Westley, who
certainly hadn't seen Jesus either, but who was now sitting proudly on the platform, swinging his knickerbockered° legs and grinning down at me, surrounded
by deacons and old women on their knees praying. God had not struck Westley
dead for taking his name in vain or for lying in the temple. So I decided that
maybe to save further trouble, I'd better lie, too, and say that Jesus had come,
and get up and be saved.

knickerbockered: Wearing the baggy shorts of the time

So I got up.   12

Suddenly the whole room broke into a sea of shouting, as they saw me rise. 13
Waves of rejoicing swept the place. Women leaped in the air. My aunt threw
her arms around me. The minister took me by the hand and led me to the
platform.

When things quieted down, in a hushed silence, punctuated by a few ec- 14
static "Amens," all the new young lambs were blessed in the name of God. Then
joyous singing filled the room.

That night, for the last time in my life but one — for I was a big boy twelve   15
years old — I cried. I cried, in bed alone, and couldn't stop. I buried my head under the quilts, but my aunt heard me. She woke up and told my uncle I was crying because the Holy Ghost had come into my life, and because I had seen Jesus.
But I was really crying because I couldn't bear to tell her that I had lied, that I
had deceived everybody in the church, that I hadn't seen Jesus, and that now I
didn't believe there was a Jesus any more, since he didn't come to help me.

Understanding the Reading

1. What is the purpose of the "special meeting for children"?
2. In what ways is Westley different from Hughes?
3. According to his aunt, why is Hughes crying? What reasons for crying does Hughes give?
4. What does Hughes learn from the events that occurred at the revival meeting?

Visualizing the Reading

Study the photo taken at a contemporary revival meeting. What do you learn about revival meetings from this photo that you have not already learned from "Salvation"?
Write a list of details gathered from your analysis of the picture that would add meaning to Hughes's essay.

Examining the Characteristics of Narrative Essays

1. What does Hughes's narration of the events reveal about revival meetings and his belief in Jesus?

2. Highlight or create a list of details that are particularly descriptive in Hughes's essay. How do these details contribute to your image of the revival meeting and the people attending it?

3. Identify the conflict that Hughes faces while attending the revival meeting. What techniques does he use to create and sustain tension in the essay?

4. Study the dialogue of Auntie Reed, the minister, and Westley. What does Hughes's use of dialogue reveal about the personalities of each character?

5. Hughes uses foreshadowing to suggest his thesis in the first two sentences of the essay. He then presents his main point at the very end of the essay. Is this an implied or a stated thesis? Do you think this treatment of thesis is effective? Why or why not?

Building Your Critical Thinking Skills: Connotative Meaning

Although all words have a literal, or *denotative*, meaning (their dictionary definition), many words also have a **connotative meaning.** This meaning expresses a feeling or idea that is associated with the word. Connotative meanings often carry a positive or negative association. Consider, for example, the word *mob*; it carries the negative association of an unruly, out-of-control crowd. Use your knowledge of connotative meaning to answer the following questions.

1. What connotation does the word *saved* have in Hughes's story? Is it positive or negative?

2. What does Hughes think his aunt means by "seeing" Jesus? How does this differ from Auntie Reed's understanding of the word?

Building Your Word Power

1. Explain the idiom "by leaps and bounds" as it is used in paragraph 1.

2. Explain the meaning of the metaphors used in paragraph 13: "sea of shouting" and "waves of rejoicing."

3. Explain the meaning of each of the following words or phrases as it is used in the reading: *dire* (para. 3), *serenely* (7), *in vain* (11), and *punctuated* (14). Refer to your dictionary as needed.

For a definition of idiom *and* metaphor, *see the chart of commonly used language features on p. 21.*

Reacting to the Topic: Discussion and Journal Writing

1. Discuss the atmosphere of the children's revival meeting and Hughes's understanding of what it means to be "brought to Jesus" (para. 1). How might this understanding have contributed to Hughes's behavior at the revival?

2. In class or in your journal, write about a religious ceremony or service that you have attended. Include a description of the atmosphere of the event and the feelings you experienced. Or write instead about some other type of nonreligious ceremony that you have attended.

Applying Your Skills: Writing Assignments

1. **Paragraph Assignment.** The story contrasts Hughes's calm waiting and the boisterous noise and action of the revival. Write a paragraph using narration about a struggle you faced while trying to remain calm and patient in a stressful situation.

2. Hughes discovers that deception is a practical way to end the evening. Write a narrative essay describing a situation from your own experience involving deception. Include an evaluation of whether you thought the deception was justified.

3. Hughes trusts his elders that he will see Jesus, but he feels disillusioned when he doesn't see anything. Write a narrative essay describing how you trusted or believed in a person only to discover that you had been misled.

4. **Combining Patterns.** The minister and congregation in "Salvation" use various forms of persuasion to convert the children. Write an essay analyzing the persuasive techniques mentioned in the essay. Include specific examples from the essay to support your thesis about whether or not these types of techniques are effective.

5. **Internet Research.** In June 2003, PBS produced a series called "This Far by Faith" about the spiritual development of African Americans over the past three hundred years. Based on your research of the show's Web site, www.pbs.org/thisfarby faith, write a summary about the series and the producers' goals in creating the project.

A View from the Bridge

Cherokee Paul McDonald

After a tour of duty in Vietnam, Cherokee Paul McDonald returned to his home town of Fort Lauderdale, Florida, where he worked as a police officer. Following ten years of policing he left the force to become a writer. His work often focuses on themes of justice, balance, and fairness. He published his first book, *The Patch*, in 1986. His memoir, *Blue Truth*, was published in 1991, and his first novel, *Summer's Room*, was released in 1994. His most recent work, *Into the Green: A Reconnaissance by Fire* (2001), is a memoir of his experiences in Vietnam. This story was first published in 1990 in *Sunshine* magazine.

As you read, notice how McDonald's use of first-person point of view leads the reader to understand the narrator's attitudes and realizations. Also pay attention to McDonald's use of dialogue. The conversations between the jogger and the boy play an important role in the development of their relationship.

Focus on Understanding   Read to discover what the jogger learns from the boy on the bridge.

Focus on the Topic   In class or in your journal, write about the problems you might encounter if you became blind. Consider in particular how your loss of sight would affect your lifestyle.

I was coming up on the little bridge in the Rio Vista neighborhood of Fort Lauderdale, deepening my stride and my breathing to negotiate the slight incline without altering my pace. And then, as I neared the crest, I saw the kid. 1

He was a lumpy little guy with baggy shorts, a faded T-shirt and heavy sweat socks falling down over old sneakers. 2

Partially covering his shaggy blond hair was one of those blue baseball caps with gold braid on the bill and a sailfish patch sewn onto the peak. Covering his eyes and part of his face was a pair of those stupid-looking '50s-style wraparound sunglasses. 3

He was fumbling with a beat-up rod and reel, and he had a little bait bucket by his feet. I puffed on by, glancing down into the empty bucket as I passed. 4

"Hey mister! Would you help me, please?" 5

The shrill voice penetrated my jogger's concentration, and I was determined to ignore it. But for some reason, I stopped. 6

With my hands on my hips and the sweat dripping from my nose I asked, "What do you want, kid?" 7

127

"Would you please help me find my shrimp? It's my last one and I've been 8 getting bites and I know I can catch a fish if I can just find that shrimp. He jumped outta my hand as I was getting him from the bucket."

Exasperated, I walked slowly back to the kid, and pointed. 9

"There's the damn shrimp by your left foot. You stopped me for *that?*" 10

As I said it, the kid reached down and trapped the shrimp. 11

"Thanks a lot, mister," he said. 12

I watched as the kid dropped the baited hook down into the canal. Then I 13 turned to start back down the bridge.

That's when the kid let out a "Hey! Hey!" and the prettiest tarpon° I'd ever 14 seen came almost six feet out of the water, twisting and turning as he fell through the air.

"I got one!" the kid yelled as the fish hit the water with a loud splash and 15 took off down the canal.

I watched the line being burned off the reel at an alarming rate. The kid's 16 left hand held the crank while the extended fingers felt for the drag° setting.

"No, kid!" I shouted. "Leave the drag alone . . . just keep that damn rod 17 tip up!"

Then I glanced at the reel and saw there were just a few loops of line left on 18 the spool.

"Why don't you get yourself some decent equipment?" I said, but before the 19 kid could answer I saw the line go slack.

"Ohhh, I lost him," the kid said. I saw the flash of silver as the fish turned. 20

"Crank, kid, crank! You didn't lose him. He's coming back toward you. 21 Bring in the slack!"

The kid cranked like mad, and a beautiful grin spread across his face. 22

"He's heading in for the pilings," I said. "Keep him out of those pilings!"° 23

The kid played it perfectly. When the fish made its play for the pilings, he 24 kept just enough pressure on to force the fish out. When the water exploded and the silver missile hurled into the air, the kid kept the rod tip up and the line tight.

As the fish came to the surface and began a slow circle in the middle of the 25 canal, I said, "Whooee, is that a nice fish or what?"

The kid didn't say anything, so I said, "Okay, move to the edge of the bridge 26 and I'll climb down to the seawall and pull him out."

When I reached the seawall I pulled in the leader, leaving the fish lying on 27 its side in the water.

"How's that?" I said. 28

"Hey, mister, tell me what it looks like." 29

"Look down here and check him out," I said. "He's beautiful." 30

But then I looked up into those stupid-looking sunglasses and it hit me. The 31 kid was blind.

"Could you tell me what he looks like, mister?" he said again. 32

"Well, he's just under three, uh, he's about as long as one of your arms," I 33 said. "I'd guess he goes about 15, 20 pounds. He's mostly silver, but the silver is

tarpon: A large, tropical fish with a silvery pattern that is caught for sport

drag: Resistance applied to the spool by the fisherman to slow a fish from pulling all the line off the reel

pilings: Large posts that support a bridge or dock

somehow made up of *all* the colors, if you know what I mean." I stopped. "Do you know what I mean by colors?"

The kid nodded. 34

"Okay. He has all these big scales, like armor all over his body. They're silver 35 too, and when he moves they sparkle. He has a strong body and a large powerful tail. He has big round eyes, bigger than a quarter, and a lower jaw that sticks out past the upper one and is very tough. His belly is almost white and his back is gunmetal gray. When he jumped he came out of the water about six feet, and his scales caught the sun and flashed it all over the place."

By now the fish had righted itself, and I could see the bright-red gills as the 36 gill plates opened and closed. I explained this to the kid, and then said, more to myself, "He's a beauty."

"Can you get him off the hook?" the kid asked. "I don't want to kill him." 37

I watched as the tarpon began to slowly swim away, tired but still alive. 38

By the time I got back up to the top of the bridge the kid had his line se- 39 cured and his bait bucket in one hand.

He grinned and said, "Just in time. My mom drops me off here, and she'll 40 be back to pick me up any minute."

He used the back of one hand to wipe his nose. 41

"Thanks for helping me catch that tarpon," he said, "and for helping me to 42 see it."

I looked at him, shook my head, and said, "No, my friend, thank you for let- 43 ting *me* see that fish."

I took off, but before I got far the kid yelled again. 44

"Hey, mister?" 45

I stopped. 46

"Someday I'm gonna catch a sailfish and a blue marlin and a giant tuna and 47 *all* those big sportfish!"

As I looked into those sunglasses I knew he probably would. I wished I 48 could be there when it happened.

Understanding the Reading

1. What is the jogger's attitude toward the boy in the beginning of the story? How does it change over the course of the story?

2. What clues does McDonald give to suggest that the boy is blind?

3. Why does it take a long time for the jogger to realize that the boy is blind?

4. What does the jogger mean when he thanks the boy for letting him "see that fish" (para. 43)?

Visualizing the Reading

Writers of narrative essays frequently use physical description, dialogue, and the telling of events to reveal their characters' personalities and to make their main point. Using the chart below, fill in what you learned about the boy, the jogger, and the fish for each of the characteristics of narrative essays used by McDonald. For each box, fill in at least two examples.

Narrative Characteristic	The Boy	The Jogger (narrator)	The Fish
Physical description			
Dialogue			
Events			

Examining the Characteristics of Narrative Essays

1. Explain the title of the essay. Who views what from the bridge? How does the title reveal the author's purpose in writing this narrative?

2. What details does McDonald use to create an impression about the boy in the first several paragraphs? How does this impression change later in the essay? What details reveal the author's changing impression as the essay develops?

3. In paragraph 30 the jogger describes the fish as "beautiful." But after realizing that the boy is blind, he uses much more vivid language to describe the fish (paras. 33–36). What effect does this change in language create — in terms of your understanding of the character, the tone of the dialogue, and the events in the story?

4. McDonald uses an implied thesis. Identify his thesis and then, in your own words, write an explicit thesis for this essay.

5. Consider the boy's optimism and the narrator's expression of faith in the boy at the end of the essay. Does this ending make an effective conclusion? Why or why not? What other conclusions would be feasible?

*For a definition of **jargon** and other terms used here, see the chart of commonly used language features on p. 21.*

Building Your Word Power

1. Every hobby and sport has its own specialized language, or *jargon*. Identify the specialized words used by McDonald that apply to fishing.

2. Evaluate the figures of speech "silver missile" (para. 24) and "scales, like armor" (para. 35). What images do these expressions create in your mind?

3. Explain the meaning of each of the following words as it is used in the reading: *negotiate* (para. 1), *crest* (1), *exasperated* (9), *slack* (21), and *played* (24). Refer to your dictionary as needed.

Building Your Critical Thinking Skills: Symbolism

One feature of language that writers commonly employ is **symbolism:** the use of one thing, word, or idea to represent another. For example, a lion could symbolize courage or a rose could represent beauty. By analyzing the symbolic meaning of certain elements in a story, the reader can gain a deeper understanding of the author's themes. Using your knowledge of symbolism, answer the following questions.

1. What is the significance of the bridge in McDonald's story?

2. Children often symbolize innocence. Does the boy in this story represent innocence? Why or why not? What do you think the boy's blindness suggests?

3. The fish is an important part of the narrative. What might it symbolize?

Reacting to the Topic: Discussion and Journal Writing

1. Discuss how you feel about helping strangers on the street. Are there circumstances under which you feel more inclined to offer assistance? less inclined? What aspects of the situation make the difference?

2. Hearing is different from listening, since listening involves paying attention. Likewise, there are differences between looking and seeing. Discuss these differences, using specific events from the essay to illustrate how the acts of *looking* and *seeing* differ, particularly in the context of this story.

Applying Your Skills: Writing Assignments

1. Paragraph Assignment. At the end of the story, the man wishes he could be there when the boy catches more sportfish. Using narration, write a paragraph about a significant event involving a friend or family member that you hope to attend one day.

2. Using narration, rewrite McDonald's story using the first person from the boy's point of view. Feel free to make up details or add events. You will need to devise a new thesis statement. (Hint: Your thesis may be that people are often rude, or it may be that rude people can change.) Plan your essay before you write, deciding at what point in the action you will begin.

3. Write a narrative essay describing a situation in which, at first, you looked but did not "see" what was happening. Be sure to describe the person or event that caused you to see things differently.

4. Combining Patterns. Brainstorm a list of your favorite places. Choose one, and write an essay that describes it to someone who is blind. Include an explanation of why this place is special to you.

5. Internet Research. Visit the Web site for the American Council of the Blind at www.acb.org or any other site that relates to blindness and visual impairment. Write an essay on what you learn about the obstacles faced by people and their families with this type of physical challenge. Be sure to include information on the types of services, products, and technology that are available to them based on what you discover on the Web site.

The Lesson

Toni Cade Bambara

Toni Cade Bambara (1939–1995) was born in New York City and spent the first ten years of her life in Harlem, a neighborhood that she credits with having a profound influence on her writing. She was educated in New York, Italy, and England. A civil rights activist who was greatly concerned with the conditions of the poor, she often focused on the experience of African American women in her writing. Despite the serious themes that she often addressed, Bambara felt that humor was important in her writing. Her collections of short stories include *Gorilla, My Love* (1972), in which this short story first appeared. She wrote numerous articles as well as film scripts, short stories, and two novels, *Salt Eaters* (1980) and *If Blessing Comes* (1987). *Deep Sightings and Rescue Missions*, her final collection of writing, was published in 1996.

As you read, pay attention to Bambara's use of tone. Notice how the first sentence sets the narrator's tone, preparing the reader for how the story will be told. Pay attention also to the author's use of dialect and informal language, and consider what they contribute to the story.

Focus on Understanding   In your reading, identify the lesson referred to in the title.

Focus on the Topic   In class or in your journal, write about a lesson you learned during childhood. Explain what you learned and how it was taught.

Back in the days when everyone was old and stupid or young and foolish and me and Sugar were the only ones just right, this lady moved on our block with nappy° hair and proper speech and no makeup. And quite naturally we laughed at her, laughed the way we did at the junk man who went about his business like he was some big-time president and his sorry-ass horse his secretary. And we kinda hated her too, hated the way we did the winos who cluttered up our parks and pissed on our handball walls and stank up our hallways and stairs so you couldn't halfway play hide-and-seek without a goddamn gas mask. Miss Moore was her name. The only woman on the block with no first name. And she was black as hell, cept for her feet, which were fish-white and spooky. And she was always planning these boring-ass things for us to do, us being my cousin, mostly, who lived on the block cause we all moved North the same time and to the same apartment then spread out gradual to breathe. And our parents would yank our heads into some kinda shape and crisp up our clothes so we'd be presentable for travel with Miss Moore, who always looked like she was going to church, though she never did. Which is just one of the things the

1

nappy: Kinky; tightly curled or twisted

133

grownups talked about when they talked behind her back like a dog. But when she came calling with some sachet she'd sewed up or some gingerbread she'd made or some book, why then they'd all be too embarrassed to turn her down and we'd get handed over all spruced up. She'd been to college and said it was only right that she should take responsibility for the young ones' education, and she not even related by marriage or blood. So they'd go for it. Specially Aunt Gretchen. She was the main gofer in the family. You got some ole dumb shit foolishness you want somebody to go for, you send for Aunt Gretchen. She been screwed into the go-along for so long, it's a blood-deep natural thing with her. Which is how she got saddled with me and Sugar and Junior in the first place while our mothers were in a la-de-da apartment up the block having a good ole time.

So this one day, Miss Moore rounds us all up at the mailbox and it's puredee 2
hot and she's knockin herself out about arithmetic. And school suppose to let up in summer I heard, but she don't never let up. And the starch in my pinafore° scratching the shit outta me and I'm really hating this nappy-head bitch and her goddamn college degree. I'd much rather go to the pool or to the show where it's cool. So me and Sugar leaning on the mailbox being surly, which is a Miss Moore word. And Flyboy checking out what everybody brought for lunch. And Fat Butt already wasting his peanut-butter-and-jelly sandwich like the pig he is. And Junebug punchin on Q.T.'s arm for potato chips. And Rosie Giraffe shifting from one hip to the other waiting for somebody to step on her foot or ask her if she from Georgia so she can kick ass, preferably Mercedes'. And Miss Moore asking us do we know what money is, like we a bunch of retards. I mean real money, she say, like it's only poker chips or monopoly papers we lay on the grocer. So right away I'm tired of this and say so. And would much rather snatch Sugar and go to the Sunset and terrorize the West Indian kids and take their hair ribbons and their money too. And Miss Moore files that remark away for next week's lesson on brotherhood, I can tell. And finally I say we oughta get to the subway cause it's cooler and besides we might meet some cute boys. Sugar done swiped her mama's lipstick, so we ready.

So we heading down the street and she's boring us silly about what things 3
cost and what our parents make and how much goes for rent and how money ain't divided up right in this country. And then she gets to the part about we all poor and live in the slums, which I don't feature. And I'm ready to speak on that, but she steps out in the street and hails two cabs just like that. Then she hustles half the crew in with her and hands me a five-dollar bill and tells me to calculate 10 percent tip for the driver. And we're off. Me and Sugar and Junebug and Flyboy hangin out the window and hollering to everybody, putting lipstick on each other cause Flyboy a faggot anyway, and making farts with our sweaty armpits. But I'm mostly trying to figure how to spend this money. But they all fascinated with the meter ticking and Junebug starts laying bets as to how much it'll read when Flyboy can't hold his breath no more. Then Sugar lays bets as to how much it'll be when we get there. So I'm stuck. Don't nobody want to go for my plan, which is to jump out at the next light and run off to the first

pinafore: Sleeveless dress or apron worn by a little girl

bar-b-que we can find. Then the driver tells us to get the hell out cause we there already. And the meter reads eighty-five cents. And I'm stalling to figure out the tip and Sugar say give him a dime. And I decide he don't need it bad as I do, so later for him. But then he tries to take off with Junebug foot still in the door so we talk about his mama something ferocious. Then we check out that we on Fifth Avenue° and everybody dressed up in stockings. One lady in a fur coat, hot as it is. White folks crazy.

Fifth Avenue: Street in New York City famous for its expensive shops

"This is the place," Miss Moore say, presenting it to us in the voice she uses 4 at the museum. "Let's look in the windows before we go in."

"Can we steal?" Sugar asks very serious like she's getting the ground rules 5 squared away before she plays. "I beg your pardon," say Miss Moore, and we fall out. So she leads us around the windows of the toy store and me and Sugar screamin, "This is mine, that's mine, I gotta have that, that was made for me, I was born for that," till Big Butt drowns us out.

"Hey, I'm going to buy that there." 6

"That there? You don't even know what it is, stupid." 7

"I do so," he say punchin on Rosie Giraffe. "It's a microscope." 8

"Whatcha gonna do with a microscope, fool?" 9

"Look at things." 10

"Like what, Ronald?" ask Miss Moore. And Big Butt ain't got the first no- 11 tion. So here go Miss Moore gabbing about the thousands of bacteria in a drop of water and the somethinorother in a speck of blood and the million and one living things in the air around us is invisible to the naked eye. And what she say that for? Junebug go to town on that "naked" and we rolling. Then Miss Moore ask what it cost. So we all jam into the window smudgin it up and the price tag say $300. So then she ask how long'd take for Big Butt and Junebug to save up their allowances. "Too long," I say. "Yeh," adds Sugar, "outgrown it by that time." And Miss Moore say no, you never outgrow learning instruments. "Why, even medical students and interns and," blah, blah, blah. And we ready to choke Big Butt for bringing it up in the first damn place.

"This here costs four hundred eighty dollars," say Rosie Giraffe. So we pile 12 up all over her to see what she pointin out. My eyes tell me it's a chunk of glass cracked with something heavy, and different-color inks dripped into the splits, then the whole thing put into a oven or something. But for $480 it don't make sense.

"That's a paperweight made of semi-precious stones fused together under 13 tremendous pressure," she explains slowly, with her hands doing the mining and all the factory work.

"So what's a paperweight?" ask Rosie Giraffe. 14

"To weigh paper with, dumbbell," say Flyboy, the wise man from the 15 East.

"Not exactly," say Miss Moore, which is what she say when you warm or 16 way off too. "It's to weigh paper down so it won't scatter and make your desk untidy." So right away me and Sugar curtsy to each other and then to Mercedes who is more the tidy type.

"We don't keep paper on top of the desk in my class," say Junebug, figuring   17
Miss Moore crazy or lyin one.

"At home, then," she say. "Don't you have a calendar and a pencil case and   18
a blotter and a letter-opener on your desk at home where you do your homework?" And she know damn well what our homes look like cause she nosys
around in them every chance she gets.

"I don't even have a desk," say Junebug. "Do we?"   19

"No. And I don't get no homework neither," say Big Butt.   20

"And I don't even have a home," say Flyboy like he do at school to keep the   21
white folks off his back and sorry for him. Send this poor kid to camp posters,
is his specialty.

"I do," says Mercedes. "I have a box of stationery on my desk and a picture   22
of my cat. My godmother bought the stationery and the desk. There's a big rose
on each sheet and the envelopes smell like roses."

"Who wants to know about your smelly-ass stationery," say Rosie Giraffe   23
fore I can get my two cents in.

"It's important to have a work area all your own so that . . ."   24

"Will you look at this sailboat, please," say Flyboy, cutting her off and   25
pointin to the thing like it was his. So once again we tumble all over each other
to gaze at this magnificent thing in the toy store which is just big enough to
maybe sail two kittens across the pond if you strap them to the posts tight. We
all start reciting the price tag like we in assembly. "Handcrafted sailboat of
fiberglass at one thousand one hundred ninety-five dollars."

"Unbelievable," I hear myself say and am really stunned. I read it again for   26
myself just in case the group recitation put me in a trance. Same thing. For
some reason this pisses me off. We look at Miss Moore and she lookin at us,
waiting for I dunno what.

"Who'd pay all that when you can buy a sailboat set for a quarter at Pop's,   27
a tube of glue for a dime, and a ball of string for eight cents? It must have a
motor and a whole lot else besides," I say. "My sailboat cost me about fifty
cents."

"But will it take water?" say Mercedes with her smart ass.   28

"Took mine to Alley Pond Park once," say Flyboy. "String broke. Lost it.   29
Pity."

"Sailed mine in Central Park and it keeled over and sank. Had to ask my fa-   30
ther for another dollar."

"And you got the strap," laugh Big Butt. "The jerk didn't even have a string   31
on it. My old man wailed on his behind."

Little Q.T. was staring hard at the sailboat and you could see he wanted it   32
bad. But he too little and somebody'd just take it from him. So what the hell.
"This boat for kids, Miss Moore?"

"Parents silly to buy something like that just to get all broke up," say Rosie   33
Giraffe.

"That much money it should last forever," I figure.   34

"My father'd buy it for me if I wanted it."   35

"Your father, my ass," say Rosie Giraffe getting a chance to finally push 36
Mercedes.

"Must be rich people shop here," say Q.T.   37

"You are a very bright boy," say Flyboy. "What was your first clue?" And he 38
rap him on the head with the back of his knuckles, since Q.T. the only one he
could get away with. Though Q.T. liable to come up behind you years later and
get his licks in when you half expect it.

"What I want to know is," I says to Miss Moore though I never talk to her, 39
I wouldn't give the bitch that satisfaction, "is how much a real boat costs? I figure a thousand'd get you a yacht any day."

"Why don't you check that out," she says, "and report back to the group?" 40
Which really pains my ass. If you gonna mess up a perfectly good swim day
least you could do is have some answers. "Let's go in," she say like she got something up her sleeve. Only she don't lead the way. So me and Sugar turn the
corner to where the entrance is, but when we get there I kinda hang back. Not
that I'm scared, what's there to be afraid of, just a toy store. But I feel funny,
shame. But what I got to be shamed about? Got as much right to go in as anybody. But somehow I can't seem to get hold of the door, so I step away from
Sugar to lead. But she hangs back too. And I look at her and she looks at me
and this is ridiculous. I mean, damn, I have never been shy about doing nothing or going nowhere. But then Mercedes steps up and then Rosie Giraffe and
Big Butt crowd in behind and shove, and next thing we all stuffed into the doorway with only Mercedes squeezing past us, smoothing out her jumper and
walking right down the aisle. Then the rest of us tumble in like a glued-together
jigsaw done all wrong. And people lookin at us. And it's like the time me and
Sugar crashed into the Catholic church on a dare. But once we got in there and
everything so hushed and holy and the candles and the bowin and the hand-
kerchiefs on all the drooping heads, I just couldn't go through with the plan.
Which was for me to run up to the altar and do a tap dance while Sugar played
the nose flute and messed around in the holy water. And Sugar kept given me
the elbow. Then later teased me so bad I tied her up in the shower and turned
it on and locked her in. And she'd be there till this day if Aunt Gretchen hadn't
finally figured I was lying about the boarder takin a shower.

Same thing in the store. We all walkin on tiptoe and hardly touchin the 41
games and puzzles and things. And I watched Miss Moore who is steady
watchin us like she waitin for a sign. Like Mama Drewery watches the sky and
sniffs the air and takes note of just how much slant is in the bird formation.
Then me and Sugar bump smack into each other, so busy gazing at the toys,
'specially the sailboat. But we don't laugh and go into our fat-lady bump-stom-
ach routine. We just stare at that price tag. Then Sugar run a finger over the
whole boat. And I'm jealous and want to hit her. Maybe not her, but I sure want
to punch somebody in the mouth.

"Watcha bring us here for, Miss Moore?"   42

"You sound angry, Sylvia. Are you mad about something?" Givin me one of 43
them grins like she tellin a grown-up joke that never turns out to be funny. And

she's lookin very closely at me like maybe she plannin to do my portrait from memory. I'm mad, but I won't give her that satisfaction. So I slouch around the store being very bored and say, "Let's go."

Me and Sugar at the back of the train watchin the tracks whizzin by large 44 then small then getting gobbled up in the dark. I'm thinkin about this tricky toy I saw in the store. A clown that somersaults on a bar then does chin-ups just cause you yank lightly at his leg. Cost $35. I could see me askin my mother for a $35 birthday clown. "You wanna who that costs what?" she'd say, cocking her head to the side to get a better view of the hole in my head. Thirty-five dollars could buy new bunk beds for Junior and Gretchen's boy. Thirty-five dollars and the whole household could go visit Grand-daddy Nelson in the country. Thirty-five dollars would pay for the rent and the piano bill too. Who are these people that spend that much for performing clowns and $1000 for toy sailboats? What kinda work they do and how they live and how come we ain't in on it? Where we are is who we are, Miss Moore always pointin out. But it don't necessarily have to be that way, she always adds then waits for somebody to say that poor people have to wake up and demand their share of the pie and don't none of us know what kind of pie she talking about in the first damn place. But she ain't so smart cause I still got her four dollars from the taxi and she sure ain't gettin it. Messin up my day with this shit. Sugar nudges me in my pocket and winks.

Miss Moore lines us up in front of the mailbox where we started from, seem 45 like years ago, and I got a headache for thinkin so hard. And we lean all over each other so we can hold up under the draggy-ass lecture she always finishes us off with at the end before we thank her for borin us to tears. But she just looks at us like she readin tea leaves. Finally she say, "Well, what did you think of F.A.O. Schwarz?"

Rosie Giraffe mumbles, "White folks crazy." 46

"I'd like to go there again when I get my birthday money," says Mercedes, 47 and we shove her out the pack so she has to lean on the mailbox by herself.

"I'd like a shower. Tiring day," say Flyboy. 48

Then Sugar surprises me by sayin, "You know, Miss Moore, I don't think all 49 of us here put together eat in a year what that sailboat costs." And Miss Moore lights up like somebody goosed her. "And?" she say, urging Sugar on. Only I'm standin on her foot so she don't continue.

"Imagine for a minute what kind of society it is in which some people can 50 spend on a toy what it would cost to feed a family of six or seven. What do you think?"

"I think," say Sugar pushing me off her feet like she never done before, 51 cause I whip her ass in a minute, "that this is not much of a democracy if you ask me. Equal chance to pursue happiness means an equal crack at the dough, don't it?" Miss Moore is besides herself and I am disgusted with Sugar's treachery. So I stand on her foot one more time to see if she'll shove me. She shuts up, and Miss Moore looks at me, sorrowfully I'm thinkin. And somethin weird is goin on, I can feel it in my chest.

"Anybody else learn anything today?" lookin dead at me. I walk away and 52
Sugar has to run to catch up and don't even seem to notice when I shrug her
arm off my shoulder.

"Well, we got four dollars anyway," she says.   53

"Uh, hunh."   54

"We could go to Hascombs and get half a chocolate layer and then go to the 55
Sunset and still have plenty money for potato chips and ice cream sodas."

"Uh, hunh."   56

"Race you to Hascombs," she say.   57

We start down the block and she gets ahead which is O.K. by me cause I'm 58
going to the West End and then over to the Drive to think this day through. She
can run if she want to and even run faster. But ain't nobody gonna beat me at
nuthin.

Understanding the Reading

1. "The Lesson" is written from the point of view of a young African American girl
   named Sylvia. Describe what you learn about the narrator as the story progresses.
2. What is it about Miss Moore that bothers Sylvia and the other children?
3. How does the outing to FAO Schwarz affect the children?
4. What are the lessons taught in the story?

Visualizing the Reading

A narrative often conveys a message through events, action, dialogue, or description of
characters. For each of the items listed in the table below, decide what it reveals, suggests, and contributes to the story. The first two have been done for you.

Event, Action, Dialogue, or Description	Significance
1. Miss Moore is the only woman on the block with no first name. (para. 1)	This suggests formality and distance; it also suggests respect.
2. "I'm really hating this nappy-head bitch and her goddamn college degree." (para. 2)	Sylvia hates what Miss Moore represents: education and civility. *(Continued)*

(Continued)	
3. Sylvia decides she needs the cab driver's tip more than he does. (para. 3)	
4. "I feel funny, shame." (para. 40)	
5. "'You sound angry, Sylvia. Are you mad about something?'" (para. 43)	
6. "Where we are is who we are, Miss Moore always pointin out." (para. 44)	
7. "Imagine for a minute what kind of society it is in which some people can spend on a toy what it would cost to feed a family of six or seven." (para. 50)	

Examining the Characteristics of Narrative Essays

1. The theme of a story is its central or dominant idea, the main point the author makes about the human experience. What broad statement about life does Bambara make? Include evidence from the story to support your interpretation.

2. Writers of literature often bend the rules of grammar and usage, using sentence fragments, ungrammatical dialogue, or unusual punctuation to create a particular effect. Why do you think Bambara chose to use so much slang, dialect, and swearing in her story? What effect does this have on your reading?

3. The plot, or central story line, of a short story is often centered on a conflict. Identify the conflict that the narrator deals with in "The Lesson" and the point of climax when the story is resolved. How does the author create and sustain tension?

4. "The Lesson" is told from the first-person point of view of Sylvia, the narrator. One potential drawback of this approach is that it does not give access to the inner thoughts of the central character, Miss Moore. Had Bambara chosen to use third-person point of view, what aspects of Miss Moore's personality would you have liked to know about?

5. Consider where the action of the story occurs. Why is place important in "The Lesson"? How does Bambara use concrete details to create a sense of place, both in the neighborhood and on Fifth Avenue?

Building Your Word Power

1. Explain the connotative, or implied, meaning of the phrase "real money" (para. 2).

2. Miss Moore is described as explaining the paper weight "with her hands doing the mining and all the factory work" (para. 13). What picture does this metaphor paint in your mind?

3. Explain the meaning of each of the following words as it is used in the reading: *saddled* (para. 1), *keeled over* (30), *wailed* (31), *liable* (38), and *boarder* (40). Refer to your dictionary as needed.

For a definition of **connotative meaning** *and* **metaphor**, *see the chart of commonly used language features on p. 21.*

Building Your Critical Thinking Skills: Colloquial Language

Colloquial language is informal, conversation-like writing. In formal research papers, most articles, and nonfiction books, this type of writing is unacceptable. However, in less formal settings and in fiction, colloquial language can add a special dimension. Characters that use slang, dialect, or "colorful" language reveal a great deal about their thoughts, attitudes, and feelings. Authors may use language that they are familiar with from their own lives, or they might do research to ensure that their characters are speaking appropriately. Use your knowledge of colloquial language to answer the following questions.

1. What can you determine about the period or setting of the story based on the language used by the characters?

2. Why doesn't Miss Moore use the same language as the children? How does this difference affect your understanding of the characters?

3. What does Bambara's use of colloquial language add to the story? Do you find it humorous? Explain your answer.

Reacting to the Topic: Discussion and Journal Questions

1. Discuss whether you would feel comfortable being a mentor to a younger person. What lessons would you offer to someone younger than yourself? How would the experience benefit you?

2. In class or in your journal, explore the various reasons why parents might want an adult outside the family to teach their child life lessons.

Applying Your Skills: Writing Assignments

1. **Paragraph Assignment.** Sylvia is surprised that she is uneasy about going into the toy store. Write a narrative paragraph about a time when your reaction to a situation surprised you.

2. Choose a person from whom you have learned something about the ways of the world. Think of one lesson you learned, and write an essay narrating that experience. Be sure to include vivid and realistic details.

3. In this story there are two groups of people: the haves and the have-nots. Think of an incident in your own life that illustrates a division between those with wealth

and power and those without. Write a narrative essay explaining how your experience demonstrates the division. In your thesis, be sure to reveal your feelings about such a division.

4. **Combining Patterns.** Sylvia exhibits a disdain for education and knowledge in "The Lesson." In an essay using illustration that includes examples from the story, evaluate and comment on Sylvia's attitude toward education. In your thesis, present a case for why Sylvia might have such a negative outlook on education. Given the outcome of the story, do you think this outlook is likely to change? Why or why not?

5. **Internet Research.** Explore the Pseudo Dictionary site at www.pseudo dictionary.com/index.php, or visit another online site dedicated to slang and colloquial language. Browse the listings of colloquial and slang words, and see what terms have recently been added. Then write an essay about the use of informal and formal language describing situations in which the use of either type would be appropriate. Use examples from the site to illustrate your points, drawing a conclusion about whether our society is too formal or informal.

Description: Portraying People, Places, and Things

WRITING QUICK START

S uppose you are moving to a large city and need to sell your car because the apartment you just rented does not include parking. You place the following advertisement in the local newspaper:

> 6-year-old VW bug. $4500 or best offer.
> Call 555-2298.

Although the ad runs for two weeks, you only get a few calls and no offers. Then a friend advises you to write a more appealing description of your unique vehicle that will make people want to contact you. Rewrite the advertisement, describing the car in a way that will convince prospective buyers to call you.

What Is Description?

Description presents information in a way that appeals to one or more of the five senses, usually with the purpose of creating a specific impression or feeling. Descriptive writing makes your ideas vivid so that the audience can almost see, hear, smell, taste, or touch what you are writing about. People use description every day. For example, in a conversation with a friend you might describe a pair of new shoes you recently bought, a flavor of ice cream you tasted last night, or a concert you attended last weekend. You will use description in many situations in college and on the job, as these examples show.

- For a *chemistry* lab report, you are asked to describe the odor and appearance of a substance made by combining two chemicals.
- As a *nurse* at a local burn treatment center, you are responsible for recording on each patient's chart the overall appearance of and change in second- and third-degree burns.

In the following lively description of a sensory experience of taste, you will feel as if you, too, are eating chilli peppers.

Eating Chilli Peppers

Jeremy MacClancy

Jeremy MacClancy (b. 1953) is an anthropologist who studies the everyday choices people make and how those choices vary from culture to culture. As professor of social anthropology at Oxford Brookes University in England, MacClancy has written on a variety of topics, but he has a particular interest in food. He chairs the United Kingdom's chapter of the International Commission on the Anthropology of Food and has edited the book *Researching Food Habits* (2003), in addition to being a noted expert on Basque food. The following essay comes from MacClancy's book *Consuming Culture: Why You Eat What You Eat* (1993).

As you read the essay, pay special attention to the sensory details that enliven MacClancy's description of how it feels to eat hot peppers. Think about how those details contribute to the overall impression he conveys.

Introduction: creates interest through questions that are answered in the essay

How come over half of the world's population have made a powerful chemical irritant the center of their gastronomic lives? How can so many millions stomach chillies?

1

Biting into a tabasco pepper is like aiming a flame-thrower at your parted lips. There might be little reaction at first, but then the burn starts to grow. A few seconds later the chilli mush in your mouth reaches critical mass and your palate prepares for liftoff. The message spreads. The sweat glands open, your eyes stream, your nose runs, your stomach warms up, your heart accelerates, and your lungs breathe faster. All this is normal. But bite off more than your body can take, and you will be left coughing, sneezing, and spitting. Tears stripe your cheeks, and your mouth belches fire like a dragon celebrating its return to life. Eater, beware!

As a general stimulant, chilli is similar to amphetamines — only quicker, cheaper, non-addictive, and beneficial to boot. Employees at the tabasco plant in Louisiana rarely complain of coughs, hay fever, or sinusitis. (Recent evidence, however, suggests that too many chillies can bring on stomach cancer.) Over the centuries, people have used hot peppers as a folk medicine to treat sore throats or inflamed gums, to relieve respiratory distress, and to ease gastritis induced by alcoholism. For aching muscles and tendons, a chilli plaster is more effective than one of mustard, with the added advantage that it does not blister the skin. But people do not eat tabasco, jalapeño, or cayenne peppers because of their pharmacological side effects. They eat them for the taste — different varieties have different flavors — and for the fire they give off. In other words, they go for the burn.

Eating chillies makes for exciting times: the thrill of anticipation, the extremity of the flames, and then the slow descent back to normality. This is a benign form of masochism, like going to a horror movie, riding a roller coaster, or stepping into a cold bath after a sauna. The body flashes danger signals, but the brain knows the threat is not too great. Aficionados, self-absorbed in their burning passion, know exactly how to pace their whole chilli eating so that the flames are maintained at a steady maximum. Wrenched out of normal routines by the continuing assault on their mouths, they concentrate on the sensation and ignore almost everything else. They play with fire and just ride the burn, like experienced surfers cresting along a wave. For them, without hot peppers, food would lose its zest and their days would seem too dull. A cheap, legal thrill, chilli is the spice of their life.

In the rural areas of Mexico, men can turn their chilli habit into a contest of strength by seeing who can stomach the most hot peppers in a set time. This gastronomic test, however, is not used as a way to prove one's machismo, for women can play the game as well. In this context, chillies are a non-sexist form of acquired love for those with strong hearts and fiery passions — a steady source of hot sauce for their lives.

---

2   Vivid comparison (simile)

Sensory details: taste and touch

Another vivid simile

3   Comparison to drug use

4

Continued use of vivid comparisons

Sensory details: taste

Another effective comparison

5

Describes use of chillis in Mexico

Conclusion: author
ends as he began, with
a question

The enjoyable sensations of a running nose, crying eyes, and dragon-   6
like mouth belching flames are clearly not for the timorous.

More tabasco, anyone?   7

Characteristics of Descriptive Essays

Successful descriptions offer readers more than a list of sensory details or a catalog of characteristics. In a good description, the details work together to create a
single dominant impression. Writers often use comparison to help readers understand the experience.

Description Uses Sensory Details

Sensory details appeal to one or more of the five senses. For example, in paragraph 2 of "Eating Chilli Peppers," MacClancy describes the physical sensations
that eating chilli peppers creates. Paragraph 3 focuses on their drug-like effects,
while paragraphs 4 and 5 emphasize their psychological effects. Throughout the
essay the writer uses vivid language that appeals to the senses of sight and taste so
that the reader can almost feel a chilli pepper burning in the mouth. By appealing
to the senses in your writing, you too can help readers experience the object, sensation, event, or person you aim to describe.

Sight. When you describe what something looks like, you help the reader create a
mental picture of it. In the following excerpt, Loren Eiseley uses visual detail to
describe what he found in a field.

> One day as I cut across the field which at that time extended on one side of our
> suburban shopping center, I found a giant slug feeding from a funnel of pink ice
> cream in an abandoned Dixie cup. I could see his eyes telescope and protrude in
> a kind of dim, uncertain ecstasy as his dark body bunched and elongated in the
> curve of the cup.
>
> LOREN EISELEY, "The Brown Wasps"

The description enables the reader to imagine the slug eating the ice cream in a
way that a bare statement of the facts — "On my way to the mall, I saw a slug in a
paper cup" — could never do. Eiseley describes shape ("funnel of pink ice cream"),
action ("bunched and elongated"), color ("pink funnel," "dark body"), and size
("giant"). Notice also how he includes specific details ("suburban shopping
center," "Dixie cup") to help readers visualize the scene.

Sound. Sound can also be a powerful descriptive tool. Can you "hear" the engines
in the following description?

They were one-cylinder and two-cylinder engines, and some were make-and-break and some were jump-spark, but they all made a sleepy sound across the lake. The one-lungers throbbed and fluttered, and the twin-cylinder ones purred and purred, and that was a quiet sound too. But now the campers all had outboards. In the daytime, in the hot mornings, these motors made a petulant, irritable sound; at night, in the still evening when the afterglow lit the water, they whined about one's ears like mosquitoes.

E. B. WHITE, "Once More to the Lake"

White conveys the sounds of the engines by using active verbs ("throbbed and fluttered," "purred and purred," "whined"), descriptive adjectives ("sleepy," "petulant," "irritable"), and a comparison ("whined about one's ears like mosquitoes").

Writers of description also use *onomatopoeia* — that is, words that approximate the sounds they describe. The words *hiss, whine, spurt,* and *sizzle* are examples.

Smell. Smells are sometimes difficult to describe, partly because there are not as many adjectives for smells as there are for sights and sounds. However, smell can be an effective descriptive device, as shown here.

Driving through farm country at summer sunset provides a cavalcade of smells: manure, cut grass, honeysuckle, spearmint, wheat chaff, scallions, chicory, tar from the macadam road.

DIANE ACKERMAN, *A Natural History of the Senses*

Notice how Ackerman lists nouns that evoke distinct odors and leaves it to the reader to imagine how they smell.

Taste. Words that evoke the sense of taste can make descriptions very lively, as in "Eating Chilli Peppers." Consider MacClancy's description of the initial taste of a chilli: "There might be little reaction at first, but then the burn starts to grow. A few seconds later the chilli mush in your mouth reaches critical mass and your palate prepares for liftoff" (para. 2).

Touch. Descriptions of texture, temperature, and weight enable a reader not only to visualize but almost to tactilely experience an object or scene. In the excerpt that follows, Annie Dillard describes the experience of holding a Polyphemus moth cocoon.

We passed the cocoon around; it was heavy. As we held it in our hands, the creature within warmed and squirmed. We were delighted, and wrapped it tighter in our fists. The pupa began to jerk violently, in heart-stopping knocks. Who's there? I can still feel those thumps, urgent through a muffling of spun silk and leaf, urgent through the swaddling of many years, against the curve of my palm. We kept passing it around. When it came to me again it was hot as a bun;

it jumped half out of my hand. The teacher intervened. She put it, still heaving and banging, in the ubiquitous Mason Jar.

ANNIE DILLARD, *Pilgrim at Tinker Creek*

Dillard describes the texture of the cocoon ("a muffling of spun silk and leaf"), its temperature ("hot as a bun"), and its weight ("heavy") to give readers an accurate sense of how it felt to hold it.

Description Uses Active Verbs and Varied Sentences

Sensory details are often best presented by using active, vivid verbs in sentences with varied structure. Look, for instance, at the active verbs in this sentence from paragraph 2 of MacClancy's essay.

The sweat glands *open,* your eyes *stream,* your nose *runs,* your stomach *warms up,* your heart *accelerates,* and your lungs *breathe* faster.

In fact, active verbs are often more effective than adverbs in creating striking and lasting impressions, as the following example demonstrates.

ORIGINAL: The team captain *proudly* accepted the award.

REVISED: The team captain *marched* to the podium, *grasped* the trophy, and *gestured* toward his teammates.

To maximize the effective expression of sensory details, be sure to use different types of sentences and to vary their lengths. Looking again at paragraph 2 in MacClancy's essay, note how he varies his sentences to make the description interesting. You should also avoid wordy or repetitive sentences, especially those with strings of mediocre adjectives or adverbs (*pretty, really, very*), which detract from the vivid impression you want to create.

Description Creates a Dominant Impression

An effective description leaves the reader with a **dominant impression** — an overall attitude, mood, or feeling about the subject. The impression may be awe, inspiration, anger, or distaste, for example. The dominant impression is the implied thesis of a descriptive essay; it suggests the author's main point about the subject.

Suppose you are writing about an old storage box in your parents' attic, and the aspect of the box you want to emphasize (your "slant") is *memories of childhood*. Given this slant, you might describe the box in several different ways, each of which would convey a different dominant impression.

A box filled with treasures from my childhood brought back memories of long, sunny afternoons playing in our backyard.

Opening the box was like lifting the lid of a time machine, revealing toys and games from another era.

When I opened the box I was eight years old again, fighting over my favorite doll with my twin sister, Erica.

Because each example provides a different impression of the contents of the storage box, each would require a different type of support — that is, only selected objects from within the box would be relevant to each impression. Also, it is significant that in all of these examples the dominant impression is stated directly rather than implied. Many times, writers rely on descriptive language to imply a dominant impression.

In "Eating Chilli Peppers," all the details evoke the thrill of eating the peppers for those who love them; as MacClancy says, "they go for the burn." The first two sentences of the essay pose the questions that the remaining paragraphs answer. The answer is the dominant impression: Eating chilli peppers is thrilling. To write an effective description you need to select details carefully, including only those that contribute to the dominant impression you want to create. Details that do not support the dominant impression can clutter the description and distract the reader. MacClancy does not clutter his description by describing the size, shape, texture, or color of chilli peppers; instead he focuses on their thrilling, fiery hotness and the side effects they cause.

Description Uses Connotative Language Effectively

As noted in Chapter 1, most words have two levels of meaning: *denotative* and *connotative*. The denotation of a word is its precise dictionary meaning (for instance, the denotation of *flag* is "a piece of cloth used as a national emblem"). Usually, however, feelings and attitudes are also associated with a word; these are the word's connotations. (A common connotation of *flag* is patriotism — love and respect for one's country.) As you write, be careful about the connotations of the words you choose. Select words that strengthen the dominant impression you are creating.

Description Uses Comparisons

When describing a person or an object, you can help readers by comparing it to something familiar. Several types of comparison are used in descriptive writing: similes, metaphors, personification, and analogies.

In a **simile** the comparison is direct and is introduced by the word *like* or *as*. For example, MacClancy uses this telling simile in "Eating Chilli Peppers": "Biting into a tabasco pepper is like aiming a flame-thrower at your parted lips."

A **metaphor** is an indirect, comparison, describing one thing as if it were another. Instead of the simile shown above, MacClancy could have used a metaphor to describe the experience of eating chillies: "Eating chilli peppers is a descent into a fiery hell."

Personification is a figure of speech in which an object is given human qualities or characteristics. "The television screen stared back at me" is an example. An **analogy** is an extended comparison in which one subject is used to explain the other. Often, a more familiar subject is used to explain one that is less familiar. For example, you might explain the elements of an essay — introduction, thesis, body, and conclusion — by comparing them to a documentary film containing those elements. Like similes and metaphors, analogies add interest to writing while making your ideas more accessible to the reader.

Description Assumes a Vantage Point

A **vantage point** is the point or position from which one writes a description. With a *fixed vantage point*, you describe what you see from a particular position. With a *moving vantage point*, you describe your subject from a number of different positions. In this way, the vantage point is similar to a movie camera: A fixed vantage point is like a stationary camera trained on a subject from one direction, whereas a moving vantage point is like a hand-held camera that moves around the subject, capturing it from many directions.

In "Eating Chilli Peppers," MacClancy uses a moving vantage point; he first reports sensations within the mouth and then moves on to other body parts. When you use a moving vantage point, be sure to alert your readers when you change positions. MacClancy gives his readers clues that his vantage point is changing. For example, in paragraph 2 he states that "the message spreads" to indicate that he is moving from the palate to sweat glands, eyes, and so forth.

Description Follows a Method of Organization

Effective descriptions, like other kinds of writing, must follow a clear method of organization in order to be easy to read. Three common methods of organization used in descriptive writing are spatial order, chronological order, and most-to-least or least-to-most order.

- When you use **spatial order**, you systematically describe a subject from top to bottom, inside to outside, or near to far away. Or you may start from a central focal point and then describe the objects that surround it. For example, in describing a college campus you might start with a building at the center of the campus, then describe the buildings next to it, and conclude by describing something on the outskirts.
- **Chronological order** works well for describing events or changes that occur in objects or places over a given period. For example, you might use chronological order to describe the changes in a puppy's behavior as it grows.
- You might use **least-to-most** or **most-to-least order** to describe the different smells in a flower garden or the sounds of an orchestra tuning up.

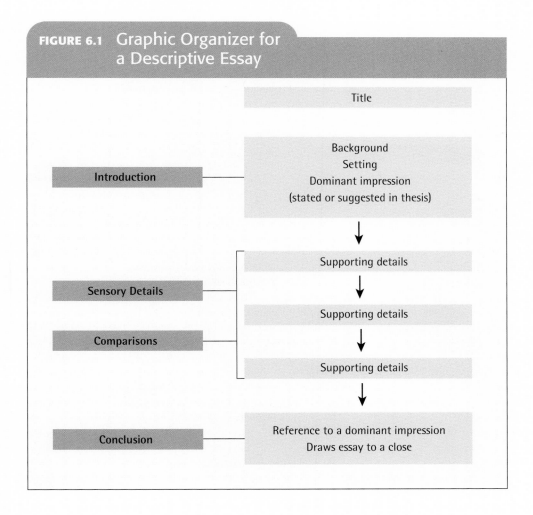

FIGURE 6.1 Graphic Organizer for a Descriptive Essay

Title

Introduction — Background / Setting / Dominant impression / (stated or suggested in thesis)

Sensory Details

Comparisons — Supporting details / Supporting details / Supporting details

Conclusion — Reference to a dominant impression / Draws essay to a close

Visualizing a Descriptive Essay

The graphic organizer in Figure 6.1 will help you visualize the elements of a description. When your primary purpose is to describe something, you'll need to follow the standard essay format — title, introduction, body, and conclusion — with slight adaptations and adjustments. Figure 6.2 is a graphic organizer based on "Eating Chilli Peppers."

When you incorporate a description into an essay that also uses other patterns of development, you will probably need to condense or eliminate one or more of these elements.

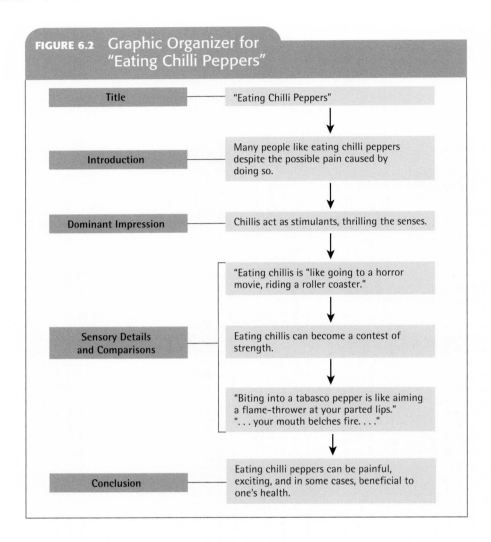

FIGURE 6.2   Graphic Organizer for "Eating Chilli Peppers"

Title — "Eating Chilli Peppers"

Introduction — Many people like eating chilli peppers despite the possible pain caused by doing so.

Dominant Impression — Chillis act as stimulants, thrilling the senses.

Sensory Details and Comparisons —

"Eating chillis is "like going to a horror movie, riding a roller coaster."

Eating chillis can become a contest of strength.

"Biting into a tabasco pepper is like aiming a flame-thrower at your parted lips."
". . . your mouth belches fire. . . ."

Conclusion — Eating chilli peppers can be painful, exciting, and in some cases, beneficial to one's health.

Writing a Descriptive Essay

To write a descriptive essay, use the following steps. Be sure to develop vivid sensory details of your subject.

Planning a Descriptive Essay

Your first step is to choose a subject. Make sure it is one you are familiar with or one you can readily observe. Also be aware that you may need to observe the object, activity, or person several times as you work through your essay.

Because almost any subject will encompass many more details than you could possibly include, you'll need to emphasize a particular slant or angle. If your subject is a person, you might focus on a character trait such as compulsiveness or sense of humor. To describe an object, you might emphasize its usefulness, value, or beauty.

Collecting Details That Describe Your Subject

Once you've decided on a slant or angle, you're ready to collect and record additional sensory details. The following suggestions will help you generate details. Also refer to the table on page 154 to stimulate your thinking.

Gathering Details for Descriptive Essays

1. Brainstorm about your subject. Record any sensory details that support the slant or angle you have chosen.
2. Try describing the subject to a friend, concentrating on your particular slant. You may discover that details come more easily during conversation. Make notes on what you said and on your friend's response.
3. Draw a quick sketch of the subject, and label the parts. You may recall additional details as you draw.
4. Divide a piece of paper or a computer file into five horizontal sections. Label the sections *sight, sound, taste, touch,* and *smell.* Work through each section in turn, systematically recording what the subject looks like, sounds like, and so forth.

Finding Comparisons and Choosing a Vantage Point

Look over your list of details. Try to think of appropriate comparisons — similes, metaphors, analogies, personification — for as many details as possible. Jot down your comparisons in the margin next to the relevant details in your list. Don't expect to find a comparison for each detail. Instead, your goal is to discover one or two strong comparisons that will be most effective.

Next, consider whether to use a fixed or moving vantage point. Think about the aspect of your subject you are emphasizing and how it can best be communicated. Ask yourself the following questions.

- What vantage point(s) will give the reader the most useful information?
- From which vantage point(s) can I provide the most revealing or striking details?

Creating a Dominant Impression

As noted earlier, think of the dominant impression as the thesis that conveys your main point and holds the rest of the essay together. It also creates a mood or feeling about the subject, which all other details in the essay explain or support.

The dominant impression you decide on should be the one about which you feel most knowledgeable and confident. It should also appeal to your audience,

Characteristics to Consider in Developing Sensory Details

Sight	Color
	Pattern
	Shape
	Size
Sound	Volume (loud or soft)
	Pitch
	Quality
Taste	Pleasant or unpleasant
	Salty, sweet, sour, or bitter
Touch	Texture
	Weight
	Temperature
Smell	Agreeable or disagreeable
	Strength

For more on support-ing your thesis, see Chapter 2, p. 39.

offer an unusual perspective, and provide new insights on the subject. Finally, keep in mind that you may need to do additional prewriting to gather support for your dominant impression. This step is similar to collecting evidence for a thesis, except the "evidence" for a descriptive essay consists of sensory details. Therefore, before drafting your essay, check to see if you have enough sensory details to support your dominant impression.

Drafting a Descriptive Essay

Once you are satisfied with your dominant impression and sensory details, you can choose the method of organization that will best support the dominant impression (see p. 150). As you draft the essay, remember that all details must support the dominant impression. For example, if you are describing the way apes in a zoo imitate one another and humans, only details about how the apes mimic people and other apes should be included. Other details, such as the condition of the apes' environment and types of animals nearby, do not belong in the essay. Be careful as well about the *number* of details you include. Too many details will tire your readers, but an insufficient number will leave them unconvinced of your main point. Select striking sensory details that make your point effectively; leave out details that tell the reader little or nothing. For example, instead of selecting five or six ordinary details to describe a concert, choose one revealing detail such as the following.

> As the band performed the final song, the lights dimmed and every single member of the audience of twelve hundred people silently held a lighted candle before his or her face.

Try also to include one or two telling metaphors or similes. If you cannot think of any, however, don't stretch to construct them. Effective comparisons usually come to mind as you examine your subject. Contrived comparisons will only lessen the impact of your essay.

As you write, remember that the sensory language you use should enable readers to re-create the person, object, or scene in their minds. Keep the following three guidelines in mind.

Guidelines for Using Sensory Language

1. **Create images that appeal to the five senses.** Your descriptions should appeal to one or more of the senses. See pages 146–48 for examples of ways to engage each of the five senses.

2. **Avoid vague, general descriptions.** Use specific, not vague, language to describe your subject.

VAGUE:	The pizza was cheaply prepared.
CONCRETE:	**The supposedly "large" pizza was miniature, with a nearly imperceptible layer of sauce, a light dusting of cheese, a few paper-thin slices of pepperoni, and one or two stray mushroom slices.**

3. **Use figures of speech and analogies effectively.** Figures of speech (similes, metaphors) analogies, and personification create memorable images that enliven your writing and capture the readers' attention.

   - Choose fresh, surprising images. Avoid overused clichés such "cold as ice" and "it's a hop, skip, and a jump away."
   - Make sure the similarity between the two items being compared is apparent. If you write "*Peter* looked like an *unpeeled tangerine*," your reader will not be able to guess what characteristics Peter shares with the tangerine. "Peter's *skin* was as dimpled as a *tangerine peel*" gives the reader a clearer idea of what Peter looks like.
   - Don't mix or combine figures of speech. Such expressions, called **mixed metaphors**, are confusing and often unintentionally humorous. For example, this sentence mixes images of a hawk and a wolf: "The fighter jet was a hawk soaring into the clouds, growling as it sought its prey."

Analyzing and Revising

If possible, set aside your draft for a day or two before rereading and revising. As you reread, focus on overall effectiveness, not on grammar and mechanics. Use the Revision Flowchart in Figure 6.3 to discover the strengths and weaknesses of your descriptive essay.

FIGURE 6.3 Revising a Descriptive Essay

QUESTIONS

REVISION STRATEGIES

1. Without looking at your essay, *write* a sentence that states the dominant impression you want to convey. Next, highlight the sentence(s) that express the *dominant impression.* Compare the two statements. Are they similar?

 NO

- Reread your essay. Make a list of the different impressions it conveys (pp. 148–49).
- Choose one impression that you have the most to say about, and brainstorm to develop additional supporting details.
- If the impressions don't seem promising, try to emphasize a new aspect of your subject or change subjects and start over.

 YES

2. Place a checkmark ✔ by each sensory detail. Does each detail support your *dominant impression?* Are your connotations appropriate?

 NO

- Eliminate irrelevant sensory details.
- Analyze the connotations of your descriptive words. For any words with inappropriate connotations, substitute words that better support the dominant impression.

 YES

3. Review the sensory details you have ✔ checkmarked. Have you used vivid language? Have you included enough to help the reader visualize the topic? Does every paragraph use either sensory details or vivid language?

NO

- Brainstorm to discover additional sensory details (see the table on p. 153).
- Replace passive verbs with active ones. Vary sentence structure.
- Tape-record the description of your subject. Play the tape and determine where more detail is needed.

 YES

QUESTIONS		REVISION STRATEGIES

4. Place brackets [ ] around each comparison—simile, metaphor, analogy, personification. Is each one fresh and effective?

 NO

- Look for and eliminate clichés.
- Brainstorm to find fresh comparisons.
- Instead of writing, try speaking to a friend or into a tape recorder to free up ideas.

 YES

5. *Write* a sentence describing the point of view you used. Does it give the clearest possible view of your subject?

 NO

- Consider other points of view. Would these make your essay more interesting?
- If your essay seems unfocused, consider switching to a single or different point of view.

 YES

6. In the margin next to each paragraph, *write* a specific part of the description on which it focuses. Is each paragraph well developed and focused on a separate part of the description?

 NO

- Consider combining closely related paragraphs.
- Split paragraphs that cover more than one part of the description.

 YES

7. Write a brief outline depicting how you have organized your details. Is it clear how the details are organized?

 NO

- Arrange your details using a different order—spatial, chronological, or most-to-least or least-to-most order.
- Experiment with several different arrangements to see which one works best.
- Add transitions to connect ideas.

YES

8. Underline the topic sentence of each paragraph. Compare the sensory details (✔) to the *topic sentence.* Does the topic sentence make clear what is being described?

 NO

- Revise so that each paragraph has a topic sentence and supporting details.

YES

(Continued)

FIGURE 6.3   *(Continued)*

QUESTIONS

REVISION STRATEGIES

9.   Draw a box around the introduction and conclusion, and reread them. Is each one effective?

 NO

- Revise your introduction and conclusion so that they meet the guidelines in Chapter 3.

 YES

10.   Print out another draft to edit and proofread before turning in your essay.

Editing and Proofreading

The last step is to check your revised essay for errors in grammar, spelling, punctuation, and mechanics. In addition, be sure to look for the types of errors you tend to make in any writing assignments, whether for this class or any other situation. For descriptive writing, pay particular attention to the punctuation of adjectives. Keep the following rules in mind.

Editing Tips and Troublespots: Description

1. **Use a comma between adjectives not joined by *and*.**

   ▸ Singh was a confident, skilled pianist.

   The order of adjectives can usually be scrambled (*skilled, confident pianist* or *confident, skilled pianist*). To be sure a comma is needed, try reversing the two adjectives. If the phrase sounds correct when the adjectives are reversed, a comma is needed.

   ▸ *Two frightened brown* eyes peered at us from under the sofa.

   You would not write *frightened two brown eyes.*

2. **Use a hyphen to connect two words that work together as an adjective before a noun.** Here are a few examples.

   ▸ *well-used* book

   ▸ *perfect-fitting* shoes

   ▸ *foil-wrapped* pizza

(Continued)

3. **Avoid misplaced modifiers** — that is, words or phrases that describe, change, qualify, or limit the meaning of another word or phrase in a sentence. Be sure your modifiers give readers a clear picture of the details you want to convey.

> *In the Caribbean, w*
> ► We visited a tremendously powerful telescope searching distant stars for
> signs of life ~~in the Caribbean.~~

> *I sent him*
> ► Hoping to get a message to John, an urgent fax ~~was sent.~~

> *carefully*
> ► The FBI monitors Web sites coming from known terrorist groups ~~carefully.~~

For more on misplaced modifiers, see Chapter 4, p. 85.

Students Write

Danielle Cruz, a twenty-five-year-old returning student, wrote the following essay for a writing class. She was asked to describe a frightening experience. As you read, look for words, phrases, and sentences that have sensory appeal and that help you see and hear what the writer experienced.

I Survived the Blackout of 2003

Danielle Cruz

There are certain events that happen in life that change how you view the world; one such event happened to me on a sweltering hot August day during the Blackout of 2003. I first became aware that something was wrong as I was lying quietly on my couch, enjoying the cold air blowing from the air conditioning vent on a sultry mid-summer day in New York City. All of a sudden, I noticed that the comforting rumble of the A/C had stopped. At the same moment, my television screen went blank, throwing my apartment into a sudden and eerie silence. I looked at my ceiling fan and saw that it was slowly spinning to a stop. My initial thought was that the check I sent to the electric company had bounced, as money had been tight. I tried to call my mother in Florida on my cell phone, but the lines were busy. For the first time, fear crept into my mind and I had an overwhelming sense that I was alone in the world.

To find out what was going on, I leashed my dog and maneuvered carefully down four flights of dark stairs and out my building. The streets were full of people staggering

1

Thesis: creates interest and identifies the topic

Sensory detail: sound

Sensory detail: sight

2

Chronological sequence continues

Sensory details:
sight

around Manhattan as if in a daze, their hands shading their eyes as they looked toward the sky. I noticed a familiar-looking woman crouched on the steps to my building with a battery-powered radio and walked over to listen to the news reports coming in. The newscasters were confused, hesitant, and uncertain as they stumbled over what was clearly breaking news. Reports were coming in of blackouts all over New York, Ohio, Pennsylvania, and even as far north as Canada. My fear intensified and I nervously wondered: *Is this a repeat of 9/11?*

The woman with the radio, whose name I found out was Patti, became the first neighbor I met since I moved to Manhattan the month before. There had been polite nodding and hesitant smiles between me and my neighbors beforehand, but no one in my building had ventured to introduce themselves to the new girl in #3F. And you can forget about meeting sane strangers on the street. In my neighborhood, everyone was always going somewhere. There were the attractive, young nannies in tight jeans push-ing carriages while cruising for construction workers, men and women in suits hurrying to work, the skinny fashionistas dressed to kill screeching on their cell phones, and the endless stream of joggers, cyclists, and dog walkers pushing through the crowd like salmon headed to spawn. Even the doormen were too busy to say hello unless you lived in their building. In my one month living here, I had found New York City to be a very lonely place. But on the day of the blackout, it seemed as though the entire city was in the same boat, lost and floating aimlessly, uncertain where to turn. There was nowhere to go, we had very little information about what was going on, and we were all scared. You could feel the fear in the air.

Sensory details:
sights and sounds

Simile: vivid
comparison

Metaphor

3

Sensory details:
sound

Patti offered to share her bowl of cherries with me. We sat on the stoop together listening to the radio as we ate sour cherries and spat the pits onto the hot sidewalk. The mayor's reassuring voice soon came over the airwaves. He calmed us, saying that he was almost sure this was not an act of terrorism and that while they did not know the cause of the blackout, it was widespread, affecting over 50 million people in the North-east. As we listened together, we heard how rescue workers were trying to help free New Yorkers stuck in the subways and elevators all over town. For the first time, I felt less afraid and felt especially lucky to be outside, not trapped in a dark and unbearably hot subway car somewhere deep below the city.

4

Chronological
sequence continues

As night fell, the tenants of my building congregated on the patio, offering the food from their warming refrigerators: spicy curry, paella, lasagna, and lots of lukewarm beer. Several neighbors donated candles to me, as I had none. As we exchanged names, I found we had lots of things in common. Like me, some had recently moved to the city, were without jobs, and were feeling as overwhelmed as I often felt. Some had very in-teresting jobs and promised to help me find one. And to my delight, some even had

5

dogs that my dog liked to play with. A few had even been to my hometown and liked it very much. As we talked, ate, and drank into the night, I felt for the first time a sense of belonging and knew that my life in New York was finally beginning.

I climbed the four flights of stairs to my apartment in the pitch dark that night, not with a sense of dread but happy at last. There would be no air conditioning on this hot August night, but with thoughts of my new friends in my mind, this inconvenience seemed minor. I lit the room with one of the lavender candles that a neighbor had given me; when it finally burned out and the sweet smell of lavender had dissipated into the sticky air, I fell asleep with a bag of half-frozen okra for a pillow, knowing that the power would soon return and that I had made friends where I previously thought there were none to be made.

6

Conclusion: refers back to introduction when she felt alone

Sensory details: smell and touch

Responding to "Students Write"

1. Describe Cruz's dominant impression about her experience. Is it stated explicitly or implied?
2. Which sensory descriptions are particularly effective? Could any be strengthened? If so, how?
3. Identify the different types of comparisons used in the essay.
4. What questions do you have about surviving the blackout that the author does not address? Would information on these issues strengthen the essay?
5. Evaluate the title, introduction, and conclusion of the essay.

Reading a Descriptive Essay

When you read descriptive essays, you are more concerned with impressions and images than with the logical progression of ideas. To get the full benefit of descriptive writing, you need to connect what you are reading to your own senses of sight, sound, smell, touch, and taste. Here are some guidelines for reading descriptive essays.

What to Look for, Highlight, and Annotate

Understanding the Reading

- Plan on reading the essay more than once. Read it a first time to get a general sense of what's going on. Then reread it, paying attention to sensory details.

- Study the introduction and conclusion. What is the purpose of each?
- Evaluate the title. What meaning does it contribute?

Examining the Characteristics of Descriptive Essays

- Be alert for the dominant impression. If it is not directly stated, ask yourself this question: "How does the author want me to feel about the subject?" Your answer will be the dominant impression the writer wants to convey.
- Highlight particularly striking details and images that you may want to refer to again or that may help you analyze the essay's effectiveness.
- Identify the author's vantage point and method of organization.
- Analyze each paragraph, deciding how it contributes to the dominant impression. In marginal annotations, summarize your findings.
- Observe how the author uses language to achieve effect; notice types of images, sentence structure, and use of and placement of adjectives and adverbs.

How to Find Ideas to Write About

Since you may be asked to write a response to a descriptive essay, keep an eye out for ideas as you read. Try to think of parallel situations that evoked similar images and feelings in you. For example, for an essay describing the peace and serenity the author experienced while sitting beside a remote lake in a forest, try to think of situations in which you felt peace and serenity or how you felt when you visited a national park or wilderness area. Perhaps you had negative feelings, such as anxiety about being in a remote spot. Such negative feelings may be worth exploring as well.

The Discus Thrower

Richard Selzer

Richard Selzer (b. 1928) is a medical doctor who has written several books and articles presenting realistic and frank descriptions of life as a medical doctor. His books include *Mortal Lessons* (1977), *Confessions of a Knife* (1979), *Raising the Dead* (1994), and *The Doctor Stories* (1998). This essay first appeared in *Harper's* magazine in 1977.

As you read, notice Selzer's use of detail. These sensory elements create a vivid picture of his patient. Also pay attention to his use of dialogue: It is important for what is *not* said as much as for what *is* said.

Focus on Understanding   Read to discover who the "Discus Thrower" is and why he is given this name.

Focus on the Topic   In class or in your journal, write about the different ways that people with terminal illness might react to their condition.

1   I spy on my patients. Ought not a doctor to observe his patients by any means and from any stance, that he might the more fully assemble evidence? So I stand in the doorways of hospital rooms and gaze. Oh, it is not all that furtive an act. Those in bed need only look up to discover me. But they never do.

2   From the doorway of Room 542 the man in the bed seems deeply tanned. Blue eyes and close-cropped white hair give him the appearance of vigor and good health. But I know that his skin is not brown from the sun. It is rusted, rather, in the last stage of containing the vile repose within. And the blue eyes are frosted, looking inward like the windows of a snowbound cottage. This man is blind. This man is also legless — the right leg missing from midthigh down, the left from just below the knee. It gives him the look of a bonsai, roots and branches pruned into the dwarfed facsimile of a great tree.

3   Propped on pillows, he cups his right thigh in both hands. Now and then he shakes his head as though acknowledging the intensity of his suffering. In all of this he makes no sound. Is he mute as well as blind?

4   The room in which he dwells is empty of all possessions — no get-well cards, small, private caches of food, day-old flowers, slippers, all the usual kickshaws of the sickroom. There is only the bed, a chair, a nightstand, and a tray on wheels that can be swung across his lap for meals.

kickshaws: Trinkets

5   "What time is it?" he asks.

6   "Three o'clock."

7   "Morning or afternoon?"

8   "Afternoon."

163

He is silent. There is nothing else he wants to know.   9

"How are you?" I say.   10

"Who is it?" he asks.   11

"It's the doctor. How do you feel?"   12

He does not answer right away.   13

"Feel?" he says.   14

"I hope you feel better," I say.   15

I press the button at the side of the bed.   16

"Down you go," I say.   17

"Yes, down," he says.   18

He falls back upon the bed awkwardly. His stumps, unweighted by legs and   19
feet, rise in the air, presenting themselves. I unwrap the bandages from the
stumps, and begin to cut away the black scabs and the dead, glazed fat with
scissors and forceps. A shard of white bone comes loose. I pick it away. I wash
the wounds with disinfectant and redress the stumps. All this while, he does not
speak. What is he thinking behind those lids that do not blink? Is he remembering a time when he was whole? Does he dream of feet? Of when his body
was not a rotting log?

He lies solid and inert. In spite of everything, he remains impressive, as   20
though he were a sailor standing athwart a slanting deck.

"Anything more I can do for you?" I ask.   21

For a long moment he is silent.   22

"Yes," he says at last and without the least irony. "You can bring me a pair   23
of shoes."

In the corridor, the head nurse is waiting for me.   24

"We have to do something about him," she says. "Every morning he orders   25
scrambled eggs for breakfast, and, instead of eating them, he picks up the plate
and throws it against the wall."

"Throws his plate?"   26

"Nasty. That's what he is. No wonder his family doesn't come to visit. They   27
probably can't stand him any more than we can."

She is waiting for me to do something.   28

"Well?"   29

"We'll see," I say.   30

The next morning I am waiting in the corridor when the kitchen delivers   31
his breakfast. I watch the aide place the tray on the stand and swing it across
his lap. She presses the button to raise the head of the bed. Then she leaves.

In time the man reaches to find the rim of the tray, then on to find the dome   32
of the covered dish. He lifts off the cover and places it on the stand. He fingers
across the plate until he probes the eggs. He lifts the plate in both hands, sets it
on the palm of his right hand, centers it, balances it. He hefts it up and down
slightly, getting the feel of it. Abruptly, he draws back his right arm as far as he
can.

There is the crack of the plate breaking against the wall at the foot of his   33
bed and the small wet sound of the scrambled eggs dropping to the floor.

And then he laughs. It is a sound you have never heard. It is something new 34
under the sun. It could cure cancer.

Out in the corridor, the eyes of the head nurse narrow. 35

"Laughed, did he?" 36

She writes something down on her clipboard. 37

A second aide arrives, brings a second breakfast tray, puts it on the night- 38
stand, out of his reach. She looks over at me shaking her head and making her
mouth go. I see that we are to be accomplices.

"I've got to feed you," she says to the man. 39

"Oh, no you don't," the man says. 40

"Oh, yes I do," the aide says, "after the way you just did. Nurse says so." 41

"Get me my shoes," the man says. 42

"Here's oatmeal," the aide says. "Open." And she touches the spoon to his 43
lower lip.

"I ordered scrambled eggs," says the man. 44

"That's right," the aide says. 45

I step forward. 46

"Is there anything I can do?" I say. 47

"Who are you?" the man asks. 48

In the evening I go once more to that ward to make my rounds. The head 49
nurse reports to me that Room 542 is deceased. She has discovered this quite by
accident, she says. No, there had been no sound. Nothing. It's a blessing, she says.

I go into his room, a spy looking for secrets. He is still there in his bed. His 50
face is relaxed, grave, dignified. After a while, I turn to leave. My gaze sweeps
the wall at the foot of the bed, and I see the place where it has been repeatedly
washed, where the wall looks very clean and very white.

Understanding the Reading

1. According to Selzer, what is wrong with the patient? What don't we know about his medical condition?

2. In paragraph 25, we learn that the head nurse is upset. What is upsetting her, and how does the doctor react to the nurse's complaints?

3. What emotion does the patient exhibit as he throws his food? Why might he feel this way?

4. How does the doctor find out that the patient has died? What is the head nurse's reaction to the patient's death? How does Selzer react to his death?

Visualizing the Reading

To analyze the descriptive elements used in Selzer's essay, complete the following graphic organizer.

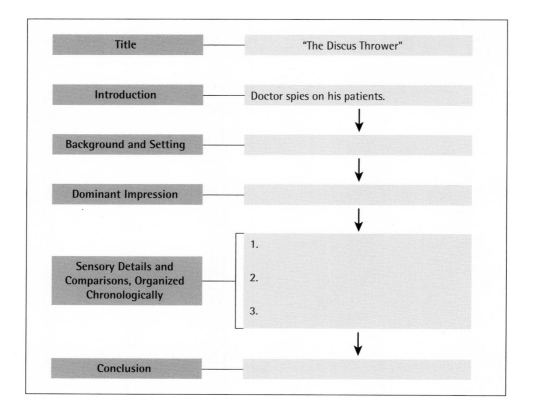

Examining the Characteristics of Descriptive Essays

1. The author does not include a stated thesis. Instead, Selzer uses description to build a single dominant impression. Identify his dominant impression. What might this tell you about his purpose for writing about this patient?

2. Highlight several sections in which sensory details are particularly effective.

3. This story is told from the vantage point of the doctor. Is this point of view effective? What does it achieve? What do you learn, and what information remains untold?

4. Evaluate the conclusion. What does the doctor notice about the patient and his room after the death? How do these details contrast with earlier descriptions of the patient and his room?

Building Your Word Power

For a definition of **connotative meaning,** *see the chart of commonly used language features on p. 21.*

1. What are the connotative meanings of the word *spy* as used in paragraphs 1 and 50?

2. Evaluate the use of figurative language in this essay. Consider the statements that liken the patient to a cottage (para. 2), a bonsai tree (2), a log (19), and a sailor (20). What do you learn about the patient from each?

3. Explain the meaning of each of the following words as it is used in the reading: *furtive* (para. 1), *shard* (19), *inert* (20), *athwart* (20), and *hefts* (32). Refer to your dictionary as needed.

Building Your Critical Thinking Skills: Tone

A writer's language often reveals his or her **tone** — how the author sounds to the readers and how he or she feels about the topic. An author establishes tone by using certain words, sentence arrangements, and formal or informal language. The author's tone affects the reader's attitude toward the topic. For example, the tone in an academic essay about the effects of littering would differ from that of a letter of complaint to a neighboring business that had repeatedly ignored requests to clean up the trash around its property. Consequently, it is important to be aware of tone and how it affects the reader's response. Use your knowledge about tone to answer the following questions.

1. How would you characterize Selzer's overall tone in "The Discus Thrower"?
2. How does the author's use of dialogue contribute to the tone of the essay?
3. How does Selzer's tone affect your reading of the situation described in the essay? How does it make you feel about doctors and nurses? How does it make you feel about the patient?

Reacting to the Topic: Discussion and Journal Writing

1. Suggest how the doctor might have approached the patient differently or offered more help and support.
2. Why does the doctor refer to himself as a spy? Are there certain things about a patient that a doctor should not know or ask?
3. The discus thrower dies quietly and alone. In class or in your journal, write about a time when you were alone and wished you had had a friend or family member nearby.

Applying Your Skills: Writing Assignments

1. **Paragraph Assignment.** Selzer focuses on one particular patient in "The Discus Thrower"; but other than the man's medical condition, we know little about him. Using descriptive details, write a paragraph that describes briefly who this man is and why he is alone at the hospital.
2. Using description, rewrite the essay from the point of view of the head nurse or the patient. Begin by establishing a background and setting for your character, feeling free to invent details. Include a dominant impression supported by sensory details.
3. Brainstorm a list of feelings you experienced when undergoing a medical procedure of some kind. What dominant impression do they suggest? Develop and support this dominant impression by writing an essay that describes your medical treatment and experience.
4. **Combining Patterns.** The doctor and the patient seem unable to communicate. Have you ever experienced a communication breakdown? Write an essay describing

the situation. Identify the problem, and explain the process by which you tried to solve your communication issues.

5. **Internet Research.** Médecins Sans Frontières (MSF), or Doctors without Borders, is an organization comprising volunteer doctors, nurses, and other health professionals that addresses health concerns in countries throughout the world. Every year the organization publishes a list of the Top Ten Most Underreported Humanitarian Stories. Look over the current report at www.doctorswithout borders.org/publications/reports/2005/top10.html, or conduct some further research about this group by doing an online search. Based on your research, write an essay describing some of the challenges faced by the people featured on this Web site. Use details from the site to support the dominant impression that you establish.

The Sweat Bath Ritual

Mary Brave Bird

Mary Brave Bird (b. 1953), also known as Mary Crow Dog, is a political activist and writer from the Rosebud Reservation in South Dakota. She has written two memoirs, *Lakota Woman* (1990) and *Ohitika Woman* (1993), about her life on the reservation and her participation with the American Indian Movement, a Native American spiritual and cultural group that grew out of the civil rights era of the 1960s. This essay is taken from *Lakota Woman*, for which Brave Bird won a National Book Award in 1991.

As you read, consider how Brave Bird uses concrete details to bring the reader directly into the sweat bath. In particular, pay attention to the physical descriptions of the lodge.

Focus on Understanding   Read to find out what a sweat bath is and what the author learns from participating in a sweat bath ritual.

Focus on the Topic   In class or in your journal, discuss why it is important for people to participate in traditional or cultural events.

Some of our medicine men always say that one must view the world 1 through the eye in one's heart rather than just trust the eyes in one's head. "Look at the real reality beneath the sham realities of things and gadgets," Leonard always tells me. "Look through the eye in your heart. That's the meaning of Indian religion."

The eye of my heart was still blind when I joined Leonard to become his 2 wife. I knew little of traditional ways. I had been to a few peyote meetings° without really understanding them. I had watched one Sun Dance,° and later the Ghost Dance° held at Wounded Knee,° like a spectator — an emotional spectator, maybe, but no different from white friends watching these dances. They, too, felt emotion. Like myself they did not penetrate through symbolism to the real meaning. I had not yet participated in many ancient rituals of our tribe — the sweat bath, the vision quest, yuwipi, the making of relatives, the soul keeping. I did not even know that these ceremonies were still being performed. There were some rituals I did not even know existed.

I had to learn about the sweat bath, because it precedes all sacred cere- 3 monies, and is at the same time a ceremony all by itself. It is probably the oldest of all our rituals because it is connected with the glowing stones, evoking thoughts of Tunka, the rock, our oldest god. Our family's sweat lodge, our oinik- aga tipi, is near the river which flows through Crow Dog's land. That is good. Pure, flowing water plays a great part during a sweat. Always at the lodge we

peyote meetings: Ceremonies giving thanks for the sacred peyote cactus; **Sun Dance:** Religious ceremony held at the summer solstice; **Ghost Dance:** Part of a religious movement begun in 1889, the Ghost Dance ceremony focuses on salvation, resurrection, and fear of white people; **Wounded Knee:** Site of the December 29, 1890, battle in which over three hundred Indian men, women, and children were massacred by American soldiers

169

can hear the river's voice, the murmur of its waters. Along its banks grows washte wikcemna, a sweet-smelling aromatic herb — Indian perfume.

The lodge is made of sixteen willow sticks, tough but resilient and easy to bend. They are formed into a beehive-shaped dome. The sweat lodges vary in size. They can accommodate anywhere from eight to twenty-four people. The bent willow sticks are fastened together with strips of red trade cloth. Sometimes offerings of Bull Durham tobacco are tied to the frame, which is then covered with blankets or a tarp. In the old days buffalo skins were used for the covering, but these are hard to come by now. The floor of the little lodge is covered with sage. In the center is a circular pit to receive the heated rocks. In building a lodge, people should forget old quarrels and have only good thoughts.

Outside the lodge, wood is piled up in a certain manner to make the fire in which the rocks will be heated — peta owihankeshni — the "fire without end" which is passed on from generation to generation. After it has blazed for a while, white limestone rocks are placed in its center. These rocks do not crack apart in the heat. They come from the hills. Some of them are covered with a spidery network of green moss. This is supposed by some to represent secret spirit writing.

The scooped-out earth from the firepit inside the lodge is formed up into a little path leading from the lodge entrance and ending in a small mound. It represents Unci — Grandmother Earth. A prayer is said when this mound is made. A man is then chosen to take care of the fire, to bring the hot rocks to the lodge, often on a pitchfork, and to handle the entrance flap.

In some places men and women sweat together. We do not do this. Among us, men and women do their sweat separately. Those taking part in a sweat strip, and wrapped in their towels, crawl into the little lodge, entering clockwise. In the darkness inside they take their towels off and hunker down naked. I was astounded to see how many people could be swallowed up by this small, waist-high, igloo-shaped hut. The rocks are then passed into the lodge, one by one. Each stone is touched with the pipe bowl as, resting in the fork of a deer antler, it is put into the center pit. The leader goes in first, sitting down near the entrance on the right side. Opposite him, at the other side of the entrance sits his helper. The leader has near him a pail full of cold, pure water and a ladle. Green cedar is sprinkled over the hot rocks, filling the air with its aromatic odor. Outside the entrance flap is a buffalo-skull altar. Tobacco ties are fastened to its horns. There is also a rack for the pipe to rest on.

Anywhere from twelve to sixty rocks can be used in this ceremony. The more rocks, the hotter it will be. Once the rocks have been passed into the lodge, the flap is closed. Inside it is dark except for the red glow of the rocks in the pit. Now the purification begins. As sage or cedar is sprinkled on the rocks, the men or women participating catch the sacred smoke with their hands, inhaling it, rubbing it all over their face and body. Then cold water is poured on the rocks. The rising cloud of white steam, "grandfather's breath," fills the lodge. A sweat has four "doors," meaning that the flap is opened four times during the purification to let some cool outside air in, bringing relief to the participants.

Everybody has the privilege to pray or speak of sacred things during the 9 ceremony. It is important that all take part in the ritual with their hearts, souls, and minds. When women have their sweats, a medicine man runs them — which is all right because it is so dark inside that he cannot see you.

The first time I was inside the oinikaga tipi, the sweat lodge, when water 10 was poured over the rocks and the hot steam got to me, I thought that I could not endure it. The heat was beyond anything I had imagined. I thought I would not be able to breathe because it was like inhaling liquid fire. With my cupped hands I created a slightly cooler space over my eyes and mouth. After a while I noticed that the heat which had hurt me at first became soothing, penetrating to the center of my body, going into my bones, giving me a wonderful feeling. If the heat is more than a person can stand, he or she can call out "Mitakuye oyasin!" — All my relatives! — and the flap will be opened to let the inside cool off a bit. I was proud not to have cried out. After the sweat I really felt newly born. My pores were opened and so was my mind. My body tingled. I felt as if I had never experienced pain. I was deliciously light-headed, elated, drunk with the spirit. Soon I began looking forward to a good sweat.

Understanding the Reading

1. What prompted Brave Bird to participate in a sweat bath ritual?
2. Describe the physical appearance of the sweat lodge.
3. What is the significance of the rocks that are placed in the lodge during the ritual?
4. What happened to the author during her first sweat, and how did she feel after it was over? What did she learn from it?

Visualizing the Reading

Compare the sweat bath shown in the photograph with the description that Mary Brave Bird gives in her essay. What additional information do you learn from the photo? What do you learn about sweat lodges from the essay that the photograph does not show?

Examining the Characteristics of Descriptive Essays

1. Create a list of senses to which Brave Bird's descriptions appeal. For each sense, include an example from the essay.
2. What method of organization does the author use to order her descriptive details? Did you find this method of organization effective? Why or why not?
3. What comparisons does the author make within the development of the description? How does this add to your understanding of the ritual?
4. How does the information about the author's background contribute to the dominant impression in the essay? What might have been Brave Bird's purpose in writing about her experience?

Building Your Word Power

For a definition of simile, see the chart of commonly used language features on p. 21.

1. To what does the expression "eye in one's heart" refer (para. 1)?
2. Explain the simile "it was like inhaling liquid fire" (para. 10).
3. Explain the meaning of each of the following words as it is used in the reading: *sham* (para. 1), *spidery* (5), *hunker down* (7), *purification* (8), and *elated* (10). Refer to your dictionary as needed.

Building Your Critical Thinking Skills: Evaluating Authors

One aspect of evaluating sources involves considering the **author's qualifications.** Readers should be aware of the author's credentials to write on a particular subject. A writer does not have to be a certified expert as long as he or she does research on that subject. However, when experts do write about their specialty, they can add special information or experience that enhances the reader's understanding of the material. Use your knowledge of the author's qualifications to answer the following questions.

1. What qualifies Mary Brave Bird to write this essay on sweat bath rituals?
2. What does she reveal about herself in the essay that enhances her authority on this subject?

Reacting to the Reading: Discussion and Journal Writing

1. Discuss your knowledge of Native Americans. How are they and their cultural traditions regarded in our society today?
2. Discuss the concept of community. What makes a community? To what communities do you belong?
3. In class or in your journal, write about a time that you participated in a traditional or cultural event. How did it feel to be part of a time-honored practice?

Applying Your Skills: Writing Assignments

1. **Paragraph Assignment.** Despite being married to a medicine man, Mary Brave Bird knew little about the traditional rituals of her tribe. Using description, write a paragraph about a situation in which someone close to you introduced you to an unfamiliar procedure, ritual, or custom.

2. The sweat bath is an ancient Native American ritual. Choose a ritual that is meaningful or important to you, and write an essay describing it. It may be a religious ritual such as a wedding or a secular ritual such as a graduation or a holiday tradition. Be sure to create a dominant impression and support it with sensory detail.

3. Write an essay that describes an object but does not name it specifically. Then have a classmate read your essay to see if he or she can name the object based on your use of description.

4. **Combining Patterns.** Write an essay comparing the sweat bath ritual and another ritual with which you are familiar. What do they have in common? How are they different?

5. **Internet Research.** Visit the Web site for the American Indians of the Pacific Northwest Digital Collection at http://content.lib.washington.edu/aipnw/index .html or another online archive of Native American artifacts and images. Choose a category from the Web site, and explore the photographs. Then write a descriptive essay explaining the characteristics of the category you chose (for example, dwellings) as portrayed in the photographs.

Po-Po in Chinatown

Eric Liu

Eric Liu (b. 1968) is a former speechwriter for President Clinton, a regular contributor to *Slate* magazine, and founder of *The Next Progressive*, a journal of Democratic politics. He has edited *Next: Young American Writers on the New Generation* (1994). In *The Accidental Asian: Notes from a Native Speaker* (1998), from which the following selection is taken, Liu writes about his experiences as a second-generation Chinese American.

As you read, notice the variety of sensory detail that Liu uses to describe Po-Po. Pay attention also to the author's use of Chinese words, and consider their effect in bringing Po-Po's character to life.

Focus on Understanding   Learn who Po-Po is and how the author is related to this character.

Focus on the Topic   In class or in your journal, write about a time when you were particularly proud of or embarrassed by a member of your family.

1   For more than two decades, my mother's mother, Po-Po, lived in a cinder-block one-bedroom apartment on the edge of New York's Chinatown. She was twenty floors up, so if you looked straight out of the main room, which faced north, one block appeared to melt into the next, all the way to the spire of the Empire State off in the distance. This was a saving grace, the view, since her own block down below was not much to look at. Her building, one of those interchangeable towers of 1970s public housing, was on the lower east side of the Lower East Side, at the corner of South and Clinton. It was, as the relators say, only minutes from the Brooklyn Bridge and South Street Seaport, although those landmarks, for all she cared, might as well have been in Nebraska. They weren't part of the world Po-Po inhabited, which was the world that I visited every few months during the last years of her life.

2   My visits followed a certain pattern. I'd get to her apartment around noon, and when I knocked on the door I could hear her scurrying with excitement. When she opened the door, I'd be struck, always as if for the first time, by how tiny she was: four feet nine and shrinking. She wore loose, baggy clothes, nylon, and ill-fitting old glasses that covered her soft, wrinkled face. It was a face I recognized from my own second-grade class photo. *Eh, Po-Po, ni hao maaa?* She offered a giggle as I bent to embrace her. With an impish smile, she proclaimed my American name in her Yoda-like° voice: *Areek*. She got a kick out of that. As she shuffled to the kitchen, where Li Tai Tai, her caregiver, was preparing lunch, I would head to the bathroom, trained to wash my hands upon entering Po-Po's home.

Yoda: A very old and respected shriveled-up creature from the Star Wars movies

174

In the small bath were the accessories of her everyday life: a frayed tooth-   3
brush in a plastic Star Trek mug I'd given her in 1979, stiff washrags and aged
pantyhose hanging from a clothesline, medicine bottles and hair dye cluttered
on the sinktop. I often paused for a moment there, looking for my reflection in
the filmy, clouded mirror, taking a deep breath or two. Then I would walk back
into the main room. The place was neat but basically grimy. Some of the
furniture — the lumpy couch, the coffee table with old magazines and congealed candies, the lawn chair where she read her Chinese newspaper through
a magnifying glass — had been there as long as I could remember. The
windowsill was crammed with plants and flowers. The only thing on the thickly
painted white wall was a calendar. *Your house looks so nice*, I'd say in a tender
tone of Mandarin that I used only with her. On a tray beside me, also surveying
the scene, was a faded black-and-white portrait of Po-Po as a beautiful young
woman dressed in Chinese costume. *Lai chi ba*, Po-Po would say, inviting me
to eat.

Invariably, there was a banquet's worth of food awaiting me on the small   4
kitchen table: *hongshao* stewed beef, a broiled fish with scallions and ginger, a
leafy green called *jielan*, a soup with chicken and winter melon and radishes,
tofu with ground pork, stir-fried shrimp still in their salty shells. Po-Po ate sparingly, and Li Tai Tai, in her mannerly Chinese way, adamantly refused to dine
with us, so it was up to me to attack this meal. I gorged myself, loosening my
belt within the half hour and sitting back dazed and short of breath by the end.
No matter how much I put down, Po-Po would express disappointment at my
meager appetite.

As I ate she chattered excitedly, pouring forth a torrent of opinions about   5
politics in China, Hong Kong pop singers, the latest developments in Taiwan.
After a while, she'd move into stories about people I'd never met, distant relations, half brothers killed by the Communists, my grandfather, who had died
when I was a toddler. Then she'd talk about her friends who lived down the "F"
train in Flushing or on the other side of Chinatown and who were dying one by
one, and she'd tell me about seeing Jesus after she'd had a cancer operation in
1988, and how this blond Jesus had materialized and said to her in Chinese, *You
are a good person, too good to die now. Nobody knows how good you are. Nobody
appreciates you as much as I do*. I would sit quietly then, not sure whether to
smile. But just as she approached the brink she would take a sip of 7 UP and
swerve back to something in the news, perhaps something about her heroine,
the Burmese dissident Aung San Suu Kyi.° She was an incredible talker, Po-Po,
using her hands and her eyes like a performer. She built up a tidal momentum,
relentless, imaginative, spiteful, like a child.

I generally didn't have much to say in response to Po-Po's commentary, save   6
the occasional Chinese-inflected *Oh?* and *Wah!* I took in the lilt of her Sichuan
accent and relied on context to figure out what she was saying. In fact, it wasn't
till I brought my girlfriend to meet Po-Po that I realized just how vague my
comprehension was. *What did she say?* Carroll would ask. *Um, something about,
something, I think, about the president of Taiwan*. Of course, I'm not sure Po-Po

Aung San Suu Kyi: A
woman who was
awarded the Nobel
Peace Prize in 1991 in
recognition of her
"non-violent struggle
for democracy and
human rights" in her
home country of
Burma

even cared whether I understood. If I interjected, she'd cut me off with a hasty *bushide — no, it's not that —* a habit I found endearing in small doses but that my mother, over a lifetime, had found maddening.

If there was a lull, I might ask Po-Po about her health, which would prompt her to spring up from her chair and, bracing herself on the counter, kick her leg up in the air. *I do this ten times every morning at five,* she would proudly say in Chinese. *Then this,* she'd add, and she would stretch her arms out like little wings, making circles with her fingertips. *And last week I had a beadache, so I rubbed each eye like this thirty-six times.* Pretty soon I was out of my chair, too, laughing, rubbing, kicking, as Po-Po schooled me in her system of exercises and home remedies. We did this every visit, like a ritual.

Time moved so slowly when I was at Po-Po's. After lunch, we might sit on the couch next to each other or go to her room so she could tell me things that she didn't want Li Tai Tai to hear. We would rest there, digesting, our conversation turning more mellow. I might pull out of my bag a small keepsake for her, a picture of Carroll and me, or a souvenir from a recent vacation. She would show me a bundle of poems she had written in classical Chinese, scribbled on the backs of small cardboard rectangles that come with travel packs of Kleenex. She would recount how she'd been inspired to write this poem or that one. Then she would open a spiral notebook that she kept, stuffed with news clippings and filled with idioms and sentences she had copied out of the Chinese newspaper's daily English lesson: *Let's get a move on. I don't like the looks of this.* At my urging, she'd read the sentences aloud, tentatively. I would praise her warmly, she would chuckle, and then she might show me something else, a photo album, a book about *qigong.*°

One day she revealed to me her own way of prayer, demonstrating how she sat on the side of her bed at night and clasped her hands, bowing as if before Buddha, repeating in fragile English, *God bless me? God bless me? God bless me?* Another time she urgently recited to me a short story that had moved her to tears, but I understood hardly a word of it. On another visit she fell asleep beside me, her glasses still on, her chin tucked into itself. And so the hours would pass, until it was time for me to go — until, that is, I decided it was time to go, for she would have wanted me to stay forever — and I would hold her close and stroke her knotted back and tell her that I loved her and that I would miss her, and Po-Po, too modest to declare her heart so openly, would nod and press a little red envelope of money into my hand and say to me quietly in Chinese, *How I wish I had wings so I could come see you where you live.*

qigong: The ancient Chinese practice of meditation and movement to achieve self-healing

Understanding the Reading

1. Describe Liu's relationship with his grandmother. In what ways is there distance between them? In what ways is closeness evident?

2. Explain Po-Po's attitude toward Liu.

3. Using examples from the essay to support your statements, describe Po-Po's lifestyle.
4. What larger issue(s) is Liu commenting on through this essay?

Visualizing the Reading

Liu conveys information about Po-Po and her surroundings by using many of the characteristics of descriptive essays. Analyze his use of these characteristics by completing the following chart. Give several examples for each type of characteristic used, including paragraph numbers for reference. The first one has been done for you.

Characteristic	Examples
Active verbs	1. "*shuffled* to the kitchen" (para. 2) 2. "I *gorged* myself" (para. 4)
Sensory details (sound, smell, touch, sight, taste)	
Varied sentences	
Comparisons	
Connotative language	

Examining the Characteristics of Descriptive Essays

1. What dominant impression about Po-Po does Liu convey? Is it stated or implied? Support your answer with examples from the reading.
2. Highlight several sections in which Liu uses Chinese words or phrases. Is your understanding of these words clear? If not, does this add or detract from your reading of the essay? Would English words have had the same impact? Why or why not?
3. In organizing his details, what method of organization does Liu use?
4. Identify particularly striking descriptive details about Po-Po that reveal her character. Include some examples of connotative language that create a positive image of her.

Building Your Word Power

1 . Evaluate the author's use of the words *attack* and *gorged* in paragraph 4. How do these descriptive words contrast with Po-Po's disappointment at Liu's "meager appetite" (para. 4)?

For a definition of **simile**, *see the chart of commonly used language features on p. 21.*

2. Liu describes Po-Po as an "incredible talker . . . using her hands and her eyes like a performer" (para. 5). Explain this simile by describing how you think Po-Po spoke.

3. Explain the meaning of each of the following words as it is used in the reading: *impish* (para. 2), *congealed* (3), *adamantly* (4), *materialized* (5), and *commentary* (6). Refer to your dictionary as needed.

Building Your Critical Thinking Skills: Selective Omissions

In developing and supporting their thesis, writers make choices about what kinds of supporting evidence to include and what to omit. Writing, then, is necessarily subjective. With each detail that an author includes, he or she could be leaving out something that might add additional meaning; these are **selective omissions**. Therefore, readers should always read between the lines and think critically about what has *not* been included. You might wonder, for example, whether Po-Po has ever visited Liu where he lives. Using your knowledge of selective omissions, answer the following questions about details not included in "Po-Po in Chinatown."

1. Liu does not tell much about himself. What additional information might he have included to help readers better understand his relationship with Po-Po?

2. The author provides a great deal of information about Po-Po but does not tell everything about her. What additional details about her life would have been useful?

3. Chinese culture is rich and complex, but Liu touches on only a few aspects of his heritage. What aspects are touched on that you would like to know more about?

Reacting to the Topic: Discussion and Journal Writing

1. Discuss the ways in which older people in your own community, family, or culture help to keep traditional ways of life alive.

2. Discuss the treatment of the elderly in the United States. Do we treat members of the oldest segment of the population with honor and respect? Cite some examples.

3. Liu and Po-Po follow the same routine during each visit. In class or in your journal, explore the possible reasons they do this. Describe a routine that you follow. It might be a daily routine or one that you follow during a holiday, for example.

Applying Your Skills: Writing Assignments

1. **Paragraph Assignment.** Write a paragraph describing a meal you have eaten (good or bad) made up of foods from a culture other than your own. Using descriptive details, re-create the experience highlighting smells, sounds, and tastes.

2. Using description, rewrite the essay from the point of view of Po-Po. Describe how she views Eric's visits. Emphasize her feelings and experience of the visits, making sure to organize your details so that they create a dominant impression.

3. Liu describes his efforts to bridge the generation gap between himself and Po-Po. Write an essay describing a personal relationship in which a generation gap exists in your own life. Be sure to include vivid and realistic sensory details.

4. **Combining Patterns.** Brainstorm a list of ways that we might honor and assist older people in our country. Pick one or more ways, and write an essay aimed at your peers in which you argue for them to get involved in helping older citizens. Conclude with your opinion on the benefits that one might reap from the experience of aiding the elderly.

5. **Internet Research.** Po-Po kept a notebook that contained idioms she wanted to learn. Visit www.goenglish.com/Index.asp or another Web site that contains English idioms. Choose five to seven idioms from the site — ideally, ones that are somehow related (for example, idioms relating to time) — and write an essay to an international student describing what an idiom is and how the idioms you chose might be used appropriately in everyday speech.

Piedra

Gary Soto

Gary Soto (b. 1952) decided while in college that he wanted to be a poet. Born and raised in Fresno, California, he has published not only poetry but also essays, plays, short stories, and novels for children and adults, including *Taking Sides* (1991), *Too Many Tamales* (1992), *Snapshots from the Wedding* (1997), and *Amnesia in a Republican County* (2003). In much of his writing Soto draws on his experiences in the Mexican American neighborhood where he grew up, but he emphasizes that most of the details and characters in his work come from his imagination rather than from his past.

This selection appears in *The Effects of Knut Hamsun on a Fresno Boy,* a collection of essays published in 2000. In this essay Soto describes the place where his family went on picnics when he was young. Notice how he uses visual details, especially color, to create an image in the reader's mind.

Focus on Understanding   Read to discover what Piedra is and why it is significant.

Focus on the Topic   In class or in your journal, write a description of a special place that you visited as a child.

The river was gray-blue when you sat on the bank, and gray when you stood on the bank, and swift and cold no matter how you looked at it in autumn. River rock splayed the water, so that it leaped white like fish; leaped up and fell back to join the gray-cold current, southward, to feed Avocado Lake.° 1

Avocado Lake: A small lake located east of Fresno, California

Minkler: A small town along Route 180, east of Fresno, California

Piedra. River of rock, place where our family went for a Saturday picnic. It was a fifteen-mile drive past plum and almond orchards, dairies, the town with its green sign, Minkler° — Population 35. *Mexicanos* pruning orange trees on ladders, and our mother's talk that if our grades didn't improve we would be like *those* people. Past cows with grassy jaws, past fallen fences, groceries, tractors itching with rust, the Griffin ranch with its mowed pasture and white fence that proclaimed he was a gentleman farmer. We gawked at his ranch, and counted his cows, which seemed cleaner, better looking than the fly-specked ones we had passed earlier. 2

I dreamed about Griffin's daughters. I imagined that their hair was tied in ponytails and bounced crazily when they rode horses in knee-high grass near the river. They were the stuff of romance novels, sad and lonely girls who were in love with a stable boy, who was also sad and lonely but too poor for the father's liking, because he himself had once been poor but now was rich and liked to whip horses, cuss, and chase gasping foxes at daybreak. 3

My dreaming stopped when the road narrowed, gravel ticked under a fender, and we began our climb through the foothills. I was scared that our step- 4

180

father would forget to turn the wheel and we would roll slowly off the cliff into the brush and flint-sharp boulders. But he always remembered in time to turn and weave the car, its tires squalling through the hills that were covered with grass and oak trees. Then — just like that — around a bend the river came into view and our ears were filled with the roar of water.

Like so many other parents, ours didn't know what to do with themselves while we played. They would gaze at the river from our picnic table, drink coffee from thermoses, keep up one-word conversations, and smoke cigarettes. They looked tired. I felt sorry for them, but not sorry enough to keep them company. I joined my brother and sister in a game of hide-and-seek in the brush that ran along the river; played hide-and-seek until it turned into a game of army that would turn into a game of nothing at all. We would just sit in the brush and overturn rocks to see what they hid. They hid glittery sand and soggy leaves, smaller rocks, bottle caps, and toads and lizards that scared us so that we let out sharp screams when they ran along our fingers. We played games that we could have played at home, but it seemed so special to be there, the river loud at our side, the fishermen shushing us, dogs knee-deep in water and drinking.

When we were called back, it was for a lunch of hot dogs and barbecue chips and soda, and then back to playing. One time, however, I didn't join my brother and sister, but went on my own to hike toward a mountain that mother said would take a long time to climb. I told her I could do it in twenty minutes. She drank coffee from the thermos cup. She didn't seem to hear me. I started off, leaving my brother and sister to call me names because I didn't want to go with them to the dam to throw rocks.

The mountain seemed so close I could touch it. I walked *forever*, as a kid would say, and climbed a barbed-wire fence that said No Trespassing, and continued on until I was out of breath. I stopped, looked back and was surprised at how far I had come. The picnic table was far below, my parents just shadows on the benches. The river was thin as a wrist, and even Friant dam seemed smaller now that the gushing water spilled noiselessly from its opened valves. I liked where I was. The wind was in my hair, the sun in the yellow grass. I sat down, hugging my knees, and scanned the hills, which were brown and tree-specked and a purplish dark where the sun did not reach; scanned the road for the roadside grocery where we had stopped to buy sodas. Except for the wind it was quiet, and I was quiet too, with just one thought, and this thought was happiness. I was happy. All the badness in my life was momentarily gone, flooded with sunlight, and I believed I could lie down in the grass *forever*. I will have my chance.

Understanding the Reading

1. This essay describes a place that Soto remembers vividly. However, he does not visit the river alone. What do we learn about the boy's family in the course of the essay?

2. Describe the behavior of both the children and the adults during the picnic. How does their behavior differ?

3. What kinds of things does the boy dream about during the trip? What do these details suggest about his age at the time? What do they suggest about his self-image?

4. How did the boy spend the afternoon during this particular visit to the river? Why was this afternoon so important to him?

Visualizing the Reading

This photograph shows a view of a river and a person interacting with it. How does this person's way of relating to a river compare with Soto's relationship to the Piedra River? What overall impression does the photograph create?

Examining the Characteristics of Descriptive Writing

1. Soto uses descriptive details to bring the Piedra River vividly to life. How does he convey the sound of the river? To which other senses does Soto appeal? Cite examples from the text.

2. The author uses descriptive details to convey a special sense of place and the feelings it inspired in him. What is Soto's dominant impression of Piedra, and how do the descriptive details contribute to this impression?

3. What type of vantage point does Soto use? Evaluate the effectiveness of this approach.

4. Rather than using a conclusion that summarizes or restates his main point, Soto describes a solo hike that he made, in effect presenting a climax — or decisive point in the events of the essay — at the very end. Do you find this approach effective? Why or why not? Consider also the last line of the essay. What do you think Soto means by "I will have my chance" (para. 7)?

*For a definition of **connotative meaning** and **imagery**, see the chart of commonly used language features on p. 21.*

Building Your Word Power

1. What is meant by "*those* people" in paragraph 2? What is the connotation of this phrase?

2. What image does the phrase "itching with rust" (para. 2) create?

3. Explain the meaning of each of the following words as it is used in the reading: *splayed* (para. 1), *ticked* (4), and *squalling* (4). Refer to your dictionary as needed.

Building Your Critical Thinking Skills: Point of View

Authors choose a **point of view** — or perspective — when deciding how to tell a story. Usually, this point of view is the first person (*I, me*) or the third person (*he, she, they*), though occasionally writers use the second person (*you, your, yours*). With the first person, the reader gets firsthand information from one character; this information includes thoughts and feelings as well as actions. With the third person, the reader finds out the motives and emotions of many characters because the action is explained from an all-encompassing view. Use your knowledge of point of view to answer the following questions.

1. What point of view does Soto use in "Piedra"?

2. How does the chosen point of view reflect more than just the boy's experience?

3. What is left out of the story as a result of using this point of view?

Reacting to the Topic: Discussion and Journal Writing

1. Discuss the ways families spend their free time. Do you think there is more or less family cohesiveness today than when you were a child?

2. What is it about lakes, rivers, and oceans that attracts people? For example, what are some emotional, social, and economic reasons for the popularity of bodies of water as "getaway" destinations?

3. In class or in your journal, describe a picnic, outing, or day trip that you went on as a child. Where did you go? Who else was there? What did you eat and do? How did it make you feel?

Applying Your Skills: Writing Assignments

1. **Paragraph Assignment.** Soto describes the boy imagining how the girls live on the Griffin ranch. Choose a public figure or celebrity who interests you, and write a paragraph describing how you imagine that person lives.

2. Using description, rewrite Soto's essay from the perspective of someone else in the story. Be sure to have this person describe the boy as he or she sees him, feeling free to make up details. Your essay should build toward a dominant impression supported with sensory details.

3. Using descriptive details, write an essay describing a place that inspires a particular feeling in you. The feeling may be happiness, awe, peacefulness, or tranquility, for example. If possible, visit the actual place to generate details for your essay. If you cannot visit the place, close your eyes and visualize yourself there. Make notes on what you "see," "hear," "smell," and "feel."

4. **Combining Patterns.** As he climbed the mountain, Soto was able to focus on only one thought. What do you have to do to free your own mind of cluttering

thoughts? Write an essay describing the process that you must undergo to free your mind. Be sure to describe its results as well.

5. Internet Research. Choose an artist or photographer who focuses on nature, such as Ansel Adams (photographer), Georgia O'Keeffe (modern painter), or Thomas Cole (eighteenth-century painter). After doing some online research about the artist, choose a particular painting or photograph or collection of images that you find especially interesting. Then write an essay in which you describe the place or scene as viewed through the artist's eyes.

Sister Flowers

Maya Angelou

Maya Angelou, a poet and author of memoirs and plays, was born Marguerite Johnson in Saint Louis, Missouri, in 1928. She spent her childhood living alternately with her grandmother in Stamps, Arkansas, and with each of her divorced parents. In addition to this instability, she endured great suffering, having been raped at age eight by her mother's boyfriend. Also, she became a mother at age sixteen. Yet she turned her experiences with racism and a dysfunctional family life into her best-known writings, the autobiographical works *I Know Why the Caged Bird Sings* (1970) and *All God's Children Need Traveling Shoes* (1986).

The narrative that follows, which comes from *I Know Why the Caged Bird Sings*, begins after a trauma that has left young Marguerite speechless. As you read, notice the rich variety of adjectives Angelou uses to describe Sister Flowers, Momma, and the locations of key events. Consider how Angelou's descriptive technique enhances her narrative.

Focus on Understanding   Read to discover who Sister Flowers is and what gift she gives to the author.

Focus on the Topic   In class or in your journal, write about some ways to make a child feel important and loved.

1   For nearly a year [after I was raped], I sopped around the house, the Store, the school and the church, like an old biscuit, dirty and inedible. Then I met, or rather got to know, the lady who threw me my first lifeline.

2   Mrs. Bertha Flowers was the aristocrat of Black Stamps.° She had the grace of control to appear warm in the coldest weather, and on the Arkansas summer days it seemed she had a private breeze which swirled around, cooling her. She was thin without the taut look of wiry people, and her printed voile° dresses and flowered hats were as right for her as denim overalls for a farmer. She was our side's answer to the richest white woman in town.

Stamps: Small town in Arkansas

voile: Soft, sheer fabric made from cotton, rayon, or wool

3   Her skin was a rich black that would have peeled like a plum if snagged, but then no one would have thought of getting close enough to Mrs. Flowers to ruffle her dress, let alone snag her skin. She didn't encourage familiarity. She wore gloves too.

4   I don't think I ever saw Mrs. Flowers laugh, but she smiled often. A slow widening of her thin black lips to show even, small white teeth, then the slow effortless closing. When she chose to smile on me, I always wanted to thank her. The action was so graceful and inclusively benign.

5   She was one of the few gentlewomen I have ever known, and has remained throughout my life the measure of what a human being can be.

Momma had a strange relationship with her. Most often when she passed 6 on the road in front of the Store, she spoke to Momma in that soft yet carrying voice, "Good day, Mrs. Henderson." Momma responded with "How you, Sister Flowers?"

familiar: Close friend

Mrs. Flowers didn't belong to our church, nor was she Momma's familiar.° 7 Why on earth did she insist on calling her Sister Flowers? Shame made me want to hide my face. Mrs. Flowers deserved better than to be called Sister. Then, Momma left out the verb. Why not ask, "How *are* you, *Mrs*. Flowers?" With the unbalanced passion of the young, I hated her for showing her ignorance to Mrs. Flowers. It didn't occur to me for many years that they were as alike as sisters, separated only by formal education.

Although I was upset, neither of the women was in the least shaken by what 8 I thought an unceremonious greeting. Mrs. Flowers would continue her easy gait up the hill to her little bungalow, and Momma kept on shelling peas or doing whatever had brought her to the front porch.

Occasionally, though, Mrs. Flowers would drift off the road and down to the 9 Store and Momma would say to me, "Sister, you go on and play." As she left I would hear the beginning of an intimate conversation. Momma persistently using the wrong verb, or none at all.

"Brother and Sister Wilcox is sho'ly the meanest — " "Is," Momma? "Is"? 10 Oh, please, not "is," Momma, for two or more. But they talked, and from the side of the building where I waited for the ground to open up and swallow me, I heard the soft-voiced Mrs. Flowers and the textured voice of my grandmother merging and melting. They were interrupted from time to time by giggles that must have come from Mrs. Flowers (Momma never giggled in her life). Then she was gone.

moors: Open, boggy highlands

heath: Grassy, uncultivated land

She appealed to me because she was like people I had never met personally. 11 Like women in English novels who walked the moors° (whatever they were) with their loyal dogs racing at a respectful distance. Like the women who sat in front of roaring fireplaces, drinking tea incessantly from silver trays full of scones and crumpets. Women who walked over the "heath"° and read morocco-bound books and had two last names divided by a hyphen. It would be safe to say that she made me proud to be Negro, just by being herself.

She acted just as refined as whitefolks in the movies and books and she was 12 more beautiful, for none of them could have come near that warm color without looking gray by comparison.

It was fortunate that I never saw her in the company of powhitefolks. For 13 since they tend to think of their whiteness as an evenizer, I'm certain that I would have had to hear her spoken to commonly as Bertha, and my image of her would have been shattered like the unmendable Humpty-Dumpty.

One summer afternoon, sweet-milk fresh in my memory, she stopped at 14 the Store to buy provisions. Another Negro woman of her health and age would have been expected to carry the paper sacks home in one hand, but Momma said, "Sister Flowers, I'll send Bailey up to your house with these things."

She smiled that slow dragging smile, "Thank you, Mrs. Henderson. I'd 15
prefer Marguerite, though." My name was beautiful when she said it. "I've been
meaning to talk to her, anyway." They gave each other age-group looks.

Momma said, "Well, that's all right then. Sister, go and change your dress. 16
You going to Sister Flower's."

The chifforobe° was a maze. What on earth did one put on to go to Mrs. 17
Flowers's house? I knew I shouldn't put on a Sunday dress. It might be sacrilegious. Certainly not a house dress, since I was already wearing a fresh one. I
chose a school dress, naturally. It was formal without suggesting that going to
Mrs. Flowers's house was equivalent to attending church.

I trusted myself back into the Store. 18

"Now, don't you look nice." I had chosen the right thing, for once. . . . 19

There was a little path beside the rocky road, and Mrs. Flowers walked in 20
front swinging her arms and picking her way over the stones.

She said, without turning her head, to me, "I hear you're doing very good 21
school work, Marguerite, but that it's all written. The teachers report that they
have trouble getting you to talk in class." We passed the triangular farm on our
left and the path widened to allow us to walk together. I hung back in the separate unasked and unanswerable questions.

"Come and walk along with me, Marguerite." I couldn't have refused even 22
if I wanted to. She pronounced my name so nicely. Or more correctly, she spoke
each word with such clarity that I was certain a foreigner who didn't understand English could have understood her.

"Now no one is going to make you talk — possibly no one can. But bear in 23
mind, language is man's way of communicating with his fellow man and it is
language alone which separates him from the lower animals." That was a totally
new idea to me, and I would need time to think about it.

"Your grandmother says you read a lot. Every chance you get. That's good, 24
but not good enough. Words mean more than what is set down on paper. It
takes the human voice to infuse them with the shades of deeper meaning."

I memorized the part about the human voice infusing words. It seemed so 25
valid and poetic.

She said she was going to give me some books and that I not only must read 26
them, I must read them aloud. She suggested that I try to make a sentence
sound in as many different ways as possible.

"I'll accept no excuse if you return a book to me that has been badly 27
handled." My imagination boggled at the punishment I would deserve if in fact
I did abuse a book of Mrs. Flowers's. Death would be too kind and brief.

The odors in the house surprised me. Somehow I had never connected Mrs. 28
Flowers with food or eating or any other common experience of common
people. There must have been an outhouse, too, but my mind never recorded it.

The sweet scent of vanilla had met us as she opened the door. 29

"I made tea cookies this morning. You see, I had planned to invite you for 30
cookies and lemonade so we could have this little chat. The lemonade is in the
icebox."

chifforobe: Furniture
that holds clothing;
has drawers and a
place to hang items

It followed that Mrs. Flowers would have ice on an ordinary day, when most 31
families in our town bought ice late on Saturdays only a few times during the
summer to be used in the wooden ice-cream freezers.

She took the bags from me and disappeared through the kitchen door. I 32
looked around the room that I had never in my wildest fantasies imagined I
would see. Browned photographs leered or threatened from the walls and the
white, freshly done curtains pushed against themselves and against the wind. I
wanted to gobble up the room entire and take it to Bailey, who would help me
analyze and enjoy it.

"Have a seat, Marguerite. Over there by the table." She carried a platter cov- 33
ered with a tea towel. Although she warned that she hadn't tried her hand at
baking sweets for some time, I was certain that like everything else about her
the cookies would be perfect.

They were flat round wafers, slightly browned on the edges and butter- 34
yellow in the center. With the cold lemonade they were sufficient for childhood's
lifelong diet. Remembering my manners, I took nice little lady-like bites off the
edges. She said she had made them expressly for me and that she had a few in
the kitchen that I could take home to my brother. So I jammed one whole cake
in my mouth and the rough crumbs scratched the insides of my jaws, and if I
hadn't had to swallow, it would have been a dream come true.

As I ate she began the first of what we later called "my lessons in living." 35
She said that I must always be intolerant of ignorance but understanding of illiteracy. That some people, unable to go to school, were more educated and
even more intelligent than college professors. She encouraged me to listen carefully to what country people called mother wit. That in those homely sayings
was couched the collective wisdom of generations.

When I finished the cookies she brushed off the table and brought a thick, 36
small book from the bookcase. I had read *A Tale of Two Cities* and found it up
to my standards as a romantic novel. She opened the first page and I heard
poetry for the first time in my life.

"It was the best of times and the worst of times . . ." Her voice slid in and 37
curved down through and over the words. She was nearly singing. I wanted to
look at the pages. Were they the same that I had read? Or were there notes,
music, lined on the pages, as in a hymn book? Her sounds began cascading
gently. I knew from listening to a thousand preachers that she was nearing the
end of her reading, and I hadn't really heard, heard to understand, a single word.

"How do you like that?"   38

It occurred to me that she expected a response. The sweet vanilla flavor was 39
still on my tongue and her reading was a wonder in my ears. I had to speak.

I said, "Yes, ma'am." It was the least I could do, but it was the most also.   40

"There's one more thing. Take this book of poems and memorize one for 41
me. Next time you pay me a visit, I want you to recite."

I have tried often to search behind the sophistication of years for the en- 42
chantment I so easily found in those gifts. The essence escapes but its aura
remains. To be allowed, no, invited, into the private lives of strangers, and
to share their joys and fears, was a chance to exchange the Southern bitter

wormwood° for a cup of mead° with Beowulf° or a hot cup of tea and milk with Oliver Twist.° When I said aloud, "It is a far, far better thing that I do, than I have ever done . . ."° tears of love filled my eyes at my selflessness.

On that first day, I ran down the hill and into the road (few cars ever came 43 along it) and had the good sense to stop running before I reached the Store.

I was liked, and what a difference it made. I was respected not as Mrs. 44 Henderson's grandchild or Bailey's sister but for just being Marguerite Johnson.

Childhood's logic never asks to be proved (all conclusions are absolute). I 45 didn't question why Mrs. Flowers had singled me out for attention, nor did it occur to me that Momma might have asked her to give me a little talking to. All I cared about was that she had made tea cookies for *me* and read to *me* from her favorite book. It was enough to prove that she liked me.

wormwood: Bitter-tasting plant; mead: Alcoholic drink made from honey; Beowulf: Heroic character from an Old English poem; Oliver Twist: Title character in a novel by Charles Dickens; "It is a far, far better thing . . .": The final words of a central character in A Tale of Two Cities by Charles Dickens

Understanding the Reading

1. How does Marguerite feel about her grandmother's interactions with Mrs. Flowers? What do these feelings reveal about Marguerite herself?

2. Which characteristics of Mrs. Flowers appeal to Marguerite? How do these traits set her apart from other people in the community?

3. What do you think Mrs. Flowers wants to accomplish with Marguerite? How does she attempt to reach this goal?

4. What does Marguerite learn from Sister Flowers?

Visualizing the Reading

Angelou uses a variety of sensory details to convey her dominant impression of Sister Flowers. Analyze her use by completing the following chart. For each sense, fill in several striking and effective examples. Include the paragraph number for reference. The first one has been done for you.

Sense	Examples
Sight	1. "Her skin was a rich black that would have peeled like a plum if snagged" (3) 2.
Taste	
Touch	
Smell	
Sound	

Examining the Characteristics of Descriptive Essays

1. "Sister Flowers" is a chapter from one of Maya Angelou's autobiographies. In this essay, what do you think Angelou is communicating about her childhood?

2. What aspects of Mrs. Flowers does Angelou describe? What method of organization does she use to order her details about Mrs. Flowers? Would another organization have been more or less effective? Explain why.

3. What is the dominant impression about Mrs. Flowers that Angelou presents? Include several examples of the details that support her dominant impression.

4. Who else is described in this story besides Mrs. Flowers? Explain how the author describes them. Is there a significant difference between the descriptions of these characters and that of Mrs. Flowers?

Building Your Critical Thinking Skills: Details

Authors often include **details** without explaining their significance. For example, Marguerite reports that Momma often uses "the wrong verb, or none at all" (para. 9). By including this detail, the narrator suggests that she is embarrassed by Momma's incorrect grammar. What does each of the following details contribute to your understanding of the person or the situation?

1. "[Mrs. Flowers] was our side's answer to the richest white woman in town" (para. 2).

2. "My [Marguerite's] name was beautiful when she said it." (para. 15)

3. "I had chosen the right thing, for once. . . ." (para. 19)

Building Your Word Power

For a definition of simile, see the chart of commonly used language features on p. 21.

1. Explain the simile used in paragraph 1: "I sopped around . . . like an old biscuit, dirty and inedible."

2. What does Mrs. Flowers mean by the phrase "mother wit" in paragraph 35?

3. Explain the meaning of each of the following words as it is used in the reading: *benign* (para. 4), *sacrilegious* (17), *infusing* (25), *leered* (32), and *aura* (42). Refer to your dictionary as needed.

Reacting to the Topic: Discussion and Journal Writing

1. At the start of the essay, we learn that Marguerite has recently been raped and was traumatized by it. Identify other childhood experiences that may create trauma.

2. Marguerite expresses pleasure and delight at being invited into the lives of strangers through literature (para. 42). When you read a story, see a movie, or watch a television show, do you feel as if you are viewing or participating in the lives of strangers? Is this participation part of the appeal of plays, movie, and novels?

3. In class or in your journal, describe an experience from your childhood (positive or negative) involving an older person that you will never forget. Explain why this experience was so meaningful to you.

Applying Your Skills: Writing Assignments

1. **Paragraph Assignment.** Mrs. Flowers throws Marguerite her "first lifeline" (para. 1). Write a paragraph describing a situation in which someone threw you a lifeline.

2. Using description, rewrite Angelou's essay from the point of view of Mrs. Flowers, Momma, or Bailey. Be sure to include a description of Marguerite, feeling free to make up details as needed. Plan your essay before you begin writing. For example, will you begin in the past or, say, just a week or a day before Mrs. Flowers started helping Marguerite?

3. When Sister Flowers reads aloud the opening paragraph of *A Tale of Two Cities*, Marguerite hears it in a new way, even though she has already read it. Write an essay describing a person, place, or situation that you came to understand and view differently after seeing it from a new perspective.

4. **Combining Patterns.** Marguerite is greatly influenced by literature; in her essay, she uses it to help describe her feelings for Mrs. Flowers. Have you ever been influenced by something you have studied, either in school or independently? Write an essay explaining what caused this influence and how it affected you.

5. **Internet Research.** Visit the official Web site for poet and author Maya Angelou at www.mayaangelou.com, or visit related sites about the author by conducting an online search. Read the biographical material on the site, and follow the links to hear audiotapes and videotapes of Maya Angelou talking about her work. As you research the site, create a list of characteristics of the author and her work. Then use these characteristics to write an essay that describes her and her work to someone who is unfamiliar with Angelou and her writing. Use descriptive details to support your dominant impression.

Illustration: Explaining with Examples

WRITING QUICK START

In a social problems class, the instructor projects the photograph shown on this page onto a screen and makes the following statement: "Environmental pollution is a growing national problem." She asks the class to think of situations similar to the one shown here that confirm this view. Using the instructor's statement as your topic sentence, write a supporting paragraph with examples that illustrate this growing problem. Begin by brainstorming a list of different types of environmental pollution that you have observed or read about, and then use several of these examples to illustrate your main point about pollution.

What Is Illustration?

Illustration is a means of using specific information to reveal the essential characteristics of a topic or to reinforce the thesis. In arguing that horror films are harmful for young viewers, for instance, you might mention several films that demonstrate objectionable qualities. Or if you are making a point about the high cost of attending a movie, you might quote prices at several movie theaters in your neighborhood. Examples make ideas concrete, often connecting them to situations within the reader's experience. Most textbooks are filled with examples for this very reason. Writers in academic and work situations commonly use illustration as well, as these examples show.

- For a *literature* class, you are assigned to write an analysis of the poet Emily Dickinson's use of metaphor. To explain your point about her metaphorical use of animals, you provide examples from several of her poems.
- You are an *elementary school reading teacher,* and as part of a request to the school board for new computer software you give several examples of how the software will benefit particular types of students.

In the following illustration essay, "Snoopers at Work," Bill Bryson uses examples to support a thesis.

Snoopers at Work

Bill Bryson

Bill Bryson (b. 1951) grew up in the United States and then lived in England from 1977 to the mid-1990s, where he wrote for newspapers and then branched out into travel writing. Bryson's travel books include *A Walk in the Woods* (1998), *In a Sunburned Country* (2000), *Bill Bryson's African Diary* (2002), and two nonfiction works about travels in the United States, *The Lost Continent* (1989) and *I'm a Stranger Here Myself* (1999).

The essays in *I'm a Stranger Here Myself* began as Sunday columns in a British newspaper, *The Mail.* In the following piece from that collection, Bryson discusses the invasion of workers' privacy by their employers. As you read, pay attention to the kinds of examples the author chooses to illustrate this disturbing trend, and notice how he uses humor to comment on the material.

Now here is something to bear in mind should you ever find yourself using a changing room in a department store or other retail establishment. It is perfectly legal — indeed, it is evidently routine — for the store to spy on you while you are trying on their clothes.

1   Introduction: opens with arresting scenario

Background
information

I know this because I have just been reading a book by Ellen Alderman and Caroline Kennedy called *The Right to Privacy,* which is full of alarming tales of ways that businesses and employers can — and enthusiastically do — intrude into what would normally be considered private affairs.   2

Specific example
relating to
introduction

The business of changing-cubicle spying came to light in 1983 when a customer trying on clothes in a department store in Michigan discovered that a store employee had climbed a stepladder and was watching him through a metal vent. (Is this tacky or what?) The customer was sufficiently outraged that he sued the store for invasion of privacy. He lost. A state court held that it was reasonable for retailers to defend against shoplifting by engaging in such surveillance.   3

Thesis

He shouldn't have been surprised. Nearly everyone is being spied on in some way in America these days. A combination of technological advances, employer paranoia, and commercial avarice means that many millions of Americans are having their lives delved into in ways that would have been impossible, not to say unthinkable, a dozen years ago. . . .   4

Topic sentence makes
generalization

Example: medical
record surveillance

Many companies are taking advantage of technological possibilities to make their businesses more ruthlessly productive. In Maryland, according to *Time* magazine, a bank searched through the medical records of its borrowers — apparently quite legally — to find out which of them had life-threatening illnesses and used this information to cancel their loans. Other companies have focused not on customers but on their own employees — for instance, to check what prescription drugs the employees are taking. One large, well-known company teamed up with a pharmaceutical firm to comb through the health records of employees to see who might benefit from a dose of antidepressants. The idea was that the company would get more serene workers; the drug company would get more customers.   5

Example: statistics that
document methods of
spying

According to the American Management Association two-thirds of companies in the United States spy on their employees in some way. Thirty-five percent track phone calls, and 10 percent actually tape phone conversations to review at leisure later. About a quarter of companies surveyed admitted to going through their employees' computer files and reading their e-mail.   6

Topic sentence: opens
with transition and
makes generalization

Example: video
surveillance

Still other companies are secretly watching their employees at work. A secretary at a college in Massachusetts discovered that a hidden video camera was filming her office twenty-four hours a day. Goodness knows what the school authorities were hoping to find. What they got were images of the woman changing out of her work clothes and into a track suit each night in order to jog home from work. She is suing and will probably get a pot of money. But elsewhere courts have upheld companies' rights to spy on their workers.   7

There is a particular paranoia about drugs. I have a friend who got a job with a large manufacturing company in Iowa a year or so ago. Across the street from the company was a tavern that was the company after-hours hangout. One night my friend was having a beer after work with his colleagues when he was approached by a fellow employee who asked if he knew where she could get some marijuana. He said he didn't use the stuff himself, but to get rid of her — for she was very persistent — he gave her the phone number of an acquaintance who sometimes sold it.

8

Example: drug use entrapment

The next day he was fired. The woman, it turned out, was a company spy employed solely to weed out drug use in the company. He hadn't supplied her with marijuana, you understand, hadn't encouraged her to use marijuana, and had stressed that he didn't use marijuana himself. Nonetheless he was fired for encouraging and abetting the use of an illegal substance.

9

Already, 91 percent of large companies — I find this almost unbelievable — now test some of their workers for drugs. Scores of companies have introduced what are called TAD rules — TAD being short for "tobacco, alcohol, and drugs" — which prohibit employees from using any of these substances at any time, including at home. There are companies, if you can believe it, that forbid their employees to drink or smoke at any time — even one beer, even on a Saturday night — and enforce the rules by making their workers give urine samples.

10

Topic sentence: continued use of statistics lends credibility to thesis

Example: TAD rules

But it gets even more sinister than that. Two leading electronics companies working together have invented something called an "active badge," which tracks the movements of any worker compelled to wear one. The badge sends out an infrared signal every fifteen seconds. This signal is received by a central computer, which is thus able to keep a record of where every employee is and has been, whom they have associated with, how many times they have been to the toilet or water cooler — in short, to log every single action of their working day. If that isn't ominous, I don't know what is.

11

Example: "active badge" tracking

However, there is one development, I am pleased to report, that makes all of this worthwhile. A company in New Jersey has patented a device for determining whether restaurant employees have washed their hands after using the lavatory. Now *that* I can go for.

12

Conclusion: humorous example ends essay on a light note

Characteristics of Illustration Essays

Effective illustration essays support a generalization with pertinent examples that maintain readers' interest and help to fulfill the author's purpose. Because an illustration essay is more than a list of examples, a well-thought-out organization is essential.

Illustration Uses Examples to Support Generalizations

Examples are effective in supporting generalizations. A **generalization** is a broad statement about a topic. Often, the thesis of an essay contains a generalization. In "Snoopers at Work," Bryson's thesis contains a generalization about how "millions of Americans are having their lives delved into in ways that would have been impossible, not to say unthinkable, a dozen years ago" (para. 4).

The following statements are generalizations because they make assertions about an entire group or category.

- Most college students are energetic, ambitious, and eager to get ahead in life.
- Gestures play an important role in nonverbal communication.
- Boys are more willing to participate in class discussions than are girls.

To explain and support any of these generalizations, you would need to provide specific examples to show how or why the statement is accurate. For instance, you could support the generalization about college students by describing several students who demonstrate energy and ambition: One student works two part-time jobs to cover tuition costs; another is the mother of two young children as well as a full-time student. However, because this general statement says, "*Most* college students are energetic . . . ," you would need to provide other types of support to accompany the examples of individual students. Relevant facts, statistics, expert opinions, anecdotes, personal observations, or descriptions could be used to show that the generalization does indeed apply to the majority of college students.

Illustration Uses Examples to Explain or Clarify

Examples are also useful for explaining an unfamiliar topic, a difficult concept, or an abstract term.

Unfamiliar Topics.   When the audience has little or no knowledge of your topic, consider using examples to help them understand it. In "Snoopers at Work," Bryson uses the example of tracking workers' visits to the toilet or water cooler to help readers understand how an "active badge" works. Similarly, note how examples are used in the following excerpt from a book by Bryson about the English language.

> The complexities of the English language are such that even native speakers cannot always communicate effectively, as almost every American learns on his first day in Britain. . . . That may be. But if the Briton and American of the twenty-second century baffle each other, it seems altogether likely that they won't confuse many others — not, at least, if the rest of the world continues expropriating words and phrases at its present rate. Already Germans talk about *ein Image Problem* and *das Cash-Flow*, Italians program their computers with *il software*, French motorists going away for a *weekend break* pause for *les refueling stops*, Poles watch *telewizja*, Spaniards have a *flirt*, Austrians eat *Big Macs*, and the Japanese go on a *pikunikku*. For better or worse, English has

become the most global of languages, the lingua franca of business, science, education, politics, and pop music.

BILL BRYSON, The Mother Tongue

Difficult Concepts.   Many concepts are difficult for readers to grasp by definition alone. For instance, readers might guess that the term *urbanization,* a key concept in sociology, has something to do with cities. Defining the concept as, say, "the process by which an area becomes part of a city" would give the readers more to go on. But examples of formerly suburban areas that have become urban would make the concept immediately understandable.

Abstract Terms.   Abstract terms refer to ideas rather than to people or to concrete things you can see and touch. Terms such as *truth* and *justice* are abstract. Because abstractions are difficult to understand, examples help to clarify them. Notice how the following passage from a communication textbook lists examples to help readers understand the term *channel.*

> **Channels** are simply the vehicles or mechanisms that transmit messages from senders to receivers. The channels that come to mind first would include sound waves (oral communication) and light waves (nonverbal communication). However, you could quickly compile a list of many other frequently used communication channels. Consider, for example, the possible channels used for written communication (memos, letters), electronic communication (radio, television), and computer-transmitted communication (email, Internet).

DAN O'HAIR ET AL., Competent Communication

In other cases, however, abstract terms mean different things to different people. In these situations you would give examples to clarify what *you* mean by the abstract term in question. Suppose you were to use the term *unfair* to describe your employer's treatment of employees; readers might have different ideas of fairness. Providing examples of you employer's unfair treatment would make the meaning clear.

Illustration Maintains Readers' Interest

Examples that give readers a glimpse of an event or a circumstance and that enable them to imagine themselves there also help to maintain interest. In "Snoopers at Work," we can visualize Bryson's example of the hidden camera filming a secretary twenty-four hours a day, recording images of her changing into her jogging clothes at the end of each workday. Similarly, Bryson's opening example about dressing room surveillance gets our attention; we want to keep reading to learn more about this and other alarming instances of loss of privacy.

Illustration Takes Purpose and Audience into Account

A successful illustration essay contains either a series of related examples or one extended example in support of its thesis. The number and type of examples depend on the writer's purpose and audience. An essay arguing that a Toyota Matrix is a better buy than a Ford Focus would need to include a series of examples to illustrate the various models, years, and options available to potential car buyers. But an essay for an audience of high school students about the consequences of dropping out of school would be perfectly fine with a single poignant example.

Likewise, audience is a key factor in deciding what type of examples to include. At times, technical examples may be appropriate; at other times, more personal or nontechnical ones are effective. For instance, suppose you want to persuade readers that the Food and Drug Administration should approve a new cancer drug. If your audience is composed of physicians, the most effective examples would include statistical studies and technical explanations of the drug's effectiveness. But if your audience is the general public, it would be better to include personal anecdotes about lives being saved and nontechnical examples of the drug's safety. Bryson, addressing the general public about surveillance techniques, uses examples that most readers are familiar with: department store changing rooms, personal records, and drug testing.

Illustration Uses Carefully Selected Examples

All examples that are used to explain a thesis should be carefully chosen. Select examples that are relevant, representative, accurate, and striking. *Relevant* examples have a direct relationship to the thesis. For example, if your essay advocates publicly funded and operated preschool programs, you should support your case with examples of successful publicly funded programs, not privately operated ones.

An example is *representative* when it shows a typical or real-life situation, not a rare or unusual one. In many cases, you will need to give several representative examples. For instance, in an essay arguing that preschool programs advance children's prereading skills, one example of an all-day, year-round preschool would not be representative of all or most other programs.

Be sure the examples you include are *accurate and specific.* Report statistics objectively, and provide enough information so that readers can evaluate the reliability of the data. In the following examples, notice how the second one provides better detail.

EXAMPLE LACKING DETAIL:	Most students in preschool programs have better language skills than children who don't attend such programs.
DETAILED EXAMPLE:	According to an independent evaluator, 73 percent of children who attended Head Start program in Clearwater had better language skills after one year of attendance than students who did not attend the program.

Remember that *striking and dramatic* examples make a strong, lasting impression on readers. Rather than simply stating that companies use spies to collect evidence against employees, Bryson uses a vivid and compelling example of a friend who was fired after being solicited by a company spy to buy marijuana (para. 8). At times, it may be necessary to conduct research to find examples outside of your knowledge and experience. For an essay on preschool programs, for example, you would need to do library or Internet research to obtain statistical information such as the 73 percent mentioned above. You might also interview a preschool administrator or teacher to gather firsthand anecdotes and opinions.

Illustration Organizes Details Effectively

In using examples to support a thesis, it is important to decide how to organize both the examples and the details that accompany them. Often, one of the methods of organization discussed in Chapter 3 will be useful: most-to-least, least-to-most, chronological, or spatial order. For instance, in an essay explaining why punk rockers dress unconventionally, the examples might be arranged spatially, starting with footwear and moving upward to illustrate outlandish hairstyles and piercings. In some instances, you may want to organize examples according to another pattern of development, such as comparison and contrast or cause and effect. For example, to support the thesis that a local department store needs to improve its customer services, you might begin by contrasting the department store with several computer stores that do have better customer services and offering examples of the services provided by each.

For more on methods of organization, see Chapter 3, p. 48.

Visualizing an Illustration Essay

The graphic organizer in Figure 7.1 will help you visualize the components of an illustration essay. The structure is straightforward: The introduction contains background information and usually includes the thesis, the body paragraphs give one or more related examples, and the conclusion presents a final statement. For an essay using one extended example — such as a highly descriptive account of an auto accident intended to persuade readers to wear seat belts — the body paragraphs would focus on the details of that one example. A graphic organizer of "Snoopers at Work," which uses numerous related examples to support the thesis, is provided in Figure 7.2.

Writing an Illustration Essay

To write an illustration essay, use the following steps. Although you will give examples to support your thesis, you may need to follow one or more of the other patterns of development to organize your examples or to relate them to one another.

Planning an Illustration Essay

Your first step is to choose a topic and then narrow it so it becomes manageable — so that it can be supported by one or more examples. For instance, if you decide to write about the effects of test anxiety, you would need to provide several examples of testing situations in which individuals "freeze" or "go blank."

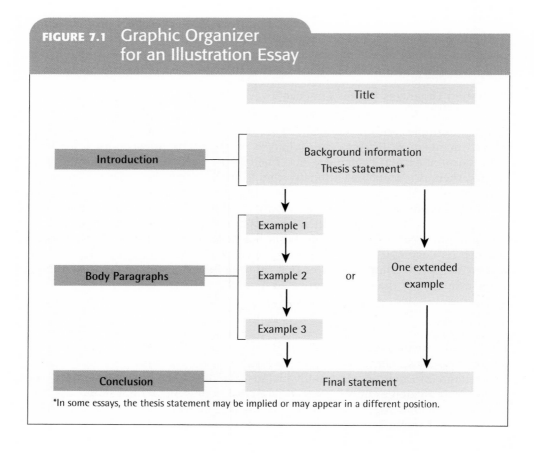

FIGURE 7.1 Graphic Organizer for an Illustration Essay

Title

Introduction — Background information / Thesis statement*

Example 1

Body Paragraphs — Example 2 or One extended example

Example 3

Conclusion — Final statement

*In some essays, the thesis statement may be implied or may appear in a different position.

Developing Your Thesis

The next step is to develop a working thesis about the narrowed topic. The thesis in an illustration essay expresses the idea that all the examples help to support. To write an effective thesis statement, use the following guidelines.

- Identify the narrowed topic of your essay.
- Make a generalization about the narrowed topic that you will support through the use of examples.

In "Snoopers at Work," Bryson makes such a generalization when he says, "A combination of technological advances, employer paranoia, and commercial avarice means that many millions of Americans are having their lives delved into in ways that would have been impossible, not to say unthinkable, a dozen years ago" (para. 4). All his examples support this thesis.

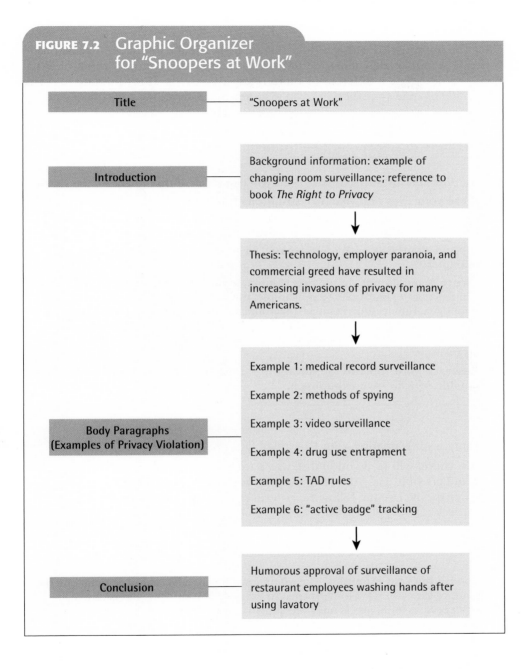

FIGURE 7.2   Graphic Organizer for "Snoopers at Work"

Title	"Snoopers at Work"
Introduction	Background information: example of changing room surveillance; reference to book *The Right to Privacy*
	Thesis: Technology, employer paranoia, and commercial greed have resulted in increasing invasions of privacy for many Americans.
Body Paragraphs (Examples of Privacy Violation)	Example 1: medical record surveillance Example 2: methods of spying Example 3: video surveillance Example 4: drug use entrapment Example 5: TAD rules Example 6: "active badge" tracking
Conclusion	Humorous approval of surveillance of restaurant employees washing hands after using lavatory

Gathering Examples for Your Essay

Once you are satisfied with your thesis statement, use the following suggestions to generate examples that illustrate it. As you brainstorm, you may think of situations that illustrate a different or more interesting thesis. Don't hesitate to revise or entirely change your thesis as you discover more about the topic.

Generating Examples for Illustration Essays

1. **Jot down all instances or situations you can think of that illustrate the thesis.**
2. **Close your eyes and visualize situations that illustrate the thesis.**
3. **Systematically review your life — year by year, place by place, or job by job — to recall situations that illustrate the thesis.**
4. **Discuss the thesis with a classmate.** Try to match or better each other's examples.
5. **Create two columns.** In the first column, write a list of words describing how you feel about your topic. (For example, the topic *cheating on college exams* might generate feelings such as anger and surprise.) In the second column, elaborate on these feelings by adding details about specific situations. (For example, you were surprised to discover that your best friend had cheated on an exam.)
6. **Research your topic in the library or on the Internet to discover examples outside of your own experience.**

Choosing and Evaluating Your Examples

Brainstorming will lead you to discover a wealth of examples — many more than you could possibly use. Your task, then, is to select the examples that will best support your thesis. Use the following criteria in choosing examples.

Guidelines for Choosing Examples to Illustrate Your Essay

1. **Choose relevant examples.** The examples you use must clearly demonstrate the point or idea you want to illustrate. An example of a student who is physically weak because of illness is not good support for the thesis that schools do not provide students with the instruction in physical education necessary to maintain a healthy lifestyle. Because lack of training in physical education is not responsible for this student's problem, the case would be irrelevant to your thesis.
2. **Choose a variety of useful examples.** If you are using more than one example, choose a variety that reveals different aspects of your topic or that contributes new information.

(Continued)

3. **Choose representative examples.** Choose typical cases, not rare or unusual ones, to illustrate your point. For the thesis about physical education, a high school all-star football player who lacks adequate strength would be an exceptional case and a nonrepresentative example. A recent graduate who did not learn to play a single sport and failed to develop a habit of regular exercise would be a more representative example.

4. **Choose striking examples.** Include examples that capture readers' attention and make a vivid impression.

5. **Choose accurate examples.** Be sure the examples are accurate. They should be neither exaggerated nor understated; they should present the situation realistically.

6. **Choose examples that will appeal to the audience.** Some examples will appeal to one type of audience more than to another type. If you want to illustrate high school graduates' lack of training in physical education for an audience of students, examples involving actual students may be most appealing, whereas expert opinion and statistics would be appropriate for an audience of parents.

Drafting an Illustration Essay

Once you are satisfied with your thesis and the examples you have chosen to illustrate it, it is time to organize your ideas and write the essay. If you are using an extended example, you might want to relate events in chronological order. If you are using several examples, you may want to order them in terms of importance or group them in categories.

For more on methods of organization, see Chapter 3, p. 48.

Once you have decided on a method of organization, the next step is to write a first draft. Here are some tips for drafting an illustration essay.

Guidelines for Writing an Illustration Essay

1. **Begin with a clear introduction.** In most illustration essays, the thesis is stated at the outset. Your introduction should also spark readers' interest and include background information about the topic.

2. **Remember that each paragraph should express one key idea; the example or examples in that paragraph should illustrate that key idea.** Develop the body paragraphs so that each one presents a single example or group of closely related examples.

3. **Use the topic sentence in each paragraph to make clear the particular idea that each example or set of examples illustrates.**

4. **Provide sufficient detail about each example.** Explain each example with vivid descriptive language. Your goal is to make readers feel as if they are experiencing or observing the situation themselves.

(Continued)

(Continued)

5. **Use transitions to move readers from one example to another.** Without transitions, your essay will seem choppy and disconnected. Use transitions such as *for example* and *in particular* to keep readers on track.

6. **End with an effective conclusion.** Your essay should conclude with a final statement that pulls your ideas together and reminds readers of your thesis. In less formal writing situations, you may end with a final example — as Bryson does in "Snoopers at Work" — as long as it effectively concludes the essay and reminds readers of the thesis.

Analyzing and Revising

If possible, set aside your draft for a day or two before rereading and revising it. As you reread and review, concentrate on organization, level of detail, and overall effectiveness — not on grammar or mechanics. Use the flowchart in Figure 7.3 to discover the strengths and weaknesses of your illustration essay.

Editing and Proofreading

For more on these and other common errors, see Chapter 4, p. 81.

The last step is to check your revised essay for errors in grammar, spelling, punctuation, and mechanics. In addition, look for the types of errors you commonly make in any writing assignments, whether for this class or any other situation. For illustration essays, pay particular attention to the following common errors.

Editing Tips and Troublespots: Illustration

1. **Avoid inconsistent verb tense.** Be consistent in the verb tense used in extended examples. For example, when citing an event from the past as an example, always use the past tense to describe it.

   ▸ Special events *are* an important part of children's lives. For example, parent visitation day at school *was* an event my daughter talked about for an entire week. Children *are* also excited by . . .

2. **Avoid inconsistent use of first, second, or third person.** Be sure to use first person (*I, me*), second person (*you*), or third person (*he, she, it, him, her*) consistently throughout your essay.

   ▸ I visited my daughter's first-grade classroom during parents' week last

   month. Each parent was invited to read a story to the class, and ~~you~~ were
   ^{we} ∧

   encouraged to ask the children questions afterward.

3. **Avoid sentence fragments.** Although professional writers such as Bill Bryson occasionally use fragments, student writers should avoid them; each sentence should have both a subject and a verb.

   ▸ Technology is becoming part of teenagers' daily lives. ~~For example, high~~
   ^{High} ∧

   school students who carry pagers
   ∧ _{are an example.}

FIGURE 7.3   Revising an Illustration Essay

QUESTIONS

REVISION STRATEGIES

1. Highlight your thesis statement. Place a checkmark by each example. Does the thesis clearly indicate the generalization that your examples support?

 NO

- Revise your thesis, focusing only on the ideas that the examples illustrate.
- Reconsider your thesis, changing your generalization so that it fits the examples.

 YES

2. Does each example explain and clarify unfamiliar topics, difficult concepts, or abstract terms?

 NO

- Circle terms that might be problematic, and see if a classmate or friend can define them.
- List terms or concepts in one column. For each item, write at least two examples in another column.

YES

3. *Write* a sentence describing your audience. Cross out any examples that won't appeal to the audience. Are there sufficient remaining examples that will appeal to the audience?

 NO

- Replace obvious, predictable examples with more striking or interesting ones.
- Replace examples that are too technical with more familiar ones.
- Add examples that represent different aspects of or viewpoints on the topic.

YES

4. *Write* a sentence stating the purpose of your essay. Cross out any examples that don't fulfill your purpose in writing. Are there sufficient remaining examples that do fulfill your purpose?

NO

- Brainstorm examples that are more appropriate to your purpose.
- Consider using more than one example or cutting back and using one extended example, depending on your purpose.

 YES

FIGURE 7.3   *(Continued)*

QUESTIONS	REVISION STRATEGIES

5. Reread each example you checked in question 2. Are your examples relevant, varied, striking, representative, and appealing?

NO ▶

- Eliminate examples that do not illustrate the thesis.
- Brainstorm or conduct research to discover relevant or more striking examples.
- Expand the examples to include more details.
- Consider adding other kinds of examples (such as expert opinion and statistics).

YES

6. <u>Underline</u> the topic sentence of each paragraph. Does one clearly make a point that the example(s) illustrates?

NO ▶

- Add topic sentences that clearly indicate the point being illustrated.
- Reorganize the essay, grouping examples according to the point or idea they illustrate.

YES

7. *Write* a brief outline detailing your method of organization. Draw brackets [ ] around each transitional word or phrase. Is your method of organization clear and effective?

NO ▶

- Review the methods of organization in Chapter 3.
- Consider using a different organizing strategy: most-to-least, least-to-most, chronological, or spatial order.
- Add transitions if the essay sounds choppy.

YES

8. Draw a box around and reread your introduction and conclusion. Is each one effective?

NO ▶

- Revise your introduction and conclusion so that they meet the guidelines in Chapter 3.

YES

9. Print out another draft to edit and proofread before turning the essay in.

Students Write

Melissa Parker, a student at Canisius College, wrote the following essay to fulfill an assignment that directed her to choose a problem facing modern society and then write an essay explaining and illustrating the problem. As you read the illustration essay, underline the examples that best explain the problems created by Internet hoaxes.

Internet Hoaxes: A Multiplying Problem

Melissa Parker

The Internet has revolutionized the spread of information around the world because of its ease of use and accessibility. Unfortunately, not all information found on the Internet is truthful or accurate. In addition to giving access to misleading informational Web sites, the Internet has seen the growth of deliberately deceptive and damaging hoaxes containing false information. Many Internet hoaxes encourage the recipient to forward them to as many people as possible. Because hoaxes can be spread on the Internet to millions of people in a short time by way of emailing, they can be especially damaging both in terms of misleading the public with false information or promises and through their adverse economic impact.

One common type of Internet hoax is the message that promises instant wealth or free merchandise. One such hoax was an email that promised free M&M's to the public. This message seemed believable because it included the name of a supposed "marketing analyst" for Mars Incorporated, the company that produces M&M's chocolate candies. The email claimed that if the Internet user forwarded the message to five friends, a tracking device would calculate how many emails had been sent out. When it reached 2,000 people, the user would receive a free case of M&M's. Promises like this of free goods or services are generally hoaxes; one would be wise to follow the old adage "if it seems too good to be true, it probably is" as a guideline when determining the credibility of any online offers.

Other Internet hoaxes play on the need of people who want to help others. For example, hoax virus warnings caution Internet users about damaging computer viruses that are spreading rapidly. These types of email messages urge Internet users to warn all of their friends about the virus. One hoax warned users of the dangers of a new "Y2K7

Title: identifies topic and suggests its importance

1

Introduction: background on Internet and hoaxes

Thesis: presents generalization

2 **Topic sentence: presents key idea and shows that examples will be grouped in categories**

Example: M&M's hoax offers clear support for thesis

3 **Topic sentence: transition to different type of hoax**

Example: Y2K7 virus

virus." According to the warning, if a person clicked on an email titled "Y2K7" from Microsoft with an .Exe file, his or her computer registry would be changed. Many users who received this warning thought it was real and passed it along to everyone in their address book. In this way, the hoax spread quickly around the world. However, no virus entitled "Y2K7" ever existed, and the only thing that was rapidly spread was the hoax itself.

Topic sentence: third type of hoax

Example: flu vaccine hoax demonstrates danger of such hoaxes

Potentially dangerous are those Internet hoaxes that supposedly offer medical advice. Like virus hoaxes, these spread quickly because people feel compelled to pass along anything that they deem "useful" information. In the fall of 2003, during the onset of an especially bad flu season, a rumor was spread via the Internet warning of a recalled batch of flu vaccine that had been contaminated. Simply by noting that the FDA had issued the recall, the creator was able to convince people that the hoax was real, potentially scaring away from receiving a flu vaccine people who were most at risk. People must be on guard to protect themselves from potentially dangerous hoaxes; when in doubt, they should should always fully research both the source and the information itself.

4

Topic sentence: transition to economic costs

Examples: mail delays, loss of time in workplace

Difficult concept is explained using easy-to-understand example

In addition to disseminating misleading and potentially dangerous information, Internet hoaxes have a real economic cost. While one might think that such messages are merely a nuisance, clogging up one's inbox, consider that if every person who received an Internet hoax forwarded it to ten people, the message would reach one million people by the sixth generation. This proves costly because it delays mail servers and costs the Internet user. Consider also the loss of time in the workplace that such messages create. If 600 employees at one company all received an Internet hoax and they all took approximately two minutes to read and forward the message to their friends and colleagues, a full twenty hours of business time would be lost. If you multiply that by an average hourly wage, the loss to the business would quickly climb to thousands of dollars.

5

Conclusion: reminds reader of thesis and offers solution

The solution is to avoid forwarding email messages that ask you to forward them to as many people as possible. If the message sounds like a hoax, it probably is one. Companies and corporations will not give individuals money or free benefits for forwarding email messages. Also, credible virus warnings do not ask recipients to forward them. If you receive a virus warning, you should research it at an anti-virus Web site to determine if it is legitimate. Likewise, contact your doctor or visit a credible medical site like the Centers for Disease Control Web site to ascertain whether a message containing health-related information is true. The Internet is flooded with hoaxes, and forwarding them through email only contributes to the problem and encourages mischief-makers to create more.

6

Responding to "Students Write"

1. Evaluate Parker's thesis statement. How does it predict the essay's organization?
2. Does Parker's introduction capture your interest? If not, can you think of more interesting ways to begin?
3. Evaluate the appropriateness, quantity, and types of examples Parker provides.
4. What do the statistics provided in paragraph 5 contribute to the essay?
5. In what way does the conclusion reemphasize the key points of the essay?

Reading an Illustration Essay

Examples are dramatic, real, and concrete, and it is easy to pay too much attention to them. Be sure to focus on the key points the examples illustrate. Here are some suggestions for reading illustration essays with a focused eye.

What to Look for, Highlight, and Annotate

Understanding the Reading

- Read the essay once to grasp its basic ideas; reread it to analyze its structure and content.
- Study the introduction and conclusion. Does the introduction present enough background information about the topic? Does the conclusion reinforce the thesis?
- What meaning does the title contribute to the essay?
- Use marginal annotations to record thoughts or questions that occur to you as you read.

Examining the Characteristics of Illustration Essays

- Identify the thesis statement. If the thesis is not directly stated, ask yourself this question: What one major point do all the examples illustrate?
- Study and highlight the examples. Note in the margin the characteristics or aspects of the thesis each example illustrates.
- Record your answers to these questions: How well do the examples explain or clarify the thesis? Did you feel convinced of the writer's thesis after reading the essay?
- Are the examples organized in order of importance, in chronological order, in spatial order, or by some other method?
- Note how the examples fit with any other patterns of development used in the essay.

How to Find Ideas to Write About

When you are asked to write a response to an illustration essay, keep an eye out for ideas to write about as you read. Try to think of similar examples from your personal experience. While reading "Snoopers at Work," for instance, you might have thought about your own experience with surveillance. You might have recalled privacy forms you filled out at the bank or doctor's office, or the presence of a video camera at your local ATM. Each of these examples could lead you to a thesis and ideas for writing.

Just Walk On By: A Black Man Ponders His Power to Alter Public Space

Brent Staples

Brent Staples (b. 1951) is a journalist who has written numerous articles, essays, and editorials as well as a memoir, *Parallel Time: Growing Up in Black and White* (1994). Staples holds a Ph.D. in psychology and has served since 1990 as editor for education, race, and culture at the *New York Times*.

This essay was first published in *Harper's* in 1986. As you read it, consider the examples Staples uses to illustrate his "power to alter public space." Notice the situations in which he is mistaken for a criminal, and consider what he says he has done in response to such misperceptions.

Focus on Understanding   Read to discover what the public space referred to in the title is and how the author has the power to "alter" it.

Focus on the Topic   In class or in your journal, discuss the ways that people use (and misuse) stereotypes. Why do you think stereotypes are so pervasive?

My first victim was a woman — white, well dressed, probably in her late 1 twenties. I came upon her late one evening on a deserted street in Hyde Park, a relatively affluent neighborhood in an otherwise mean, impoverished section of Chicago. As I swung onto the avenue behind her, there seemed to be a discreet, uninflammatory distance between us. Not so. She cast back a worried glance. To her, the youngish black man — a broad six feet two inches with a beard and billowing hair, both hands shoved into the pockets of a bulky military jacket — seemed menacingly close. After a few more quick glimpses, she picked up her pace and was soon running in earnest. Within seconds she disappeared into a cross street.

That was more than a decade ago. I was twenty-two years old, a graduate 2 student newly arrived at the University of Chicago. It was in the echo of that ter-rified woman's footfalls that I first began to know the unwieldy inheritance I'd come into — the ability to alter public space in ugly ways. It was clear that she thought herself the quarry of a mugger, a rapist, or worse. Suffering a bout of insomnia, however, I was stalking sleep, not defenseless wayfarers. As a softy who is scarcely able to take a knife to a raw chicken — let alone hold one to a person's throat — I was surprised, embarrassed, and dismayed all at once. Her flight made me feel like an accomplice in tyranny. It also made it clear that I was indistinguishable from the muggers who occasionally seeped into the area from the surrounding ghetto. That first encounter, and those that followed,

211

signified that a vast, unnerving gulf lay between nighttime pedestrians — particularly women — and me. And I soon gathered that being perceived as dangerous is a hazard in itself. I only needed to turn a corner into a dicey situation, or crowd some frightened, armed person in a foyer somewhere, or make an errant move after being pulled over by a policeman. Where fear and weapons meet — and they often do in urban America — there is always the possibility of death.

In that first year, my first away from my hometown, I was to become thoroughly familiar with the language of fear. At dark, shadowy intersections, I could cross in front of a car stopped at a traffic light and elicit the *thunk, thunk, thunk, thunk* of the driver — black, white, male, or female — hammering down the door locks. On less traveled streets after dark, I grew accustomed to but never comfortable with people crossing to the other side of the street rather than pass me. Then there were the standard unpleasantries with policemen, doormen, bouncers, cab-drivers, and others whose business it is to screen out troublesome individuals *before* there is any nastiness. 3

I moved to New York nearly two years ago and I have remained an avid night walker. In central Manhattan, the near-constant crowd cover minimizes tense one-on-one street encounters. Elsewhere — in SoHo, for example, where sidewalks are narrow and tightly spaced buildings shut out the sky — things can get very taut indeed. 4

After dark, on the warrenlike streets of Brooklyn where I live, I often see women who fear the worst from me. They seem to have set their faces on neutral, and with their purse straps strung across their chests bandolier-style,° they forge ahead as though bracing themselves against being tackled. I understand, of course, that the danger they perceive is not a hallucination. Women are particularly vulnerable to street violence, and young black males are drastically overrepresented among the perpetrators of that violence. Yet these truths are no solace against the kind of alienation that comes of being ever the suspect, a fearsome entity with whom pedestrians avoid making eye contact. 5

It is not altogether clear to me how I reached the ripe old age of twenty-two without being conscious of the lethality nighttime pedestrians attributed to me. Perhaps it was because in Chester, Pennsylvania, the small, angry industrial town where I came of age in the 1960s, I was scarcely noticeable against a backdrop of gang warfare, street knifings, and murders. I grew up one of the good boys, had perhaps a half-dozen fistfights. In retrospect, my shyness of combat has clear sources. 6

As a boy, I saw countless tough guys locked away; I have since buried several, too. They were babies, really — a teenage cousin, a brother of twenty-two, a childhood friend in his mid-twenties — all gone down in episodes of bravado played out in the streets. I came to doubt the virtues of intimidation early on. I chose, perhaps unconsciously, to remain a shadow — timid, but a survivor. 7

The fearsomeness mistakenly attributed to me in public places often has a perilous flavor. The most frightening of these confusions occurred in the late 1970s and early 1980s, when I worked as a journalist in Chicago. One day, rush- 8

bandolier-style: over the shoulder and across the chest, as a soldier wears a belt of ammunition

ing into the office of a magazine I was writing for with a deadline story in hand, I was mistaken for a burglar. The office manager called security and, with an ad hoc posse,° pursued me through the labyrinthine halls, nearly to my editor's door. I had no way of proving who I was. I could only move briskly toward the company of someone who knew me.

ad hoc posse: a group formed with whatever people happen to be present for the purpose of apprehending a criminal

Another time I was on assignment for a local paper and killing time before an interview. I entered a jewelry store on the city's affluent Near North Side. The proprietor excused herself and returned with an enormous red Doberman pinscher straining at the end of a leash. She stood, the dog extended toward me, silent to my questions, her eyes bulging nearly out of her head. I took a cursory look around, nodded, and bade her good night. 9

Relatively speaking, however, I never fared as badly as another black male journalist. He went to nearby Waukegan, Illinois, a couple of summers ago to work on a story about a murderer who was born there. Mistaking the reporter for the killer, police officers hauled him from his car at gunpoint and but for his press credentials would probably have tried to book him. Such episodes are not uncommon. Black men trade tales like this all the time. 10

Over the years, I learned to smother the rage I felt at so often being taken for a criminal. Not to do so would surely have led to madness. I now take precautions to make myself less threatening. I move about with care, particularly late in the evening. I give a wide berth to nervous people on subway platforms during the wee hours, particularly when I have exchanged business clothes for jeans. If I happen to be entering a building behind some people who appear skittish, I may walk by, letting them clear the lobby before I return, so as not to seem to be following them. I have been calm and extremely congenial on those rare occasions when I've been pulled over by the police. 11

And on late-evening constitutionals I employ what has proved to be an excellent tension-reducing measure: I whistle melodies from Beethoven and Vivaldi and the more popular classical composers. Even steely New Yorkers hunching toward nighttime destinations seem to relax, and occasionally they even join in the tune. Virtually everybody seems to sense that a mugger wouldn't be warbling bright, sunny selections from Vivaldi's *Four Seasons*. It is my equivalent of the cowbell that hikers wear when they know they are in bear country. 12

Understanding the Reading

1. Explain how Staples has the power to alter public space. How does this ability affect his life?

2. How did Staples manage to escape the violence of the "angry industrial town" (para. 6) where he grew up?

3. Staples considers himself a "survivor" (para. 7). To what does he attribute his survival?

4. What does Staples do to make his presence less threatening to others?

Visualizing the Reading

Review the reading and supply the missing information in the following graphic organizer.

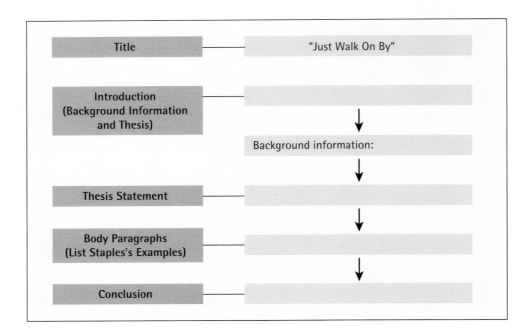

Examining the Characteristics of Illustration Essays

1. Identify Staples's thesis. Is the generalization adequately supported by relevant examples? Why or why not?
2. What audience do you think Staples is writing for? What do you think his purpose is? How does his use of examples relate to this purpose?
3. Cite an example used by Staples that is particularly striking or dramatic. Explain why it makes such a strong impression on you.
4. Cite several examples of the author's descriptive language. How does his use of vivid language contribute to the effectiveness of his examples?
5. Many of the paragraphs in this essay begin with clearly stated topic sentences. Identify at least one topic sentence, and list the kinds of support offered for it. Do you feel that the support is sufficient? Why or why not?

Building Your Word Power

For a definition of **connotative meaning,** *see the chart of commonly used language features on* *p. 21.*

1. A *warren* is a group of connected burrows where rabbits live. Discuss the connotative meanings of the phrase "warrenlike streets" (para. 5).

2. Explain the meaning of the phrase "unwieldy inheritance" used in the context of paragraph 2.

3. Explain the meaning of each of the following words as it is used in the reading: *uninflammatory* (para. 1), *billowing* (1), *quarry* (2), *wayfarers* (2), *lethality* (6), and *constitutionals* (12). Refer to your dictionary as needed.

Building Your Critical Thinking Skills: Cause and Effect Relationships

A **cause and effect relationship** describes how two or more actions relate to each other. In an illustration essay, an author may use examples to explain the reasons or motives and/or the results or consequences of an event or series of events. Use your knowledge of cause and effect relationships to answer the following questions.

1. Paragraph 1 describes the first time that Staples realized how his presence had the power to alter the "public space" around him. According to the example, what caused his "first victim" to start running?

2. Paragraphs 6 and 7 describe the author's upbringing on the streets of Chester, Pennsylvania. How did the experience growing up in this tough neighborhood affect him?

Reacting to the Topic: Discussion and Journal Writing

1. Discuss some other ways that people can "alter public space."

2. Discuss ways in which you could have altered or did alter your behavior or appearance to make others around you more comfortable.

3. In class or in your journal, discuss a time when you had an irrational fear or uncomfortable feeling in response to someone else. Was the feeling justified?

Applying Your Skills: Writing Assignments

1. **Paragraph Assignment.** Write a paragraph that illustrates how people sometimes judge a person by his or her appearance. Begin with a topic sentence that makes a generalization about whether it is ever appropriate to judge people by the way they look, and include an example or two to support your main point.

2. Rewrite Staples's essay from his "first victim's" point of view, using illustrative techniques. Include a thesis that makes a generalization, and provide supporting examples. You might include the woman's background, past experiences, and mental condition. Consider discussing of how the experience of encountering Staples on the street affected her and whether she changed her behavior as a result of the experience.

3. Staples speaks of an "alienation that comes of being ever the suspect" (para. 5). Have you experienced separation or alienation, or observed someone else being excluded or alienated from a group? Write an essay about a situation involving alienation, using carefully selected examples to support a thesis about your experience.

4. **Combining Patterns.** Staples describes himself as a "survivor" (para. 7) of the streets he grew up on. In a sense, everyone is a survivor of certain decisions or

circumstances that, if played out differently, might have resulted in misfortunes or, at least, a different direction in life. Write an essay using illustration that explains how and why you or someone you know is a survivor.

5. Internet Research. Visit the American Civil Liberties Union Web site at www.aclu.org. Click on "Racial Equality," and then under "Racial Equality Issues" go to the Racial Profiling page. Here you will find a complaint form for people who think they were stopped by the police simply because of their race or ethnic background. After reading the complaint form carefully, write an essay describing the form and its use. Your audience is other college students. Be sure to include examples from the form to illustrate its purpose and contents. Alternatively, conduct your own online search on racial profiling, and then write an essay using examples that illustrates your main point about the prevalence of and legal issues associated with the problem.

Abs and the Adolescent

Rita Kempley

Rita Kempley is a journalist and staff writer for the *Washington Post*, where she often covers film and television. She won a fellowship from the Alicia Patterson Foundation in 2002 to study and write about sexual mythology in American cinema. In this piece, from the *Post*'s October 22, 2003, edition, Kempley discusses the effects of media images on teen and preteen boys.

As you read "Abs and the Adolescent," notice the way Kempley uses direct quotations — both from boys affected by the phenomenon she is describing and from experts in various fields. Think about how the material she chooses to include supports her main point.

Focus on Understanding   Read to discover what kind of adolescent behavior this essay addresses.

Focus on the Topic   In class or in your journal, explore the importance of physical fitness and exercise in your own life.

Naked from the waist up, waxed, ripped, tanned and impossibly handsome, the Abercrombie & Fitch Adonis° stares into the mall from the store's entryway. His body language is as seductive as it is challenging. "You are never going to look like me," he seems to say.

Apparently it is a challenge the company's target group — teens, preteens and even younger children — can't resist. Of course, most won't look like the poster boy. Fashion models, pop icons and rock stars wouldn't look so godlike either without personal trainers, hours in the gym and expensive grooming.

A decade or so ago, 10-year-old boys couldn't have cared less about their physiques. "Today more boys than we know or can imagine are as affected by the physical attributes they see in media and advertising" as girls are, says psychologist William Pollack, author of "Real Boys" and "Real Boys' Voices."

"Women used to complain, 'I'm just a piece of meat.' Now boys are actually making themselves into beefcake," says Pollack of the beauty culture. "Once it was said males could walk around with potbellies and still get dates — some still do — but the new mantra is: 'If you don't look good, the girls won't look at you and the popular boys will see you as inferior.'"

Joe Friedman, a seventh-grader at Charles E. Smith Jewish Day School, has a girlfriend he met in April, but the 12-year-old is taking no chances. Joe, who was shopping at Montgomery Mall recently with his mother, Seena Sussman, lifts weights at home and at a fitness center with his father. "I'm pushing for big muscles," says the 12-year-old, who pumps three or four times every two weeks.

Adonis: extremely good-looking youth in Greek mythology; today the term refers to any very handsome male

217

Joe started lifting really light weights when he was 7 and says he can now 6
bench-press 80 pounds. His girlfriend likes his muscles, particularly his biceps,
he says, laughing. "I mean they're not like watermelons or anything, but you
can see the definition."

His ultimate goal: "To get even bigger." 7

Little Joe is not alone. 8

Sociologist Michael Kimmel, author of "Manhood in America," observes, 9
"There have been dramatic changes in what constitutes muscularity and masculinity. Look at Lou Ferrigno as the Hulk as compared to the animated character in the new movie. He would be incapable of walking if his thighs were that
big.

"Arnold Schwarzenegger may have been the top bodybuilder of his era, but 10
he is really small now, disappointingly so," says Kimmel after seeing him back-
stage at a charity fundraiser. "And GI Joe Extreme's biceps are now as big as the
waist of the action figure that came out in the 1960s." If Joe were blown up to
human size, the boy toy would have a biceps circumference of 26 inches, more
than 11 inches greater than those of a committed weightlifter, according to
Roberto Olivardia, co-author of "The Adonis Complex: The Secret Crisis of
Male Body Obsession." Olivardia has tracked men's growing interest in self-
image from the late '70s to now, what he calls "a tide of regard for their bodies."

Personal trainers such as Bryan Wynn, 24, who works at Washington's 11
Northwest Sport & Health, report that they are working with younger clients
these days. "Strength training gives them confidence and prepares them to participate in their sport" of choice, he says. Even if their sport is only chasing
girls.

"Most males want to look good for the females," says Wynn, teasing a timid 12
13-year-old client. The boy ducks his head and gets into a staring contest with
his sneakers. Though it's hard to believe, this painfully shy youngster has become more outgoing since he began strength training this past summer.

Fabian Navidi-Kasmai, a sixth-grader at Janney Elementary School in 13
Northwest Washington, is enrolled in another fitness center program designed
for 9- to-11-year-olds. He rides a stationary bike, lifts light weights and does a
short series of lunges and squats. "It energizes me. It is one of the things that
make a bad day good. . . . I haven't been doing it long enough to see muscles,
but I can feel them," he says.

Not to worry for now. Middle school girls aren't as demanding as all that. 14

Melanie Hanson, a 13-year-old student at Alice Deal Junior High, doesn't 15
want a brawny beau. "He just has to be a little taller than me," she says.

"And not really fat," adds her friend Deborah Samuels, also 13. 16

Arthur Olinga, a sophomore at Woodrow Wilson, has been weight training 17
since he was 12 and it shows. On most nights, he spends three hours working
out in the fitness center atop his apartment building. "Some guys work out just
to see themselves in the mirror, but I do it to keep myself healthy and strong for
sports," says Olinga, who adds in passing that a man's abdominal six-pack°
"shows a little sexy side of himself."

abdominal six-pack:
refers to the *rectus
abdominis* muscle in
the abdomen; when
highly developed, it
shows prominently as
six distinct bulges

Brady Blade, athletic director of Bethesda–Chevy Chase High School, says, 18
"The weight room used to be the jocks' refuge, but no more. When you wanted
to show off your manhood, sports were the way to go 10 years ago. You no
longer need to be an athlete to define your masculinity.

"We've always known girls were concerned about how they looked. The 19
guys got a pass, but now they are judged by their looks, too. In spring, I can't
believe how many boys show up [for school] with their shirts off," Blade says.
"The boys noticed the girls were dressing like pop tarts and asked themselves:
'Why shouldn't I show what I've got?' "

Alas, six-packs are no longer enough, according to Wynn and other train- 20
ers. Now there are eight- and 12-packs, he says, indicating the space south of
his rib cage.

"Marketers have persuaded males, as they had females, they are flawed," 21
says Olivardia. "Our society is so focused on imagery, it was almost inherent
that this was going to happen to males.

"Today males buy more products because they are also dissatisfied with 22
their bodies. Their concern with appearance puts them on the same negative treadmill that females are on. They become narcissistic° in hopes that
someone will love them. You see teenagers spending hours a day in the gym,
taking steroids and still complaining about how small they are," Olivardia
says.

> narcissistic: showing excessive self-admiration or self-centeredness

Antonia Baum, a Chevy Chase psychiatrist who treats athletes of all ages 23
and aspirations, also cites the corrupting influence of body-baring fashions for
tweens, music videos and computer games. "More and more middle school children are working out for aesthetic reasons. A growing percentage abuse ana-
bolic steroids with great peril," Baum says. The aesthetic negatives, which
range from acne to shrunken testicles, seem likely to negate the alleged allure
of all that bulk, she adds.

For most kids, the goal isn't to be a Mr. Universe.° 24

> Mr. Universe: the winner of an international body-building competition

Take Alex Cox, a lanky 15-year-old from the District who goes to the gym 25
with his mother. While she sweats upstairs on the aerobic equipment, he works
out in the weight room. He grimaces and grunts as he pushes through one more
set of quad exercises.

Alex doesn't work out to excess and disdains supplements. All he wants to 26
do, he says, is get stronger so he can improve his soccer game.

What about impressing the girls? 27

"That is an extra benefit," he says, blushing into the roots of his red hair. 28

Understanding the Reading

1. According to the essay, what population group is becoming very body conscious?
2. Why is this happening? Who has created this new ideal?

3. In what ways do the youngsters in this essay try to achieve physical perfection?

4. Kempley uses a quote that describes the subjects of her essay as being on the "same negative treadmill that females are on" (para. 22). Explain what this means. What negative aspects of this obsession does the author mention?

Visualizing the Reading

Study the photo. What concerns might this boy have about his appearance? How does the photograph reinforce Kempley's thesis? Could the photo be used to further illustrate any of the other main points of her essay? Identify the paragraph(s).

Examining the Characteristics of Illustration Essays

1. What generalization about the topic does Kempley support in her essay?

2. What kinds of examples does she use to illustrate her thesis? Are the examples relevant, representative, and accurate? Why or why not?

3. Are any types of information *not* included that would have made the author's illustration more compelling? Please explain.

4. Kempley concludes with an example and a quotation. Is this approach effective? Why or why not?

Building Your Word Power

For a definition of **metaphor***, see the chart of commonly used language features on p. 21.*

1. What is meant by the metaphor "I'm just a piece of meat" as used in paragraph 4?

2. Explain the phrase "jocks' refuge" as used in paragraph 18.

3. Explain the meaning of each of the following words as it is used in the reading: *mantra* (para. 4), *biceps* (6), *brawny* (15), *aspirations* (23), and *disdains* (26). Refer to your dictionary as needed.

Building Your Critical Thinking Skills: Evaluating Sources

Authors include different types of source material to support their thesis. This material can come from online and library research, interviews, or the authors' personal observations. Critical readers must evaluate these sources carefully because some types of information may be more reliable and appropriate than others. For example, in an article about global warming, data from studies by scientists would be more reliable than an author's own observation that summers seem warmer now than when she was a child. When **evaluating sources,** be sure to consider the date of publication, the qualifications of the author, the level of detail, and the appropriateness of the source for the audience. Using your skills in evaluating sources, answer the following questions.

1. Create a list of the types of sources that Kempley uses to support her thesis. How reliable do you think they are?

2. Using your list of sources, identify where you might go to verify the information from each one. Are any sources used here that could provide even more information about the topic? If so, which ones would they be?

Reacting to the Reading: Discussion and Journal Writing

1. Discuss our society's obsession with beauty and personal appearance. How does this obsession manifest itself in our culture, and what effect does it have on you and your peers?

2. Many of the people interviewed for this article were in high school or middle school. Discuss the pressure for physical perfection that these youths face today. Is this a new trend, or have young people always been concerned about appearance?

3. In class or in your journal, discuss a time when you paid extra close attention to your appearance. Was the added effort worth it?

Applying Your Skills: Writing Assignments

1. **Paragraph Assignment.** Kempley mentions that some celebrities are "godlike" in appearance. Choose a famous person you admire for reasons other than style, image, and looks. In an illustration paragraph, write about one of this person's admirable characteristics, using one or two examples to support your topic sentence.

2. Make a generalization about college men and their attention to personal appearance. Then write an illustration essay to support your thesis, using relevant and clear examples from your own experience and observations. Conclude with your overall thoughts on our society's emphasis on fitness and good looks.

3. Advertisers target specific groups for their products. Identify one of these groups, and write an essay explaining how advertisers target it. (Hint: The group may be based on age, sex, educational or income level, profession, or ethnic or religious affiliation.) Support your generalizations with relevant examples from advertising.

4. **Combining Patterns.** Spend some time "people watching," paying attention to how different types of people look, act, and interact with one another. Identify two different "types" of people, such as jocks and young mothers. In an essay, make a generalization about these two types and their behavior as it corresponds to their

personal appearance. Use the information from your observations to illustrate and support your generalization and to compare and contrast the differences between the two groups.

5. Internet Research. Most people associate eating disorders with teenage girls and young women, but conditions like anorexia nervosa and bulimia are increasingly affecting young men as well. Research the information at the Anorexia Nervosa and Related Eating Disorders, Inc. (ANRED) Web site at www.anred.com/males.html or at another site pertaining to eating disorders in men. Using illustration, write an essay that includes a thesis based on a generalization from your research. Support your thesis with examples and evidence from the Web site.

If You Are What You Eat, Then What Am I?

Geeta Kothari

Geeta Kothari (b. 1928) is a lecturer in the English department at the University of Pittsburgh, where she also directs the writing center. She is the editor of the collection *Did My Mama Like to Dance? and Other Stories about Mothers and Daughters* (1994). Many of her short works of fiction and nonfiction that appeared in many anthologies, newspapers, and journals have focused on poverty, third world development, politics in India, and world peace.

As an American of South Asian descent, Kothari explains that she feels neither completely American nor completely Indian. In this essay, which appeared in *Best American Essays 2000*, consider how she uses the examples of foods that she eats — and does not eat — to illustrate her claims about her American and Indian cultural background.

Focus on Understanding As you read, discover how the author associates food with her identity.

Focus on the Topic In class or in your journal, describe your experiences tasting ethnic foods or other unusual foods.

The first time my mother and I open a can of tuna, I am nine years old. We 1 stand in the doorway of the kitchen, in semidarkness, the can tilted toward daylight. I want to eat what the kids at school eat: bologna, hot dogs, salami — foods my parents find repugnant because they contain pork and meat byproducts, crushed bone and hair glued together by chemicals and fat. Although she has never been able to tolerate the smell of fish, my mother buys the tuna, hoping to satisfy my longing for American food.

Indians, of course, do not eat such things. 2

The tuna smells fishy, which surprises me because I can't remember any- 3 one's tuna sandwich actually smelling like fish. And the tuna in those sandwiches doesn't look like this, pink and shiny, like an internal organ. In fact, this looks similar to the bad foods my mother doesn't want me to eat. She is silent, holding her face away from the can while peering into it like a half-blind bird.

"What's wrong with it?" I ask. 4

She has no idea. My mother does not know that the tuna everyone else's 5 mothers made for them was tuna *salad*.

"Do you think it's botulism?"° 6

I have never seen botulism, but I have read about it, just as I have read 7 about but never eaten steak and kidney pie.

botulism: poisoning caused by a toxin in improperly canned or cooked foods

223

There is so much my parents don't know. They are not like other parents, 8
and they disappoint me and my sister. They are supposed to help us negotiate
the world outside, teach us the signs, the clues to proper behavior: what to eat
and how to eat it.

We have expectations, and my parents fail to meet them, especially my 9
mother, who works full-time. I don't understand what it means, to have a
mother who works outside and inside the home; I notice only the ways in which
she disappoints me. She doesn't show up for school plays. She doesn't make
chocolate-frosted cupcakes for my class. At night, if I want her attention, I have
to sit in the kitchen and talk to her while she cooks the evening meal, attentive
to every third or fourth word I say.

We throw the tuna away. This time my mother is disappointed. I go to 10
school with tuna eaters. I see their sandwiches, yet cannot explain the discrepancy between them and the stinking, oily fish in my mother's hand. We do not
understand so many things, my mother and I.

amoebic dysentery: intestinal infection caused by a parasite in contaminated food or water

When we visit our relatives in India, food prepared outside the house is care- 11
fully monitored. In the hot, sticky monsoon months in New Delhi and Bombay,
we cannot eat ice cream, salad, cold food, or any fruit that can't be peeled.
Definitely no meat. People die from amoebic dysentery,° unexplained fevers,
strange boils on their bodies. We drink boiled water only, no ice. No sweets except for jalebi, thin fried twists of dough in dripping hot sugar syrup. If we're
caught outside with nothing to drink, Fanta, Limca, Thums Up (after Coca-Cola
is thrown out by Mrs. Gandhi)[1] will do. Hot tea sweetened with sugar, served
with thick creamy buffalo milk, is preferable. It should be boiled, to kill the
germs on the cup.

My mother talks about "back home" as a safe place, a silk cocoon frozen in 12
time where we are sheltered by family and friends. Back home, my sister and I do
not argue about food with my parents. Home is where they know all the rules. We
trust them to guide us safely through the maze of city streets for which they have
no map, and we trust them to feed and take care of us, the way parents should.

Finally, though, one of us will get sick, hungry for the food we see our 13
cousins and friends eating, too thirsty to ask for a straw, too polite to insist on
properly boiled water.

At my uncle's diner in New Delhi, someone hands me a plate of aloo tikki, 14
fried potato patties filled with mashed channa dal and served with a sweet and
a sour chutney. The channa, mixed with hot chilies and spices, burns my tongue
and throat. I reach for my Fanta, discard the paper straw, and gulp the sweet
orange soda down, huge drafts that sting rather than soothe.

When I throw up later that day (or is it the next morning, when a stom- 15
achache wakes me from deep sleep?), I cry over the frustration of being singled
out, not from the pain my mother assumes I'm feeling as she holds my hair back

[1]In 1977, Coca-Cola withdrew from India after the government, led by Indira Ghandi,
asked the company to divulge its formula and use an Indian manufacturer.

from my face. The taste of orange lingers in my mouth, and I remember my lips touching the cold glass of the Fanta bottle.

At that moment, more than anything, I want to be like my cousins. 16

In New York, at the first Indian restaurant in our neighborhood, my father orders with confidence, and my sister and I play with the silverware until the steaming plates of lamb biryani arrive. 17

What is Indian food? my friends ask, their noses crinkling up. 18

Later, this restaurant is run out of business by the new Indo-Pak-Bangladeshi combinations up and down the street, which serve similar food. They use plastic cutlery and Styrofoam cups. They do not distinguish between North and South Indian cooking, or between Indian, Pakistani, and Bangladeshi cooking, and their customers do not care. The food is fast, cheap, and tasty. Dosa, a rice flour crepe stuffed with masala° potato, appears on the same trays as chicken makhani. 19

Now my friends want to know, Do you eat curry at home? 20

One time my mother makes lamb vindaloo for guests. Like dosa, this is a South Indian dish, one that my Punjabi° mother has to learn from a cookbook. For us, she cooks everyday food — yellow dal, rice, chapati, bhaji. Lentils, rice, bread, and vegetables. She has never referred to anything on our table as "curry" or "curried," but I know she has made chicken curry for guests. Vindaloo, she explains, is a curry too. I understand then that curry is a dish created for guests, outsiders, a food for people who eat in restaurants. 21

I look around my boyfriend's freezer one day and find meat: pork chops, ground beef, chicken pieces, Italian sausage. Ham in the refrigerator, next to the homemade bolognese sauce. Tupperware filled with chili made from ground beef and pork. 22

He smells different from me. Foreign. Strange. 23

I marry him anyway. 24

He has inherited blue eyes that turn gray in bad weather, light brown hair, a sharp pointy nose, and excellent teeth. He learns to make chili with ground turkey and tofu, tomato sauce with red wine and portobello mushrooms, roast chicken with rosemary and slivers of garlic under the skin. 25

He eats steak when we are in separate cities, roast beef at his mother's house, hamburgers at work. Sometimes I smell them on his skin. I hope he doesn't notice me turning my face, a cheek instead of my lips, my nose wrinkled at the unfamiliar, musky smell. 26

I have inherited brown eyes, black hair, a long nose with a crooked bridge, and soft teeth with thin enamel. I am in my twenties, moving to a city far from my parents, before it occurs to me that jeera, the spice my sister avoids, must have an English name. I have to learn that haldi = turmeric, methi = fenugreek. What to make with fenugreek, I do not know. My grandmother used to make methi roti for our breakfast, cornbread with fresh fenugreek leaves served with a lump 27

masala: a mixture of spices used in Indian cooking

Punjabi: from the Punjab, a region in northwestern India

of homemade butter. No one makes it now that she's gone, though once in a while my mother will get a craving for it and produce a facsimile ("The cornmeal here is wrong") that only highlights what she's really missing: the smells and tastes of her mother's house.

I will never make my grandmother's methi roti or even my mother's unsatisfactory imitation of it. I attempt chapati; it takes six hours, three phone calls home, and leaves me with an aching back. I have to write translations down: jeera = cumin. My memory is unreliable. But I have always known garam = hot. 28

If I really want to make myself sick, I worry that my husband will one day leave me for a meat-eater, for someone familiar who doesn't sniff him suspiciously for signs of alimentary infidelity. 29

Indians eat lentils. I understand this as absolute, a decree from an unidentifiable authority that watches and judges me. 30

So what does it mean that I cannot replicate my mother's dal? She and my father show me repeatedly, in their kitchen, in my kitchen. They coach me over the phone, buy me the best cookbooks, and finally write down their secrets. Things I'm supposed to know but don't. Recipes that should be, by now, engraved on my heart. 31

Living far from the comfort of people who require no explanation for what I do and who I am, I crave the foods we have shared. My mother convinces me that moong is the easiest dal to prepare, and yet it fails me every time: bland, watery, a sickly greenish yellow mush. These imperfect imitations remind me only of what I'm missing. 32

But I have never been fond of moong dal. At my mother's table it is the last thing I reach for. Now I worry that this antipathy toward dal signals something deeper, that somehow I am not my parents' daughter, not Indian, and because I cannot bear the touch and smell of raw meat, though I can eat it cooked (charred, dry, and overdone), I am not American either. 33

I worry about a lifetime purgatory in Indian restaurants where I will complain that all the food looks and tastes the same because they've used the same masala. 34

Understanding the Reading

1. Describe the foods that the author's family eats and those they avoid. Why are the foods that her family finds "repugnant" important to Kothari?

2. How does Kothari describe the conditions in India? What health precautions does her family take when visiting relatives there?

3. In the beginning of the essay, Kothari relates an event from childhood when her mother tried to serve tuna to satisfy Kothari's "longing for American food" (para. 1). What does this story tell you about the author's relationship with her mother?

4. What food conflicts does the author have with her husband? How has he accommodated her food preferences?

Visualizing the Reading

Analyze the effectiveness of Kothari's examples by completing the following chart. For each example, indicate what information it adds to your knowledge of Kothari or her family's culinary habits. The first one has been done for you.

Example	What It Illustrates
Tuna story (para. 1–10)	Illustrates the difference between American and Indian foods, and reveals the mother's inability to grasp American ways.
Visiting relatives in India (para. 11–13)	
Visit to uncle's diner in New Delhi (para.14–16)	
Visit to Indian restaurant in New York (para. 17–19)	
Boyfriend's food preferences (para. 22–26)	
Author's attempts to cook Indian food (para. 27–32)	

Examining the Characteristics of Illustration Essays

1. Identify the main point of Kothari's essay. What generalization about the topic does she make?

2. What types of examples does Kothari use to support her main point? Were there any striking or dramatic examples that made an especially strong or lasting impression on you? Identify them, and explain how they maintained your interest.

3. What techniques does the author use to help convey difficult or abstract concepts, such as food items that might be unfamiliar to the reader. Was her explanation sufficient, or is there anything you wished that she had explained in more detail? If so, what?

4. What method of development does Kothari use to organize her examples?

5. Identify some other methods of development that Kothari uses.

Building Your Word Power

1. Evaluate the use of the similes "like an internal organ" and "like a half-blind bird" in paragraph 3. How do these figures of speech reveal Kothari's attitude toward American food and toward her mother in an unfamiliar culture?

*For a definition of **simile** and **connotative meaning**, see the chart of commonly used language features on p. 21.*

2. The word *home* has different connotative meanings for the author and for her mother. Compare and contrast the different connotative meanings.

3. Explain the meaning of each of the following words as it is used in the reading: *repugnant* (para. 1), *discrepancy* (10), *monsoon* (11), *facsimile* (27), and *alimentary* (29). Refer to your dictionary as needed.

Building Your Critical Thinking Skills: Drawing Conclusions

When you draw a conclusion, you make a reasoned decision or opinion based on relevant evidence or facts. For example, you might conclude that your relationship with a friend has changed because she has not called you, ignores you on campus, and seems to be developing new friendships. Using your knowledge about drawing conclusions, answer the following questions.

1. What conclusions does Kothari draw about her mother? What do these add to the essay?

2. Kothari draws a conclusion about her own ability to cook Indian food. What is it? How does this lead to her conclusion about her identity at the end of the essay?

Reacting to the Reading: Discussion and Journal Writing

1. What foods, if any, do you find repugnant or disgusting? Why?

2. In what sense, beyond ethnic identity, do you become what you eat? (Hint: What does a snack food junkie become? What does a heavy alcohol user become?) In class or in your journal, explore this idea. Consider both the physical and the abstract implications of becoming what you eat.

Applying Your Skills: Writing Assignments

1. **Paragraph Assignment.** Kothari marries her boyfriend even though he eats a lot of meat. Using one or two examples to support a generalization made in your topic sentence, write a paragraph explaining why you are accepting of someone even though they do or believe something that displeases you.

2. Brainstorm a list of foods that you loved as a child and a list of foods you hated. In an essay, analyze whether your tastes have changed since then and whether a certain person or experience influenced that change. Include a generalization about your food preferences today, along with relevant and interesting examples to support it.

3. Kothari defines her identity partially through food. What other factors contribute to one's identity? Using illustration, write an essay describing the factors that you consider important in defining yourself. Include relevant examples from your own experience that explain each factor and support a generalization about your identity.

4. **Combining Patterns.** As a child, the author struggled with trying to fit in with her American friends. Write an essay that describes a situation in which you had to try to fit in. Include examples that illustrate how you felt alienated and relevant sensory details that describe the steps you took to become accepted.

5. Internet Research. The Centers for Disease Control and Prevention maintains a Web site that includes health information for travelers. Visit the page for Travelers to the Indian Subcontinent at www.cdc.gov/travel/indianrg.htm, or conduct your own online research about the health risks associated with travel to this region. Using illustration, write an essay about some of the topics covered on the site. Include examples about the health risks that support a broader generalization about traveling to India. Conclude with some suggestions for readers regarding travel to India.

Goin' Gangsta, Choosin' Cholita: Claiming Identity

Nell Bernstein

Nell Bernstein (b. 1965) is a freelance journalist who writes frequently about current issues affecting young people and their families. Her pieces have appeared in *Glamour, Health, Mother Jones,* and *Salon.com,* and her work has won several awards, including a media fellowship from the Center on Crime, Communities, and Culture of the Open Society Institute. She is the author of *A Rage to Do Better: Listening to Young People from the Foster Care System* (2000).

The following is an excerpt from an essay that originally appeared in 1994 in *West* magazine, the Sunday supplement to the *San Jose Mercury News.* In the piece, Bernstein discusses several California teenagers as examples of the way Americans' understanding of ethnic and racial identity continues to evolve.

Focus on Understanding   Identify the *cholita* mentioned in the title.

Focus on the Topic   In class or in your journal, write about why some young people might want to alter their cultural identities.

Her lipstick is dark, the lip liner even darker, nearly black. In baggy pants, 1
a blue plaid Pendleton, her bangs pulled back tight off her forehead, 15-year-old
April is a perfect cholita, a Mexican gangsta girl.

But April Miller is Anglo. "And I don't like it!" she complains. "I'd rather be 2
Mexican."

April's father wanders into the family room of their home in San Leandro, 3
California, a suburb near Oakland. "Hey, cholita," he teases. "Go get a suntan.
We'll put you in a barrio° and see how much you like it."

A large, sandy-haired man with "April" tattooed on one arm and "Kelly" — 4
the name of his older daughter — on the other, Miller spent 21 years working in
a San Leandro glass factory that shut down and moved to Mexico a couple of
years ago. He recently got a job in another factory, but he expects NAFTA° to
swallow that one, too.

"Sooner or later we'll all get nailed," he says. "Just another stab in the back 5
of the American middle class."

Later, April gets her revenge: "Hey, Mr. White Man's Last Stand," she teases. 6
"Wait till you see how well I manage my welfare check. You'll be asking me for
money."

A once almost exclusively white, now increasingly Latin and black working- 7
class suburb, San Leandro borders on predominantly black East Oakland. For

barrio: the Spanish-speaking section of a city

NAFTA (North American Free Trade Agreement): an agreement among North American countries to ease restrictions on the exchange of goods and services

230

decades, the boundary was strictly policed and practically impermeable. In 1970 April Miller's hometown was 97 percent white. By 1990 San Leandro was 65 percent white, 6 percent black, 15 percent Hispanic, and 13 percent Asian or Pacific Islander. With minorities moving into suburbs in growing numbers and cities becoming ever more diverse, the boundary between city and suburb is dissolving, and suburban teenagers are changing with the times.

In April's bedroom, her past and present selves lie in layers, the pink walls   8 of girlhood almost obscured, Guns N' Roses and Pearl Jam posters overlaid by rappers Paris and Ice Cube. "I don't have a big enough attitude to be a black girl," says April, explaining her current choice of ethnic identification.

What matters is that she thinks the choice is hers. For April and her friends,   9 identity is not a matter of where you come from, what you were born into, what color your skin is. It's what you wear, the music you listen to, the words you use — everything to which you pledge allegiance, no matter how fleetingly.

The hybridization of American teens has become talk show fodder, with   10 "wiggers" — white kids who dress and talk "black" — appearing on TV in full gangsta regalia. In Indiana a group of white high school girls raised a national stir when they triggered an imitation race war at their virtually all-white high school last fall simply by dressing "black."

In many parts of the country, it's television and radio, not neighbors, that   11 introduce teens to the allure of ethnic difference. But in California, which demographers predict will be the first state with no racial majority by the year 2000,[1] the influences are more immediate. The California public schools are the most diverse in the country: 42 percent white, 36 percent Hispanic, 9 percent black, 8 percent Asian.

Sometimes young people fight over their differences. Students at virtually   12 any school in the Bay Area can recount the details of at least one "race riot" in which a conflict between individuals escalated into a battle between their clans. More often, though, teens would rather join than fight. Adolescence, after all, is the period when you're most inclined to mimic the power closest at hand, from stealing your older sister's clothes to copying the ruling clique at school.

White skaters and Mexican would-be gangbangers listen to gangsta rap and   13 call each other "nigga" as a term of endearment; white girls sometimes affect Spanish accents; blond cheerleaders claim Cherokee ancestors.

"Claiming" is the central concept here. A Vietnamese teen in Hayward, an-   14 other Oakland suburb, "claims" Oakland — and by implication blackness — because he lived there as a child. A law-abiding white kid "claims" a Mexican gang he says he hangs with. A brown-skinned girl with a Mexican father and a white mother "claims" her Mexican side, while her fair-skinned sister "claims" white. The word comes up over and over, as if identity were territory, the self a kind of turf.

[1]According to the California State Census, the state's racial makeup in 2000 was 46.7% White, 32.4% Hispanic, 11.1% Asian or Pacific Islander, 6.4% Black, 0.5% American Indian, and 2.9% two or more races.

At a restaurant in a minimall in Hayward, Nicole Huffstutler, 13, sits with her 15
friends and describes herself as "Indian, German, French, Welsh, and,
um . . . American": "If somebody says anything like 'Yeah, you're just a pecker-
wood, I'll walk up and I'll say 'white pride!' 'Cause I'm proud of my race, and I
wouldn't wanna be any other race."

"Claiming" white has become a matter of principle for Heather, too, who 16
says she's "sick of the majority looking at us like we're less than them."
(Hayward schools were 51 percent white in 1990, down from 77 percent in
1980, and whites are now the minority in many schools.)

Asked if she knows that nonwhites have not traditionally been referred to 17
as "the majority" in America, Heather gets exasperated: "I hear that all the time,
every day. They say, 'Well, you guys controlled us for many years, and it's time
for us to control you.' Every day."

When Jennifer Vargas — a small, brown-skinned girl in purple jeans who 18
quietly eats her salad while Heather talks — softly announces that she's "mostly
Mexican," she gets in trouble with her friends.

"No, you're not!" scolds Heather. 19

"I'm mostly Indian and Mexican," Jennifer continues flatly. "I'm very 20
little . . . I'm mostly . . ."

"Your mom's white!" Nicole reminds her sharply. "She has blond hair." 21

"That's what I mean," Nicole adds. "People think that white is a bad thing. 22
They think that white is a bad race. So she's trying to claim more Mexican than
white."

"I have very little white in me," Jennifer repeats. "I have mostly my dad's 23
side, 'cause I look like him and stuff. And most of my friends think that me and
my brother and sister aren't related, 'cause they look more like my mom."

"But you guys are all the same race, you just look different," Nicole insists. 24
She stops eating and frowns. "OK, you're half and half each what your parents
have. So you're equal as your brother and sister, you just look different. And you
should be proud of what you are — every little piece and bit of what you are.
Even if you were Afghan or whatever, you should be proud of it."

Will Mosley, Heather's 17-year-old brother, says he and his friends listen to rap 25
groups like Compton's Most Wanted, NWA, and Above the Law because they
"sing about life" — that is, what happens in Oakland, Los Angeles, anyplace but
where Will is sitting today, an empty Round Table Pizza in a minimall.

"No matter what race you are," Will says, "if you live like we do, then that's 26
the kind of music you like."

And how do they live? 27

"We don't live bad or anything," Will admits. "We live in a pretty good 28
neighborhood, there's no violence or crime. I was just . . . we're just city people,
I guess."

Will and his friend Adolfo Garcia, 16, say they've outgrown trying to be 29
something they're not, "When I was 11 or 12," Will says, "I thought I was becoming a big gangsta and stuff. Because I liked that music, and thought it was

the coolest, I wanted to become that. I wore big clothes, like you wear in jail. But then I kind of woke up. I looked at myself and thought, 'Who am I trying to be?'"

They may have outgrown blatant mimicry, but Will and his friends remain 30 convinced that they can live in a suburban tract house with a well-kept lawn on a tree-lined street in "not a bad neighborhood" and still call themselves "city" people on the basis of musical tastes. "City" for these young people means crime, graffiti, drugs. The kids are law-abiding, but these activities connote what Will admiringly calls "action." With pride in his voice, Will predicts that "in a couple of years, Hayward will be like Oakland. It's starting to get more known, because of crime and things. I think it'll be bigger, more things happening, more crime, more graffiti, stealing cars."

"That's good," chimes in 15-year-old Matt Jenkins, whose new beeper — an 31 item that once connoted gangsta chic but now means little more than an active social life — goes off periodically. "More fun."

The three young men imagine with disdain life in a gangsta-free zone. "Too 32 bland, too boring," Adolfo says. "You have to have something going on. You can't just have everyday life."

"Mowing your lawn," Matt sneers. 33

"Like Beaver Cleaver's house," Adolfo adds. "It's too clean out here." 34

Not only white kids believe that identity is a matter of choice or taste, or 35 that the power of "claiming" can transcend ethnicity. The Manor Park Locos — a group of mostly Mexican-Americans who hang out in San Leandro's Manor Park — say they descend from the Manor Lords, tough white guys who ruled the neighborhood a generation ago.

They "are like our . . . uncles and dads, the older generation," says Jesse 36 Martinez, 14. "We're what they were when they were around, except we're Mexican."

"There's three generations," says Oso, Jesse's younger brother. "There's 37 Manor Lords, Manor Park Locos, and Manor Park Pee Wees." The Pee Wees consist mainly of the Locos' younger brothers, eager kids who circle the older boys on bikes and brag about "punking people."

Unlike Will Mosley, the Locos find little glamour in city life. They survey the 38 changing suburban landscape and see not "action" or "more fun" but frightening decline. Though most of them are not yet 18, the Locos are already nostalgic, longing for a Beaver Cleaver past that white kids who mimic them would scoff at.

Walking through nearly empty Manor Park, with its eucalyptus stands, its 39 softball diamond and tennis courts, Jesse's friend Alex, the only Asian in the group, waves his arms in a gesture of futility. "A few years ago, every bench was filled," he says. "Now no one comes here. I guess it's because of everything that's going on. My parents paid a lot for this house, and I want it to be nice for them. I just hope this doesn't turn into Oakland."

Glancing across the park at April Miller's street, Jesse says he knows what 40 the white cholitas are about. "It's not a racial thing," he explains. "It's just all the most popular people out here are Mexican. We're just the gangstas that every-one knows. I guess those girls wanna be known."

Not every young Californian embraces the new racial hybridism. Andrea 41 Jones, 20, an African American who grew up in the Bay Area suburbs of Union City and Hayward, is unimpressed by what she sees mainly as shallow mimicry. "It's full of posers out here," she says. "When *Boyz N the Hood* came out on video, it was sold out for weeks. The boys all wanna be black, the girls all wanna be Mexican. It's the glamour."

Driving down the quiet, shaded streets of her old neighborhood in Union 42 City, Andrea spots two white preteen boys in Raiders jackets and hugely baggy pants strutting erratically down the empty sidewalk. "Look at them," she says. "Dislocated."

She knows why. "In a lot of these schools out here, it's hard being white," 43 she says. "I don't think these kids were prepared for the backlash that is going on, all the pride now in people of color's ethnicity, and our boldness with it. They have nothing like that, no identity, nothing they can say they're proud of.

"So they latch onto their great-grandmother who's a Cherokee, or they take 44 on the most stereotypical aspects of being black or Mexican. It's beautiful to ap-preciate different aspects of other people's culture — that's like the dream of what the 21st century should be. But to garnish yourself with pop culture stereotypes just to blend — that's really sad."

Roland Krevocheza, 18, graduated last year from Arroyo High School in 45 San Leandro. He is Mexican on his mother's side, Eastern European on his fa-ther's. In the new hierarchies, it may be mixed kids like Roland who have the hardest time finding their place, even as their numbers grow. (One in five mar-riages in California is between people of different races.) They can always be called "wannabes," no matter what they claim.

"I'll state all my nationalities," Roland says. But he takes a greater interest 46 in his father's side, his Ukrainian, Romanian, and Czech ancestors. "It's more unique," he explains. "Mexican culture is all around me. We eat Mexican food all the time, I hear stories from my grandmother. I see the low-riders and stuff. I'm already part of it. I'm not trying to be; I am."

His darker-skinned brother "says he's not proud to be white," Roland adds. 47 "He calls me 'Mr. Nazi.'" In the room the two share, the American flags and the reproduction of the Bill of Rights are Roland's; the Public Enemy poster be-longs to his brother.

Roland has good reason to mistrust gangsta attitudes. In his junior year in 48 high school, he was one of several Arroyo students who were beaten up outside the school at lunchtime by a group of Samoans who came in cars from Oakland. Roland wound up with a split lip, a concussion, and a broken tail-bone. Later he was told that the assault was "gang-related" — that the Samoans were beating up anyone wearing red.

"Rappers, I don't like them," Roland says. "I think they're a bad influence 49 on kids. It makes kids think they're all tough and bad."

Those who, like Roland, dismiss the gangsta and cholo styles as affectations 50 can point to the fact that several companies market overpriced knock-offs of "ghetto wear" targeted at teens.

But there's also something going on out here that transcends adolescent 51 faddishness and pop culture exoticism. When white kids call their parents "racist" for nagging them about their baggy pants; when they learn Spanish to talk to their boyfriends; when Mexican-American boys feel themselves descended in spirit from white "uncles"; when children of mixed marriages insist that they are whatever race they say they are, all of them are more than just confused.

They're inching toward what Andrea Jones calls "the dream of what the 52 21st century should be." In the ever more diverse communities of Northern California, they're also facing the complicated reality of what their 21st century will be.

Meanwhile, in the living room of the Miller family's San Leandro home, the 53 argument continues unabated. "You don't know what you are," April's father has told her more than once. But she just keeps on telling him he doesn't know what time it is.

Understanding the Reading

1. What does racial or ethnic identity mean to April Miller? According to Bernstein, by what standards does Miller define herself?

2. What reasons does Bernstein propose to explain why the teenagers developed such attitudes about their racial and ethnic identity?

3. According to the author and the people interviewed for this essay, what role does music play in the formation of cultural identity?

4. How do the young people profiled in the essay change their attitudes toward identity as they grow older, as evidenced by Will Mosley and Adolfo Garcia?

Visualizing the Reading

Bernstein uses interviews with different teenagers as the examples that illustrate her thesis. In the following chart or one like it, record what each example illustrates. Also consider how the information contributes to Bernstein's thesis about identity. The first one has been done for you.

Teenager(s)	What the Example Illustrates
April Miller (para. 1–9, 53)	She is Anglo but "claims" a Mexican identity; feels that the choice of ethnic identification is hers.
Nicole Huffstutler, Heather, and Jennifer Vargas (para. 15–24)	
Will Mosley, Adolfo Garcia, and Matt Jenkins (para. 25–34)	
Jesse Martinez, Oso Martinez, and Alex (para. 36–40)	
Andrea Jones (para. 41–44, 52)	
Roland Krevocheza (para. 45–49)	

Examining the Characteristics of Illustration Essays

1. What generalization does Bernstein make and support in this essay?

2. *Identity* is an abstract term. How does Bernstein make this term real and understandable?

3. Evaluate Bernstein's use of illustration: Are the examples relevant and representative? striking and dramatic? Does she include enough examples? Explain your responses.

4. Bernstein uses the example involving April Miller in the introduction and conclusion. Is this strategy effective? Why or why not?

Building Your Word Power

1. Explain the figurative expression "Sooner or later we'll all get nailed" used by April's father (para. 5). What might this reveal about his own self-image?

2. Explain the meaning of the word *claiming* as it is used in the essay. In what ways does the author aid the reader in understanding this unfamiliar term?

3. Explain the meaning of each of the following words as it is used in the reading: *impermeable* (para. 7), *hybridization* (10), *fodder* (10), *connoted* (31), and *affectations* (50). Refer to your dictionary as needed.

Building Your Critical Thinking Skills: Alternative Viewpoints

Writers sometimes include **alternative viewpoints** in order to present another side of their topic or to provide depth and contrast to the ideas they are discussing. If you encounter a different viewpoint, be sure to evaluate its purpose and relevance and determine what it contributes to the essay's thesis. Does the author include the viewpoint simply to acknowledge alternative points of view, or does the writer explain why he or she disagrees with it? Consider also whether additional viewpoints are omitted that you would have liked the writer to address. Using your knowledge of alternative viewpoints, answer the following questions.

1. Which teenagers offer an alternative viewpoint to April's views? What is this viewpoint, and how is it presented?

2. What alternative viewpoints does Andrea Jones offer? How do her comments about identity contribute to Bernstein's thesis?

3. Are any alternative viewpoints *not* included in Bernstein's article that you would have liked to read about? Why might the author have omitted such views in favor of the ones she included?

Reacting to the Reading: Discussion and Journal Writing

1. Have you observed teenagers claiming an ethnic or a racial stereotype? How do they look and behave? What seems to motivate them?

2. In class or in your journal, discuss why you agree or disagree with this statement: "Teenagers who establish their identities by copying members of racial or ethnic groups only strengthen unwanted stereotypes."

Applying Your Skills: Writing Assignments

1. **Paragraph Assignment.** In the reading, identity is related to clothing. Using examples, write a paragraph about what you wear and how it reflects your personality and self-image.

2. Using illustration, write an essay about the power of peer pressure. Begin by explaining the concept of peer pressure, using examples from your own experience to support your thesis.

3. Music is important to many of the teens in Bernstein's essay. Write an illustration essay explaining the role of music in your own life. Include relevant examples, such as specific pieces of music or artists, to support your thesis.

4. **Combining Patterns.** Brainstorm a list of reasons why some young people choose to alter their cultural identities. Using cause and effect, write an essay that explains

this phenomenon. Support your reasons with examples that illustrate your main point.

5. Internet Research. Visit the Glass Houses Web site, funded in part by the University of California, Riverside, at www.cmp.ucr.edu/students/GlassHouses/. Explore the site, visiting all the rooms, to experience the life of a Mexican American woman who grew up in California during the 1960s. Then write an essay on the subject of cultural assimilation and identity. Or, if you prefer, research online the terms *cultural identity* and *cultural assimilation* using a search engine like Google. Presenting examples from your research, support a thesis that makes a generalization about cultural assimilation in this country.

What I Wouldn't Do

Dorianne Laux

Dorianne Laux, who was born in Maine in 1952, had managed a gas station, cooked in a sanatorium, cleaned houses, and made donuts before she began taking classes at a local junior college and attending poetry workshops. A single mother, Laux went to California with her daughter in 1983 to attempt a writing career. Because of her work she won scholarships, and she earned a B.A. in 1988. She published her first book of poems, *Awake*, in 1990. At present she teaches in the creative writing program at the University of Oregon.

In the following poem from Laux's 1994 collection *What We Carry*, the speaker provides snapshots of work at a series of unglamorous jobs. As you read, notice what the speaker has found satisfying about the work, and consider what was different about the job that the speaker "quit / after the first shift." To grasp the full meaning of Laux's poem, it is important to pay attention to the sound and meaning of individual words and to consider how all the words work together to convey the theme.

Focus on Understanding   Read to discover what job the author wouldn't do and her reasons for not doing it.

Focus on the Topic   In class or in your journal, write about the kinds of jobs that interest you and the kinds that you would hate to do. Why are some more appealing than others?

The only job I didn't like, quit
after the first shift, was selling
subscriptions to *TV Guide* over the phone.
Before that it was fast food, all
the onion rings I could eat, handing   5
sacks of deep fried burritos through
the sliding window, the hungry hands
grabbing back. And at the laundromat,
plucking bright coins from a palm
or pressing them into one, kids   10
screaming from the bathroom and twenty
dryers on high. Cleaning houses was fine,
polishing the knick-knacks of the rich.
I liked holding the hand-blown glass bell
from Czechoslovakia up to the light,   15
the jewelled clapper swinging lazily

from side to side, its foreign,
A-minor ping. I drifted, an itinerant,°

itinerant: someone who travels from place to place to find work

from job to job, the sanatorium
where I pureed peas and carrots   20
and stringy beets, scooped them,
like pudding, onto flesh-colored
plastic plates, or the gas station
where I dipped the ten-foot measuring stick
into the hole in the blacktop,   25
pulled it up hand over hand
into the twilight, dripping
its liquid gold, pink-tinged.
I liked the donut shop best, 3 AM,
alone in the kitchen, surrounded   30
by sugar and squat mounds of dough,
the flashing neon sign strung from wire
behind the window, gilding my white uniform
yellow, then blue, then drop-dead red.
It wasn't that I hated calling them, hour   35
after hour, stuck in a booth with a list
of strangers' names, dialing their numbers
with the eraser end of a pencil and them
saying hello. It was that moment
of expectation, before I answered back,   40
the sound of their held breath,
their disappointment when they realized
I wasn't who they thought I was,
the familiar voice, or the voice they loved
and had been waiting all day to hear.   45

Understanding the Reading

1. What sorts of jobs has the author held? What do they have in common?
2. What was Laux's favorite job, and why did she like it? What didn't she like about the job referred to in the title?
3. How satisfied do you think the author was with her various jobs? What information from the poem leads you to this conclusion?

Visualizing the Reading

When analyzing a poem, it is often helpful to begin by identifying the features universal to all poems. To grasp the structure and content of Laux's poem, identify the following features by completing this chart or one like it.

Feature	"What I Wouldn't Do"
Narrator (Who is speaking in the poem?)	
Audience (To whom is the poem addressed?)	
Subject (What is the subject of the poem?)	
Tone (What feelings does the narrator express about her subject?)	
Thesis (What main point does the narrator express about her subject?)	
Examples (What examples support the thesis?)	

Examining the Characteristics of Illustration Essays

1. Poems express a main point, or theme, about the human experience. Because themes are often unstated and several interpretations may be possible, it is up to the reader to uncover the poet's theme and purpose in writing. What is Laux trying to express in this poem? What unstated generalization about work do her examples support? In your answer, consider alternative interpretations.

2. Evaluate the writer's use of illustration. What types of examples support her generalization about work? Are the examples relevant and representative? Does Laux include enough examples? Explain your responses.

3. What senses does the author appeal to in her choice of details to describe each job? Give examples.

4. Consider the use of transition. How does Laux make the transition from example to example in her poem? Does this approach differ from the use of transition in an essay? Please explain.

Building Your Word Power

1. Discuss the connotative meanings of the word *job*.
2. What does the figure of speech "hungry hands" mean in line 7?
3. Explain the meaning of each of the following words as it is used in the reading: *knick-knacks* (line 13), *sanatorium* (19), and *gilding* (33). Refer to your dictionary as needed.

*For a definition of **connotative meaning**, see the chart of commonly used language features on p. 21.*

Building Your Critical Thinking Skills: Analyzing Poetry

Poetry differs from essays and other forms of literature because it is written in lines and stanzas, instead of paragraphs, and complete sentences are not always used. Because of this unique format, ideas in poems are often expressed in compact and concise language, and reading and **analyzing a poem** may take as much time and effort as analyzing an essay or short story. To fully grasp the meaning of a poem, it is important to pay attention to the sound and meaning of individual words and to consider how all the words work together to convey meaning. After reading "What I Wouldn't Do" several times, use your knowledge of analyzing poetry to answer the following questions.

1. How does Laux use language to create an effect? Consider the connotations, or shades of meaning, of words in her poem. How does her use of descriptive language contribute to her message?

2. What emotional atmosphere or mood does Laux create? For example, do you sense foreboding, excitement, or contentment?

Reacting to the Reading: Discussion and Journal Writing

1. Discuss the importance of liking your job. Should your job add meaning to your life, or is it just a way to earn money?

2. In class or in your journal, discuss your idea of a fantasy job — one that you think would be pure fun. Would you consider trying this job in the future?

Applying Your Skills: Writing Assignments

1. Paragraph Assignment. Write a paragraph using examples from your own experience about a job that has influenced your career goals in either a negative or a positive way.

2. Rewrite the poem as an illustration essay. Be sure to begin with a generalization about work that you can support with the examples that Laux includes. Feel free to make up details or add events. As you write, pay attention to your paragraphs, making sure to include clear topic sentences and to use transitions between different types of examples. Conclude with an effective statement reflecting on the jobs or looking toward the future.

3. Brainstorm a list of service-oriented occupations that you encounter in your daily life. Based on this list, make a generalization about these jobs — for example, "Working with the public can be very rewarding." Write an illustration essay supporting your generalization with relevant and interesting examples from your observations about these occupations. Include vivid sensory details. Conclude with your thoughts about the importance and future of service occupations.

4. Combining Patterns. When workers begin a new job, they must go through a process when they learn what will be expected of them and how to do the job effectively. In an essay, describe a process you had to undergo in learning a new job. Include specific examples from your experience that illustrate and support a thesis about the necessary steps to be successful in this job.

5. Internet Research. Consider the career path that you have chosen or one that you are considering. Visit a job posting site such as www.monster.com, and research the job possibilities of your chosen career area. Then write an illustration essay about the various career tracks available for your chosen area. Explain each track by using examples from the Web site.

Process Analysis: Explaining How Something Works or Is Done

WRITING QUICK START

This photograph shows a college student dealing with a familiar problem — money management. Earning, saving, budgeting, and spending money is an important skill and a process that can lead to financial success or ruin. Write a paragraph describing your own process in deciding how to spend and/or save the money you earn. Include the steps you follow when budgeting your money each month.

243

What Is Process Analysis?

The paragraph you have just written followed a pattern of development called **process analysis.** A process analysis explains in step-by-step fashion how something works, is done, or is made. Process analyses provide people with practical information (such as directions for assembling something) or inform people about things that affect them (such as an explanation of how a medication works). Regardless of the purpose, the information in a process analysis must be accurate, clear, and easy to follow.

Process analysis is a common type of writing in college and on the job, as these examples show.

- In a *chemistry* lab report, you summarize the procedure you followed in preparing a solution or conducting an experiment.
- As an *engineer* at a water treatment plant, you must write for your supervisor an explanation of how the city's drinking water is tested and treated for contamination.

There are two basic types of process analysis essays.

- A *how-to essay* explains how something works or is done for readers *who want or need to perform the process*.
- A *how-it-works essay* explains how something works or is done for readers *who want to understand the process but not actually perform it*.

At times, you may read or write essays that contain elements of both types of process analysis. In writing about how a car alarm system works, for example, you might find it necessary to include explicit instructions on how to activate and deactivate the system. The following essay exemplifies the second type of process analysis: a how-it-works essay.

How the Oscars Work

Melissa Russell-Ausley and Tom Harris

Melissa Russell-Ausley has worked as a staff writer for the informational Web site HowStuffWorks.com. Tom Harris, who has also served as a staff writer for the site, is currently its editorial director. HowStuffWorks, which was started in North Carolina by a computer science teacher, strives "to clearly explain technology, biology, and the world in a way that is interesting and accessible to anyone who wants to learn."

In the article that follows, Russell-Ausley and Harris explain the history and workings of the Academy Awards. As you read, notice how the authors break down the category of "the Oscars" into smaller, more manageable parts, such as the organization of the Academy of Motion Picture Arts and Sciences and the history of the awards ceremony. Pay attention to the authors' detailed, step-by-step analysis of the complex process of picking Oscar winners.

Every spring, the movie industry gears up for its biggest celebration: the Academy Awards, more commonly known as the Oscars. There is extensive press coverage of the event, even down to the arrival of the stars; flash bulbs and microphones abound as the nominees and other famous, well-dressed guests make their way down the "red carpet," flanked by cheering onlookers. The Oscars aren't just for Hollywood's most powerful and glamorous, though — millions of people tune in every year to root for their favorite movies and actors, check out the incredible clothing on display, or maybe just catch any embarrassing podium mishaps as they happen.

Let's take a look at the organization behind the Oscars, see what the "Academy" actually is, and learn how Oscars are awarded.

The Academy

So many Oscar winners gush, "I would like to thank the Academy" that it's become a cliché. But what is the Academy, anyway? And why should it be thanked?

The Academy, in this case, is the Academy of Motion Picture Arts and Sciences, a professional honorary society formed in 1927. In spirit, the Academy is something like the Phi Beta Kappa Society or National Honor Society. It's an organization dedicated to promoting excellence in a particular field (filmmaking). Just like similar organizations, it has many members connected to that field (more than 5,000 filmmaking professionals).

You must be invited by the Academy to become a member. Different branches of the Academy (focusing on different aspects of the filmmaking world) have their own standards of eligibility for potential members.

The Academy is involved in a lot of different projects — from film preservation to developing new film technology — but it's best known for its yearly awards ceremony. The purpose of the Academy Awards is to promote excellence in filmmaking by honoring extraordinary achievements from the previous year.

Members of the Academy, including actors, producers, directors and a variety of other film craftsmen, choose who will receive the awards that

Margin annotations:

1   Introduction

2   Thesis: suggests order in which ideas will be presented

3   Headings announce topics and make information easy to locate

4   Background information about the Academy

5

6

7

year by casting ballots. So when a winner thanks the Academy, he or she is really thanking all their professional peers who collectively decided to bestow the honor. They're also thanking the organization as a whole, which decided to hand out awards in the first place.

All about Oscar

We generally think of the entire Academy Awards ceremony as "the Oscars," but Oscar is really just a nickname for the actual award statuettes and their image.

When MGM art director Cedric Gibbons and sculptor George Stanley created the statuette in 1928, the Academy referred to it as the Academy Award of Merit. It didn't take on the name Oscar until the 1930s.

There are several stories about the nickname's origin, and nobody is completely sure of the truth. The Academy supports this version: In the early '30s, an Academy librarian named Margaret Herrick remarked that the statue looked like her Uncle Oscar. The name stuck, and the Academy staff began referring to the statue as "Oscar." In 1934, Sidney Skolsky mentioned the nickname in a column on Katharine Hepburn's first Best Actress win. The name caught on, and the Academy officially adopted it in 1939.

Picking the Winners

The first stage in selecting Oscar winners is narrowing all the possible honorees in a given year down to five nominees for each award category. To be eligible for nominations in any of the feature film categories, a movie must meet these basic requirements:

- It must be more than 40 minutes long.
- Its public premiere must have been in a movie theater, during the appropriate calendar year (during 2003, for the 76th Academy Awards).
- It must have premiered in 35mm or 70mm film format or in 24-frame, progressive scan digital format.
- It must have played in an L.A. County theater, for paid admission, for seven consecutive days, beginning in the appropriate calendar year.

If a producer or distributor would like their eligible film to be considered for an Oscar nomination, they must submit an Official Screen Credits form. This form lists the production credits for all related Oscar categories. The Academy collects these forms and lists the submitted films in the "Reminder List of Eligible Releases." In January, the Academy mails a nomination ballot and a copy of the "Reminder List" to each Academy member.

For most of the award categories, only Academy members in that particular field are allowed to vote for nominees (that is, only directors sub-

Margin notes:

Background information about "Oscar"

Topic sentence: suggests chronological organization and gives overview of steps 1–3

Step 1: films are submitted

Step 2: Academy members select nominees

Paragraph numbers: 8, 9, 10, 11, 12, 13

mit nominations for best director and only editors submit nominations for best editor). Foreign film and documentary nominees are chosen by special screening groups made up of Academy members from all branches, and everybody gets to select best picture nominees. Foreign film nominees are selected from a list of films submitted by foreign nations. Every foreign country can only submit one film per year.

An Academy member can select five nominees per category, ranked in order of preference. For most categories, voters write in only the film title. For acting categories, the voters pick specific actors. It's up to the individual Academy voters to decide whether an actor should be nominated for leading role or supporting role. An actor can't be nominated for both categories for a single performance, however. The Academy assigns the nominee to whichever category the nominee qualifies for first. Producers often take out ads in Variety and other major movie industry magazines to suggest nominees for particular categories.

Academy members typically have a couple of weeks to submit their choices for nominees. Once the ballots are in, the accounting firm PricewaterhouseCoopers tabulates the nominee ballot votes in secrecy. Soon after, the Academy announces the nominees in an early morning press conference at the Samuel Goldwyn Theatre in Beverly Hills. A week or so later, the Academy mails final ballots to all Academy members. Members have two weeks to return the ballots, and then the "polls" are closed. PricewaterhouseCoopers tabulates the votes in absolute secrecy and seals the results.

While all this is going on, production companies are sinking considerable funds into campaigning for their contenders. The Academy condones any efforts to get Academy members to see the films, but restricts production companies from mailing out inappropriate incentives. Production companies are allowed to send Academy members video copies of contender films, and to organize special screenings of their films.

After all the ballots are in, and the votes are counted, it all comes down to the big night itself. The Oscars is a night of honoring big-budget entertainment, and, appropriately, it is [a] big-budget entertainment event, itself. Every year, hundreds of workers, including carpenters, artists, musicians, cameramen and chefs, work days on end preparing for the big show. The result, in a good year, is a vibrant, glamorous celebration of all things Hollywood.

14

15   Step 3: nominee ballots are tabulated and nominees announced

Step 4: ballots are distributed to Academy members

16   Step 5: production companies campaign for their films

17   Conclusion and Step 6: ballots are counted and winners announced at Academy Awards Ceremony

Characteristics of Process Analysis Essays

A process analysis essay should include everything a reader needs to know to understand or perform the process. In addition to presenting an explicit thesis, the essay should provide a clear, step-by-step description of the process, define key terms, provide necessary background information, describe equipment needed to perform the process, supply adequate detail, and — for a how-to essay — anticipate and offer help with potential problems.

Process Analysis Usually Includes an Explicit Thesis Statement

A process analysis usually contains a clear thesis that identifies the process to be discussed and suggests the writer's attitude or approach toward it. The thesis statement also tells why the process is important or useful. In "How the Oscars Work," for instance, Russell-Ausley and Harris state: "Let's take a look at the organization behind the Oscars, see what the 'Academy' actually is, and learn how Oscars are awarded" (para. 2). Thesis statements for how-to process analyses suggest the usefulness or importance of the process. In a how-it-works essay, the writer either reveals why the information is worth knowing or makes an assertion about the nature of the process itself.

HOW-TO THESIS: **Switching to a low-carbohydrate diet can improve weight control dramatically.**

HOW-IT-WORKS THESIS: **Although understanding the grieving process will not lessen the grief that you experience after the death of a loved one, knowing that your experiences are normal does provide some comfort.**

Process Analysis Is Organized Chronologically

The steps or events in a process analysis are usually organized in chronological order — that is, the order in which the steps are completed. Think of process analysis as being organized by the clock or calendar. A process essay presents what happens first in time, then next in time, and so forth. In "How the Oscars Work," the authors explain chronologically the process through which Oscars are awarded.

On occasion, the steps of a process may not have to occur in any particular order. For example, in an essay on how to resolve a dispute between two co-workers, the order may depend on the nature of the dispute. In this type of situation, a logical progression of recommended actions should be used, such as starting with informal or simple steps and progressing to more formal or complex ones.

Process Analysis Defines Technical Terms

In most cases, you can assume the audience is not familiar with technical terms associated with the process you are describing. In a process essay, be sure to define specialized terms. In describing how cardiopulmonary resuscitation (CPR) works, for instance, you would need to explain the meanings of such terms as *airway*, *sternum*, and *cardiac compression*. In "How the Oscars Work," which was first published online, a link is provided to a Web site that explains the technical phrase "24-frame, progessive scan digital format."

Process Analysis Provides Background Information

In some process analysis essays, readers may need background information to fully understand the process. For example, in an explanation of how CPR works, general readers might need to know how the heart functions before they can understand how pressing down on a person's breastbone propels blood into the arteries. In "How the Oscars Work," Russell-Ausley and Harris give background information that reveals how the Academy Awards statuettes came to be called Oscars.

Process Analysis Describes Necessary Equipment

When special equipment is needed to perform or understand the process, you should describe the equipment. If necessary, you should also mention where to obtain it. For example, in explaining how to use a computer system to readers unfamiliar with computers, you would need to describe the keyboard, monitor, printer, and so forth. "How the Oscars Work" includes information on forms and ballots, the equipment involved in Oscar nominations and awards.

Process Analysis Provides an Appropriate Level of Detail

In deciding the level of detail to include in a process analysis essay, be careful not to overwhelm readers with too many technical details. For example, an essay about how to perform CPR written by and for physicians would be highly technical; but it would be less technical if written for paramedics, and even less so if written for a friend who is considering whether to enroll in a CPR course. At the same time, include enough detail to show readers how to perform the steps of the CPR process.

Keep in mind that essays explaining technical or scientific processes benefit from sensory details and figures of speech to make the writing lively and interesting. Rather than giving dry technical details, try using descriptive language.

Process Analysis Anticipates Trouble Spots and Offers Solutions

Especially in a how-to essay, you need to anticipate potential trouble spots or areas of confusion and offer advice on how to avoid or resolve them. A how-to essay should also alert readers to difficult, complicated, or critical steps. In the following paragraph, notice that the authors caution readers about problems to avoid in both phases of a sit-up exercise. They also urge readers to use a padded floor mat.

> The bent-knee sit-up test is probably the best-known field test available to evaluate abdominal muscle endurance. Begin by lying on your back with your arms crossed on your chest. Your knees should be bent at approximately

90-degree angles, with your feet flat on the floor. The complete sit-up is performed by bringing your chest up to touch your knees and returning to the original lying position. . . . Sit-up tests are generally considered to be relatively safe fitness tests, but two precautions should be mentioned. First, avoid undue stress on your neck during the "up" phase of the exercise. That is, let your abdominal muscles do the work; do not whip your neck during the sit-up movement. Second, avoid hitting the back of your head on the floor during the "down" phase of the sit-up. Performance of the test on a padded mat is helpful.

Scott K. Powers and Stephen L. Dodd, *Total Fitness and Wellness*, 3rd ed.

Visualizing a Process Analysis Essay

The graphic organizer in Figure 8.1 shows the basic organization of a process analysis essay. When your primary purpose is to explain a process, you should follow this format. The introduction should include background information and present the thesis statement. The body paragraphs should explain the steps of the process in chronological order. The conclusion should draw the essay to a satisfying close and refer back to the thesis. The graphic organizer in Figure 8.2 is based on the reading "How the Oscars Work."

When you incorporate process analysis into an essay by using one or more patterns of development, briefly introduce the process and then move directly to the steps involved. If the process is complex, consider adding a summary of it before the transition back to the main topic.

Writing a Process Analysis Essay

The following steps will help you write a process analysis essay. It may be a how-to or a how-it-works essay. Although you will focus on process analysis, you may need to integrate one or more other patterns of development.

Planning a Process Analysis Essay

The first step is to select a process to write about. Be sure to keep the following tips in mind.

- For a how-to essay, choose a process that you can visualize or actually perform as you write. Keep the object or equipment nearby for easy reference. In explaining how to scuba dive, for example, it may be helpful to have your scuba equipment in front of you.

- For a how-it-works essay, choose a topic about which you have background knowledge or for which you can find adequate information. Unless you are experienced in woodworking, for example, do not try to explain how certain stains produce different effects on different kinds of wood.

FIGURE 8.1 Graphic Organizer for a Process Analysis Essay

	Title
Introduction	Background information
	Thesis statement*
	↓
	Step 1
	↓
	Step 2
Body: Steps in the Process	↓
	Step 3
	↓
	Step 4
	↓
Conclusion	Draws essay to a close and refers back to the thesis

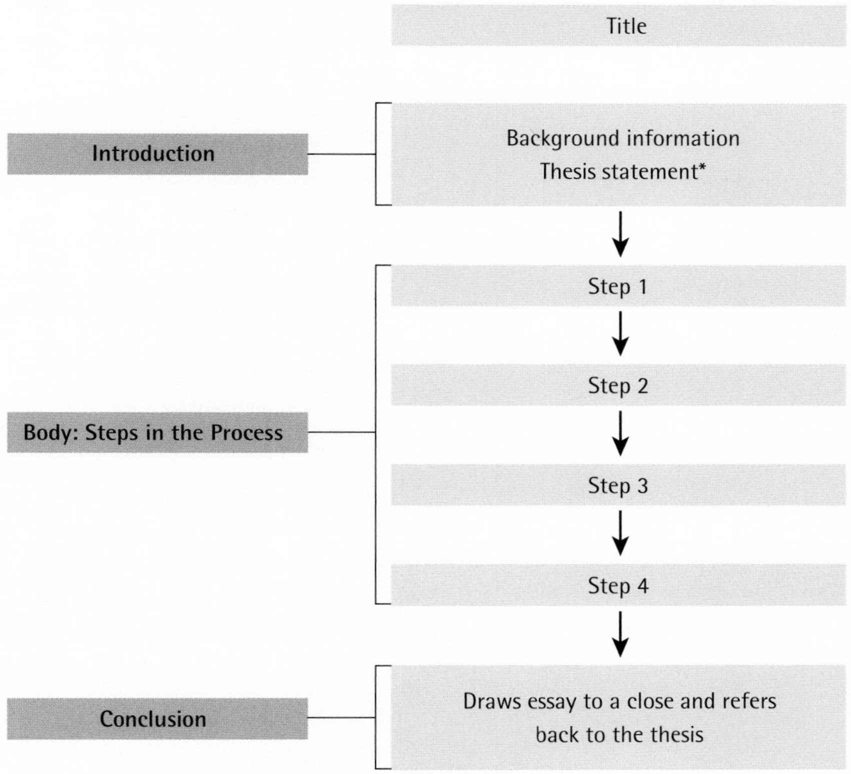

*In some essays, the thesis statement may be implied or may appear in a different position.

- Choose a topic that is useful and of interest to readers. For example, unless you can find a way to make an essay about how to do the laundry interesting, do not write about it.

Developing Your Thesis

Once you have chosen a process to write about, the next step is to develop a working thesis. As noted earlier, the thesis of a process analysis essay tells readers *why* the process is important, beneficial, or relevant to them (see p. 248). In a how-to essay on jogging, for instance, your thesis might be: "Jogging, an excellent aerobic activity, provides both exercise and a chance for solitary reflection." Note how the benefits of the activity are clearly stated in the thesis statement.

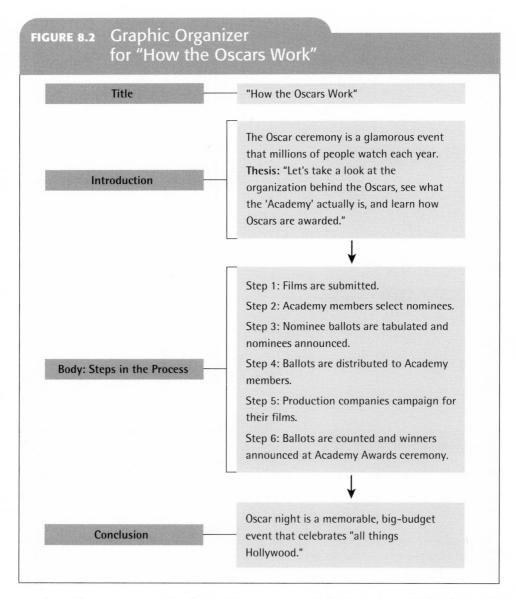

FIGURE 8.2 Graphic Organizer for "How the Oscars Work"

Title → "How the Oscars Work"

Introduction → The Oscar ceremony is a glamorous event that millions of people watch each year. **Thesis:** "Let's take a look at the organization behind the Oscars, see what the 'Academy' actually is, and learn how Oscars are awarded."

Body: Steps in the Process →
Step 1: Films are submitted.
Step 2: Academy members select nominees.
Step 3: Nominee ballots are tabulated and nominees announced.
Step 4: Ballots are distributed to Academy members.
Step 5: Production companies campaign for their films.
Step 6: Ballots are counted and winners announced at Academy Awards ceremony.

Conclusion → Oscar night is a memorable, big-budget event that celebrates "all things Hollywood."

Considering your particular audience is especially important in developing a thesis for a process analysis because what may be of interest or importance to one audience may be of little interest to another audience.

Listing the Steps and Gathering Details

Once you are satisfied with your working thesis statement, it is time to list the steps in the process and to gather appropriate and interesting details. You will probably need to do additional prewriting at this point to generate ideas and details that help explain the process. Use the following suggestions.

Generating Details for a Process Analysis Essay

1. **List the steps in the process as they occur to you, keeping these questions in mind.**
   - What separate actions are involved?
   - What steps are obvious to me but may not be obvious to someone unfamiliar with the process?
   - What steps, if omitted, will lead to problems or failure?
2. **Describe the process aloud into a tape recorder, and then take notes as you play back the recording.**
3. **Discuss the process with classmates to see what kinds of details they need to know about it.**
4. **Generate details for the steps you are describing by doing additional prewriting or conducting research online or in the library.** Make sure to have sufficient detail about unfamiliar terms, equipment, and trouble spots. If you are explaining how to hike in the Grand Canyon, for example, you might include details about carrying sufficient water and dressing in layers.

Drafting a Process Analysis Essay

Once you have an effective thesis and enough details to explain the steps in the process, it is time to organize your ideas and draft the essay. For a process that involves fewer than ten steps, you can usually arrange the steps in chronological order, devoting one paragraph to each step (as Russell-Ausley and Harris do in "How the Oscars Work"). However, for a process with ten or more steps, divide them into three or four major groups.

After organizing the steps, you are ready to write a first draft. Use the following guidelines.

Guidelines for Writing a Process Analysis Essay

1. **Write an effective introduction.** The introduction usually presents the thesis statement and includes necessary background information. It should also capture the readers' interest and focus their attention on the process. For some essays, you may want to explain that the process you are describing is related to

(Continued)

(Continued)

other processes and ideas (for example, the process of jogging is related to running). For a lengthy or complex process, consider including an overview of the steps or providing a brief introductory list.

2. **Include reasons for the steps.** Unless the reason is obvious, explain why each step or group of steps is important and necessary. In explaining why a step is important, consider including a brief anecdote as an example.

3. **Consider using graphics.** For a process involving many complex steps, consider using a drawing or diagram to help readers visualize each step. Remember, however, that a graphic is no substitute for a clearly written explanation.

4. **Consider adding headings.** Headings divide the body of a lengthy or complicated process analysis into manageable segments. They also call attention to the main topics and signal readers that a change in topic is about to occur.

5. **Use transitions.** To avoid writing a process analysis that sounds monotonous, use transitions such as *before*, *next*, and *finally*.

6. **Use an appropriate tone.** Your tone should be appropriate for your audience and purpose. In some situations a direct, matter-of-fact tone is appropriate; at other times an emotional or humorous tone may be suitable.

7. **Write a satisfying conclusion.** An essay that ends with the final step in the process may sound incomplete. In the conclusion, you might emphasize the value or importance of the process, describe situations in which it is useful, or offer a final amusing or emphatic comment or anecdote.

Analyzing and Revising

If possible, wait at least a day before rereading and revising your draft. As you reread, concentrate on the organization and your ideas, not on grammar or mechanics. Use the flowchart in Figure 8.3 to guide your analysis.

Editing and Proofreading

The last step is to check your revised essay for errors in grammar, spelling, punctuation, and mechanics. In addition, be sure to look for errors that you tend to make in any writing assignments, whether for this class or any other situation. As you edit and proofread your process analysis essay, watch out for two grammatical errors in particular: comma splices and shifts in verb mood.

FIGURE 8.3 Revising a Process Analysis

QUESTIONS

REVISION STRATEGIES

1. Highlight your thesis statement. Does it make clear the importance of the process you are discussing? **NO**

- Ask yourself: "Why do I need to know this process? Why is it important?" Incorporate the answers into your thesis statement.

 YES

2. *Number* the steps or groups of the process in the margin of your paper. Are they organized in chronological order (or in some other logical progression)? **NO**

- Visualize or actually complete the process to discover the best order in which to do it.
- Study your graphic organizer or outline to determine if any steps are out of order.

 YES

3. Place an ✗ beside any technical terms you have used. Is each unfamiliar term defined? **NO**

- Define technical terms for your readers.
- Ask a classmate to read your definitions of unfamiliar terms, and revise if clarification is necessary.

 YES

4. Place brackets [ ] around any background information you provided in the introduction. Is it sufficient? Is an overview of the process needed? **NO**

- Give an example of a situation in which the process might be used.
- Explain that related processes and ideas depend on the process you are describing.

 YES

5. Draw a box around any equipment you have mentioned. Have you mentioned all necessary equipment? **NO**

- Describe equipment you have overlooked.
- Describe equipment that might be unfamiliar to readers.

 YES

(Continued)

FIGURE 8.3   *(Continued)*

QUESTIONS	REVISION STRATEGIES

6. Place checkmarks ✔ beside key details of the process. Have you included an appropriate level of detail?

→ **NO**

- Add or delete background information in the introduction.
- Add or delete definitions of technical terms.
- Add or delete details.

↓ **YES**

7. For a how-to essay, <u>double underline</u> sections where you have anticipated problems and difficulties for readers. Are these sections clear and reassuring?

→ **NO**

- Add more detail about critical steps.
- Warn readers about confusing or difficult steps.
- Offer advice on what to do if things go wrong.

↓ **YES**

8. <u>Underline</u> each topic sentence. Does each paragraph contain a topic sentence? Does the topic sentence focus each paragraph on a separate step or group of steps?

→ **NO**

- Revise so each paragraph has a topic sentence and supporting details.
- Ask a classmate whether more or less detail is needed for each step.

↓ **YES**

9. Draw a (circle) around and reread your introduction and conclusion. Is each one effective?

→ **NO**

- Revise your introduction and conclusion so that they meet the guidelines in Chapter 3.

↓ **YES**

10. Print out another draft to edit and proofread before turning your essay in.

Editing Tips and Troublespots: Process Analysis

1. **Avoid comma splices.** A comma splice occurs when two independent clauses are joined only by a comma. To correct comma splices, do the following.

   Add a coordinating conjunction (*and, but, for, nor, or, so,* or *yet*).

   ▸ The first step in flower arranging is to choose an attractive container,
   but
   ∧ the container should not be the focal point of the arrangement.

   Change the comma to a semicolon.

   ▸ Following signs is one way to navigate a busy airport, looking for a map
   ∧
   is another.

For more on these and other common errors, see Chapter 4, p. 81.

   Divide the sentence into two sentences.

   ▸ To place a long-distance call using a credit card, first dial 0 and the ten-
   . Next
   digit number, ~~next~~ punch in your credit card number and PIN.
   ∧

   Subordinate one clause to the other.

   After you have placed
   ▸ ~~Place~~ the pill on the cat's tongue, hold its mouth closed, rubbing its chin
   ∧ until it swallows the pill.

2. **Avoid shifts in verb mood.** A verb can have three *moods* — the indicative mood (used for ordinary statements and to ask questions), the imperative mood (used for orders, advice, and directions), and the subjunctive mood (used for statements contrary to fact or for wishes and recommendations). When writing a process analysis, be sure to use a consistent mood throughout your essay.

   ▸ The firefighters told the third-grade class about procedures to follow if a fire occurred in their school. They emphasized that children should leave
   children should
   the building quickly. Also, ∧ move at least 100 feet away from the
   building.

Students Write

Kyle Mares was a student at Crafton Hills Community College in California when he wrote the following essay. He was asked to explain a process that he had mastered. As you read, consider if the steps outlined in the essay clearly explain the process of creating a Web site.

Creating Your Own Web Site

Kyle Mares

Title: identifies topic

Introduction: explains importance and usefulness of topic

Thesis: identifies key steps in process

Despite the challenges involved, there are many advantages to publishing your own Web site on the World Wide Web. For example, having your résumé available online for potential employers to view can showcase your technical savvy, and a Web site built around your personal interests and concerns can connect you to any like-minded person with Internet access. To create your own Web site and reap the benefits associated with having one, you need to follow a five-step process that includes: planning, designing, creating content, testing and reviewing, and finally publishing and promoting your Web site.

Step 1: planning your site consists of three steps, suggesting chronological order

First stage of planning: three options for deciding where to publish

Advice for beginners

To start, you will need to plan your Web site by considering where to publish it, how to build it, and what it will contain. It is important to consider where you will publish it because each option offers different benefits and drawbacks. The first option is to use free Web publishing through an Internet service provider like AOL or Earthlink. Even though these "hosting" services are free, they provide limited storage space for your files and they insert advertisements into your Web pages, affecting your layout. The second option is a fee-based, or dedicated, hosting service like DreamHost or Yahoo Geocities. These offer more storage space, professional design advice, and a greater degree of freedom and flexibility, but there is a cost to use these services. The third option is to purchase your own Web server, but although this gives you ultimate control over your site, a server is incredibly expensive and requires a constant connection to the Internet. For beginners, the best option is to publish through one of the free hosting services that offers the most server space and the fewest restrictions. Many colleges also host their students' personal Web pages for free without inserting advertisements, so be sure to check with your school first to see if this is an option.

Second stage of planning: how to build it

Background information about how HTML works

Suggests systems that can be used to do the process

After determining where to publish your site, you need to plan how you will build it. There are two ways to build a Web site: You can create code in HTML (Hypertext Markup Language), or you can use an authoring program. HTML is the computer language designers use to create Web sites. When Web browsers read a Web page, they convert the HTML coding into the page you see. Learning to write HTML is very challenging, but it is a useful and marketable skill. However, if learning HTML seems too difficult, you can use an authoring program like FrontPage or Dreamweaver. These computer programs work like word processing programs and allow you to build a Web page without knowing how to use HTML. Therefore, using an inexpensive authoring program is the easiest way for beginners to build their site.

The last step in planning your Web site is to create a site map -- a diagram of all the pages on the site. You can use a word processing program to create your diagram, or merely sketch it out on a pad of paper. Like a roadmap, a site map shows the basic structure of your site, allowing you to follow it when implementing design and content.

Once you have a site map, you are ready to begin designing the site. The design of your Web site is crucial because a poorly designed site discourages people from visiting it. A good design should attract and capture your audience's attention. There are a wide variety of design details to consider, such as use of navigation bars, color, font, visuals, and links. To keep your reader oriented, make sure that the overall design is consistent from page to page. You can achieve this through the use of repeated headers, footers, and sidebars. Before you begin, it is a good idea to spend some time visiting other sites on the Web, noting both good and poor applications of design elements and creating a list of what design features might work on your site. When designing your site, check each page thoroughly to ensure that the layout, colors, navigation tools, links, and other design elements are clear and easy to follow. Problems like unclearly labeled links may require changes to fix them, but it is much better to catch a mistake and correct it early in the design process than to publish a flawed Web site and receive a torrent of complaint emails.

Once you have a basic design in place, you are ready to create content. Content is the material on the Web site, the unique text and graphics for every page. Keep your users interested by offering compelling information in a wide variety of formats, including figures, visuals, sound and video clips, or articles and analysis that they may not find anywhere else. However, even the fanciest graphics and images won't hold someone's attention if there is no significant content, so be sure to invest just as much time developing the words for your site as you did in planning and designing it. To keep your site fresh and to keep people returning to it, you may need to update it regularly with new text and data. Your topic will determine how often to update your site. For example, if your site deals with an upcoming election, you should update as often as new information becomes available. This process takes time because you will have to check the entire site every time you update it, but the labor involved is well worth it in order to keep the content relevant, fresh, and interesting for your audience.

The final step before launching your Web site is to test and review all aspects of the site to ensure that everything performs as it should. In doing so, you may find that certain elements and features do not work as intended, and that you need to find creative solutions. It is a good idea to have a friend review your site, to see if he or she has any difficulty navigating the pages. Test all details on your pages to make them as

4   Third stage of planning: making site map

Simile helps reader understand how site map works

5   Step 2: designing your site

Useful design tip

Points out potential problem

6   Step 3: create content

7   Step 4: test and review

Practical advice

user-friendly as possible, and don't be afraid to visit other sites to see how they handle various problems and obstacles.

Step 5: publish and promote the site

Once you are satisfied with your Web site, you are ready to publish and promote it.   8
To launch the site, follow your hosting service's instructions for publishing. To make others aware of your site's existence, you can publicize your Web site by submitting it to search engines and Web rings, online links of similar Web sites. Offer to exchange links with people who run similar pages so that readers from the community you are trying to reach learn of your Web site. Depending on the subject of your site, consider posting its address, or URL, on related message boards and newsgroups to create interest, or even place an ad for it in your college newspaper. This extra effort will ensure that others will visit and make use of your site.

Technical term is defined

Conclusion: reemphasizes benefits of creating your own Web site

Although a lot of time and effort are necessary to build your own Web site, the cre-   9
ative process is richly rewarding. In the Information Age, Web expertise is a valuable skill, and each step in designing Web pages will teach you new techniques and skills that can be used in a wide variety of careers. There are incredible opportunities for people who take a hands-on approach to the World Wide Web, and by publishing your own pages you'll gain valuable experience that will benefit you in your future endeavors.

Responding to "Students Write"

1. Evaluate the writer's thesis statement and introduction. How do they indicate why making a personal Web site might be useful and important?

2. Where are the potential trouble spots in the process that Mares identifies?

3. Evaluate the essay's level of detail. Do you think you could create a Web site by following Mares's instructions? If not, where is additional detail needed?

4. Does Mares's conclusion bring the essay to a satisfying close? Why or why not?

Reading a Process Analysis Essay

Process analysis is a common method of explaining; it is often used in textbooks (including this one) and in other forms of academic writing. To read a process analysis effectively, use the following suggestions.

What to Look for, Highlight, and Annotate

Understanding the Reading

- For a complex or especially important process, outline or draw a graphic organizer of the steps. Try explaining each step in your own words without referring to the text.

- For a how-to essay, imagine yourself carrying out the process as you read.
- Annotate the sections that summarize complex steps.

Examining the Characteristics of Process Analysis Essays

- Look for and highlight the thesis statement. Discover why the author thinks the process is important or useful.
- Identify the organizational structure. Does the author list steps chronologically or according to a different type of organization?
- Highlight or underline each step or group of steps. Then, using a different colored highlighter or an asterisk (*), mark steps that the author warns are difficult or troublesome.
- Highlight or use a symbol to mark new terms as they are introduced.
- Annotate any sections that pertain to special equipment needed to perform or understand the process.
- For a how-to essay, look for difficulties you might experience in trying to follow the process, and write down any further information you would need to successfully complete the process.
- For a how-it-works essay, identify details that still need to be added to better understand the process.

How to Find Ideas to Write About

Look for ideas to write about *as you read*. Record your ideas and impressions as marginal annotations. Think about why you want or need to understand the process. Consider situations in which you can apply the information. Consider also how other processes are the same and/or different from the one in the essay. If metaphors or analogies come to mind, such as the similarity of a dream catcher to a spider's web, make a note of them. Finally, evaluate the usefulness and completeness of the information provided.

You and Improved

Matthew Gilbert

Reporter Matthew Gilbert (b. 1958) has written about pop culture for the *Boston Globe* since 1987 and has served as chief television critic for the newspaper since 1997. He graduated from Connecticut College and abandoned a stint in law school to get a master's degree in English literature at the University of New Hampshire. He has worked on staff for a number of magazines, including *Boston Review*. The article that follows first appeared on the *Globe*'s online site, Boston.com, in November 2003.

In "You and Improved," Gilbert analyzes the television trend toward makeover shows. He notes that at the time this piece was written, over forty makeover series — in which people try to perfect their homes, lifestyles, consumer choices, and even their bodies and faces — were available to television viewers. As you read, notice how Gilbert uses humorous questions and comments to critique the makeover concept.

Focus on Understanding   As you read, identify the how the author feels about makeover shows.

Focus on the Topic   In class or in your journal, explore the popularity of makeover TV shows. Why do you think people watch them?

As endless holiday socializing looms, it's time to scrutinize, criticize, revise, and, finally, if you truly want to be Martha Stewart lily-in-a-glass-bowl perfect, accessorize.   1

That's the narrative cycle of TV's many, many makeover series, from *Trading Spaces*, *What Not to Wear*, and *Queer Eye for the Straight Guy* to the great giant in its field, *Buff Brides*. Hosted by telegenic° "experts," these reality shows promise to overhaul and upgrade every surface of your existence, to eliminate the embarrassing "before" in favor of the tasteful happily ever "after." They offer you a helping hand out of your big-nosed, tacky-shirted, ugly-couched, Charlie Brown–treed° life, and into a gleaming fantasy of good taste and home entertainment.   2

The classic makeover process goes something like this: 3

(1) Scrutinize your home. Look closely. Is it an inelegant mess, with peeling wallpaper in the den and sour milk in the refrigerator? Are your kitchen cabinets stocked unimaginatively, lined only with macaroni and cheese and the poor man's protein fix, canned tuna?   4

(2) Criticize your appearance. Do you see a week of gray days under your eyes, and are you contemplating the sale of your skin to a leather factory? And your teeth: Does someone have a very special fondness for butterscotch? Have   5

telegenic: suited for appearance on television

Charlie Brown–treed: refers to a scene in *A Charlie Brown Christmas* where Charlie Brown buys an ugly, real Christmas tree that everyone makes fun of

262

you considered becoming one of the 10,000 people who have applied to have their face rearranged on *Extreme Makeover?*

(3) Criticize your wardrobe, too — the fraying khakis, the horribly saggy loafers, the ancient (but not "vintage") T-shirts. Are you actually going out in public in such infantile baseball caps? What will you wear to the holiday office party? And your white socks: How queer (and un-*Queer*) are they? 6

(4) Pause to revise, to rethink, to renovate. Is there a way out of this disgrace? What would the Fab Five advise? 7

Watch several of the more than 40 makeover shows on TV. Read a few remake-your-life books and scan the fashion magazines. Search high and low culture for a better-looking way to live in the world. Jot down ideas. Cut out photo fantasies. Feel the future. 8

Feel your wallet. Go to the beauty salons, the specialty-food markets, the furniture stores. Buy products — especially the ones named on the shows. Deck yourself in layers of fashion. 9

Purchase the tickets to your happiness. 10

(5) And, finally, accessorize. Adopt the little flourishes that can make — or break — the whole gestalt.° Are you ready to select a pocket square, more commonly known as a handkerchief, and casually stuff it in your pocket? Sartorial° splendor is in the details. 11

Makeover mania. It's a definitively American phenomenon. While many of the popular makeover TV series originated in England, they naturally suit the traditional American hunger for transformation and self-realization. They are built for dreamers and yearners, for people who want to become something else, something better. 12

And there's nothing terribly wrong with making over, as long as you keep it in perspective. After all, you can alter every surface in your life, from your face to your coffee table, and still be unhappy. A flawlessly glazed turkey does not guarantee you'll have a lot to be thankful for at the Thanksgiving table. 13

Makeover shows may assert that if you heed their directives, you will find contentment and self-esteem. But, really, they don't address the insecurities that lead so many people to the makeover process in the first place. The exactly right scarf may look regal, but it will only make you queen for a day. It isn't going to fill the hole in the middle of your self-esteem, just patch it temporarily, in time for the New Year's bash. 14

And if you're not careful, the hunger for makeover information can lead you further away from self-realization. It can chain you to a standard of beauty and behavior that isn't right for you, one to which you will always compare yourself negatively. We are steeped in the tyranny of the glossy magazine spreads, which present models, interior designs, and cozy holiday images that are idealized and unreal. But in reality there is nothing absolute about attractiveness; it's subjective and personal. One man's ceiling mural is another man's bore. 15

So listen to the televised advice, collect the magazine clippings, and then throw it all out and do what you want. Develop your unique style, your particular vision of beauty, and not someone else's. 16

gestalt: the arrangement of parts into a perfectly complete whole

sartorial: having to do with tailors or tailored clothing

Understanding the Reading

1. Identify the five steps in Gilbert's tongue-in-cheek makeover process.
2. According to Gilbert, why do people like makeover shows?
3. In his opinion, when are people especially likely to feel that they need a makeover?
4. Gilbert seems to indicate that he favors makeovers, but later he reveals his true purpose for writing. State his purpose in your own words, and explain the drawbacks of watching such shows.

Visualizing the Reading

To analyze the process described in Gilbert's essay, complete the following graphic organizer by filling in the blank boxes.

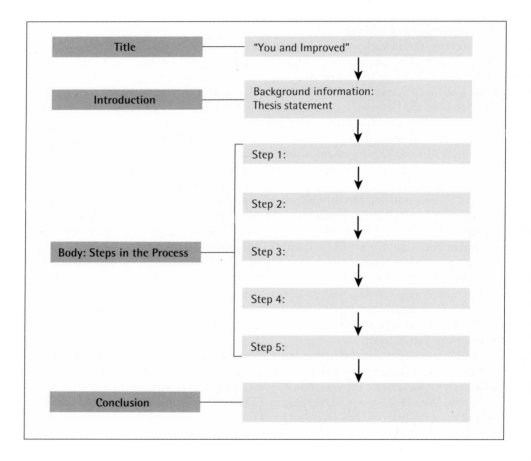

Title	"You and Improved"
Introduction	Background information: Thesis statement
Body: Steps in the Process	Step 1:
	Step 2:
	Step 3:
	Step 4:
	Step 5:
Conclusion	

Examining the Characteristics of Process Analysis Essays

1. What is the author's thesis? Would you identify this as a how-to essay or a how-it-works essay? Explain your answer.

2. What background information does Gilbert present? Is there enough for you to understand the process? Why or why not?

3. Process analysis essays usually follow a chronological organization. What organizational technique does Gilbert use here? Why do you think he used this technique in ordering the steps in his process?

4. Provide some examples of the author's use of detail in describing the makeover process. What kinds of sensory details and figures of speech make his writing lively and interesting?

Building Your Word Power

1. What is the connotative meaning of *vintage* as used in paragraph 6?

2. What does the author mean in paragraph 15 when he writes, "We are steeped in the tyranny of the glossy magazine spreads"?

3. Explain the meaning of each of the following words as it is used in the reading: *looms* (para. 1), *scrutinize* (1), *infantile* (6), *yearners* (12), and *heed* (14). Refer to your dictionary as needed.

For a definition of **connotative meaning,** *see the chart of commonly used language features on p. 21.*

Building Your Critical Thinking Skills: Humor

One of the techniques that writers use is humor. Some writers are humorists — specialists in making jokes and writing funny essays. Other writers simply incorporate bits of humor to create an informal tone or to lighten a serious topic. Still other writers use a bitter type of humor called sarcasm to make fun of something or someone. Regardless of the type of humor, it is important to recognize when a writer is using humor and to consider the purpose. Because humor can be a matter of personal taste, you may need to read a passage a few times to determine if the author's intent is indeed humorous. Using your skills in identifying humor, answer the following questions.

1. Consider the tone of Gilbert's essay. Would you say that he uses sarcasm in outlining the process of makeover shows, or is his intent lighter and more informal? Why do you think he uses humor in this essay?

2. How does Gilbert combine humor with process analysis? Include specific examples from the essay.

Reacting to the Reading: Discussion and Journal Writing

1. Discuss your opinion of makeovers. Do they serve a useful purpose? Can people go too far in their quest for a makeover?

2. Discuss the media's role in how we form opinions of ourselves. Are we too concerned with looking like the people we see on TV, in films, and in magazines?

3. In class or in your journal, explain something you wanted to change about yourself but then learned to accept.

Applying Your Skills: Writing Assignments

1. **Paragraph Assignment.** Gilbert writes that people seek makeovers to patch holes in their self-esteem. Write a paragraph describing a few steps that you might take to improve your self-esteem.

2. Write an essay about one change you would like to make in your life. Provide background information about why you'd like to make this change. Using an appropriate level of detail, describe the process you would follow to accomplish the change.

3. Watch a makeover show on television. Then write an essay describing the process you observed. In your introduction and conclusion, address and evaluate the participant's intent and overall satisfaction with the makeover.

4. Combining Patterns. Analyze your lifestyle as a consumer. Which possessions are important to you, and which ones are superficial? Choose one that is of outstanding value to you, and write an essay about it. Describe it with sensory details so readers can visualize it. Explain the processs through which you acquired it, and give reasons for its importance to you.

5. Internet Research. Visit the Web sites for several currently popular makeover shows, or research several of those mentioned in Gilbert's article. Review the rules for applying to be on the show, and then write a summary of the application process that includes details from your research.

Campus Racism 101

Nikki Giovanni

The poet Yolanda Cornelia "Nikki" Giovanni (b. 1943) grew up in Cincinnati, Ohio, and attended Fisk University, where she served as editor of the literary magazine. After graduation she organized Cincinnati's Black Arts Festival and began to make a name for herself as an activist and writer. Although Giovanni is best known for her poetry — she has published fourteen collections of poems — she has also written children's books and nonfiction works during her thirty-year literary career. At present she is a professor of English at Virginia Tech.

The following selection comes from *Racism 101* (1994), a nonfiction book. As you read the essay, notice the way Giovanni uses a question-and-answer technique to emphasize her understanding of the problems faced by black students at predominantly white colleges. In addition, notice the rules she lays out for students at such schools, and consider how her advice would benefit them.

Focus on Understanding   Read to discover Giovanni's advice for black college students attending predominantly white colleges.

Focus on the Topic   In class or in your journal, address this question: Does racism exist on your campus? Explain.

There is a bumper sticker that reads: TOO BAD IGNORANCE ISN'T PAINFUL. I like 1 that. But ignorance is. We just seldom attribute the pain to it or even recognize it when we see it. Like the postcard on my corkboard. It shows a young man in a very hip jacket smoking a cigarette. In the background is a high school with the American flag waving. The caption says: "Too cool for school. Yet too stupid for the real world." Out of the mouth of the young man is a bubble enclosing the words "Maybe I'll start a band." There could be a postcard showing a jock in a uniform saying, "I don't need school. I'm going to the NFL or NBA." Or one showing a young man or woman studying and a group of young people saying, "So you want to be white." Or something equally demeaning. We need to quit it.

I am a professor of English at Virginia Tech. I've been here for four years, 2 though for only two years with academic rank. I am tenured, which means I have a teaching position for life, a rarity on a predominantly white campus. Whether from malice or ignorance, people who think I should be at a predominantly Black institution will ask, "Why are you at Tech?" Because it's here. And so are Black students. But even if Black students weren't here, it's painfully obvious that this nation and this world cannot allow white students to go through higher education without interacting with Blacks in authoritative positions. It is equally clear that predominantly Black colleges cannot accommodate the numbers of Black students who want and need an education.

Is it difficult to attend a predominantly white college? Compared with what? Being passed over for promotion because you lack credentials? Being turned down for jobs because you are not college-educated? Joining the armed forces or going to jail because you cannot find an alternative to the streets? Let's have a little perspective here. Where can you go and what can you do that frees you from interacting with the white American mentality? You're going to interact; the only question is, will you be in some control of yourself and your actions, or will you be controlled by others? I'm going to recommend self-control.

What's the difference between prison and college? They both prescribe your behavior for a given period of time. They both allow you to read books and develop your writing. They both give you time alone to think and time with your peers to talk about issues. But four years of prison doesn't give you a passport to greater opportunities. Most likely that time only gives you greater knowledge of how to get back in. Four years of college gives you an opportunity not only to lift yourself but to serve your people effectively. What's the difference when you are called nigger in college from when you are called nigger in prison? In college you can, though I admit with effort, follow procedures to have those students who called you nigger kicked out or suspended. You can bring issues to public attention without risking your life. But mostly, college is and always has been the future. We, neither less nor more than other people, need knowledge. There are discomforts attached to attending predominantly white colleges, though no more so than living in a racist world. Here are some rules to follow that may help:

Go to class. No matter how you feel. No matter how you think the professor feels about you. It's important to have a consistent presence in the classroom. If nothing else, the professor will know you care enough and are serious enough to be there.

Meet your professors. Extend your hand (give a firm handshake) and tell them your name. Ask them what you need to do to make an A. You may never make an A, but you have put them on notice that you are serious about getting good grades.

Do assignments on time. Typed or computer-generated. You have the syllabus. Follow it, and turn those papers in. If for some reason you can't complete an assignment on time, let your professor know before it is due and work out a new due date — then meet it.

Go back to see your professor. Tell him or her your name again. If an assignment received less than an A, ask why, and find out what you need to do to improve the next assignment.

Yes, your professor is busy. So are you. So are your parents who are working to pay or help with your tuition. Ask early what you need to do if you feel you are starting to get into academic trouble. Do not wait until you are failing.

Understand that there will be professors who do not like you; there may even 10 be professors who are racist or sexist or both. You must discriminate among your professors to see who will give you the help you need. You may not simply say, "They are all against me." They aren't. They mostly don't care. Since you are the one who wants to be educated, find the people who want to help.

Don't defeat yourself. Cultivate your friends. Know your enemies. You can- 11 not undo hundreds of years of prejudicial thinking. Think for yourself and speak up. Raise your hand in class. Say what you believe no matter how awkward you may think it sounds. You will improve in your articulation and confidence.

Participate in some campus activity. Join the newspaper staff. Run for of- 12 fice. Join a dorm council. Do something that involves you on campus. You are going to be there for four years, so let your presence be known, if not felt.

You will inevitably run into some white classmates who are troubling because 13 they often say stupid things, ask stupid questions — and expect an answer. Here are some comebacks to some of the most common inquiries and comments:

Q: What's it like to grow up in a ghetto? 14
A: I don't know. 15

Q: (from the teacher) Can you give us the Black perspective on Toni Morrison,° 16 Huck Finn,° slavery, Martin Luther King, Jr., and others?
A: I can give you *my* perspective. (Do not take the burden of 22 million people 17 on your shoulders. Remind everyone that you are an individual, and don't speak for the race or any other individual within it.)

Q: Why do all the Black people sit together in the dining hall? 18
A: Why do all the white students sit together? 19

Q: Why should there be an African-American studies course? 20
A: Because white Americans have not adequately studied the contributions of 21 Africans and African-Americans. Both Black and white students need to know our total common history.

Q: Why are there so many scholarships for "minority" students? 22
A: Because they wouldn't give my great-grandparents their forty acres and the 23 mule.°

Q: How can whites understand Black history, culture, literature, and so forth? 24
A: The same way we understand white history, culture, literature, and so forth. 25 That is why we're in school: to learn.

Toni Morrison: well-known contemporary black American writer and winner of the 1993 Nobel Prize for Literature; **Huck Finn:** character in *The Adventures of Huckleberry Finn* by Mark Twain, a novel controversial in some circles today for its language and portrayal of the slave Jim

forty acres and the mule: policy after the Civil War giving freed slaves 40 acres of land and a mule, although very few freed slaves ever received what was promised

Q: Should whites take African-American studies courses?   26

A: Of course. We take white-studies courses, though the universities don't call   27
them that.

Comment: When I see groups of Black people on campus, it's really intimi-   28
dating.

Comeback: I understand what you mean. I'm frightened when I see white stu-   29
dents congregating.

Comment: It's not fair. It's easier for you guys to get into college than for other   30
people.

Comeback: If it's so easy, why aren't there more of us?   31

Comment: It's not our fault that America is the way it is.   32

Comeback: It's not our fault, either, but both of us have a responsibility to   33
make changes.

It's really very simple. Educational progress is a national concern; educa-   34
tion is a private one. Your job is not to educate white people; it is to obtain an
education. If you take the racial world on your shoulders, you will not get the
job done. Deal with yourself as an individual worthy of respect, and make
everyone else deal with you the same way. College is a little like playing grown-
up. Practice what you want to be. You have been telling your parents you are
grown. Now is your chance to act like it.

Understanding the Reading

1. Why does Giovanni think her presence is important at Virginia Tech?

2. What are some of the challenges that black students face at predominantly
   white colleges? How does this experience equip a black person for life after college?

3. In her rules for black students to follow, Giovanni includes a number of points
   relating to professors. Why is it important for students to meet their professors,
   and how should black students cultivate and maintain a relationship with
   them?

4. According to the author, what is a black student's most imporant job in college?

Visualizing the Reading

An effective process analysis identifies trouble spots and offers solutions. By listing typical questions and possible answers, Giovanni identifies the trouble spots and problems black students may experience on predominately white college campuses. Using
this chart or one like it, identify the potential trouble spots suggested by each question
that Giovanni poses. The first one has been done for you.

Question	Potential Trouble Spot
"What's it like to grow up in a ghetto?" (para. 14)	Racial stereotyping; some students assume all black people live in a ghetto.
"Can you give us the Black perspective on Toni Morrison, Huck Finn, . . ." (para. 16)	
"Why do all the Black people sit to-gether in the dining hall?" (para. 18)	
"Why should there be an African-American studies course?" (para. 20)	
"Why are there so many scholarships for 'minority' students?" (para. 22)	
"How can whites understand Black history, culture, literature, and so forth?" (para. 24)	
"Should whites take African-American studies courses?" (para. 26)	

Examining the Characteristics of Process Analysis Essays

1. How does the title, "Campus Racism 101," suggest the author's purpose in writing this essay?

2. Identify the essay's thesis statement. How does the author reveal her thesis?

3. How does Giovanni make readers understand the importance of the process she recommends?

4. How does the background information included in the essay both establish the author's qualifications for writing about racism and help readers understand the process that she explains?

5. Describe Giovanni's tone. Does it strengthen the essay and make it appealing to her audience? Why or why not?

Building Your Word Power

1. Consider Giovanni's use of the emotionally charged word *nigger* in paragraph 4. How does its use affect your reading of the essay and your understanding of the author's tone?

2. What are the different connotative meanings of the word *discriminate* (para. 10)? How does the author use the word in this essay?

*For a definition of **connotative meaning**, see the chart of commonly used language features on p. 21.*

3. Explain the meaning of each of the following words as it is used in the reading: *malice* (para 2), *authoritative* (2), *cultivate* (11), *articulation* (11), and *inevitably* (13). Refer to your dictionary as needed.

Building Your Critical Thinking Skills: Point of View

Point of view is the perspective from which an essay is written. When the first-person point of view is used (*I, me, mine, ours*), the story is told as if the writer is the speaker. In the second-person point of view (*you, yours*), the author addresses readers directly. The third-person point of view (*he, she, they*) is more distant. Using your knowledge of point of view, answer the following questions.

1. What point of view does Giovanni use? How does it reinforce her message?
2. How does the point of view affect your reaction to the essay? Did you feel as if you were part of Giovanni's audience or excluded from it?

Reacting to the Reading: Discussion and Journal Writing

1. Discuss whether minority students should receive preferential treatment in the awarding of scholarships.
2. In class or in your journal, write a list of questions or comments from friends or family that reveal how they do not understand you or misinterpret who you are or what you do.

Applying Your Skills: Writing Assignments

1. **Paragraph Assignment.** One of the author's recommendations is, "Meet your professors." Write a paragraph explaining the steps you would take in following this recommendation.
2. Write a how-to essay aimed at fellow students that addresses the challenges of a particular aspect of college life, such as relationships with roommates or professors, studying, socializing, or test taking. Include a thesis statement that identifies the process and suggests your attitude or approach toward it.
3. Think about a time when someone judged you unfairly on the basis of how you look, your ethnicity, or some other characteristic. Write an essay about that experience using process analysis. For example, you might explain the process you went through in responding to that person, or how you attempted to change his or her opinion of you.
4. **Combining Patterns.** Giovanni makes a comparison between prison and college. Using a different type of institution (for example, high school, religion, the military, a place of employment), write a comparison between it and college. Once you've established your comparison, include a list of advice for students that offers a process for making the most of the similarities between the two institutions.
5. **Internet Research.** Explore the "Storming the Gates of Knowledge" site from the University of Virginia (www.virginia.edu/woodson/projects/kenan/) or any other Web site that documents the stories of minority students who challenged a school's policies regarding race or sexual identity. Using examples from your research, write an essay that describes the processes these people undertook in order to gain entrance to the school. Pay particular attention to any documents that are linked because newspaper articles, letters, court papers, and other primary sources are strong pieces of evidence that will bolster your thesis.

Dater's Remorse

Cindy Chupack

Cindy Chupack (b. 1965) served as an executive producer and, frequently, a writer for the HBO show *Sex and the City*. She trained as a journalist at Northwestern University because she wanted to make a living as a writer, but she found that journalism did not suit her. After working in advertising, Chupack contributed a personal essay to *New York Woman* magazine that attracted the attention of a television writer who encouraged her to create sitcom scripts. She now divides her time between Los Angeles and New York.

This selection appears in a collection of Chupack's writings titled *The Between Boyfriends Book* (2003). As you read, notice the way Chupack builds her humorous analogy between shopping and dating, from her opening description of her telephone-company "suitors" to her conclusion: *Caveat emptor* — "Let the buyer beware."

Focus on Understanding   Read to discover what dater's remorse is and what advice the author offers to avoid it.

Focus on the Topic   In class or in your journal, write about advice that you have received or given about dating.

1   I never imagined this would happen, but three men are fighting over me. They call me repeatedly. They ply me with gifts. They beg me for a commitment. Yes, they're just AT&T, MCI, and Sprint salesmen interested in being my long-distance carrier, but what I'm relishing — aside from the attention — is the sense that I am in complete control.

2   In fact, just the other day my ex (phone carrier, that is) called to find out what went wrong. Had I been unhappy? What would it take to win me back? Turns out all it took was two thousand frequent flier miles. I switched, just like that. I didn't worry about how my current carrier would feel, or how it might affect my Friends and Family. Now if only I could use that kind of healthy judgment when it comes to my love life.

3   The unfortunate truth is that while most of us are savvy shoppers, we're not sufficiently selective when looking for relationships, and that's why we often suffer from dater's remorse. Perhaps we should try to apply conventional consumer wisdom to men as well as merchandise. How satisfying love might be if we always remembered to:

4   *Go with a classic, not a trend.* We all know it's unwise to spend a week's salary on vinyl hip-huggers. But when it comes to men, even the most conservative among us occasionally invests in the human equivalent of a fashion fad.

The furthest I ever strayed from a classic was during college. I wrote a paper about the Guardian Angels, those street toughs who unofficially patrol inner-city neighborhoods, and being a very thorough student, I ended up dating one. He wore a red beret and entertained me by demonstrating martial arts moves in my dorm room. I remember telling my concerned roommate how he was *sooo* much more interesting than those boring MBA° types everybody else was dating. Of course, what initially seemed like a fun, impulse buy turned out to require more of an emotional investment than I was willing to make. It took me two months to break up with him — two months of getting persistent late-night calls, angry letters, and unannounced visits to my dorm room door, which I envisioned him kicking down someday. The good thing about MBAs: They're familiar with the expression "Cut your losses."

MBA: Master of Business Administration, an advanced business degree

Beware of the phrase "Some assembly required." Anyone who has tried to follow translated-from-Swedish directions for putting together a swivel chair understands that when you've got to assemble something yourself, the money you save isn't worth the time you spend. The same goes for men. Many women think that even though a guy is not exactly "together," we can easily straighten him out. The fact is that fixer-uppers are more likely to stay forever flawed, no matter what we do. My friend Jenny fell for a forty-one-year-old bachelor, despite the fact that he spent their first few dates detailing his dysfunctional family and boasting that he went to the same shrink as the Menendez brothers.° "Six weeks later, when he announced he couldn't handle a relationship, it shouldn't have surprised me," says Jenny, who now looks for men requiring a little less duct tape.

5

Menendez brothers: two brothers who were convicted in 1996 of killing their parents

Make sure your purchase goes with the other things you own. I once fell in love with a very expensive purple velvet couch, and I seriously considered buying it, even though it would mean getting my cat declawed, and I had signed an agreement when I adopted her that I would never do that. But the couch . . . the couch . . . I visited it a few more times, but I didn't buy, and not just out of sympathy for my cat. I realized that if I owned that couch, I'd have to replace all my comfy, old stuff with new furniture equal in quality and style to the purple couch. Men can be like that, too. You're drawn to them because they're attractively different, but being with them may mean changing your entire life. For example, while dating a long-distance bicyclist, my friend Janet found herself suddenly following his training regimen: bowing out of social events just as the fun began, rising at an hour at which she normally went to bed, and replacing fine dining with intensive carbo-loading. And the only bike she ever rode was the stationary one at the gym.

6

Check with previous owners. Once beyond age twenty-five, most men would have to be classified as secondhand, and we all know how risky it is to buy used merchandise. Therefore, it's up to you to do some basic consumer research. Find out how many previous owners your selection has had. If he's such a steal, why is he still on the lot? Is it because his exterior is a bit unsightly, or because he's fundamentally a lemon? (Before becoming too critical, bear in mind that *you* are still on the lot.)

7

Caveat emptor.° Following these guidelines won't guarantee a great rela-   8
tionship, but it will help you cut down on the number of times you feel dater's
remorse. Obviously looking for a husband is a bit more complicated than
choosing a major appliance, but since there are no lifetime guarantees or lemon
laws for men, it pays to be a savvy shopper.

Caveat emptor: Latin
phrase meaning "Let
the buyer beware"

Understanding the Reading

1. How does the author's relationship with long distance phone companies relate to
   the topic of dating?
2. According to Chupack, what can happen when you date someone who is "the human equivalent of a fashion fad" (para. 4)?
3. Explain the connection between dating and buying furniture. Why does the author
   advise women to stay away from "fixer-uppers" (para. 5)?
4. What assumption does the author make about her readers as revealed in the final
   paragraph?

Visualizing the Reading

Chupack explains the process of avoiding dater's remorse by comparing it to shopping.
Evaluate her analogy by matching up the steps. The first one has been done for you.

Step	Shopping Analogy	Dating Advice
1	"Go with a classic, not a trend." (para. 4)	Avoid men who are radically different from the types you usually date.
2	"Beware of the phrase 'Some assembly required.'" (para. 5)	
3	"Make sure your purchase goes with the other things you own." (para. 6)	
4	"Check with previous owners." (para. 7)	
5.	"Caveat emptor." (para. 8)	

Examining the Characteristics of Process Analysis Essays

1. Chupack's thesis involves dating as well as shopping. Identify her thesis, and evaluate the effectivess of her comparison.

2. What type of organization does Chupack use to order the steps in her process analysis essay? If the essay is not organized chronologically, does the author use any sort of logical progression such as starting with simple steps and progressing to more complex ones? Is her type of organization effective? Why or why not?

3. Evaluate the author's level of detail. Is it detailed enough to be of practical use?

4. Is Chupack's reference to lemon laws a satisfying conclusion? Why or why not?

Building Your Word Power

1. Explain the various ways the word *lot* is used in paragraph 7.

*For a definition of **connotative meaning**, see the chart of commonly used language features on p. 21.*

2. What is the connotative meaning of *secondhand* and *used merchandise* as used in paragraph 7?

3. Explain the meaning of each of the following words as it is used in the reading: *relishing* (para. 1), *conventional* (3), *classic* (4), *envisioned* (4), *dysfunctional* (5), and *regimen* (6). Refer to your dictionary as needed.

Building Your Critical Thinking Skills: Analogies

An **analogy** is a comparison in which an author illustrates one point, thing, or situation by likening it to another. For example, in "Campus Racism 101" Nikki Giovanni compares college to a prison and describes the ways the two institutions are similar. Be sure to evaluate analogies in order to determine whether they are appropriate and effective. How closely are the two concepts related? Do the two ideas have enough in common? For what purpose is the analogy used? Using your skills in identifying and evaluating analogies, answer the following questions.

1. How does Chupack develop her analogy? Analyze each part. Do all the aspects of the analogy make sense? Explain.

2. Are there ways in which shopping and dating differ? If yes, how? Does the author address these? Why or why not?

Reacting to the Reading: Discussion and Journal Writing

1. Discuss some experiences you or a friend have had with dating. How difficult is it to find someone compatible?

2. Write a journal entry about a successful relationship that you have now or had in the past. What made this relationship work out so well?

Applying Your Skills: Writing Assignments

1. Paragraph Assignment. Chupack warns readers about men who are "fixer-uppers" (para. 5). Think of a person from your own experience who "required some assembly." In a paragraph, list the steps that this person would need to follow to repair flaws in his or her personality or lifestyle.

2. Write an essay aimed at high school seniors about starting and maintaining friendships at college. Point out the differences and similarities in the social structures of high school and college, and then use process analysis to give advice on how to meet people on campus. Provide examples from your own experiences or those of your friends.

3. Write a process analysis essay offering your own advice on dating or marriage. Present suggestions for maintaining a workable and satisfying relationship. Include potential trouble spots and advice on how to avoid or resolve them. Title your essay "How to Make a Relationship Work."

4. Combining Patterns. Chupack advises readers to "go with a classic, not a trend" when choosing dating partners. Brainstorm a list of situations other than dating in which the same advice might apply. Choose one and write a pattern essay using examples that explains why this advice applies. Where applicable, include process analysis, comparison and contrast, or description.

5. Internet Research. Conduct online research about "speed dating." In a how-it-works essay, explain what speed dating is and outline the steps that one must follow to participate in this activity. Include background information about the process and interesting and relevant details to keep readers informed and interested. In your essay, address your own feelings about speed dating. What are its advantages and disadvantages over traditional ways of meeting people?

How to Defend Someone You Know Is Guilty

David Feige

David Feige (b. 1965) spent nearly twenty years as a public defender in Washington, D.C., and New York City, representing clients unable to afford a lawyer. He has pursued a parallel career as a writer, publishing articles in the *New York Times* and *Slate*, among other publications, and he also serves as a commentator on National Public Radio. In 2003 he won a Soros Justice Fellowship to complete a book on defending poor clients.

"How to Defend Someone You Know Is Guilty" first appeared in the *New York Times Magazine* in April 2001. Notice that Feige spends less time analyzing the legal steps involved in defense and more time discussing his commitment to the job — a job that must be done, he points out, if the legal system is to provide justice.

Focus on Understanding   Read to discover the explanation that the author gives for defending guilty people.

Focus on the Topic   In class or in your journal, write about some reasons why people choose to enter public service occupations — like the job of public defender described in the essay.

rap sheet: a record of arrests

I loved Kevin. He had a rap sheet° that ran to 30 pages and a crack addiction to which he had completely surrendered — but to me, he was wonderful. Kevin was bald with a scar running across the forehead and had the thin, resilient frame of a man who has spent many nights seeking shelter in out-of-the-way places. I remember the night I met him. Back in the pens behind the courtroom, amid three dozen men, stood Kevin, shot by the cops, clad only in a green hospital smock and a big bandage. Having shot him, the police seized his clothes and charged him with trying to rob an undercover police officer. 1

Most people suspect that criminal-defense lawyers, especially canny ones, help their clients come up with a defense. They introduce themselves and in sonorous tones say: "Kevin, you have been charged with robbery in the second degree. Before you say anything let me tell you this: There are three defenses to robbery . . ." While some lawyers do this, it couldn't be further from my approach. 2

Imagine for a moment that you are poor, poorly educated, black and charged with a crime. A big loud white lawyer you've never seen before comes in telling you he has been assigned by the court to defend you. Almost no sane person would admit their guilt or even tell much of the truth to such a stranger. 3

So when I sit down, for the first time, across from someone charged with a serious crime, I rarely bother with "the facts."

Instead I spend my time trying to build trust — explaining who I am and why the hell I'd be in a windowless place that smells of urine, defending someone who supposedly robbed someone else. I explain how I work, what the client can expect and what the charges are. I try to learn about them, their families, their living conditions. In certain cases, I will try to get the names of witnesses so I can start an investigation. But I will rarely address their participation directly at this point. I have spent too long in the system to believe that people tell me the truth at first anyway. The truth is often the only thing my clients have left once the handcuffs go on. It's precious, not something they part with often or easily.

Eventually, of course, the facts become critical. By the time we reach the trial, I need a clear defense that I can explain to a jury in a sentence or two. Ultimately, there are only two basic defenses — "the ID" (they have the wrong guy) and the "what happened" (it was self-defense; it was a fight, not a robbery) — and which one I use depends on what my client eventually tells me. I take the defenses as I take my clients — as they are.

That goes for appearances too. My office has a closet full of secondhand suits and ties to share with clients who can't afford them, but in Kevin's case, as many others, putting him in a suit would look like a lie. Kevin was a homeless crack addict. He walked and talked and dressed like exactly what he was. So rather than try to "fix" Kevin, I tried to make a jury understand him.

During our first conversation, more than anything, Kevin was confused. All he wanted to tell me was that he had just bought some crack and was on his way to smoke it when, out of nowhere, he was shot. The police, on the other hand, had a detailed description of a drug deal gone wrong — an undercover cop attacked with a screwdriver and forced, in self-defense, to open fire. Kevin's case, independent of anything he said, presented a nice defense: the police were lying to cover up a bad shoot. But the fact that there was a plausible defense — even the fact that the cops had shot Kevin — had little to do with my connection to the case. (In fact, Kevin eventually pleaded guilty to attempted criminal sale of a controlled substance and was sentenced to what was effectively time served.) Like all of my clients, I'd defend Kevin happily, guilty or innocent.

Few public defenders have ever escaped a cocktail party without being confronted with "the question": How do you defend someone who is guilty? And out in the world, in public, we lie all the time. We offer abstract answers full of half-truths. I do this, too. I do it because the truth is too hard to explain. I say that I choose sides based on politics and ideology. I believe in the Constitution, and I think in terms of proof, not guilt. I tell them that trial work is fun, and that like most longtime public defenders, I can't imagine incarcerating people for a living.

But the half I don't tell is that having chosen sides, it becomes easy for me. It's as simple as this: I care about the person I know. In most cases, the complainant is an abstraction to me. His victimization is an abstraction. My client, on the other hand, is very human and very real. It is his tears I see, his hand I hold and his mother I console. I understand my clients like no one else in the system. I empathize with my clients the way everyone else in the system empathizes with the complainants. And ultimately, I do to the complainants what the rest of the system does to my client. I dehumanize them. I learn their facts and statistics from police reports, but I don't linger over their faces. "At TPO" — time and place of occurrence — "perp did threaten UC#4225 with a screwdriver." That's the victim. Somewhere behind that language is the person that prosecutors and cops and judges and politicians and friends and family all rally around.

What I see instead, through the bars of the cramped interview booth, is   10
Kevin: a 46-year-old man who lived from day to day and pipe to pipe by stealing car radios and cassette tapes, who has a family he loves but is too embarrassed to visit and a girlfriend whose addiction he feels responsible for. And as he sits there and we talk and I learn about what he likes and where he sleeps and how he recently lost his favorite uncle to gunfire, that's when the battle lines are drawn. That's when he becomes real and the victim abstract. Ultimately, the thing that I have so much trouble explaining to people is that when I get to know them, I just really, really like my clients.

So defending the reviled, even those who are guilty, is not some mental   11
trick, nor even a moral struggle for me. I don't lack imagination or willfully close my eyes to another's suffering. Rather, the reality of my clients — their suffering, their fear — is more vivid to me than that of the victims. My clients are the ones left exposed. They are the ones who are hated. They are the ones who desperately need my protection. Everyone else can look out for the victims. And they do, of course.

And that leaves me to look after Kevin.   12

Understanding the Reading

1. Explain what we learn about the author and his beliefs. What are Feige's reasons for defending the "guilty"?

2. How does the author feel about the victims of the crimes in which his clients are involved? How does this contrast with his feelings toward the perpetrators of crimes?

3. Explain what Kevin did and how Feige planned to defend him.

Visualizing the Reading

Study the photograph of a man breaking into a car. What advice would you offer this person in finding a lawyer to defend him? What characteristics in a lawyer should he look for? Based on Feige's explanation of the process of defending someone who is guilty, how might Feige approach a defense of this man?

Examining the Characteristics of Process Analysis Essays

1. Identify Feige's thesis. What main process does the author describe? What other processes are also described?
2. What details about Kevin does the author provide? Why are these important?
3. How does the author organize the steps in his essay?
4. What trouble spots or problems does Feige identify? What solutions does he offer?
5. Did you find the conclusion satisfying? Had Feige chosen to include additional information about Kevin and the outcome of his trial, would the conclusion have been strengthened? Why or why not?

Building Your Word Power

1. What does the phrase "putting him in a suit would look like a lie" mean (para. 6)?
2. Evaluate the author's use of legal jargon. What does this contribute to the essay?
3. Explain the meaning of each of the following words as it is used in the reading: *resilient* (para. 1), *canny* (2), *sonorous* (2), *incarcerating* (8), and *reviled* (11). Refer to your dictionary as needed.

*For a definition of **jargon**, see the chart of commonly used language features on p. 21.*

Building Your Critical Thinking Skills: Facts and Opinions

Authors often combine facts and opinions in their writing. The distinction between what is an established fact or verifiable statement and what is an opinion or a personal thought or idea can sometimes be difficult to make. Authors often express their beliefs so strongly and convincingly that readers might mistake them for facts. For example, someone writing about the role of the military in the United States today might state that our nation needs a strong defense to combat terrorism. Many readers would take this as fact, but it is an opinion. However, any statistics and data used in the essay to show the relationship between terrorism and military power would be facts. Any opinions used in the essay should be examined so that they are not mistaken for facts, no matter how convincing. Use your knowledge of fact and opinion to mark the following statements from Feige's essay as Fact (F) or Opinion (O).

_____   1. "Having shot him, the police seized his clothes and charged him with trying to rob an undercover police officer" (para. 1).

_____   2. "It's precious, not something they part with often or easily" (para. 4).

_____   3. "Kevin was a homeless crack addict" (para. 6).

_____   4. "And out in the world, in public, we lie all the time" (para. 8).

_____   5. "They are the ones who are hated" (para. 11).

Reacting to the Reading: Discussion and Journal Writing

1. Do we have courts of *law* or courts of *justice*? Consider the connotative meanings of these words, and discuss your view of the legal system in the United States.

2. Discuss whether you would feel comfortable defending someone you knew was guilty.

3. In class or in your journal, discuss a time when someone came to your defense for a nonlegal matter.

Applying Your Skills: Writing Assignments

1. **Paragraph Assignment.** Write a paragraph about a time when you helped someone with a problem. Briefly describe the process you followed in helping this person.

2. Brainstorm a list of issues facing our society today, such as the high cost of legal services for illegal immigrants or mandatory sentencing for drug use. Choose one issue, and write a process analysis essay describing steps that could be taken to combat the problem. Be sure to provide enough introductory and background information so that the reader fully understands the issue.

3. Feige uses first-person point of view, allowing readers to know what the process means to him personally. Using first-person point of view, write a how-it-works essay that describes a process you are emotionally connected to. For example, if you are active in playing music, you could write a process analysis essay explaining how practice and performance work while at the same time addressing why this process has meaning for you.

4. **Combining Patterns.** Feige admits to offering half-truths about his reasons for defending those who are guilty. Write an argumentation essay evaluating whether telling half-truths is the equivalent of lying. Support your argument with examples or situations that illustrate your thesis.

5. **Internet Research.** Do some online research about what happens when someone is arrested and facing charges (one place to look for information is Find Law's

"Stages of a Criminal Case" at http://criminal.findlaw.com/crimes/criminal _stages.html). Then write an essay describing the process that people go through once they have been charged with a crime. Be sure to include necessary background information about the legal process, and explain technical legal terms. Feel free to use examples from an actual crime that has been in the news to illustrate the steps in the process.

Inside the Engine

Tom and Ray Magliozzi

Tom (b. 1938) and his younger brother Ray (b. 1947) Magliozzi, better known to their listening audience as Click and Clack, the Tappet Brothers, are the award-winning hosts of *Car Talk* on National Public Radio. After graduating from MIT, the brothers opened The Good News Garage in their hometown of Cambridge, Massachusetts. In 1977 they appeared on a local radio station to talk about cars. This appearance led to *Car Talk*, a call-in radio show that is now broadcast nationally to over 4.1 million listeners every week. The show has a devoted following because of the brothers' use of humor as they offer automobile repair advice mixed in with laughter and life lessons all learned on the job at their own auto repair shop.

This selection was taken from *Car Talk*, a book published in 1991 featuring some of the best advice from the brothers' radio show. The authors begin with a story about a customer. As you read, notice how effectively they explain complex terms and technology in order to make their how-it-works essay easy to understand.

Focus on Understanding   Read to discover what processes the authors of "Inside the Engine" address.

Focus on the Topic   In class or in your journal, write about a problem you or someone you know has experienced with automobile use, operation, repair, or maintenance.

1   A customer of ours had an old Thunderbird that he used to drive back and forth to New York to see a girlfriend every other weekend. And every time he made the trip he'd be in the shop the following Monday needing to get something fixed because the car was such a hopeless piece of trash. One Monday he failed to show up and Tom said, "Gee, that's kind of unusual." I said jokingly, "Maybe he blew the car up."

2   Well, what happened was that he was on the Merritt Parkway in Connecticut when he noticed that he had to keep the gas pedal all the way to the floor just to go 30 m.p.h., with this big V-8 engine,° and he figured something was awry.

V-8 engine: powerful engine so called because of its eight cylinders arranged in two rows situated at right angles to each other

3   So he pulled into one of those filling stations where they sell gasoline and chocolate-chip cookies and milk. And he asked the attendant to look at the engine and, of course, the guy said, "I can't help you. All I know is cookies and milk." But the guy agreed to look anyway since our friend was really desperate. His girlfriend was waiting for him and he needed to know if he was going to

284

make it. Anyway, the guy threw open the hood and jumped back in terror. The engine was glowing red. Somewhere along the line, probably around Hartford, he must have lost all of his motor oil. The engine kept getting hotter and hotter, but like a lot of other things in the car that didn't work, neither did his oil pressure warning light. As a result, the engine got so heated up that it fused itself together. All the pistons melted, and the cylinder heads deformed, and the pistons fused to the cylinder walls, and the bearings welded themselves to the crankshaft — oh, it was a terrible sight! When he tried to restart the engine, he just heard a *click, click, click* since the whole thing was seized up tighter than a drum.

That's what can happen in a case of extreme engine neglect. Most of us   4
wouldn't do that, or at least wouldn't do it knowingly. Our friend didn't do it knowingly either, but he learned a valuable lesson. He learned that his girlfriend wouldn't come and get him if his car broke down. Even if he offered her cookies and milk.

The oil is critical to keeping things running since it not only acts as a lu-   5
bricant, but it also helps to keep the engine cool. What happens is that the oil pump sucks the oil out of what's called the sump (or the crankcase or the oil pan), and it pushes that oil, under pressure, up to all of the parts that need lubrication.

The way the oil works is that it acts as a cushion. The molecules of oil ac-   6
tually separate the moving metal parts from one another so that they don't directly touch; the crankshaft *journals*, or the hard parts of the crankshaft, never touch the soft connecting-rod *bearings* because there's a film of oil between them, forced in there under pressure. From the pump.

It's pretty high pressure too. When the engine is running at highway speed,   7
the oil, at 50 or 60 pounds or more per square inch (or about 4 bars, if you're of the metric persuasion — but let's leave religion out of this), is coursing through the veins of the engine and keeping all these parts at safe, albeit microscopic, distances from each other.

But if there's a lot of dirt in the oil, the dirt particles get embedded in these   8
metal surfaces and gradually the dirt acts as an abrasive and wears away these metal surfaces. And pretty soon the engine is junk.

It's also important that the motor oil be present in sufficient quantity. In   9
nontechnical terms, that means there's got to be enough of it in there. If you have too little oil in your engine, there's not going to be enough of it to go around, and it will get very hot, because four quarts will be doing the work of five, and so forth. When that happens, the oil gets overheated and begins to burn up at a greater than normal rate. Pretty soon, instead of having four quarts, you have three and a half quarts, then three quarts doing the work of five. And then, next thing you know, you're down to two quarts and your engine is glowing red, just like that guy driving to New York, and it's chocolate-chip cookie time.

In order to avoid this, some cars have gauges and some have warning lights; 10 some people call them "idiot lights." Actually, we prefer to reverse it and call them "idiot gauges." I think gauges are bad. When you drive a car — maybe I'm weird about this — I think it's a good idea to look at the road most of the time. And you can't look at the road if you're busy looking at a bunch of gauges. It's the same objection we have to these stupid radios today that have so damn many buttons and slides and digital scanners and so forth that you need a co-pilot to change stations. Remember when you just turned a knob?

Not that gauges are bad in and of themselves. I think if you have your 11 choice, what you want is idiot lights — or what we call "genius lights" — and gauges too. It's nice to have a gauge that you can kind of keep an eye on for an overview of what's going on. For example, if you know that your engine typically runs at 215 degrees and on this particular day, which is not abnormally hot, it's running at 220 or 225, you might suspect that something is wrong and get it looked at before your radiator boils over.

On the other hand, if that gauge was the only thing you had to rely on and 12 you didn't have a light to alert you when something was going wrong, then you'd look at the thing all the time, especially if your engine had melted on you once. In that case, why don't you take the bus? Because you're not going to be a very good driver, spending most of your time looking at the gauges.

Incidentally, if that oil warning light ever comes on, shut the engine off! We 13 don't mean that you should shut it off in rush-hour traffic when you're in the passing lane. Use all necessary caution and get the thing over to the breakdown lane. But don't think you can limp to the next exit, because you can't. Spend the money to get towed and you may save the engine.

It's a little-known fact that the oil light does *not* signify whether or not you 14 have oil in the engine. The oil warning light is really monitoring the oil *pressure*. Of course, if you have no oil, you'll have no oil pressure, so the light will be on. But it's also possible to have plenty of oil and an oil pump that's not working for one reason or another. In this event, a new pump would fix the problem, but if you were to drive the car (saying, "It must be a bad light, I just checked the oil!") you'd melt the motor.

So if the oil warning light comes on, even if you just had an oil change and 15 the oil is right up to the full mark on the dipstick and is nice and clean — don't drive the car!

Here's another piece of useful info. When you turn the key to the "on" posi- 16 tion, all the little warning lights *should light up:* the temperature light, the oil light, whatever other lights you may have. Because that is the *test mode* for these lights. If those lights *don't* light up when you turn the key to the "on" position (just before you turn it all the way to start the car), does that mean you're out of oil? No. It means that something is wrong with the warning light itself. If the light doesn't work then, it's not going to work at all. Like when you need it, for example.

One more thing about oil: overfilling is just as bad as underfilling. Can you [17] really have too much of a good thing? you ask. Yes. If you're half a quart or even a quart overfilled, it's not a big deal, and I wouldn't be afraid to drive the car under those circumstances. But if you're a quart and a half or two quarts or more overfilled, you could have so much oil in the crankcase that the spinning crankshaft is going to hit the oil and turn it into suds. It's impossible for the pump to pump suds, so you'll ruin the motor. It's kind of like a front-loading washing machine that goes berserk and spills suds all over the floor when you put too much detergent in. That's what happens to your motor oil when you overfill it.

With all this talk about things that can go wrong, let's not forget that mod- [18] ern engines are pretty incredible. People always say, "You know, the cars of yesteryear were wonderful. They built cars rough and tough and durable in those days."

Horsefeathers.° [19]   horsefeathers: nonsense

The cars of yesteryear were nicer to look at because they were very indi- [20] vidualistic. They were all different, and some were even beautiful. In fact, when I was a kid, you could tell the year, make, and model of a car from a hundred paces just by looking at the taillights or the grille.

Nowadays, they all look the same. They're like jellybeans on wheels. You [21] can't tell one from the other. But the truth is, they've never made engines as good as they make them today. Think of the abuse they take! None of the cars of yesteryear was capable of going 60 or 70 miles per hour all day long and taking it for 100,000 miles.

Engines of today — and by today I mean from the late '60s on up — are far [22] superior. What makes them superior is not only the design and the metallurgy, but the lubricants. The oil they had thirty years ago was lousy compared to what we have today. There are magic additives and detergents and long-chain polymers and what-have-you that make them able to hold dirt in suspension and to neutralize acids and to lubricate better than oils of the old days.

There aren't too many things that will go wrong, because the engines are [23] made so well and the tolerances are closer. And aside from doing stupid things like running out of oil or failing to heed the warning lights or overfilling the thing, you shouldn't worry.

But there's one word of caution about cars that have timing belts: Lots of [24] cars these days are made with overhead camshafts. The camshaft, which opens the valves, is turned by a gear and gets its power from the crankshaft. Many cars today use a notched rubber *timing belt* to connect the two shafts instead of a chain because it's cheaper and easy to change. And here's the caveat: *If you don't change it and the belt breaks, it can mean swift ruin to the engine.* The pistons can hit the valves and you'll have bent valves and possibly broken pistons.

So you can do many hundreds of dollars' worth of damage by failing to [25] heed the manufacturer's warning about changing the timing belt in a timely manner. No pun intended. For most cars, the timing belt replacement is somewhere between $100 and $200. It's not a big deal.

I might add that there are many cars that have rubber timing belts that will 26 *not* cause damage to the engine when they break. But even if you have one of those cars, make sure that you get the belt changed, at the very least, when the manufacturer suggests it. If there's no specific recommendation and you have a car with a rubber belt, we would recommend that you change it at 60,000 miles. Because even if you don't do damage to the motor when the belt breaks, you're still going to be stuck somewhere, maybe somewhere unpleasant. Maybe even Cleveland! So you want to make sure that you don't fall into that situation.

Many engines that have rubber timing belts also use the belt to drive the 27 water pump. On these, don't forget to change the water pump when you change the timing belt, because the leading cause of premature belt failure is that the water pump seizes. So if you have a timing belt that drives the water pump, get the water pump out of there at the same time. You don't want to put a belt in and then have the water pump go a month later, because it'll break the new belt and wreck the engine.

The best way to protect all the other pieces that you can't get to without 28 spending a lot of money is through frequent oil changes. The manufacturers recommend oil changes somewhere between seven and ten thousand miles, depending upon the car. We've always recommended that you change your oil at 3,000 miles. We realize for some people that's a bit of an inconvenience, but look at it as cheap insurance. And change the filter every time too.

And last but not least, I want to repeat this because it's important: Make 29 sure your warning lights work. The oil pressure and engine temperature warning lights are your engine's lifeline. Check them every day. You should make it as routine as checking to see if your zipper's up. You guys should do it at the same time.

What you do is, you get into the car, check to see that your zipper's up, and 30 then turn the key on and check to see if your oil pressure and temperature warning lights come on.

I don't know what women do.   31

Understanding the Reading

1. Why did their customer's car break down? What lesson relating to this story do the authors teach?

2. Why is oil so important to a car? What does a car's oil warning light mean when it goes on?

3. What problem do the authors associate with gauges?

4. What do the authors say is the best way to protect your car?

Visualizing the Reading

"Inside the Engine" includes practical advice for keeping your car operating properly. Use the following chart to summarize the how-to advice offered in each of these paragraphs. The first one has been done for you.

Paragraph	How-to Advice
13	Shut the engine off if the oil warning light comes on.
16	
17	
24	
26	
27	
28	

Examining the Characteristics of Process Analysis Essays

1. Identify the thesis statement. Does it state why the process is important or useful to readers?

2. Analyze the level of detail in the selection. Is it appropriate, or do the authors include unecessary technical details? Please explain.

3. Through what techniques do the authors make the topic interesting and understandable? What level of knowledge and mechanical saavy do the authors assume their readers possess?

4. What potential trouble spots or areas of confusion do the authors identify? Are their suggested solutions easy to understand? Why or why not?

5. What techniques do the authors use to make technical terms understandable to readers who lack mechanical knowledge?

Building Your Word Power

1. The oil is described as "coursing through the veins of the engine" (para. 7). How does this use of personification enhance the story?

2. Evaluate the similes "like a front-loading washing machine" (para. 17) and "like jellybeans on wheels" (para. 21) How effective are they in helping you understand the term or concept being described?

3. Explain the meaning of each of the following words as it is used in the reading: *lubricant* (para. 5), *limp* (13), *metallurgy* (22), *neutralize* (22), and *caveat* (24). Refer to your dictionary as needed.

For the definition of **personification** *and* **simile***, see the chart of commonly used language features on p. 21.*

Building Your Critical Thinking Skills: Evaluating Authors

Authors who are experts in a certain field offer not only factual information but also professional opinion. Generally readers who believe that an author is an expert will accept the advice without much question. However, it is important to evaluate a published opinion by assessing whether the author is indeed an expert in his or her field. Evaluating an author involves reviewing any background information included or conducting a quick online search about the author, as well as determining whether the author's expertise includes the area in which he or she is giving advice. Using your skills in evaluating authors, answer the following questions.

1. Are the authors of "Inside the Engine" qualified to give professional car advice? Why or why not?

2. Do the authors offer advice about anything outside their realm of expertise? If so, what is it, and do you trust it?

Reacting to the Reading: Discussion and Journal Writing

1. Discuss why good car repair advice is hard to find.

2. Have you ever listened to *Car Talk* on National Public Radio? If so, how would you describe the program to someone who has never heard the show? Based on your description, would you say that this essay is typical of how the Magliozzi brothers approach automotive issues on their show?

3. Discuss the authors' attitude toward the increasing complexity of technology. Do you agree or disagree with their asssessment?

Applying Your Skills: Writing Assignments

1. **Paragraph Assignment.** Write a how-to paragraph that briefly describes the process of applying for and obtaining a driver's license in your state.

2. Write a how-it-works process analysis essay explaining how a machine that you use every day works. For example, you could explain how the elevator in your building works or how a microwave oven operates. Depending on your level of knowledge about the machine, it may be necessary to do a bit of research. Be sure to include a thesis and an explanation of the steps in the process, using relevant and apppropriate details. Personalize your essay by describing how the item impacts your daily life.

3. Brainstorm a list of people whom you have gone to for advice. Choose one and write a process analysis essay about seeking advice from this person. For example, you may have sought the help of a guidance counselor when applying to colleges. Describe the process you undertook in identifying whom to approach for help, how you arranged a meeting, any preparation that you did before the meeting, and the type of advice given. Be sure to include a conclusion that explains the process and how the advice ultimately affected you.

4. **Combining Patterns.** Do you think men understand better than women how cars and machinery work? In an argumentation essay, defend your position on this issue, using examples from your own experience that illustrate how men and women approach the process of fixing their cars differently.

5. Internet Research. Visit the *Car Talk* Web site at www.cartalk.com. Explore the site and then choose a process that is explained there — for example, how to set your side-view mirrors so that there is no blind spot. In your own words, write a process analysis essay that explains the steps to a group of new drivers. Be sure to define technical terms, and use sensory details and figures of speech to keep your writing lively and interesting.

Comparison and Contrast: Showing Similarities and Differences

WRITING QUICK START

The photograph on this page shows two scenes of the same country road. Study the photograph and make two lists: the ways the scenes are similar and the ways they are different. Include details about the setting. Then write a paragraph that answers these questions: How are these two scenes the same, and how are they different?

What Are Comparison and Contrast?

As you discovered in writing your paragraph about the scenes of the country road, using **comparison and contrast** involves looking at both similarities and differences. For example, when you compare and contrast two used cars, you might consider how they are similar in terms of size, body type, and gas mileage, and how they are different in terms of price, color, and engine size. You will find many occasions to use comparison and contrast in the writing you do in college and on the job, as these examples show.

- For a course in *criminal justice,* your instructor asks you to compare organized crime in three societies: Italy, Japan, and Russia.
- As a *computer technician* for a pharmaceutical firm, you are asked to compare and contrast several notebook computers and recommend one the company should purchase.

Most comparison and contrast essays use one of two primary methods of organization: point by point or subject by subject. In subject-by-subject organization, the writer describes the key points or characteristics of one subject before moving on to those of the other subject. Point-by-point organization is used in the following essay by Joseph Sobran, "Patriotism or Nationalism?" Here the author moves back and forth between two subjects (patriotism and nationalism), comparing them on the basis of several key points.

Patriotism or Nationalism?

Joseph Sobran

Joseph Sobran was a child-care worker at a mental hospital in Michigan when he was introduced to William F. Buckley Jr., who invited him to join the staff of the *National Review.* Sobran spent over twenty years at the magazine, including eighteen as senior editor. Sobran currently writes a nationally syndicated newspaper column and publishes *Sobran's,* a newsletter of his own essays and columns.

"Patriotism or Nationalism?" is Sobran's column from October 16, 2001, shortly after the terrorist attacks on New York City and Washington, D.C. As you read, notice the way he begins with a quotation that helps to define the terms he is contrasting. Pay attention, too, to the other quotations — mainly slogans — that he uses to depict the different feelings of nationalists and patriots.

This is a season of patriotism, but also of something that is easily mistaken for patriotism; namely, nationalism. The difference is vital.

1 Thesis: emphasis will be on differences

G.K. Chesterton once observed that Rudyard Kipling, the great poet 2
of British imperialism, suffered from a "lack of patriotism." He explained:
"He admires England, but he does not love her; for we admire things with
reasons, but love them without reasons. He admires England because she
is strong, not because she is English."

Quotation helps explain nationalism

In the same way, many Americans admire America for being strong, 3
not for being American. For them America has to be "the greatest country
on earth" in order to be worthy of their devotion. If it were only the 2nd-
greatest, or the 19th-greatest, or, heaven forbid, "a 3rd-rate power," it
would be virtually worthless.

This is nationalism, not patriotism. Patriotism is like family love. You 4
love your family just for being your family, not for being "the greatest family on earth" (whatever that might mean) or for being "better" than other
families. You don't feel threatened when other people love their families
the same way. On the contrary, you respect their love, and you take comfort in knowing they respect yours. You don't feel your family is enhanced
by feuding with other families.

Uses analogy to family love to explain patriotism

While patriotism is a form of affection, nationalism, it has often been 5
said, is grounded in resentment and rivalry; it's often defined by its enemies and traitors, real or supposed. It is militant by nature, and its typical
style is belligerent. Patriotism, by contrast, is peaceful until forced to
fight.

Point of comparison: nature and style

The patriot differs from the nationalist in this respect too: he can 6
laugh at his country, the way members of a family can laugh at each
other's foibles. Affection takes for granted the imperfection of those it
loves; the patriotic Irishman thinks Ireland is hilarious, whereas the Irish
nationalist sees nothing to laugh about.

Continuation of family analogy

The nationalist has to prove his country is always right. He reduces 7
his country to an idea, a perfect abstraction, rather than a mere home. He
may even find the patriot's irreverent humor annoying.

Patriotism is relaxed. Nationalism is rigid. The patriot may loyally de- 8
fend his country even when he knows it's wrong; the nationalist has to insist that he defends his country not because it's his, but because it's right.
As if he would have defended it even if he hadn't been born to it! The nationalist talks as if he just "happens," by sheer accident, to have been a native of the greatest country on earth — in contrast to, say, the pitiful
Belgian or Brazilian.

Point of comparison: degree of flexibility

Because the patriot and the nationalist often use the same words, they 9
may not realize that they use those words in very different senses. The
American patriot assumes that the nationalist loves this country with an
affection like his own, failing to perceive that what the nationalist really
loves is an abstraction — "national greatness," or something like that. The

Point of comparison: attitude toward each other

American nationalist, on the other hand, is apt to be suspicious of the patriot, accusing him of insufficient zeal, or even "anti-Americanism."

When it comes to war, the patriot realizes that the rest of the world can't be turned into America, because his America is something specific and particular — the memories and traditions that can no more be transplanted than the mountains and the prairies. He seeks only contentment at home, and he is quick to compromise with an enemy. He wants his country to be just strong enough to defend itself.

10   Point of comparison: war and international relations

But the nationalist, who identifies America with abstractions like *freedom* and *democracy*, may think it's precisely America's mission to spread those abstractions around the world — to impose them by force, if necessary. In his mind, those abstractions are universal ideals, and they can never be truly "safe" until they exist, unchallenged, everywhere; the world must be made "safe for democracy" by "a war to end all wars." We still hear versions of these Wilsonian themes. Any country that refuses to Americanize is "anti-American" — or a "rogue nation." For the nationalist, war is a welcome opportunity to change the world. This is a recipe for endless war.

11

In a time of war hysteria, the outraged patriot, feeling his country under attack, may succumb to the seductions of nationalism. This is the danger we face now.

12   Conclusion: puts discussion in context of 9/11 and danger of nationalism

Characteristics of Comparison and Contrast Essays

When writers use comparison and contrast, they consider subjects with characteristics in common, examining similarities, differences, or both. Whether used as the primary pattern of development or alongside another pattern, comparison and contrast can help writers achieve their purpose and make a clear point about their subjects.

Comparison and Contrast Has a Clear Purpose

A comparison and contrast essay usually has one of three purposes: *to express ideas, to inform,* or *to persuade.* In "Patriotism or Nationalism?" the author highlights the differences between the two schools of thought in order to persuade his readers that nationalism is dangerous. "The difference is vital" (para. 1), warns Sobran. Regardless of the purpose of a comparison and contrast essay, it should be made clear to readers.

Comparison and Contrast Considers Shared Characteristics

You have probably heard the familiar expression, "You can't compare apples and oranges." Although it is overused, the cliché makes a useful point about comparisons: You cannot compare two unlike things unless they have something in common. Apples and oranges can be compared if they share at least one characteristic — nutritional value, for instance. When making a comparison, then, a writer needs to choose a **basis of comparison** — the common characteristics on which to base the essay.

A Comparison and Contrast Essay Fairly Examines Similarities, Differences, or Both

Depending on their purpose, writers of comparison and contrast essays may focus on similarities, differences, or both. In an essay intended to *persuade* readers that performers Britney Spears and Jennifer Lopez have much in common in terms of talent and cultural influence, the writer would focus on similarities — hit records, millions of fans, and parts in movies. However, an essay intended to *inform* readers about the singers would probably cover both similarities and differences, discussing the singers' different childhoods or singing styles. In "Patriotism or Nationalism?" Sobran attempts to persuade readers to avoid the "seductions of nationalism" (para. 12) by concentrating on the differences between nationalism and patriotism.

An essay focusing on similarities often mentions a few differences, usually in the introduction, to let readers know the writer is aware of them. Conversely, an essay that focuses on differences might mention a few similarities. This technique gives the writer greater credibility because it indicates that his or her knowledge of the subject is not one-sided.

Whether you cover similarities, differences, or both in an essay, you should strive to treat your subjects fairly. Relevant information should not be purposely omitted to show one subject in a more favorable light. In an essay about Britney Spears and Jennifer Lopez, for instance, you would not leave out information about Spears's charity work in an effort to make Lopez appear to be a nicer person.

Comparison and Contrast Makes a Point

Regardless of the purpose of a comparison and contrast essay, its main point should spark readers' interest rather than bore them with a mechanical listing of similarities or differences. This main point can serve as the thesis, or the thesis can be implied in the writer's choice of details. In "Patriotism or Nationalism?" Sobran states his main point in the first paragraph, signaling to readers that he will concentrate on the differences between the two terms.

An explicit thesis has three functions.

1. It identifies the *subjects* being compared or contrasted.
2. It suggests whether the focus is on *similarities, differences,* or *both*.
3. It states the *main point* of the comparison and contrast.

Notice how the following sample theses meet the above criteria. Note, too, that each thesis suggests why the comparison and contrast is meaningful.

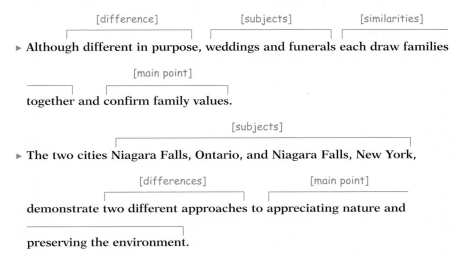

[difference]   [subjects]   [similarities]

▶ **Although different in purpose, weddings and funerals each draw families**

[main point]

together and confirm family values.

[subjects]

▶ **The two cities Niagara Falls, Ontario, and Niagara Falls, New York,**

[differences]   [main point]

demonstrate two different approaches to appreciating nature and

preserving the environment.

Comparison and Contrast Considers a Sufficient Number of Significant Characteristics and Details

A comparison and contrast essay considers various points or characteristics on which to discuss both subjects. These **points of comparison** should be significant as well as relevant to the essay's purpose and thesis. Although the number of points of comparison can vary by topic, usually at least three or four significant points are needed to support a thesis. Each point should be fully described or explained so readers can fully grasp the thesis.

A writer may use sensory details, dialogue, examples, expert testimony, and other kinds of detail in a comparison and contrast essay. Consider the following paragraph:

> Certain events are parallel, but compared with Hugh's, my childhood was unspeakably dull. When I was seven years old, my family moved to North Carolina. When he was seven years old, Hugh's family moved to the Congo. We had a collie and a house cat. They had a monkey and two horses named Charlie Brown and Satan. I threw stones at stop signs. Hugh threw stones at crocodiles. The verbs are the same, but he definitely wins the prize when it comes to nouns and objects. An eventful day for my mother might have involved a trip to the dry cleaner or a conversation with the potato-chip deliveryman. Asked one ordinary Congo afternoon what she'd done with her day, Hugh's mother answered that she and a fellow member of the Ladies' Club had visited a leper colony on the outskirts of Kinshasa. No reason was given for the expedition, though chances are she was staking it out for a future field trip.
>
> DAVID SEDARIS, *Me Talk Pretty One Day*

Notice how Sedaris uses lively and interesting details to contrast his childhood from that of his friend Hugh. Note too that each subject is treated fairly to better support the author's main point about his "dull" childhood.

Visualizing a Comparison and Contrast Essay

Suppose you want to compare two houses (House A and House B) built by the same architect for the purpose of evaluating how the architect's style has changed over time. After brainstorming ideas, you decide to base your essay on these points of comparison: layout, size, building materials, and landscaping. You could organize the essay in one of two ways: subject by subject or point by point.

Subject-by-Subject Organization

In a *subject-by-subject organization*, you would first discuss all points about House A — its layout, size, building materials, and landscaping. Then you would do the same for House B. This pattern is shown in the graphic organizer in Figure 9.1.

Point-by-Point Organization

In a *point-by-point organization*, you would first discuss the layout of each house, then their size, then their building materials, and finally their landscaping. You would go back and forth between the two houses, noting similarities and differences between them on each point of comparison. You can visualize this pattern as shown in the graphic organizer in Figure 9.2.

The essay "Patriotism or Nationalism?" uses a point-by-point organization. Now that you have read the essay, study the graphic organizer for it in Figure 9.3.

Writing a Comparison and Contrast Essay

To write a comparison and contrast essay, use the following steps. Although you will focus on comparing and contrasting subjects, you may need to integrate one or more other patterns of development into your essay.

Planning a Comparison and Contrast Essay

The first step is to choose specific subjects to write about. You may want to compare subjects that are concrete (such as two public figures) or abstract (such as teaching styles or views on an issue). Be sure, in any case, to choose subjects with which you have some firsthand experience or that you are willing to learn about through research. Also choose subjects that interest you. It will be more fun writing about them, and your enthusiasm will enliven your essay.

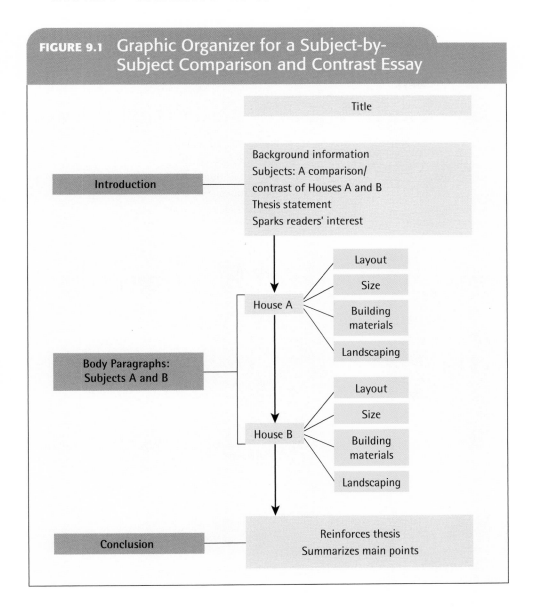

FIGURE 9.1   Graphic Organizer for a Subject-by-Subject Comparison and Contrast Essay

Choosing a Basis of Comparison and a Purpose

After selecting your subjects, you need to establish a basis of comparison and a purpose for writing. To compare or contrast two well-known football players — a quarterback and a linebacker — you could compare them on the basis of the positions they play, describing the skills and training needed for each position. Your purpose in this instance would be to *inform* readers about the two positions.

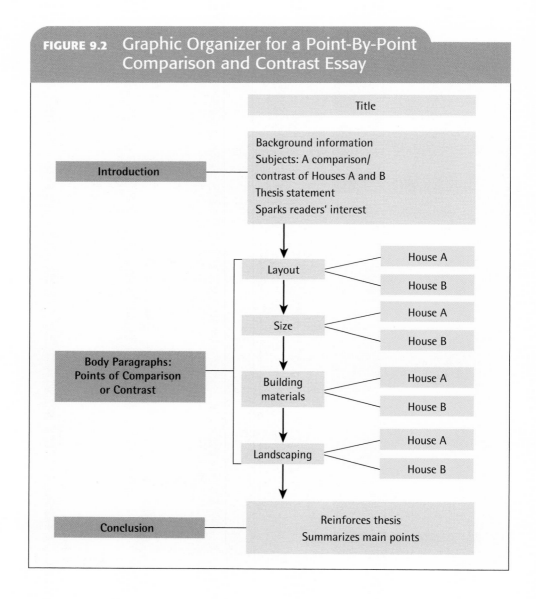

FIGURE 9.2   Graphic Organizer for a Point-By-Point Comparison and Contrast Essay

Alternatively, you could base the comparison on their performances on the field; in this case, your purpose might be to *persuade* readers to accept your evaluation of both players and your opinion on who is the better athlete. Other bases of comparison might be the players' media images, contributions to their respective teams, or service to the community.

Once you have a basis of comparison and a purpose, try to state them clearly in a few sentences. Refer to these sentences throughout the process of writing your essay to keep on track.

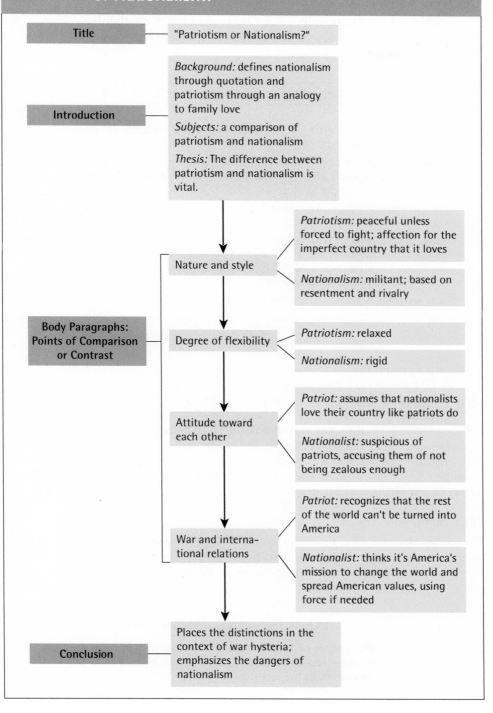

FIGURE 9.3 Graphic Organizer for "Patriotism or Nationalism?"

Title — "Patriotism or Nationalism?"

Introduction —
Background: defines nationalism through quotation and patriotism through an analogy to family love

Subjects: a comparison of patriotism and nationalism

Thesis: The difference between patriotism and nationalism is vital.

Body Paragraphs: Points of Comparison or Contrast —

Nature and style
Patriotism: peaceful unless forced to fight; affection for the imperfect country that it loves
Nationalism: militant; based on resentment and rivalry

Degree of flexibility
Patriotism: relaxed
Nationalism: rigid

Attitude toward each other
Patriot: assumes that nationalists love their country like patriots do
Nationalist: suspicious of patriots, accusing them of not being zealous enough

War and international relations
Patriot: recognizes that the rest of the world can't be turned into America
Nationalist: thinks it's America's mission to change the world and spread American values, using force if needed

Conclusion — Places the distinctions in the context of war hysteria; emphasizes the dangers of nationalism

Discovering Similarities and Differences and Generating Details

The next step is to discover how your two subjects are similar, how they are different, or both. You can approach this task in a number of ways.

Generating Details for a Comparison and Contrast Essay

1. **Create a two-column list of similarities and differences.** Jot down ideas in the appropriate column.
2. **Ask a classmate to help you brainstorm aloud by mentioning only similarities; then counter each similarity with a difference.** Take notes as you brainstorm, or tape-record your session.
3. **For concrete subjects, try visualizing them.** Take notes on what you "see," or draw a sketch of the subjects.
4. **Create a scenario in which your subjects interact.** For example, if your topic is automobiles of the 1920s and 2004, imagine taking your great-grandfather, who owned a Model T Ford, for a drive in a 2004 luxury car. How would he react? What would he say?
5. **Do research on your two subjects at the library or on the Internet.**

For more on brainstorming and other prewriting techniques, see Chapter 2, p. 29.

Keep in mind that your readers will need plenty of details to grasp the similarities and differences between the subjects. Vivid description, interesting examples, and appropriate facts will make your subjects seem real.

To maintain an even balance between the two subjects, do some brainstorming, freewriting, or library or Internet research to gather roughly the same amount of detail for each. This guideline is especially important if your purpose is to demonstrate that Subject A is preferable to or better than Subject B. Readers will become suspicious if you provide plenty of detail about Subject A and only sketchy information about Subject B.

Developing Your Thesis

The thesis statement for a comparison and contrast essay needs to fulfill the three criteria noted earlier: It should identify the subjects; suggest whether you will focus on similarities, differences, or both; and state your main point. In addition, the thesis should tell why your comparison and contrast of the two subjects is important or useful. Look at the following sample thesis statements.

WEAK:	The books by Robert Parker and Sue Grafton are similar.
REVISED:	The novels of Robert Parker and Sue Grafton are popular because readers are fascinated by the intrigues of witty, independent private detectives.

The first thesis is weak because it presents the two subjects in isolation, without placing the comparison within a context or giving readers a reason to care about it. The second thesis provides a basis for comparison and indicates why the similarity is worth reading about. As you develop your thesis, consider what large idea or worthwhile point the comparison demonstrates.

Selecting Points of Comparison

With your thesis in mind, review your notes and try to identify the points or characteristics by which you can best compare your subjects. For example, if your thesis involves evaluating the performance of the two football players, you would probably select various facts and details about their training, the plays they make, and their records. Think of points of comparison as the main similarities or differences that support your thesis. Make sure to have enough points of comparison to support the thesis and enough details to develop those points. If necessary, do additional brainstorming.

Drafting a Comparison and Contrast Essay

Before you begin writing, decide whether you will use a point-by-point or a subject-by-subject organization. To select a method of organization, consider the complexity of your subjects and the length of your essay. You may also need to experiment with the two approaches to see which one works better. It is a good idea to make an outline or draw a graphic organizer at this stage. To experiment with different methods of organization, create a new computer file for each possibility and try each one out.

Here are a few other points to consider when deciding what method of organization to use.

- The subject-by-subject method tends to emphasize the larger picture, whereas the point-by-point method emphasizes details and specifics.
- The point-by-point method often works better for lengthy essays because it keeps both subjects current in the reader's mind.
- The point-by-point method is usually preferable for complicated or technical subjects.

After choosing a method of organization, your next step is to write a first draft. Use the following guidelines.

Guidelines for Writing a Comparison and Contrast Essay

1. **Write an effective introduction.** The introduction should spark readers' interest, present your subjects, state your thesis, and include any background information readers may need.

(Continued)

(Continued)

2. **For a point-by-point essay, work back and forth between the two subjects, generally mentioning the subjects in the same order.** If both subjects share a particular characteristic, then you may want to mention the two subjects together.

3. **For a point-by-point essay, arrange the points of comparison carefully.** Start with the clearest, simplest points and then move on to more complex ones.

4. **For a subject-by-subject essay, cover the same points for both subjects.** Address the points of comparison for each subject in the same order for both halves of your essay.

5. **For a subject-by-subject essay, include a clear statement of transition when you switch from one subject to the other.**

6. **Use analogies.** An **analogy** is a special type of comparison in which a familiar subject is used to explain a less familiar one. For example, a writer could explain the evolution of the universe by comparing it to the stages of a human being's life. In this sense analogies differ from similes and metaphors, in which comparisons are based on a single shared point.

7. **Use transitions to alert readers to the organization of the essay and to shift between subjects or new points of comparison.** To move between subjects, use transitional words and phrases such as *similarly, in contrast, on the one hand . . . on the other hand,* and *not only . . . but also.*

8. **Write a satisfying conclusion.** The conclusion should offer a final comment on the comparison and contrast, reminding readers of your thesis. For a lengthy or complex essay, it is a good idea to summarize the main points as well.

Analyzing and Revising

If possible, set your draft aside for a day or two before rereading and revising it. As you reread, concentrate on your ideas and not on grammar or mechanics. Use the flowchart in Figure 9.4 to guide your analysis of the draft's strengths and weaknesses.

Editing and Proofreading

For more on these and other common errors, see Chapter 4, p. 81.

The last step is to check your revised essay for errors in grammar, spelling, punctuation, and mechanics. In addition, be sure to look for errors that you tend to make in any writing assignments, whether for this class or any other situation. As you edit and proofread your comparison and contrast essay, watch out for the types of errors discussed on page 307.

FIGURE 9.4 Revising a Comparison and Contrast Essay

QUESTIONS

REVISION STRATEGIES

1. Highlight your thesis statement. Does it identify the subjects being compared and state the main point? Does it (or nearby sentences) express a clear purpose — to express ideas, inform, or persuade?

 NO

- Revise your thesis using the suggestions on p. 73.
- Brainstorm a list of reasons why the comparison is important. Make the most promising reason your purpose.
- If you cannot discover why the comparison is important, broaden or narrow your topic or choose a new one.

YES

2. Mark a checkmark ✔ next to the sentences that focus on similarities. Mark an ✘ next to the sentences that focus on differences. Do you examine similarities and differences fairly? Is each similarity or difference significant, and does each one support the thesis?

 NO

- Add details to provide a more balanced examination.
- If you have trouble thinking of similar or opposing points, conduct research or ask a classmate to suggest ideas.
- Delete any similarities or differences that do not directly support your thesis.
- Review your prewriting to see if you overlooked any significant details about your subjects.

YES

3. *Write* the basis of comparison at the top of your paper. Is the basis of comparison clear? Does it clearly relate to your thesis?

 NO

- Ask a friend or classmate to help you think of a clear or new basis for comparison.

YES

4. Draw a circle around the shared characteristics on which you base the essay. Do you include at least one characteristic for each paragraph?

 NO

- Use *who, what, where, when,* and *how* questions to generate characteristics about your subjects or to find those common to both.

 YES

(Continued)

FIGURE 9.4 *(Continued)*

QUESTIONS

REVISION STRATEGIES

5. <u>Underline</u> the topic sentence of each paragraph. Does each paragraph have a topic sentence? Is each paragraph focused on a separate point or shared characteristic?

 NO

- Follow the guidelines for writing clear topic sentences (p. 55).
- Split paragraphs that focus on more than one point or characteristic.
- Consider combining closely related paragraphs.

 YES

6. Draw a <u>wavy underline</u> under the concrete details in each paragraph. Are there enough details to make your comparisons vivid and interesting? Do all details relate to the topic sentences and shared characteristics?

NO

- Add or delete details as necessary.
- Review your prewriting to see if you overlooked any significant points or details.
- Research your subject to generate additional details or examples.

 YES

7. Draw a brief diagram of the organization of the essay. Did you use either point-by-point or subject-by-subject organization throughout the entire essay? Is that clear to the reader?

NO

- Study your diagram to find inconsistencies or gaps.
- Reorganize your essay, using only one method of organization consistently.

 YES

8. Draw a box around your introduction and conclusion. Does the introduction provide a context for the comparison? Is the conclusion satisfying and relevant to the comparison?

NO

- Revise the introduction to meet the guidelines in Chapter 3.
- Review what the comparison suggests; then revise the conclusion.
- Propose an action or way of thinking that is appropriate in light of the comparison.
- Revise the conclusion to meet the guidelines in Chapter 3.

YES

9. Print out another draft to edit and proofread before turning your essay in.

Editing Tips and Troublespots: Comparison and Contrast

1. **Look at adjectives and adverbs and their degrees of comparison** — *positive* (the form that describes without comparing), *comparative,* and *superlative.* Make sure to change the form of adjectives and adverbs when comparing two items (comparative), and three or more items (superlative). The following examples show how adjectives and adverbs change forms.

	ADJECTIVES	ADVERBS
POSITIVE	sharp	early
COMPARATIVE	sharper	earlier
SUPERLATIVE	sharpest	earliest

▸ Both *The Village* and *The Sixth Sense* were suspenseful movies, but I liked

   The Sixth Sense ~~best.~~ *better*

▸ George, Casey, and Bob all play basketball badly, but Bob's game is ~~worse.~~ *worst*

2. **Use correlative conjunctions properly.** Make sure that items linked by correlative conjunctions (conjunctions used in pairs such as *either . . . or, neither . . . nor, not only . . . but also*) are in the same grammatical form.

▸ The Grand Canyon is not only a spectacular tourist attraction but also

   ~~scientists consider it~~ a useful geological record. *for scientists.*

Students Write

Heather Gianakos was a first-year student when she wrote the following comparison and contrast essay for her composition course. Although she has always enjoyed the two styles of cooking she chose to discuss, she needed to do some research in the library and on the Internet to learn more about their history. As you read the essay, observe how Gianakos integrates information from sources into her essay.

Border Bites

Heather Gianakos

Chili peppers, tortillas, tacos: All these foods belong to the styles of cooking
known as Mexican, Tex-Mex, and Southwestern. These internationally popular styles

Title: suggests topic in interesting, indirect way

1

often overlap; sometimes it can be hard to tell which style a particular dish belongs to. Two particular traditions of cooking, however, play an especially important role in the kitchens of Mexico and the American Southwest: native-derived Mexican cooking ("Mexican"), and Anglo-influenced Southwestern cooking, particularly from Texas ("Southwestern"). The different traditions and geographic locations of the inhabitants of Mexico and of the Anglo-American settlers in the Southwest have resulted in subtle, flavorful differences between the foods featured in Mexican and Southwestern cuisine.

Thesis statement: focus will be on differences

Many of the traditions of Southwestern cooking grew out of difficult situations -- cowboys and ranchers cooking over open fires, for example. Chili, which can contain beans, beef, tomatoes, corn, and many other ingredients, was a good dish to cook over a campfire because everything could be combined in one pot. Dry foods, such as beef jerky, were a convenient way to solve food storage problems and could be easily tucked into saddlebags. In Mexico, <u>by contrast,</u> fresh fruits and vegetables such as avocados and tomatoes were widely available and did not need to be dried or stored. They could be made into spicy salsa and guacamole. Mexicans living in coastal areas could also enjoy fish and lobster dishes <u>(Jamison and Jamison 5)</u>.

First point of comparison: availability of ingredients

Transitional phrase alerts reader to shift between subjects

2

<u>Corn</u> has been a staple in the American Southwest and Mexico since the time of the Aztecs, who made tortillas (flat, unleavened bread, originally made from stone-ground corn and water) similar to the ones served in Mexico today <u>(Jamison and Jamison 5)</u>. Southwesterners, often of European descent, adopted the tortilla but often prepared it with wheat flour, which was easily available to them. Wheat-flour tortillas are now used in both Mexican and Southwestern cooking, but corn is usually the primary grain in dishes with pre-colonial origins. Tamales (whose name derives from a word in Nahuatl, the Aztec group of languages) are a delicious example: A hunk of cornmeal dough, sometimes combined with ground meat, is wrapped in corn husks and steamed. In Southwestern cooking, corn is often used for leavened corn bread, which is made with corn flour rather than cornmeal and can be flavored with jalapeños or back bacon.

Second point of comparison: use of corn

Sources provide historical background

3

Meat of various kinds is often the centerpiece of both Mexican and Southwestern tables. However, although <u>chicken,</u> beef, and pork are staples in both traditions, they are often prepared quite differently. Fried chicken rolled in flour and dunked into sizzling oil or fat is a popular dish throughout the American Southwest. In traditional Mexican cooking, <u>however,</u> chicken is often cooked more slowly, in stews or baked dishes, with a variety of seasonings, including ancho chiles, garlic, and onions.

Third point of comparison: preparation of chicken

Transitional phrase

4

Ever since Southwestern cattle farming began with the early Spanish missions in Texas, <u>beef</u> has been eaten both north and south of the border. In Southwestern cooking, steak--flank, rib eye, or sirloin--grilled quickly and served rare is often a chef's

Fourth point of comparison: preparation of beef

5

crowning glory. In Mexican cooking, beef may be combined with vegetables and spices and rolled into a fajita or served ground in a taco. For a Mexican food purist, in fact, the only true fajita is made from skirt steak, although Mexican food as it is served in the United States often features chicken fajitas.

In Texas and the Southwest United States, barbecued <u>pork ribs</u> are often prepared in barbecue cookoffs, similar to chili-cooking competitions (Raven 1). However, while the BBQ is seen as a Southwestern specialty, barbecued ribs as they are served in Southwestern-themed restaurants today actually come from a Hispanic and Southwest Mexican tradition dating from the days before refrigeration: Since pork fat, unlike beef fat, has a tendency to become rancid, pork ribs were often marinated in vinegar and spices and then hung to dry. Later the ribs were basted with the same sauce and grilled (Campa 278). The resulting dish has become a favorite both north and south of the border, although in Mexican cooking, where beef is somewhat less important than in Southwestern cooking, pork is equally popular in many other forms, such as chorizo sausage.

6   Fifth point of comparison: preparation of pork

Sources provide details

Cooks in San Antonio or Albuquerque would probably tell you that the food they cook is as much Mexican as it is Southwestern. Regional cuisines in such areas of the Southwest as New Mexico, southern California, and Arizona feature elements of both traditions; chimichangas, deep-fried burritos, actually originated in Arizona (Jamison and Jamison 11). Food lovers who sample regional specialties, however, will note, and savor, the contrast between the spicy, fried or grilled, beef-heavy style of Southwestern food and the richly seasoned, corn- and tomato-heavy style of Mexican food.

7   Conclusion: refers back to regional differences discussed in introduction and summarizes differences in taste

Works Cited

Campa, Arthur L. *Hispanic Culture in the Southwest.* Norman: U of Oklahoma P, 1979.

Jamison, Cheryl Alters, and Bill Jamison. *The Border Cookbook.* Boston: Harvard Common, 1995.

Raven, John. "Competition Barbecuing." *Texas Cooking* Apr. 1998. 9 June 1998 <http://www.texascooking.com/features/apr98ravencompetition.htm>.

Responding to "Students Write"

1. What is Gianakos's purpose in writing the essay? How effectively does she present and support her thesis?

2. What method of organization does Gianakos use?

3. Consider Gianakos's points of comparison. How effective is she in presenting details to support each point? What types of examples and sensory details describe each characteristic?

4. How does Gianakos's use of sources contribute to the essay?

Reading a Comparison and Contrast Essay

Reading a comparison and contrast essay is somewhat different from reading other kinds of essays. First, the essay contains two or more subjects, instead of one. Second, the subjects are being compared, contrasted, or both, so you must follow the author's points of comparison between or among them. Use the following guidelines to read comparison and contrast essays effectively.

What to Look for, Highlight, and Annotate

Understanding the Reading

- Read the essay once to get an overall sense of how it develops. Determine whether it uses point-by-point or subject-by-subject organization. Knowing the method of organization will help you move through the essay more easily.
- Review the essay by drawing a graphic organizer (see the graphic organizers on pp. 299 and 300). This activity will help you learn and recall the key points.

Examining the Characteristics of Comparison and Contrast Essays

- Identify and highlight the thesis statement, if it is stated explicitly. Use it to guide your reading: What does it tell you about the essay's purpose, direction, and organization?
- As you read, watch for the points of comparison that the writer makes. Highlight each point as you discover it.
- Identify whether each point of comparison focuses on similarities, differences, or both.

How to Find Ideas to Write About

To respond to or write about a comparison and contrast essay, consider the following strategies.

- Compare the subjects by using a different basis of comparison. If, for example, an essay compares or contrasts athletes in various sports on the basis of salary, you could compare them according to the training required for each sport.
- For an essay that emphasizes differences, consider writing about similarities, and vice versa. For example, in response to an essay on the differences between two late-night television hosts, you might write about their similarities.
- To write an essay that examines one point of comparison in more depth, you might do research to discover further information or interview an expert on the topic.

We've Got the Dirt on Guy Brains

Dave Barry

Dave Barry, who holds an English degree from Haverford College, began his professional writing career covering local events for a Pennsylvania newspaper. In 1983 he began writing a humor column for the *Miami Herald* that appeared in more than five hundred newspapers; Barry stopped writing the column in 2004. Barry has written twenty-five books; plays lead guitar in the Rock Bottom Remainders, a rock band made up of well-known writers such as Stephen King and Amy Tan; and received a Pulitzer Prize for Commentary in 1988.

"We've Got the Dirt on Guy Brains" originally appeared in November 2003. As you read, pay attention to the comparisons Barry draws between male and female brains and the "evidence" he uses to back up his humorous points. In addition, notice how he presents and refutes "opposing viewpoints" (supposedly from irate readers of a previous column).

Focus on Understanding   Read to discover what the author is trying to convey about the way men think versus the way women think.

Focus on the Topic   In class or in your journal, discuss differences that you have noticed between the thinking patterns of men and women.

1   I like to think that I am a modest person. (I also like to think that I look like Brad Pitt naked, but that is not the issue here.)

2   There comes a time, however, when a person must toot his own personal horn, and for me, that time is now. A new book has confirmed a theory that I first proposed in 1987, in a column explaining why men are physically unqualified to do housework. The problem, I argued, is that men — because of a tragic genetic flaw — cannot see dirt until there is enough of it to support agriculture. This puts men at a huge disadvantage against women, who can detect a single dirt molecule 20 feet away.

3   This is why a man and a woman can both be looking at the same bathroom commode, and the man — hindered by Male Genetic Dirt Blindness (MGDB) — will perceive the commode surface as being clean enough for heart surgery or even meat slicing; whereas the woman can't even *see* the commode, only a teeming, commode-shaped swarm of bacteria. A woman can spend two hours cleaning a toothbrush holder and still not be totally satisfied; whereas if you ask a man to clean the entire New York City subway system, he'll go down there with a bottle of Windex and a single paper towel, then emerge 25 minutes later, weary but satisfied with a job well done.

When I wrote about Male Genetic Dirt Blindness, many irate readers complained that I was engaging in sexist stereotyping, as well as making lame excuses for the fact that men are lazy pigs. All of these irate readers belonged to a gender that I will not identify here, other than to say: Guess what, ladies? There is now scientific proof that I was right. 4

This proof appears in a new book titled *What Could He Be Thinking? How a Man's Mind Really Works.* I have not personally read this book, because, as a journalist, I am too busy writing about it. But according to an article by Reuters,° the book states that a man's brain "takes in less sensory detail than a woman's, so he doesn't see or even feel the dust and household mess in the same way." Got that? We can't see or feel the mess! We're like: "What snow tires in the dining room? Oh, *those* snow tires in the dining room." 5

And this is only one of the differences between men's and women's brains. Another difference involves a brain part called the "cingulate gyrus," which is the sector where emotions are located. The Reuters article does not describe the cingulate gyrus, but presumably in women it is a structure the size of a mature cantaloupe, containing a vast quantity of complex, endlessly recalibrated emotional data involving hundreds, perhaps thousands, of human relationships; whereas in men it is basically a cashew filled with NFL highlights. 6

In any event, it turns out that women's brains secrete more of the chemicals "oxytocin" and "serotonin," which, according to biologists, cause humans to feel they have an inadequate supply of shoes. No, seriously, these chemicals cause humans to want to bond with other humans, which is why women like to share their feelings. Some women (and here I am referring to my wife) can share as many as three days' worth of feelings about an event that took eight seconds to actually happen. We men, on the other hand, are reluctant to share our feelings, in large part because we often don't have any. Really. Ask any guy: A lot of the time, when we look like we're thinking, we just have this low-level humming sound in our brains. That's why, in male-female conversations, the male part often consists entirely of him going "hmmmm." This frustrates the woman, who wants to know what he's really thinking. In fact, what he's thinking is, literally, "hmmmm." 7

So anyway, according to the Reuters article, when a man, instead of sharing feelings with his mate, chooses to lie on the sofa, holding the remote control and monitoring 750 television programs simultaneously by changing the channel every one-half second (pausing slightly longer for programs that feature touchdowns, fighting, shooting, car crashes or bosoms) his mate should *not* come to the mistaken conclusion that he is an insensitive jerk. In fact, he is responding to scientific biological brain chemicals that require him to behave this way for scientific reasons, as detailed in the scientific book *What Could He Be Thinking? How a Man's Mind Really Works,* which I frankly cannot recommend highly enough. 8

In conclusion, no *way* was that pass interference. 9

Reuters: an international news and financial information service providing reports and stories to the media

Understanding the Reading

1. How does the author describe himself?
2. What was Barry's original claim regarding men's ability to do housework? What new proof does he offer to back up this claim?
3. What information does Barry give from the book he mentions? What other sources does he cite in his essay?
4. Give two examples of the types of situations in which Barry feels men and women differ in their thinking.

Visualizing the Reading

Evaluate the essay's content and organization by completing the following graphic organizer.

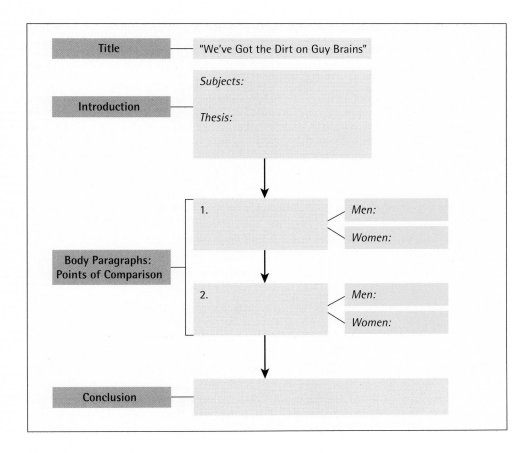

Examining the Characteristics of Comparison and Contrast Essays

1. Consider Barry's purpose in writing. What basis of comparison does he use to convey his message?

2. What is Barry's thesis? What characteristics about men and women does he emphasize to support this idea?

3. Evaluate the examples. Does Barry give enough examples to compare and contrast each characteristic? Are his details relevant and interesting? Explain.

4. Does Barry organize his essay point by point or subject by subject? Would the essay be equally effective if the other method were used? Why or why not?

Building Your Word Power

For a definition of al-lusion and imagery, see the chart of commonly used language features on p. 21.

1. Explain the allusion to Brad Pitt in paragraph 1.

2. Barry describes the "cingulate gyrus" as a "cantaloupe" and a "cashew" (para. 6). Explain the effectiveness of these images in the context of the essay.

3. Explain the meaning of each of the following words as it is used in the reading: *modest* (para. 1), *teeming* (3), *irate* (4), *recalibrated* (6), and *secrete* (7). Refer to your dictionary as needed.

Building Your Critical Thinking Skills: Humor

When encountering humor in an essay, readers must evaluate the purpose and appropriateness of the statements that are intended to be funny. Writers use humor in different ways: to entertain, to lighten the tone of an otherwise serious essay, or to expose the negative side of an issue through *sarcasm* — bitter or dark humor. If you do not appreciate an author's humor, do not be concerned. Humor is often a matter of personal taste. Use your skills in identifying and evaluating humor to answer the following questions.

1. Why do you think Barry uses humor in this essay? How does the use of humor relate to the subject matter?

2. How would the essay be different if it had been written without humor? Would it be as effective? Explain.

3. Do you think this essay is funny? Why or why not? Support your answer.

Reacting to the Reading: Discussion and Journal Writing

1. Discuss your reaction to Barry's essay. Do you agree with his assessment of male and female thinking patterns?

2. Barry uses humor to discuss the perennial "battle of the sexes." How does humor help or hinder discussions about sensitive issues?

3. In class or in your journal, explain your personal living style. Are you a "neat freak" or a slob, or somewhere in between? Has this ever caused a problem with your roommate or siblings? Explain.

Applying Your Skills: Writing Assignments

1. Paragraph Assignment. Write a paragraph comparing two people you know in terms of their attitudes toward "dirt."

2. Barry claims that men are unqualified to do housework. What other activities do you think either men or women seem less qualified to do than the opposite sex? Write an essay describing one such activity and comparing and contrasting men's and women's ability to perform it.

3. Find a few comic strip artists or political cartoonists that you like. Read their work in newspapers and magazines, and select two favorites. Then write an essay that compares and contrasts the two by focusing on similarities, differences, or both.

4. Combining Patterns. Write an essay describing the division of housework in your childhood home or in the household you currently maintain. Who was or is responsible for chores such as cooking, cleaning, and yard work? How was this decided? Include an argument for or against this type of arrangement.

5. Internet Research. Visit the online site for *The Onion* humor news magazine at www.theonion.com/ or another site that spoofs current events. Find a story in this humor magazine that is based on a real current event, and then use cnn.com or another online news source to find the nonsatirical version of the story. Write an essay describing the differences and similarities in the two accounts. Be sure to give background information on the story and explain how the humorous version gives insight or makes a political comment.

A Taste of Snow

Jeanne Wakatsuki Houston

Jeanne Wakatsuki Houston, an American of Japanese descent, is the award-winning author of *Farewell to Manzanar* (1973), *Don't Cry, It's Only Thunder* (1984), and *Beyond Manzanar* (1985), from which the following essay is taken. She was a child during World War II, when Japanese Americans — under suspicion after the bombing of Pearl Harbor — were forced to sell their property and belongings and relocate to internment camps for the duration of the war. Her family spent those years at Manzanar, a crowded camp surrounded by barbed wire in the cold high-desert climate of northern California.

In "A Taste of Snow," Houston compares the Christmas when she first saw snow, while the family was interned at Manzanar, with a happier Christmas spent at the family home in Ocean Park in the warm southern part of California. As you read, notice the key points Houston makes about each place and how her two concluding paragraphs pull together the comparison of the two Christmases.

Focus on Content   Read to discover in what ways the two places described in the essay are different.

Focus on the Topic   In class or in your journal, discuss your memories of two celebrations of the same holiday in different years. How were they the same? How did they differ?

Owens Valley: arid valley located in northern California near the Sierra Nevada Mountains

I first saw snow one Christmas when I lived in the high desert of Owens Valley,° California. I was nine years old. It was during the Second World War, the first winter my family and I spent at Manzanar. When the crystal flakes floated down, like translucent coconut chips dancing in the breeze, I ran out into the clear area between the barracks, twirling and dancing and opening my mouth to catch the powdery ice. The snow reminded me of cotton candy, wispy and delicate, and gone with one whisk of the tongue.

I was surprised by the sharp coldness of the air and somehow disappointed that such beauty had its price to be paid — icy feet and hands, and uncomfortable wetness when the snow melted upon contact with my clothes and face. Still, the utter loveliness of this new phenomenon was so overpowering I soon forgot my discomfort.

getas: Japanese wooden raised sandals for outdoor wear

Other people began coming out of the barracks into a transformed world. Some carried brightly colored Japanese parasols and wore high wooden getas° to raise their stockinged feet above the snow. It was odd not to hear the "kata-kata" clatter of wooden clogs scraping across sand and gravel. The blanket of snow muffled sound and thickened the thin planed roofs of the barracks, softening the stark landscape of white on white. It was strangely soothing to me, silent and tranquil. I found myself moved to tears.

This particular imprint in my memory is easily explained. Before being sent 4 to Manzanar we lived in Ocean Park, on Dudley Avenue, a block from the beach. Ocean Park Pier was my playground. All the kids in the neighborhood played ball and skated along the wide cement promenade that bordered the beach from Ocean Park to Venice.

Memories of Ocean Park are warm ones of sunshine, hot days on the beach, 5 building sand castles, playing Tarzan and Jungle Girl, jumping off lifeguard stands and spraining ankles. Fourth of July was a balmy evening of crowds milling around the pier waiting for fireworks to spray the sky with luminous explosives. Easter was as colorful as the many-hued eggs the local service club buried in the sand for the kids to uncover. And Christmas was just another version of this type of buoyant, high-spirited celebration my family enjoyed before the war. In my memory Christmas morning seemed always sunny and clear. Strolling along the promenade in my orange-flowered dress and white high-topped shoes, pushing the doll carriage Santa left under the big tree in our living room, I proudly displayed myself and my gifts as did the other children of the neighborhood. My oldest brother Bill, who was then in his twenties, walked with me and helped me feed popcorn to the pigeons warbling and pecking around our feet. Then he rushed me off in his old blue roadster to visit his girlfriend Molly, who played the violin while he sang, and I slept.

The Manzanar War Relocation Center, photographed sometime between 1942 and 1945.

Like a story within a story, or a memory within a memory, I cannot think 6
of one memorable Christmas, but of these two. They are yin and yang, each necessary to appreciate the other. I don't remember Christmas trees in Manzanar.
But we gathered driftwood from the creeks that poured down from the nearby
Sierras and across the high desert. With these we improvised. In my mind's eye
they co-exist: a lush, brilliantly lit fir tree; and a bare manzanita limb embellished with origami cranes.

To this day, when I travel in the high country, I can cry seeing nature's ex- 7
quisite winter garb and remembering my first taste of snow.

Understanding the Reading

1. Why was the author living in Owens Valley?
2. Why was Houston so interested in the snow?
3. What was Houston's life like before she went to Manzanar?

Visualizing the Reading

Analyze Houston's use of subject-by-subject organization by identifying the different
points of comparison in her essay. The first one has been done for you.

Points of Comparison	Manzanar	Ocean Park
Location	The high desert of Owens Valley, California	Dudley Avenue, a block from the beach
Temperature/weather		
Impression of landscape		
Christmas		

Examining the Characteristics of Comparison and Contrast Essays

1. Comparison and contrast essays usually have one of three purposes: to express
   ideas, to inform, or to persuade. Is Houston's purpose clear? If not, why do you
   think she wrote the essay?

2. Does the author use an implied or explicit thesis? Identify how the thesis is revealed, and evaluate its effectiveness.

3. Evaluate the subject-by-subject organization. Would the comparison be as effective
   with a point-by-point organization? Why or why not?

4. Evaluate the number and variety of details that the author uses. To what senses does Houston appeal through these details? Give examples.

5. What other patterns of development does Houston use? How do these contribute to the essay?

Building Your Word Power

1. What does the author mean by the figure of speech "beauty had its price to be paid" (para. 2)?

2. Houston states that the two Christmases exist "like . . . a memory within a memory" (para. 6). What does this simile mean?

3. Explain the meaning of each of the following words as it is used in the reading: *planed* (para. 3), *balmy* (5), *luminous* (5), *buoyant* (5), and *embellished* (6). Refer to your dictionary as needed.

For a definition of simile, *see the chart of commonly used language features on p. 21.*

Building Your Critical Thinking Skills: Symbolism

A common feature of language that writers often use is **symbolism.** A symbol is a thing, word, or idea that suggests more than its literal meaning. For example, water often implies purification, and elderly characters often suggest wisdom. To recognize symbols, look for objects that are given a particular or unusual emphasis. Be sure not only to analyze the obvious symbols in a reading, but also to consider the symbolic meanings of other events, people, or objects that are mentioned. In this way, you can better understand the author's main point. Using your knowledge of symbols, answer the following questions.

1. Consider the significance of Christmas in the reading. What does it symbolize for the author?

2. What does snow symbolize for the author?

3. Houston mentions several specific places. Name these locations, and identify what they might symbolize in the context of the reading.

Reacting to the Reading: Discussion and Journal Writing

1. Discuss the importance of holidays in our society. What drives our desire to celebrate?

2. In class or in your journal, discuss the importance of place. Do you have strong memories of a particular place from your childhood? If possible, compare this memory to what you now know about this place.

Applying Your Skills: Writing Assignments

1. **Paragraph Assignment.** In a paragraph, briefly compare two days that had very different types of weather. You might contrast a cold, rainy afternoon with a hot, sultry evening, for example. For each, include a brief explanation of how the weather affected your mood.

2. Write an essay about two holiday or birthday celebrations that you have experienced. Compare and contrast the two events using relevant and interesting details. Be sure to establish a thesis based on the nature of the events. For example, you might choose the best and worst birthday parties you have ever had, stating as your thesis that not all birthdays are happy. Use your conclusion to offer some insight into celebrations in general.

3. Create a list of your favorite places. Write an essay comparing and/or contrasting two of them. Mention how these places make you feel, what memories they provoke, and details about how they look and significant events that happened there in the past.

4. **Combining Patterns.** Houston vividly recalls her first encounter with snow. Write an essay describing in detail the first time you saw some natural phenomenon, event, or place that had a lasting impression on you. Using sensory details, explain what was special about this occurrence, using comparisons to other "first" encounters to highlight the differences and to explain why this one was especially memorable.

5. **Internet Research.** Using an Internet browser, find two Web sites devoted to Manzanar, such as the two National Park Service Web sites for the Manzanar National Historic Site: www.nps.gov/manz/home.htm and www.nps.gov/manz/index.htm. Look over the sites carefully, making notes about their purpose and content. Then write a comparison and contrast essay about the two sites. Be sure to include examples that would help someone decide which one is better for planning a visit, conducting research, or developing a visual image of the setting. Conclude with your thoughts on the use of the Internet to inform the public about Manzanar.

East vs. West: One Sees the Big Picture, the Other Is Focused

Sharon Begley

Sharon Begley spent twenty-five years working for *Newsweek* magazine, beginning as a science writer and eventually holding the position of general editor. She has won numerous awards for articles discussing complex scientific concepts in clear, understandable language. She is currently science editor for the *Wall Street Journal*, where this article originally appeared in 2003.

In "East vs. West," Begley explains a surprising new theory that human beings do not all think and understand the world in the same way. Notice how she uses vivid examples, ranging from personal observations to the results of scientific studies, to clarify the differences between Eastern and Western views of the world. Note also that she includes evidence that cross-cultural understanding can reduce differences in thinking.

Focus on Understanding   As you read, identify the new theory among scholars of human thought.

Focus on the Topic   In class or in your journal, write about the differences you perceive among people of different cultures.

You ask two new acquaintances to tell you about themselves. The Japanese gent describes himself as "outgoing with his family," "competitive on the soccer field" and "serious at work." The Briton doesn't parse it so finely, saying he is "friendly, intellectual and goal-driven."

Then you ask each to decide which two — of a panda, a monkey and a banana — go together. The Japanese man selects the monkey and the banana; the Brit, the panda and the monkey.

Like many scholars of human thought since at least Hume° and Locke,° today's cognitive psychologists tend to be "universalists," assuming that everyone perceives, thinks and reasons the same way. "There has long been a widespread belief among philosophers and, later, cognitive scientists that thinking the world over is basically the same," says psychologist Howard Gardner of Harvard University in Cambridge, Mass. Although there have always been dissenters, the prevailing wisdom held that a Masai° hunter, a corporate raider and a milkmaid all see, remember, infer and think the same way.

But an ever-growing number of studies challenge this assumption. "Human cognition is not everywhere the same," concludes psychologist Richard E. Nisbett of the University of Michigan, Ann Arbor, in his new book, "The Geography of Thought: How Asians and Westerners Think Differently . . . and

Hume: David Hume (1711–1776), an influential Scottish philosopher; **Locke:** John Locke (1632–1704), a British philosopher, physician, and political activist

Masai: East African tribe located primarily in Kenya and Tanzania

321

Why." Instead, he says, "the characteristic thought processes of Asians and Westerners differ greatly."

The book compares people from East Asia (Korea, China and Japan) with Westerners (from Europe, the British Commonwealth and North America).   5

As the monkey-panda example shows, Westerners typically see categories (animals) where Asians typically see relationships (monkeys eat bananas). Such differences in thinking can trip up business and political relationships.   6

The cognitive differences start with basic sensory perception. In one study, Michigan's Taka Masuda showed Japanese and American students pictures of aquariums containing one big fast-moving fish, several other finned swimmers, plants, rock and bubbles. What did the students recall? The Japanese spontaneously remembered 60% more background elements than did the Americans. They also referred twice as often to relationships involving background objects ("the little frog was above the pink rock").   7

The difference was even more striking when the participants were asked which, of 96 objects, had been in the scene. When the test object was shown in the context of its original surroundings, the Japanese did much better at remembering correctly whether they had seen it before. For the Americans, including the background was no help; they had never even seen it.   8

"Westerners and Asians literally see different worlds," says Prof. Nisbett. "Westerners pay attention to the focal object, while Asians attend more broadly — to the overall surroundings and to the relations between the object and the field." These generalizations seem to hold even though Eastern and Western countries each represent many different cultures and traditions.   9

Because of their heightened perception of surroundings, East Asians attribute causality less to actors than to context. Little wonder, then, that West and East see North Korea's nuclear threats very differently. "Understanding how other people think and see the world is crucial in international disputes," says psychologist Robert Sternberg of Yale University in New Haven, Conn.   10

Divergent East-West thinking also has produced some tense business conflicts. In the 1970s, Japanese refiners, having signed a contract to buy sugar from Australia for $160 a ton, asked to renegotiate after world prices dropped. The Aussies refused. To the Asians, changing circumstances dictated changes in agreements; to the Westerners, a deal was a deal.   11

One striking east-west difference centers on drawing inferences. Imagine a line graph plotting economic growth in which the rate of growth accelerates (that is, the line gets steeper to the right). Researchers asked college students in Ann Arbor and Beijing whether they thought the growth rate would go up, go down, or stay the same. The Americans were more likely to predict a continued rise, extrapolating trends, than were the Chinese, who saw trends as likely to reverse.   12

Westerners prefer abstract universal principles; East Asians seek rules appropriate to a situation. For example, when researchers in the Netherlands asked people what to do about an employee whose work has been subpar for a year after 15 years of exemplary service, more than 75% of Americans and Canadians said to let her go; only 20% of Singaporeans and Koreans agreed.   13

Cognitive differences likely originate in child rearing and social practices, but 14 are far from hard-wired: Asians living in the West and Westerners in Asia often find that their cognitive style goes native. Similarly, bicultural people, like those in Hong Kong with its British and Chinese history, show thinking patterns intermediate between East and West. That's a model that workplaces might do well to emulate, says Prof. Nisbett: The more cultural diversity and, hence, thinking styles in a workforce, the likelier it is to see problems clearly and solve them.

Understanding the Reading

1. What do modern cognitive psychologists assume about human thought?
2. What did the aquarium experiment show?
3. How do Eastern and Western ways of thinking differ?
4. According to the author, how are thinking patterns affected in people living away from their native cultures? How might an understanding of this be of benefit to businesses?

Visualizing the Reading

To evaluate the points of comparison between Easterners and Westerners in Begley's article and to analyze the supporting evidence provided for each, complete the following chart. The first one has been done for you.

Point of Comparison	Supporting Evidence
1. **Sensory perception:** Japanese remember more background elements than do Americans.	Study conducted in Michigan in which students were shown photos of aquariums
2. **Remembering objects:**	
3. **Business dealings:**	
4. **Drawing inferences:**	
5. **Abstract principles vs. situational rules:**	

Examining the Characteristics of Comparison and Contrast Essays

1. Consider the author's purpose: What does Begley want to demonstrate about Eastern and Western thought? Is her purpose clear? Explain.
2. Identify the author's thesis. Evaluate its effectiveness in identifying the subjects being compared and in clarifying the focus of the comparison: similarities, differences, or both.

3. What main ideas make up the basis of Begley's comparison? Does she provide enough points of comparison? Are they sufficiently explained? What do the details of the various studies add to the comparison?

4. What background information about human thought does Begley provide? Is it sufficient for you to understand the comparison? If not, what additional material would you have liked?

5. Evaluate Begley's organization. Is her essay organized point by point or subject by subject? Would a different type of organization be more or less effective? Explain your answer.

Building Your Word Power

*For a definition of **idiom**, see the chart of commonly used language features on p. 21.*

1. Explain the phrase "parse it so finely" as used in paragraph 1. If the meaning is not clear within the context of the paragraph, look up *parse* in your dictionary.

2. Explain the idiom "hard-wired" as used in paragraph 14.

3. Explain the meaning of each of the following words as it is used in the reading: *cognitive* (para. 3), *prevailing* (3), *causality* (10), *extrapolating* (12), and *emulate* (14). Refer to your dictionary as needed.

Building Your Critical Thinking Skills: Evaluating Sources

Authors often use information from other sources to support their main ideas. Such information usually comes from research studies, personal experience, quotations, observations, and other articles, books, and news reports. Because not all sources are equally reliable, readers should evaluate all outside sources used by an author. Begin by determining where the source material came from and whether it can be trusted. For example, a scientific study published by a known university would likely be more trustworthy than the opinion voiced in a newspaper editorial. Consider also whether the source applies directly to the subject of the essay. Using your skills in evaluating source material, answer the following questions.

1. What types of source material does Begley use? How reliable do you think these sources are? How might you verify them or find more information about them?

2. How does the choice of sources relate to Begley's purpose and tone?

Reacting to the Reading: Discussion and Journal Writing

1. Discuss Begley's thesis. In your experience, have you come across these differences in thinking between Easterners and Westerners?

2. Explore how cultural differences might affect international relations or business dealings.

3. In class or in your journal, discuss your sensory perception. What types of things do you notice about people or situations? What types of things do you ignore or overlook? Mention a few examples of times when this was an advantage or a disadvantage.

Applying Your Skills: Writing Assignments

1. **Paragraph Assignment.** Write a paragraph describing one or more ways in which you differ from or are similar to a friend, classmate, or family member in how you approach a task. You might write about how you study for an exam or how you clean your room, for example.

2. Write an essay comparing and contrasting the thought processes of two people you know well. Consider these factors: Are they logical? Do they make snap decisions? Do they weigh facts or rely on emotions? Do they focus on facts or see the big picture? Be sure to include background information about your subjects, a clear thesis, and sufficient details arranged point by point or subject by subject.

3. Think of a place where you frequently walk, and list what you remember seeing in that area. Then go to the actual place and take notes as you walk, recording everything you see. Compare the list of what you remembered to the list of what is really there. Analyze your results. Do you focus on details such as buildings or plants, or do you see the whole picture — what type of neighborhood it is, for example? Write an essay that compares and contrasts your results. Conclude with what you learned from this experiment.

4. **Combining Patterns.** Begley states that differences in thinking can affect business relationships. Write a narrative essay about a work or school experience in which you describe how someone's way of thinking caused a misunderstanding or differed from your own. Compare or contrast the actual handling of the situation to the way you might have managed it to achieve a better outcome.

5. **Internet Research.** Diet differs tremendously between Western and Eastern countries. Visit the Food and Nutrition Information Center at www.nal.usda.gov/fnic, or find another online site to review the USDA food pyramid. Compare the food allowances with the Asian Diet Pyramid (located in the "ethnic/cultural food guide pyramid" section of the FNIC site). Write a comparison and contrast essay about the differences and similarities between these two diets. In your opinion, is one diet healthier than another? Explain your view.

A Case of "Severe Bias"

Patricia Raybon

Patricia Raybon, a former reporter and feature writer for the *Denver Post,* is currently an associate professor at the University of Colorado's School of Journalism and Mass Communication in Boulder. She is also an award-winning author whose personal essays have appeared in the *New York Times Magazine, USA Today,* and other publications, as well as on National Public Radio's *Weekend Edition.* She won a Christopher Award for her book, *My First White Friend* (1996).

This selection originally appeared in 1989 in *Newsweek.* As you read, consider the way Raybon contrasts media images of black Americans with the reality of their lives, emphasizing what black Americans are *not.* Notice that she also compares media images of black and white Americans to determine the messages conveyed about each group.

Focus on Understanding   Read to discover what the "severe bias" is.

Focus on the Topic   In class or in your journal, write about biases in the media. Are certain types of media more likely than others to perpetuate certain stereotypes?

This is who I am not. I am not a crack addict. I am not a welfare mother. I am not illiterate. I am not a prostitute. I have never been in jail. My children are not in gangs. My husband doesn't beat me. My home is not a tenement. None of these things defines who I am, nor do they describe the other black people I've known and worked with and loved and befriended over these forty years of my life.   1

Nor does it describe most of black America, period.   2

Yet in the eyes of the American news media, this is what black America is: poor, criminal, addicted, and dysfunctional. Indeed, media coverage of black America is so one-sided, so imbalanced that the most victimized and hurting segment of the black community — a small segment, at best — is presented not as the exception but as the norm. It is an insidious practice, all the uglier for its blatancy.   3

In recent months, I have observed a steady offering of media reports on crack babies, gang warfare, violent youth, poverty, and homelessness — and in most cases, the people featured in the photos and stories were black. At the same time, articles that discuss other aspects of American life — from home buying to medicine to technology to nutrition — rarely, if ever, show blacks playing a positive role, or for that matter, any role at all.   4

Day after day, week after week, this message — that black America is dysfunctional and unwhole — gets transmitted across the American landscape. Sadly, as a result, America never learns the truth about what is actually a wonderful, vibrant, creative community of people.   5

Most black Americans are *not* poor. Most black teenagers are *not* crack addicts. Most black mothers are *not* on welfare. Indeed, in sheer numbers, more *white* Americans are poor and on welfare than are black. Yet one never would deduce that by watching television or reading American newspapers and magazines.   6

Why do the American media insist on playing this myopic, inaccurate picture game? In this game, white America is always whole and lovely and healthy, while black America is usually sick and pathetic and deficient. Rarely, indeed, is black America ever depicted in the media as functional and self-sufficient. The free press, indeed, as the main interpreter of American culture and American experience, holds the mirror on American reality — so much so that what the media say is *is,* even if it's not that way at all. The media are guilty of a severe bias and the problem screams out for correction. It is worse than simply lazy journalism, which is bad enough; it is inaccurate journalism.   7

For black Americans like myself, this isn't just an issue of vanity — of wanting to be seen in a good light. Nor is it a matter of closing one's eyes to the very real problems of the urban underclass — which undeniably is disproportionately black. To be sure, problems besetting the black underclass deserve the utmost attention of the media, as well as the understanding and concern of the rest of American society.   8

But if their problems consistently are presented as the *only* reality for blacks, any other experience known in the black community ceases to have validity, or to be real. In this scenario, millions of blacks are relegated to a sort of twilight zone,° where who we are and what we are isn't based on fact but on image and perception. That's what it feels like to be a black American whose lifestyle is outside of the aberrant behavior that the media present as the norm.   9

For many of us, life is a curious series of encounters with white people who want to know why we are "different" from other blacks — when, in fact, most of us are only "different" from the now common negative images of black life. So pervasive are these images that they aren't just perceived as the norm, they're *accepted* as the norm.   10

I am reminded, for example, of the controversial Spike Lee film *Do the Right Thing*° and the criticism by some movie reviewers that the film's ghetto neighborhood isn't populated by addicts and drug pushers — and thus is not a true depiction.   11

In fact, millions of black Americans live in neighborhoods where the most common sights are children playing and couples walking their dogs. In my own inner-city neighborhood in Denver — an area that the local press consistently describes as "gang territory" — I have yet to see a recognizable "gang" member or any "gang" activity (drug dealing or drive-by shootings), nor have I been the victim of "gang violence."   12

twilight zone: reference to Rod Serling's classic science fiction/fantasy television show (1959–1964) that featured strange and bizarre events

Do the Right Thing: 1989 Spike Lee movie about a hot summer day in a Brooklyn neighborhood when racial tensions explode into violence

Yet to students of American culture — in the case of Spike Lee's film, the 13 movie reviewers — a black, inner-city neighborhood can only be one thing to be real: drug-infested and dysfunctioning. Is this my ego talking? In part, yes. For the millions of black people like myself — ordinary, hard-working, law-abiding, tax-paying Americans — the media's blindness to the fact that we even exist, let alone to our contributions to American society, is a bitter cup to drink. And as self-reliant as most black Americans are — because we've had to be self-reliant — even the strongest among us still crave affirmation.

I want that. I want it for my children. I want it for all the beautiful, healthy, 14 funny, smart black Americans I have known and loved over the years.

And I want it for the rest of America, too. 15

I want America to know us — all of us — for who we really are. To see us in 16 all of our complexity, our subtleness, our artfulness, our enterprise, our specialness, our loveliness, our American-ness. That is the real portrait of black America — that we're strong people, surviving people, capable people. That may be the best-kept secret in America. If so, it's time to let the truth be known.

Understanding the Reading

1. What do we learn about the author's life from the reading?
2. What types of media outlets does Raybon accuse of being biased?
3. Cite several examples of the bias that Raybon describes.
4. Explain why, according to Raybon, negative images of blacks are damaging to black people.

Examining the Characteristics of Comparison and Contrast Essays

1. Identify Raybon's thesis. Consider whether the author is writing to *express ideas,* to *inform,* or to *persuade.* What does she want readers to understand about the media portrayal of black people as a result of reading this essay?
2. How does the author introduce the subjects of this comparison and contrast essay? What background information does she provide?
3. In her comparison, the author identifies all the things she and other black Americans are *not.* Is this a useful technique? Why or why not?
4. Does the author use point-by-point or subject-by-subject organization? Evaluate its effectiveness.
5. What points of comparison does Raybon offer to support her thesis? Does she concentrate on differences, similarities, or both? Give examples.

Visualizing the Reading

Study the photo on the next page. Raybon's essay contrasts the images of black people as presented by the media with the reality of most black Americans' experiences.

Create a list of features of this family's lifestyle that Raybon would agree is typical of black Americans. How might she have used this photo as an example to support her thesis?

Building Your Word Power

1. Explain the different connotative meanings of the phrase "black America" in the context of the first three paragraphs.

2. What does the phrase "free press" mean in paragraph 7? How does it "[hold] the mirror on American reality"?

3. Explain the meaning of each of the following words as it is used in the reading: *insidious* (para. 3), *blatancy* (3), *myopic* (7), *aberrant* (9), and *enterprise* (16). Refer to your dictionary as needed.

*For a definition of **connotative meaning,** see the chart of commonly used language features on p. 21.*

Building Your Critical Thinking Skills: Cause and Effect Relationships

When authors want to explain how certain actions relate to each other, they use **cause and effect** relationships. For example, in an essay comparing the pros and cons of land lines versus cell phones, a writer might begin by describing the benefit of having a cell phone on hand in the case of a flat tire. The writer might then contrast this with accident statistics illustrating the dangerous consequences of using a cell phone while driving. Cause and effect relationships can be used to answer simple questions or to delve into motives and complex reasons. When you encounter this type of writing, evaluate the relationship to make sure that the causes and effects really do relate to each other and that they are relevant to the main thesis. Using your knowledge of cause and effect relationships, answer the following questions.

1. According to Raybon, what is the effect of the "severe bias" in the media?
2. Read the last paragraph of the essay. What effect does the author hope her essay will have on America?

Reacting to the Reading: Discussion and Journal Writing

1. Discuss the images of black Americans and other people of color in movies, television, and advertising. Would you say that Raybon's complaints against the news media apply to other popular media as well? Explain.
2. In class or in your journal, discuss the news sources you rely on. How do you find out what is happening on campus and in your city, country, and world? How do you know whether this news is reliable?

Applying Your Skills: Writing Assignments

1. **Paragraph Assignment.** Choose a family member, teacher, or other important person in your life whose role in the family or job is often stereotyped by the media. In a paragraph, briefly compare how this person is similar to or different from the media stereotype (mother, younger sibling, coach, etc.).
2. Think of a message that the media transmit to Americans. (To get ideas, watch television commercials or look through articles and advertisements in magazines.) For example, the media portray desirable women as thin and good-looking. Write an essay comparing the message with the reality in American life.
3. Write an essay using comparison and contrast about biases toward college students that everyday working people don't encounter. Choose a basis of comparison, and write a thesis that makes the purpose of your essay clear. Include an explanation of the source of the bias, and discuss how these attitudes may be overcome.
4. **Combining Patterns.** Write an essay defining yourself by explaining what you are *not*, as Raybon did in paragraphs 1 and 6. Compare or contrast this definition of yourself with how you imagine others perceive you. Use relevant and interesting examples, relying on narrative or descriptive techniques, to support your thesis.
5. **Internet Research.** Conduct some online research on the effects of the media on popular culture. One in-depth source is the Web site for "The Merchants of Cool: A Report on the Marketing of Pop Culture for Teenagers," a 2001 PBS *Frontline* production, at www.pbs.org/wgbh/pages/frontline/shows/cool. Research the techniques by which the media market "cool" to young people, and then write an essay, using examples from your research, that compares and contrasts the different techniques used to market pop culture. Include a thesis that takes a stance for or against the types of marketing described in your essay.

Sex, Lies, and Conversation

Deborah Tannen

Deborah Tannen was born in Brooklyn, New York, in 1945. She holds a Ph.D. in linguistics from the University of California, Berkeley, and is currently a professor at Georgetown University. Tannen has written several award-winning and best-selling books about communication and language, including *I Only Say This Because I Love You* (2000), in which she examines communication between family members. In addition to writing for many national publications, she has appeared on several major television programs and has lectured to students and business people all around the world.

The following essay first appeared in the *Washington Post* in 1990. Notice how the author begins with a personal example, immediately catching the reader's interest. Pay attention also to her use of supporting evidence.

Focus on Understanding   Read to discover how communication styles differ between men and women.

Focus on the Topic   In class or in your journal, discuss differences you have observed between the way men and women communicate.

I was addressing a small gathering in a suburban Virginia living room — a women's group that had invited men to join them. Throughout the evening, one man had been particularly talkative, frequently offering ideas and anecdotes, while his wife sat silently beside him on the couch. Toward the end of the evening, I commented that women frequently complain that their husbands don't talk to them. This man quickly concurred. He gestured toward his wife and said, "She's the talker in our family." The room burst into laughter; the man looked puzzled and hurt. "It's true," he explained. "When I come home from work I have nothing to say. If she didn't keep the conversation going, we'd spend the whole evening in silence." 1

This episode crystallizes the irony that although American men tend to talk more than women in public situations, they often talk less at home. And this pattern is wreaking havoc with marriage. 2

The pattern was observed by political scientist Andrew Hacker in the late '70s. Sociologist Catherine Kohler Riessman reports in her new book *Divorce Talk* that most of the women she interviewed — but only a few of the men — gave lack of communication as the reason for their divorces. Given the current divorce rate of nearly 50 percent, that amounts to millions of cases in the United States every year — a virtual epidemic of failed conversation. 3

In my own research, complaints from women about their husbands most often focused not on tangible inequities such as having given up the chance for 4

331

a career to accompany a husband to his, or doing far more than their share of daily life-support work like cleaning, cooking, social arrangements, and errands. Instead, they focused on communication: "He doesn't listen to me." "He doesn't talk to me." I found, as Hacker observed years before, that most wives want their husbands to be, first and foremost, conversational partners, but few husbands share this expectation of their wives.

In short, the image that best represents the current crisis is the stereotypical cartoon scene of a man sitting at the breakfast table with a newspaper held up in front of his face, while a woman glares at the back of it, wanting to talk. 5

Linguistic Battle of the Sexes

How can women and men have such different impressions of communication in marriage? Why the widespread imbalance in their interests and expectations? 6

In the April issue of *American Psychologist,* Stanford University's Eleanor Maccoby reports the results of her own and others' research showing that children's development is most influenced by the social structure of peer interactions. Boys and girls tend to play with children of their own gender, and their sex-separate groups have different organizational structures and interactive norms.° 7

norms: behavior that is typical of a group or culture

I believe these systematic differences in childhood socialization make talk between women and men like cross-cultural communication, heir to all the attraction and pitfalls of that enticing but difficult enterprise. My research on men's and women's conversations uncovered patterns similar to those described for children's groups. 8

For women, as for girls, intimacy is the fabric of relationships, and talk is the thread from which it is woven. Little girls create and maintain friendships by exchanging secrets; similarly, women regard conversation as the cornerstone of friendship. So a woman expects her husband to be a new and improved version of a best friend. What is important is not the individual subjects that are discussed but the sense of closeness, of a life shared, that emerges when people tell their thoughts, feelings, and impressions. 9

Bonds between boys can be as intense as girls', but they are based less on talking, more on doing things together. Since they don't assume talk is the cement that binds a relationship, men don't know what kind of talk women want, and they don't miss it when it isn't there. 10

Boys' groups are larger, more inclusive, and more hierarchical, so boys must struggle to avoid the subordinate position in the group. This may play a role in women's complaints that men don't listen to them. Some men really don't like to listen, because being the listener makes them feel one-down, like a child listening to adults or an employee to a boss. 11

But often when women tell men, "You aren't listening," and the men protest, "I am," the men are right. The impression of not listening results from misalignments in the mechanics of conversation. The misalignment begins as 12 soon as a man and a woman take physical positions. This became clear when I studied videotapes made by psychologist Bruce Dorval of children and adults talking to their same-sex best friends. I found that at every age, the girls and women faced each other directly, their eyes anchored on each other's faces. At every age, the boys and men sat at angles to each other and looked elsewhere in the room, periodically glancing at each other. They were obviously attuned to each other, often mirroring each other's movements. But the tendency of men to face away can give women the impression they aren't listening even when they are. A young woman in college was frustrated: Whenever she told her boyfriend she wanted to talk to him, he would lie down on the floor, close his eyes, and put his arm over his face. This signaled to her, "He's taking a nap." But he insisted he was listening extra hard. Normally, he looks around the room, so he is easily distracted. Lying down and covering his eyes helped him concentrate on what she was saying.

Analogous to the physical alignment that women and men take in conversation is their topical alignment. The girls in my study tended to talk at length about one topic, but the boys tended to jump from topic to topic. The second-grade girls exchanged stories about people they knew. The second-grade boys teased, told jokes, noticed things in the room, and talked about finding games to play. The sixth-grade girls talked about problems with a mutual friend. The sixth-grade boys talked about 55 different topics, none of which extended over more than a few turns. 13

Listening to Body Language

Switching topics is another habit that gives women the impression men aren't listening, especially if they switch to a topic about themselves. But the evidence of the 10th-grade boys in my study indicates otherwise. The 10th-grade boys sprawled across their chairs with bodies parallel and eyes straight ahead, rarely looking at each other. They looked as if they were riding in a car, staring out the windshield. But they were talking about their feelings. One boy was upset because a girl had told him he had a drinking problem, and the other was feeling alienated from all his friends. 14

Now, when a girl told a friend about a problem, the friend responded by asking probing questions and expressing agreement and understanding. But the boys dismissed each other's problems. Todd assured Richard that his drinking was "no big problem" because "sometimes you're funny when you're off your butt." And when Todd said he felt left out, Richard responded, "Why should you? You know more people than me." 15

Women perceive such responses as belittling and unsupportive. But the boys seemed satisfied with them. Whereas women reassure each other by implying, "You shouldn't feel bad because I've had similar experiences," men do so by implying, "You shouldn't feel bad because your problems aren't so bad." 16

There are even simpler reasons for women's impression that men don't listen. Linguist Lynette Hirschman found that women make more listener- 17 noise, such as "mhm," "uhuh," and "yeah," to show "I'm with you." Men, she found, more often give silent attention. Women who expect a stream of listener-noise interpret silent attention as no attention at all.

Women's conversational habits are as frustrating to men as men's are to 18 women. Men who expect silent attention interpret a stream of listener-noise as overreaction or impatience. Also, when women talk to each other in a close, comfortable setting, they often overlap, finish each other's sentences, and anticipate what the other is about to say. This practice, which I call "participatory listenership," is often perceived by men as interruption, intrusion, and lack of attention.

A parallel difference caused a man to complain about his wife, "She just 19 wants to talk about her own point of view. If I show her another view, she gets mad at me." When most women talk to each other, they assume a conversationalist's job is to express agreement and support. But many men see their conversational duty as pointing out the other side of an argument. This is heard as disloyalty by women, and refusal to offer the requisite support. It is not that women don't want to see other points of view, but that they prefer them phrased as suggestions and inquiries rather than as direct challenges.

In his book *Fighting for Life*, Walter Ong points out that men use "agonis- 20 tic" or warlike, oppositional formats to do almost anything; thus discussion becomes debate, and conversation a competitive sport. In contrast, women see conversation as a ritual means of establishing rapport. If Jane tells a problem and June says she has a similar one, they walk away feeling closer to each other. But this attempt at establishing rapport can backfire when used with men. Men take too literally women's ritual "troubles talk," just as women mistake men's ritual challenges for real attack.

The Sounds of Silence

These differences begin to clarify why women and men have such different ex- 21 pectations about communication in marriage. For women, talk creates intimacy. Marriage is an orgy of closeness: you can tell your feelings and thoughts, and still be loved. Their greatest fear is being pushed away. But men live in a hierarchical world, where talk maintains independence and status. They are on guard to protect themselves from being put down and pushed around.

This explains the paradox of the talkative man who said of his silent wife, 22 "She's the talker." In the public setting of a guest lecture, he felt challenged to show his intelligence and display his understanding of the lecture. But at home, where he has nothing to prove and no one to defend against, he is free to remain silent. For his wife, being home means she is free from the worry that something she says might offend someone, or spark disagreement, or appear to be showing off; at home she is free to talk.

The communication problems that endanger marriage can't be fixed by me- 23 chanical engineering. They require a new conceptual framework about the role of talk in human relationships. Many of the psychological explanations that have become second nature may not be helpful, because they tend to blame either women (for not being assertive enough) or men (for not being in touch with their feelings). A sociolinguistic approach by which male–female conversation is seen as cross-cultural communication allows us to understand the problem and forge solutions without blaming either party.

Once the problem is understood, improvement comes naturally, as it did to the young woman and her boyfriend who seemed to go to sleep when she wanted to talk. Previously, she had accused him of not listening, and he had refused to change his behavior, since that would be admitting fault. But then she learned about and explained to him the differences in women's and men's habitual ways of aligning themselves in conversation. The next time she told him she wanted to talk, he began, as usual, by lying down and covering his eyes. When the familiar negative reaction bubbled up, she reassured herself that he really was listening. But then he sat up and looked at her. Thrilled, she asked why. He said, "You like me to look at you when we talk, so I'll try to do it." Once he saw their differences as cross-cultural rather than right and wrong, he independently altered his behavior. 24

Women who feel abandoned and deprived when their husbands won't listen to or report daily news may be happy to discover their husbands trying to adapt once they understand the place of small talk in women's relationships. But if their husbands don't adapt, the women may still be comforted that for men, this is not a failure of intimacy. Accepting the difference, the wives may look to their friends or family for that kind of talk. And husbands who can't provide it shouldn't feel their wives have made unreasonable demands. Some couples will still decide to divorce, but at least their decisions will be based on realistic expectations. 25

In these times of resurgent ethnic conflicts, the world desperately needs cross-cultural understanding. Like charity, successful cross-cultural communication should begin at home. 26

Understanding the Reading

1. What does the opening anecdote about the man at a women's group illustrate?
2. What differences in communication are observable between young girls and boys?
3. In what ways does body language differ between men and women? How do these differences affect communication between the sexes?
4. What can men and women do to overcome the communication problems described by Tannen?

Visualizing the Reading

Tannen includes different types of evidence to support her thesis. Analyze and evaluate the purpose of the supporting evidence by completing the following chart. The first one has been done for you.

Evidence	Purpose
Reference to political scientist Andrew Hacker (para. 3)	Gives legitimacy to the thesis and demonstrates that the thesis is not a new idea
Sociologist Catherine Kohler Riessman's observations from her book *Divorce Talk* (para. 3)	
The author's own research (para. 4)	
American Psychologist article by Stanford University's Eleanor Maccoby (para. 7)	
Psychologist Bruce Dorval's videotapes (para. 12)	
The author's own research (para. 13–16)	
Linguist Lynette Hirschman's research (para. 17)	
Reference to *Fighting for Life* by Walter Ong (para. 20)	

Examining the Characteristics of Comparison and Contrast Essays

1. What is Tannen's thesis about gender communication? Is it effectively placed? Why or why not?

2. What method of organization does Tannen use? Why do you think she chose it? Would the essay be as effective with a different organizational plan? Explain.

3. Identify the points of comparison that Tannen uses to support her thesis. Does she focus on similarities, differences, or both? Does she treat her subjects fairly? Explain.

4. In explaining the communication differences between men and women, Tannen explores the causes of these differences. How does this information strengthen the essay?

Building Your Word Power

For a definition of jargon, see the chart of commonly used language features on p. 21.

1. What sort of image does the phrase "wreaking havoc" (para. 2) bring to mind?

2. Tannen, a linguist, uses some linguistic jargon even though she is writing for the general public. Highlight these terms and evaluate their effectiveness. Are they a benefit or a detriment to your understanding of the essay?

3. Explain the meaning of each of the following words as it is used in the reading: *crystallizes* (para. 2), *hierarchical* (11), *requisite* (19), *paradox* (22), and *resurgent* (26). Refer to your dictionary as needed.

Building Your Critical Thinking Skills: Original Sources

Sometimes when authors are reporting on research for a general audience, they do not provide full citations for the work — that is, the original sources — they mention. For example, they may cite a journal or an author, but not the date of the publication, title, or other information usually provided in academic or scholarly texts. While authors sometimes omit full bibliographic information because they assume most readers will not be interested in reading the original source, some readers would like to do further research. Original sources can often be accessed through library databases and catalogs. For a book, the library catalog is the place to start. For journal articles, use a journal database to obtain the full text or to locate the specific issue. Using your knowledge of finding original sources, answer the following questions.

1. Review the list of sources included in the Visualizing the Reading activity on p. 335. Next to each one, indicate whether full (e.g., author, title, date, publisher), incomplete (e.g., author and title but no date or publisher), or no source information has been given.

2. Using the same list, jot down your ideas on how to find the original sources mentioned in the essay. For example, you might use your library catalog to locate Catherine Kohler Riessman's book *Divorce Talk*.

Reacting to the Reading: Discussion and Journal Writing

1. Discuss the importance of clear communication in a relationship you have experienced.

2. Discuss how Tannen's findings are similar to or different from those of Dave Barry as expressed in "We've Got the Dirt on Guy Brains" (p. 311).

3. In class or in your journal, describe an incident from your own experience that confirms or contradicts Tannen's findings.

Applying Your Skills: Writing Assignments

1. **Paragraph Assignment.** Analyze your own friendships with members of the opposite sex. In a paragraph, explain whether your communication fits the pattern Tannen describes.

2. Tannen provides many points of comparison to support her thesis. Choose one of them and expand it into a comparison and contrast essay of your own. Develop the point of comparison by using information from your own experiences. For example, you could show how differences in body language do indeed reflect a common communication pattern.

3. Think of a college class in which discussion is encouraged or required. What differences do you notice between how men and women in the class communicate? Consider how they phrase and ask questions, their body language in class, how

they address and interact with the professor, length and tone of comments, and so forth. Write a comparison and contrast essay reporting your findings.

4. Use Tannen's essay as a basis for observing how men and women communicate around you. Write a comparison and contrast essay that examines what you observed in relation to what Tannen describes. For each of Tannen's points of comparison, explain whether you agree or disagree with her findings on the basis of this exercise and your own knowledge and experience.

5. Combining Patterns. Tannen's essay addresses differences in communication between men and women. Consider how communication is similar or different between two other groups — parents and teenagers, employers and employees, or twenty-year-olds and forty-year-olds, for example. Then write an essay that defines each group and compares or contrasts their differences or similarities. Include descriptive details and narration to help readers "see" your subjects. Conclude with possible reasons for the differences you observed.

6. Internet Research. Using a search engine, look for articles on communication between men and women. For example, the *Purdue News* includes a short article on this subject at http://news.uns.purdue.edu/UNS/html4ever/2004/040217.Mac George.sexroles.html. After choosing an article, write an essay that compares and contrasts it with Tannen's report. Are their findings similar or different? If they disagree, why might their findings differ?

Classification and Division: Explaining Categories and Parts

WRITING QUICK START

S tudy this photograph of a grocery store. Notice how similar items on the shelves are grouped together. Think of a favorite store that you frequent, and write a paragraph describing for someone who has never been there how the different categories of merchandise are arranged. Be sure to identify all the categories clearly.

What Are Classification and Division?

The paragraph you have just written uses **classification,** a method of development that explains the categories or groups into which a given subject can be divided. You use classification every day to organize things and ideas. Your dresser drawers and kitchen cabinets are probably organized by categories — with socks and sweatshirts in different drawers, and pots and glasses in different cabinets. Classification, then, is a process of sorting people, things, or ideas into groups or categories to make them more understandable. For example, your college classifies course offerings by schools, divisions, and departments. Imagine how difficult it would be to find courses in a catalog or schedule if it were arranged alphabetically instead of by categories.

Division is similar to classification; but instead of involving numerous items being grouped into categories, division involves *one* item being broken down into parts. Thus, for example, the humanities department at your college may be divided into English, modern languages, and philosophy, and the modern language courses might be further divided into Spanish, French, Chinese, and Russian. Division is closely related to process analysis (see Chapter 8) because they both involve breaking things down into smaller parts.

A classification or division essay explains a topic by describing types or parts. For example, a classification essay might explore types of advertising: direct mail, radio, television, newspaper, and so forth. A division essay might describe the parts of an art museum: exhibit areas, museum store, visitor services desk, and the like. You will find many occasions to use these patterns of development in the writing you do in college and the workplace, as these examples show.

- For a course in *anatomy and physiology*, you are asked to review the structure and parts of the human ear by identifying the function of each part.

- While working as a *facilities planner*, you are asked to conduct a feasibility study of several new sites. You begin by sorting the sites into three categories: within-state, out-of-state, and out-of-country.

In the following essay, Judith Viorst classifies the kinds of friendship she has experienced or observed.

Friends, Good Friends — Such Good Friends

Judith Viorst

Judith Viorst has written poetry, nonfiction, a novel, and twelve children's books, including *Alexander and the Terrible, Horrible, No Good, Very Bad Day* (1972). She is a graduate of the Washington Psychoanalytic Institute and has won several awards for her work, which often addresses psychological aspects of human behavior. Viorst was a contributing editor for over twenty-five years at *Redbook*, where this essay first appeared in 1977. She lives in Washington, D.C.

In "Friends, Good Friends — Such Good Friends," Viorst categorizes types of friendships. Note that even though she differentiates friends according to the depth of feelings and trust they share, she also accords each type some importance. As you read, notice how many examples Viorst includes, both from her own experience and from the experiences of others.

Women are friends, <u>I once would have said</u>, when they totally love and support and trust each other, and bare to each other the secrets of their souls, and run — no questions asked — to help each other, and tell harsh truths to each other (no, you can't wear that dress unless you lose ten pounds first) when harsh truths must be told.

Women are friends, <u>I once would have said</u>, when they share the same affection for Ingmar Bergman, plus train rides, cats, warm rain, charades, Camus, and hate with equal ardor Newark and Brussels sprouts and Lawrence Welk and camping.

In other words, <u>I once would have said</u> that a friend is a friend all the way, but now I believe that's a narrow point of view. For the friendships I have and the friendships I see are conducted at many levels of intensity, serve many different functions, meet different needs, and range from those as all-the-way as the friendship of the soul sisters mentioned above to that of the most nonchalant and casual playmates.

Consider these varieties of friendship:

1. Convenience friends. These are women with whom, if our paths weren't crossing all the time, we'd have no particular reason to be friends: a next-door neighbor, a woman in our car pool, the mother of one of our children's closest friends, or maybe some mommy with whom we serve juice and cookies each week at the Glenwood Co-op Nursery.

Convenience friends are convenient indeed. They'll lend us their cups and silverware for a party. They'll drive our kids to soccer when we're sick. They'll take us to pick up our car when we need a lift to the garage. They'll even take our cats when we go on vacation. As we will for them.

But we don't, with convenience friends, ever come too close or tell too much; we maintain our public face and emotional distance. "Which means," says Elaine, "that I'll talk about being overweight but not about being depressed. Which means I'll admit being mad but not blind with rage. Which means that I might say that we're pinched this month but never that I'm worried sick over money."

But which doesn't mean that there isn't sufficient value to be found in these friendships of mutual aid, in convenience friends.

Margin annotations:

1 — Introduction: presents contrast to her previous way of looking at friends

2 — Details such as Bergman (Swedish film director), Camus (French writer), and Welk (host of a popular TV show of the 60s and 70s) help define friends

3 — Thesis

4

5 — Category 1

6 — Concrete examples

7

8

Category 2

2. Special-interest friends. These friendships aren't intimate, and they needn't involve kids or silverware or cats. Their value lies in some interest jointly shared. And so we may have an office friend or a yoga friend or a tennis friend or a friend from the Women's Democratic Club. 9

Effective use of dialogue

"I've got one woman friend," says Joyce, "who likes, as I do, to take psychology courses. Which makes it nice for me — and nice for her. It's fun to go with someone you know and it's fun to discuss what you've learned, driving back from the classes." And for the most part, she says, that's all they discuss. 10

"I'd say that what we're doing is *doing* together, not being together," Suzanne says of her Tuesday-doubles friends. "It's mainly a tennis relationship, but we play together well. And I guess we all need to have a couple of playmates." 11

I agree. 12

My playmate is a shopping friend, a woman of marvelous taste, a woman who knows exactly *where* to buy *what*, and furthermore is a woman who always knows beyond a doubt what one ought to be buying. I don't have the time to keep up with what's new in eyeshadow, hemlines, and shoes and whether the smock look is in or finished already. But since (oh, shame!) I care a lot about eyeshadow, hemlines, and shoes, and since I don't *want* to wear smocks if the smock look is finished, I'm very glad to have a shopping friend. 13

Category 3

Use of narrative to
explain the category

3. Historical friends. We all have a friend who knew us when . . . maybe way back in Miss Meltzer's second grade, when our family lived in that three-room flat in Brooklyn, when our dad was out of work for seven months, when our brother Allie got in that fight where they had to call the police, when our sister married the endodontist from Yonkers, and when, the morning after we lost our virginity, she was the first, the only, friend we told. 14

The years have gone by and we've gone separate ways and we've little in common now, but we're still an intimate part of each other's past. And so whenever we go to Detroit we always go to visit this friend of our girlhood. Who knows how we talked before our voice got un-Brooklyned. Who knows what we ate before we learned about artichokes. And who, by her presence, puts us in touch with an earlier part of ourself, a part of ourself it's important never to lose. 15

"What this friend means to me and what I mean to her," says Grace, "is having a sister without sibling rivalry. We know the texture of each other's lives. She remembers my grandmother's cabbage soup. I remember the way her uncle played the piano. There's simply no other friend who remembers those things." 16

Category 4

4. Crossroads friends. Like historical friends, our crossroads friends are important for *what was* — for the friendship we shared at a crucial, now past, time of life. A time, perhaps, when we roomed in college to- 17 gether; or worked as eager young singles in the Big City together; or went together, as my friend Elizabeth and I did, through pregnancy, birth, and that scary first year of new motherhood.

Concrete examples

Crossroads friends forge powerful links, links strong enough to endure with not much more contact than once-a-year letters at Christmas. And out of respect for those crossroad years, for those dramas and dreams we once shared, we will always be friends.

18

5. Cross-generational friends. Historical friends and crossroads friends seem to maintain a special kind of intimacy — dormant but always ready to be revived — and though we may rarely meet, whenever we do connect, it's personal and intense. Another kind of intimacy exists in the friendships that form across generations in what one woman calls her daughter–mother and her mother–daughter relationships.

19 Category 5

Evelyn's friend is her mother's age — "but I share so much more than I ever could with my mother" — a woman she talks to of music, of books and of life. "What I get from her is the benefit of her experience. What she gets — and enjoys — from me is a youthful perspective. It's a pleasure for both of us."

20 Use of dialogue gives concrete example

I have in my own life a precious friend, a woman of 65 who has lived very hard, who is wise, who listens well; who has been where I am and can help me understand it; and who represents not only an ultimate ideal mother to me but also the person I'd like to be when I grow up.

21 Personal example

In our daughter role we tend to do more than our share of self-revelation; in our mother role we tend to receive what's revealed. It's another kind of pleasure — playing wise mother to a questing younger person. It's another very lovely kind of friendship.

22

6. Part-of-a-couple friends. Some of the women we call our friends we never see alone — we see them as part of a couple at couples' parties. And though we share interests in many things and respect each other's views, we aren't moved to deepen the relationship. Whatever the reason, a lack of time or — and this is more likely — a lack of chemistry, our friendship remains in the context of a group. But the fact that our feeling on seeing each other is always, "I'm *so* glad she's here" and the fact that we spend half the evening talking together says that this too, in its own way, counts as a friendship.

23 Category 6

(Other part-of-a-couple friends are the friends that came with the marriage, and some of these are friends we could live without. But sometimes, alas, she married our husband's best friend; and sometimes, alas, she *is* our husband's best friend. And so we find ourself dealing with her, somewhat against our will, in a spirit of what I'll call *reluctant* friendship.)

24 Inclusion of exception to the category adds credibility

7. Men who are friends. I wanted to write just of women friends, but the women I've talked to won't let me — they say I must mention man–woman friendships too. For these friendships can be just as close

25 Category 7

and as dear as those that we form with women. Listen to Lucy's description of one such friendship:

Contrast to female
friendships

"We've found we have things to talk about that are different from what he talks about with my husband and different from what I talk about with his wife. So sometimes we call on the phone or meet for lunch. There are similar intellectual interests — we always pass on to each other the books that we love — but there's also something tender and caring too." 26

In a couple of crises, Lucy says, "he offered himself for talking and for helping. And when someone died in his family he wanted me there. The sexual, flirty part of our friendship is very small, but *some* — just enough to make it fun and different." She thinks — and I agree — that the sexual part, though small, is always *some*, is always there when a man and a woman are friends. 27

It's only in the past few years that I've made friends with men, in the sense of a friendship that's *mine*, not just part of two couples. And achieving with them the ease and the trust I've found with women friends has value indeed. Under the dryer at home last week, putting on mascara and rouge, I comfortably sat and talked with a fellow named Peter. Peter, I finally decided, could handle the shock of me minus mascara under the dryer. Because we care for each other. Because we're friends. 28

Sensory details

8. There are medium friends, and pretty good friends, and very good friends indeed, and these friendships are defined by their level of intimacy. And what we'll reveal at each of these levels of intimacy is calibrated with care. We might tell a medium friend, for example, that yesterday we had a fight with our husband. And we might tell a pretty good friend that this fight with our husband made us so mad that we slept on the couch. And we might tell a very good friend that the reason we got so mad in that fight that we slept on the couch had something to do with that girl that works in his office. But it's only to our very best friends that we're willing to tell all, to tell what's going on with that girl in his office. 29

Category 8

The best of friends, I still believe, totally love and support and trust each other, and bare to each other the secrets of their souls, and run — no questions asked — to help each other, and tell harsh truths to each other when they must be told. 30

Conclusion: affirms
value of best friends

But we needn't agree about everything (only 12-year-old girl friends agree about *everything*) to tolerate each other's point of view. To accept without judgment. To give and to take without ever keeping score. And to *be* there, as I am for them and as they are for me, to comfort our sorrows, to celebrate our joys. 31

Characteristics of Classification and Division Essays

A successful classification or division essay is meaningful to its audience. The writer uses one principle of classification or division, with exclusive categories or parts that are broad enough to include all members of the group.

Classification and Division Group or Divide Ideas According to One Principle

To sort items into groups, a writer must decide how to categorize them. For example, birds could be classified in terms of size, habitat, or diet, while microwave ovens could be classified by price, size, or manufacturer. For a division essay, the writer must decide into what parts to divide the topic. A journalist writing about a new aquarium could divide the topic according to type of fish displayed, suitability for children of different ages, or quality of the exhibits.

To develop an effective set of categories or parts, a writer must choose one principle of classification or division and use it consistently throughout the essay or within a particular section of the essay. For instance, a college president might classify professors by age or teaching style, but he or she would not mix categories by classifying some professors by age and others by teaching style. The president could, however, classify all professors by age in the first part of a report and then by teaching style in another part. In "Friends, Good Friends — Such Good Friends," Viorst uses the principle of types of friendship to categorize the friends she has known and observed.

Once a writer chooses an appropriate principle of classification or division, the next step is to identify a manageable number of categories or parts. An essay classifying birds according to diet, for example, might address five or six types of diet, not twenty. Likewise, an essay dividing aquarium exhibits according to suitability for children might address four or five categories.

Classification and Division Are Meaningful to an Audience

Because several different bases — or principles — can be used to categorize any particular group, the writer's purpose will determine the principle of classification that is choosen. The personnel director of a college might classify professors by age in preparing a financial report that projects upcoming retirements, whereas a student writing a paper about effective teaching methods might categorize professors by teaching style. To develop a meaningful classification, therefore, focus on your readers and your purpose. When your purpose is to inform, choose a principle of classification that will interest your readers. If, for instance, you want to inform parents about the types of day-care centers in the local area, you could classify the centers according to the services they offer because your readers would be looking for that information.

Division essays, too, are guided by purpose and audience. For example, a journalist who divides aquarium exhibits according to their suitability for children of different ages might be writing to persuade readers that the aquarium is primarily designed for children. His audience might be readers of the leisure section of the local newspaper.

Classification Uses Categories and Division Uses Parts That Are Exclusive and Comprehensive

Categories or parts should not overlap. In other words, a particular item or person should fit into no more than one category. A familiar example is age: The age categories *25 to 30* and *30 to 35* are not mutually exclusive because someone who is thirty years old would fit into both. The second category should be changed to *31 to 35*. In an essay about the nutritional value of pizza, you could divide the topic into carbohydrates, proteins, and fats, but you would not add a separate category for saturated fat because that is already contained in the fats category.

Categories or parts should also be comprehensive. In a division essay, all the major parts of an item should be included. In a classification essay, the categories need to include all the items in the group or all the major items. Each member of the group should fit into one category or another. For example, an essay categorizing fast-food restaurants according to type of food served would have to include a category for pizza because a fair number of fast-food establishments in most areas do indeed carry pizza on their menus.

Classification and Division Fully Explain Each Category or Part

A classification or division essay contains adequate detail so that each category or part can be well understood. In the following excerpt from a student essay on types of sales, the writer describes one source of consumer purchases — vending machines. Notice how the student begins with some background and an explanation of how vending machines work before talking about the advantages of this type of sales. She concludes with details about the types of products one can buy from a vending machine.

> While automatic vending machines have been around since the turn of the century, the accessibility and low overhead associated with them continue to make them a popular sales option. To make a purchase, the consumer simply inserts cash and the machine dispenses the product. This makes vending machines cost effective because they do not require sales staff or a high-maintenance selling floor. They are also accessible twenty-four hours a day and can be placed in convenient locations, such as hotels, malls, and office buildings. A wide assortment of goods can now be purchased through vending machines: from steaming hot coffee to calorie-packed snacks, everyday items like stamps and subway tokens, and even travel insurance at airports.

Descriptive details such as these enable readers to "see" the writer's categories or parts.

Classification and Division Develop a Thesis

The thesis statement in a classification or division essay identifies the topic and may reveal the principle used to classify or divide it. In most cases, the writer also suggests why the classification or division is relevant or important. In "Friends, Good Friends — Such Good Friends," for example, prior to stating her thesis Viorst says she no longer believes that all friends fit into one group — thus implying the importance of her classification. Here are a few other examples of thesis statements.

CLASSIFICATION ESSAY: **Most people consider videos a form of entertainment; however, videos can also serve educational, commercial, and political functions.**

DIVISION ESSAY: The Grand Canyon is divided into two distinct geographical areas, the North Rim and the South Rim; each offers different views, facilities, and climatic conditions.

Visualizing a Classification or Division Essay

The graphic organizer in Figure 10.1 outlines the basic organization of a classification or division essay. The introduction announces the topic, gives background information, and states the thesis. The body paragraphs explain the categories or parts and their characteristics. The conclusion brings the essay to a satisfying close by reinforcing the thesis and offering a new insight on the topic. The graphic organizer in Figure 10.2 is based on the reading "Friends, Good Friends — Such Good Friends."

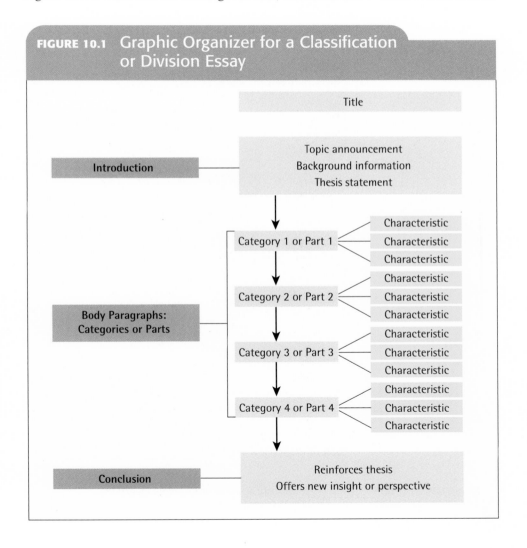

FIGURE 10.1 Graphic Organizer for a Classification or Division Essay

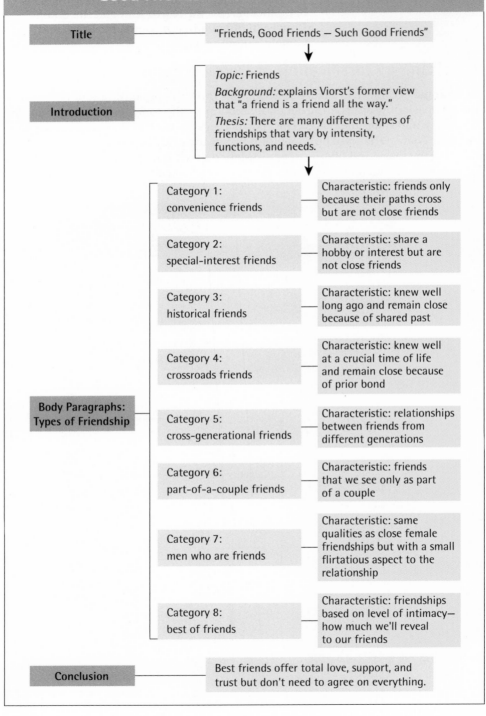

FIGURE 10.2 Graphic Organizer for "Friends, Good Friends — Such Good Friends"

Title — "Friends, Good Friends — Such Good Friends"

Introduction
Topic: Friends
Background: explains Viorst's former view that "a friend is a friend all the way."
Thesis: There are many different types of friendships that vary by intensity, functions, and needs.

Body Paragraphs: Types of Friendship

Category 1: convenience friends — Characteristic: friends only because their paths cross but are not close friends

Category 2: special-interest friends — Characteristic: share a hobby or interest but are not close friends

Category 3: historical friends — Characteristic: knew well long ago and remain close because of shared past

Category 4: crossroads friends — Characteristic: knew well at a crucial time of life and remain close because of prior bond

Category 5: cross-generational friends — Characteristic: relationships between friends from different generations

Category 6: part-of-a-couple friends — Characteristic: friends that we see only as part of a couple

Category 7: men who are friends — Characteristic: same qualities as close female friendships but with a small flirtatious aspect to the relationship

Category 8: best of friends — Characteristic: friendships based on level of intimacy— how much we'll reveal to our friends

Conclusion — Best friends offer total love, support, and trust but don't need to agree on everything.

Writing a Classification or Division Essay

To write a classification or division essay, use the following steps. Although you will focus primarily on classifying or dividing your subject, you may need to integrate one or more other patterns of development.

Planning a Classification or Division Essay

Your first step is to choose a subject to classify or divide. Once you've done so, you need to come up with details about the subject and its categories or parts.

Generating Details

Often it works best to generate details first and then use the details to identify categories or parts. Begin with one or more of the following strategies for generating details about your topic.

Generating Details for a Classification or Division Essay

1. **Visit a place where you can observe the topic or the people associated with it.** For example, to generate details about sports fans, attend a sporting event or watch one on television. Make notes on or tape-record what you see and hear. Be specific; record conversations, physical characteristics, behaviors, and so forth.

2. **Discuss the topic with a classmate or friend.** Focus on the qualities and characteristics of the topic.

3. **Brainstorm a list of all the features or characteristics of the topic.**

4. **Draw a map or diagram that illustrates the topic's features and characteristics.**

5. **Conduct library or Internet research to discover facts, examples, and other details about the topic.**

Choosing a Principle of Classification or Division

Your next task is to decide which principle or basis on which to classify or divide the subject. Read through your details, looking for shared features or characteristics. If the topic is highway drivers, for instance, you could classify them by gender, age, type of car driven, or driving habits. Your principle of classification or division should be interesting and meaningful to the audience. It should also enable you to make a worthwhile point about the classification or division. For the essay on highway drivers, you might decide to classify drivers according to their driving habits, focusing on annoying or unsafe habits that you have observed. Experiment with several principles of classification or division until you find one that fits your purpose and audience.

Choosing Categories or Parts

With your principle of classification or division in mind, use the following suggestions to determine categories or parts.

Guidelines for Choosing Categories or Parts

1. **Make sure most or all members of the group fit into one of the categories; few, if any, members should be left out.** For example, in a division essay about parts of a baseball stadium, you would not exclude the infield or the bleachers.

2. **Be sure the categories are exclusive; each group member should fit into one category only.** For example, in a classification essay about annoying driving habits, the categories of reckless drivers and aggressive drivers would overlap, so exclusive categories should be used instead.

3. **Create specific categories or parts that will engage your readers.** For example, a division essay on players' facilities in a baseball stadium — dugout, locker room, and bullpen — would be more interesting to sports fans than an essay describing different seating sections of the stadium.

4. **Once you establish categories or parts, you may need to do additional brainstorming or some other type of prewriting to generate enough details to explain each category or part adequately.**

5. **Choose descriptive names that emphasize the distinguishing feature of each category or part.** For example, in the essay classifying highway drivers with annoying habits, you might assign names like "I-own-the-road" drivers and "I'm-daydreaming" drivers.

Identifying the Key Features of Each Category or Part

Once you have a workable list of categories or parts, go back to the details and identify key features. These are the features that you will use to explain and differentiate each category or part. Recall how Viorst, in "Friends, Good Friends — Such Good Friends," clearly describes the major characteristics of each type of friendship she has experienced or observed.

Consider again the categories of annoying highway drivers. You might distinguish each type of driver by the key characteristics listed here.

"I-OWN-THE-ROAD" DRIVERS: Inconsiderate of other drivers; weave in and
out of traffic; honk horns or flash lights to intimidate others into letting them pass

"I'M-DAYDREAMING" DRIVERS: Fail to observe other drivers; fail to signal when changing lanes; wander over the dividing line or onto the shoulder

As you identify characteristics for each category or part, you may find that two categories or parts overlap or that a category or part is too broad. Do not hesitate to create, combine, or eliminate categories or parts as you work.

For some classification or division essays, it may be easier to start with categories or parts and then fill in the details. In other words, you may want to reverse — to some extent — the process just described. If you do so, be sure not to skip any steps.

Developing Your Thesis

Once you choose categories or parts and are satisfied with your details, it is time to develop a thesis. Remember that the thesis statement should identify the topic and reveal the principle of division or classification. In most cases, it should also suggest why the classification or division is useful or important. Avoid writing a thesis statement that merely announces the categories, as in "There are four kinds of . . ." Notice how the following weak thesis has been strengthened by showing both what the categories are and why they are important.

WEAK: There are four types of insurance that most people can purchase.

REVISED: If you understand the four common types of insurance — health, home, life, and auto — you will be able to make sure that you, your family members, and your property are protected.

Draft your thesis and then check your prewriting to make sure there are enough details to support the thesis. If necessary, do some additional prewriting to gather more supporting details. In addition, keep in mind that a lengthy or complex topic may require a more elaborate thesis and introduction; you may need to provide more detailed information about the principle of classification or division or its importance.

Drafting a Classification or Division Essay

After evaluating categories or parts and reviewing your thesis, you are ready to organize your ideas and draft the essay. Choose the method of organization that best suits your purpose. One method that works well in classification essays is the least-to-most arrangement whereby categories are addressed in increasing order of importance or from least to most common, difficult, or frequent. Spatial order often works well in division essays, as does order of importance. In describing the parts of a baseball stadium, you might move from stands to playing field (spatial order). In writing about the parts of a hospital, you might describe the most important areas first (operating rooms and emergency room) and then move to less important facilities (waiting rooms and cafeteria).

For more on methods of organization, see Chapter 3, p. 48.

Once you decide how to organize your categories or parts, the next step is to write a first draft. Use the following guidelines.

Guidelines for Writing a Classification or Division Essay

1. **Write an effective introduction.** The introduction, which usually includes the thesis statement, should provide background information and explain further, if needed, the principle of classification or division. It might also suggest why the classification or division is significant.

2. **Explain each category or part.** Begin by defining each category or part, taking into account the complexity of the topic and the background knowledge of the audience. For example, in a division essay about a baseball stadium, you might need to define *infield* and *outfield* if the audience includes a large number of people who are not sports fans.

3. **Provide details that describe each category or part**. Be sure to show how each category or part is distinct from the others. Include a wide range of details — sensory details, personal experiences, examples, and comparisons and contrasts.

4. **Generally, allow one or more paragraphs for each category or part.**

5. **Use transitions.** Your readers need transitions to keep on track as you move from one category or part to another. Transitions such as "the *third* category of . . . ," "an *additional* characteristic of . . . ," and "it *also* contains . . ." will help to distinguish key features between and within categories or parts.

6. **Provide roughly the same amount and kind of detail and description for each category or part.** For instance, if you give an example of one type of mental disorder, then you should give an example for every other type discussed in the essay.

7. **Consider adding headings or lists to make the categories or parts clear and distinct.** Headings or lists can be especially useful if there are a large number of categories or parts.

8. **Consider adding a visual such as a diagram or flowchart to make your system of classification or division clearer for the readers.**

9. **Write a satisfying conclusion.** The conclusion should do more than just repeat categories or parts. It should bring the essay to a satisfying close, reemphasizing the thesis or offering a new insight or perspective on the topic. If you have trouble finding an appropriate way to conclude, return to your statement about why the classification or division is significant and try to elaborate on it.

Analyzing and Revising

If possible, set your draft aside for a day or two before rereading and revising it. As you review the draft, focus on content and ideas, not on grammar, punctuation, or mechanics. Use the flowchart in Figure 10.3 to guide your analysis of the strengths and weaknesses in your draft essay.

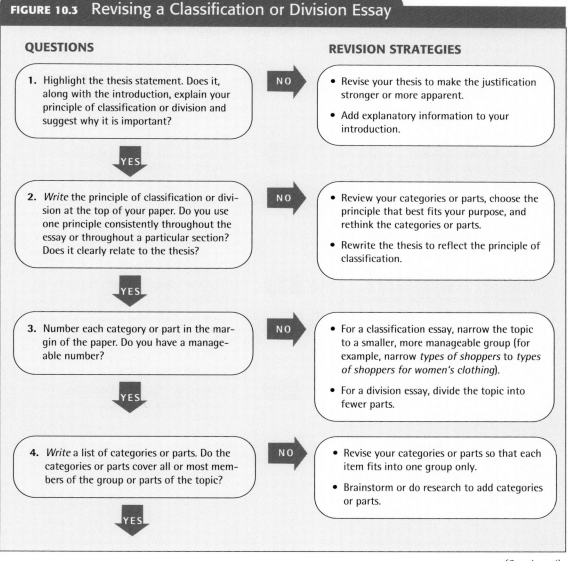

FIGURE 10.3 Revising a Classification or Division Essay

QUESTIONS

REVISION STRATEGIES

1. Highlight the thesis statement. Does it, along with the introduction, explain your principle of classification or division and suggest why it is important?

   NO →
   - Revise your thesis to make the justification stronger or more apparent.
   - Add explanatory information to your introduction.

   YES ↓

2. *Write* the principle of classification or division at the top of your paper. Do you use one principle consistently throughout the essay or throughout a particular section? Does it clearly relate to the thesis?

   NO →
   - Review your categories or parts, choose the principle that best fits your purpose, and rethink the categories or parts.
   - Rewrite the thesis to reflect the principle of classification.

   YES ↓

3. Number each category or part in the margin of the paper. Do you have a manageable number?

   NO →
   - For a classification essay, narrow the topic to a smaller, more manageable group (for example, narrow *types of shoppers* to *types of shoppers for women's clothing*).
   - For a division essay, divide the topic into fewer parts.

   YES ↓

4. *Write* a list of categories or parts. Do the categories or parts cover all or most members of the group or parts of the topic?

   NO →
   - Revise your categories or parts so that each item fits into one group only.
   - Brainstorm or do research to add categories or parts.

   YES ↓

(Continued)

FIGURE 10.3 *(Continued)*

QUESTIONS	REVISION STRATEGIES

5. Place checkmarks ✔ beside the details that explain each category or part. Does your essay fully explain the key features of each category or part? (If it reads like a list, answer "No.")

 NO

- Brainstorm or do research to discover more details.
- Add examples, definitions, facts, and expert testimony to improve your explanations.

 YES

6. *Sketch* a brief outline of the organization used to structure the essay. Is the organization clear? Are the categories or parts organized in a way that suits your purpose?

 NO

- Draw a graphic organizer to evaluate the present organization.
- Refer to Chapter 3 to discover an organizing plan.

 YES

7. Underline the topic sentence of each paragraph. Is each paragraph focused on a separate category or part?

 NO

- Consider combining closely related paragraphs.
- Split paragraphs that cover more than one category or part.

 YES

8. Draw a box around the conclusion. Does it offer a new insight or perspective on the topic?

 NO

- Ask yourself: "So what? What does this mean?" Build your answers into the conclusion.

YES

9. Print out another draft to edit and proofread before turning your essay in.

Editing and Proofreading

The last step is to check your revised essay for errors in grammar, spelling, punctuation, and mechanics. In addition, watch out for the types of errors you tend to make in any writing assignments, whether for this class or any other situation. When editing a classification or division essay, pay attention to two particular kinds of grammatical error: choppy sentences and omitted commas following introductory elements.

For more on these and other common errors, see Chapter 4, p. 81.

Editing Tips and Troublespots: Classification and Division

1. **Avoid short, choppy sentences,** which can make a classification or division sound dull and mechanical. Try combining a series of short sentences and varying sentence patterns and lengths.

   ▶ Working dogs are another one of the American Kennel Club's breed categories. ~~These include German shepherds and sheep-herding dogs.~~

   , such as German shepherds and sheep-herding dogs,

   ▶ ~~One~~ standard type of writing instrument ~~is the fountain pen.~~ ~~It~~ is sometimes messy and inconvenient to use. It often leaks.

   The fountain pen, one

2. **Use a comma to separate introductory words, phrases, and clauses from the rest of the sentence.**

   ▶ When describing types of college students be sure to consider variations in age.

   Although there are many types of cameras most are easy to operate.

Students Write

Ryan Porter was a first-year student when he wrote the following essay in response to an assignment for his writing course. He is an avid reader of car magazines and enjoys antique cars, especially cars of the 1950s. As you read the essay, identify the basis of classification and the categories he uses, and annotate your reactions to his details.

Motor Heads

Ryan Porter

Interest-catching title

Introduction: establishes importance of the topic

Details add interest

Thesis: includes principle of classification

Category 1: aficionados

Concrete examples help readers unfamiliar with the topic understand type

Simile adds detail

Category 2: gear heads; topic sentence contains helpful examples

As you probably realize, we live in an automobile-oriented society; car culture is everywhere. Can you really say that you don't care about cars or that you are not a car lover on some level? Although your interest may be merely practical, there are multitudes of people who are car nuts to some degree.

You see them on Sundays in spring, gathered around the glittering external exhaust pipes of a classic Duesenberg dual-cowl phaeton parked on the fairway at an antique auto show, or on Saturday nights in summer in a fast-food parking lot, jostling each other to peek at the chromed engine bay of a chopped and channeled '56 Chevy Bel Air. You see them bunched up at the parts counter at Pep Boys or poring over the car magazines at Borders Books. These are the motor heads or the car nuts; and like all nuts, they come in many varieties, each identifiable by the kind of car that they worship.

The first variety, the aficionado, is usually wealthy or has pretensions of wealth. Aficionados own classic cars from the 1920s and 1930s, such as the fabled Duesenberg, Hispano-Suiza, Packard, or Bentley. If they own more than one, you might hear them talk of the cars in their "stable," as if these machines were thoroughbred horses. These autos are extremely valuable -- often selling at auction for hundreds of thousands of dollars -- and can be considered part of their investment portfolios. Because of this, aficionados rarely, if ever, drive their cars, preferring instead to have the vehicles trailered to shows. Aficionados never actually put a wrench to any lug nut on one of their classic cars; instead they hire a mechanic who specializes in maintaining antiques and classics. Aficionados treat their classic cars like fine crystal. Maybe they should collect crystal instead; it takes up less room and is a lot easier to maintain.

The second type of car nut, the gear head, can be seen sporting grease-smeared T-shirts with faded Camaro, Mustang, or Corvette logos. Unlike the aficionados, the gear heads are ready, willing, and able to thrust a wrench-wielding hand into the engines of their Camaros, Mustangs, or Corvettes. They can disassemble a turbo hydramatic transmission and then reassemble it, at a moment's notice. They have wrenches in their jeans pocket. Gear heads seem to have ESP when it comes to automobile engines. A gear head can pop open the hood of your car, listen with head cocked and eyes closed for a second or two, and tell you that you have nine hundred miles left on your timing belt. You say, "Sure I do, buddy." Five weeks later you're stranded on the side of the road as a friendly police officer observes, "Sounds like the timing belt is gone." When most people think of a car nut, it is the gear head who comes to mind. Hollywood has been using the gear head in movies and television shows for decades: James Dean in the 1950s, the Fonz in the 1970s, and Tim Allen in *Home Improvement* in the 1990s. On a practical level, you may not ever want to be a gear head, but you'd want your brother-in-law to be one.

Use of humor lightens tone and engages reader

On a more specialized level, there is the make-specific car nut. This is not your Uncle Walter, who always drove Fords and swore by them. The make-specific car nuts go far beyond that, knowing every detail about every model of one specific brand of automobile. They might love Porsches, for instance, rattling off observations like, "The '96 Turbo's machined rather than cast cylinder fins dissipate hot air better than those of the Carrera 2." Make-specific car nuts bore their friends to tears with descriptions of the differences between the drip-rail moldings on the 1959 versus 1960 Oldsmobile Super 88 Vista Cruiser sedans. Upon spotting two old Woodstock-era Volkswagen (VW) Beetles putt-putting down the road, the make-specific car nut will handily determine the year they were made. It's eerie; everyone knows you can't tell one year's vintage VW from another. Make-specific car nuts dress like you and me, except they wear accessories -- tie clips, cuff links, pens, and dress shirts -- adorned with their favorite car's logo. Will coffee served in a Firebird mug really stay warm longer?

5 Category 3: make-specific car nuts

Helpful details

Orphan-make hoarders are the twin of make-specific car nuts, except orphan-make hoarders love only the cars manufactured by companies no longer in business. They are determined to collect every model of every Packard or Kaiser-Frazer ever produced. Usually residing in rural areas, the hoarder often owns a thirty-acre parcel of land upon which are parked a hundred or more examples of the make in various stages of decomposition, not one of which is drivable. Do you need the horn-ring for a 1951 Studebaker President Land Cruiser? The orphan-make hoarder has fourteen of them.

6 Category 4: orphan-make hoarders

Humorous details add interest

Finally, closer in orbit to our own planet, we have the wishful thinkers. They read *Road & Track, Car and Driver,* and *Automobile* every month and dream of someday owning a Ferrari Testarossa or Porsche 911 Turbo. Wishful thinkers drag their families or friends to car shows, auto races, and antique auto events. You find them in auto showrooms whenever a new model is introduced, demanding to road-test the new BMW roadster or Mustang GT that they have no intention of buying. The salespeople call them "tire-kickers." The wishful thinker owns a five-year-old Honda Civic sedan.

7 Category 5: wishful thinkers

As you can see, car nuts cross all social and economic levels, reflecting the diversity of our society. You probably know a car nut or may be one yourself. America is a nation in love with the automobile. Whatever their variety, car nuts take that love to the next level: obsession.

8 Conclusion: refers back to thesis and makes final statement about car obsession

Responding to "Students Write"

1. How does the writer establish the importance or meaningfulness of his classification?
2. Porter uses classification to discuss the different types of "motor heads." What other patterns of development does he use to develop each category?
3. Evaluate the title, introduction, and conclusion.
4. Consider Porter's tone. What kind of audience does he address? If his audience were different, would the use of humor be equally effective? Explain.

Reading a Classification or Division Essay

A classification or division essay is usually highly organized and relatively easy to follow. Use the following suggestions to read classification essays, division essays, or any writing that uses classification or division.

What to Look for, Highlight, and Annotate

Understanding the Reading

- Read the essay once to get a general sense of the flow. Then reread it, paying attention to the different categories or parts used.
- Study the introduction and conclusion. What is the purpose of each?
- Evaluate the title. Does it contribute any meaning to the essay?

Examining the Characteristics of Classification and Division Essays

- Highlight the thesis statement, the principle of classification, and the name or title of each category or part.
- Look for visual clues, such as italics or boldface print, to identify the categories or parts.
- Use a different color highlighter or annotations to identify the key features of each category.
- Mark important definitions and vivid examples for later reference.
- Add annotations indicating where you find a category or part confusing or where you think more detail is needed.

How to Find Ideas to Write About

To gain a different perspective on the reading, think of other ways of classifying or dividing the topic. For example, consider an essay that classifies types of exercise programs at health clubs according to the benefits for cardiovascular health. Such exercise programs could also be classified according to cost, degree of strenuousness, type of exercise, and so forth.

A classification or division essay provides the reader with one particular viewpoint on the subject. Be sure to keep in mind that it is *only* one viewpoint. Once you identify alternative viewpoints, choose one to write about.

A Brush with Reality: Surprises in the Tube

David Bodanis

David Bodanis is a journalist and academic trained in mathematics, physics, and economics. He has taught postgraduate social science survey courses at Oxford, consulted with businesses on energy policy and sustainable development, and written several books, including *The Body Book* (1984), *The Secret Garden* (1992), and *The Secret Family* (1997).

The following essay is from *The Secret House* (1986), a book that examines the foods eaten and products consumed by a family over the course of a day. In this piece, Bodanis examines the substances that are put together to make toothpaste. Notice the deadpan tone he uses to describe ingredient after unappetizing ingredient and the words he chooses in order to leave the desired stomach-churning impression on readers.

Focus on Understanding   Read to discover what the "surprises" are.

Focus on the Topic   In class or in your journal, write about the different criteria you use for choosing products such as toothpaste and shampoo.

Into the bathroom goes our male resident, and after the most pressing need 1 is satisfied it's time to brush the teeth. The tube of toothpaste is squeezed, its pinched metal seams are splayed, pressure waves are generated inside, and the paste begins to flow. But what's in this toothpaste, so carefully being extruded out?

Water mostly, 30 to 45 percent in most brands: ordinary, everyday simple 2 tap water. It's there because people like to have a big gob of toothpaste to spread on the brush, and water is the cheapest stuff there is when it comes to making big gobs. Dripping a bit from the tap onto your brush would cost virtually nothing; whipped in with the rest of the toothpaste the manufacturers can sell it at a neat and accountant-pleasing $2 per pound equivalent. Toothpaste manufacture is a very lucrative occupation.

Second to water in quantity is chalk: exactly the same material that school- 3 teachers use to write on blackboards. It is collected from the crushed remains of long-dead ocean creatures. In the Cretaceous° seas chalk particles served as part of the wickedly sharp outer skeleton that these creatures had to wrap around themselves to keep from getting chomped by all the slightly larger other ocean creatures they met. Their massed graves are our present chalk deposits.

The individual chalk particles — the size of the smallest mud particles in 4 your garden — have kept their toughness over the aeons,° and now on the tooth-brush they'll need it. The enamel outer coating of the tooth they'll have to face is the hardest substance in the body — tougher than skull, or bone, or nail. Only the chalk particles in toothpaste can successfully grind into the teeth during brushing, ripping off the surface layers like an abrading wheel° grinding down a boulder in a quarry.

The craters, slashes, and channels that the chalk tears into the teeth will 5 also remove a certain amount of build-up yellow in the carnage, and it is for that polishing function that it's there. A certain amount of unduly enlarged extra-abrasive chalk fragments tear such cavernous pits into the teeth that future decay bacteria will be able to bunker down there and thrive; the quality control people find it almost impossible to screen out these errant super-chalk pieces, and government regulations allow them to stay in.

In case even the gouging doesn't get all the yellow off, another substance is 6 worked into the toothpaste cream. This is titanium dioxide. It comes in tiny spheres, and it's the stuff bobbing around in white wall paint to make it come out white. Splashed around onto your teeth during the brushing it coats much of the yellow that remains. Being water soluble it leaks off in the next few hours and is swallowed, but at least for the quick glance up in the mirror after finishing it will make the user think his teeth are truly white. Some manufacturers add optical whitening dye — the stuff more commonly found in washing machine bleach — to make extra sure that that glance in the mirror shows reassuring white.

These ingredients alone would not make a very attractive concoction. They 7 would stick in the tube like a sloppy white plastic lump, hard to squeeze out as well as revolting to the touch. Few consumers would savor rubbing in a mixture of water, ground-up blackboard chalk, and the whitener from latex paint first thing in the morning. To get around that finicky distaste the manufacturers have mixed in a host of other goodies.

To keep the glop from drying out, a mixture including glycerine glycol — related to the most common car antifreeze ingredient — is whipped in with the 8 chalk and water, and to give that concoction a bit of substance (all we really have so far is wet colored chalk) a large helping is added of gummy molecules from the seaweed Chondrus Crispus. This seaweed ooze spreads in among the chalk, paint, and antifreeze, then stretches itself in all directions to hold the whole mass together. A bit of paraffin oil (the fuel that flickers in camping lamps) is pumped in with it to help the moss ooze keep the whole substance smooth.

With the glycol, ooze, and paraffin we're almost there. Only two major 9 chemicals are left to make the refreshing, cleansing substance we know as toothpaste. The ingredients so far are fine for cleaning, but they wouldn't make much of the satisfying foam we have come to expect in the morning brushing.

To remedy that, every toothpaste on the market has a big dollop of detergent added too. You've seen the suds detergent will make in a washing machine. 10 The same substance added here will duplicate that inside the mouth. It's not particularly necessary, but it sells. The only problem is that by itself this ingredient tastes, well, too like detergent. It's horribly bitter and harsh. The chalk put

abrading wheel: a tool that wears down material by applying friction and pressure from a rotating disk

in toothpaste is pretty foul-tasting too for that matter. It's to get around that gustatory discomfort that the manufacturers put in the ingredient they tout perhaps the most of all. This is the flavoring, and it has to be strong. Double rectified peppermint oil is used — a flavorer so powerful that chemists know better than to sniff it in the raw state in the laboratory. Menthol crystals and saccharin or other sugar simulators are added to complete the camouflage operation.

Is that it? Chalk, water, paint, seaweed, antifreeze, paraffin oil, detergent, 11 and peppermint? Not quite. A mix like that would be irresistible to the hundreds of thousands of individual bacteria lying on the surface of even an immaculately cleaned bathroom sink. They would get in, float in the water bubbles, ingest the ooze and paraffin, maybe even spray out enzymes to break down the chalk. The result would be an uninviting mess. The way manufacturers avoid that final obstacle is by putting something in to kill the bacteria. Something good and strong is needed, something that will zap any accidentally intrudant bacteria into oblivion. And that something is formaldehyde — the disinfectant used in anatomy labs.

So it's chalk, water, paint, seaweed, antifreeze, paraffin oil, detergent, pep- 12 permint, formaldehyde, and fluoride (which can go some way towards preserving children's teeth) — that's the usual mixture raised to the mouth on the toothbrush for a fresh morning's clean. If it sounds too unfortunate, take heart. Studies show that thorough brushing with just plain water will often do as good a job.

Understanding the Reading

1. What are the ingredients in toothpaste?
2. Why did the author include information about the origins of chalk?
3. What is in toothpaste to inhibit the growth of bacteria?
3. What does the author present as a final thought on the subject? What does this imply about his feelings about toothpaste?

Visualizing the Reading

Analzye the effectiveness of Bodanis's division essay by completing the graphic organizer on the opposite page.

Examining the Characteristics of Classification and Division Essays

1. Analyze the effectiveness of using an implied thesis. Is the author's purpose in writing clear? Why or why not?
2. How successful is Bodanis is presenting his categories? Is the division of the ingredients in toothpaste complete? Do any parts overlap?

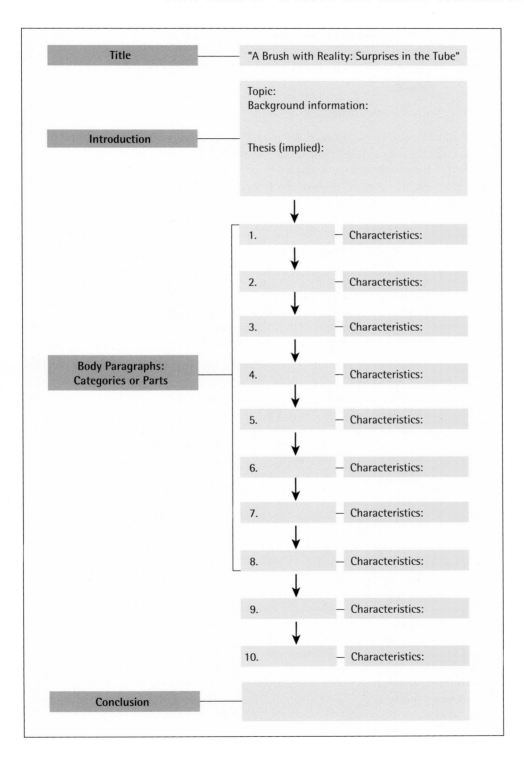

Title — "A Brush with Reality: Surprises in the Tube"

Introduction —
Topic:
Background information:

Thesis (implied):

Body Paragraphs:
Categories or Parts —
1. — Characteristics:
2. — Characteristics:
3. — Characteristics:
4. — Characteristics:
5. — Characteristics:
6. — Characteristics:
7. — Characteristics:
8. — Characteristics:
9. — Characteristics:
10. — Characteristics:

Conclusion —

3. Name some especially effective details that are included for each category. Are some parts better explained than others? Explain your answer.

4. Did you find the conclusion satisfying? Is there additional information that you would find helpful?

Building Your Word Power

1. What does the author mean by the phrase "reassuring white" in paragraph 6?

2. Evaluate the expressions "finicky distaste" and "host of other goodies" (para. 7). What is the author trying to express?

3. Explain the meaning of each of the following words as it is used in the reading: *splayed* (para. 1), *lucrative* (2), *errant* (5), *gustatory* (10), and *tout* (10). Refer to your dictionary as needed.

Building Your Critical Thinking Skills: Drawing Conclusions

When drawing conclusions, one makes reasoned decisions or opinions on the basis of available facts. Sometimes authors draw conclusions throughout an essay. For example, in an article about methods of food preservation, the author might draw conclusions about the ease, safety, or prevalence of the method, as each is discussed. Conclusions can also serve as a way to transition from one category to another. Using your knowledge about drawing conclusions, answer the following questions.

1. What conclusion does Bodanis draw about the fact that water is the most plentiful ingredient in toothpaste?

2. Throughout the essay, Bodanis refers repeatedly to the consumers of toothpaste. Reread paragraphs 6, 7, and 10. What conclusion is he drawing about consumers?

3. Just as the thesis is implied, the main conclusion is not stated directly. Based on his use of details, what conclusion do you think Bodanis is drawing about the use of toothpaste?

Reacting to the Reading: Discussion and Journal Writing

1. Discuss the role of dental hygiene in our society. Why do we place such great importance on our teeth?

2. Discuss the strategies that manufacturers use to make their products appealing to consumers.

3. In class or in your journal, explore the various reasons why some people choose to buy "natural" personal care products.

Applying Your Skills: Writing Assignments

1. **Paragraph Assignment.** Bodanis helps us see an everyday item in a new way. Pick an ordinary prepared food; using the ingredients label, write a classification or division paragraph to reveal a new way of seeing that food.

2. Conduct a study of one advertising medium: TV, radio, the Internet, newspapers, or magazines. Take notes on what you see, hear, and read. Then write a classifica-

tion essay describing the different types of ads according to aspects such as content, intended audience, or placement. Be sure to indicate what effect the ads had on you.

3. How much do people know about what they consume and use? Choose a common processed food or household product, and ask three to five friends to tell you what they think is in it, taking notes on their comments. Then compare their answers to the actual ingredients. Write a classification or division essay describing the degrees of knowledge people have about this food or product. Make recommendations about how we can learn more about what we eat and use.

4. Combining Patterns. Write an essay about something that you used to eat, do, or believe in until you found out something about it that made you change your mind. In addition to explaining the cause of this change, classify the ways that others react to this food, substance, activity, or belief. For example, you might categorize people as "uninformed," "in denial," or "anti-smoking activists" in terms of their reactions to smoking.

5. Internet Research. Choose a product that you use daily, such as shampoo or deodorant. Using the label of ingredients as a starting point, use the Internet to research what the product really contains. Then write a division essay that identifies the product's components and explains each, as Bodanis does for toothpaste.

The Seven Ages of Walking

Elizabeth Wray

Elizabeth Wray is a freelance writer living in San Francisco. She has written numerous articles about health, travel, and family issues for a variety of publications. In addition, she has worked extensively in theater as a playwright and critic.

This article originally appeared in the November/December 2003 issue of *Body and Soul*. Here, Wray develops an analogy borrowed from Shakespeare's *As You Like It*, which describes life as consisting of seven ages, moving from infancy through childhood, youth, adulthood, middle age, old age, and a final second infancy. As you read, note the detailed examples of "ages of walking" that Wray draws from her own life and the lives of the people she knows best — her family.

Focus on Understanding As you read, identify the ways in which walking mirrors the stages in life.

Focus on the Topic In class or in your journal, write about the different functions of walking. When is it more than just a means of getting from place to place?

Two years ago my 84-year-old father went for a walk in the neighborhood, a walk he'd been taking twice a day for the past 10 years. Thirteen hours later, the police found him wandering near the freeway some 15 miles from the two-flat house we share in San Francisco. He was thirsty and a little tired, had no idea where he'd been or what he'd done, but seemed in good spirits about the whole experience, whatever it was. This was one of those existential moments when everything shifts. 1

After that, my mother began to walk with my father twice a day, reporting that he was either silent; delighted by babies, dogs, and airplanes; or quoting Shakespeare like a youngster might chant nursery rhymes. My mother was once again walking a toddling family member, just as she'd done with me in the 1950s. 2

Walking, like life, has its stages and repetitive patterns, and in middle age, in the comings and goings of my family over the past 19 years, I've experienced most of them. My father's old classroom crony, Jaques° from *As You Like It*, outlined the seven ages of man. There's a progression as well to walking through life. 3

Toddlerhood

Walking gives us a way to be in the world, and we discover this early, after months of sitting like baby Buddhas, observing the world as it passes. Once we join in, it doesn't take long to crawl, stand, step, fall, step, step, waddle, and run 4

Jaques: Shakespeare character from the play *As You Like It* who gives a famous speech about man's seven ages ("*All the world's a stage . . .*")

to reach for the world with a pure sense of wonder. A monarch butterfly, a bright-purple thistle, a squeaking screen door, catalpa leaves patterning the light on the front porch, a snail marking a trail across the sidewalk, mud in March, its dark, uncensored taste.

In the first few years of life, we walk into immediate experience, goalless, guileless, short-legged explorers of the human condition. 5

Childhood

Children develop and refine basic walking skills into a whole repertoire of movement through space: hop, skip, twirl, slide, gallop. Our ways of locomotion will never be as goofily complex as they are in childhood. Kids move with abandon, often for no other reason than that it makes them feel good. 6

"Walk, don't run" are the pointless words adults use to try to stave off the inevitable. Kids run through locked arms playing Red Rover, run back to tag base, run in the halls and up the aisles, busting through doors to explore a wider world. Even dreamy children run between daydreams. My mother ran five miles between Gadsden and Attalla, Alabama, for a month one summer just to read *Gone With the Wind* without interruption on her aunt's front porch. Like dogs, children run just to run. 7

They also learn to run for goals — soccer goals and the finish line — but also more complex goals, like the one my son, Kit, learned as a kindergartner playing "Kissy Girls," in which the girls were "it" and the boys, if caught, were made to endure their kisses. Kit, who went on to win field-day races, was always the first one caught. 8

Teens & Twenties

Now, at 14, my son's childhood is ending, and kids are slowing down. In sixth grade, he explained to me when I made the mistake of using the childish word "recess." "Mom, in middle school we don't have recess, we walk the halls." The arbiters of cool, teenagers walk to a social beat. It's a big responsibility, and part of this burden of cool is to walk, swagger, or shake it in a particular way. Walking is a way of saying who they are. This is the age of independent exploration, and even though running isn't cool, teenagers and twentysomethings can't walk fast enough to keep up with their curiosity about an expanding world that's their stage for self-discovery. 9

Although at this age social walking is rampant, it's also the beginning of walking by oneself, contemplating a new job, a new love, existence. At 22, I took my first walks alone, truly existentially alone, along the Hudson River, pondering whether to quit my editorial job and become even poorer by "doing theater" full-time. As a freshman in college, my daughter, Anava, walks along the Mississippi River, fretting over whether she's giving up too much of life on the pre-med track. 10

Thirties

I was working in the theater at the time I became a parent, rehearsing every night, up late, flying around the country, moving too fast to think most days. I 11 was in desperate need of slowing down. As a new mother, I rediscovered reflective time as I pushed my daughter in a heavy stroller slowly up a neighborhood hill, learning the names of the wildflowers — goldfields, blue flax — that romanced me on my plodding way.

Walking with infants, or with a friend to a neighborhood café when I could 12 get away, became a solace, contemplative time in the midst of busy mother-wife-working-woman days. But as infants grow up, parents become more and more reliant on cars to haul kids and their equipment and friends, groceries, and Goodwill° bags. and to do a thousand other errands of the young middle years. Walking fades to the background, becoming a quaint pastime, almost forgotten. As for running, if I did it at all, it was around the block for exercise between dropping the kids at school and the first meeting of the day.

Goodwill: a nonprofit organization that raises money through household donations to help people with disabilities develop job skills and find employment

Forties & Fifties

This is the age in which walking becomes both exercise and meditation prac- 13 tice. For me, it goes something like this. My teenagers are mostly taking care of themselves. My own youth is fading fast. I feel like running again, but ouch, my knees aren't working so great anymore. I settle for a fast walk because it feels good and it takes me places — up Goat Hill after dark, panting with my black retriever, Mu, watching the city shimmer below. After Mu died, I continued to take night walks, considering things like how to make more money so that I could put two kids through college.

Walking for exercise in the middle years can also be serious fun, rekindling 14 the urge to run, hop, skip, trot, twirl, and the rest of the childhood repertoire. We all work this out in different ways — running, jogging, playing handball, skiing. I dance twice a week, mostly samba. I think of dancing as walking with sublime intent, muscles coaxed by music, just as the voice can grow from talking into song.

Then there's walking for causes, something my baby-boomer generation 15 was practically weaned on. Many of us, myself included, got busy with our own lives and dropped out of these group-cause walks for years. Now, in middle age, many of us are once again walking with our children in antiwar, breast cancer cure, and AIDS marches.

Sixties

In the next decade or two, as I and my fellow boomers approach and enter our 16 sixties, I see my possible walking future reflected in my mother's life. When she retired, she moved from Oklahoma to San Francisco with my father and my grandmother and into the downstairs flat of my Victorian. My mother became an avid walker, dividing much of her walking time between her toddler grandson and her aged mother. Kit's tiny, restless hands clutched her legs — the home base he needed to push off from and return to. Linked to a soft, wrinkled arm, she watched over her slow, bent mother, whose eyes were always downcast to the troublesome pavement as she summoned up stories of long ago. I saw her as an usher — ushering in and ushering out — slowing her pace to theirs and learning from them what it was like to be both very young and very old.

Old Age

Last year at 80, her cancer in remission, my mother still walked my father, lost 17
without her. On a quiet street at midday, he paused to say, "So still." And she
stood with him, absorbing the stillness around and between them. "I'm with
him," she told me, "but I'm also restless. I hate my soundless crepe-soled shoes.
I long for high heels and the way I used to make them click. I still have the impulse to run. If I weren't afraid of falling. I'd run like the wind."

This year, my mother gone, I'm the one who walks my father. Recently, he 18
stopped in a sunny spot and said, "Oooh, it's warm right here." For a few moments, we floated in that warmth, on our goalless walk, walking and sensing, just
to feel good. Flashbacks of a hundred other walks flooded through me, walks with
my mother, children, friends, and lovers, in which we'd slow our pace and fall
back into silence as our senses took over: scent of lilac, *ok-a-lee* trill of red-winged
blackbird, rainy mist on closed eyelids. Once again, I'd walked into a wondrous
moment. Standing there treading the warmth with my father, I felt alive as my old
dog Mu, who for years stopped me on our hillside walks to take in as much as
possible — ears perked, nostrils distended — for as long as we could.

Understanding the Reading

1. What are the stages of walking described in the essay?
2. How is walking important in our early lives? in our later lives?
3. What information does the author reveal about herself?
4. According to the reading, how can walking be useful to us?

Visualizing the Reading

Analyze Wray's classification of the stages of walking by completing the following
chart. For each category, identify the function(s) of walking during that particular life
stage. The first one has been done for you

Life Stage	Function(s)
Toddlerhood	To explore the world
Childhood	
Teens and twenties	
Thirties	
Forties and fifties	
Sixties	
Old age	

Examining the Characteristics of Classification and Division Essays

1. Identify Wray's thesis. What principle of classification does she use? How does this principle relate to her own life?

2. Evaluate Wray's choice of categories. Would you agree that each stage is exclusive and comprehensive? Explain.

3. How are the categories organized? Explain why or why not this arrangement makes sense.

4. What other patterns of development does Wray use? How do these contribute to the essay?

5. Consider the effect of the personal details from the author's own family. Why do you think Wray included these details to explain each stage?

Building Your Word Power

*For a definition of **allusion** and **connotative meaning**, see the chart of commonly used language features on p. 21.*

1. Explain the allusion to the "human condition" in paragraph 5.

2. Why does the word *recess* (para. 9) now sound childish to the author's son? What connotative meaning does this word have for him?

3. Explain the meaning of each of the following words as it is used in the reading: *guileless* (para. 5), *abandon* (6), *arbiters* (9), *solace* (12), and *treading* (18). Refer to your dictionary as needed.

Building Your Critical Thinking Skills: Analogies

An analogy is a comparison in which a writer illustrates one point, thing, or situation by likening it to another. You can use an analogy either as part of the essay or as a way to make comparisons within the essay. Analogies are useful because they help make complicated ideas and concepts easier to understand. Be sure to evaluate analogies to determine if they are reliable and believable. For an analogy to be effective, the connection between the two things being compared should be clear. Using your skills in evaluating analogies, answer the following questions.

1. How does Wray use the analogy to the seven ages of man from *As You Like It* in her essay? Is it appropriate in this context?

2. In paragraph 16, Wray makes an analogy between her mother and an "usher." Is this analogy clear and believable? Why or why not?

Reacting to the Reading: Discussion and Journal Writing

1. Discuss the different ways that families deal with child care and elder care. How does our society support (or not support) families in these situations?

2. Discuss whether you agree that teenagers are the "arbiters of cool" (para. 9).

3. In class or in your journal, describe your earliest childhood memories. Who cared for you as a young child? What relationships were important to you at that point in your life?

Applying Your Skills: Writing Assignments

1. **Paragraph Assignment.** Write a paragraph in which you invent and classify the stages of the teenage years. Identify each stage by name, and include a brief definition that sums up the main characteristic of this period in a teenager's development.

2. Write a classification or division essay about your life and the lives of people you know in terms of stages. These stages could be the same as Wray's, or you might focus on different ones such as educational stages or stages of relationships. Whatever you choose, be sure to clearly state in your thesis what you intend to describe. Use relevant supporting details that are manageable in number and scope.

3. Choose another activity or interest (other than walking), and create an analogy to life stages. You might consider sports, fashion, or collecting, for example. Write a classification or division essay explaining your analogy.

4. **Combining Patterns.** Consulting Wray's classification, identify your current "stage of walking" and evaluate whether your own experience is similar to her description. Write an argumentation essay agreeing or disagreeing with Wray's description of the role of walking. Using narration and description, include examples from your own life to support your argument.

5. **Internet Research.** Visit a Web site that ranks something, such as the American Podiatric Medical Association's list of the best walking cities at www .apma.org/s_apma/doc.asp?CID=18&DID=17913 or *US News and World Report*'s annual list of best colleges at www.usnews.com/usnews/edu/college/rankings/ rankindex_brief.php. Do you agree with the rankings? What criteria did the site use for the rankings? Using similar types of criteria, write a classification essay that ranks things in your own life. For example, if you researched the site about the best walking cities, you might write about walking in your community or on your campus, explaining what makes your area a good or bad place to walk. Be sure to illustrate your points with relevant examples.

The Men We Carry in Our Minds

Scott Russell Sanders

Scott Russell Sanders (b. 1945) grew up in a working-class family in Tennessee and Ohio, went to Brown University on a scholarship, and graduated first in his class. He has written novels, short stories, and children's books, but he is best known for his work in nonfiction, for which he has won numerous awards. Four of his personal essays have been included in volumes of *Best American Essays*, annual collections of outstanding nonfiction work. Sanders is a Distinguished Professor of English at Indiana University.

This essay was originally published in 1984 in the *Milkweed Chronicle* and later appeared in Sanders's collection *The Paradise of Bombs* (1987). As you read, think about the common features he sees in the familiar men from his youth, the "warriors and toilers" he describes. Notice how class differences give the author and the women he meets at college completely different perceptions of men.

Focus on Understanding   Read to discover how the men mentioned in the title influenced the author.

Focus on the Topic   In class or in your journal, discuss the ways that an individual's upbringing can affect his or her future.

The first men, besides my father, I remember seeing were black convicts and white guards, in the cottonfield across the road from our farm on the outskirts of Memphis. I must have been three or four. The prisoners wore dingy gray-and-black zebra suits, heavy as canvas, sodden with sweat. Hatless, stooped, they chopped weeds in the fierce heat, row after row, breathing the acrid dust of boll-weevil° poison. The overseers wore dazzling white shirts and broad shadowy hats. The oiled barrels of their shotguns flashed in the sunlight. Their faces in memory are utterly blank. Of course those men, white and black, have become for me an emblem of racial hatred. But they have also come to stand for the twin poles of my early vision of manhood — the brute toiling animal and the boss. [1]

When I was a boy, the men I knew labored with their bodies. They were marginal farmers, just scraping by, or welders, steel workers, carpenters; they swept floors, dug ditches, mined coal, or drove trucks, their forearms ropy with muscle; they trained horses, stoked furnaces, built tires, stood on assembly lines wrestling parts onto cars and refrigerators. They got up before light, worked all day long whatever the weather, and when they came home at night they looked as though somebody had been whipping them. In the evenings and on weekends they worked on their own places, tilling gardens that were lumpy [2]

boll-weevil: relating to a type of beetle that destroys cotton plants

with clay, fixing broken-down cars, hammering on houses that were always too drafty, too leaky, too small.

The bodies of the men I knew were twisted and maimed in ways visible and invisible. The nails of their hands were black and split, the hands tattooed with scars. Some had lost fingers. Heavy lifting had given many of them finicky backs and guts weak from hernias. Racing against conveyor belts had given them ulcers. Their ankles and knees ached from years of standing on concrete. Anyone who had worked for long around machines was hard of hearing. They squinted, and the skin of their faces was creased like the leather of old work gloves. There were times, studying them, when I dreaded growing up. Most of them coughed, from dust or cigarettes, and most of them drank cheap wine or whiskey, so their eyes looked bloodshot and bruised. The fathers of my friends always seemed older than the mothers. Men wore out sooner. Only women lived into old age.

As a boy I also knew another sort of men, who did not sweat and break down like mules. They were soldiers, and so far as I could tell they scarcely worked at all. During my early school years we lived on a military base, an arsenal in Ohio, and every day I saw GIs in the guardshacks, on the stoops of barracks, at the wheels of olive drab Chevrolets. The chief fact of their lives was boredom. Long after I left the Arsenal I came to recognize the sour smell the soldiers gave off as that of souls in limbo. They were all waiting — for wars, for transfers, for leaves, for promotions, for the end of their hitch — like so many braves waiting for the hunt to begin. Unlike the warriors of older tribes, however, they would have no say about when the battle would start or how it would be waged. Their waiting was broken only when they practiced for war. They fired guns at targets, drove tanks across the churned-up fields of the military reservation, set off bombs in the wrecks of old fighter planes. I knew this was all play. But I also felt certain that when the hour for killing arrived, they would kill. When the real shooting started, many of them would die. This was what soldiers were *for*, just as a hammer was for driving nails.

Warriors and toilers: those seemed, in my boyhood vision, to be the chief destinies for men. They weren't the only destinies, as I learned from having a few male teachers, from reading books, and from watching television. But the men on television — the politicians, the astronauts, the generals, the savvy

3

4

5

lawyers, the philosophical doctors, the bosses who gave orders to both soldiers and laborers — seemed as remote and unreal to me as the figures in tapestries. I could no more imagine growing up to become one of these cool, potent creatures than I could imagine becoming a prince.

A nearer and more hopeful example was that of my father, who had escaped from a red-dirt farm to a tire factory, and from the assembly line to the front office. Eventually he dressed in a white shirt and tie. He carried himself as if he had been born to work with his mind. But his body, remembering the earlier years of slogging work, began to give out on him in his fifties, and it quit on him entirely before he turned sixty-five. Even such a partial escape from man's fate as he had accomplished did not seem possible for most of the boys I knew. They joined the Army, stood in line for jobs in the smoky plants, helped build highways. They were bound to work as their fathers had worked, killing themselves or preparing to kill others.

A scholarship enabled me not only to attend college, a rare enough feat in my circle, but even to study in a university meant for the children of the rich. Here I met for the first time young men who had assumed from birth that they would lead lives of comfort and power. And for the first time I met women who told me that men were guilty of having kept all the joys and privileges of the earth for themselves. I was baffled. What privileges? What joys? I thought about the maimed, dismal lives of most of the men back home. What had they stolen from their wives and daughters? The right to go five days a week, twelve months a year, for thirty or forty years to a steel mill or a coal mine? The right to drop bombs and die in war? The right to feel every leak in the roof, every gap in the fence, every cough in the engine, as a wound they must mend? The right to feel, when the layoff comes or the plant shuts down, not only afraid but ashamed?

I was slow to understand the deep grievances of women. This was because, as a boy, I had envied them. Before college, the only people I had ever known who were interested in art or music or literature, the only ones who read books, the only ones who ever seemed to enjoy a sense of ease and grace were the mothers and daughters. Like the menfolk, they fretted about money, they scrimped and made-do. But, when the pay stopped coming in, they were not the ones who had failed. Nor did they have to go to war, and that seemed to me a blessed fact. By comparison with the narrow, ironclad days of fathers, there was an expansiveness, I thought, in the days of mothers. They went to see neighbors, to shop in town, to run errands at school, at the library, at church. No doubt, had I looked harder at their lives, I would have envied them less. It was not my fate to become a woman, so it was easier for me to see the graces. Few of them held jobs outside the home, and those who did filled thankless roles as clerks and waitresses. I didn't see, then, what a prison a house could be, since houses seemed to me brighter, handsomer places than any factory. I didn't realize — because such things were never spoken of — how often women suffered from men's bullying. I did learn about the wretchedness of abandoned wives, single mothers, widows; but I also learned about the wretchedness of lone men. Even then I could see how exhausting it was for a mother to cater all day to the needs of young children. But if I had been asked, as a boy, to choose between tending a baby and tending a machine, I think I would have chosen the baby. (Having now tended both, I know I would choose the baby.)

So I was baffled when the women at college accused me and my sex of having cornered the world's pleasures. I think something like my bafflement has been felt by other boys (and by girls as well) who grew up in dirt-poor farm country, in mining country, in black ghettos, in Hispanic barrios, in the shadows of factories, in Third World nations — any place where the fate of men is as grim and bleak as the fate of women. Toilers and warriors. I realize now how ancient these identities are, how deep the tug they exert on men, the undertow of a thousand generations. The miseries I saw, as a boy, in the lives of nearly all men I continue to see in the lives of many — the body-breaking toil, the tedium, the call to be tough, the humiliating powerlessness, the battle for a living and for territory.

When the women I met at college thought about the joys and privileges of men, they did not carry in their minds the sort of men I had known in my childhood. They thought of their fathers, who were bankers, physicians, architects, stockbrokers, the big wheels of the big cities. These fathers rode the train to work or drove cars that cost more than any of my childhood houses. They were attended from morning to night by female helpers, wives and nurses and secretaries. They were never laid off, never short of cash at month's end, never lined up for welfare. These fathers made decisions that mattered. They ran the world.

The daughters of such men wanted to share in this power, this glory. So did I. They yearned for a say over their future, for jobs worthy of their abilities, for the right to live at peace, unmolested, whole. Yes, I thought, yes yes. The difference between me and these daughters was that they saw me, because of my sex, as destined from birth to become like their fathers, and therefore as an enemy to their desires. But I knew better. I wasn't an enemy, in fact or in feeling. I was an ally. If I had known, then, how to tell them so, would they have believed me? Would they now?

Understanding the Reading

1. What types of men does the author describe?
2. Why did Sanders envy women when he was a boy? How did his view of women change while he was in college?
3. How was the author different from the other students at his university?
4. As a child, what did Sanders expect to be when he grew up?

Visualizing the Reading

Analyze the effectiveness of Sanders's classification essay by completing the following graphic organizer.

Title	"The Men We Carry in Our Minds"

Introduction	Topic: Background information: Thesis (implied):

	1.	— Characteristics:
Body Paragraphs: Categories or Parts	2.	— Characteristics:
	3.	— Characteristics:
	4.	— Characteristics:

Conclusion	

Examining the Characteristics of Classification and Division Essays

1. Identify Sanders's thesis statement. On what bases does he create categories? How does he organize them? Analyze the effectiveness of the author's choices.

2. Identify one category that you find particularly effective. What kinds of details does Sanders supply that help you "see" this category?

3. Are there any categories in this essay that are not fully explained or that overlap with others? Explain.

4. Classification or division is often used in conjunction with other types of writing. What other patterns of development does Sanders use in this essay?

5. How does the conclusion reaffirm the thesis? What insight does Sanders offer in the conclusion?

Building Your Word Power

1. Underline some of the descriptive words in paragraph 3 relating to factory work. What do these words emphasize about this type of work?

2. Evaluate the author's use of the figurative expressions "the sour smell the soldiers gave off as that of souls in limbo" (para. 4) and "the men on television . . . as remote and unreal . . . as the figures in tapestries" (para. 5). Are these similes effective? Why or why not?

3. Explain the meaning of each of the following words as it is used in the reading: *emblem* (para. 1), *finicky* (3), *slogging* (6), *undertow* (9), and *tedium* (9). Refer to your dictionary as needed.

For a definition of simile, see the chart of commonly used language features on p. 21.

Building Your Critical Thinking Skills: Evaluating Titles

In evaluating a title, readers should consider how the title relates to the thesis and whether it is appropriate to that particular type of writing. Although all good titles reflect the purpose, audience, and tone of the reading, writers use different techniques to capture readers' attention at the outset via the title. In academic writing, the title is usually straightforward and describes the essay's content, such as *The Use of Vitamin B Therapy in Patients over the Age of 75*. Sometimes a question is posed, such as *Terrorism: Just How Worried Should We Be?* More informal writing styles may use other techniques including humor, catchy phrases, or shocking information, such as *Violent Media Is Good for Kids*. Using your knowledge of evaluating titles, answer the following questions.

1. What is the meaning of Sanders's title?

2. Evaluate the appropriateness and effectiveness of the reading's title. If you do not find it to be effective, suggest some alternative titles.

Reacting to the Reading: Discussion and Journal Writing

1. "The Men We Carry in Our Minds" describes a time over thirty-five years ago. Discuss whether Sanders's views of men and women are still applicable today.

2. Sanders's essay ends with two questions. How do you think he would answer them? How would you?

3. In class or in your journal, discuss what you thought as a child you would be when you grew up.

Applying Your Skills: Writing Assignments

1. **Paragraph Assignment.** Write a paragraph classifying the various roles that women assume in today's families.

2. Brainstorm a list of the occupations held by people in your family, neighborhood, and your friends' families when you were growing up. Create categories for these types of professions, and write a classification essay describing these different kinds of jobs. Address how you felt the occupations affected family life and whether gender was a significant factor. If applicable, conclude with your thoughts on how these people affected your college and career choices.

3. Write a division essay discussing the ingredients of job success. Analyze the components of jobs that you have held: What skills, knowledge, and mind-set did they require? Use examples from your own job experiences so that readers can easily understand each part of your essay.

4. Combining Patterns. Examine gender differences on your campus. For example, what is the ratio of men to women in certain majors or on the faculty? Are there any special organizations or programs just for women or men? In an essay for the student newspaper, use classification to categorize the information that you discovered. Supporting your position with concrete examples, argue for or against more efforts for gender equality on campus.

5. Internet Research. Classification is used throughout the Internet to organize and sort material on Web sites. Visit a historical archive such as the one sponsored by the U.S. Department of Labor entitled "A Pictorial Walk through the 20th Century: Honoring the U.S. Miner," at www.msha.gov/century/century.htm. Review the materials included in the archive, and evaluate how the site categorizes and organizes information. For example, the Web site honoring the U.S. miner includes pictures and text sorted by different types of miners (Irish, African American, children, etc.). Based on your research, write a classification essay about what you learned. Explain some of the different categories included on the site, using examples from the archive along with sensory details to help your reader "see" the information. Your thesis should identify the Web site and the categories used and explain why this information is important.

The Ways of Meeting Oppression

Martin Luther King Jr.

Martin Luther King Jr. (1929–1968) was America's best-known civil rights leader of the 1960s. While serving as pastor of the Dexter Avenue Church in Montgomery, Alabama, King helped to organize the 1955–1956 Montgomery bus boycott to protest the arrest of a black woman, Rosa Parks, who had refused to give up her seat to a white passenger. King worked tirelessly for civil rights for black Americans for over a decade, advocating a policy of nonviolent resistance to racism and segregation. His struggle for civil rights was honored with a Nobel Prize for Peace in 1964. King was assassinated on April 4, 1968, in Memphis, Tennessee.

Among King's writings is *Stride toward Freedom* (1958), his book about the bus boycott, from which the following essay was taken. As you read, pay attention to the way King draws on other authorities — such as the Bible, Shakespeare, and philosophy — to convince readers of the need for nonviolent resistance to oppression.

Focus on Understanding   As you read, identify the different ways to meet oppression.

Focus on the Topic   In class or in your journal, write about a time when you witnessed a person or group of people dealing with oppression, or a personal experience that you had with oppression.

Oppressed people deal with their oppression in three characteristic ways. One way is acquiescence: the oppressed resign themselves to their doom. They tacitly adjust themselves to oppression, and thereby become conditioned to it. In every movement toward freedom some of the oppressed prefer to remain oppressed. Almost 2800 years ago Moses set out to lead the children of Israel from the slavery of Egypt to the freedom of the promised land. He soon discovered that slaves do not always welcome their deliverers. They become accustomed to being slaves. They would rather bear those ills they have, as Shakespeare pointed out, than flee to others that they know not of. They prefer the "fleshpots of Egypt"° to the ordeals of emancipation.

There is such a thing as the freedom of exhaustion. Some people are so worn down by the yoke of oppression that they give up. A few years ago in the slum areas of Atlanta, a Negro guitarist used to sing almost daily: "Been down so long that down don't bother me." This is the type of negative freedom and resignation that often engulfs the life of the oppressed.

But this is not the way out. To accept passively an unjust system is to cooperate with that system; thereby the oppressed become as evil as the

"fleshpots of Egypt": biblical reference to districts or establishments offering sensual pleasure or entertainment

1

2

3

379

oppressor. Noncooperation with evil is as much a moral obligation as is cooperation with good. The oppressed must never allow the conscience of the oppressor to slumber. Religion reminds every man that he is his brother's keeper. To accept injustice or segregation passively is to say to the oppressor that his actions are morally right. It is a way of allowing his conscience to fall asleep. At this moment the oppressed fails to be his brother's keeper. So acquiescence — while often the easier way — is not the moral way. It is the way of the coward. The Negro cannot win the respect of his oppressor by acquiescing; he merely increases the oppressor's arrogance and contempt. Acquiescence is interpreted as proof of the Negro's inferiority. The Negro cannot win the respect of the white people of the South or the peoples of the world if he is willing to sell the future of his children for his personal and immediate comfort and safety.

A second way that oppressed people sometimes deal with oppression is to resort to physical violence and corroding hatred. Violence often brings about momentary results. Nations have frequently won their independence in battle. But in spite of temporary victories, violence never brings permanent peace. It solves no social problem; it merely creates new and more complicated ones.   4

Violence as a way of achieving racial justice is both impractical and immoral. It is impractical because it is a descending spiral ending in destruction for all. The old law of an eye for an eye leaves everybody blind. It is immoral because it seeks to humiliate the opponent rather than win his understanding; it seeks to annihilate rather than to convert. Violence is immoral because it thrives on hatred rather than love. It destroys community and makes brotherhood impossible. It leaves society in monologue rather than dialogue. Violence ends by defeating itself. It creates bitterness in the survivors and brutality in the destroyers. A voice echoes through time saying to every potential Peter,° "Put up your sword." History is cluttered with the wreckage of nations that failed to follow this command.   5

If the American Negro and other victims of oppression succumb to the temptation of using violence in the struggle for freedom, future generations will be the recipients of a desolate night of bitterness, and our chief legacy to them will be an endless reign of meaningless chaos. Violence is not the way.   6

The third way open to oppressed people in their quest for freedom is the way of nonviolent resistance. Like the synthesis in Hegelian philosophy,° the principle of nonviolent resistance seeks to reconcile the truths of two opposites — acquiescence and violence — while avoiding the extremes and immoralities of both. The nonviolent resister agrees with the person who acquiesces that one should not be physically aggressive toward his opponent; but he balances the equation by agreeing with the person of violence that evil must be resisted. He avoids the nonresistance of the former and the violent resistance of the latter. With nonviolent resistance, no individual or group need submit to any wrong, nor need anyone resort to violence in order to right a wrong.   7

It seems to me that this is the method that must guide the actions of the Negro in the present crisis in race relations. Through nonviolent resistance the Negro will be able to rise to the noble height of opposing the unjust system   8

Peter: one of Christ's apostles who drew his sword to defend Christ from arrest, but Christ, the voice cited by King, responded by directing Peter to put away his sword

Hegelian philosophy: Hegel (1770–1831) was a German philosopher who proposed that truth is reached by stating a thesis, developing a contradictory antithesis, and combining and resolving them into a coherent message, or synthesis while loving the perpetrators of the system. The Negro must work passionately and unrelentingly for full stature as a citizen, but he must not use inferior methods to gain it. He must never come to terms with falsehood, malice, hate, or destruction.

Nonviolent resistance makes it possible for the Negro to remain in the South and struggle for his rights. The Negro's problem will not be solved by running away. He cannot listen to the glib suggestion of those who would urge him to migrate en masse to other sections of the country. By grasping his great opportunity in the South he can make a lasting contribution to the moral strength of the nation and set a sublime example of courage for generations yet unborn. 9

By nonviolent resistance, the Negro can also enlist all men of good will in his struggle for equality. The problem is not a purely racial one, with Negroes set against whites. In the end, it is not a struggle between people at all, but a tension between justice and injustice. Nonviolent resistance is not aimed against oppressors but against oppression. Under its banner consciences, not racial groups, are enlisted. 10

Understanding the Reading

1. According to King, why do some people prefer to remain oppressed?
2. Which response to oppression does King consider cowardly?
3. Why is violence an impractical method for achieving racial justice? Why, according to King, is it also immoral?
4. What are the "truths" of acquiescence and violence? How does the principle of nonviolent resistance reconcile these truths?

Examining the Characteristics of Classification and Division Essays

1. Identify King's thesis statement. Does it reveal why the classification is relevant or important? If not, how does King present this information?
2. Consider the organization of the essay. Why do you think King presents acquiescence, violence, and nonviolent resistance in that order?
3. Are the categories in the essay exclusive and comprehensive? That is, do the types of responses to oppression not overlap with one another? Does King provide a similar amount and kind of detail for each category? Explain.
4. Identify how King uses transitions to help readers stay on track as they move from one category to another.
5. What other patterns of development does King use within each category?

Visualizing the Reading

The three photos above show different responses to being an African American in the 1930s and the 1960s. The first image shows Martin Luther King Jr. waving to the crowd at the civil rights march in Washington, D.C., on August 28, 1963. The second image shows a group of Black Panthers, a militant black organization, in 1969. The final photograph shows a man drinking from a segregated water fountain in Oklahoma City in 1939. According to King's categories for "meeting oppression," how would you classify the actions shown in these photos? Can you think of other ways to classify these images, either together or separately?

Building Your Word Power

1. Explain the religious allusions to "his brother's keeper" (para. 3) and "an eye for an eye" (para. 5). How does King use allusions like these to support his statements? Considering the author's background and purpose, why might he rely on so many biblical allusions to convey his message?

2. Choose two of the following words or phrases that have strong connotative meanings. Define these words, and discuss their effect on the reader's response to King's message: *slaves* (para. 1), *brother's keeper* (3), *coward* (3), annihilate (5), *perpetrators* (8).

3. Explain the meaning of each of the following words as it is used in the reading: *acquiescence* (para. 1), *emancipation* (1), *corroding* (4), *monologue* (5), and *synthesis* (7). Refer to your dictionary as needed.

For a definition of allusion and connotative meaning, see the chart of commonly used language features on p. 21.

Building Your Critical Thinking Skills: Figures of Speech

A **figure of speech** is a comparison that makes sense creatively or imaginatively, but not literally. Figures of speech are useful tools because they help writers create vivid images for readers while helping them understand the idea or concept by comparing it to something familiar. There are many different types of figures of speech, but the most common are *simile, metaphor*, and *personification*. Be sure to evaluate figures of speech to determine whether they are effective: How closely are the two concepts related? Do the two ideas have enough in common? To what purpose is the figure of speech used? Using your knowledge of evaluating figures of speech, assess the effectiveness of this writing strategy by explaining King's use of figurative language in each of the following examples.

For a definition of simile, metaphor, and personification, see Chapter 6, pp. 149–50.

1. "the yoke of oppression" (para. 2)
2. "negative freedom" (para. 2)
3. "to sell the future" (para. 3)
4. "a descending spiral" (para. 5)
5. "the wreckage of nations" (para. 5)
6. "a desolate night of bitterness" (para. 6)

Reacting to the Reading: Discussion and Journal Writing

1. Discuss violence as a response to oppression. Can you think of any situation in which violent behavior might be justified?

2. King discusses acquiescence as a response to oppression. Think of a time when you chose to acquiesce to a situation rather than oppose it. Why did you choose to acquiesce? Would you do things differently if you were in the same situation again?

Applying Your Skills: Writing Assignments

1. **Paragraph Assignment.** In a paragraph, outline three possible responses to a particular situation, ending with the one you consider most appropriate. You might, for example, explain the different responses to finding a wallet full of money on the street.

2. Do you agree with King that there are three basic responses to oppression? Write an essay based on your own experiences that explores and classifies other possible

responses to oppression or conflict. (Hint: Be sure to define your use of the word *oppression* so that it applies to the situations you are describing.)

3. What avenues does your college offer to students who experience difficulty dealing with depression, a particular course, or a living situation? Write an essay using division that explains the different aspects of the health and counseling services at your college.

4. **Combining Patterns.** Choose one of King's classifications (acquiescence, violence, nonviolent resistance), and write an essay arguing that this "way of meeting oppression" is appropriate in certain situations. Explain the different categories for your reader, and describe one particular situation (real or imagined) where you would advocate the use of this approach.

5. **Internet Research.** Use the World Wide Web to research some famous leaders' approach to oppression or conflict. You might consider Malcolm X, Mahatma Gandhi, the Dalai Lama, Mother Teresa, Franklin D. Roosevelt, or Joan of Arc. Write an essay that classifies the different leadership styles of at least three individuals and explores the success or failure of their approach to oppression or conflict.

Profile of a Terrorist

Cindy C. Combs

Cindy C. Combs is an internationally known expert on terrorism and a professor of political science at the University of North Carolina in Charlotte. She is the author of *Terrorism in the Twenty-First Century* (2003), a leading textbook on terrorism, from which this excerpt was taken. Combs has also coauthored the *Encyclopedia of Terrorism* (2002) and lectured widely on the subject.

In "Profile of a Terrorist," Combs breaks down categories of terrorists and analyzes what motivates each group and what each expects to gain from an act of terror. As you read, notice in what ways the types of terrorists are different and similar. Combs also explains why understanding the differences is crucially important for those who hope to prevent future attacks.

Focus on Understanding   Read to discover why it is important to understand the different types of terrorists.

Focus on the Topic   In class or in your journal, explore your thoughts and concerns about terrorism *prior to* September 11, 2001.

What kind of person becomes a terrorist? Perhaps an understanding of the 1 dynamics of becoming a terrorist will increase our understanding of this phenomenon. . . . Terrorist acts are committed for a wide variety of causes. It is also true that a variety of individuals and groups commit terrorist acts. Although studying all such persons in detail is not feasible, a brief analysis of some of the important characteristics of modern terrorists might be informative.

The political world changed a great deal in the last two decades of the twen- 2 tieth century. These political changes have influenced the type of persons more likely to be recruited into terrorist groups. A study of the type of individuals known to be drawn to terrorism in the twentieth century will, perhaps, help us to predict the most probable type of twenty-first century terrorist. This could be an extremely useful tool for governments and institutions that must plan to cope with terrorism.

Why do people become terrorists? Are they crazy? Are they thrill seekers? 3 Are they religious fanatics? Are they ideologues?° Is there any way to tell who is likely to become a terrorist?

This final question provides a clue as to why political scientists and gov- 4 ernment officials are particularly interested in the psychological factors relating to terrorism. If one could identify the traits most closely related to a willingness to use terrorist tactics, then one would be in a better position to predict, and prevent, the emergence of terrorist groups.

ideologues: people who blindly follow a certain set of theories

385

Unfortunately, identifying such traits is not easy. Just as not all violence is   5
terrorism, and not all revolutionaries are terrorists, not all persons who commit
acts of terrorism are alike. Frederick Hacker suggested three categories of persons who commit terrorism: *crazies, criminals,* and *crusaders.* He notes that an
individual carrying out a terrorist act is seldom "purely" one type or the other
but that each type offers some insights into why an individual will resort to
terrorism.[1]

Understanding the individual who commits terrorism is vital, not only for   6
humanitarian reasons, but also to decide how best to deal with those individuals *while they are engaged in terrorist acts.* From a law enforcement perspective,
for example, it is important to appreciate the difference between a criminal and
a crusading terrorist involved in a hostage-taking situation. Successful resolution of such a situation often hinges on understanding the mind of the individual perpetrating the crime.

Let us consider the three categories of terrorists suggested by Hacker: cra-   7
zies, criminals, and crusaders. For the purposes of this study, we need to establish loose descriptions of these three types. Hacker offers some useful ideas on
what is subsumed under each label. **Crazies,** he suggests, are *emotionally disturbed individuals who are driven to commit terrorism "by reasons of their own
that often do not make sense to anybody else."*

Criminals, on the other hand, *perform terrorist acts for more easily under-*   8
stood reasons: personal gain. Such individuals transgress the laws of society
knowingly and, one assumes, in full possession of their faculties. Both their motives and their goals are usually clear, if still deplorable, to most of humanity.

This is not the case with the crusaders. These individuals commit terrorism   9
for reasons that are often unclear both to themselves and to those witnessing
the acts. Their ultimate goals are frequently even less understandable. Although
such individuals are usually idealistically inspired, their idealism tends to be a
rather mixed bag of half-understood philosophies. **Crusaders,** according to
Hacker, *seek not personal gain, but prestige and power for a collective cause.* They
commit terrorist acts in the belief "that they are serving a higher cause," in
Hacker's assessment.

What difference does it make what kind of terrorist is behind the machine   10
gun or bomb? To the law enforcement personnel charged with resolving the
hostage situation, it can be crucial to know what type of person is controlling
the situation. Criminals, for instance, can be offered sufficient personal gains
or security provisions to induce them to release the hostages. Crusaders are far
less likely to be talked out of carrying out their threats by inducements of personal gains, because to do so they would have to betray, in some sense, that
higher cause for which they are committing the action.

For the same reason, it is useful to security agents to know what type of in-   11
dividual is likely to commit a terrorist act within their province. A criminal, for

[1]Frederick J. Hacker, *Crusaders, Criminals, Crazies: Terror and Terrorism in Our Time*
(New York: Norton, 1976, pp. 8–9).

example, would be more likely to try to smuggle a gun aboard an airline than a bomb, because the criminal usually anticipates living to enjoy the reward of his or her illegal activities. Crusaders, however, are more willing to blow themselves up with their victims, because their service to that higher cause often carries with it a promise of a reward in the life to come.

The distinction between criminals and crusaders with respect to terrorism 12 needs some clarification. Clearly, when anyone breaks the law, as in the commission of a terrorist act, he or she becomes a criminal, regardless of the reason for the transgression. The distinction between criminal and crusader, though, is useful in understanding the differences in the motives and goals moving the person to commit the act.

The majority of the individuals and groups carrying out terrorist acts in the 13 world in the last decade of the twentieth and the beginning of the twenty-first century have been crusaders. This does not mean that there are not occasional instances in which individuals who, reacting to some real or perceived injury, decide to take a machine gun to the target of their anger or kidnap or destroy anyone in sight. Nor does it mean that there are not individual criminals and criminal organizations that engage in terrorist activities.

Nonetheless, the majority of individuals who commit modern terrorism 14 are, or perceive themselves to be, crusaders. According to Hacker, the typical crusading terrorist appears to be normal, no matter how crazy his or her cause or how criminal the means he or she uses for this cause may seem. He or she is neither an idiot nor a fool, neither a coward nor a weakling. Instead, the crusading terrorist is frequently a professional, well trained, well prepared, and well disciplined in the habit of blind obedience to a cause.

The following table indicates a few dramatic differences between the types 15 of terrorists Hacker profiles. One is that crusaders are the least likely to negotiate a resolution to a crisis, both because such action can be viewed as a betrayal of a sublime cause and because there is little that the negotiator can offer,

HACKER'S TYPOLOGY° OF TERRORISTS

typology: the study or systematic classification of types

TYPE OF TERRORIST	MOTIVE/GOAL	WILLING TO NEGOTIATE?	EXPECTATION OF SURVIVAL
Crazy	Clear only to perpetrator	Possible, but only if negotiator can understand motive and offer hope/alternatives	Strong, but not based on reality
Criminal	Personal gain/profit	Usually, in return for profit and/or safe passage	Strong
Crusader	"Higher cause" (usually a blend of religious and political)	Seldom, because to do so could be seen as a betrayal of the cause	Minimal, because death offers reward in an afterlife

because neither personal gain nor safe passage out of the situation are particularly desired by true crusaders. Belief in the cause makes death not a penalty, but a path to reward and glory; therefore, the threat of death and destruction can have little punitive value. What can a police or military negotiator offer to a crusader to induce the release of hostages or the defusing of a bomb?

Similar problems exist with crazies, depending on how much in touch with reality such an individual is at the time of the incident. Negotiation is difficult, but not impossible, if the negotiator can ascertain the goal/motive of the perpetrator and offer some hope (even if it is not real) of success in achieving that goal by other, less destructive means. One of the critical elements is that crazies, according to Hacker's evaluation, have a limited grip on the reality that they themselves may die in the course of this action. Thus, the threat of death by a superior force carries diminished weight if the perpetrator cannot grasp the fact that he or she may die in this encounter. Just as very young children find the reality of death a difficult concept to grasp, Hacker suggests that crazies offer serious difficulties for negotiators because they often cannot grasp this reality. 16

Criminals, then, are the preferred perpetrators, because they will negotiate; their demands are generally logical (although often outrageous) and are based in terms that can be met or satisfied with rational alternatives. Criminals know that they can be killed and have a strong belief/desire to live to enjoy the rewards of the actions they are taking. Thus, negotiators have specific demands to be bartered, and their "clients" can be expected to recognize superior force and to respond accordingly in altering demands and resolving the incident. 17

These differences are critically important in at least two contexts: (1) resolving situations in which hostages are held by terrorists and (2) establishing security measures and training for vulnerable targets. The type of terrorist engaged in the incident significantly impacts the successful resolution of the situation. Hostage negotiators need to know whether they are dealing with a crusader or a criminal, to know whether negotiation has any potential. If the individual(s) perpetrating the crime are crusaders, then an immediate hostage rescue attempt may be more appropriate than the initiation of a negotiation process. 18

In terms of security devices and training, the profiles become even more vital. The events of September 11, 2001, illustrate dramatically the consequences of training and equipping for the wrong type of perpetrators. The pilots of airlines in the United States had been trained to respond to attempts to take over flights as hostage situations and thus were engaged in trying to keep the situation calm and to "talk down" the plane, to initiate a hostage release without violence. But the individuals engaged in the takeover were crusaders, not criminals or crazies, who did not plan to live through the incidents. Only the passengers on the flight that crashed in Pennsylvania were able to offer substantial resistance — perhaps in part because they had not been trained to assume that a peaceful resolution could be negotiated with hostage takers. 19

This does not suggest that the pilots and crew were not vigilant and did not 20 make every effort to save the lives of the passengers. But because the profile they had been trained to respond to did not match that with which they were confronted, they were unable to respond successfully to the demands of the situation. Thus, inaccurate profiling in pilot training was a serious contributing factor to the sequence of events on that day.

To political scientists, as well as to military, police, and other security and 21 intelligence units assigned the task of coping with terrorism, an understanding of the type of person likely to commit acts of terrorism is invaluable. As our understanding of a phenomenon increases, our ability to predict its behavior with some accuracy also increases. Thus, as we try to understand who terrorists are and what they are like, we should increase our ability to anticipate their behavior patterns, thereby increasing our ability to respond effectively and to prevent more often the launching of successful terrorist attacks.

Understanding the Reading

1. According to the author, what are the differences among "crazy," "criminal," and "crusader" terrorists?
2. Describe the typical outcome of each type of terrorist situation.
3. Why does the author mention the pilots of the plane that crashed in Pennsylvania?
4. Why does the author want law enforcement agencies to know more about terrorists?

Visualizing the Reading

Wanted by Interpol
BIN LADEN, Usama

Using Frederick Hacker's categories of terrorists, decide what type of terrorist Osama Bin Laden is. Write a paragraph explaining how he fits the category you have chosen.

Examining the Characteristics of Classification and Division Essays

1. Identify and evaluate the author's thesis. Does it state the principle of classification used in the essay? Explain.

2. Identify where in the essay Combs names the categories used in her classification. Are enough details provided for each category? Do any of the categories overlap? Explain.

3. Evaluate the usefulness of Frederick Hacker's table on page 387. How do this and other references to Hacker's work aid in your understanding of the essay's classification?

4. Evaluate the conclusion. Compare Combs's restatement of the thesis in the conclusion to its presentation at the beginning of the essay. Is a stronger version presented in the final paragraph? Explain.

Building Your Word Power

For a definition of **idiom**, *see the chart of commonly used language features on p. 21.*

1. Explain the idiom "mixed bag" in paragraph 9.

2. Evaluate the figurative expression "blind obedience" (para. 14). What picture does the expression create in your mind?

3. Explain the meaning of each of the following words as it is used in the reading: *emergence* (para. 4), *transgress* (8), *faculties* (8), *deplorable* (8), *sublime* (15), and *punitive* (15). Refer to your dictionary as needed.

Building Your Critical Thinking Skills: Author's Purpose

To determine the **author's purpose** for writing an essay, you must consider the intended audience, the author's background, and both the stated and unstated reasons for writing. For example, is the author trying to convince you of something or just explain it? Does the author present more than one side of an issue or a strong opinion in favor of only one side? Authors' purposes vary widely, from reporting new academic research to writing to inform or persuade, or even just to entertain. Using what you know about identifying the author's purpose, answer the following questions.

1. Who is the intended audience for this reading? Are there parts of this reading that members of this audience might not understand?

2. Is Combs attempting to convince readers of something? If so, what is it?

3. Does Combs present more than one view of the issue? If so, how does she accomplish this?

Reacting to the Reading: Discussion and Journal Writing

1. Discuss the government's role in protecting us against terrorism. Has it done enough? If not, what should it be doing, and how far should it go in areas such as civil liberties?

2. Discuss Hacker's typology. How useful do you think it is? Is there another type of terrorist that you would add?

3. Refer back to the "Focus on the Topic" question on page 385. In class or in your journal, discuss how your attitude toward terrorism has changed since September 11, 2001.

Applying Your Skills: Writing Assignments

1. Paragraph Assignment. Choose a group of people and, in a paragraph, classify them into types along with a brief description of each type. (Hint: You might choose shoppers, drivers, parents, sales clerks, etc.)

2. The essay presents Hacker's typology of terrorists. In a similar vein, create a typology of college instructors or of college students. Identify at least three categories, and write a classification essay describing your categories.

3. Consider your response to the events of September 11, 2001. Then recall how others responded; consider people you know as well as what you saw, heard, and read in the media. Develop categories of response, and write an essay explaining those categories.

4. Combining Patterns. Write an essay describing and analyzing the long-term effects of the September 11, 2001, terrorist attacks. Limit your essay to the effects on a certain group or area such as law enforcement, travel and tourism, or awareness in your community. Use classification to group the different types of responses to the attacks.

5. Internet Research. Visit the Web site for the Department of Homeland Security at www.dhs.gov. Then write a division essay explaining the different parts and purposes of the agency, which was founded in response to the new challenges of terrorism after the September 11 attacks.

Chapter

11

Definition: Explaining What You Mean

WRITING QUICK START

The photograph on this page shows members of a popular band performing on stage. What kind of music do you like to listen to? Choose one of your favorite musicians or musical groups, and write a paragraph defining the type of music they play. Imagine you are explaining it to someone who is unfamiliar with that type of music, using examples and sensory details to help define exactly how this musical act sounds.

What Is a Definition?

A **definition** explains what a term means or which meaning is intended when a word has several different meanings. You might define *slicing* to someone unfamiliar with golf, or the term *koi* to someone unfamiliar with tropical fish. If you call a friend a *nonconformist*, she might ask exactly what you mean; or you and a friend might disagree over what constitutes *feminism*. Clearly, definitions are an important part of daily communication.

When members of a group share a set of terms with commonly understood meanings, communication is simplified. For example, many sports and hobby enthusiasts have their own special vocabulary: Hockey fans know terms such as *high-sticking, icing, puck,* and *blueline*; cooking enthusiasts know terms such as *sauté, parboil,* and *fillet*. Members of professions and academic fields of study also have specialized terminology: A surgeon, for example, does not ask a surgical nurse for "the small, straight knife with the thin, sharp blade"; he or she simply asks for a *scalpel*. As you can see, terms and meanings make communication precise, helping to avoid misunderstandings and confusion.

Many academic and work situations require that you write or learn definitions, as the following examples illustrate.

- On an exam for a *health and fitness course*, you find the following short-answer question: "Define the term *wellness*."
- As a *chemical engineer* responsible for your department's compliance with the company's standards for *safety* and *work efficiency*, you write a brief memo to your staff defining each term.

In the following essay, Mary Pipher defines the term *cultural brokers*.

Cultural Brokers

Mary Pipher

Mary Pipher (b. 1947), a clinical psychologist, is the author of several books on American culture and its effects on mental health. She is widely known for her best-selling book *Reviving Ophelia* (1994), which explores the psychology of adolescent girls. She has also written about the elderly and the importance of community. In *The Middle of Everywhere* (2002), Pipher discusses the difficulties that refugees face when adjusting to a new culture.

In the following excerpt from *The Middle of Everywhere*, Pipher defines what it means to be a "cultural broker" for newcomers. As you read, notice how cultural brokers' duties resemble — and differ from — those of schoolteachers (who, according to Pipher, often serve as cultural brokers). What items surprise you on Pipher's list of things that she has taught newcomers?

Introduction: uses
comparison and
contrast to describe
difficulties that
immigrants face

The United States is a series of paradoxes for newcomers. Every plus   1
is married to a minus. It is the land of opportunity and yet the opportunity is often to work in a meatpacking plant. Newcomers have fled war
zones for the safety of our country but, in the United States, they often
find themselves in our most dangerous neighborhoods. They are in a
country with sophisticated health and mental health care but often cannot afford even the most basic treatments. They come for our wonderful
educational system, but often their children are educated by television
and learn all the wrong lessons. And finally, they come because of the
generosity of the American people, and yet once here, they must deal with
an unfriendly and grossly inefficient INS [Immigration and Natural-
ization Service].

Introduction of the
term

Brief definition

From the moment refugees arrive they are offered ideas about how to   2
spend their time, energy, and money. There are two main ways refugees
are educated. One is through the media and ads that are omnipresent. The
second is through <u>cultural brokers</u> — schoolteachers, caseworkers, public
health nurses, and American friends who may teach them to make inten-
tional decisions about what to accept and what to reject in America.
<u>Cultural brokers help ease people into each other's cultures.</u> Foucault
wrote that "information is power." Cultural brokers give newcomers information that directly translates into power. . . .

Thesis: establishes
need for cultural
brokers

Right away, refugees must deal with housing, transportation, and le-   3
gal status, as well as work, health, and mental health issues. These external factors have a great deal to do with a refugee's later success in
America. Cultural brokers can make a tremendous difference.

Suggests most-to-
least organization

Distinguishing
characteristic:
educators provide
information

The <u>most important cultural brokers are schoolteachers.</u> Schools are   4
the frontline institution for acculturation, where children receive solid information about their new world. Almost all refugee families have a
tremendous respect for education and educators. And our schools do not
let them down. I have met many heroic teachers who, among their other
responsibilities, become the antidotes to media and ads. One ELL
[English Language Learners] teacher told me, "We're all there is between
them and Howard Stern and Eminem."

Distinguishing
characteristic: teach
judgement and
moderation

Concrete examples

<u>Cultural brokers can teach the difference between *need* and *want* and</u>   5
<u>also the meaning of the word *enough*.</u> They can teach, as Bebe Moore
Campbell said, that "Everything good to you ain't good for you." They can
teach, as Paul Gruchow put it, that "Labor saving machines delivered not
so much freedom from drudgery as enslavement to creditors." Gruchow
also wrote, "Wealth is fully as capable of corrupting the soul as is poverty.
What makes people happy in small doses is not necessarily good in large
amounts. Too much candy, alcohol, leisure time, and shopping choices all
make people miserable."

<u>Cultural brokers encourage families to read, go to museums, draw, learn to play an instrument, and to find a place of worship or a community center.</u> They encourage them to walk on our prairies, fish in our lakes, and ride bikes on our trails. If refugees learn only from television, they will end up unhealthy, stressed, rushed, addicted, and broke.

<u>Cultural brokers teach Budgeting 101.</u> In their home countries, many refugees have not had to manage their desires because never before has there been enough. Cultural brokers try to teach intentionality, that is, thoughtfulness about choices. Intentionality requires a moral center, accurate information, and the skills to implement good decisions.

<u>A cultural broker has information on everything</u> — what schools are the best, where to go fishing or buy lemongrass, where to find work or buy a used car, and how to change a tire. A cultural broker knows whom to call about INS problems and where to get free legal aid and tax assistance. Cultural brokers understand local resources and have a commitment to helping newcomers avoid mistakes that can slow down their adjustment. Below is a list of things that, as a cultural broker, I have taught newcomers.

How to order food in a café

How to use escalators, stairs, elevators, and revolving doors

How to cross streets with traffic lights

How to feed a traffic meter

How to drive — what signs and signals mean, how to start a car, defensive driving as a concept

What is the length of a human life in America

How to use a water fountain

How to tell time and use an alarm clock, a watch, a calendar, and an appointment book

How to work a bike lock and a combination lock

How to put on a bike helmet and why helmets are important

How to check the oil and put gas in a car

How to write a check and balance a checkbook

How to peel an orange and eat watermelon

What to put in a refrigerator

How to bake a frozen pizza and use Shake 'n Bake to cook chicken

How to mix juice

That most Americans shower daily

What a doctor is doing — taking a temperature, blood pressure, drawing blood

What are dangerous situations — don't ride with strangers and don't walk around alone at night

---

Marginal annotations:

6 — Distinguishing characteristic: encourage active participation

Cause and effect

7 — Distinguishing characteristic: teach budgeting and decision making

8 — Distinguishing characteristic: source of information

Concrete examples illustrate what cultural brokers teach

Why we don't give money to phone or door-to-door solicitors . . .

What *homesick* means

What a washing machine is

What aluminum foil is

Why American parents talk to babies

What animals pork and beef come from

What a tissue is

What a rocking chair is

What a dinosaur is

Why we shouldn't litter

How to eat an ice-cream cone

Distinguishing characteristic: accompanies immigrants and serves as guide

One aspect of being a cultural broker is being an introducer. Cultural brokers can attend every first meeting between a refugee and a caseworker, doctor, banker, or employer. Just being present as a supportive friend helps these first meetings, often filled with anxiety on all sides, go more smoothly. If a local person accompanies newcomers to their first Jazz in June, contra dance, or GED [General Equivalency Degree] session, the newcomers may later return alone. Without a guide, certain things never seem to happen on their own.   9

Value and importance of cultural brokers

Having a cultural broker can make a tremendous difference in how successfully a new family adapts to America. People come here traumatized, and the trauma doesn't end with arrival. Without guidance and support, it's difficult to survive.   10

Conclusion: song lyric reaffirms the importance of cultural brokers

Every newcomer needs someone who knows how to get things done locally. Communities are nuanced cultures, and the nuances are precisely what newcomers need help with. Songwriter Greg Brown might have been speaking of cultural brokers when he wrote, "Your hometown is where you know what the deal is. You may not like it, but you understand it."   11

Characteristics of Definition Essays

There will be many occasions to use definition in your writing. For example, when you suspect your reader may not understand a key term, offer a brief definition. Often, however, a standard definition will not be sufficient to explain a complex idea. At times you may need a paragraph or an entire essay to define a single term. For instance, if you had to define the term *happiness*, you would probably have trouble coming up with a brief definition because the emotion is experienced in a variety of situations. In an essay-length piece of writing, however, you could explore the term and explain all that it means to you. Such a lengthy, detailed definition is an **extended definition**.

Definitions Often Include a Brief Explanation of the Term

Almost any kind of essay will include a brief definition of an important **term**. Even in an extended definition essay, it is useful to include a brief definition to help readers begin to grasp the concept. A brief or standard definition (the kind found in a dictionary) consists of three parts:

- the *term* itself
- the *class* to which the term belongs
- the *characteristics* that distinguish the term from all others in its class

For example, a *wedding band* is a piece of jewelry. "Jewelry" is the **class**, or group, of objects that includes wedding bands. To show how a wedding band differs from other members of that class, you would need to define its **distinguishing charac-teristics** — the features that make it different from other types of jewelry. You could say that a wedding band is a ring, often made of gold, that the groom gives to the bride or the bride gives to the groom during a marriage ceremony. Likewise, you might explain that a *Dalmatian* (the term) is a "breed of dog" (the class to which the term belongs) that originated in Dalmatia and is known for its short, smooth coat with black or dark brown spots (distinguishing characteristics).

Guidelines for Writing a Standard Definition

1. **Describe the class as specifically as possible.** In the preceding example, no-tice that for *Dalmatian* the class is not "animal" or "mammal," but "breed of dog." Narrowing the class will make it easier for readers to understand the term.

2. **Do not use the term (or forms of the term) as part of your definition.** Synonyms may be helpful as substitutes for a term. For example, do not write, "*Mastery* means that one has *mastered* a skill." In place of *mastered*, you could use *learned*.

3. **Include enough distinguishing characteristics so that readers will not mistake the term for something similar within the class.** If you define *an-swering machine* as "a machine that records messages," your definition would be incomplete because other machines (such as computers) also record messages.

4. **Do not limit the definition so much that it becomes inaccurate.** Defining *bacon* as "a smoked, salted meat from a pig that is served at breakfast" would be too limited because bacon is also served at other mealtimes (at lunch, for instance, as part of a bacon, lettuce, and tomato sandwich) and other salted, smoked pork products are sometimes served at breakfast (ham, for instance).

Look at the following definition of the term *bully*, taken from a magazine ar-ticle on the topic. As you read it, study the highlighting and marginal notes.

Term

Three characteristics

Distinguishes this
term from similar
terms

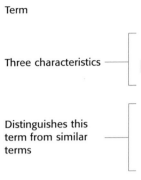

The term *bully* does not have a standard definition, but Dan
Olweus, professor of psychology at the University of Bergen,
has honed the definition to three core elements — bullying
involves a pattern of *repeated aggressive behavior* with *negative intent* directed from one child to another where there is
a *power difference.* Either a larger child or several children
pick on one child, or one child is clearly more dominant
than the others. Bullying is not the same as garden-variety
aggression; although aggression may involve similar acts, it
happens between two people of equal status. By definition,
the bully's target has difficulty defending him- or herself,
and the bully's aggressive behavior is intended to cause distress.

Example of power
difference

HARA ESTROFF MARANO, *"Big. Bad. Bully."*

Definition Is Specific and Focused

An extended definition focuses on a specific term and discusses it in detail. In her
essay, Pipher concentrates on defining the specific term *cultural brokers*. She explains who cultural brokers are, how they aid refugees, and why they are so important to immigrant families. Pipher does not sidetrack readers by discussing
other aspects of immigrants' lives.

Definition Makes a Point

The thesis of an extended definition essay often includes a brief standard definition of the term and tells why it is worth reading about, as in the following:
"Produced by the body, hormones are chemicals that are important to physical as
well as emotional development."

Sometimes, however, writers separate the brief definition from their thesis. In
"Cultural Brokers," for instance, Pipher defines the term briefly in paragraph 2
("Cultural brokers help ease people into each other's cultures") but states her thesis in paragraph 3: "Cultural brokers can make a tremendous difference [in how
well refugees succeed in America]."

Definition Uses Other Patterns of Development

To explain the meaning of a term, writers usually integrate one or more patterns
of development. Here are some examples of how other patterns might be used in
an extended definition.

- *Narrate* a term's origins (or etymology) or a story that demonstrates its use
  (Chapter 5).
- *Describe* the item a term stands for (Chapter 6).
- Offer examples to *illustrate* how a term is used (Chapter 7).
- Explain how something works — its *process* (Chapter 8).
- *Compare* or *contrast* a term to similar terms (Chapter 9).
- *Classify* a term within a category, or *divide* it into parts (Chapter 10).

- Examine the *causes* or *effects* of a term (Chapter 12).
- *Argue* in favor of a particular definition of a term (Chapter 13).

In "Cultural Brokers," for example, Pipher uses several patterns of development. She describes what cultural brokers do, illustrates with examples such as school-teachers, and contrasts the education refugees receive via the media to that received from cultural brokers.

Definition Includes Sufficient Distinguishing Characteristics and Details

An extended definition includes enough distinguishing characteristics and details so that readers can fully understand the term. Pipher provides detailed descriptions of many characteristics of cultural brokers. Consider this example: "A cultural broker has information on everything — what schools are the best, where to go fishing or buy lemongrass, where to find work or buy a used car, and how to change a tire" (para. 8).

Definition May Use Negation and Address Misconceptions

When the term being defined is so similar to other terms in the same class that it can be confused with them, a writer may use negation to explain how the term is different from the others. For example, in an essay defining *rollerblading*, you might clarify how it is unlike *rollerskating*, which involves a different type of wheeled boot that allows different kinds of motions. This strategy is known as **negation** because it involves explaining what a term *is not* as well as what it *is*. You can also use negation to clarify personal meanings. In defining what she means by *cultural brokers*, Pipher uses examples from the media to show what cultural brokers *don't* do.

In addition, an extended definition may need to address popular misconceptions about the term. In an essay defining *plagiarism*, for instance, you might correct the mistaken idea that plagiarism only involves passing off another writer's entire paper as your own, whereas it actually also includes using other writers' quotes or general phrases and not giving them credit.

Visualizing a Definition Essay

The graphic organizer in Figure 11.1 shows the basic organization of an extended definition essay. The introduction announces the term, provides background information, and usually includes the thesis statement (which briefly defines the term and indicates its significance). The body paragraphs, which are organized according to one or more patterns of development, present the term's distinguishing characteristics along with supporting details. The conclusion refers back to the thesis and brings the essay to a satisfying close, perhaps by citing a memorable quotation, making a final observation, or indicating a new direction of thought. Figure 11.2 is a graphic organizer based on the reading "Cultural Brokers."

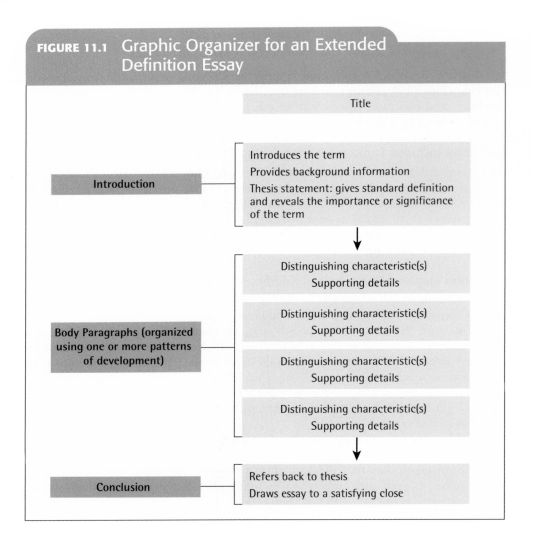

FIGURE 11.1 Graphic Organizer for an Extended Definition Essay

Title

Introduction
- Introduces the term
- Provides background information
- Thesis statement: gives standard definition and reveals the importance or significance of the term

Body Paragraphs (organized using one or more patterns of development)
- Distinguishing characteristic(s)
  Supporting details
- Distinguishing characteristic(s)
  Supporting details
- Distinguishing characteristic(s)
  Supporting details
- Distinguishing characteristic(s)
  Supporting details

Conclusion
- Refers back to thesis
- Draws essay to a satisfying close

Writing a Definition Essay

To write a definition essay, use the following steps. Although you will focus on definition, you will need to integrate one or more other patterns of development into your essay.

Planning a Definition Essay

The first step is to select a topic and narrow it to a more specific term. For example, the term *celebrity* is probably too broad a topic for a brief essay, but it can be narrowed to a particular type of celebrity, such as *sports celebrity*, *Hollywood*

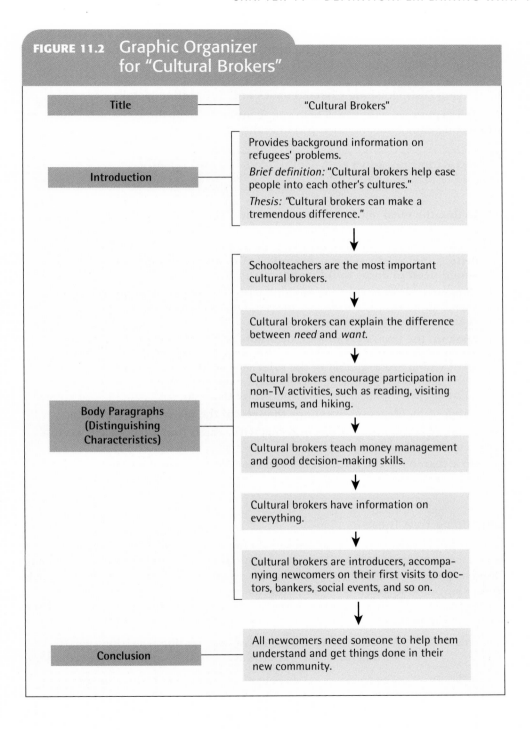

FIGURE 11.2 Graphic Organizer for "Cultural Brokers"

Title — "Cultural Brokers"

Introduction —
Provides background information on refugees' problems.
Brief definition: "Cultural brokers help ease people into each other's cultures."
Thesis: "Cultural brokers can make a tremendous difference."

Body Paragraphs (Distinguishing Characteristics) —
Schoolteachers are the most important cultural brokers.

Cultural brokers can explain the difference between *need* and *want*.

Cultural brokers encourage participation in non-TV activities, such as reading, visiting museums, and hiking.

Cultural brokers teach money management and good decision-making skills.

Cultural brokers have information on everything.

Cultural brokers are introducers, accompanying newcomers on their first visits to doctors, bankers, social events, and so on.

Conclusion —
All newcomers need someone to help them understand and get things done in their new community.

celebrity, *local celebrity*, or *political celebrity*. Consider your readers as well. When the audience is unfamiliar with the term, you will need to explain it in greater detail than when the audience already is familiar with it.

Identifying Distinguishing Characteristics and Supporting Details

The following suggestions will help you identify distinguishing characteristics and supporting details for the term you intend to define.

Generating Distinguishing Characteristics and Details for a Definition Essay

1. **Define the term out loud for a classmate.** Then discuss the term with your classmate, making notes about anything that was unclear.
2. **Brainstorm a list of (a) words that describe your term, (b) people and actions that might serve as examples of it, and (c) everything a person would need to know to fully understand it.**
3. **Observe a person who is associated with the term or who performs some aspect of it.** Take notes on your observations, including the qualities and characteristics of what you see.
4. **Look up the term's etymology, or origin, in the *Oxford English Dictionary*, *A Dictionary of American English*, or *A Dictionary of Americanisms*, all of which are available in the reference section of your library.** Take notes; the word's etymology may indicate some of its characteristics and details that give you ideas on how to organize the essay.
5. **Think of incidents or situations that reveal the meaning of the term.**
6. **Think of similar and different terms with which your readers are likely to be more familiar.**
7. **Do a search for the term on the Internet.** Visit three or four Web sites, and take notes on what you discover.

Developing Your Thesis

Once you have gathered distinguishing characteristics and supporting details for your term, you are ready to develop a thesis. It is a good idea to include a brief standard definition within the thesis and an explanation of why your extended definition is useful, interesting, or important.

Notice how the following weak thesis statement can be revised to reveal the writer's main point.

> WEAK: Wireless cable is a means of transmitting television signals through the air by microwave.

> REVISED: The future of wireless cable, a method of transmitting television signals through the air using microwaves, is uncertain.

Avoid statements that begin "Friendship is when . . ." or "Laziness is when . . ."; instead, name the class to which the term belongs (see p. 397).

WEAK:	Discrimination is when a person is treated unfairly because of the group or class to which that person belongs.
REVISED:	Discrimination is an unfair attitude taken against a person because he or she belongs to a particular group or class.

Notice that both of the preceding revised theses include a standard definition as well as an assertion about the term.

Drafting a Definition Essay

Once you have evaluated your term's distinguishing characteristics, supporting details, and the thesis, it is time to organize your ideas and draft your essay.

To a considerable extent, the organization of a definition essay depends on the pattern(s) of development you decide to use (see the examples on pp. 398–99). With your pattern(s) firmly in mind, think about how to organize your term's characteristics and details. For example, an essay *classifying* different types of marathon runners would probably follow a least-to-most or most-to-least organization, whereas an essay *narrating* a story about marathon runners might be most effectively related in chronological order.

For more on methods of organization, see Chapter 3, p. 48.

Once you have decided on a method of organization, use the following guidelines to draft the essay.

Guidelines for Writing a Definition Essay

1. **Include enough details.** Be sure to include sufficient information to enable readers to understand each characteristic.

2. **Consider including the etymology of the term.** The etymology, or origin, of a term may be of interest to readers. Alternatively, you might include a brief history of the term in your introduction or elsewhere.

3. **Use transitions.** When moving from characteristic to characteristic, be sure to use transitional words or phrases to signal each change. The transitions *another*, *also*, and *in addition* are especially useful in extended definitions.

4. **Write an effective introduction and a satisfying conclusion.** Your introduction should introduce the term, provide background information, and state the thesis, including a justification of why the topic is important. When introducing the term, it may be helpful to use negation, explaining what the term *is* and *is not*. Your conclusion should reinforce the thesis and draw the essay to a satisfying close.

Analyzing and Revising

If possible, set your draft aside for a day or two before rereading and revising it. As you review it, concentrate on your ideas and organization, not on grammar or mechanics. Use the flowchart in Figure 11.3 to discover the strengths and weaknesses of your definition essay.

FIGURE 11.3   Revising a Definition Essay

QUESTIONS

REVISION STRATEGIES

1. Highlight your thesis statement. Does it include a brief definition of the term? Does it indicate why your extended definition is useful, interesting, or important?

NO →

- Use the guidelines on p. 397 to identify the class and distinguishing characteristics of the term.
- Write a standard definition, and incorporate it into the thesis.
- Ask yourself, "Why is this definition worth reading about?" Add your answer to the thesis.

↓ **YES**

2. *Number* the parts of your extended definition in the margin. Do these parts make the definition specific and focused?

NO →

- Delete any details that do not help to define the term.
- Narrow the term further. For example, the broad term *leisure-time activities* could be narrowed to *television addiction*.

↓ **YES**

3. Place checkmarks ✔ beside the distinguishing characteristics of your definition. Do they make the term distinct from similar terms?

NO →

- Do additional research or prewriting to discover more characteristics and details.

↓ **YES**

4. *Write* the name of the pattern(s) of development used in your essay. Does it connect the details and help explain the term's distinguishing characteristics?

NO →

- Review the list of patterns on pages 398–99.
- Think of useful details, examples, and comparisons.
- Consider adding a narrative.
- Explain a process related to the term.
- Classify the term, or explain its causes or effects.

↓ **YES**

QUESTIONS		REVISION STRATEGIES
5. Draw brackets [ ] around sections where you use negation or address misconceptions. Does each section eliminate possible misunderstandings?	NO →	• Revise your explanation of what the term is not. • Add facts or expert opinion to correct readers' mistaken notions about the term.
↓ YES		
6. <u>Underline</u> the topic sentence of each paragraph. Does each paragraph focus on a particular characteristic? Is each paragraph well developed?	NO →	• Consider combining closely related paragraphs. • Split paragraphs that cover more than one characteristic. • Be sure each body paragraph has a topic sentence and supporting details (see Chapter 3).
↓ YES		
7. Draw a box around the introduction and conclusion. Does the introduction provide necessary background information? Does the conclusion offer a satisfying close?	NO →	• Add background information that sets a context for the term you are defining. • Revise the introduction and conclusion so that they meet the guidelines presented in Chapter 3 (pp. 61–64).
↓ YES		
8. Print out another draft to edit and proofread before turning your essay in.		

Editing and Proofreading

The final step is to check your revised essay for errors in grammar, spelling, punctuation, and mechanics. In addition, look for the types of errors you commonly make in any writing, whether for this class or any other situation. As you edit and proofread your definition essay, watch out for the following types of errors commonly found in this type of writing.

For more on these and other common errors, see Chapter 4, p. 81.

Editing Tips and Troublespots: Definition

1. **Make sure to avoid awkward expressions such as** *is when* **or** *is where* **in defining the term.** Name the class to which the term belongs.

   > are reduced-priced dinners served in
   > ► Early-bird specials ~~is when~~ restaurants ~~offer reduced-price dinners~~ late in
   >   the afternoon and ^early in the evening.

   > a transaction in which funds from one investment are transferred
   > ► A rollover is ~~where an employee transfers money from one retirement~~
   >   ^
   >   to another, often without the holder of the funds taking possession of them.
   >   ~~account to another.~~
   >   ^

2. **Make sure subjects and verbs agree in number.** When two subjects are joined by *and*, the verb should be plural.

   > excite
   > ► The upbeat rhythm <u>and</u> intense lyrics of hip-hop music ~~excites~~ the crowd,
   >   ^
   >   making people want to get up and dance.

   When two nouns are joined by *or*, the verb should agree with the noun closest to it.

   > is
   > ► For most birds, the markings <u>or</u> wing span ~~are~~ easily observed with a pair
   >   ^
   >   of good binoculars.

   When the subject and verb are separated by a prepositional phrase, the verb should agree with the subject, not with the noun in the phrase.

   > are
   > ► The features of a hot-air balloon ~~is~~ best learned by studying the attached
   >   ^
   >   diagram.

Students Write

Geneva Lamberth was a first-year student at Canisius College when she wrote the following essay in response to an assignment for her writing class. As you read, highlight the characteristics of eating disorders that Lamberth identifies.

Eating Disorders: Serious and Legitimate Illnesses

Geneva Lamberth

Today's society is weight-obsessed. The ideals of Western culture coupled with certain psychological issues increase one's susceptibility to developing an eating disorder. Those who are afflicted with these disorders are vulnerable to a variety of health complications, some of which can lead to death. Because so many individuals are susceptible to or suffering from these potentially fatal conditions, it is important to understand that eating disorders are legitimate medical illnesses caused by a combination of emotional and physical factors characterized by an obsession with weight, food, and appearance.

Males and females of all ages are vulnerable to eating disorders. According to the Harvard Eating Disorders Center (HEDC), more than five million Americans suffer from eating disorders (HEDC, screen 5). Eating disorders, however, are most common in adolescents and in young-adult females. In fact, most victims of eating disorders are members of middle or upper class families -- families in which there is undue emphasis on physical appearance. These women may feel they must take unusual steps to stay thin and be able to wear fashionable clothes, both of which contribute to presenting the "right" appearance.

The cause of eating disorders includes multiple factors. Genetic, physiological, familial, and sociocultural factors influence the individual, affecting his/her personality and rendering him/her more or less vulnerable to developing an eating disorder. Dieting is the most common behavior that precedes an eating disorder. Indeed, the diet industry is a huge business in the United States, making weight ideals so pervasive that even young children are self-conscious and afraid of being fat.

Anorexia nervosa and bulimia nervosa are the most widely recognized types of eating disorders. Those afflicted with anorexia nervosa suffer from "an intense preoccupation with weight and shape" and "the relentless pursuit of thinness," according to Beaumont, author of "The Clinical Presentation of Anorexia and Bulimia Nervosa" (151). Because they are terrified of the prospect of gaining weight, anorexic individuals under-eat, avoid high-calorie foods, and often subject themselves to strenuous exercise. As a result, they may become malnourished and emaciated, which can lead to failures of the endocrine system. Bulimia is characterized by a cycle of bingeing and purging. While the bulimic individual tries to restrain herself from eating, there are sessions of

---

Title: straightforward and direct

1 Introduction: opens with interest-provoking statement

Thesis: defines term while making a point about its importance

2 First distinguishing characteristic: source citation adds concrete detail

3 Second distinguishing characteristic: cause and effect used to explore factors for eating disorders

4 Third distinguishing characteristic: classification used to discuss different types

Cause and effect used to explain the cycle of bulimia

over-eating, or binge eating, that are followed by intense guilt feelings. To relieve the tension, the bulimic individual performs compensatory, or purging, behaviors that can include self-induced vomiting and laxative abuse. Unlike those who suffer from anorexia, a bulimic individual's weight tends to fall within the range of normal. However, certain aspects of her digestive system are compromised, and her daily social contacts are affected by her often secretive behavior. While the manifestations of these two disorders vary, they are both rooted in deep-seated issues of self-esteem; only with consistent and prolonged treatment can sufferers hope to break the cycle of the disease.

Third distinguishing characteristic: classification used to explain different treatments

Treatment of eating disorders can include one or more of the following: (1) cognitive-behavioral and educational therapy, (2) psychodynamic, feminist, and family therapy, and/or (3) hospital and pharmacological treatments (Garfinkel and Garner xiii-xiv). The first type of approach emphasizes increasing awareness, nutritional counseling, and supervised exercise. This approach works best with individuals afflicted with bulimia nervosa. The second approach utilizes psychotherapy to work on changing the patient's body image and feelings toward the disease. The third approach relies on in-patient and drug treatments. This approach is used when the individual suffers from serious health complications. Treatments are always chosen according to the type and severity of the disorder and must be tailored to meet the needs of the individual.

5

Conclusion: reiterates importance of the topic

Because so many people suffer from eating disorders and because the effects can be so detrimental, it is important that we become informed about what eating disorders are, what the warning signs are, and how to prevent and treat them. Information about eating disorders can be accessed through many mediums, from the Internet to books and periodicals, and even documentaries. Also, there are many organizations dedicated to providing information about the treatment and awareness of these disorders, further demonstrating the prevalence of these disorders in our society. Until our cultural ideals change, we are all vulnerable to eating disorders and the physical and psychological risks associated with them.

6

Works Cited

Beaumont, P. "The Clinical Presentation of Anorexia and Bulimia Nervosa." *Eating Disorders and Obesity*. Ed. K. Brownell and C. Fairburn. New York: Guilford, 1995.

Garfinkel, P., and D. Garner, eds. *Handbook of Treatment for Eating Disorders*. New York: Guilford, 1997.

Harvard Eating Disorders Center. 13 Oct. 2004. Harvard Medical School. 20 Oct. 2004 <http://www.hedc.org/>.

Responding to "Students Write"

1. Lamberth does not include examples of individuals suffering from the disorders she describes. How would such examples enhance or detract from the essay?
2. Do you think the three options for treating eating disorders are sufficiently explained? What further information, if any, would be useful?
3. Lamberth uses a straightforward title. Try suggesting an alternative, more creative title that would still indicate the seriousness of the subject matter.
4. Evaluate the effectiveness of the introduction and conclusion. In what other ways could the topic have been introduced? What other techniques for concluding could Lamberth have used?

Reading a Definition Essay

When preparing to read a definition essay of a term that is unfamiliar or unusual, it may be helpful to check its standard dictionary meaning for some background and context. If, for example, you are about to read an essay defining the term *revenge*, the dictionary meaning would reveal various facets of the concept: punishment, retaliation, and spite. Then, as you read the essay, you can determine which facets the author addresses. It may also be helpful to think of what the term means to you, and then look for similarities and differences between your own definition and that of the author.

What to Look for, Highlight, and Annotate

Understanding the Reading

- Read the essay once to get a general sense of what's being defined. Then reread it, paying attention to the distinguishing characteristics of the extended definition.
- Evaluate the title, introduction, and conclusion. What is the purpose of each?
- Make sure that you understand how the term differs from similar terms, especially those presented in the same article or chapter. If a textbook or article does not explain sufficiently how two or more terms differ, check a standard dictionary. If the difference is still unclear, check a subject dictionary.

Examining the Characteristics of Definition Essays

- Highlight the thesis statement, and identify why the subject is worth reading about.
- As you read the definition, identify the class and highlight or underline the distinguishing characteristics. Mark any that are unclear or incomplete.
- Many students find it useful to highlight definitions using a special color of pen or highlighter, or to designate them with annotations. You might use *V* for vocabulary, *Def.* for definition, or some other annotation.

How to Find Ideas to Write About

As you read an extended definition or an article containing brief definitions, jot down any additional characteristics or examples that come to mind. When responding to the article, you might indicate how the definition could be expanded to include these additional characteristics or examples. You might also try the following strategies.

- Think of other terms in the same class.
- Try to relate the definitions to your own experience. Where or when have you observed the characteristics described? Your personal experiences might be useful in an essay in which you agree with or challenge the writer's definitions.
- If the writer has not already done so, you might use negation to expand the meaning of the term, or you might explore its etymology.

Spanglish

Janice Castro, Dan Cook, and Christina Garcia

Janice Castro, a former senior correspondent for *Time* magazine and editor of *Time.com*, is currently an assistant professor of new media at Northwestern University's Medill School of Journalism. Along with *Time* writers Dan Cook and Christina Garcia, Castro wrote the following article for a special feature on Latinos in a 1985 issue of *Time* magazine.

In "Spanglish," the authors define a blend of English and Spanish that is becoming increasingly familiar to Americans of all ethnicities. As you read, notice the examples that demonstrate the prevalence of Spanglish. How do they show the increasing acceptance of Spanglish among Americans who speak Spanish — and among those who don't?

Focus on Understanding Read to discover what Spanglish is and who speaks it.

Focus on the Topic In class or in your journal, write a list of common words or phrases that you know come from other languages.

1 In Manhattan a first-grader greets her visiting grandparents, happily exclaiming, "Come here, *siéntate!*" Her bemused grandfather, who does not speak Spanish, nevertheless knows she is asking him to sit down. A Miami personnel officer understands what a job applicant means when he says, "*Quiero un* part time." Nor do drivers miss a beat reading a billboard alongside a Los Angeles street advertising CERVEZA — SIX PACK!

2 This free-form blend of Spanish and English, known as Spanglish, is common linguistic currency° wherever concentrations of Hispanic Americans are found in the U.S. In Los Angeles, where 55% of the city's 3 million inhabitants speak Spanish, Spanglish is as much a part of daily life as sunglasses. Unlike the broken-English efforts of earlier immigrants from Europe, Asia, and other regions, Spanglish has become a widely accepted conversational mode used casually — even playfully — by Spanish-speaking immigrants and native-born Americans alike.

> **linguistic currency:** acceptable and widespread language

3 Consisting of one part Hispanicized English, one part Americanized Spanish, and more than a little fractured syntax, Spanglish is a bit like a Robin Williams comedy routine: a cracking line of cross-cultural patter straight from the melting pot. Often it enters Anglo homes and families through children, who pick it up at school or at play with their young Hispanic contemporaries. In other cases, it comes from watching TV; many an Anglo child watching *Sesame Street* has learned *uno dos tres* almost as quickly as one two three.

4 Spanglish takes a variety of forms, from the Southern California Anglos who bid farewell with the utterly silly "*hasta la* bye-bye" to the Cuban-American

411

drivers in Miami who *parquean* their *carros*. Some Spanglish sentences are mostly Spanish, with a quick detour for an English word or two. A Latino friend may cut short a conversation by glancing at his watch and excusing himself with the explanation he must "*ir al* supermarket."

Many of the English words transplanted in this way are simply handier   5
than their Spanish counterparts. No matter how distasteful the subject, for example, it is still easier to say "income tax" than *impuesto sobre la renta*. At the same time, many Spanish-speaking immigrants have adopted such terms as VCR, microwave, and dishwasher for what they view as largely American phenomena. Still other English words convey a cultural context that is not implicit in the Spanish. A friend who invites you to *lonche* most likely has in mind the brisk American custom of "doing lunch" rather than the languorous afternoon break traditionally implied by *almuerzo*.

Mainstream Americans exposed to similar hybrids of German, Chinese, or   6
Hindu might be mystified. But even Anglos who speak little or no Spanish are somewhat familiar with Spanglish. Living among them, for one thing, are 19 million Hispanics.[1] In addition, more American high school and university students sign up for Spanish than any other foreign language.

Only in the past ten years, though, has Spanglish begun to turn into a na-   7
tional slang. Its popularity has grown with the explosive increases in U.S. immigration from Latin American countries. English has increasingly collided with Spanish in retail stores, offices, and classrooms, in pop music, and on street corners. Anglos whose ancestors picked up such Spanish words as *rancho, bronco, tornado*, and *incommunicado*, for instance, now freely use such Spanish words as *gracias, bueno, amigo*, and *por favor*.

Among Latinos, Spanglish conversations often flow more easily from   8
Spanish into several sentences of English and back.

Spanglish is a sort of code for Latinos: the speakers know Spanish, but their   9
hybrid language reflects the American culture in which they live. Many lean to shorter, clipped phrases in place of the longer, more graceful expressions their parents used. Says Leonel de la Cuesta, an assistant professor of modern languages at Florida International University in Miami: "In the U.S., time is money, and that is showing up in Spanglish as an economy of language." Conversational examples: *taipiar* (type) and *winshi-wiper* (windshield wiper) replace *escribir a máquina* and *limpiaparabrisas*.

Major advertisers, eager to tap the estimated $134 billion in spending   10
power wielded by Spanish-speaking Americans, have ventured into Spanglish to promote their products. In some cases, attempts to sprinkle Spanglish through commercials have produced embarrassing gaffes. A Braniff airlines ad that sought to tell Spanish-speaking audiences they could settle back *en* (in) luxuriant *cuero* (leather) seats, for example, inadvertently said they could fly without clothes (*encuero*). A fractured translation of the Miller Lite slogan told

---

[1]According to the 2002 Census, there were 37.4 million Hispanics in the United States.

readers the beer was "Filling, and less delicious." Similar blunders are often made by Anglos trying to impress Spanish-speaking pals. But if Latinos are amused by mangled Spanglish, they also recognize these goofs as a sort of friendly acceptance. As they might put it, *no problema*.

Understanding the Reading

1. Why has the addition of Spanish words to the English language caught on more than that of other languages from Asia or Europe?
2. Give an example from the reading of an English word that is easier to use than its Spanish equivalent. How is this a benefit to Spanish speakers in America?
3. How have advertisers used Spanglish to tap into the buying power of Spanish-speaking Americans? Citing examples from the text, explain how this tactic has created some embarrassing gaffes.
4. According to the authors, how do Latinos react to the misuse of Spanglish? How might they express their reaction in Spanglish?

Visualizing the Reading

Review the reading, and supply the missing information in the following graphic organizer.

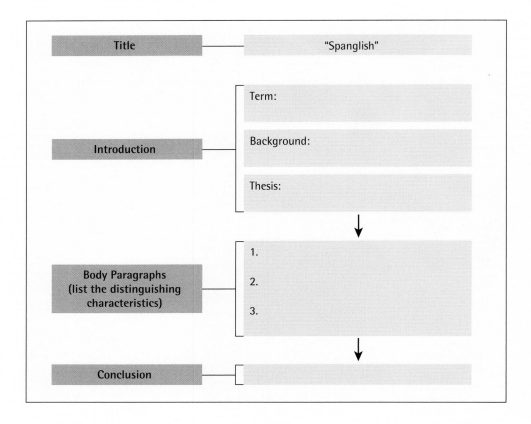

Examining the Characteristics of Definition Essays

1. Identify the standard definition of *Spanglish*. Do the authors identify the class to which the term belongs and the characteristics that distinguish it? Explain.

2. What main point do the authors make about Spanglish? According to the authors, why is this term worth reading about?

3. How do the authors expand the definition of Spanglish beyond the second paragraph? Do they include sufficient distinguishing characteristics and details to support the extended definition? Explain.

4. "Spanglish takes a variety of forms" (para. 4). What are these forms, and how are they defined within the essay? How do these details contribute to the extended definition as a whole?

5. Identify the patterns of development used by the authors, and explain how these techniques help to clarify the term. Did you find the techniques helpful? Why or why not?

Building Your Word Power

1. Using context clues, define the following Spanish words as used in the essay. If necessary, consult a Spanish-English dictionary: *siéntate* (para. 1), *quiero un* (1), *cerveza* (1), *uno dos tres* (3), *parquean* (4), *carros* (4), *ir al* (4), *almuerzo* (5), and *bronco* (7).

2. Explain the connotative meanings of the words *explosive* and *collided* as used in paragraph 7. What effect do these words have in describing the prevalence of Spanglish?

3. Explain the meaning of each of the following words as it is used in the reading: *syntax* (para. 3), *contemporaries* (3), *convey* (5), *languorous* (5), *clipped* (9) *tap* (10), *wielded* (10), and *gaffes* (10). Refer to your dictionary as needed.

For a definition of ***connotative meaning***, *see the chart of commonly used language features on p. 21.*

Building Your Critical Thinking Skills: Tone

The **tone** of a piece of writing reflects to the author's overall feeling toward the material and the audience; it is conveyed through word choice, sentence arrangement, and formal or informal use of language. For example, a letter about a class picnic to members of your class would have a casual, friendly tone, whereas a piece of technical writing for a biotechnology company would have a formal, serious tone. The author's tone affects the readers' attitude toward the topic. For instance, someone might become very emotional after reading an impassioned letter to the editor about the rising cost of housing. For that reason, it is important to be aware of the author's tone when reading. Using your knowledge of tone, answer the following questions about Spanglish.

1. What is the overall tone of the essay? How does this tone make you feel about Spanglish?

2. How do the first and last paragraphs contribute to the tone?

3. Identify any other tones used in the essay. Are there different tones that the authors could have used effectively for this topic? Explain.

Reacting to the Reading: Discussion and Journal Writing

1. Discuss your own familiarity with Spanglish. How often do you come in contact with this "language"? Are there certain situations in which you hear Spanglish more than others?

2. Brainstorm a list of factors that contribute to the use of foreign words and phrases in America.

3. In class or in your journal, discuss the growing Hispanic influence in American society. Consider the Hispanic influences on food, music, or pop culture, for example.

Applying Your Skills: Writing Assignments

1. **Paragraph Assignment.** In a paragraph, define your style of language. Are you a native speaker of English? Do you speak with an accent? Do you use slang? Do you incorporate words from languages other than your native language?

2. Pick a word with multiple meanings, such as *love* or *feminism*. Brainstorm a list of the different meanings and ways that the word is used. You might also want to research its etymology or origins. Then write a definition essay using the information you gathered. Be sure to include a clear thesis statement and a satisfying conclusion.

3. Many social groups develop their own slang words and specialized terminology. Choose a group that you are familiar with or part of (football fans, engineering students, hip-hop fans, etc.), and write an essay defining and describing the language used by this group.

4. Combining Patterns. Consider the foreign words or phrases used in advertisements, business names, names of streets and towns, and everyday speech. Then write an illustration essay about the prevalence of foreign words in American English, using examples to support a thesis that defines the term *foreign* and makes a point about how common foreign words and phrases are in American English.

5. Internet Research. Conduct online research about Spanglish and Ebonics (also known as Black English) and the role of these dialects in bilingual education. One source is a radio report entitled "Spanglish in Schools? Sounds Loco!" that aired on National Public Radio: www.npr.org/about/nextgen/interns/interns/ie03/show.html. Using this and other online sources, write a definition essay about bilingual education and the controversy over dialects like Spanglish and Ebonics in schools.

One Term Says It All: "Shut Up!"

Shelly Branch

Shelly Branch is a journalist specializing in personal finance. She is a staff reporter for the *Wall Street Journal*, a contributor to *Money*, and the author of *Dollar Pinching: A Consumer's Guide to Smart Spending* (1996).

The *Wall Street Journal* article that follows discusses the changing fortunes of the phrase "Shut up!" Once considered rude, the phrase has taken on a hip, new, non-negative meaning. As you read, notice the wide range of experts Branch cites to explain how these words are used today: Among those who have capitalized on the new acceptance of this exclamation are not only linguistics professors and dictionary editors but also authors, television writers, and marketing specialists.

Focus on Understanding   As you read, identify the usage of "Shut up!" that the author describes.

Focus on the Topic   In class or in your journal, identify some words or phrases with new meanings that have entered our language recently.

1   As chief of staff to a California assemblyman, Bob Hartnagel chooses his words carefully — especially when his boss is around. But once the coast is clear, he can't resist tossing off a playful "Shut up!" to his colleagues. "It's kind of an exclamation point to whatever's going on," says Mr. Hartnagel, 32 years old. "If it's met with a smile, you proceed. If there's a gasp . . . you refrain."

2   Not too many years ago, the unrude use of "Shut up!" might have baffled linguists and just about everybody else. But the term has now made its way from schoolgirl chatter to adult repartee and into movies and advertising. People use it as much to express disbelief, shock and joy as to demand silence. In some circles, it has become the preferred way to say "Oh my God!" "Get out of town!" and "No way!" all at once.

3   A recent ad for Hyundai's Elantra shows a young woman sparring with a dealer. "Shut up!" screams the woman, who pokes the man in the chest each time he points out a feature that sounds too good to be true.

4   Editors of the *New Oxford American Dictionary* are considering a new entry for "Shut up!" in the next edition. "I think we should add it because it appears to be widespread," says senior editor Erin McKean. Already, she has mulled possible definitions: "used to express amazement or disbelief" and "oh, so true!"

5   Shut up! is the latest example of a linguistic phenomenon called amelioration, whereby a word or phrase loses its negative associations over time. A classic example is "nice," which meant "stupid" up through the 13th century. Recent flip-flops include "bad" (as in good) and "dope" (as in great). "Words

417

that were once considered rude are now included in regular conversation, but in a context that lets you know it's not impolite," says Connie Eble, professor of English at the University of North Carolina at Chapel Hill and the author of "Slang and Sociability." "They become so generalized that the shock value wears off."

Words with rich semantic connotations "typically have the possibility to   6
mean their opposite when used in an ironic or joking context," adds Bert Vaux, an associate professor of linguistics at Harvard University.

In the case of the Elantra ad, copy writers at the Richards Group in Dallas   7
settled on the line while cramming last Memorial Day weekend for snappy, youthful expressions. At first, they considered having the actress say something like, "no way," or "you're kidding," but were inspired by the irreverent lingo that staff people in their twenties had been shouting across the agency's open-office cubicles.

"There's a very fine line between being funny and obnoxious," says creative   8
director Mike Malone, who was nervous about offending Hyundai's older deal-ers. "But every time we said 'Shut up!' it just sounded funnier." He knew he had a hit on his hands, he says, when the agency showed the TV spot to a group of Hyundai dealers in their fifties and they burst out laughing. "After the meeting, they were all walking around telling each other to shut up," says Mr. Malone.

To ensure the proper tone for their ad, writers for the Hyundai spot audi-   9
tioned more than 200 actresses. "We were getting a really annoying read," says writer Kevin Paetzel, who wanted the character to have a more endearing qual-ity. "The trick is to hit the 'sh' very hard."

The most effective enunciation also places a full stop between "shut" and   10
"up." Excitable types pitch their voices higher on the word "up." (Mr. Hartnagel adds "right now!" when he's feeling acutely peppy.) Spoken in haste, the phrase loses what linguists call its "rhythmic features." Then, it can sound too much like an affront.

Once considered base, "shut up" has a long, distinguished history.   11
According to the *Oxford English Dictionary,* an early documented use, in 16th-century England, was a figurative one, meaning "to withhold one's money or kindness from a person." In 1840, the *New Orleans Picayune* printed the first known slang/imperative use of "shut up," when a reporter referred to an offi-cer's demand for a Dutchman to be quiet.

More recently, children's author Meg Cabot has given the phrase a literary   12
twist. Her title character in "The Princess Diaries" favors it to express geeky teenage delight. Disney screenwriters were so fond of the princess's breezy use of the term that they wove it prominently into the movie adaptation. "Shut up!" even landed in the promotional trailer for the film. "I've had a lot of letters from parents thanking me sarcastically for introducing 'shut up!' to their kids' vo-cabulary," says Ms. Cabot.

The origins of the newest usage have fueled some debate. Ms. Cabot says   13
she picked it up a few years ago from schoolgirls on Manhattan's Lower East Side. An earlier adopter of the phrase was the character Elaine on "Seinfeld." In a 1992 episode written by Larry David called "The Pez Dispenser," Jerry tells

a story about a man who splashed Gatorade on his head, got pneumonia and dropped dead. Elaine responds: "Shut up!" In subsequent episodes, Elaine tells people to "Shut up!" all the time — but she really means it. Writers had her intone the hip version just twice, according to Paul McFedries, a language writer and founder of the online site "The Word Spy" who has studied the complete body of Seinfeld scripts.

The fact that "Shut up!" seems to resonate particularly with women doesn't 14 surprise word whizzes. "Women tend to use more conversational movers than men," says dictionary editor Ms. McKean, who also edits "Verbatim," a language quarterly. "These are little phrases that help keep the dialogue going."

Though some people don't like the phrase ("I think it just sounds rude," 15 says actress Drew Barrymore), plenty of professional types are hooked. Says Dawn Jackson, a 32-year-old communications manager in San Francisco, "There are just times when nothing else can express the level of shock, surprise, you name it, that you're feeling."

Understanding the Reading

1. What is the new use of "Shut up!" as described by Branch? Give some examples of its different uses from the essay.
2. Why did the Elantra ad writers decide to use "Shut up!"? What concern did they have about this phrase, and how was their concern alleviated?
3. What example does the author provide for the use of "Shut up!" on television?
4. According to the article, what is the history of the phrase "Shut up!" What source does Branch cite where you could read more about the evolution of this phrase?

Visualizing the Reading

To define a term, writers frequently make use of other methods of development. Analyze Branch's use of other methods by completing the following chart. The first one has been done for you.

Method of Development	Example
Process	The author explains how to pronounce the phrase (para. 9–10).
Narration	
Description	
Illustration	
Comparison and contrast	

Examining the Characteristics of Definition Essays

1. What is Branch's thesis? Evaluate its effectiveness by identifying whether or not it includes a brief definition of the term and an explanation of why the term is worth reading about.

2. In paragraphs 9 and 10, Branch explains the way to pronounce "Shut up!" Why is this explanation important to a full understanding of the current use of the term?

3. Branch includes the history of the phrase "Shut up!" Describe some of the other ways that Branch defines the term.

4. Using examples from the essay to support your view, explain whether the author's definition includes sufficient distinguishing characteristics and details.

5. How effective are the essay's introduction and conclusion? Does the author provide sufficient background material in the introduction, and does she reinforce the thesis in the conclusion? Explain.

Building Your Word Power

For a definition of ***connotative meaning,*** *see the chart of commonly used language features on p. 21.*

1. Explain the connotative meaning of the phrases "schoolgirl chatter" and "adult repartee" as used in paragraph 2.

2. Why are parents thanking children's author Meg Cabot "sarcastically" (para. 12)?

3. Explain the meaning of each of the following words as it is used in the reading: *mulled* (para. 4), *semantic* (6), *endearing* (9) *affront* (10), and *base* (11). Refer to your dictionary as needed.

Building Your Critical Thinking Skills: Inferences

Writers do not always state directly everything that they are trying to communicate. Therefore, readers must make **inferences**, or informed guesses about what is not known on the basis of what *is* known. Making inferences involves "reading between the lines" to determine the deeper meaning behind a phrase, passage, or entire reading. For example, in an essay about corporate corruption, an author might make statements about his own situation that would lead you to infer that he was personally hurt by recent corporate wrongdoing. Using your inference skills, answer the following questions.

1. What can you infer about Hartnagel's relationship with the California assemblyman he works for (para. 1)? Why won't he say "Shut up!" when the assemblyman is around?

2. Make an inference as to why you think more than two hundred actresses had to be auditioned for the Elantra spot (para. 9).

Reacting to the Reading: Discussion and Journal Writing

1. Discuss the role of spoken language among today's youth. How important is it to use the correct lingo?

2. Discuss how television ads use popular language and culture to sell products.

3. In class or in your journal, explore your own speech habits. What popular phrases do you use frequently? In what situations, if any, do you avoid using them?

Applying Your Skills: Writing Assignments

1. **Paragraph Assignment.** Choose an expression that would be appropriate and acceptable to use among friends but *not* with a different group or person, such as an employer or a professor. Write a paragraph explaining its meaning and the circumstances under which it would not be appropriate.

2. Choose a word that means or suggests something different to you than it does to someone of an older generation. For example, *gay* to an elderly aunt may suggest something happy and brilliant, while to you it means "homosexual." Write a definition essay explaining the word's various meanings over time.

3. Write a definition essay about a hip, new phrase that you have heard people using. Be sure to explain what it means, when you first heard it, and any other meanings it may have had in the past. Use examples from your own experiences and observations to provide sufficient defining characteristics and examples. Conclude with your thoughts on the future use of this phrase.

4. Write an essay defining the characteristics of the "perfect job" you hope to hold after graduation. Your audience is your instructor.

5. **Combining Patterns.** Brainstorm a list of situations you have been in where language played an important role in how the situation developed. For example, an argument with a roommate might have gone in various directions depending on the words you chose. Pick one situation, and write an essay that narrates the experience and explains how word choice contributed to its resolution. Be sure to explain whether any of the words or phrases used at the time had connotative meanings or definitions that caused the misunderstanding. Conclude with your thoughts on how different word choices might have caused the outcome to change.

6. **Internet Research.** Visit the sites for *The Word Spy* at www.wordspy.com and *Verbatim* at www.verbatimmag.com, both mentioned in the reading. Look over the sites carefully, and write an essay that defines the purpose of each. Use comparison and contrast to describe how each site differs in its treatment of language issues. Be sure to include examples from each site to support your main point.

Web Logs Get Personal

William Plasencia

William Plasencia is a contributing writer for *Hispanic*, an online magazine specializing in the interests and needs of the Hispanic community in the United States. His articles usually focus on aspects of technology and culture — or on a combination of the two, as in the following article from November 2003.

In "Web Logs Get Personal," Plasencia discusses blogging, a phenomenon in which computer users write entries in online "diaries" that can be read (and, often, commented on) by other users. As you read, notice how Plasencia uses direct quotations and personal stories to emphasize users' emotional connections to the blogs they read and write.

Focus on Understanding   Read to discover what a Web log is and what the author says about Web log users.

Focus on the Topic   In class or in your journal, explore what you know about blogs.

Used to be that personal diaries were best kept locked and hidden from prying eyes. The Internet, however, is increasingly taking those personal expressions, opinions, and yearnings, and laying them bare for the world to see. Known as Web logs, or blogs, these online snapshots into the minds of their owners range from simple diaries of the mundane day-to-day to full-fledged forums for news, opinion, and even photographs, peppered with commentary from the visitors that read them. 1

"I get a place to vent where I can tell people about experiences that I've had, and I can share things with a wide array of people from all over the world," says an Atlanta-based technology consultant, about his Web log. "There's a bit of narcissism there, knowing that people are coming to my blog to see what I have to say. But it also can be extremely cathartic. I've written about very personal issues and gotten responses from people on the other side of the world with words of encouragement and similar stories." 2

Blogging is not just for technophiles. Everyone from housewives to executives and artists are taking advantage of the dozens of services and software programs available to build and maintain a Web log. Blogger, Blogspot, and the newly launched TypePad are some of the easiest and most popular, and they are examples of hosted services that use a familiar Web browser to give you access to your Web log either at no cost or for a small ongoing fee. If you already host your website at home, there are dozens of free software programs, such as MovableType, pMachine, and Bloxsom, that will let you construct and personalize a Web log of your own. 3

Lorena Haldeman, 33, a writer and editor from Gainesville, Florida, updates her Web log every day to mostly keep her friends and family up to date on 4

422

her life. She says she reads "blogs by folks who seem to be people I'd like to hang out with in real life. Interaction with them is sort of the icing on the cake — it's a charge."

The Internet initially held out the promise of being a great equalizing 5 medium. But in recent years, much of that initial enthusiasm has died down as commercial interests have made the Internet their own. Blogging is seen by many as a powerful push to once again give people a voice using tools that used to be the purview of rich corporations and media outlets.

"A blog can be a way to write on personal issues; if you are shy or intro- 6 verted, it can be a safe way to expose your ideas or personal experiences without the fear of criticism," says a Latin American blogger who goes by the nickname BlaBla. "There are search engines to find blogs by region, subject, etc. This points to the fact that communities and relationships are important to bloggers."

Roberto J. Torres, a professor of sociology at St. Lawrence University, 7 Canton, New York, and a blogger himself, says the community aspects of Web logs became hugely evident after the terrorist attacks of September 11.

"What happened on my blog immediately after 9/11: An entire community 8 of friends from the Web came together to talk about the implications of this event and its ramifications for U.S. action and policy. This virtual discussion was valuable not only for me personally, but also for others who were participating in the exchange. I think that we all found something through the blog and the Web itself that we weren't finding locally in our flesh-and-blood relationships."

Understanding the Reading

1. Why do people create and maintain Web logs? What kinds of people read them?
2. Identify two ways that people use Web logs.
3. What computer requirements are necessary in order to have a Web log?
4. According to the reading, how do blogs relate to the original intent of the Internet?

Examining the Characteristics of Definition Essays

1. Identify Plasencia's thesis statement. How does it suggest the importance or usefulness of Web logs?
2. Does the author use a particular organizational method to present the distinguishing characteristics of the term? Does his extended definition include sufficient details to fully explain *blogging*? Explain.
3. The author includes details about the individuals quoted in the article. Does this additional information strengthen his definition? Why or why not?
4. What other patterns of development besides definition does Plasencia use? How do these contribute to the essay?
5. Evaluate the author's conclusion. Why does he end with the reference to the events of 9/11?

Visualizing the Reading

Examine the author's use of definition by completing the following graphic organizer.

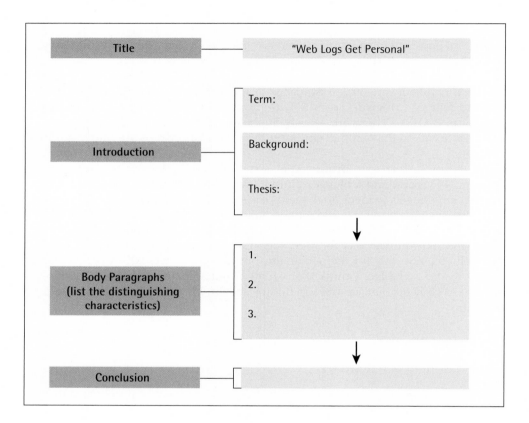

Building Your Word Power

1. The words *blog, blogging,* and *blogger* are examples of new words entering our language. Define each one.
2. What does the author mean by the word *peppered* as used in paragraph 1?
3. Explain the meaning of each of the following words as it is used in the reading: *mundane* (para. 1), *narcissism* (2), *cathartic* (2), *technophiles* (3), *purview* (5), *introverted* (6), and *ramifications* (8). Refer to your dictionary as needed.

Building Your Critical Thinking Skills: Evaluating Sources

When proving a point or explaining an idea, authors often use information from other sources to support their main ideas. This evidence varies according to topic, audience, and purpose; but it can include personal experience, research findings, expert opinion, and information from articles, books, and news reports. Because not all sources are equally reliable, the process of evaluating sources is important to determine whether supporting evidence is relevant and credible. Begin by determining where the source material came from and whether it can be trusted. For example, medical statistics from a Web site with known ties to a major tobacco company might not be as trustworthy as those from an impartial university study in a published paper about the effects of secondhand smoke. Make sure also that all sources cited clearly support the thesis. Using your skills in evaluating sources, answer the following questions.

1. Make a list of the types of supporting evidence that Plasencia uses. How reliable do you find them to be?

2. How closely does the supporting evidence relate to the thesis?

3. How could you find out more about the people whose experiences are mentioned in the article?

Reacting to the Reading: Discussion and Journal Writing

1. Discuss the use of the Internet. How has this technology enhanced our lives? Are there any downsides to this technology?

2. In class or in your journal, write several days' worth of journal entries as if you were hosting a daily Web log. Then discuss your experiences in writing for an "audience."

Applying Your Skills: Writing Assignments

1. **Paragraph Assignment.** Consider your comfort level with computers and technology. Classify yourself as a technophile, a technophobe, or something (some other term) that falls in between these extremes. Then write a paragraph defining the term as it relates to your degree of computer savvy.

2. Brainstorm a list of computer-related terms. Pick one, and describe it in a definition essay written for older adults who have very little experience with computers. Explain the term as simply and yet as thoroughly as possible. In creating your definition, you may need to use other patterns of development such as comparison and contrast or classification and division.

3. Write an essay defining an important concept in a field of study, perhaps from one of your other courses. Your audience is other students not enrolled in the course.

4. **Combining Patterns.** Both diaries and Web logs use writing to convey ideas and feelings. Using comparison and contrast, write an essay exploring the benefits of these different types of personal writing. Begin your essay by defining the terms you will compare. If relevant, include examples from your own experience with diaries or blogs.

5. **Internet Research.** Conduct research of the different types of blogs available online. Two directories that are good places to start are www.blogwise.com and www.blogarama.com. Narrow your search to a particular kind of blog, such as political or music blogs; then, in a definition essay, explain its distinguishing characteristics. Use examples from your research to support a thesis about the relevance and importance of this type of blog.

The Meanings of a Word

Gloria Naylor

Gloria Naylor (b. 1950), the daughter of uprooted Mississippi sharecroppers, grew up in New York City. As a young adult, she became an active member of the Jehovah's Witnesses. She left the group at age twenty-five and began taking college classes while working as a switchboard operator. After reading a novel by an African American woman, Naylor discovered a passion for writing fiction. Her first novel, *The Women of Brewster Place* (1982), won numerous awards and became a television movie. Since then Naylor, who still lives in New York, has written several other novels and works of nonfiction.

The essay below first appeared in the *New York Times* in 1986. Notice not only that the word Naylor defines means different things when spoken by a white boy and by members of Naylor's family, but that it also changes meaning according to how each family member uses it. Consider how Naylor supports her point that "consensus gives [words] true power."

Focus on Understanding   As you read, identify which word the title refers to and what the author realizes about its meaning.

Focus on the Topic   Have you ever been called an insulting name? If so, write a journal entry about your experience. If not, write about an imaginary situation in which you react to an insulting name.

Language is the subject. It is the written form with which I've managed to keep the wolf away from the door and, in diaries, to keep my sanity. In spite of this, I consider the written word inferior to the spoken, and much of the frustration experienced by novelists is the awareness that whatever we manage to capture in even the most transcendent passages falls far short of the richness of life. Dialogue achieves its power in the dynamics of a fleeting moment of sight, sound, smell, and touch.

I'm not going to enter the debate here about whether it is language that shapes reality or vice versa. That battle is doomed to be waged whenever we seek intermittent reprieve from the chicken and egg dispute. I will simply take the position that the spoken word, like the written word, amounts to a nonsensical arrangement of sounds or letters without a consensus that assigns "meaning." And building from the meanings of what we hear, we order reality. Words themselves are innocuous; it is the consensus that gives them true power.

I remember the first time I heard the word *nigger*. In my third-grade class, our math tests were being passed down the rows, and as I handed the papers to a little boy in back of me, I remarked that once again he had received a much lower mark than I did. He snatched his test from me and spit out that word. Had he called me a nymphomaniac° or a necrophiliac,° I couldn't have been more puzzled. I didn't know what a nigger was, but I knew that whatever it meant, it was something he shouldn't have called me. This was verified when I raised my hand, and in a loud voice repeated what he had said and watched the teacher scold him for using a "bad" word. I was later to go home and ask the inevitable question that every black parent must face — "Mommy, what does *nigger* mean?"

And what exactly did it mean? Thinking back, I realize that this could not have been the first time the word was used in my presence. I was part of a large extended family that had migrated from the rural South after World War II and formed a close-knit network that gravitated around my maternal grandparents. Their ground-floor apartment in one of the buildings they owned in Harlem was a weekend mecca for my immediate family, along with countless aunts, uncles, and cousins who brought along assorted friends. It was a bustling and open house with assorted neighbors and tenants popping in and out to exchange bits of gossip, pick up an old quarrel, or referee the ongoing checkers game in which my grandmother cheated shamelessly. They were all there to let down their hair and put up their feet after a week of labor in the factories, laundries, and shipyards of New York.

Amid the clamor, which could reach deafening proportions — two or three conversations going on simultaneously, punctuated by the sound of a baby's crying somewhere in the back rooms or out on the street — there was still a rigid set of rules about what was said and how. Older children were sent out of the living room when it was time to get into the juicy details about "you-know-who" up on the third floor who had gone and gotten herself "p-r-e-g-n-a-n-t!" But my parents, knowing that I could spell well beyond my years, always demanded that I follow the others out to play. Beyond sexual misconduct and death, everything else was considered harmless for our young ears. And so among the anecdotes of the triumphs and disappointments in the various workings of their lives, the word *nigger* was used in my presence, but it was set within contexts and inflections that caused it to register in my mind as something else.

In the singular, the word was always applied to a man who had distinguished himself in some situation that brought their approval for his strength, intelligence, or drive:

"Did Johnny *really* do that?"

"I'm telling you, that nigger pulled in $6,000 of overtime last year. Said he got enough for a down payment on a house."

When used with a possessive adjective by a woman — "my nigger" — it became a term of endearment for her husband or boyfriend. But it could be more than just a term applied to a man. In their mouths it became the pure essence of manhood — a disembodied force that channeled their past history of struggle and present survival against the odds into a victorious statement of being: "Yeah, that old foreman found out quick enough — you don't mess with a nigger."

nymphomaniac: a woman with an uncontrollable sex drive; **necrophiliac:** a person who is obsessed with or excited by dead bodies

In the plural, it became a description of some group within the community 10 that had overstepped the bounds of decency as my family defined it. Parents who neglected their children, a drunken couple who fought in public, people who simply refused to look for work, those with excessively dirty mouths or unkempt households were all "trifling niggers." This particular circle could forgive hard times, unemployment, the occasional bout of depression — they had gone through all of that themselves — but the unforgivable sin was a lack of self-respect.

A woman could never be a "nigger" in the singular, with its connotation of 11 confirming worth. The noun *girl* was its closest equivalent in that sense, but only when used in direct address and regardless of the gender doing the addressing. *Girl* was a token of respect for a woman. The one-syllable word was drawn out to sound like three in recognition of the extra ounce of wit, nerve, or daring that the woman had shown in the situation under discussion.

"G-i-r-l, stop. You mean you said that to his face?" 12

But if the word was used in a third-person reference or shortened so that it 13 almost snapped out of the mouth, it always involved some element of communal disapproval. And age became an important factor in these exchanges. It was only between individuals of the same generation, or from any older person to a younger (but never the other way around), that *girl* would be considered a compliment.

I don't agree with the argument that use of the word *nigger* at this social 14 stratum of the black community was an internalization of racism. The dynamics were the exact opposite: the people in my grandmother's living room took a word that whites used to signify worthlessness or degradation and rendered it impotent. Gathering there together, they transformed *nigger* to signify the varied and complex human beings they knew themselves to be. If the word was to disappear totally from the mouths of even the most liberal of white society, no one in that room was naive enough to believe it would disappear from white minds. Meeting the word head-on, they proved it had absolutely nothing to do with the way they were determined to live their lives.

So there must have been dozens of times that *nigger* was spoken in front of 15 me before I reached the third grade. But I didn't "hear" it until it was said by a small pair of lips that had already learned it could be a way to humiliate me. That was the word I went home and asked my mother about. And since she knew that I had to grow up in America, she took me in her lap and explained.

Understanding the Reading

1. What does the author think about written language?

2. What prompted the little boy to use the word *nigger*? What was the young Naylor's reaction to his use of the word?

3. Describe the author's childhood as we can infer it from the reading.

4. According to Naylor, what is the difference between a white person's and a black person's use of the word *nigger*?

Visualizing the Reading

To define a term, writers frequently make use of other methods of development besides definition. Analyze how Naylor uses other methods by completing the following chart. The first one has been done for you.

Method of Development	Example
Narration	Naylor tells the story of her experience in third grade (para. 3).
Description	
Illustration	
Cause and effect	
Classification	

Examining the Characteristics of Definition Essays

1. Identify the author's thesis. Does Naylor include a brief definition in it? If not, how does the thesis relate to the extended definition that follows?

2. Identify some of the distinguishing characteristics that Naylor uses to explain her extended definition. Why do you suppose she includes detailed descriptions of her own family gatherings?

3. What other word is defined in the essay? Why does Naylor include a definition of this term?

4. Authors of extended definitions often address popular misconceptions. In your view, does Naylor use this technique to explain the different meanings of the word *nigger*? Explain.

5. Evaluate the essay's conclusion. What is the effect of the last sentence?

Building Your Word Power

1. Explain the allusion to the "chicken and egg" dispute (para. 2).

2. Naylor's essay explores the different connotative meanings of the word *nigger*. Explain the connotations of these other words as used by Naylor: *bad* (para. 3), *hear* (15).

For a definition of allusion and connotative meaning, see the chart of commonly used language features on p. 21.

3. Explain the meaning of each of the following words as it is used in the reading: *intermittent* (para. 2), *reprieve* (2), *essence* (9), *internalization* (14), and *rendered* (14). Refer to your dictionary as needed.

Building Your Critical Thinking Skills: Comparison and Contrast

Authors use **comparison and contrast** to show similarities and differences between the ideas, people, places, or arguments about which they are writing. This technique is useful in definition essays because it places terms into a context with which readers may already be familiar. When evaluating comparisons and contrasts, identify what basis of comparison, or common characteristics between two things, the writer uses. Applying your skills in evaluating comparison and contrast, answer the following questions.

1. What comparisons and contrasts does Naylor make between written and spoken language?
2. How did the author's family and friends compare and contrast different types of black people?
3. Naylor compares and contrasts the black use of *nigger* with the white use. What factors characterize each type of use?

Reacting to the Reading: Discussion and Journal Writing

1. Most children learn the expression "sticks and stones may break my bones, but names will never hurt me," but some people say that "a sharp tongue cuts forever." Discuss the meaning of these two sayings, and consider which one seems to ring truer in our society today.
2. In class or in your journal, discuss a time when you had to ask your parents or some other adult for an explanation of a word or for advice in resolving a conflict.

Applying Your Skills: Writing Assignments

1. **Paragraph Assignment.** Naylor's essay shows that language can be used to humiliate. Choose a word or phrase that demonstrates how language can be used to uplift or comfort. In a paragraph, define the term or phrase and briefly explain its use.
2. Brainstorm a list of issues that currently affect our society. Choose one, and write an essay that defines the problem. Be sure to use appropriate examples and clear distinguishing characteristics. Conclude with some possible solutions.
3. Naylor says she must have heard the word *nigger* while growing up but really "heard" it for the first time in third grade. Think of a word, phrase, or expression that you had heard but never thought about until a situation called attention to it. Write an essay defining the word or phrase and explaining the circumstances by which it came to your attention.
4. **Combining Patterns.** Children who taunt and make fun of other children are often considered bullies. Write a definition essay that defines *bullies* and explains how victims, parents, and school officials can respond. Use narration, illustration,

comparison and contrast, or other patterns of development to support your main point.

5. Internet Research. Naylor's essay deals with her introduction to discrimination. Using the Internet, research some antidiscrimination sites such as the education area of the American-Arab Anti-Discrimination Committee Web site at www.adc.org/index.php?id=203 or the site for the National Association for the Advancement of Colored People at www.naacp.org. Use your research to write a definition essay about a concept found on these Web sites pertaining to discrimination in America.

Spinning

Gina Kolata

Gina Kolata (b. 1948), a science writer for the *New York Times*, is a passionate fan of exercise. She is the author of *Ultimate Fitness: The Quest for Truth about Exercise and Health* (2003), a book that aims to dispel myths about fitness.

   In the following chapter from *Ultimate Fitness*, Kolata defines "Spinning," an exercise trend involving high-resistance workouts on stationary bicycles. Notice that she provides very detailed information, describing everything from the appropriate shoes to the setup of the bike, to clarify the essentials of Spinning for readers who are unfamiliar with the concept.

Focus on Understanding   Read to discover what Spinning is and why the author decided to take a Spinning class.

Focus on the Topic   In class or in your journal, write about a time when you tried a new sport or activity for the first time.

1   I have become an acute observer of my heart. I know how fast it beats when I am standing around at the gym. I know how fast it beats when I exercise hard enough to be out of breath. I know its maximum rate and I know how quickly that falls when I stop exercising.

2   My almost obsessive fascination with monitoring my heart began not because I thought there was anything wrong with it but because I discovered Spinning. It is a sport that has led me into a world of heart-rate training that I barely knew existed. It is a world that uses the heart as a way to assess the body and the effects of exercise, and raises questions such as: Where do the formulas for calculating your maximum heart rate come from? Can they be trusted? And: Is there a special "fat-burning zone" where your heart is beating at just the right rate so you burn the most fat possible when you exercise?

3   But those questions were farthest from my mind on the cold evening in November of 2000 when I first stepped into a Spinning room. I was there to accompany my husband, Bill, who had decided that Spinning might be a solution to his annual funk. Bill only likes one type of exercise — bicycling; and only one type of bicycling — road riding, as opposed to mountain biking. Every year, the pattern is the same. In September, when it gets dark so early that he can't ride his bike after work, he starts to feel downcast. By January, when it gets truly cold and the roads get so slushy or icy that he no longer wants to ride outside even on weekends, he gets even more discouraged. While others might say they feel glum because it's winter, with its short days that force you to go to work in the darkness and return home after the sun sets, Bill attributes his gray moods

to an inability to exercise the way he wants to. For months on end, he is relegated to riding stationary bikes at the gym. And, as he is quick to tell me, those computer-controlled exercise machines are not only boring but they do not look or feel like a real road bike.

That year, Bill decides he wants to try something new. He's been noticing 4
the Spinning classes in a little glass-walled area just behind the treadmills at our gym. There, in a darkened room, on stationary bikes that look remotely like road bikes, he sees sweaty people pedaling away to music, led by an instructor at the front of the room. It is hard to tell just what is going on, since the instructor always turns off the lights when the class starts, but the class seems to do more than simply sit back and pedal their bikes. They also rise from their seats to stand straight up, and sometimes to pedal leaning forward over the handlebars. The only alternative being a LifeCycle,° Bill reasons, what does he have to lose?

LifeCycle: a brand of stationary bicycle

At the very least curious, I join him, and we arrive with our mandatory wa- 5
ter bottles and sweat towels. We are also wearing special bicycling shoes, which clip directly to the pedals to afford us the most efficient motion — as your foot rises, your shoe pulls the pedal up. We are ready to learn the mechanics of Spinning.

The bikes are set in sturdy metal frames, and have only one wheel, a heavy 6
metal flywheel, in front. But that's okay, because you're not going anywhere on these bikes. You adjust the seat's height by moving it up or down on a post, and you adjust its distance from the handlebars by sliding it forward or backward along a metal bar. The handlebars point forward like a bull's horns, and you can move them higher or lower. The seat is narrow and hard, like the seat on a racing bike. There is a cage on the bike frame, in front of and below the seat, where you can slip a plastic bottle of water. There also is a round knob on the frame, just below the fork that holds the front wheel, that you can turn to increase or decrease the resistance on the pedals. The way it works is when you turn the knob for more resistance, on either side of the front wheel, pads close in, pressing against the wheel with variable pressure. The pads, about three inches long and about an inch and a half wide, are made of fiber that has the texture of industrial carpeting. They slow the wheel by friction as they push against it, and the more you turn the resistance knob, the harder they press against the wheel. Your job is to overcome the force of friction that they generate. It is like trying to ride a bike with the brake on; the harder you push on the brake, the harder you will have to pedal to turn the wheel.

You set up your bike so it fits you. The seat must be high enough so that 7
when you extend your leg, with your foot on the pedal, your leg should be extended, but not so much that your knee is locked. The angle between the upper part of your leg and the lower part of your leg should be about twenty degrees. Your handlebars can be one or two inches above or below your seat, depending on your preference. When you reach out for the handlebars, your arms should be extended but your elbows must not be locked.

In class, you sit, stand, or lean forward on your bike, pedaling in time to the 8 music. You turn the knob that increases or decreases the resistance while you simulate climbing a hill or sprinting on a flat stretch of road — or, sometimes, sprinting up a hill. If you put your mind to it, turning the resistance knob enough and pedaling fast enough so that you are exerting real effort, you can get a hard, heart-pounding workout, we discover. It can be as difficult as a fast run; and, I learn, it can make me feel as good.

So, to our great surprise, Bill and I become Spinning enthusiasts, taking the 9 forty-minute classes two, three, even four nights a week. Sometimes, we find ourselves setting an alarm and waking up early on Saturday mornings to take Spinning classes. At our gym, those weekend classes are crowded, and because some bikes are better than others, the only way to be sure you have the best Spinning experience is to come an hour or so before class and drape your towel over the bike you want. While you wait for the class to begin, you lift weights.

One Thursday night, after we've been taking Spinning classes for a few 10 weeks, Anna Hess, the instructor, takes me aside. This warm blonde is also a personal trainer and a marathon runner, and it shows. A short and compact powerhouse, Anna seems driven to inspire the class to take Spinning seriously, not just pedaling along at a low resistance, as most people seem to do, but working at a precisely measured pace. She has us tap our knee with each pedal stroke and count how many times per minute we turn the pedals, making sure we keep up our cadence. She admonishes us to keep track of our heart rates, if not with a heart-rate monitor, then by putting a finger to the carotid artery in our necks and counting our pulse.

Anna wanted to tell me about a special Spinning class that is being planned 11 at another gym where she also teaches. It is going to be a four-hour Spinning climb, called Mount Everest, and we can sign up for it if we want to, training at our gym and the gym where the ride will take place. Are we interested?

Bill demurs, wondering how much time and effort he really wants to devote 12 to this indoor sport and wondering why anyone would want to spend four hours in a hot little room, on a Spinning bike, with the resistance turned up, simulating a climb. I, however, am all for it. How could we not do it, I ask Bill. I think of it as a form of Extreme Spinning and decide that it will be, at the very least, memorable. It will also be an opportunity to test our physical limits. I remember what my son, Stefan, says about my running programs. "The way you run is so boring," he tells me. "It's like you're always between seasons, never training for anything." This is our chance to see if we can go from forty-minute classes to a four-hour climb.

We sign up for the class. We have about two months to train. 13

The first thing we have to do, Anna tells us, is get heart-rate monitors. They 14 are mandatory for the Mount Everest ride. I'd always questioned why I would want one. To use it, you strap an elastic band around your chest. In front is a plastic strip with two flat sections that you wet with water so they maintain a tight contact with your chest. They contain sensors that pick up your heart's electrical signals, convert them into radiowave signals, and transmit them to a device that looks like a wristwatch that displays the data in terms of heart beats per minute. I've seen them on men who are running shirtless. They had seemed absurd to me — with this wide strap across their chests, like a sort of mini-bra. I wondered where a woman would put the strap. Across her breasts? I could not imagine it. But it turns out that you can put the strap just below your bra. It began to seem a little less weird, although still definitely a bit extreme.

Now that I'm taking Spinning classes, however, I can see why heart-rate 15 monitors make sense. If you want to improve — and that, after all, is the point of training — you have to have some way of assessing your performance objectively. If you run, you can get a pretty good idea of what kind of a workout you did — you can see how far you ran and how long it took you. But Spinning is so abstract, it offers no such gauge. You cannot even try to guess at your effort by how hard you are breathing — the music is so loud, you cannot hear yourself breathe. And you can't tell how hard you are working by how hot you become because the temperature can vary in the little room, and you may or may not be near a fan to cool yourself.

What you want to know is your effort, your watts, a unit of power that is 16 the equivalent of calories burned over time. Spinning bikes are not designed with wattmeters, so you are left with two indirect measures of your effort. One is your cadence, how quickly you are pushing the pedals. If you keep the resistance constant, the faster you move the pedals, the harder you are working. There is, however, a problem with using cadence, and it is one that shows up in every Spinning class I've ever been in. I see people who are pedaling away, at astonishing rates, but with virtually no resistance on their flywheels. Once you start pedaling with the resistance knob turned to zero, the heavy wheel will turn fast on its own, from its own momentum. Although your pedals are whirling, you are essentially just going along for the ride. You are putting out almost no effort, and burning almost no calories, even though it looks like you are blazing along at an impressive speed.

That leaves heart rate as a measure of effort. It is an indirect indicator, be- 17 cause although your heart beats faster and faster as your effort gets greater and greater, the relationship is linear only at the lower levels of effort. As your effort increases, the heart rate creeps toward a plateau, your maximum heart rate. That means you can increase your effort, burning more calories, and see only a tiny change in how quickly your heart is beating. It is a bit frustrating — the harder you work, the less effect you see in your heart rate — and when you are working hardest, you'd like to be rewarded with a real rise in your beats per minute. But with this limitation: the higher your heart rate, the more calories you are turning and the harder you are working. . . . Knowing it helps me exercise more vigorously. One night, I realized why it matters to me.

As I was leaving a Spinning class, I heard a young woman talking to the in- 18 structor, Arline Lohli. It was her first class, she said, and she was bored. In aerobics classes, she had to pay rapt attention to keep up with the steps and the dancelike patterns, but in Spinning you can spend five minutes just standing up straight and pedaling. Suddenly, I understood why Spinning is different for me and why I love it so much. It is because in Spinning I challenge myself by seeing how intensely I can push myself. And the higher I keep my heart rate, the more exhilarated I feel. It is that experience that draws me to exercise, and it is that feeling I start to crave when I go more than a few days between vigorous exercise sessions. It is a sensation that is hard to describe to someone who has not experienced it — it combines euphoria with a sort of clear-headedness and a feeling that I have somehow moved into another zone, like the feeling you might get when you are totally absorbed in your work, or in playing a musical instrument. It does not always come in a Spinning class, but I know that it can happen, and the way to get there is to strive for intense exertion. Being able to monitor my heart rate lets me work harder longer, and that is what helps get me to that state where I feel so good.

Understanding the Reading

1. What type of exercise does the author's husband, Bill, prefer above all others?
2. To what does Bill attribute his annual depression?
3. How does Kolata describe the bicycles that are used for Spinning? How should a bike fit its rider?
4. Why would you want to increase or decrease the resistance on a bike in Spinning class?

Visualizing the Reading

Reread the description of the bicycles used for Spinning and how to ride them (para. 6–8). Do the distinguishing characteristics and examples used in Kolata's extended definition match up with what you see in this photograph? Compare and contrast your imagined experience of the riders in this picture with that of Kolata and her husband.

Examining the Characteristics of Definition Essays

1. Kolata uses an implied thesis in "Spinning." Express her thesis in your own words, and evaluate the effectiveness of the implied-thesis technique.

2. List the distinguishing characteristics of Spinning. Does the author include enough characteristics and details so that you understand what Spinning is?

3. Kolata uses an extended definition to explain an important tool related to Spinning. What is the name of this tool, and how effective is Kolata's definition of it?

4. What patterns of development, other than definition, does the author use? How does she distinguish Spinning from exercising on stationary bikes like LifeCycles?

Building Your Word Power

1. Define the word *funk* as it is used in paragraph 3, underlining the words and phrases that provide a clue to its meaning.

2. Evaluate the simile "like the feeling you might get when you are totally absorbed in your work, or in playing a musical instrument" (para. 18). Does this figure of speech convey the feeling that the author experiences while Spinning? If not, can you suggest some different similes that would better express the sensation to someone who doesn't enjoy their work or play an instrument?

   For a definition of simile, *see the chart of commonly used language features on p. 21.*

3. Explain the meaning of each of the following words as it is used in the reading: *downcast* (para. 3), *relegated* (3), *mandatory* (5), *exerting* (8), *enthusiasts* (9), *demurs* (12), and *cadence* (16). Refer to your dictionary as needed.

Building Your Critical Thinking Skills: Author's Purpose

Authors write to inform, to persuade, to entertain, or for a combination of these or other purposes. To determine the **author's purpose** you should consider the intended audience, the author's background, and any stated or unstated reasons for writing. Identify whether more than one side of an issue is presented or if the author leans toward a particular viewpoint. Is he or she trying to convince you of something or just explain it? Using what you know about identifying the author's purpose, answer the following questions.

1. This essay comes from a chapter in Kolata's book, *Ultimate Fitness: The Quest for Truth about Exercise and Health*. What does this title indicate about the author's purpose in writing?

2. Examine how Kolata treats the subject of Spinning. At the end of the essay, did you feel as though she was trying to convince you to take up Spinning, or that she was merely trying to explain the sport to you? Support your answer with examples from the essay.

Reacting to the Reading: Discussion and Journal Writing

1. Discuss other types of indoor exercises that simulate outdoor sports.

2. In class or in your journal, describe the benefits of a particular kind of exercise or activity to someone who is unfamiliar with it.

Applying Your Skills: Writing Assignments

1. **Paragraph Assignment.** Write a paragraph defining the feeling you get after exercising or doing a favorite activity. Give it a name such as "runner's high," for example, and briefly list some of its characteristics.

2. Write an essay defining a form of exercise or activity that you enjoy. Include a description of equipment that is necessary for the exercise, such as goggles or running shoes. Be sure to describe your personal history with the activity, such as when and why you first started doing it and what you gain from it.

3. Kolata says she has an "almost obsessive fascination" with monitoring her heart rate. Brainstorm a list of things that fascinate you or about which you are obsessive. For example, you might be fascinated by shoes or sports cars, or you might be obsessive about neatness or correctness. Choose one, and write an essay that defines your fascination or obsession.

4. **Combining Patterns.** The author mentions that Spinning classes are set to music. Based on your own musical preferences, write an essay using cause and effect in which you propose an ideal "soundtrack" for a sport or activity that you enjoy, discussing how the music and songs affect you. Begin your essay with a definition of your ideal soundtrack.

5. **Internet Research.** The American Heart Association presents a wealth of information about exercise and other elements of an active lifestyle on its Web site: www.justmove.org/myfitness/active.cfm. Research this site or one like it; then, on the basis of your research, write a definition essay about one of the concepts or terms described there. Use examples from the site and from your own experience to develop the essay.

Cause and Effect: Using Reasons and Results to Explain

WRITING QUICK START

Assume you are a journalist for your local newspaper reporting on a natural disaster that occurred in a nearby town. Your immediate task is to write a brief article to accompany the photograph shown on this page. Write a paragraph telling readers why the disaster occurred and what happened as a result of it. For the purpose of this activity, make up a plausible account of the event that led up to the scene depicted in the photograph.

439

What Are Causes and Effects?

A **cause and effect** essay, also called a **causal analysis**, analyzes (1) *causes* (why an event or phenomenon happens), (2) *effects* (what happens because of the event or phenomenon), or (3) both causes and effects. The essay generally shows how one event or phenomenon brings about another: Losing your car keys (the *cause*) leads you to be late for class (the *effect*).

Many everyday occasions require the use of causal analyses. If your child is injured in an accident, the doctor may ask what effects the accident had on your child. In a note to a manufacturer, you may need to explain how a product is defective and why you deserve a refund. You will have many occasions to use causal analysis in college and on the job, as indicated in the following examples.

- For an essay exam in your *twentieth-century history* course, you are required to discuss the causes of U.S. involvement in the Korean conflict.
- For your job as an *investment analyst*, you need to explain to a client why a certain company was profitable this year.

In the following essay, Deb Aronson explains why contact with nature relieves stress and aids healing.

How Nature Heals Us

Deb Aronson

Deb Aronson is a freelance writer based in Urbana, Illinois. The following essay appeared in the July/August 2003 issue of *Science & Spirit* magazine and was reprinted in the November/December 2003 issue of *Utne*.

Introduction: introduces topic and poses question that essay will answer

Thesis

Background information about types of attention

Can contact with nature relieve anxiety and stress, aid healing, and increase concentration? It appears that it can, even when "contact" is defined in the loosest way. Some researchers now suggest that passive contact with nature, like looking at trees from a car, can be as therapeutic as a walk in the woods. It appears that nature can really provide nurture — for the young and old, healthy and sick, alike.

Here's why.

"We have two kinds of attention," says Andrea Faber Taylor, an environmental psychologist and postdoctoral research associate at the University of Illinois. The first is the "directed attention" we call on for tasks that require focus, like driving or doing our taxes. Directed attention tends to be tiring, however, and fatigue affects our ability to make good decisions and control destructive impulses. The best way to restore directed attention is to give it a rest by shifting to the second type, "involuntary attention," which we display when we watch a fire or meditate, for instance. <u>Looking at nature is another activity that gives our directed attention a chance to recover.</u>

    For example, Roger Ulrich and his colleagues at Texas A&M University found that people who commuted along scenic roads recovered more quickly from stressful driving conditions than those who saw billboards, buildings, and parking lots. Ulrich also noted something he termed an "inoculation" effect: <u>Drivers who had taken the scenic route responded more calmly to stressful situations later on.</u> Ulrich also looked at patients recovering from gallbladder surgery. <u>The patients who could see trees from their hospital beds needed fewer painkillers and had shorter hospital stays than those who looked out on brick walls.</u>

    So, with all our efforts to alleviate stress — from aerobics and yoga to anti-anxiety pills — maybe the key is as simple as a garden. In fact, even a little bit of green seems to make a big impact. Some studies suggest that a houseplant or even a picture of nature can convey similar benefits.

    "It used to be that we looked at cataclysmic events, like divorce or loss of a job, as stressors," says Kathleen Wolf of the College of Forest Resources at the University of Washington. "But now we are seeing that our daily lives have constant small stressors, and the cumulative effect is significant. Consequently, even small, incremental contacts with nature in our daily lives are beneficial."

    In her study, Andrea Faber Taylor looked at children living in Chicago's notorious Robert Taylor Homes housing project. The children she studied were all from the same socioeconomic bracket; all were African American; all lived in virtually identical apartments to which their families had been randomly assigned; and all lived on the second, third, or fourth floors, the best levels for viewing nature. The only difference was that some apartments overlooked trees and grass while others overlooked pavement.

    <u>Girls who could see nature from their windows were better able to concentrate, and to control impulsive behavior, as measured in standard psychological tests.</u> These behaviors tend to help children resist peer pressure and sexual pressure, and help in other challenging situations.

    "Our theory was that public housing is a very fatiguing environment," says Faber Taylor. "It turns out that small amounts of greenery seem to make a big difference. You don't have to live in Sherwood Forest[1] to enjoy nature's benefits."

    By creating more green spaces, particularly in urban areas, we could minimize, or at least buffer, the stresses of everyday life and the long-term costs in mental and physical health associated with stress. Now that's a magic bullet.

[1]An ancient forest in England, said to be the home of Robin Hood.

Margin annotations:

- Cause and effect A
- 4 — Research study cited to support cause and effect B
- Cause and effect C
- 5 — Recognizes and dispels common assumptions about how to relieve stress
- 6
- 7 — Research study adds credibility
- 8 — Cause and effect D
- Additional benefits
- 9
- 10 — Conclusion: calls for creation of more green spaces

Characteristics of Cause and Effect Essays

A causal analysis has a clear purpose: to explain causes or effects, or both. In addition, a cause and effect essay includes a thesis, follows a logical organizational plan, develops each cause or effect fully, and may recognize or dispel readers' assumptions about the topic.

Causal Analysis Focuses on Causes, Effects, or Both

In deciding whether to consider causes, effects, or both, it is important to distinguish the causes from the effects. Some are relatively easy to identify.

CAUSE   EFFECT
You get a flat tire.   ⟶   You are late for work.

In more complex situations, however, the causes and effects are less clear. For example, the causes for a weight problem are complex, and causes may not always be clearly separable from effects. Some people have an obsession with dieting (*effect*) because they have a poor body image (*cause*). Yet an obsession with dieting (*cause*) can lead to a poor body image (*effect*).

To identify causes and effects, think of causes as the *reasons that something happened* and effects as the *results of the thing that happened*.

CAUSE   EFFECT
Event X happened because . . .   ◄— EVENT X —►   The result of event X was . . .

Multiple Causes and Effects. Causal analysis can be complex when it deals with an event or phenomenon that has multiple causes, effects, or both. Indeed, several causes may produce a single effect. For example, you probably chose the college you attend now (*one effect*) for a number of reasons, including the availability of courses in your major, the cost of tuition, the reputation of the school, and its distance from your home (*multiple causes*).

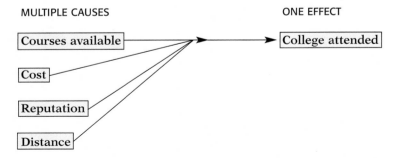

Alternatively, one cause may have several effects. For instance, your decision to quit your part-time job (*one cause*) will result in more study time, less pressure, and less spending money (*multiple effects*).

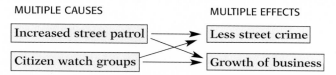

Related events or phenomena may have both multiple causes and multiple effects. For instance, an increase in the number of police officers patrolling the street in urban areas along with the formation of citizen watch groups (*multiple causes*) will result in less street crime and the growth of small businesses (*multiple effects*).

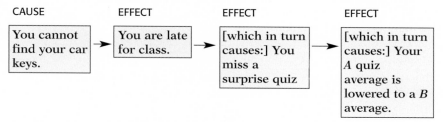

Chains of Events. In some cases a series of events forms a chain in which each event is both the effect of what happened before it and the cause of the next event. In other words, a simple event can produce a chain of consequences.

CAUSE	EFFECT	EFFECT	EFFECT
You cannot find your car keys.	You are late for class.	[which in turn causes:] You miss a surprise quiz	[which in turn causes:] Your *A* quiz average is lowered to a *B* average.

Once you clearly separate causes and effects, you can decide whether to focus on causes, effects, or both.

Causal Analysis Has a Clear Purpose

A cause and effect essay may be expressive, but more often it is informative, persuasive, or both. In an essay about the effects of the death of a close relative, for example, you would express your feelings about the person by showing how the loss affected you. However, an essay describing the sources (*causes*) of the pollution of a local river could be primarily informative, or it could be informative and persuasive if it also stressed the positive results (*effects*) of enforcing anti-pollution laws.

Some cause and effect essays have more than one purpose. For example, an essay may examine the causes of academic cheating (*informative*) and propose policies that would alleviate the problem (*persuasive*). In "How Nature Heals Us,"

Aronson informs readers about the effects of contact with nature, but she also suggests that creating more green space in urban areas might be beneficial.

Causal Analysis Includes a Clear Thesis Statement

Most cause and effect essays have a clear thesis statement that identifies the topic, makes an assertion about that topic, and suggests whether the essay will focus on causes, effects, or both.

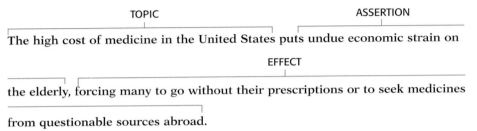

When you write cause and effect essays for college classes, be sure to cover these three items in a one-sentence thesis. Professional writers, however, occasionally express their theses in a less direct way, using two or more sentences. In "How Nature Heals Us," Aronson states her topic in a question (line 1) and then makes her assertion in the answer to it a few lines later: "It appears that nature can really provide nurture — for the young and old, healthy and sick, alike."

Causal Analysis Follows a Logical Organization

A cause and effect essay is organized logically and systematically. It may present causes or effects in chronological order — the order in which they happened. Consider this paragraph from a history book that uses chronological order to describe the effects of the tactics of the vastly outnumbered Seminole Indians against U.S. troops in the Second Seminole War.

> General Winfield Scott took charge, but his columns of troops, marching impressively into Seminole territory, found no one. They became tired of the mud, the swamps, the heat, the sickness, the hunger — the classic fatigue of a civilized army fighting people on their own land. No one wanted to face Seminoles in the Florida swamps. In 1836, 103 commissioned officers resigned from the regular army, leaving only forty-six. In the spring of 1837, Major General Jesup moved into the war with an army of ten thousand, but the Seminoles just faded into the swamps, coming out from time to time to strike at isolated forces.
>
> HOWARD ZINN, *A People's History of the United States*

In other situations, a causal analysis may use a most-to-least or least-to-most order to sequence the causes or effects according to a particular characteristic. In "How Nature Heals Us," Aronson uses most-to-least order, first discussing the most obvious types of exposure to nature (driving on scenic roads) before moving on to less obvious contacts (viewing trees from an apartment window).

Causal Analysis Explains Each Cause or Effect Fully

A causal analysis presents each cause or effect in a detailed and understandable way, using examples, facts, descriptions, comparisons, statistics, and/or anecdotes. Aronson uses several of these elements to give readers a convincing explanation of the effects of contact with nature. She uses examples to support her analysis (para. 3 and 5); she describes a comparative study on children living in a housing project (para. 7–9); and she includes quotations and data by researchers to support her main point (para. 4, 6).

For most cause and effect essays, you will need to research the topic to locate evidence that will support the thesis. In an essay about the effects on children of viewing violence on television, for instance, you might need to locate research or statistics that document changes in children's behavior after watching violent programs. In addition to statistical data, expert opinion is often used as evidence. For example, to support a thesis that reading aloud to preschool children helps them develop prereading skills, you might cite the opinions of reading specialists or psychologists who specialize in child development.

Causal Analysis May Recognize or Dispel Readers' Assumptions

Some cause and effect essays recognize or dispel popular ideas that readers assume to be true. For example, an essay on the effects of capital punishment might attempt to dispel the notion that it is a deterrent to crime. In "How Nature Heals Us," Aronson tries to dispel the notion that people need aerobics, yoga, or anti-anxiety pills to relieve stress (para. 5).

Recognizing the causes or effects that readers assume to be most important, regardless of whether your essay supports or refutes them, lends credibility. In an informative essay, this recognition conveys the impression that nothing has been overlooked. In a persuasive essay, it reassures readers that other viewpoints have been recognized.

Visualizing a Cause and Effect Essay

The graphic organizers in Figures 12.1, 12.2, and 12.3 show the basic organization of three types of causal analysis essays. All three types include an introduction (which identifies the event, provides background information, and states a thesis) as well as a conclusion. Notice that causes are presented before effects. Although this is the typical arrangement, writers sometimes reverse it, discussing effects first and then causes to create a sense of drama or surprise. Figure 12.4 is a graphic organizer based on the reading "How Nature Heals Us."

When you incorporate causes, effects, or both into an essay that is not primarily a causal analysis, you can adapt one of these organizational plans to suit your purpose.

FIGURE 12.1   Graphic Organizer for an Essay on Causes or Effects

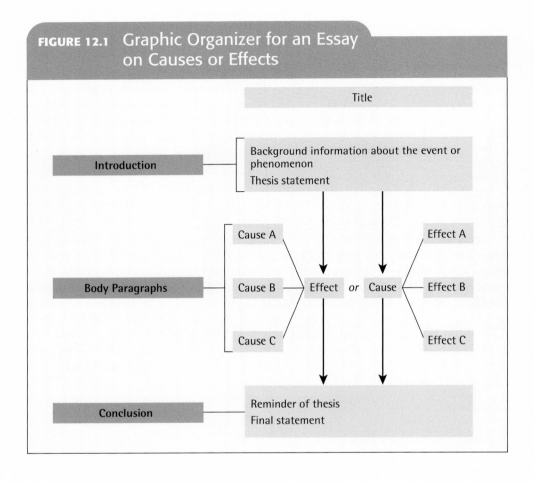

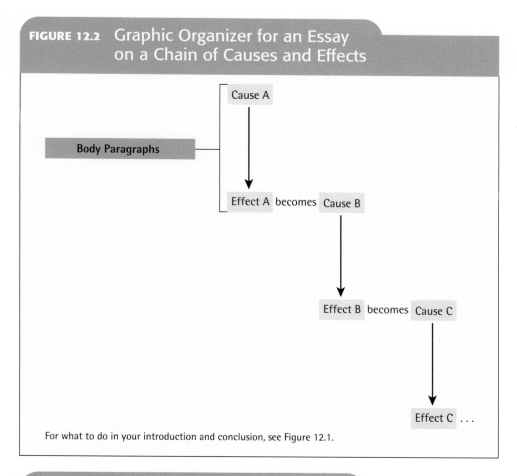

FIGURE 12.2 Graphic Organizer for an Essay on a Chain of Causes and Effects

For what to do in your introduction and conclusion, see Figure 12.1.

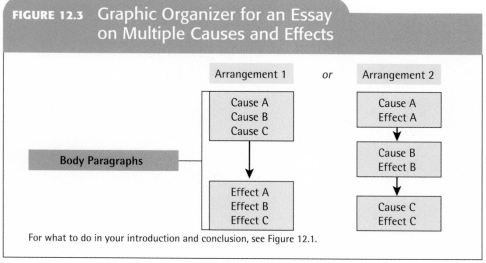

FIGURE 12.3 Graphic Organizer for an Essay on Multiple Causes and Effects

For what to do in your introduction and conclusion, see Figure 12.1.

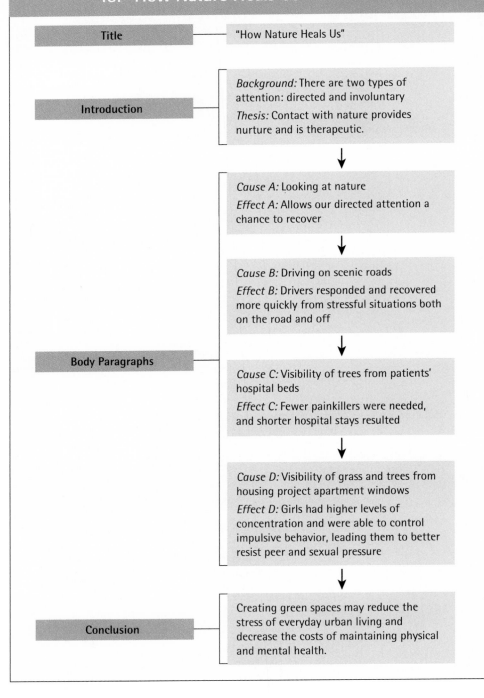

FIGURE 12.4 Graphic Organizer for "How Nature Heals Us"

Title	"How Nature Heals Us"
Introduction	*Background:* There are two types of attention: directed and involuntary *Thesis:* Contact with nature provides nurture and is therapeutic.
Body Paragraphs	*Cause A:* Looking at nature *Effect A:* Allows our directed attention a chance to recover
	Cause B: Driving on scenic roads *Effect B:* Drivers responded and recovered more quickly from stressful situations both on the road and off
	Cause C: Visibility of trees from patients' hospital beds *Effect C:* Fewer painkillers were needed, and shorter hospital stays resulted
	Cause D: Visibility of grass and trees from housing project apartment windows *Effect D:* Girls had higher levels of concentration and were able to control impulsive behavior, leading them to better resist peer and sexual pressure
Conclusion	Creating green spaces may reduce the stress of everyday urban living and decrease the costs of maintaining physical and mental health.

Writing a Cause and Effect Essay

To write a cause and effect essay, use the following steps. Although you will focus primarily on causal analysis, you will probably need to integrate one or more other patterns of development.

Planning a Cause and Effect Essay

The first step is to select an event or phenomenon to write about. Be sure to choose one with which you are familiar or about which you can find information in the library or on the Internet. Then decide on your purpose and whether to focus on causes, effects, or both. Keep the length of your essay in mind as you think about these issues. It would be unrealistic, for example, to try to discuss both the causes and the effects of child abuse in a five-page paper.

Discovering Causes and Effects

The next step is to discover causes, effects, or both. You can approach this task in a number of ways.

Generating Causes, Effects, or Both for a Cause and Effect Essay

1. **Write your topic in the middle of a page, turning the page sideways to allow extra space.** Brainstorm all possible causes and effects, writing causes on the left and effects on the right.
2. **Replay the event in your mind.** Focus on one or both of these questions: "Why did the event happen?" and "What happened as a result of it?" Make notes on the answers.
3. **Try asking questions and writing assertions about the problem or phenomenon.** Did a chain of events cause the phenomenon? What effects are not so obvious?
4. **Discuss your topic with a classmate or friend.** Ask his or her opinion on the topic's causes, effects, or both.
5. **Research your topic in the library or on the Internet.** Make notes on possible causes and effects, or print out copies of the relevant Web pages you discover.
6. **Ask a friend or classmate to interview you about the topic.** Assume you are an expert on the topic; try to explain causes, effects, or both as clearly as possible. Have your friend critique your answers, taking notes on his or her feedback to get ideas.

Identifying Primary Causes and Effects

Once you have a list of causes or effects (or both), the next task is to sort through them and decide which ones are *primary*, or most important. For example, if your topic is the possible effects of television violence on young viewers, two primary effects might be an increase in aggressive behavior and a willingness to accept violence as normal. Less important, or *secondary*, effects might include learning inappropriate or offensive words and spending less time viewing family-oriented shows. In essays about controversial issues, primary causes or effects may differ depending on the writer's interests.

Use the following questions to help you decide which causes and effects are most important.

Causes

- What are the most obvious and immediate causes?
- What cause(s), if eliminated, would drastically change the event, problem, or phenomenon?

Effects

- What are the obvious effects of the event, problem, or phenomenon?
- Which effects have the most serious consequences? For whom?

After you identify primary and secondary causes and effects, examine them to be sure you have not overlooked any *hidden* causes or effects. For example, if a child often reports to the nurse's office complaining of a stomachache, a parent may assume that the child has digestive problems. However, a closer study of the behavior may reveal that the child is worried about attending a physical education class and that the stomachaches are the result of stress and anxiety. The physical education class is the hidden cause. As you analyze causes and effects, do not assume that the most obvious or simplest explanation is the only one.

For more on faulty reasoning, see Chapter 13, p. 498.

You should also be on the lookout for assumptions that involve errors in reasoning. For example, just because Event A precedes Event B, Event A is not necessarily the cause of Event B. Suppose you decide against having a cup of coffee one morning, and later that day you score higher than ever before on a political science exam. Although one event followed the other in time, you cannot assume that reducing your coffee intake caused the high grade. To avoid such errors, look for evidence that one event did indeed cause the other.

Once you feel confident about your list of causes and effects, you need to provide a complete explanation of each primary cause or effect that will be included in the essay. To do so, you'll probably use one or more other patterns of development. For example, you may need to narrate events, present descriptive details, define important terms, explain unfamiliar processes, include examples, or make comparisons to explain unfamiliar concepts. At this point, it is a good idea to do some additional prewriting or research to gather evidence to support the causes, effects, or both. Try to discover several types of evidence, including facts, expert opinion, personal observation, quotations, and statistics.

Developing Your Thesis

Once you are satisfied with the causes and effects and the evidence you have generated to support them, the next step is to develop a working thesis. As noted earlier, the thesis for a causal analysis identifies the topic, makes an assertion about the topic, and tells whether the essay will focus on causes, effects, or both.

Use the following tips to write a clear thesis statement.

Guidelines for Writing a Thesis for a Cause and Effect Essay

1. **State the cause and effect relationship.** Do not leave it to the reader to figure out the causal relationship. In the following example, note that the original thesis is weak and vague, whereas the revision makes the cause and effect connection explicit by using the word *because* and by including necessary information.

   ▶ Breathing paint fumes in a closed environment can be dangerous. People *[for people]* suffering from asthma and emphysema are particularly vulnerable. *[because their lungs are especially sensitive to irritants.]*

2. **Avoid overly broad or absolute assertions.** Such statements are difficult or impossible to support.

   ▶ Drugs are the root *[a major]* cause of inner-city crime.

3. **Use qualifying words.** Unless a cause and effect relationship is well established and accepted, qualify your thesis statement.

   ▶ Overemphasizing competitive sports is *[may be]* harmful to the psychological development of young children.

4. **Avoid an overly assertive or dogmatic tone.** The tone of your essay, including the thesis, should be confident but not overbearing. You want readers to accept your ideas but not to be put off by an arrogant tone.

   ▶ There is no question *[Substantial evidence suggests]* that American youths have changed in response to the culture in which they live.

Drafting a Cause and Effect Essay

Once you have evaluated the cause and effect relationship and thesis, it is time to organize your ideas and draft your essay. Review Figures 12.1, 12.2, and 12.3 to find the graphic organizer that is closest to your essay's basic structure. Then choose a method of organization that will present your ideas effectively (see p. 444).

After you decide how to organize the essay, the next step is to write a first draft. Use the following guidelines to draft your essay.

Guidelines for Writing a Cause and Effect Essay

1. **Write an effective introduction.** Your introduction should identify the topic and causal relationship as well as draw readers into the essay.
2. **Provide well-developed explanations.** Be sure to provide sufficient evidence that the causal relationship exists. Offer a number of reasons and choose a variety of types of evidence (examples, statistics, expert opinion, etc.). Try to develop each cause or effect into a detailed paragraph with a clear topic sentence.
3. **Use strong transitions.** Use a transition each time you move from an explanation of one cause or effect to an explanation of another. Transitional words and phrases that are useful in cause and effect essays include *because, since, as a result*, and *therefore*.
4. **Avoid overstating causal relationships.** When writing about causes and effects, avoid words and phrases that overstate the causal relationship, such as *it is obvious, without doubt, always*, and *never*. These words and phrases wrongly suggest that a causal relationship is absolute and without exception. Instead, use words and phrases that qualify, such as *it is possible, it is likely*, and *most likely*.
5. **Write a satisfying conclusion.** Your conclusion may remind readers of the thesis and draw the essay to a satisfying close. You might also summon the readers to action, as Aronson does at the end of "How Nature Heals Us" when she calls for creating more green space in urban areas.

Analyzing and Revising

If possible, set your draft aside for a day or two before rereading and revising it. As you review the draft, concentrate on how you organize and present your ideas, not on grammar, punctuation, or mechanics. Use the flowchart in Figure 12.5 to guide your analysis of the strengths and weaknesses of your draft.

Editing and Proofreading

For more on these and other common errors, see Chapter 4, p. 81.

The final step is to check your revised essay for errors in grammar, spelling, punctuation, and mechanics. In addition, check for the types of errors you commonly make in any writing assignments, whether for this class or any other situation. As you edit and proofread your causal analysis essay, watch out for two types of errors commonly found in this type of writing: wordy sentences and mixed constructions. See the box on page 455 for more on these common errors.

FIGURE 12.5   Revising a Cause and Effect Essay

QUESTIONS

1. Highlight your thesis. Does it express a qualified, manageable assertion? (Can you prove the thesis?)

NO →

- Use mapping or questioning to narrow the topic (see Chapter 2, pp. 30 and 32).
- Revise to focus only on primary causes or effects.
- Add qualifying words or phrases to the thesis.

↓ YES

2. Reread your thesis statement. Is the purpose of your essay clear?

NO →

- Decide whether you want to express yourself, inform your readers, or persuade your readers. Revise the thesis to do so.

↓ YES

3. Place a checkmark ✓ by each cause. Mark an ✖ by each effect. Does the essay clearly focus on causes, effects, or both?

NO →

- Reconsider whether you want to explain causes, effects, or both. Will the essay be skimpy if you focus on only one? Will it be too complicated if you discuss both?

↓ YES

4. Place brackets [ ] around the explanation for each cause or effect. Is each one explained fully?

NO →

- Add anecdotes or observations from personal experience.
- Add relevant details and examples.
- Research the topic to locate more facts, research studies, statistics, and expert opinion.

↓ YES

5. *Draw* a graphic organizer or *write* a brief outline of your major topics. Do your ideas progress logically?

NO →

- Compare your organizer or outline to the graphics organizers on pages 447–48. Look for places where you can rearrange causes, effects, or both.
- Use one of the organizers on pages 447–48 as a model for reorganizing the cause, effects, or both.

↓ YES

(Continued)

FIGURE 12.5 *(Continued)*

QUESTIONS		REVISION STRATEGIES

6. *Write* the order of presentation (chronological, least-to-most, or most-to-least) you used at the top of the essay. Is the order clear and effective?

 NO

- Choose a different order, and rearrange your draft.

 YES

7. Draw a circle around sections where you have recognized or dispelled readers' assumptions. Are these sections complete and effective?

NO

- Discuss popular ideas readers might assume about the topic, and either support or challenge them.

 YES

8. <u>Underline</u> each topic sentence. Is each paragraph focused on a separate cause or effect?

NO

- Be sure each paragraph has a topic sentence and supporting details (see Chapter 3).
- Consider combining closely related paragraphs.
- Split paragraphs that cover more than one cause or effect.

 YES

9. Draw a box around the introduction and conclusion. Are they effective?

NO

- Revise the introduction and conclusion so that they meet the guidelines in Chapter 3 (pp. 61–63).

 YES

10. Print another copy to edit and proofread before turning the essay in.

Editing Tips and Troublespots: Cause and Effect

1. **Look for and revise wordy sentences.** When explaining causal relationships, writers often use complex and compound-complex sentences (sentences with multiple dependent and independent clauses). Because such sentences can become wordy and confusing, you should look for ways to eliminate empty phrases and simplify your wording.

   > Certain types of computer
   > ▸ ~~As you are already well aware,~~ viruses ~~of certain types in a computer file~~
   >   ∧
   >   often create errors that you cannot explain ~~in documents~~ and may eventually result in lost data.

2. **Revise to eliminate mixed constructions.** A mixed construction occurs when a writer connects phrases, clauses, or both that do not work together logically and that cause confusion in meaning.

   >   Although   Samantha
   > ▸ ~~Samantha, although~~ she was late for work, ~~but~~ was not reprimanded by
   >   ∧   ∧
   >   her boss.

   Using both *although* and *but* makes this a mixed construction. To avoid mixed constructions, check words that join phrases and clauses. Pay attention to prepositions and conjunctions. Also, check to be sure that the subjects of every sentence can perform the action described by the verb. If not, revise the sentence by supplying the appropriate verb.

   >   discourage
   > ▸ Higher academic standards ~~ignore~~ gifted but underprepared athletes who
   >   ∧
   >   are motivated to improve their academic skills.

(**Students Write**)

Nathan Nguyen was a first-year liberal arts major when he wrote this essay in response to an assignment for his writing class. He was asked to explain the causes and effects of a current social problem. As you read, notice how Nguyen carefully presents the effects of legalizing gambling and how these effects in turn had other unforeseen effects.

Gambling on Our Future

Nathan Nguyen

Title: suggests importance of topic

Introduction: opening example catches readers' interest

Marge Simpson is a junkie. Are you surprised? Marge has always been the moral an- [1] chor that kept *The Simpsons* squarely in the mainstream. She was the stay-at-home mom that tempered Lisa's progressive politics, the sober wife that supported Homer during his drunken misadventures, and the upstanding citizen that taught Bart how to live in society. If Marge had an intravenous drug habit, Americans everywhere would be up in arms. But it's just gambling, and in this day and age, few things are more mainstream. In fact, inspired by the huge revenues generated by Las Vegas, states are turning to gambling to finance their ailing educational systems and urban centers. As states open up their laws to all kinds of gambling, it has become more widespread and convenient, leading to an increase in addiction and problem gambling.

Thesis: suggests that essay will focus on chain of events

First event: Nevada legalizes gambling

The passage of the 1931 bill allowing gambling in Nevada was originally designed [2] to generate revenue for the state and its ailing educational system. The result was little less than a phenomenon, establishing Las Vegas as a tourist playground and a symbol of American decadence, but also changing forever the way politicians tax the people. Gambling and tourism in Las Vegas is now a $13 billion-a-year industry, and tax income from Las Vegas accounts for 43% of the state's income (Las Vegas Facts and History, screen 1). The economic boon to the state was watched enviously by lawmakers around the country; over time, what was once viewed as sinful has captured the dreams and imaginations of politicians and constituents alike.

Effects in Nevada

Second event in chain of events: other states legalize gambling

Desperate to re-create the rags-to-riches story of Las Vegas, cities and states across [3] the country have entered the business of gambling. According to the journal *American Family Physician*, "in 1978 only two states had legalized gambling; in 1998, however, only two states had not legalized gambling" (Unwin, Davis, and De Leeuw 741). The business of legalized gambling takes many forms. For example, a landmark Supreme Court decision in 1987 opened up the door to Native American gaming on tribal lands. The ensuing boost to economic development on some of these lands has caught the imagination of other impoverished areas. Struggling urban centers, such as Detroit, Oakland and St. Louis, are considering legalizing gambling in the hopes of bringing money in from the wealthy suburbs to revitalize decaying downtown districts. But gambling is not confined to casinos alone. Thirty-eight states now have casinos of a sort in every grocery, convenience store, and gas station, in the form of the lottery. With the advent of Internet gaming, "casinos" can now be reached from every household and office in the country. The problem now is not how to find legal gambling, but how to escape it.

Effect of legalization: gambling has become widespread

The dramatic acceptance of state lotteries across the nation has had the largest impact on how Americans view gambling. The lottery, like its big brother Las Vegas, was originally set up to subsidize state educational systems. Since 1964 when New Hampshire began its lottery, states have turned to lotteries as a way of increasing revenues without raising taxes. While the revenues of state-run lotteries are often lauded, according to the *Final Report* of the National Gambling Impact Study Commission, the "actual contributions are exceedingly modest" (2-4). Furthermore, lotteries are a form of regressive taxation, or a tax that takes a higher percentage of income from the poor than from higher-income groups. Despite this, Americans continue to support the lottery, making it one of the top forms of gambling in the country. According to the National Gambling Impact Study Commission's report, 86% of Americans have admitted to gambling at least once in their lives (1-1). But as "states have become active agents for the expansion of gambling," public welfare has taken a backseat to revenue raising (3-4).

The abundance of opportunities to gamble has created more compulsive gamblers by exposing people to an "illness" they might not otherwise have developed, and by giving reformed gamblers more chances to fall off the wagon. While most gamblers are able to do it healthily, a majority of the benefit derived from gambling is at the expense of the ill. A study by Duke University professors Charles Clotfelter and Philip Cook found that "5 percent of lottery players account for 51 percent of total lottery sales." Their research indicates that those who make under $10,000 spend "more than any other income group" and that lotteries rely on players who are "disproportionably poor, black, and have failed to complete a high school education" (*Final Report* 7-10). People joke that it is a tax on the stupid, but in fact it is a tax on hope. A study by researchers at Harvard Medical School "concluded that 'pathological' gaming, the severest level, has jumped more than 50 percent among adults since 1977" (Cromie, screen 1). College students are particularly vulnerable, precisely because they are more prone to taking risk than other groups and because people who begin gambling at a young age are at a much higher risk for developing a gambling problem later in life (*Final Report* 4-12). The rising rates in problem gambling correspond to the growth of legalized gambling across the country.

The promise of a Las Vegas miracle has lured states into expanding gambling and putting a mini Vegas in every 7-11 store. As states increasingly turn to gambling, more people are exposed to it, a cycle that leads to ever-rising rates of problem gambling and addiction. The hope of a Vegas miracle lures people, often poor and occasionally very sick, to a casino, to the lottery, or to online betting. The trickle-down effect from this is the often unseen side to the promise of the big jackpot: bankruptcy, job loss, divorce, alcoholism, drug addiction, and welfare are just some of the costs associated with

4 Third event in chain of events: lotteries have increased the acceptance of gambling

Cites statistics and expert opinion

5 Fourth event in chain of events: gambling has become societal problem

Research study documents appeal of gambling to the poor

Effect: increase in gambling addiction

6 Conclusion: restates chain of events and emphasizes thesis

Use of gambling jargon suggests author's opinion of the trend

gambling addiction. The question then is, are states willing to gamble with our future? For now, the trend continues, but the odds of winning are a million to one.

Works Cited

Cromie, William J. "Gambling Addictions on Increase." *Harvard University Gazette* 11 Dec. 1997. 21 Oct. 2004 <http://www.news.harvard.edu/gazette/1997/12.11/GamblingAddicti.html>.

Final Report. 3 Aug. 1999. National Gambling Impact Study Commission. 21 Oct. 2004 <http://govinfo.library.unt.edu/ngisc/index.html>.

Las Vegas Facts and History. 2000–03. Robos Las Vegas Guide. 16 Oct. 20004 <http://www.angelfire.com/tx/roboworld/facts.html>.

Unwin, Brian K., Mark K. Davis, and Jason B. De Leeuw. "Pathologic Gambling." *American Family Physician* 3 (2000): 741-49.

Responding to "Students Write"

1. Suggest an alternative title that more directly suggests the essay's thesis.
2. Evaluate Nguyen's introduction. Is the opening reference to Marge Simpson an effective strategy? How would it appeal to those who are unfamiliar with *The Simpsons?* Discuss alternative ways to introduce the topic.
3. Nguyen does not include examples of real people and their gambling addictions. Would real-life examples strengthen the essay? Why or why not?
4. Nguyen concludes by reiterating his thesis. What alternative ways might he have chosen to end the essay?

Reading a Cause and Effect Essay

Reading cause and effect essays requires critical thinking and analysis as well as close attention to detail. The overall questions to keep in mind are these: What is the relationship between the events or phenomena the writer is describing and the proposed causes or effects? Has the writer conveyed this relationship accurately and completely?

Use the following suggestions when reading text that deals with causes and effects.

What to Look for, Highlight, and Annotate

Understanding the Reading

- Read the essay once to get an overview. Then read the essay again, annotating causes or effects. Be sure to mark any relationships that are unclear or that are not supported by sufficient evidence.

- Use a graphic organizer to understand a complex causal relationship, sorting causes from effects (see Figures 12.1, 12.2, and 12.3). Fill in the organizer as you read.

- Consider the title of the essay. Does it suggest anything about causal relationships?

- What do the introduction and conclusion contribute to the essay?

Examining the Characteristics of Cause and Effect Essays

- Identify the author's thesis. Look for evidence suggesting that a causal relationship actually exists.

- Make a specific effort to distinguish between causes and effects. Mark or highlight causes in one color, effects in another.

- Distinguish between primary and secondary causes or effects, especially in a lengthy or complex essay. Try marking primary causes *PC* and secondary causes *SC*.

- Be alert for key words that signal a causal relationship. Phrases like "one impact of" and "a result of" signal effects, while phrases like "one source of" or "motivated by" indicate causes. A writer may not always use obvious transitional words and phrases.

- Establish the sequence of events for an essay that is not organized chronologically. Some authors may discuss the effect(s) before presenting the causes. Other authors may not mention key events in the order they occurred. Understanding a causal relationship sometimes requires putting events in order.

How to Find Ideas to Write About

To respond to or write about a cause and effect essay, consider the following strategies.

- If the essay discusses the causes of an event, a phenomenon, or a problem, consider writing about the effects, or vice versa.

- Think of other possible causes or effects.

- For a chain of events essay, imagine what might have happened if the chain had been broken at some point.

- Consider the secondary causes or effects the writer does not mention.

- Write about a cause and effect relationship from your own life that is similar to one in the essay.

The Honesty Virus

Clive Thompson

Clive Thompson (b. 1968), a contributing writer for *Wired*, the *New York Times Magazine*, and the *Boston Globe*, writes frequently about politics, technology, and culture. He spent the year 2002 as a Knight Science-Journalism Fellow at the Massachusetts Institute of Technology. Thompson also maintains the Web log *Collision Detection*.

In "The Honesty Virus," an article that appeared in the *New York Times Magazine* in 2004, Thompson discusses findings that defy conventional wisdom about the Internet. As you read, consider the reasons Thompson presents for the surprising amount of honesty in online personal writing. How well do his conclusions fit with your own experiences?

Focus on Understanding   Read to discover what causes people to be more truthful when they communicate online.

Focus on the Topic   In class or in your journal, write about an unusual, interesting, or revealing experience with online communication.

Everyone tells a little white lie now and then. But a Cornell professor recently claimed to have established the truth of a curious proposition: We fib less frequently when we're online than when we're talking in person. Jeffrey Hancock asked 30 of his undergraduates to record all of their communications — and all of their lies — over the course of a week. When he tallied the results, he found that the students had mishandled the truth in about one-quarter of all face-to-face conversations, and in a whopping 37 percent of phone calls. But when they went into cyberspace, they turned into Boy Scouts: only 1 in 5 instant-messaging chats contained a lie, and barely 14 percent of e-mail messages were dishonest. 1

Obviously, you can't make sweeping generalizations about society on the basis of college students' behavior. (And there's also something rather odd about asking people to be honest about how often they lie.) But still, Hancock's results were intriguing, not least because they upend some of our primary expectations about life on the Net. 2

Wasn't cyberspace supposed to be the scary zone where you couldn't trust anyone? Back when the Internet first came to Main Street, pundits worried that the digital age would open the floodgates of deception. Since anyone could hide behind an anonymous Hotmail address or chat-room moniker, Net users, we were warned, would be free to lie with impunity. Parents panicked and frantically cordoned off cyberspace from their children under the assumption that anyone lurking out there in the ether was a creep until proved otherwise. And to a certain extent, the fear seemed justified. According to Psych 101, we're 3 more likely to lie to people when there's distance between us — and you can't get much more distant than a hot-chat buddy in Siberia who calls himself 0minous-1.

Why were those fears unfounded? What it is about online life that makes us more truthful? It's simple: We're worried about being busted. In "real" life, after all, it's actually pretty easy to get away with spin. If you tell a lie to someone at a cocktail party or on the phone, you can always backtrack later and claim you said no such thing. There's probably no one recording the conversation unless you're talking to Linda Tripp° (in which case you've clearly got other problems).

On the Internet, though, your words often come back to haunt you. The digital age is tough on its liars, as a seemingly endless parade of executives are learning to their chagrin. Today's titans of industry are laid low not by ruthless competitors but by prosecutors gleefully waving transcripts of old e-mail, filled with suggestions or subterfuge. Even Microsoft was tripped up by old e-mail messages and you would figure its employees would know better. This isn't a problem for only corporate barons. We all read the headlines; we know that in cyberspace our words never die, because machines don't forget. "It's a cut-and-paste culture," as Hancock put it (though he told me that on the phone, so who knows? There's only a 63 percent chance he really meant it).

Indeed, the axiom that machines never forget is built into the very format of e-mail — consider that many e-mail programs automatically "quote" your words when someone replies to your message. Every day, my incoming e-mail reminds me of the very words I wrote yesterday, last week or even months ago. It's as if the gotcha politics of Washington were being brought to bear on our everyday lives. Every time I finish an e-mail message, I pause for a few seconds to reread it before I hit "send" just to make sure I haven't said something I'll later regret. It's as if I'm constantly awaiting the subpoena. And it's not only e-mail that records our deeds for future scrutiny. Before going on a first date, people Google their partners to see what they can learn. Mobile phones take photographs. The other day I saw an ad promoting the world's first "terabyte" hard drive for consumers' use: it can store two years' worth of continuous music, or about 200 million pieces of average-size e-mail. In a couple of years, that sort of hardware will be standard issue in even the cheapest Dell computer. We are facing an age in which virtually nothing will be forgotten.

Maybe this helps explain why television programs like *C.S.I.*° have become so popular. They're all about revealing the sneaky things that people do. We watch with fascination and unease as scientists inspect the tiniest of clues — a stray hair on a car seat, a latent fingerprint on a CD-ROM. After you've seen high-tech cops rake over evidence from a crime scene with ultraviolet light and luminol and genetic sequencers enough times, you get the message: Watch out, punk. We've got files on you. Forensic science has become the central drama of pop culture, and its popularity may well increase our anxieties about technology. So no wonder we're so careful to restrict our lying to low-fi environments. We have begun to behave like mobsters, keenly suspicious of places that might

4

5

6

7

Linda Tripp: the woman who secretly recorded Monica Lewinsky's conversations detailing her sexual relationship with former president Bill Clinton

C.S.I.: Crime Scene Investigation, a popular television show

be bugged, conducting all of our subterfuge in loud restaurants and lonely parks, where we can meet one on one.

Still, it's not only the fear of electronic exposure that drives us to tell the truth. There's something about the Internet that encourages us to spill our guts, often in rather outrageous ways. Psychologists have noticed for years that going online seems to have a catalytic effect on people's personalities. The most quiet and reserved people may become deranged loudmouths when they sit behind the keyboard, staying up until dawn and conducting angry debates on discussion boards with total strangers. You can usually spot the newbies in any discussion group because they're the ones WRITING IN ALL CAPS — they're tripped out on the Internet's heady combination of geographic distance and pseudo-invisibility.   8

One group of psychologists found that heated arguments — so-called flame-war fights, admittedly a rather fuzzy category — were far more common in online discussion boards than in comparable face-to-face communications. Another researcher, an Open University U.K. psychologist named Adam Joinson, conducted an experiment in which his subjects chatted online and off. He found that when people communicated online, they were more likely to offer up personal details about themselves without any prompting. Joinson also notes that the Samaritans, a British crisis-line organization, has found that 50 percent of those who write in via e-mail express suicidal feelings, compared with only 20 percent of those who call in. This isn't because Net users are more suicidally depressed than people offline. It's just that they're more comfortable talking about it — "disinhibited," as the mental-health profession would say.   9

Who knew? When the government created the Internet 30 years ago, it thought it was building a military tool. The Net was supposed to help the nation survive a nuclear attack. Instead, it has become a vast arena for collective therapy — for a mass outpouring of what we're thinking and feeling. I spend about an hour every day visiting blogs, those lippy Web sites where everyone wants to be a pundit and a memoirist. (Then I spend another hour writing my own blog and adding to the cacophony.) Stripped of our bodies, it seems, we become creatures of pure opinion.   10

Our impulse to confess via cyberspace inverts much of what we think about honesty. It used to be that if you wanted to know someone — to really know and trust them — you arranged a face-to-face meeting. Our culture still fetishizes physical contact, the shaking of hands, the lubricating chitchat. Executives and politicians spend hours flying across the country merely for a five-minute meeting, on the assumption that even a few seconds of face time can cut through the prevarications of letters and legal contracts. Remember when George W. Bush first met Vladimir Putin,° gazed into his eyes and said he could trust him because he'd acquired "a sense of his soul"?   11

Vladimir Putin: president of Russia, elected in 2000

So much for that. If Bush really wanted the straight goods, he should have met the guy in an AOL chat room. And maybe, in the long run, that's the gratifying news. As more and more of our daily life moves online, we could find ourselves living in an increasingly honest world, or at least one in which lies have   12 ever more serious consequences. Bush himself can't put old statements about W.M.D.° behind him partly because so many people are forwarding his old speeches around on e-mail or posting them on Web sites. With its unforgiving machine memory, the Internet might turn out to be the unlikely conscience of the world.

W.M.D.: weapons of mass destruction

Understanding the Reading

1. What were the results of Cornell professor Jeffrey Hancock's study of his students' online behavior?
2. According to Thompson, why is the digital age "tough on its liars" (para. 5)?
3. What causes people to be honest when they are online?
4. How is online communication different from offline communication? What is it about the Internet that encourages people to communicate differently?

Visualizing the Reading

To analyze the causal relationships used in Thompson's essay, complete the graphic organizer by filling in the blank boxes.

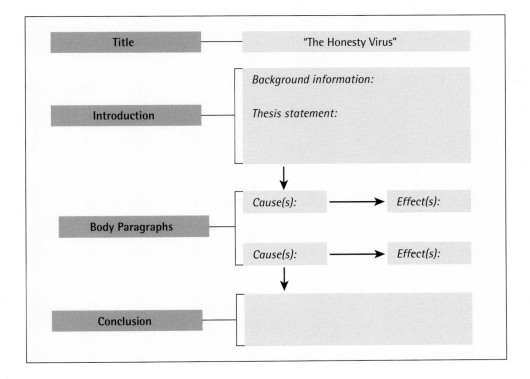

Examining the Characteristics of Cause and Effect Essays

1. Is the author's purpose in writing informative, persuasive, or both? Explain.

2. Identify Thompson's thesis statement. If he uses two or more sentences to convey his main point, express his thesis in your own words.

3. What types of evidence does the author use to support his thesis? Does he explain each cause and effect fully and in an understandable way? Suggest why or why not.

4. What popular assumption about the Internet is Thompson seeking to dispel? How effective is his essay in dispelling these fears about online communication?

5. What other patterns of development besides cause and effect does the author use?

Building Your Word Power

1. Identify what the prefix *pseudo-* means, and then explain the meaning of *pseudo-invisibility* as used in paragraph 8.

2. Find three synonyms (words that have similar meanings) for *lying* in the essay.

3. Explain the meaning of each of the following words as it is used in the reading: *up-end* para. (2), *moniker* (3), *impunity* (3), *axiom* (6), *catalytic* (8), and *cacophony* (10). Refer to your dictionary as needed.

Building Your Critical Thinking Skills: Tone

Tone reflects the way the author sounds to the readers or the way the author feels about the topic. Writers establish tone through formal or informal use of language, sentence arrangements, and word choice. An author's tone can reflect many emotions — from anger to joy, to fear, and so on. For example, the tone of an essay about the causes and effects of the melting of the polar ice cap might be passionate and alarming. Because the author's tone affects the readers' attitude toward the topic, it is important to be aware of tone. Using your knowledge about tone, answer the following questions.

1. Underline several words or phrases that contribute to the overall tone of Thompson's essay. How would you describe its tone?

2. Does the author's tone seem appropriate for his subject? Why or why not?

3. Reread the last two paragraphs of the essay. How would you categorize the author's tone toward politicians? What does this reveal about his own attitudes?

Reacting to the Reading: Discussion and Journal Writing

1. How do your online experiences compare to the ones described in the essay? Do you agree or disagree that people are more honest and more "disinhibited" (para. 9) online?

2. Do you agree that the popularity of forensic science as shown on programs like *C.S.I.* may increase our anxiety about technology? Explain your answer.

3. Technology is advancing in such a way that cameras may eventually become standard equipment on computer systems, enabling us to see each other as we com-

municate. Discuss whether people will continue to be as honest or as open about personal details if we are no longer "stripped of our bodies" (para. 10).

Applying Your Skills: Writing Assignments

1. Paragraph Assignment. The author describes why he thinks people are more honest online. Write a paragraph giving other possible reasons that people might be more open about personal details when communicating online.

2. Thompson asserts that "[w]e are facing an age in which virtually nothing will be forgotten" (para. 6). What are the positive and negative aspects of this kind of future? Write an essay exploring the consequences of a lasting, permanent memory of all our actions and words.

3. The author refers to "the Internet's heady combination of geographic distance and pseudo-invisibility" (para. 8). What effects have you noticed as a result of the relative anonymity of the Internet? Write an essay in which you discuss how the Internet causes people to communicate differently.

4. Combining Patterns. The essay opens with the statement, "Everyone tells a little white lie now and then." How prevalent is lying among people you know? Is lying ever acceptable? Is there a difference between white lies and those of a more serious nature? Write an essay that explores on the causes and effects of lying. Using examples from your own experience, explore the multiple effects or chain of events that resulted from a single lie. Include a thesis that makes an assertion about the consequences of lying.

5. Internet Research. Using a search engine, research "netiquette," or online etiquette — the dos and don'ts of communicating online. One place to start is the online version of *Netiquette* by Virginia Shea at http://albion.com/netiquette/book/index.html. Choose an aspect of online communication, such as business or romantic correspondence, and write an essay explaining the causes and effects of both proper and improper behavior for this type of online communication. Use examples from your research to support a thesis about the importance of following a code of conduct when communicating online.

When Plug Is Pulled on the Digital Age, the Basics Black Out

Susan Warren and Melanie Trottman

Susan Warren and Melanie Trottman are staff writers for the *Wall Street Journal*. This article appeared on the front page on August 18, 2003, four days after much of the northeastern United States had experienced a massive power outage.

In this article, Warren and Trottman focus not on the causes of the power outage — human error and an aging electrical grid — but on its surprising effects. In a world more and more driven by technology, electricity is increasingly needed to complete tasks that could once have been done mechanically or by hand. Consider all of the unplanned-for and extremely inconvenient problems that the authors list as the results of a blackout in the modern era.

Focus on Understanding   Read to discover what the "Digital Age" is.

Focus on the Topic   In class or in your journal, describe what would be the biggest inconvenience to you in a power outage.

For the better part of a decade, the digital dream has been a wireless, cashless, instantly connected society. But when the lights went out on Thursday, the Electronic Age blew a fuse. When you're unplugged, even very simple tasks became impossible. 1

Weary travelers at Detroit Metro Airport couldn't coax water from the bathroom sinks because the electronic eyes didn't work. Companies with electronic cash registers tried to make do with paper, pencil and sometimes, the calculators built into cellphones. Hotels had to dislodge guests because electronic keycards and locks couldn't be programmed. Phones fancied up with caller ID, built-in answering machines and cordless capability were silent. 2

At Charlys restaurant in Manhattan, the gas ovens were working and the pizza boxes were folded. But proprietor George Zamfotis, 47 years old, couldn't make pies because his electric cheese-shredder was out of commission. He never saw the sense in keeping a manual grater around. 3

"We do so much cheese, it just wouldn't work," he says. He didn't make pizzas until Friday afternoon, when he got a delivery of shredded cheese. 4

The toys and tools of the 21st century, from electronic address books to toilets that flush on their own, weren't even conceived in the huge blackouts of 1965 and 1977, and were far less common in the Western outage in 1996. This time, with numerous gadgets of convenience unworkable, many people found themselves lacking the simplest necessities — like matches, battery-powered 5

Satellite photo taken at night during the blackout of August 14, 2003.

radios, flashlights and old-style communication devices tethered to the wall by short cords and called telephones.

"When you get to the point where you can't wash your hands, you can't go 6 to the bathroom, you can't get a drink of water in a tall building above the fifth floor, you're getting into some not-so-humorous things," says Ralph Wyndrum, who has spent his life designing electrical systems and is now a vice president for the Institute of Electrical and Electronics Engineers Inc., a professional association.

Shirley Saunders of Queens, N.Y., thought she was being clever during the 7 blackout when she found a neighborhood grocery store that used an old-fashioned cash register. But the cashier couldn't weigh her potatoes and yams because the scale was electronic.

Back at home, the 65-year-old Ms. Saunders, a retired nurse, luckily found 8 matches from her daughter's 1990 wedding, so she was able to see by candlelight. But she kept walking into the kitchen to check the time on her microwave's digital clock. "I'd say, 'Oh, dummy. The lights are off.' But then I did it again. Old habits die hard."

Eventually, she dusted off an old transistor radio. It kept her company 9 through the night and reminded her not to fall asleep with candles burning.

Not having working elevators or water pumps in high-rise buildings might 10 be expected without electricity. But Angela Jones, a Manhattan fashion assistant, was surprised to discover even her gas-fired stove has an electric ignition to spark flame. She could have lit the stove with matches, but she'd never thought to stock them. Dinner was canned tuna on Melba toast.

At Diamond Cuts Salon and Barber Shop in Times Square, some customers 11 were only half-sheared when the electric trimmers cut out with the power, says co-owner Mike Santos. Scissors wouldn't work on popular styles like a "fade," where the sides are cut closer than the top.

With cordless phones dead, many turned to their cellphones. Some found 12 the networks jammed. Some of those who could use their cellphones then remembered they couldn't plug them in for recharging. Some resorted to driving around in their cars to recharge their phones, but that yielded another problem: Electronic gasoline pumps weren't working, so empty tanks couldn't be refilled.

With no cab in sight when he arrived at La Guardia Airport Thursday night, 13 New York hotel sales manager Greg Kooser, 37, took the first bus that came along — to Stamford, Conn.

At a darkened Marriott Hotel, it took an hour for the desk clerk to check him 14 in manually, and hours more before hotel staff could escort him to his room, guiding him through the pitch-black halls with a glow-stick. The electronic door locks were down, so staff had to use a master key to open rooms for guests one at a time. "It's amazing how a loss of power can ruin your day," he said.

Sitting with her roommate in her darkened Manhattan apartment on 15 Thursday night, Hope Tannenbaum, 26, talked through the night about "all the things that we can't do" and why they should have a battery-operated radio. "It's a good thing that candles are so trendy right now," she said, realizing she wouldn't have had any candles if she hadn't followed the fad.

Old-fashioned cash gained new value, too. Long lines formed at pay 16 phones, with some people walking away in frustration when their credit cards wouldn't work. Dead ATMs weren't helping, either.

"The toughest part was paying cash for beers in the airport," says Jim 17 Riordan, 42, a sales director from Columbus, Ohio, who was stranded at Detroit's Metro Airport. "The message is: Never go cashless."

Regular old phones worked just fine — if you were lucky enough to have a 18 plain-Jane model. After walking and hitchhiking home from his stranded train, New York energy consultant Larry Goldstein realized the three cordless phones in his home weren't working. He resorted to making calls from the bathroom, which had a simple phone wired directly into the wall. "Unfortunately," he said, "a lot of people we tried to call didn't have a phone in their bathroom."

Eduardo Velez practiced an ancient brand of retailing to help keep 19 RadioShack's store on 21st Street and Park Avenue in Manhattan open Friday. He hand-wrote sales invoices and accepted only cash from customers.

The Fort Worth, Texas, chain reported strong sales of battery-powered 20 radios, flashlights and old-style phones across about 500 stores affected by the blackout. RadioShack Corp. said it was rushing tractor-trailer loads of emergency supplies from a Maryland warehouse to its affected Northeast stores, activating a plan normally triggered by storms and other disasters.

Mr. Velez reassured customers that regular landlines will function when the 21 lights are off. "I had to explain that telephone lines do carry a little bit of current," he said.

Understanding the Reading

1. How did the effects of this widespread power outage differ from those of previous ones?

2. What were some of the more difficult aspects of the blackout for the shopkeepers cited in the article?

3. Phone use was a common problem during the blackout. What specific problems did people have, and how did they try to get around these difficulties?

4. In addition to candles, what other technique did the hotel employees use to combat the darkness?

Visualizing the Reading

Analyze the chain of events caused by the blackout; as detailed by the authors, many effects led to other effects. See if you can list all the effects cited in the essay. The first one has been done for you.

Cause ⟶	Effects Become Causes ⟶	Effects
Northeast Blackout of 2003	1. Company cash registers wouldn't work 2. 3. 4.	1. Had to make do with paper and pencils 2. 3. 4.

Examining the Characteristics of Cause and Effect Essays

1. Consider the authors' purpose in writing. What message about technology do they communicate?

2. What is the essay's thesis? State it in your own words.

3. What kinds of details do the authors use to explain the causes and effects of the blackout? How do the details support the authors' thesis and purpose? Explain.

4. What pattern of development besides cause and effect do the authors use? How does this technique contribute to the essay?

5. The authors do not include a conclusion. How effective is their ending? What kind of information or suggestions could they have included in a formal conclusion?

Building Your Word Power

1. What does the phrase "digital dream" mean in the context of paragraph 1?

2. Explain what the phrase "plain-Jane model" in paragraph 18 means.

3. Explain the meaning of each of the following words as it is used in the reading: *dislodge* (para. 2), *tethered* (5), *yielded* (12), and *triggered* (20). Refer to your dictionary as needed.

Building Your Critical Thinking Skills: Identifying Assumptions

Writers often make **assumptions** about audience and topic. At times they assume something about their readers — who they are, what they believe, or what they want to read; at other times they recognize or dispel ideas that their readers may assume to be true. Critical readers should identify writers' assumptions about audience and topic in order to evaluate their theses and supporting evidence. For example, in an article about treating back pain for a holistic health magazine, the author might assume that readers are already familiar with and value holistic approaches and therefore may not need a full explanation or justification of the treatment. Alternatively, an article on holistic health for a popular women's magazine may attempt to dispel readers' assumptions that holistic practices are unsafe or risky. Using your skills in identifying assumptions, answer the following questions.

1. Considering that the essay was first published in the *Wall Street Journal*, a business and financial newspaper, what assumptions might the authors have made about the interests and concerns of their audience?

2. How do the authors' assumptions about their readers' interests and concerns influence the examples that they include? What examples seem specifically targeted toward business people?

3. The writers begin with a statement about the "digital dream" of a wireless and connected society. What assumption about this "dream" do they seek to dispel?

Reacting to the Reading: Discussion and Journal Writing

1. Discuss the different ways of coping in a crisis. Consider snowstorms, traffic jams, and similar events that affect large numbers of people. What characteristics tend to emerge when people face situations like these?

2. In class or in your journal, discuss a blackout that you experienced. How long did it last? Were you prepared? How did you feel? Did the experience change you in any way?

Applying Your Skills: Writing Assignments

1. **Paragraph Assignment.** Choose a type of emergency such as a hurricane, flood, or terrorist threat. Using cause and effect, write a paragraph anticipating the effects of such a catastrophe; include your thoughts about how the event would directly affect you and your family.

2. Evaluate our society's reliance on technology. Have computers, cell phones, and other electronic devices made our lives easier and more fun, or harder and more work? or just different? Write a cause and effect essay exploring your conclusions.

3. As you go through your day on campus or at work, make note of everything you do that requires the use of electricity. What would happen during a power outage? Write a cause and effect essay to report your findings.

4. **Combining Patterns.** Brainstorm a list of people you know who would be great to have around during an emergency. Pick three people from your list, and describe the likely effects of their presence in a difficult situation. Include the reasons you

chose them, considering their personalities, characteristics, and past experiences, as you compare and contrast their usefulness in an emergency.

5. **Internet Research.** Visit the Together We Prepare site from the American Red Cross at www.redcross.org/prepare/index_a.asp or conduct your own online research about preparing for a disaster. Then write a cause and effect essay about what to do in an emergency. Describe the possible causes and effects of different types of disasters, and identify the appropriate preparations for each type.

The Wounds That Can't Be Stitched Up

Ruth Russell

Ruth Russell wrote the following essay for an assignment in a community college writing class. In 1999, it was published in *Newsweek* in "My Turn," a column that features personal essays submitted by readers.

"The Wounds That Can't Be Stitched Up" tells the harrowing story of the author's pair of encounters with the same drunk driver. Pay attention to the details Russell includes about the accident and the injuries suffered by her mother, sister, and brother. Notice that the consequences of the accident for the drunk driver are not what the author expected them to be.

Focus on Understanding   As you read, identify what the wounds mentioned in the title are.

Focus on the Topic   In class or in your journal, write about the dangers of drunk driving. Do you know what the drinking and driving laws in your state are? Have you or a friend ever had an experience with a drunk driver?

1   It was a mild December night. Christmas was only two weeks away. The evening sky was overcast, but the roads were dry. All was quiet in our small town as I drove to my grandmother's house.

2   I heard the sirens first. Red lights and blue lights strobed in tandem. Ambulances with their interiors lit like television screens in a dark room flew by, escorted by police cruisers on the way to the hospital.

3   When I arrived at my gram's, she was on the porch steps struggling to put on her coat. "Come on," she said breathlessly, "your mother has been in an accident." I was 17 then, and it would take a long time before sirens lost their power to reduce me to tears.

4   Twenty-three years have passed, but only recently have I realized how deeply affected I was by events caused by a drunk driver so long ago.

5   When the accident occurred, my youngest brother was 8. He was sitting in the back seat of our family's large, sturdy sedan. The force of the crash sent him flying headlong into the back of the front seat, leaving him with a grossly swollen black eye. He was admitted to the hospital for observation. He didn't talk much when I visited him that night. He just sat in the bed, a lonely little figure in a darkened hospital room.

6   My sister, who was 12, was sitting in the front seat. She confided to me later how much she missed the beautiful blue coat she'd been wearing at the time. It was an early Christmas present, and it was destroyed beyond repair by the medical personnel who cut it off her body as they worked to save her life. She had

472

a severely fractured skull that required immediate surgery. The resulting facial scar became for our family a permanent reminder of how close she came to dying that night.

My mother was admitted to the intensive-care unit to be stabilized before her multiple facial cuts could be stitched up. Dad tried to prepare me before we went in to see her by telling me that she looked and sounded worse than she was. One eye was temporarily held in place by a bandage wrapped around her head. Her lower lip hideously gaped, exposing a mouthful of broken teeth. Delirious, she cried out for her children and apologized for an accident she neither caused nor could have avoided. An accident that happened when her car was hit head-on by a drunk driver speeding down the wrong side of the road in a half-ton truck with no headlights.

My dad, my brothers, my sister and I spent Christmas at the hospital visiting my mother. Sometimes she was so out of it from medication that she barely recognized us. We celebrated two of my brothers' birthdays — one only days after Christmas — and the other in early January there too.

I remember watching the police escort the drunk driver out of the hospital the night of the accident. He looked about 35 years old, but his face was so distorted by rage and alcohol that I could only guess. A bandaged wrist was his only visible injury. He kept repeating that he'd done nothing wrong as several officers tried to get him into the cruiser waiting outside the emergency-room exit.

The man was jailed over the weekend and lost his license for 30 days for driving while intoxicated. I don't know if that was his first alcohol-related traffic violation, but I know it wasn't the last. Now and then I'd see his name in the court log of our local paper for another DWI, and wonder how he could still be behind the wheel.

Sometimes when I tell this story, I'd be asked in an accusatory tone if my mom and siblings were wearing seat belts. I think that's a lot like asking a rape victim how she was dressed. The answer is no. This all happened before seat-belt-awareness campaigns began. In fact, if they had been in a smaller car, seat belts or not, I believe my mother and sister would have died.

Many local people who know the driver are surprised when they hear about the accident, and they are quick to defend him. They tell me he was a war hero. His parents aren't well. He's an alcoholic. Or my favorite: "He's a good guy when he doesn't drink."

Two years ago I discovered this man had moved into my apartment building. I felt vaguely apprehensive, but I believed the accident was ancient history. Nothing could have prepared me for what happened next.

It was a mild afternoon, just a few days before Christmas. I had just started down the back staircase of the building, on my way to visit my son, when I recognized my neighbor's new pickup truck as it roared down the street. The driver missed the entrance to our shared parking lot. He reversed crookedly in the road, slammed the transmission into forward, then quickly pulled into his parking space. Gravel and sand flew as he stomped on the brakes to halt his truck just inches from where I stood frozen on the staircase. As he staggered from his vehicle, he looked at me and asked drunkenly, "Did I scare you?"

Understanding the Reading

1. Describe what happened in the accident and how it affected Russell's family.
2. What happened to the man who hit the author's family? How do the local people in Russell's town feel about him?
3. Where does the man who hit Russell's family end up living? Under what circumstances does Russell meet him the second time?
4. Explain the meaning of the title.

Visualizing the Reading

Evaluate the cause and effect relationships in the reading by completing the following diagram. Record as many immediate and long-term effects as you can identify, adding additional boxes if needed.

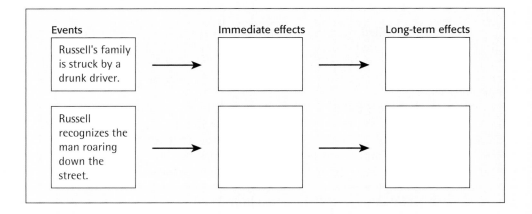

Examining the Characteristics of Cause and Effect Essays

1. What is the author's thesis? Does her essay focus on causes, effects, or both? Explain.
2. How does Russell organize her essay?
3. What types of details does the author use to fully explain the effects of the accident?
4. What other pattern of development besides cause and effect does the author use to organize the events? How does this pattern contribute to her message?

Building Your Word Power

1. What is the "power" that the author refers to in paragraph 3?
2. Explain the meaning of each of the following words as it is used in the reading: *strobed* (para. 2), *tandem* (2), *headlong* (5), *grossly* (5), and *apprehensive* (13). Refer to your dictionary as needed.

Building Your Critical Thinking Skills: Author's Purpose

Authors write for a variety of purposes — to inform, to persuade, to entertain, or for a combination of these or other purposes Writers may also write to express their feelings or for emotional release. To determine the **author's purpose** you must consider the intended audience, the author's background, and both the stated and unstated reasons for writing. Is more than one side of an issue presented, or does the author lean toward a particular viewpoint? Is the writer trying to convince you of something, or just explain it? Using what you know about identifying the author's purpose, answer the following questions.

1. The author states that twenty-three years have passed since the accident. Using clues from the reading, explain why she might write about something that happened so long ago.
2. Paragraph 11 begins with the phrase "Sometimes when I tell this story." What does this transition indicate about the author's purpose in writing? Later in the same paragraph, she defends her family. Why does she do this?
3. Examine how Russell treats the subject of the drunk driver. What does this treatment suggest about her purpose in writing?

Reacting to the Reading: Discussion and Journal Writing

1. Discuss the use and abuse of alcohol in our society. Why do people drink? How much is too much?
2. Describe a traumatic event that you or someone you know experienced. Explain its short- and long-term effects.
3. In class or in your journal, discuss how different people express emotions.

Applying Your Skills: Writing Assignments

1. **Paragraph Assignment.** It took Russell many years to realize how deeply the accident affected her. Write a paragraph describing an event that deeply affected your life.
2. Some people think that the government should ban the advertising of all alcoholic beverages. Such a ban would include television ads and athletic sponsorships. Write a cause and effect essay about the potential effects of such a ban. Use examples from your own experience and observations to support a clear thesis.
3. Brainstorm a list of issues and problems associated with alcoholism. Narrow your list to a specific topic (binge drinking, for example), and write a cause and effect essay that explains the issue. If it is relevant, you might write about a personal

experience that you or a friend had with alcoholism. Conclude with some suggestions for people (or their friends and family) who are struggling with alcohol addiction.

4. **Combining Patterns.** Brainstorm a list of events in your life that you can attribute to luck or chance. You might, for example, think of situations in which you were in the right place at the right time or in the wrong place at the wrong time. Write an essay exploring the role of chance and luck in your own life. Use cause and effect in combination with narration, description, or another pattern of development to support a thesis about your experience.

5. **Internet Research.** Prohibition (1919–1933) was the period in U.S. history when all manufacturing, import, export, transportation, and sales of alcohol were forbidden. Using the Internet, research this period and write a cause and effect essay that explores the successes and failures of the Prohibition movement. One place to start would be the collection of materials available online from the Westerville Public Library in Ohio about the Anti-Saloon League, a group that was pivotal in pushing for the congressional amendment that legalized Prohibition. The Web site is at www.wpl.lib.oh.us/AntiSaloon.

Changing My Name after Sixty Years

Tom Rosenberg

Tom Rosenberg was born in Germany and moved to the United States with his family during the Nazi era, when he was six years old. After graduating from the University of Pittsburgh he joined the Marines and fought in the Korean War; thereafter he spent almost thirty years working as a political consultant. He published his first novel, *Phantom on His Wheel*, in 2000. This essay was published in *Newsweek* as a "My Turn" column on July 17, 2000.

In "Changing My Name after Sixty Years," Rosenberg discusses the stigma of being a Jewish refugee before World War II and its effect on him and his family. As you read, consider his reasons for spending most of his life as Tom Ross — and for his decision to readopt his birth name.

Focus on Understanding   Read to discover why the author decided to change his name.

Focus on the Topic   In class or in your journal, explore how you feel about your own name. Does it have any cultural or religious significance? If you are an unmarried woman, do you plan on changing it if you get married? Would you consider changing it for other reasons?

1   My parents left Nazi Germany in 1938, when I was 6 and my mother was pregnant with my sister. They arrived in America with a lot of baggage — guilt over deserting loved ones, anger over losing their home and business, and a lifelong fear of anti-Semitism.°

2   Shortly thereafter, whether out of fear, a desire to assimilate or a combination of both, they changed our family name from Rosenberg to Ross. My parents were different from the immigrants who landed on Ellis Island and had their names changed by an immigration bureaucrat. My mother and father voluntarily gave up their identity and a measure of pride for an Anglicized name.

3   Growing up a German-Jewish kid in the Bronx in the 1940s, a time when Americans were dying in a war fought in part to save Jews from the hated Nazis, was difficult. Even my new name failed to protect me from bigotry; the neighborhood bullies knew a "sheenie"° when they saw one.

4   The bullying only intensified the shame I felt about my family's religious and ethnic background. I spent much of my youth denying my roots and vying for my peers' acceptance as "Tom Ross." Today I look back and wonder what kind of life I might have led if my parents had kept our family name.

5   In the '50s, I doubt Tom Rosenberg would have been accepted as a pledge by Theta Chi, a predominantly Christian fraternity at my college. He probably

anti-semitism: hatred toward or prejudice against Jewish people

sheenie: an extremely offensive slang term for a Jewish person

477

would have pledged a Jewish fraternity or had the self-confidence and conviction to ignore the Greek system altogether. Tom Rosenberg might have married a Jewish woman, stayed in the East and maintained closer ties to his Jewish family.

As it was, I moved west to San Francisco. Only after I married and became a father did I begin to acknowledge my Jewish heritage. 6

My first wife, a liberal Methodist, insisted that I stop running from Judaism. For years we attended both a Unitarian church and a Jewish temple. Her open-minded attitude set the tone in our household and was passed on to our three kids. As a family, we celebrated Christmas and went to temple on the High Holidays.° But even though my wife and I were careful to teach our kids tolerance, their exposure to either religion was minimal. Most weekends, we took the kids on ski trips, rationalizing that the majesty of the Sierra was enough of a spiritual experience. 7

So last year, when I decided to tell my children that I was legally changing my name back to Rosenberg, I wondered how they would react. We were in a restaurant celebrating the publication of my first novel. After they toasted my tenacity for staying with fiction for some 30 years, I made my announcement: "I want to be remembered by the name I was born with." 8

I explained that the kind of discrimination and stereotyping still evident today had made me rethink the years I'd spent denying my family's history, years that I'd been ashamed to talk about with them. The present political climate — the initiatives attacking social services for immigrants, bilingual education, affirmative action — made me want to shout "I'm an immigrant!" My children were silent for a moment before they smiled, leaned over and hugged me. 9

The memories of my years of denial continued to dog me as I told friends and family that I planned to change my name. The rabbi at the Reform temple that I belong to with my second wife suggested I go a step further. "Have you thought of taking a Hebrew first name?" he asked. 10

He must have seen the shocked look on my face. I wondered, is he suggesting I become more religious, more Jewish? "What's involved?" I asked hesitatingly. 11

The rabbi explained that the ceremony would be simple and private, just for family and friends. I would make a few remarks about why I had selected my name, and then he would say a blessing. 12

It took me a moment to grasp the significance of what the rabbi was proposing. He saw my name change as a chance to do more than reclaim a piece of my family's history; it was an opportunity to renew my commitment to Jewish ideals. I realized it was also a way to give my kids the sense of pride in their heritage that they had missed out on as children. 13

A few months later I stood at the pulpit in front of an open, lighted ark, flanked by my wife and the rabbi. Before me stood my children, holding their children. I had scribbled a few notes for my talk, but felt too emotional to use them. I held on to the lectern for support and winged it. 14

High Holidays: a sacred and important ten-day period in Judaism that begins with Rosh Hashanah and ends with Yom Kippur

"Every time I step into a temple, I'm reminded that Judaism has survived 15
for 4,000 years. It's survived because it's a positive religion. My parents, your
grandparents, changed their name out of fear. I'm changing it back out of pride.
I chose the name Tikvah because it means hope."

Understanding the Reading

1. What motivated the author's parents to change their name? How did this differ
   from the way that other immigrants' names were changed?
2. What religions and religious institutions has the author been associated with? How
   did these religious affiliations contribute to the way he raised his children?
3. Why did the author decide to change his name?
4. What did the rabbi propose, and how does the author respond to this suggestion?

Visualizing the Reading

Evaluate the cause and effect relationships in the reading by completing the following
diagram. Record as many causes and effects as you can identify, adding additional
boxes if needed.

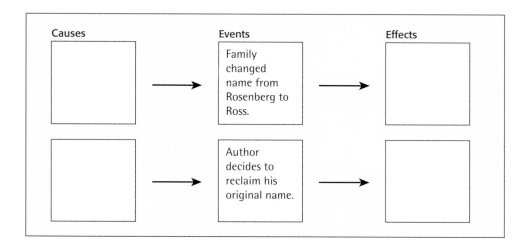

Causes	Events	Effects
	Family changed name from Rosenberg to Ross.	
	Author decides to reclaim his original name.	

Examining the Characteristics of Cause and Effect Essays

1. Consider Rosenberg's purpose in writing about his experience. Is his essay expressive, informative, persuasive, or a combination of these? Explain, identifying
   points in the text to support your answer.
2. What is the author's implied thesis?

3. How do the causes and effects that you identified in the Visualizing the Reading activity relate to Rosenberg's thesis and purpose for writing? Why does the author include personal details about his marriages and religious practices?

4. What additional information could the author have provided about his decision-making process? Would this have enhanced the effectiveness of the essay? Why or why not?

5. What narrative technique does Rosenberg use for his conclusion? How effective is it? Explain.

Building Your Word Power

*For a definition of **connotative meaning** and **idiom**, see the chart of commonly used language features on p. 21.*

1. What is the connotative meaning of the word *baggage* as used in paragraph 1?

2. Explain the idiom "continued to dog me" as used in paragraph 10.

3. Explain the meaning of each of the following words as it is used in the reading: *bigotry* (para. 3), *conviction* (5), *tenacity* (8), and *flanked* (14). Refer to your dictionary as needed.

Building Your Critical Thinking Skills: Inferences

Inferences are reasoned guesses about something unknown that are made on the basis of available information. For example, if it is snowing heavily outside and you find your classroom locked, you can infer that the class has been canceled because of the storm. Using your skills in making inferences, identify with a checkmark which of the following are *reasonable* inferences based on the information in the essay.

_____   1. Rosenberg joined a predominantly Christian fraternity because Jewish fraternities would not accept him.

_____   2. Rosenberg would approve if his children wanted to change their names.

_____   3. Rosenberg's relationship with his first wife contributed to his decision to change his name.

_____   4. Rosenberg is an active member of his temple.

Reacting to the Reading: Discussion and Journal Writing

1. Discuss the role of religion in family life today. Is the old saying "the family that prays together stays together" true?

2. In class or in your journal, describe a time when you had to tell your family some very important news. How did they react? How did the experience make you feel?

Applying Your Skills: Writing Assignments

1. **Paragraph Assignment.** Using cause and effect, write a paragraph describing a time when you changed something about yourself. What caused you to make such a change? After you had made the change, were you satisfied with the result? Explain.

2. Brainstorm a list of reasons that people turn to religion or undertake a spiritual journey. Think of the possible effects that can occur after someone chooses this type of path. Organize your ideas into a causal analysis. Provide supporting evidence and details from your own observations and experiences or from any research you wish to do.

3. Rosenberg's essay addresses the effect of assimilation. Using cause and effect, write an essay that explores how assimilation can both help and hurt immigrant cultures in the United States.

4. Combining Patterns. What's in a name? Brainstorm a list of businesses or product names (you may find it helpful to flip through the yellow pages or magazine advertisements). Using classification, group these names into categories. For example, some businesses are named after the people who founded them, while other businesses state clearly what they do or sell. Using these categories, write an essay about the effect of a name in terms of sales and advertising appeal.

5. Internet Research. Look up your name and the names of some friends or family members at the Social Security Administration's Baby Name Page at www.ssa.gov/OACT/babynames/. Has your name become more or less popular over time? Do you notice any trends? Next, research some Web sites that give naming tips. For example, visit the Healthy Start Coalition of Orange County's Web site at www.healthystartorange.org/index.asp?p=i&ArticleID=115. Finally, write an essay about the effect that names have on children. Use personal observations, experience, and information from your online research as support for your thesis.

The Clan of One-Breasted Women

Terry Tempest Williams

Terry Tempest Williams (b. 1955) is a naturalist, environmental activist, and award-winning writer who has twice testified before Congress about women's health and environmental links to cancer. Williams has written many pieces for a wide variety of publications as well as several books, including a children's book, *The Secret Language of Snow* (1984), and an analysis of folklore, *Pieces of Shell: A Journey to Navajo Land* (1984). In 1991 she published *Refuge: An Unnatural History of Family and Place*, a memoir about the rise of the Great Salt Lake, the flooding of the Bear River Migratory Bird Refuge, and her mother's diagnosis with ovarian cancer, believed to be caused by exposure to radiation from the atomic tests of the 1950s and 60s.

This essay about the cancer that has ravaged her family was originally published as the epilogue to *Refuge*. Williams starts with a very personal description of the effect that cancer has had in her family. Notice how this sets the tone for her intimate, honest essay. Also, pay attention to the primary and secondary causes she identifies and how she uses vivid and interesting language to explain them.

Focus on Understanding   Read to discover what the author means by "the clan of one-breasted women" referred to in the title.

Focus on the Topic   In class or in your journal, write about a time when you did not go along with what others expected you to think or do. Explain the issue and its outcomes.

1   I belong to a Clan of One-Breasted Women. My mother, my grandmothers, and six aunts have all had mastectomies. Seven are dead. The two who survive have just completed rounds of chemotherapy and radiation.

2   I've had my own problems: two biopsies for breast cancer and a small tumor between my ribs diagnosed as a "borderline malignancy."

3   This is my family history.

4   Most statistics tell us breast cancer is genetic, hereditary, with rising percentages attached to fatty diets, childlessness, or becoming pregnant after thirty. What they don't say is living in Utah may be the greatest hazard of all.

5   We are a Mormon family with roots in Utah since 1847. The "word of wisdom" in my family aligned us with good foods — no coffee, no tea, tobacco, or alcohol. For the most part, our women were finished having their babies by the time they were thirty. And only one faced breast cancer prior to 1960. Traditionally, as a group of people, Mormons have a low rate of cancer.

Is our family a cultural anomaly? The truth is, we didn't think about it. 6
Those who did, usually the men, simply said, "bad genes." The women's attitude
was stoic. Cancer was part of life. On February 16, 1971, the eve of my mother's
surgery, I accidentally picked up the telephone and overheard her ask my grandmother what she could expect.

"Diane, it is one of the most spiritual experiences you will ever encounter." 7
I quietly put down the receiver. 8

Two days later, my father took my brothers and me to the hospital to visit 9
her. She met us in the lobby in a wheelchair. No bandages were visible. I'll never
forget her radiance, the way she held herself in a purple velvet robe, and how
she gathered us around her.

"Children, I am fine. I want you to know I felt the arms of God around me." 10
We believed her. My father cried. Our mother, his wife, was thirty-eight 11
years old.

A little over a year after Mother's death, Dad and I were having dinner to- 12
gether. He had just returned from St. George, where the Tempest Company was
completing the gas lines that would service southern Utah. He spoke of his love
for the country, the sandstoned landscape, bare-boned and beautiful. He had
just finished hiking the Kolob trail in Zion National Park. We got caught up in
reminiscing, recalling with fondness our walk up Angel's Landing on his fiftieth
birthday and the years our family had vacationed there.

Over dessert, I shared a recurring dream of mine. I told my father that for 13
years, as long as I could remember, I saw this flash of light in the night in the
desert — that this image had so permeated my being that I could not venture
south without seeing it again, on the horizon, illuminating buttes and mesas.

"You did see it," he said. 14
"Saw what?" 15
"The bomb. The cloud. We were driving home from Riverside, California. 16
You were sitting on Diane's lap. She was pregnant. In fact, I remember the day,
September 7, 1957. We had just gotten out of the Service. We were driving
north, past Las Vegas. It was an hour or so before dawn, when this explosion
went off. We not only heard it, but felt it. I thought the oil tanker in front of us
had blown up. We pulled over and suddenly, rising from the desert floor, we saw
it, clearly, this golden-stemmed cloud, the mushroom. The sky seemed to vi-
brate with an eerie pink glow. Within a few minutes, a light ash was raining on
the car."

I stared at my father. 17
"I thought you knew that," he said. "It was a common occurrence in the 18
fifties."

It was at this moment that I realized the deceit I had been living under. 19
Children growing up in the American Southwest, drinking contaminated milk
from contaminated cows, even from the contaminated breasts of their mothers,
my mother — members, years later, of the Clan of One-Breasted Women.

It is a well-known story in the Desert West, "The Day We Bombed Utah," or 20
more accurately, the years we bombed Utah: above ground atomic testing in

Nevada took place from January 27, 1951 through July 11, 1962. Not only were the winds blowing north covering "low-use segments of the population" with fallout and leaving sheep dead in their tracks, but the climate was right. The United States of the 1950s was red, white, and blue. The Korean War was raging. McCarthyism° was rampant. Ike° was it, and the cold war was hot. If you were against nuclear testing, you were for a communist regime.

McCarthyism: period of anticommunism in the late 1940s and 1950s named for Senator Joseph McCarthy; **Ike:** Dwight D. Eisenhower, the thirty-fourth U.S. president (1953–1961)

Much has been written about this "American nuclear tragedy." Public 21 health was secondary to national security. The Atomic Energy Commissioner, Thomas Murray, said, "Gentlemen, we must not let anything interfere with this series of tests, nothing."

Again and again, the American public was told by its government, in spite 22 of burns, blisters, and nausea, "It has been found that the tests may be conducted with adequate assurance of safety under conditions prevailing at the bombing reservations." Assuaging public fears was simply a matter of public relations. "Your best action," an Atomic Energy Commission booklet read, "is not to be worried about fallout." A news release typical of the times stated, "We find no basis for concluding that harm to any individual has resulted from radioactive fallout."

On August 30, 1979, during Jimmy Carter's presidency, a suit was filed, 23 *Irene Allen* v. *The United States of America*. Mrs. Allen's case was the first on an alphabetical list of twenty-four test cases, representative of nearly twelve hundred plaintiffs seeking compensation from the United States government for cancers caused by nuclear testing in Nevada.

Irene Allen lived in Hurricane, Utah. She was the mother of five children 24 and had been widowed twice. Her first husband, with their two oldest boys, had watched the tests from the roof of the local high school. He died of leukemia in 1956. Her second husband died of pancreatic cancer in 1978.

In a town meeting conducted by Utah Senator Orrin Hatch, shortly before 25 the suit was filed, Mrs. Allen said, "I am not blaming the government, I want you to know that, Senator Hatch. But I thought if my testimony could help in any way so this wouldn't happen again to any of the generations coming up after us . . . I am happy to be here this day to bear testimony of this."

God-fearing people. This is just one story in an anthology of thousands.   26

On May 10, 1984, Judge Bruce S. Jenkins handed down his opinion. Ten of 27 the plaintiffs were awarded damages. It was the first time a federal court had determined that nuclear tests had been the cause of cancers. For the remaining fourteen test cases, the proof of causation was not sufficient. In spite of the split decision, it was considered a landmark ruling. It was not to remain so for long.

In April 1987, the Tenth Circuit Court of Appeals overturned Judge 28 Jenkins's ruling on the ground that the United States was protected from suit by the legal doctrine of sovereign immunity, a centuries-old idea from England in the days of absolute monarchs.

In January 1988, the Supreme Court refused to review the Appeals Court 29 decision. To our court system it does not matter whether the United States government was irresponsible, whether it lied to its citizens, or even that citizens died from the fallout of nuclear testing. What matters is that our government is immune: "The King can do no wrong."

In Mormon culture, authority is respected, obedience is revered, and inde- 30
pendent thinking is not. I was taught as a young girl not to "make waves" or "rock the boat."

"Just let it go," Mother would say. "You know how you feel, that's what 31
counts."

For many years, I have done just that — listened, observed, and quietly 32
formed my own opinions, in a culture that rarely asks questions because it has all the answers. But one by one, I have watched the women in my family die common, heroic deaths. We sat in waiting rooms hoping for good news, but always receiving the bad. I cared for them, bathed their scarred bodies, and kept their secrets. I watched beautiful women become bald as Cytoxan, cisplatin, and Adriamycin were injected into their veins. I held their foreheads as they vomited green-black bile, and I shot them with morphine when the pain became inhuman. In the end, I witnessed their last peaceful breaths, becoming a midwife to the rebirth of their souls.

The price of obedience has become too high. 33

The fear and inability to question authority that ultimately killed rural 34
communities in Utah during atmospheric testing of atomic weapons is the same fear I saw in my mother's body. Sheep. Dead sheep. The evidence is buried.

I cannot prove that my mother, Diane Dixon Tempest, or my grandmothers, 35
Lettie Romney Dixon and Kathryn Blackett Tempest, along with my aunts developed cancer from nuclear fallout in Utah. But I can't prove they didn't.

My father's memory was correct. The September blast we drove through in 36
1957 was part of Operation Plumbbob, one of the most intensive series of bomb tests to be initiated. The flash of light in the night in the desert, which I had always thought was a dream, developed into a family nightmare. It took fourteen years, from 1957 to 1971, for cancer to manifest in my mother — the same time, Howard L. Andrews, an authority in radioactive fallout at the National Institutes of Health, says radiation cancer requires to become evident. The more I learn about what it means to be a "downwinder," the more questions I drown in.

What I do know, however, is that as a Mormon woman of the fifth genera- 37
tion of Latter-day Saints, I must question everything, even if it means losing my faith, even if it means becoming a member of a border tribe among my own people. Tolerating blind obedience in the name of patriotism or religion ultimately takes our lives.

When the Atomic Energy Commission described the country north of the 38
Nevada Test Site as "virtually uninhabited desert terrain," my family and the birds at Great Salt Lake were some of the "virtual uninhabitants."

One night, I dreamed women from all over the world circled a blazing fire 39
in the desert. They spoke of change, how they hold the moon in their bellies and

wax and wane with its phases. They mocked the presumption of even-tempered beings and made promises that they would never fear the witch inside themselves. The women danced wildly as sparks broke away from the flames and entered the night sky as stars.

And they sang a song given to them by Shoshone grandmothers: 40

Ah ne nah, nah	Consider the rabbits
nin nah nah —	How gently they walk on the earth —
ah ne nah, nah	Consider the rabbits
nin nah nah —	How gently they walk on the earth —
Nyaga mutzi	We remember them
oh ne nay —	We can walk gently also —
Nyaga mutzi	We remember them
oh ne nay —	We can walk gently also —

The women danced and drummed and sang for weeks, preparing themselves for what was to come. They would reclaim the desert for the sake of their children, for the sake of the land.

A few miles downwind from the fire circle, bombs were being tested.   41
Rabbits felt the tremors. Their soft leather pads on paws and feet recognized the shaking sands, while the roots of mesquite and sage were smoldering. Rocks were hot from the inside out and dust devils hummed unnaturally. And each time there was another nuclear test, ravens watched the desert heave. Stretch marks appeared. The land was losing its muscle.

The women couldn't bear it any longer. They were mothers. They had suf-   42
fered labor pains but always under the promise of birth. The red hot pains beneath the desert promised death only, as each bomb became a stillborn. A contract had been made and broken between human beings and the land. A new contract was being drawn by the women, who understood the fate of the earth as their own.

Under the cover of darkness, ten women slipped under a barbed-wire fence   43
and entered the contaminated country. They were trespassing. They walked toward the town of Mercury, in moonlight, taking their cues from coyote, kit fox, antelope squirrel, and quail. They moved quietly and deliberately through the maze of Joshua trees. When a hint of daylight appeared they rested, drinking tea and sharing their rations of food. The women closed their eyes. The time had come to protest with the heart, that to deny one's genealogy with the earth was to commit treason against one's soul.

At dawn, the women draped themselves in mylar, wrapping long streamers   44
of silver plastic around their arms to blow in the breeze. They wore clear masks, that became the faces of humanity. And when they arrived at the edge of Mercury, they carried all the butterflies of a summer day in their wombs. They paused to allow their courage to settle.

The town that forbids pregnant women and children to enter because of ra-   45
diation risks was asleep. The women moved through the streets as winged messengers, twirling around each other in slow motion, peeking inside homes and

watching the easy sleep of men and women. They were astonished by such still-ness and periodically would utter a shrill note or low cry just to verify life.

The residents finally awoke to these strange apparitions. Some simply 46
stared. Others called authorities, and in time, the women were apprehended by
wary soldiers dressed in desert fatigues. They were taken to a white, square
building on the other edge of Mercury. When asked who they were and why
they were there, the women replied, "We are mothers and we have come to reclaim the desert for our children."

The soldiers arrested them. As the ten women were blindfolded and hand- 47
cuffed, they began singing:

> *You can't forbid us everything*
> *You can't forbid us to think —*
> *You can't forbid our tears to flow*
> *And you can't stop the songs that we sing.*

The women continued to sing louder and louder, until they heard the voices of
their sisters moving across the mesa:

> *Ah ne nah, nah*
> *nin nah nah —*
> *Ah ne nah, nah*
> *nin nah nah —*
> *Nyaga mutzi*
> *oh ne nay —*
> *Nyaga mutzi*
> *oh ne nay —*

"Call for reinforcements," one soldier said.

"We have," interrupted one woman, "we have — and you have no idea of 48
our numbers."

I crossed the line at the Nevada Test Site and was arrested with nine other 49
Utahns for trespassing on military lands. They are still conducting nuclear tests
in the desert. Ours was an act of civil disobedience. But as I walked toward the
town of Mercury, it was more than a gesture of peace. It was a gesture on behalf of the Clan of One-Breasted Women.

As one officer cinched the handcuffs around my wrists, another frisked my 50
body. She found a pen and a pad of paper tucked inside my left boot.

"And these?" she asked sternly. 51

"Weapons," I replied. 52

Our eyes met. I smiled. She pulled the leg of my trousers back over my boot. 53

"Step forward, please," she said as she took my arm. 54

We were booked under an afternoon sun and bused to Tonopah, Nevada. It 55
was a two-hour ride. This was familiar country. The Joshua trees standing their
ground had been named by my ancestors, who believed they looked like
prophets pointing west to the Promised Land. These were the same trees that

bloomed each spring, flowers appearing like white flames in the Mojave. And I recalled a full moon in May, when Mother and I had walked among them, flushing out mourning doves and owls.

The bus stopped short of town. We were released.   56

The officials thought it was a cruel joke to leave us stranded in the desert   57 with no way to get home. What they didn't realize was that we were home, soul-centered and strong, women who recognized the sweet smell of sage as fuel for our spirits.

Understanding the Reading

1. What is the recurring dream cited by Williams at the start of the essay? What does she learn from her father about this vision?
2. According to Williams, what caused the cancer in her family?
3. What factors made it easy for the government to conduct nuclear tests in Utah in the 1950s and 1960s? How did the government respond to the rise in cancer rates years later?
4. What dream does the author describe toward the end of the essay? How does this story relate to the action that she and other protesters take?

Visualizing the Reading

The photograph above shows the devastating effects of the explosion of a nuclear bomb in Hiroshima, Japan, on August 6, 1945, which destroyed the city. This image was the first of five photos taken by a resident of Hiroshima immediately after the atomic bombing. The explosion marked the end of World War II and the beginning of the nuclear era. How do the effects of the nuclear fallout shown here relate to the effects of the bomb tests that Williams describes? Compare your reactions to the photo and to Williams's essay. What similar and what different issues do they address? What does the photograph suggest about the changing direction of military tactics and their effects on civilians that might be related to the government's treatment of civilians in "The Clan of One-Breasted Women"?

Examining the Characteristics of Cause and Effect Essays

1. What main point does the author make, and how does that relate to her purpose in writing?

2. Identify the causes and effects discussed in Williams's essay. Is each cause and effect explained in a detailed and understandable way? Does she provide sufficient supporting evidence to prove the existence of a causal relationship between events? Explain.

3. Evaluate the author's use of descriptive language. Highlight several examples in which she expresses her thoughts through sensory details.

4. What other patterns of development does the author use? How do these patterns enhance the causal analysis?

5. Consider Williams's conclusion. In what ways does it reinforce her main assertion about the topic? Do you find this ending to be satisfying? Why or why not?

Building Your Word Power

1. Explain the doublespeak that Williams quotes, such as "low-use segments of the population" (para. 20) and "virtually uninhabited desert terrain" (para. 38).

2. What is the meaning of the metaphor "becoming a midwife to the rebirth of their souls" (para. 32)?

3. Explain the meaning of each of the following words as it is used in the reading: *aligned* (para. 5), *anomaly* (6), *permeated* (13), *assuaging* (22), *manifest* (36), and *cinched* (50). Refer to your dictionary as needed.

*For a definition of **doublespeak**, and **metaphor**, see the chart of commonly used language features on p. 21.*

Building Your Critical Thinking Skills: Facts and Opinions

Because authors often include both **facts** and **opinions** in their writing, it is up to the reader to distinguish between what are true and verifiable facts and what are opinions or statements of belief. Because authors often express their views so convincingly, the distinction between what is an established fact and what is a personal opinion can sometimes be difficult to make. For example, a writer might present a causal relationship between the cuts to after-school programs for teens and a corresponding rise in petty crime. This view would be an opinion unless it were accompanied, for example, by data showing a clear relationship between the two events. No matter how convincing they seem, all opinions should be evaluated and examined so that they are not mistaken for facts. Use your knowledge of fact and opinion to mark whether the following statements from the article are Facts (F) or Opinions (O).

_____ 1. "Most statistics tell us breast cancer is genetic." (para. 4)

_____ 2. ". . . living in Utah may be the greatest hazard of all." (para. 4)

_____ 3. "Within a few minutes, a light ash was raining on the car." (para. 16)

_____ 4. "Irene Allen lived in Hurricane, Utah." (para. 24)

_____ 5. "Tolerating blind obedience in the name of patriotism or religion ultimately takes our lives." (para. 37)

_____ 6. "Ours was an act of civil disobedience." (para. 49)

Reacting to the Reading: Discussion and Journal Writing

1. Discuss the development and testing of nuclear weapons. Should any country be allowed to continue to possess and develop them? What restrictions and safeguards should apply?

2. Discuss the notion of blind obedience. Do you agree or disagree with Williams's statement that "[t]olerating blind obedience in the name of patriotism or religion ultimately takes our lives" (para. 37)? Defend your position.

Applying Your Skills: Writing Assignments

1. **Paragraph Assignment.** Williams held the memory of the bomb's flash from when she was a very young child. Using cause and effect, write a paragraph about one of your earliest memories. Why do you think it remains so vivid for you?

2. Brainstorm a list of situations in which you did — or were tempted to — question authority. Choose one, and write a cause and effect essay about the situation, your motivation, and its outcomes.

3. Brainstorm a list of ways that government affects your life. Choose one, and write a cause and effect essay for your classmates describing the policy, law, or agency and how it influences you. Be sure to fully explain the multiple causes and effects, and recognize or dispel any assumptions your readers might have about this role of government.

4. **Combining Patterns.** Write a letter to the editor of your local newspaper explaining the possible effects of a proposed change in your community. Using argument, urge citizens to take action for or against it.

5. **Internet Research.** Since the time of the atomic bomb tests described in the essay, new and equally dangerous threats to public safety have evolved. Using cause and effect, write an essay that explores the threats civilian populations face today from nuclear weapons and other weapons of mass destruction. To keep your topic manageable, narrow it to a single issue such as the threats posed by biological weapons. A few Web sources to get you started are George W. Bush's statement on the National Strategy to Combat Weapons of Mass Destruction site at www.whitehouse.gov/news/releases/2002/12/20021211-8.html, the Department of Homeland Security site at www.dhs.gov/dhspublic/display?theme=17, and the site for the Federation of American Scientists, an organization dedicated to ending the arms race, at www.fas.org.

Argumentation: Supporting a Claim

WRITING QUICK START

Study the image of the public service poster. Identify the issue that it addresses and the position that it takes. How effective is it in conveying this message? In what ways is it convincing? Write a paragraph that could be used in place of the poster. Make a statement about the issue, and give several reasons to support it.

You scan me:

You think I'm just another pot-smoking teenage Well, you're wrong. I'm an artist, a therapist, and the last time I took a hit was in kickboxing. Drugs aren't me. My life. My decision.

i am
MY ANTI-DR

What Is an Argument?

The paragraph you have just written makes an argument. It makes a claim about drug use and supports it with reasons. In everyday conversation, an argument can be a heated exchange of ideas between two people; for example, college room-mates might argue over who should clean the sink or who left the door unlocked last night. An effective **argument** is a logical, well-thought-out presentation of ideas that makes a claim about an issue and supports that claim with reasons and evidence. An ineffective argument may be an irrational, emotional release of feelings and frustrations. Many sound arguments, however, combine emotion with logic. A casual conversation can also take the form of a reasoned argument, as in the following sample dialogue.

> **DAMON:** I've been called for jury duty. I don't want to go. They treat jurors so badly!
>
> **MARIA:** Why? Everyone should do it.
>
> **DAMON:** Have you ever done it? I have. First of all, they force us to serve, whether we want to or not. And then they treat us like criminals. Two years ago I had to sit all day in a hot, crowded room with other jurors while the TV was blaring. I couldn't read, study, or even think! No wonder people will do anything to get out of it.

Damon argues that jurors are treated unfairly. He offers two reasons to support his claim and uses his personal experience to support the second reason (that jurors are treated "like criminals"), which also serves as an emotional appeal to Maria.

An argument has three basic parts: an **issue**, a **claim**, and **support**. In the pre-ceding exchange between Damon and Maria, for instance, "fairness of jury duty" is the issue, "jury duty is unfair" is the claim, and Damon's two reasons are the support. In most arguments it is also important to argue against opposing view-points, which is known as **refutation**. Although this example does not include a refutation, Maria might have said that jury duty gives citizens the privilege of par-ticipating in the justice system. How might Damon have refuted her view?

The ability to construct and write sound arguments is an important skill in many aspects of life. Political, social, and economic issues, for instance, are often resolved through public and private debate. Knowing how to construct an effec-tive argument is also essential to success in college and on the job, as these ex-amples show.

- For a *health science* course, you write an essay claiming that the results of genetic testing, which can predict a person's likelihood of contracting serious diseases, should be kept confidential.

- As a *lawyer* representing a client whose hand was seriously injured on the job, you must argue to a jury that your client deserves compensation for the work-related injury.

The following essay presents an argument about the effectiveness of the prison system.

Why Prisons Don't Work

Wilbert Rideau

Wilbert Rideau was born in Lawtell, Louisiana, in 1942 and grew up in the deeply segregated South of the 1940s and 1950s. At age nineteen he was convicted of murder and sentenced to death. His original conviction was overturned by the Supreme Court on account of a biased jury, but in retrials held in 1964 and 1970 he was reconvicted. In 1973, a year after the Supreme Court ruled the death penalty unconstitutional, Rideau was resentenced to life in prison. In January 2005, a jury found Rideau guilty of manslaughter, but not of murder. Because Rideau had already served the maximum sentence for manslaughter, he was released from prison. While on death row Rideau began writing. He has written numerous articles for *Anglolite,* the newsletter for the Louisiana State Penitentiary at Angola. He has also written columns about prison life, coauthored a criminal justice textbook, and collaborated on a number of documentaries including *The Farm,* which was nominated for an Oscar and won the best documentary award at the Sundance Film Festival in 1998.

This essay appeared in *Time* magazine on March 21, 1994. As you read, notice how Rideau uses his knowledge of and experience in the Louisana prison system to build his argument.

1   I was among thirty-one murderers sent to the Louisiana State Penitentiary in 1962 to be executed or imprisoned for life. We weren't much different from those we found here, or those who had preceded us. We were unskilled, impulsive, and uneducated misfits, mostly black, who had done dumb, impulsive things — failures, rejects from the larger society. Now a generation has come of age and gone since I've been here, and everything is much the same as I found it. The faces of the prisoners are different, but behind them are the same impulsive, uneducated, unskilled minds that made dumb, impulsive choices that got them into more trouble than they ever thought existed. The vast majority of us are consigned to suffer and die here so politicians can sell the illusion that permanently exiling people to prison will make society safe.

Introduction: background information about author

2   Getting tough has always been a "silver bullet," a quick fix for the crime and violence that society fears. Each year in Louisiana — where excess is a way of life — lawmakers have tried to outdo each other in legislating harsher mandatory penalties and in reducing avenues of release. The only thing to do with criminals, they say, is get tougher. They have. In

the process, the purpose of prison began to change. The state boasts one of the highest lockup rates in the country, imposes the most severe penalties in the nation, and vies to execute more criminals per capita than anywhere else. This state is so tough that last year, when prison authorities here wanted to punish an inmate in solitary confinement for an infraction, the most they could inflict on him was to deprive him of his underwear. It was all he had left.

Extreme example appeals to readers' sense of decency

If getting tough resulted in public safety, Louisiana citizens would be the safest in the nation. They're not. Louisiana has the highest murder rate among states. Prison, like the police and the courts, has a minimal impact on crime because it is a response after the fact, a mop-up operation. It doesn't work. The idea of punishing the few to deter the many is counterfeit because potential criminals either think they're not going to get caught or they're so emotionally desperate or psychologically distressed that they don't care about the consequences of their actions. The threatened punishment, regardless of its severity, is never a factor in the equation. But society, like the incorrigible criminal it abhors, is unable to learn from its mistakes.

Thesis

Reason 1: this punishment doesn't deter criminals

3

Prison has a role in public safety, but it is not a cure-all. Its value is limited, and its use should also be limited to what it does best: isolating young criminals long enough to give them a chance to grow up and get a grip on their impulses. It is a traumatic experience, certainly, but it should be only a temporary one, not a way of life. Prisoners kept too long tend to embrace the criminal culture, its distorted values and beliefs; they have little choice — prison is their life. There are some prisoners who cannot be returned to society — serial killers, serial rapists, professional hit men, and the like — but the monsters who need to die in prison are rare exceptions in the criminal landscape.

Recognizes that prison does have value

Reason 2: prisoners adopt criminal lifestyle and values

4

Crime is a young man's game. Most of the nation's random violence is committed by young urban terrorists. But because of long, mandatory sentences, most prisoners here are much older, having spent fifteen, twenty, thirty, or more years behind bars, long past necessity. Rather than pay for new prisons, society would be well served by releasing some of its older prisoners who pose no threat and using the money to catch young street thugs. Warden John Whitley agrees that many older prisoners here could be freed tomorrow with little or no danger to society. Release, however, is governed by law or by politicians, not by penal professionals. Even murderers, the most feared by society, pose little risk. Historically, for example, the domestic staff at Louisiana's Governor's mansion has been made up of murders, hand-picked to work among the chief-of-state and his family. Penologists have long known that murder is almost always a once-in-a-lifetime act. The most dangerous criminal is the one who has

Reason 3: most crimes are committed by young men

Appeal to authority

Compelling evidence

5

not yet killed but has a history of escalating offenses. He's the one to watch.

<u>Rehabilitation can work.</u> Everyone changes in time. The trick is to influence the direction that change takes. The problem with prisons is that they don't do more to rehabilitate those confined in them. The convict who enters prison illiterate will probably leave the same way. Most convicts want to be better than they are, but education is not a priority. This prison houses 4,600 men and offers academic training to 240, vocational training to a like number. Perhaps it doesn't matter. About 90 percent of the men here may never leave this prison alive.

6 · Reason 4: prisons don't do enough to rehabilitate prisoners

Statistics offer concrete evidence

The only effective way to curb crime is for society to work to prevent the criminal act in the first place, to come between the perpetrator and crime. Our youngsters must be taught to respect the humanity of others and to handle disputes without violence. It is essential to educate and equip them with the skills to pursue their life ambitions in a meaningful way. As a community, we must address the adverse life circumstances that spawn criminality. These things are not quick, and they're not easy, but they're effective. Politicians think that's too hard a sell. They want to be on record for doing something now, something they can point to at reelection time. So the drumbeat goes on for more police, more prisons, more of the same failed policies.

7 · Conclusion: offers call for action

Ever see a dog chase its tail?

8 · Ends with note of frustration

Characteristics of Argument Essays

All arguments are concerned with issues. In developing an argument essay you need to narrow or limit the issue, analyze the audience, make a clear and specific claim about the issue, and give reasons and evidence to support the claim. In addition, you should follow a logical line of reasoning, use emotional appeals appropriately, and acknowledge, accommodate, and/or refute opposing views.

Argument Focuses on a Narrowed Issue

An **issue** is a controversy — a problem or idea about which people disagree. In choosing an issue, therefore, be sure it is arguable — that is, one that people have differing opinions on. For example, arguing that education is important in today's job market is pointless because people generally agree on that issue. It is worthwhile, however, to argue the merits of a liberal arts education versus technical training as preparation for after-graduation employment.

Depending on the issue you choose and the intended audience, your readers may need background information. In an argument to your classmates about the awarding of organ transplants, for example, you would give information about the scarcity of organ donors versus the number of people who need transplants.

In addition, the issue you choose should be narrow enough to address adequately in an essay-length argument. Rideau, in "Why Prisons Don't Work," makes it clear that his argument will be limited to *one* aspect of imprisonment — its effectiveness in making society safe. When you narrow the issue, your thesis will be more precise and your evidence more specific. You will also be able to provide more effective arguments against an opposing viewpoint. A detailed and specific argument is a strong argument, leaving no "holes" or gaps for opponents to uncover.

Argument States a Specific Claim in a Thesis

To build a convincing argument, you need a clear and specific **claim** — a statement that tells readers your position on the issue. If writing arguments is new to you, it is usually best to state your claim in a strong thesis early in the essay. Doing so will help keep your argument on track. As you gain experience in writing arguments, you can experiment with placing the thesis later in the essay. In "Why Prisons Don't Work," Rideau makes a clear, specific claim in paragraph 3: "Prison, like the police and the courts, has a minimal impact on crime because it is a response after the fact, a mop-up operation."

Here is an example of how a general claim can be narrowed into a clear and specific thesis statement.

GENERAL: The use of animals in testing should be prohibited.

SPECIFIC: The testing of cosmetics and skin-care products on animals should be prohibited.

While all arguments make and support a claim, some also call for action. An essay opposing human cloning, for example, might argue for a ban on that practice and urge readers to take action against it, such as by voicing their opinions in letters to congressional representatives.

Regardless of the argument, be careful about the way you state your claim. Avoid a general or absolute statement; the claim will be more convincing if you qualify or limit it. The following example shows how a generalization might be revised by adding qualifying words.

> ▸ Unclear definitions and guidelines ~~are~~ *may be* responsible for the confusion between sexual harassment and mere insensitivity.

Argument Depends on Careful Audience Analysis

Because an argument is intended to influence readers' thinking, it is important to determine how familiar the audience is with the issue. Then decide whether the audience will likely agree with your claim, be neutral about or waver on it, or disagree with it.

Agreeing Audiences. When writing for an audience that will likely agree with your claim, the focus is usually on urging readers to take action. Instead of presenting large amounts of evidence, concentrate on reinforcing your shared viewpoint and building emotional ties with the audience. By doing so, you encourage readers to act on their beliefs.

Neutral or Wavering Audiences. Neutral readers may be somewhat familiar with the issue, but they usually do not have strong feelings about it. In fact, they may have questions about it, misunderstandings about it, or no interest in it. In writing for this type of audience, be straightforward. Emphasize the importance of the issue, and offer explanations that clear up possible misunderstandings. Your goals are to establish your credibility, engender readers' trust, and present solid evidence in support of your claim.

Disagreeing Audiences. The most challenging type of audience is the disagreeing audience because they believe their position is correct and are not eager to accept your views. They may also distrust you because you don't share their views on something they care deeply about.

In writing to a disagreeing audience, the goal is to persuade readers to consider your views on the issue. Be sure to follow a logical line of reasoning. Rather than stating your claim early in the essay, for this type of audience it may be more effective to build slowly to your thesis. First establish **common ground** — a basis of trust and goodwill — with readers by mentioning interests, concerns, and experiences that you all share. Then, when you state your claim, the audience may be more open to considering your argument.

In "Why Prisons Don't Work," Rideau is writing for a mostly disagreeing audience. He establishes common ground with his readers by talking about the crimes that do merit life in prison and by using his personal experience in the criminal justice system to explain why prisons do not act as a deterrent for criminals.

Argument Presents Reasons Supported by Convincing Evidence

In developing an argument, you need to have reasons for making a claim. A **reason** is a general statement that backs up a claim; it answers the question, "Why do I have this opinion about the issue?" You also need to support each reason with evidence. Suppose, for example, you argue that high school uniforms should be mandatory for three reasons: The uniforms (1) reduce clothing costs for parents, (2) eliminate distractions in the classroom, thus improving academic performance, and (3) reduce peer pressure. Each reason would need to be supported by evidence — facts, statistics, examples, personal experience, or expert testimony. Carefully linking evidence to reasons helps readers to see how the evidence supports the claim.

Be sure to choose reasons and evidence that will appeal to your audience. In the argument about mandatory school uniforms, high school students would probably not be impressed by the first reason — reduced clothing costs for parents — but they might consider the second and third reasons if you cite evidence that appeals to them, such as personal anecdotes from students. For an audience of parents, however, facts and statistics about reduced clothing costs and improved academic performance would be appealing types of evidence.

In "Why Prisons Don't Work," Rideau offers several reasons for his claim and supports them with evidence. For instance, one reason is that random violence is committed by young people; therefore, older prisoners could safely be released. Rideau supports this reason with an example of ex-cons serving as domestic staff at the governor's mansion.

Argument Follows a Logical Line of Reasoning

The reasons and evidence in an argument should follow a logical line of reasoning. The most common types of reasoning — induction and deduction — use evidence in different ways to arrive at a conclusion.

Inductive reasoning starts with specific evidence and moves to a generalization or a conclusion. Rideau uses inductive reasoning: He provides different types of evidence that prisons don't work and then concludes with an explanation of the only effective way to prevent crime.

Deductive reasoning begins with observations or statements that are generally accepted as true. If the statements are accepted as true, then the conclusion must also be true. Suppose, for instance, that you were arguing to increase funding for the early childhood program in your town. You might start with the generally accepted observation that the federal Head Start program has helped at-risk children prepare for school. On the basis of this observation, you could build an argument for the funding of your local program.

Argument Avoids Errors in Reasoning

In an argument essay a writer may inadvertently introduce fallacies, or errors in reasoning or thinking. Several types of fallacies can weaken an argument and call into question the believability of supporting evidence. Following is a brief review of the most common types of faulty reasoning.

Circular reasoning, also called **begging the question**, occurs when a writer simply repeats the claim in different words and uses the rewording as evidence. The statement "*Cruel* and unusual experimentation on helpless animals is *inhumane*" is an example.

A **hasty generalization** occurs when the writer draws a conclusion based on insufficient evidence. If you were to taste three pieces of chocolate cake and then conclude that all chocolate cakes are overly sweet, you would be making a hasty generalization.

A **sweeping generalization** is a claim that something applies to all situations without exception. To claim that all cameras are easy to use is a sweeping generalization.

A **false analogy** results when a writer compares two situations that are not sufficiently similar. Just because two items or events are alike in *some* ways does not mean they are alike in *all* ways. If you wrote, "A human body needs rest after strenuous work, and a car needs rest after a long trip," you would be falsely comparing the human body with an automobile.

A **non sequitur** (which means "it does not follow") occurs when no logical relationship exists between two or more connected ideas. For example, the comment "Because my sister is rich, she will make a good parent" is non sequitur because no logical relationship exists between wealth and good parenting.

A **red herring** distracts readers from the main issue by raising an irrelevant point. For example, suppose you are arguing that television commercials for alcoholic beverages should be banned. To mention that some parents actually give sips of alcohol to their children creates a red herring, distracting readers from the issue of television commercials.

A **post hoc fallacy** occurs when a writer assumes that Event A caused Event B simply because B followed A. For example, the claim "Student enrollment fell dramatically this semester because of the recent appointment of the new college president" is a post hoc fallacy because other factors might have contributed to the decline in enrollment (such as changes in the economy or in the availability of financial aid).

An **either-or fallacy** argues that there are only two sides to an issue — and that only one of them is correct. For instance, on the issue of legalizing drugs, a writer may argue that all drugs must be *either* legalized *or* banned, ignoring other positions (such as legalizing marijuana use for cancer patients undergoing chemotherapy).

Argument Appeals to Readers' Needs and Values

Although an effective argument relies mainly on credible evidence and logical reasoning, emotional appeals can support and enhance a sound argument. **Emotional appeals** are directed toward readers' needs and values. **Needs** may be biological or psychological (food and drink, sex, a sense of belonging, and esteem, for example). **Values** are principles or qualities that readers consider important, worthwhile, or desirable (honesty, loyalty, privacy, and patriotism, for example). In "Why Prisons Don't Work," Rideau appeals to the human need for personal safety. He also appeals to the values of fairness and human decency, citing the example of the convict who had nothing left but his underwear.

Argument Recognizes Opposing Views

Recognizing or countering opposing arguments forces you to think hard about your own claims — and perhaps adjust them. In addition, readers will be more willing to consider your claim if you take their point of view into account. There are three methods of recognizing opposing views in an argument essay: acknowledgment, accommodation, and refutation.

When you **acknowledge** an opposing viewpoint, you admit that it exists and that you have given it serious consideration. For example, in paragraph 2 of "Why Prisons Don't Work," Rideau acknowledges an opposing view held by lawmakers who feel that "[t]he only thing to do with criminals . . . is get tougher."

When you **accommodate** an opposing viewpoint, you acknowledge readers' concerns, accept some of them, and incorporate them into your own argument. Just before he states his claim, Rideau accommodates the opposing view that "[t]here are some prisoners who cannot be returned to society" (para. 4).

When you **refute** an opposing viewpoint, you demonstrate the weakness of the opponent's argument. Consider how the author refutes an opposing viewpoint in the following paragraph:

> At the core of the argument that we should resist all government regulation of speech is the ideal that the best cure for bad speech is good, that ideas that affirm equality and the worth of all individuals will ultimately prevail. This is an empty ideal unless those of us who would fight racism are vigilant and unequivocal in that fight. We must look for ways to offer assistance and support to students whose speech and political participation are chilled in a climate of racial harassment.
>
> Charles R. Lawrence III, "On Racist Speech"

Here the author refutes a common view of free speech. By acknowledging and refuting this view, the author strengthens his own argument that recognizes the downside of unchecked freedom of speech.

Visualizing an Argument Essay

The graphic organizer in Figure 13.1 will help you analyze arguments as well as plan those that you write yourself. Unlike the graphic organizers in the preceding chapters, this organizer does not necessarily show the order in which an argument may be presented. Some arguments, for example, may begin with a claim, whereas others may start with evidence or opposing viewpoints. Regardless of your argument's sequence, you can adapt this organizer to fit your essay. Note, however, that not every element will appear in every argument. Some arguments, such as those written for an agreeing audience, may not deal with opposing viewpoints. The graphic organizer in Figure 13.2 is based on the reading "Why Prisons Don't Work."

FIGURE 13.1 Graphic Organizer for an Argument Essay

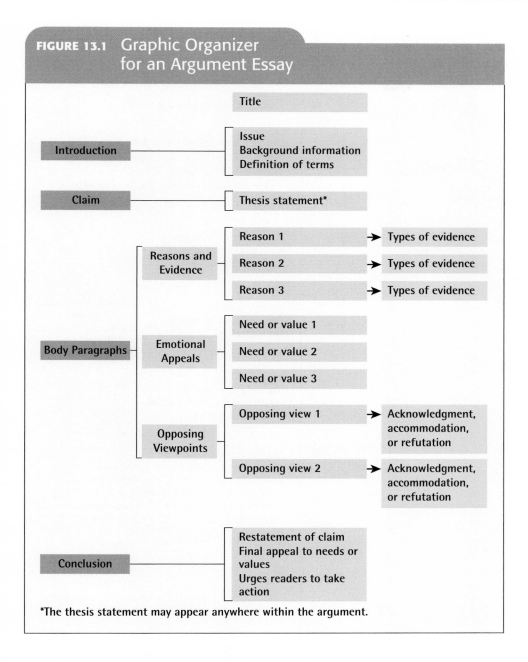

*The thesis statement may appear anywhere within the argument.

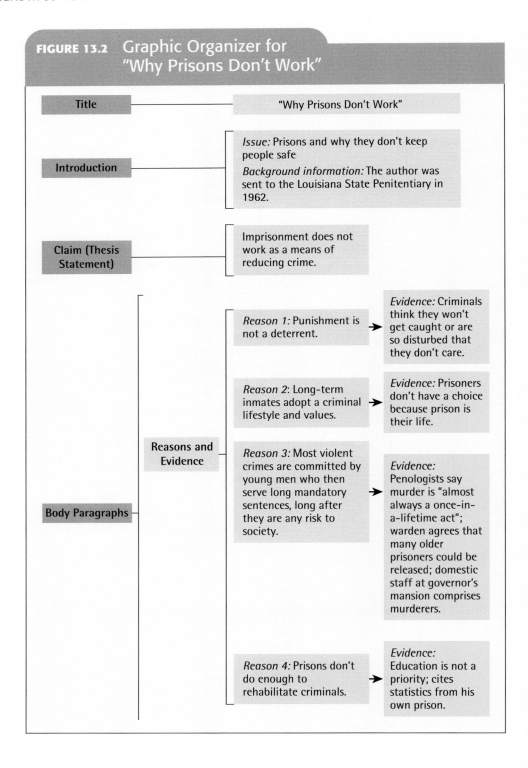

FIGURE 13.2 Graphic Organizer for "Why Prisons Don't Work"

Title	"Why Prisons Don't Work"
Introduction	*Issue:* Prisons and why they don't keep people safe *Background information:* The author was sent to the Louisiana State Penitentiary in 1962.
Claim (Thesis Statement)	Imprisonment does not work as a means of reducing crime.

Body Paragraphs — **Reasons and Evidence**

Reason 1: Punishment is not a deterrent. → *Evidence:* Criminals think they won't get caught or are so disturbed that they don't care.

Reason 2: Long-term inmates adopt a criminal lifestyle and values. → *Evidence:* Prisoners don't have a choice because prison is their life.

Reason 3: Most violent crimes are committed by young men who then serve long mandatory sentences, long after they are any risk to society. → *Evidence:* Penologists say murder is "almost always a once-in-a-lifetime act"; warden agrees that many older prisoners could be released; domestic staff at governor's mansion comprises murderers.

Reason 4: Prisons don't do enough to rehabilitate criminals. → *Evidence:* Education is not a priority; cites statistics from his own prison.

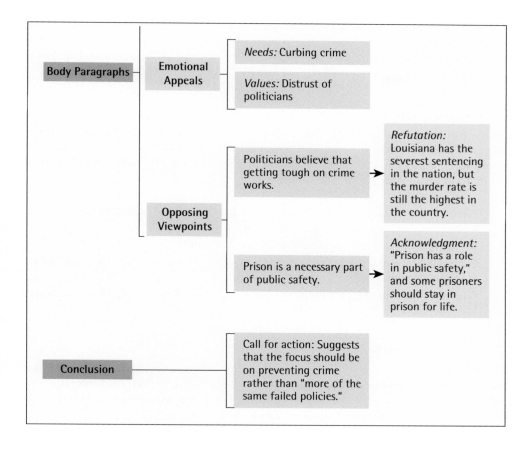

Writing an Argument Essay

To write an argument essay, use the following steps. In presenting support for your argument, you will probably need to use one or more other patterns of development.

Planning an Argument Essay

The first step is to choose an issue that interests you and that you want to learn more about. Also consider how much you already know about the topic; if you choose an unfamiliar issue, you will need to conduct extensive research. To discover a workable issue, try some of the prewriting strategies discussed in Chapter 2. Regardless of issue you choose, make sure that it is arguable and that it is narrow enough for an essay-length argument.

Considering Your Audience

Once you choose an issue, be sure to consider the audience. The reasons and the types of evidence you offer, the needs and values to which you appeal, and the common ground you establish all depend on the audience. Use the following questions to analyze your intended readers.

- What do my readers already know about the issue? What do they still need to know?
- Do my readers care about the issue? Why or why not?
- Is my audience an agreeing, neutral or wavering, or disagreeing audience? What opinions do they have on the issue?
- What do I have in common with my readers? What shared views or concerns can I use to establish common ground?

Developing a Claim in Your Thesis

Research is often an essential part of developing an argument. Reading what others have written on the issue helps you gather crucial background information, reliable evidence, and alternative viewpoints. For many arguments, you will need to consult both library and Internet sources.

After doing research about the issue, your views on it may soften, harden, or change in some other way. For instance, research on the mandatory use of seat belts may turn up statistics, expert testimony, and firsthand accounts of lives saved by seat belts in automobile accidents, leading you to reconsider your earlier view opposing mandatory use. Therefore, before developing a thesis and making a claim, consider your views on it in light of your research.

As noted earlier, the thesis for an argument essay makes a claim about the issue. As you draft your thesis, be careful to avoid general statements that are not arguable. Instead, clearly state your claim about the issue. Note the difference between a vague statement and a specific claim in the following examples.

VAGUE: **In recent years, U.S. citizens have experienced an increase in credit card fraud.**

SPECIFIC: **Although the carelessness of merchants and electronic tampering contribute to the problem, U.S. consumers are largely to blame for the recent increase in credit card fraud.**

The first example merely states a fact and is not a valid thesis for an argument. The second example makes a specific claim about an issue that is arguable.

Considering Opposing Viewpoints

Once you are satisfied with your claim and reasons and evidence, you are ready to consider opposing viewpoints; it is time to decide how to acknowledge, accommodate, and/or refute them. If you fail to at least acknowledge opposing viewpoints, readers may assume you did not think the issue through or that you dismissed alternative views without seriously considering them. In some situations, you may choose merely to acknowledge opposing ideas. At other times, you may need to accommodate opposing views, refute them, or both.

Create a list of all the pros and cons on your issue, if you haven't already done so. Then make another list of all possible objections to your argument. Try to group the objections to form two or more points of opposition.

To acknowledge an opposing viewpoint without refuting it, you can mention the opposition in your claim, as shown in this claim about enforcing speed limits.

▶ **Although speed limit laws are intended to save lives, the conditions that apply to specific highways should be taken into account in enforcing them.**

The opposing viewpoint mentioned here is that speed limits save lives. By including it as part of the claim, you show that you take it seriously.

To accommodate an opposing viewpoint, find a portion of the opposing argument that you can build into your own argument. One common way to accommodate readers' objections is to suggest alternative causes for a particular situation. For example, suppose your argument defends the competency of most high school teachers. You suspect, however, that some readers think the quality of most high school instruction is poor and attribute it to teachers' laziness or lack of skill. You can accommodate this opposing view by recognizing that there are some high schools in which poor instruction is widespread. You could then suggest that the problem is often owing to a lack of instructional supplies and the disruptive behavior of students rather than to teachers' incompetence.

If you choose to argue that an opposing view is not sound, you must refute it by pointing out problems or flaws in your opponent's reasoning or evidence. Check to see if your opponent uses faulty reasoning or fallacies. To refute an opponent's evidence, use one or more of the following guidelines.

Guidelines for Refuting Evidence

1. **Give a counterexample, or exception, to the opposing view.** For instance, if an opponent argues that dogs are protective, give an example of a situation in which a dog did not protect its owner.
2. **Question the opponent's facts.** If an opponent claims that few professors give essay exams, present statistics demonstrating that a significant percentage of professors do give essay exams.

(Continued)

(Continued)

3. **Demonstrate that an example is not representative.** If an opponent argues that professional athletes are overpaid and cites the salaries of two famous quarterbacks, cite statistics showing that these salaries are not representative of all professional athletes.

4. **Demonstrate that the examples are insufficient.** If an opponent argues that horseback riding is a dangerous sport and offers two examples of riders who were seriously injured, point out that two examples are not sufficient proof.

5. **Question the credibility of an authority.** If an opponent quotes a television personality on welfare reform, point out that she is not a sociologist or public policy expert and therefore is not an authority on welfare reform.

6. **Question outdated examples, facts, or statistics.** If an opponent presents evidence that is not recent on the need for more campus parking, you can argue that the situation has changed (for example, enrollment has declined, bus service has increased).

7. **Present the full context of a quotation or group of statistical evidence.** If an opponent quotes an authority selectively or cites incomplete statistics from a research study linking sunburn and skin cancer, the full context may show that your opponent has "edited" the evidence to suit his or her claim.

Drafting an Argument Essay

You are now ready to organize your ideas and draft your essay. Organizing and drafting an argument involve deciding on a line of reasoning, choosing a method of organization, and developing the essay accordingly.

To develop a method of organization, you need to decide on the line of reasoning you want to follow. As discussed earlier, two common lines of reasoning are *induction* and *deduction*. Inductive reasoning begins with evidence and moves to a conclusion. Deductive reasoning starts with an observation that most people accept and shows how a certain conclusion follows from it. As you plan your argument, you may decide to use one or both lines of reasoning to arrive at your conclusion; this decision will influence the way you organize your essay.

Here are four common ways to organize an argument.

METHOD I	METHOD II	METHOD III	METHOD IV
Claim/thesis	Claim/thesis	Support	Opposing viewpoints
Support	Opposing viewpoints	Opposing viewpoints	Support
Opposing viewpoints	Support	Claim/thesis	Claim/thesis

The method you choose depends on your particular audience, purpose, and issue. In some situations, it may be best to state your claim at the outset. At other times, stating the claim at the end of the argument may be more effective. You also need to decide whether to present reasons and supporting evidence before or after you discuss opposing viewpoints. Finally, decide the order in which you will discuss your reasons and supporting evidence: Will you arrange them from strongest to weakest? from most to least obvious? from familiar to unfamiliar?

Once you have chosen a method of organization, it is time to write the first draft. Use the following guidelines.

Guidelines for Writing an Argument Essay

1. **Write an effective introduction.** The introduction should identify the issue and offer background information based on the audience's knowledge and experience. Many argument essays also include a thesis in the introduction, where the writers make their *claim*. To engage your readers, you might relate a personal experience, make an attention-getting remark, or recognize a counterargument.

2. **Establish an appropriate tone.** The tone should depend on the issue and claim as well as the audience. For serious issues such as the death penalty, you would probably use a serious, even somber tone. For a call-to-action argument, you might use an energetic, enthusiastic tone. For a disagreeing audience, you might use a friendly, nonthreatening tone. Be sure to avoid overly forceful or dogmatic language that allows no room for opposing viewpoints (such as "It is obvious that . . ."). Also avoid language that may insult or alienate your readers ("Anyone who thinks . . . is . . .").

3. **Clearly state the reasons for your claim, and provide supporting evidence.** Each reason can be used to anchor the evidence that follows it. One approach is to use each reason as a topic sentence. The rest of the paragraph and perhaps those that follow would then consist of evidence supporting that particular reason.

4. **Cite the sources of your research.** As you present the evidence, you must include a citation for each quotation, summary, or paraphrase of ideas or information you borrowed from sources.

5. **Use transitions to help the readers follow your argument.** Make sure you use transitions to move clearly from reason to reason, as in "*Also relevant* to the issue . . ." and "*Furthermore*, it is important to consider. . . ." Also, be certain to distinguish your reasons and evidence from those of the opposition. Use a transitional sentence such as "Those opposed to the death penalty claim . . ." to indicate that you are about to introduce an opposing viewpoint. A transition such as "Contrary to what those in favor of the death penalty maintain . . ." can be used to signal a refutation.

6. **Write a satisfying conclusion.** You can end an argument essay in a number of different ways, such as restating the thesis, making a final appeal to values, projecting into the future, urging a specific action, or calling for further research. Choose the strategy that will have the strongest impact on your particular audience.

Analyzing and Revising

If possible, set your draft aside for a day or two before rereading and revising it. Then, as you review your draft, focus on discovering weak areas and on strengthening the overall argument, not on grammar or mechanics. Use the flowchart in Figure 13.3 to guide your analysis.

FIGURE 13.3 Revising an Argument Essay

QUESTIONS

1. Draw a circle around the portion of the essay where you introduce the issue. Is the issue defined? Is enough information provided? Is the issue sufficiently narrow?

NO →

YES ↓

2. Highlight the thesis. Is the claim stated clearly and specifically in the thesis?

NO →

YES ↓

3. Who is the audience? *Write* a brief description of their characteristics. Is your essay targeted to the intended audience? Do you appeal to those readers' needs and values?

NO →

YES ↓

REVISION STRATEGIES

- Ask a friend who is unfamiliar with the issue to ask you questions about it or to tell you what else he or she needs to know.
- Write as if you are introducing the issue to a reader who has never heard of it before.
- Use mapping or questioning to limit the issue (see Chapter 2, pp. 30 and 32).

- Without looking at your essay, write a one-sentence summary of what it is intended to prove.
- Try limiting the issue and claim to make it more specific.
- Add a qualifying word or phrase (*for example, may, possibly*) to the thesis.

- Examine each reason and piece of evidence. If it will not appeal to the audience, consider replacing it.
- Try to discover common needs, values, and experiences you share with the readers. Add appeals based on those needs, values, and experiences.
- If the audience is unfamiliar with the issue, add more background information.

QUESTIONS	REVISION STRATEGIES

4. Place a checkmark ✔ by each reason that supports the claim. Are the reasons and evidence convincing? Do they directly relate to the thesis?

 NO

- State each reason clearly; then present evidence to support it.
- Brainstorm or conduct research to discover more reasons or stronger evidence.

 YES

5. Put *numbers* in the margins of your paper to show the progression of the argument. Does each step follow a logical progression? Are there any errors in reasoning?

 NO

- Check the progression of your argument and your use of inductive and deductive reasoning by creating an outline or graphic organizer.
- Check for and omit faulty reasoning and fallacies.

YES

6. *Write* the method of organization used. Is the organization clear? Is it effective for the argument?

 NO

- Experiment with one or more other methods of organization (see Chapter 3, p. 48).

YES

7. Bracket [ ] sections that present opposing viewpoints. Do you acknowledge, accommodate, and/or refute opposing viewpoints?

NO

- Try acknowledging an opposing view in your statement or claim.
- Ask a classmate to help you find a portion of an opposing argument that could be built into your argument.
- Look for ways to refute an opponent's evidence.

YES

(Continued)

FIGURE 13.3   *(Continued)*

QUESTIONS   **REVISION STRATEGIES**

8. <u>Underline</u> the topic sentence of each paragraph. Is each paragraph well developed and focused on a separate part of the argument?

NO →
- Be sure each paragraph has a topic sentence and supporting evidence (see Chapter 3).
- Consider combining closely related paragraphs.
- Consider splitting a paragraph that covers more than one part of the argument.

↓ YES

9. Draw a box around the introduction and conclusion. Do they follow the guidelines on page 507? Are the introduction and conclusion effective?

NO →
- Revise the introduction and conclusion so that they meet the guidelines on page 507 and in Chapter 3 (pp. 61–64).

↓ YES

10. Print a copy of your essay to edit and proofread before turning the essay in.

Editing and Proofreading

For more on these and other common errors, see Chapter 4, p. 81.

The last step is to check your revised essay for errors in grammar, spelling, punctuation, and mechanics. In addition, be sure to look for the types of errors you tend to make in any writing, whether for this class or any other situation. As you edit and proofread, look out for the following two grammatical errors in particular.

Editing Tips and Troublespots: Argument

1. **Make sure to use the subjunctive mood correctly.** Because argument essays often address what would or might happen in the future, you will often use the subjunctive mood, which expresses a wish, suggestion, or condition contrary to fact. When using the verb *be* to speculate about conditions in the future, remember to say *were* in place of *was* to indicate a hypothetical situation.

(Continued)

▸ If all animal research was outlawed, progress in the control of human

were

diseases would be slowed dramatically.

2. **Look for and correct pronouns that don't refer back to a clear antecedent.**
A pronoun must refer to another noun or pronoun, called its *antecedent*. The
pronoun's antecedent should be clearly named, not just implied.

▸ Children of divorced parents often are shuttled between two homes, and

this lack of stability

that can be confusing and disturbing to them.

Students Write

Rudy De La Torre published this essay in *The Daily Aztec*, the student newspaper
for San Diego State University. De La Torre addresses the issue of ethnicity. As you
read, observe how he takes a position on ethnic heritage and supports it with reasons and evidence.

Ethnic Definitions Hinder Society's Enlightenment

Rudy De La Torre

How many times have you heard the question posed "So . . . what are you?" This
question comes up often especially when people are discussing race, ethnicity, or heritage. Often times this question is used as a tool to get to know someone -- an
icebreaker, if you will. If someone sees a person who looks kind of dark, yet has almond-
shaped eyes and blonde hair, then the question "What are you?" arises. This inquiry is
then supposed to end all suspense and wonder and enclose that individual into a tidy
little category that is easy to define.

Some people say that we have come far in terms of diversity and that we as a society are able to look past color tones and eye shapes to truly define a person's character.
But if that's true, then why do we ask the same questions and give the same answers
that we did 30 years ago? Even I answer what I am with a typical ethnic-based answer.

1   Introduction: opening question builds interest

2   Recognizes opposing viewpoint

Rarely have I responded to the "What are you" question with "sports fan," "future educator," "borderline socialist" or "upper lower-class only child of a single mother."

Americans are so stuck in a comfort zone of "tolerance" that they think that by asking this question, they are contributing to a diversity which has never been seen before in all of mankind. But when diversity is only limited to ethnicity, race, and color, we stigmatize and diminish the importance of other differences, such as taste in recreation, political orientations and even socioeconomic backgrounds. I would be able to relate a lot more to an individual if he would tell me what type of economic background he comes from rather than what ethnicity he chooses to identify himself with.

I am not saying that we should completely abandon telling others our ethnicity or our historical backgrounds. What I am saying, however, is that we need to stop putting them in the forefront of identifying who is who among our peers. Nearly 400 years ago, people would respond to the "What are you" question with their religious affiliation, while 600 years ago, people would refer to their class standing in society ("I am a peasant," or "I am a lord"). Throughout history, humans have felt the need to use one category to label themselves and others, leading to one-dimensional relationships between the haves and the have-nots, the powerful and the powerless. Today, we see similar relationships based upon ethnicities and physical racial features. To promote diversity, we make sure our campuses are full of students who are all colors, shapes, and sizes. If one color begins to dominate, we suddenly start to complain and demand equal rights.

The only true solution to all of this bickering is to make yourself a three-dimensional individual and to force others to see you in the same way. If others insist on knowing your ethnic heritage, ask them what difference it would make. If you are proud of your ethnicity, then continue to be so. However, make sure that you focus on putting more pride into what you do for your society, and less onto what nation your ancestors came from. When I die, I want people to talk about me being a good man, a hard worker, and a caring member of society. I want my epitaph to read "Rudy De La Torre: He changed many lives," not "Rudy De La Torre: In this grave lies a Mexican."

Margin annotations:

Reason

Claim

Historical evidence

Conclusion: appeals to action and ends with personal statement

Paragraph numbers: 3, 4, 5

Responding to "Students Write"

1. De La Torre's title suggests his thesis clearly, but it is lengthy and rather formal. Brainstorm a few alternative titles that would be catchier and more interesting.

2. Do the author's references to historical responses to the "What are you?" question strengthen or weaken his argument? Explain.

3. De La Torre opens with a personal question addressed to the reader. Is this an effective strategy? In what other ways could he introduce the issue of ethnicity?

4. De La Torre's conclusion offers a very personal ending to a serious essay. Is the reference to his epitaph an effective strategy? Why or why not?

Reading an Argument Essay

Reading arguments requires careful attention and analysis, so you should plan on reading an argument several times. Read it once to get an overview. Then read it several times more to analyze and critique it.

What to Look for, Highlight, and Annotate

Understanding the Reading

- Before reading, create two columns for pros and cons about the issue, and list as many ideas as you can in each column. By thinking in this way before reading, you may be less influenced by the writer's appeals and more likely to maintain an open mind and an objective, critical viewpoint.

For more on previewing, see Chapter 1, p. 6.

- Consider the meaning of the title. It may suggest the focus of the essay or even be a direct statement or synopsis of the claim, as in Rideau's essay, "Why Prisons Don't Work."

- Highlight the issue, and notice how the writer introduces it and any background information. Highlight definitions of key terms.

- If you find an argument difficult to follow, fill in a graphic organizer (see Fig. 13.1) to help clarify the steps as you read.

- Some authors and publications are known for a particular point of view, so be sure to read all headnotes, footnotes, and citations to determine where and when the essay was first published and what qualifies the author to write on the subject. If the publication or author has a particular viewpoint or audience — such as liberal or conservative — you can sometimes predict the stand an essay will take on a particular issue.

Examining the Characteristics of Argument Essays

- Identify and highlight the writer's claim. Notice any qualifying or limiting words.

- Study and highlight the types of evidence used to support the claim — facts, statistics, expert opinion, examples, and personal experience. Is the evidence relevant, accurate, current, and typical? Does the writer state reasons before introducing evidence? Add annotations indicating your initial reactions to or questions about the reasons or evidence.

- Analyze the needs and values to which the writer appeals.

- Determine whether the argument is organized effectively. Does the writer follow a logical line of reasoning? Evaluate the writer's observations and conclusions, and note any logical fallacies.

- Does the writer acknowledge, accommodate, or refute opposing views? Highlight each instance.

How to Find Ideas to Write About

Because you may be asked to write a response to an argument, watch for ideas to write about as you read.

- **Record additional supporting evidence.** Use annotations to record additional examples, personal experiences, or other evidence that comes to mind in support of the claim. These ideas may be helpful in writing your own essay in support of this writer's claim, or they might provide a start for a paper on just one aspect of the writer's argument.

- **Note opposing viewpoints and evidence.** Record events or phenomena that do not support the claim or that contradict one of the author's reasons. Keep the following question in mind: "When would this not be true?" The ideas you generate may be useful in writing an essay that supports an opposing claim.

- **Think of related issues.** Consider issues similar to the one under discussion. You may notice, for example, that the line of reasoning applied to the issue of "riding the bus rather than driving" may in part be applicable to the issue of "walking rather than riding."

A Good Death

Carol Bernstein Ferry

Carol Bernstein Ferry (1924–2001) distributed millions of dollars to various causes and charities during her lifetime. An advocate of legalized euthanasia, she chose to commit suicide by taking sleeping pills in the presence of her family after she was diagnosed with a terminal illness at the age of 76. She wrote the following piece explaining her decision and her support for a legal right to die. The essay appeared in *The Nation* in September 2001, three months after Ferry's suicide.

In "A Good Death," Ferry uses her own example to explain why a rational and well-adjusted adult might choose suicide instead of a slow death from cancer and emphysema. Notice how she anticipates counterarguments and responds to them. Observe that her beliefs, which she describes, make suicide an acceptable alternative, and note her response to those who see her choice as immoral.

Focus on Understanding   Read to discover why Ferry believes her suicide is "a good death."

Focus on the Topic   In class or in your journal, explore your feelings about assisted suicide. Should doctors be allowed to assist terminally ill patients in committing suicide? What factors are important to consider in this issue?

If my death can contribute to an understanding of euthanasia,° then I want it to do so. That is why I am writing this letter, explaining why I choose to take active steps to end my life rather than waiting for death to come gradually. With this letter I also want to make it clear that, although I have the support and tacit agreement of my children and close friends, no one but myself will take the steps that cause death. It is unfortunate that I must say this; our laws are at a destructive point just now, so if anyone other than myself actually causes my death, that person will be liable to conviction as a felon. What an absurdity! To help someone facing a time — whether short or long — of pain and distress, whose death coming bit by bit can cause major sorrow and anxiety to family and friends, not to mention the medical help, quite useless, that must be expended in order to maintain a bearable level of pain — that this sensible deed can be construed a crime is a blot on our legal system and on our power of thought.

I have known since last June that I am terminally ill. Emphysema, a tumor in my chest and recently a new tumor near my pelvis put it beyond question that I am on the way to death. This seems to me in no way a tragedy — I am, after all, 76 years old — but a natural ending. I don't feel called upon to suffer

> euthanasia: the act of killing or assisting in the death of someone who is very ill

515

until the last minute of a creeping death, nor do I want to put my children through such a time, so I am choosing to make a finish while I am still able to function.

I've had a lucky life. I've had a lot of joy; I've had enough sorrow to know   3
that I'm a member in good standing of the human race; I have tried to make myself useful. I have nothing to complain about, certainly not death. I feel lucky now, in that I have been given a somewhat definite span of life ahead. Once the approximate limit of that span — six months to a year from last June — got absorbed into my brain, many problems floated away. I no longer have to worry about death, as it is with me now. Every day is a treat, an extra gift, the positive side of the expression Borrowed Time. It is my hope that people close to me, especially my children, can also enjoy this relaxed attitude toward something that is, after all, inevitable. The idea that I can probably manage to have a peaceful and relatively painless ending is a comfort. For that probability to be a certainty would be the best comfort of all. But that certainty could only come if I were to have the help of a second person, and that I will not have, as under present law that person would be in immediate danger.

The moral beauty of suffering for its own sake is important to many, for   4
reasons that I find unfathomable. Religious pressure, the idea that God enjoys our suffering, is beyond me. And the terrible attitude of our lawmakers and politicians, considering that any help toward a painless death should be punished, is a source of wonder and shame. A few states — notably Oregon and Maine — are trying to change their laws to allow the administration of painkilling medicine even if it hastens the moment of death. Even this moderate and humane act is being fought in legislatures of some states and in the Senate. The idea that human life is sacred no matter the condition or the desire of the person seems to me irrational.

The people who think that it is immoral to make a rational decision about   5
ending life certainly have the right to consider their own death in this light and to endure to the very end whatever pain awaits them and their families. But they have flowed over into the idea that it is their right also to control those others of us who view the matter differently. There are societies here and there that do not put up roadblocks when a person decides to end life. However, the idea that each person's life is his own is too radical or too abstruse for consumption in the United States. This is the attitude that I hope will change, and soon. It is the attitude that I hope to help soften by explaining that my suicide plan is bringing me and those close to me a measure of security that my life can end in as spirited a way as possible.

I appreciate everyone who has been involved in encouraging me, including   6
those who have not encouraged me but who have withstood the temptation to reprimand me. My decision has been arrived at after many years of contemplation, not quickly or casually. I hope it will help others to feel all right about preferring a peaceful, benign path into death.

Understanding the Reading

1. Why does Ferry plan to commit suicide?

2. Will anyone be assisting Ferry in her death? What reason does she give for choosing this plan?

3. Explain how Ferry feels about the life she has lived. How does she view the time she has left?

4. According to Ferry, what are the barriers to dying in peace? What attitude toward assisted suicide does she hope to change by writing this article?

Visualizing the Reading

To review the content and organization of the reading, complete the graphic organizer on the next page. Before you begin, it might be helpful to review the explanation of reasons and evidence, emotional appeals, and opposing viewpoints on pages 497–500.

Examining the Characteristics of Argument Essays

1. What type of audience is Ferry writing for: agreeing, neutral or wavering, or disagreeing? How can you tell? Explain your answer.

2. How effectively does Ferry present her claim? Explain how her thesis qualifies her support of assisted suicide.

3. Consider the reasons that Ferry uses to support her claim. How do the details of her personal life relate to her argument?

4. How does Ferry address opposing viewpoints? Do you think she successfully recognizes or counters these viewpoints? Why or why not?

5. Does Ferry use inductive or deductive reasoning to order her argument? Is this method of organization logical given the subject matter? Explain.

Building Your Word Power

1. Discuss the connotative meaning of the word *death*.

2. What is meant by the idiom "put up roadblocks" as used in paragraph 5?

3. Explain the meaning of each of the following words as it is used in the reading: *tacit* (para. 1), *expended* (1), *unfathomable* (4), *abstruse* (5), and *benign* (6). Refer to your dictionary as needed.

*For a definition of **connotative meaning** and **idiom**, see the chart of commonly used language features on p. 21.*

Building Your Critical Thinking Skills: Evaluating Letters

Many newspapers have a "Letters to the Editor" section where readers comment on current issues. Some of these letters are well-crafted arguments, while others are overly emotional or sensational. Evaluating letters involves carefully separating fact from opinion and identifying the writers' possible bias. Readers should also consider the audience for whom each letter is intended and determine whether the letter appropriately recognizes and addresses the audience's needs. Using your skills in evaluating letters, answer the following questions. (Continued on p. 519.)

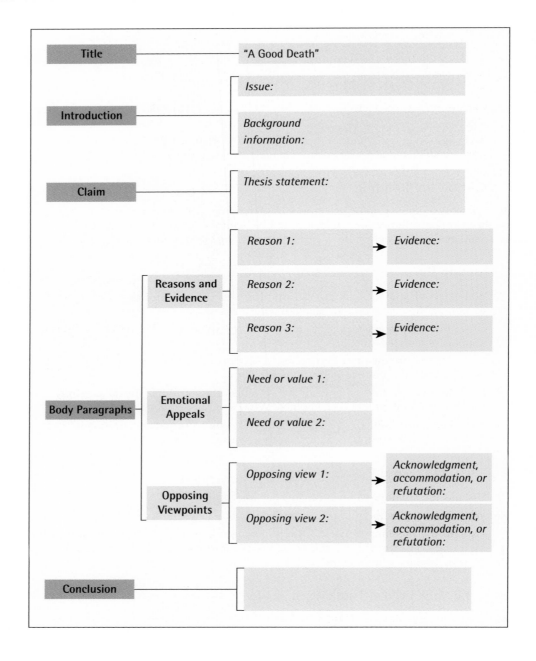

Title — "A Good Death"

Introduction — Issue:

Background information:

Claim — Thesis statement:

Body Paragraphs

Reasons and Evidence — Reason 1: → Evidence:

Reason 2: → Evidence:

Reason 3: → Evidence:

Emotional Appeals — Need or value 1:

Need or value 2:

Opposing Viewpoints — Opposing view 1: → Acknowledgment, accommodation, or refutation:

Opposing view 2: → Acknowledgment, accommodation, or refutation:

Conclusion

(Continued from p. 517.)

1. What opinions does Ferry express? What facts does she offer to support her view?

2. What biases does she reveal?

3. To what audience is her letter addressed? How effectively does Ferry address the needs and values of those readers?

Reacting to the Reading: Discussion and Journal Writing

1. Discuss euthanasia, suicide, and assisted suicide. How do these differ? Do you think there should be legal means for terminally ill people to end their lives? Explain your position.

2. In class or in your journal, discuss activists. Do you consider Ferry to be an activist? What makes some people decide to take a public stand on a cause?

Applying Your Skills: Writing Assignments

1. Paragraph Assignment. Ferry writes, "the idea that each person's life is his own is too radical or too abstruse for consumption in the United States" (para. 5). In a paragraph, explain why you agree or disagree with this statement.

2. Government often legislates how we live and act. Choose an issue, such as seat belt use or the drinking age, over which the government has control. In an essay, argue in support of reasons why the current law is either intrusive or legitimate and reasonable. Be sure to include evidence to support your claim, and recognize opposing viewpoints.

3. Write a letter to your congressional representative explaining your position on euthanasia. Urge your representative to develop, propose, and support a law that supports your position on the issue.

4. Combining Patterns. Ferry states that she had both joy and sorrow in her life. Consider the relationship between happiness and sadness. Is it necessary to experience one in order to appreciate the other? Write an argument essay in response to this question. Compare and contrast a happy and a sad experience from your own life as you build your argument.

5. Internet Research. Use the Internet to research the laws on assisted suicide in Oregon or in Holland. Choose a particular segment of the law that you find interesting or controversial. Write an argument essay about this segment of the law or another issue related to euthanasia that you discovered through your research. You might begin by visiting the following Web site: www.internationaltaskforce.org.

Athletics 101: A Change in Eligibility Rules Is Long Overdue

Frank Deford

Frank Deford (b. 1938), a member of the National Association of Sportscasters and Sportswriters' Hall of Fame, has been on the staff of *Sports Illustrated* for more than thirty years. He also works as a television sports correspondent and provides a regular commentary on National Public Radio's *Morning Edition*. Deford has written twelve books, including two that were made into movies. His peers have named him Sportswriter of the Year six times.

In the following *Sports Illustrated* essay from 2001, Deford argues against the "antiquated amateur rules" governing eligibility to play college and professional sports. Notice the analogies he uses to convince readers that his argument is reasonable. In addition, note his inclusion of historical material to explain the origin of the amateur rules — and the impact of his statement that amateurism was originally designed to give the privileged an unfair advantage.

Focus on Understanding   As you read, identify what the author thinks about the current eligibility rules in college athletics.

Focus on the Topic   In class or in your journal, explore your own view on whether colleges should pay athletes for playing sports like football and basketball that have a national audience.

As the NBA draft approaches, there is, anew, a great deal of weeping and 1 wailing and gnashing of teeth about the poor basketball players who will be deprived of more higher education if they opt to turn pro after high school or after only a year or two of college.

Curiously, no one seemed very upset about Tiger Woods's° educational loss 2 when he departed Stanford early. There were no cries of academic anguish when Pete Sampras, Andre Agassi, and Venus and Serena Williams° went on tour instead of on campus — and never is anybody disturbed by the hundreds of baseball prospects who abandon schooling every year for the minor leagues. But, of course, deeply concerned educators do care about the minds of basketball and football players because those just happen to be the only two sports that draw big-ticket crowds and rich television contracts for the universities. Similarly, the NFL and NBA want prospects to play in college so they build up their box-office appeal before moving up to the pros.

The answer to this cynical dilemma is very simple, of course. Throw out all 3 the antiquated amateur rules. After a player is drafted, he should be allowed to stay in school and play college basketball or football for up to four seasons.

Tiger Woods: a professional golfer

Pete Sampras, Andre Agassi, Venus and Serena Williams: professional tennis players

520

Who cares whether he's been paid money? Who cares whether his daddy, the school's athletic scholarship program, or the Indiana Pacers is paying his tuition?

Look at it this way: A student who wants a career in radio is praised if he   4
gets a summer internship at a radio station. When he comes back to college in the fall nobody says *well, son, you can't work at the college radio station anymore because you're a radio pro.* Are sports professionals any different from that — or any different from the kid who makes money singing in a dance band on weekends and then is allowed to sing for free in the college glee club on weekdays? Does he soil the other members of the chorus who aren't good enough to get paid?

There's a student at Princeton named Chris Young who was signed to play   5
in the Pittsburgh Pirates's farm system during the summer. As a result, he is not only banned from playing on his school's baseball team in the spring, but because he is a summer *baseball* intern, he is banned from playing *basketball* for Princeton in the winter. This is like prohibiting a published student poet from writing for the college newspaper.

But these nutty rules are affirmed by the Ivy League presidents, some of our   6
brightest educators. When it comes to sports, though, even our smartest people go bonkers.

To be sure, some athletes who come to college with great sums of bonus   7
money will goof off and do nothing but play their sport. So what? That's already all too often the case. But then, some kids with huge trust funds go to college and play video games. And some make Phi Beta Kappa.

It's time we admitted that this idiotic system of amateur athletic eligibility   8
is nothing but a vestige of a nineteenth century arrangement from a class system in another country. It was created in the 1800s by the English swells to restrict young working men from competing against the leisure classes. It has no relevance in twenty-first century America.

Open up college sports to all eligible students. Stop caring about who's pay-   9
ing the bills, and everybody — pro leagues and colleges alike — will be happier, nobody will be hurt, and a great deal of the sham and hypocrisy of sport will be instantly eliminated.

Understanding the Reading

1. According to the author, why do educators, the NFL, and the NBA care more about the eligibility of basketball and football players than the eligibility of golfers and tennis players?

2. What reasons does Deford offer in support of changing eligibility rules?

3. What comparison does the author make between athletes and students who serve as interns?

4. According Deford, why were the eligibility rules originally established?

Visualizing the Reading

Deford uses a number of non-sports-related examples to build his case against amateur rules. Analyze these comparisons by completing the following chart. The first one has been done for you.

Example	What It Contributes to the Argument
Tiger Woods	Shows that the golf community is not concerned about the issue of amateur rules
Pete Sampras, Andre Agassi, and Venus and Serena Williams	
Baseball prospects abandoning school for the minor leagues	
Radio internship	
College singer making money in a dance band	
Chris Young of Princeton	

Examining the Characteristics of Argument Essays

1. This article originally appeared in *Sports Illustrated*. What types of people read this magazine, and how does Deford address this audience to convince them of his argument?

2. Identify Deford's claim. Is his thesis clear and effective? Explain.

3. What types of evidence does the author use to support his argument? How might this evidence appeal to his audience? Do his reasons and evidence adequately support his claim? Why or why not?

4. What emotional appeals to needs and values does Deford use to support his claim?

5. Deford acknowledges the opposing view that athletes who are paid bonus money "will goof off and do nothing but play their sport" (para. 7). What method does he use to counter this view, and is the technique successful? Explain.

Building Your Word Power

1. What does the author mean by "cries of academic anguish" in paragraph 2?

2. Explain the slang term "go bonkers" in paragraph 6.

3. Explain the meaning of each of the following words as it is used in the reading: *antiquated* (para. 3), *affirmed* (6), *vestige* (8), and *hypocrisy* (9). Refer to your dictionary as needed.

Building Your Critical Thinking Skills: Tone

When writing an argument, an author uses language to appeal to readers' emotions or intellect. This use of language often reveals the author's **tone**: how the author sounds to the readers and how he or she feels about the topic. Tone can be established through word choice, sentence arrangements, or the informal or formal use of language. The tone of an argument essay is important because it affects the readers' attitude toward the topic. Using your knowledge about tone, answer the following questions.

1. Deford describes the eligibility rules in college athletics as *antiquated*, *nutty*, and *idiotic*. How do these words contribute to the tone of his argument?

2. Find examples where Deford uses sarcasm to discredit the people who support eligibility rules.

3. Do you find the tone to be amusing? condescending? alienating? What risks are associated with using such a tone?

Reacting to the Reading: Discussion and Journal Writing

1. Discuss the advantages and disadvantages of eliminating eligibility rules for college athletics.

2. If college athletes were paid to play their sport, how do you think college athletics would change? Would such a change have positive or negative effects? Explain.

Applying Your Skills: Writing Assignments

1. **Paragraph Assignment.** Write a paragraph describing a rule, law, or policy that you think is antiquated or inappropriate. It might be a campus rule or policy, or a local, state, or national law. Include a reason why it is outdated or not sensible.

2. Rewrite Deford's article for a different audience. Depending on the audience you choose, your tone might be different. For example, what tone would be most appropriate to persuade a college president? After establishing your audience, you may need to conduct library or Internet research to add supporting reasons and evidence. Alternatively, you might take the opposite side of the debate and argue to retain eligibility requirements for college athletes.

3. Deford mentions "the sham and hypocrisy of sport" (para. 9). Brainstorm a list of other things that you consider hypocritical (for example, educational testing or the objectivity of the media). Choose one, and write an impassioned argument in the style of Deford's essay that seeks to debunk the myths surrounding the issue.

4. **Combining Patterns.** What other groups on college campuses (for example, minorities, scholarship students, artists) would benefit from preferential treatment? Using description, explain the distinguishing characteristics of this group, and in an essay argue why they deserve or could benefit from preferential treatment.

5. **Internet Research.** The National Collegiate Athletic Association (NCAA) is a voluntary organization dedicated to "the sound administration of intercollegiate athletics." Conduct some research about this group at www.ncaa.org or use the Internet to research the work of this association. Narrow your research to one particular topic relating to the NCAA, such as the effect of Title IX and gender equality in college athletics or the NCAA's drug testing policy, and write an argument essay for or against this policy.

I Have a Dream

Martin Luther King Jr.

Martin Luther King Jr. (1929–1968) was one of the planners and organizers of the 1963 March on Washington for Jobs and Freedom to promote civil rights for African Americans. That year, King was heavily involved in the nonviolent protests against segregation in Birmingham, Alabama, where peaceful marchers had faced police dogs and fire hoses turned on them by order of the city's police chief. Television footage of attacks on protesters had won sympathy for the cause. Subsequently more than 250,000 marchers came to Washington, D.C., to express support for civil rights — the largest demonstration for any cause in the nation's history up to that time.

On August 28, 1963, King was the final speaker at the march. He roused the crowd with a stirring speech, "I Have a Dream," on the steps of the Lincoln Memorial. As you read the speech, which was reportedly improvised, note King's masterful use of repetition. In addition, pay attention to the imagery he uses to include all Americans in his vision.

Focus on Understanding   Read to discover what the dream referred to in the title is.

Focus on the Topic   In class or in your journal, discuss your perceptions of the state of race relations in our country.

Emancipation Proclamation: 1862 act issued by Abraham Lincoln during the Civil War to free the slaves in states that had seceded from the Union

Five score years ago, a great American, in whose symbolic shadow we stand, signed the Emancipation Proclamation.° This momentous decree came as a great beacon light of hope to millions of Negro slaves who had been seared in the flames of withering injustice. It came as a joyous daybreak to end the long night of captivity. 1

But one hundred years later, we must face the tragic fact that the Negro is still not free. One hundred years later, the life of the Negro is still sadly crippled by the manacles of segregation and the chains of discrimination. One hundred years later, the Negro lives on a lonely island of poverty in the midst of a vast ocean of material prosperity. One hundred years later, the Negro is still languishing in the corners of American society and finds himself an exile in his own land. So we have come here today to dramatize an appalling condition. 2

In a sense we have come to our nation's Capitol to cash a check. When the architects of our republic wrote the magnificent words of the Constitution and the Declaration of Independence, they were signing a promissory note to which every American was to fall heir. This note was a promise that all men would be guaranteed the unalienable rights of life, liberty, and the pursuit of happiness. 3

It is obvious today that America has defaulted on this promissory note insofar as her citizens of color are concerned. Instead of honoring this sacred ob- 4 ligation, America has given the Negro people a bad check; a check which has come back marked "insufficient funds." But we refuse to believe that the bank of justice is bankrupt. We refuse to believe that there are insufficient funds in the great vaults of opportunity of this nation. So we have come to cash this check — a check that will give us upon demand the riches of freedom and the security of justice. We have also come to this hallowed spot to remind America of the fierce urgency of *now*. This is no time to engage in the luxury of cooling off or to take the tranquilizing drug of gradualism. *Now* is the time to make real the promises of Democracy. *Now* is the time to rise from the dark and desolate valley of segregation to the sunlit path of racial justice. *Now* is the time to open the doors of opportunity to all of God's children. *Now* is the time to lift our nation from the quicksands of racial injustice to the solid rock of brotherhood.

It would be fatal for the nation to overlook the urgency of the moment and   5 to underestimate the determination of the Negro. This sweltering summer of the Negro's legitimate discontent will not pass until there is an invigorating autumn of freedom and equality. 1963 is not an end, but a beginning. Those who hope that the Negro needed to blow off steam and will now be content will have a rude awakening if the nation returns to business as usual. There will be neither rest nor tranquility in America until the Negro is granted his citizenship rights. The whirlwinds of revolt will continue to shake the foundations of our nation until the bright day of justice emerges.

But there is something I must say to my people who stand on the warm   6 threshold which leads into the palace of justice. In the process of gaining our rightful place we must not be guilty of wrongful deeds. Let us not seek to satisfy our thirst for freedom by drinking from the cup of bitterness and hatred. We must forever conduct our struggle on the high plane of dignity and discipline. We must not allow our creative protest to degenerate into physical violence. Again and again we must rise to the majestic heights of meeting physical force with soul force. The marvelous new militancy which has engulfed the Negro community must not lead us to a distrust of all white people, for many of our white brothers, as evidenced by their presence here today, have come to realize that their destiny is tied up with our destiny and their freedom is inextricably bound to our freedom. We cannot walk alone.

And as we walk, we must make the pledge that we shall march ahead. We   7 cannot turn back. There are those who are asking the devotees of civil rights, "When will you be satisfied?" We can never be satisfied as long as the Negro is the victim of the unspeakable horrors of police brutality. We can never be satisfied as long as our bodies, heavy with the fatigue of travel, cannot gain lodging in the motels of the highways and the hotels of the cities. We cannot be satisfied as long as the Negro's basic mobility is from a smaller ghetto to a larger one. We can never be satisfied as long as a Negro in Mississippi cannot vote and a Negro in New York believes he has nothing for which to vote. No, no, we are not satisfied, and we will not be satisfied until justice rolls down like waters and righteousness like a mighty stream.

I am not unmindful that some of you have come here out of great trials and 8
tribulations. Some of you have come fresh from narrow jail cells. Some of you
have come from areas where your quest for freedom left you battered by the
storms of persecution and staggered by the winds of police brutality. You have
been the veterans of creative suffering. Continue to work with the faith that un-
earned suffering is redemptive.

Go back to Mississippi, go back to Alabama, go back to South Carolina, go 9
back to Georgia, go back to Louisiana, go back to the slums and ghettoes of our
northern cities, knowing that somehow this situation can and will be changed.
Let us not wallow in the valley of despair.

I say to you today, my friends, that in spite of the difficulties and frustra- 10
tions of the moment I still have a dream. It is a dream deeply rooted in the
American dream.

I have a dream that one day this nation will rise up and live out the true 11
meaning of its creed: "We hold these truths to be self-evident; that all men are
created equal."°

I have a dream that one day on the red hills of Georgia the sons of former 12
slaves and the sons of former slaveowners will be able to sit down together at
the table of brotherhood.

I have a dream that the state of Mississippi, a desert state sweltering with 13
the heat of injustice and oppression, will be transformed into an oasis of freedom and justice.

I have a dream that my four little children will one day live in a nation 14
where they will not be judged by the color of their skin but by the content of
their character.

I have a dream today. 15

I have a dream that the state of Alabama, whose governor's lips are 16
presently dripping with the words of interposition° and nullification, will be
transformed into a situation where little black boys and black girls will be able
to join hands with little white boys and white girls and walk together as sisters
and brothers.

I have a dream today. 17

I have a dream that one day every valley shall be exalted, every hill and 18
mountain shall be made low, the rough places will be made plain, and the
crooked places will be made straight, and the glory of the Lord shall be revealed, and all flesh shall see it together.

This is our hope. This is the faith with which I return to the South. With 19
this faith we will be able to hew out of the mountain of despair a stone of hope.
With this faith we will be able to transform the jangling discords of our nation
into a beautiful symphony of brotherhood. With this faith we will be able to
work together, to pray together, to struggle together, to go to jail together, to
stand up for freedom together, knowing that we will be free one day.

This will be the day when all of God's children will be able to sing with new 20
meaning.

"We hold these truths to be self-evident; that all men are created equal": famous line from the Declaration of Independence

interposition: controversial view that the states have the right to decide if the federal government has exceeded its power

My country, 'tis of thee
Sweet land of liberty,
    Of thee I sing:
Land where my fathers died,
Land of the pilgrims' pride,
From every mountainside
    Let freedom ring.

And if America is to be a great nation this must become true. So let free- 21
dom ring from the prodigious hilltops of New Hampshire. Let freedom ring
from the mighty mountains of New York. Let freedom ring from the heighten-
ing Alleghenies of Pennsylvania!

Let freedom ring from the snowcapped Rockies of Colorado! 22

Let freedom ring from the curvaceous peaks of California! 23

But not only that; let freedom ring from Stone Mountain of Georgia! 24

Let freedom ring from Lookout Mountain of Tennessee! 25

Let freedom ring from every hill and molehill of Mississippi. From every 26
mountainside, let freedom ring.

When we let freedom ring, when we let it ring from every village and every 27
hamlet, from every state and every city, we will be able to speed up that day
when all of God's children, black men and white men, Jews and Gentiles,
Protestants and Catholics, will be able to join hands and sing in the words of
the old Negro spiritual, "Free at last! free at last! thank God almighty, we are
free at last!"

Understanding the Reading

1. According to King, what problems do African Americans still face one hundred
   years after the signing of the Emancipation Proclamation?

2. Explain King's analogy to a bad check. What does he say that America owes the
   Negro people?

3. For what purpose does King urge his followers to return to Mississippi, Alabama,
   and other states and communities?

4. What must still happen in order for America "to be a great nation" (para. 21)? In a
   sentence or two, summarize King's dream.

Visualizing the Reading

Evaluate King's use of figurative language by completing the following chart. For each
figurative expression listed, explain what it means and how it strengthens King's argument. The first one has been done for you.

Figurative Expression	Meaning
". . . we have come to our nation's Capitol to cash a check." (para. 3)	Implies an obligation between the words of the Constitution and the Declaration of Independence and the rights of the Negro. Use of this analogy gives the cause a sense of importance and legitimacy.
"*Now* is the time to lift our nation from the quicksands of racial injustice to the solid rock of brotherhood." (para. 4)	
"The whirlwinds of revolt will continue to shake the foundations of our nation until the bright day of justice emerges." (para. 5)	
"Let us not seek to satisfy our thirst for freedom by drinking from the cup of bitterness and hatred." (para. 6)	
"You have been the veterans of creative suffering." (para. 8)	
"With this faith we will be able to transform the jangling discords of our nation into a beautiful symphony of brotherhood." (para. 19)	

Examining the Characteristics of Argument Essays

1. King delivered "I Have a Dream" to a crowd assembled for a civil rights march. What kind of audience is King addressing — agreeing, neutral or wavering, or disagreeing — and how does that affect his argument?

2. What claim does King make? How does he present it?

3. What kinds of reasons and evidence does King use to support his claim? Are his details convincing and persuasive? Why or why not?

4. Identify the needs and values that King appeals to. How effectively do these emotional appeals strengthen his argument? Explain.

5. What opposing viewpoints does King address? Explain how he recognizes and counters them.

For a definition of **imagery**, *see the chart of commonly used language features on p. 21.*

Building Your Word Power

1. Evaluate the light and dark imagery in the first paragraph.

2. Explain the meaning of each of the following words as it is used in the reading: *score* (para. 1), *manacles* (2), *unalienable* (3), *defaulted* (4), *hallowed* (4), *nullification* (16), *hew* (19), and *hamlet* (27). Refer to your dictionary as needed.

Building Your Critical Thinking Skills: Evaluating Speeches

A well-written speech captures the readers' attention and keeps them interested. Because speeches are written to be spoken, most speechwriters keep complicated information and facts to a minimum. Speechwriters often use repetition, using catchphrases over and over for effect and to ensure that listeners remember key points. Many speeches build to a climax at the end, enabling the speaker to emphasize the main point while urging support for a cause and, when appropriate, a call for action. Because the power of a speaker can have a tremendous effect on listeners, it is often better to *read* the text of a speech; this enables you to analyze its content without being influenced by the actual presence and manner of delivery of the speaker. When reading, evaluate the language and any repeated phrases or terms to determine if they are truly relevant to the argument or if they are merely devices to draw the listener in. Using your knowledge of evaluating speeches, answer the following questions.

1. How does King capture the attention of his audience?

2. What repeated words and catchphrases does he use? Do they help build his argument, or are they merely devices to engage the listener? Explain.

3. Evaluate the conclusion of the speech. What final impression does it make? Explain how it appeals to values, projects into the future, or urges listeners to take action — or a combination of all three.

Reacting to the Reading: Discussion and Journal Writing

1. Discuss what you know about the civil rights movement in America. What has been accomplished since the 1960s, and what remains to be done?

2. Martin Luther King Jr. was a charismatic leader who galvanized people to take action. Are there any similar figures today to whom people look for leadership? Choose one figure and compare him or her to King.

Applying Your Skills: Writing Assignments

1. **Paragraph Assignment.** King says that "we have come to our nation's Capitol to cash a check" (para. 3). Write a paragraph arguing for a debt that is owed to you or one that you owe to someone else. Do not limit your argument to debts of money.

2. How far have Americans come in avoiding judging people by the color of their skin? Has skin color been replaced by other factors (for example, income, age, sex, health, housing, education)? Choose a factor indicating that inequality still exists in this nation, and write an argument essay that demonstrates its existence and suggests a remedy.

3. As a pivotal figure in the civil rights movement, King rallied hundreds of thousands of people to action. As citizens, it is our obligation to become involved if we want

to effect change. One of the simplest levels of involvement is to vote, yet voting rates have been in decline since the 1960s. In an essay, argue for the importance of voting. Your audience is young voters in their late teens and early twenties.

4. Combining Patterns. Brainstorm a list of factors that contribute to the American Dream. Then, in an essay, define the term "American Dream" and take a position about one's ability to achieve it. For example, you might argue that it has changed since King's time, that it is impossible to fulfill, or that it should be the goal of every American.

5. Internet Research. Listen to some speeches from the History Channel's speech archive at www.historychannel.com/speeches/archive1.html or another Web site that archives historical speeches. Browse the collection, and choose one that uses argument to call people to action. Evaluate its effectiveness, and then write an essay that argues why or why not the speech continues to have relevance today. To better understand the context of the speech, it may be necessary to conduct further online research about the historical circumstances surrounding this speech.

Organ Donation: Should People Be Allowed to Sell Their Organs?

In 1954 doctors accomplished the first successful kidney transplant from a donor to a recipient. Since then, advances in medical science have enabled doctors to do what was once considered impossible, from the first successful heart transplant in 1968 to the first successful living donor liver transplant in 1989. In the case of some organs, such as the kidney, the donor can continue to live without the organ, so the donor is alive and healthy when the organ is taken ("harvested"). For most organs, however, such as the heart, the donor must be brain dead before an organ can be harvested. The medical advances that make such transplants possible also give rise to controversies, as doctors increasingly must address ethical issues such as how to define death and who should receive access to the limited supply of organs.

Because the demand for organs far outweighs the supply of potential donors, many patients who would likely survive with a new organ die while waiting for one to become available. This situation gives rise to another issue: whether allowing the sale of organs would motivate people who wouldn't otherwise donate an organ to do so. Generally, for moral and ethical reasons, the medical community has shied away from this strategy to boost the supply of available organs; but some doctors, medical ethicists, and others are beginning to reconsider this option as perhaps the only alternative to increase the supply of organs for sick and dying patients.

Is the sale of organs morally justified if the only alternative is the death of thousands of people each year while waiting for a donor organ? The two following readings present opposing viewpoints on this issue. As you read, identify the reasons each author offers in support of his position.

How Much Is That Kidney in the Window?

Bruce Gottlieb

Bruce Gottlieb left a position as staff writer for *Slate.com* and author of its "Pundit Central" and "Explainer" columns in 1999 to attend Harvard Law School. After graduating in 2002 he joined a law firm in Washington, D.C., where he focuses on state and federal telecommunication regulation. In addition to practicing law, Gottlieb still works regularly as a freelance writer. His work has appeared in numerous publications, including the *New York Times Magazine*, the *Wall Street Journal*, and *The New Republic*, where this essay first appeared in 2000.

In the following essay, Gottlieb raises what he calls the "familiar arguments" against legalizing the sales of kidneys for transplants; then he answers each argument. As you read, observe how he addresses ethical concerns and points out what he says are logical fallacies in the arguments against allowing organ sales from living donors. Think about the type of argument he uses and about the position from which he begins his argument.

Focus on Understanding   Read to discover how the author feels about the sale of kidneys.

Focus on the Topic   In class or in your journal, explore your thoughts about organ donation. If someone close to you needed a kidney transplant, would you donate one of yours? Would your reaction to this request be different if you didn't know the person?

Eight years ago, an article appeared in an obscure Israeli medical journal, *Medicine and Law*, arguing that American citizens should be permitted to sell their kidneys. This would require changing federal law, which since 1984 has made selling any organ, even one's own, a felony punishable by up to five years in jail. The author of the article was a Michigan pathologist named Jack Kevorkian.°

Jack Kevorkian: a doctor imprisoned in 1999 for giving a fatally ill man a lethal injection instead of treating him; a leading figure in the assisted-suicide movement

Kevorkian's argument was that the current system of accepting kidneys only from dead patients and Good Samaritan donors provides too few kidneys. While this was true even then, the situation is worse today. As of April 30, there were 44,989 people on the waiting list for a kidney transplant. About 2,300 of them will die this year while waiting. If kidney sales were permitted, Kevorkian argued, these lives would almost certainly be saved.

He may be right. In recent years, economists and economically minded lawyers at the University of Chicago and Yale Law School have made similar arguments. The idea was endorsed two years ago in the pages of *The Lancet*° by a group of prominent transplant surgeons from Harvard Medical School and hospitals in Canada and England. Of course, legalizing kidney sales remains a fringe view, both within the medical profession and outside it. But that needs to change.

The Lancet: an international journal that publishes medical research and news

There are several familiar arguments against legalizing kidney sales, beginning with the idea that giving up a kidney is too dangerous for the donor. But, popular though this argument is, the statistics don't bear it out — at least relative to other risks people are legally permitted to assume. In terms of effect on life expectancy, donating one of your two kidneys is more or less equivalent to driving an additional 16 miles to work each day. No one objects to the fact that ordinary jobs — like construction or driving a delivery van — carry roughly similar risks.

Another common objection is that government ought to encourage altruism, not profit seeking. But from the perspective that matters — the recipient's — this distinction is irrelevant, so long as the donated kidney works. It's not as if the point of kidney transplants were to improve the donor's karma. Moreover, kidneys from cadavers function for eight years, on average, whereas those from live donors last 17 years. (The reason is that kidneys can be "harvested" from live donors in circumstances less hectic than death and that donors and recipients can be better matched.)

This brings us to the most powerful objection to the sale of kidneys — that, in practice, it would result in the poor selling parts of their bodies to the rich. But in today's health care economy that probably wouldn't be the case. For several decades, Congress has mandated that Medicare pay the medical bills of any patient — of any age — who requires dialysis.° Transplant surgery and postsurgical drug treatment are expensive, yes, but they're nothing compared to dialysis, which costs about $40,000 per year. That's a savings of $40,000 per year for the 17 years or so during which a transplanted kidney will function. In other words, insurers and the federal government would probably be happy to buy a kidney for anyone who needs one. They'd even be willing to pay donors considerable sums — $50,000, $100,000, or more. (Indeed, according to one estimate, if kidneys could be found for all the patients now on dialysis, Medicare would break even after just two years.)

6

At these prices, there would be no shortage of sellers. The government could enforce price floors to keep competitive sellers from bidding down the going rate for kidneys. And given the amount of money involved, it seems downright contradictory to argue that the poor should be prevented from taking the deal on the grounds that poverty is unfair. The solution to poverty is anyone's guess, but restricting poor people's economic opportunities definitely isn't the answer. Nor is it enough to say that there are better and more humane ways of leveling the distribution of wealth than allowing kidney sales. To argue against kidney selling, one must provide a better practical way of helping the disadvantaged. It does a poor person who wishes to sell his kidney no favors to tell him instead to lobby Congress for an increase in the minimum wage or a more egalitarian tax code. Besides, the kidney waiting list contains a disproportionate share of minorities. Thirty-five percent of the people on the waiting list are black; twelve percent are Hispanic. If the point of the current law is to temper the effects of income inequality, asking racial minorities to shoulder an unequal share of the burden is surely a step in the wrong direction.

7

Sure, critics will say that allowing kidney sales is the beginning of a slippery slope towards selling other, more essential organs. This, of course, would be a moral disaster, since it would mean legalizing serious maiming (selling eyes) or even murder (selling hearts or lungs). But the very outrageousness of this will keep it from happening. A slippery-slope argument is convincing only when it shows that the slipping would be either inevitable (for example, that legalizing abortion when a condom breaks means people would be less careful about birth control, thereby increasing abortions) or unconscious (outlawing child porn would lead to outlawing *Lolita*, since bureaucrats can't tell the difference). But it's easy for legislators to draft a law that clearly allows kidney selling but forbids other forms of organ selling. (Kidneys are fairly unique in that,

8

dialysis: a medical procedure whereby wastes and toxins are removed from the blood when the kidneys cannot perform this function

while everybody has two, somebody with just one can lead an almost entirely normal life.) And it seems implausible that a member of Congress would mistake public approval of kidney sales for approval of economic transactions that leave sellers dead or partially blind.

Nicholas L. Tilney, a Harvard Medical School professor and transplant surgeon, wrote a paper in 1989 against kidney selling. He says this is still the view of "100 out of 100 transplant surgeons." But in 1998 — as the kidney shortage became more acute — he coauthored, along with other surgeons, lawyers, and philosophers, the provocative *Lancet* paper that argued for legalizing kidney sales. "We debated this question for about two years before writing that piece," says Tilney. "All of us transplanters, and I'm sure the public, have this tremendous gut reaction against it. That was sort of our initial reaction. And then, when we all got around and really thought about this and talked about it, our thinking began to change." 9

The prospect of someone going under the knife to earn a down payment on a new house or to pay for college is far from pleasant. But neither is the reality of someone dying because a suitable kidney can't be found. The free market may be the worst way to allocate kidneys. The worst, that is, except for all the other alternatives. 10

Understanding the Reading

1. Why does Gottlieb favor organ sales?
2. Why does he think that the kidney is the only organ for which sales should be legalized?
3. What populations would be most affected if there were an increase in available kidneys?
4. How did the doctors mentioned in the article come to change their minds about kidney sales?

Visualizing the Reading

To review the content and organization of the reading, complete the graphic organizer on the next page. Before you begin, it might be helpful to review the explanation of reasons and evidence, emotional appeals, and opposing viewpoints on pages 497–500.

Examining the Characteristics of Argument Essays

1. In your opinion, is Gottlieb successful in presenting his case to what is probably a mostly disagreeing audience? Why or why not?
2. Consider the author's claim. Is it a claim of fact, value, or policy? Explain how you know.
3. In what order does Gottlieb arrange the opposing viewpoints? Does he acknowledge, accommodate, or refute these viewpoints with logic and relevant evidence? Explain.

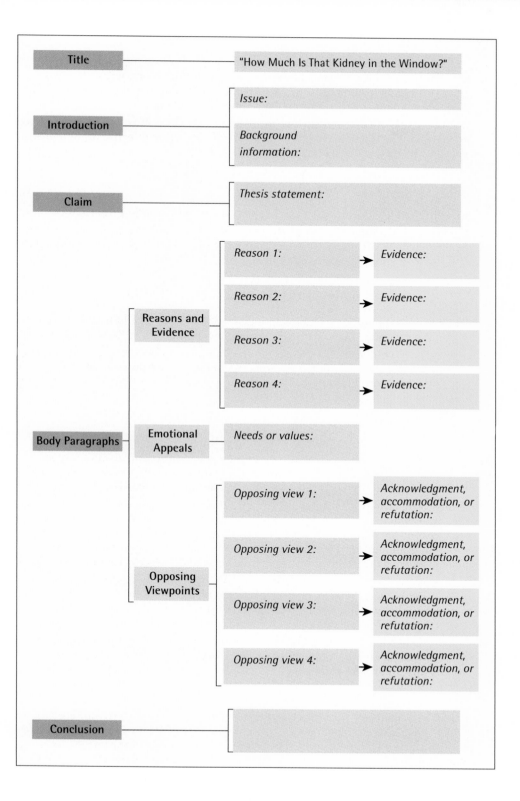

4. Identify the author's use of evidence. How does his use of statistics affect your acceptance of his argument? Does the mention of a controversial figure like Jack Kevorkian help or hinder Gottlieb's arguments? Explain.

5. Most of the essay is devoted to refuting opposing viewpoints, while very few reasons in support of organ sales are given directly. Is this an effective argument strategy, despite the lack of reasons?

Building Your Word Power

For a definition of **idiom,** *see the chart of commonly used language features on p. 21.*

1. Explain the idioms "slippery slope" (para. 8) and "gut reaction" (para. 9).

2. Explain the meaning of each of the following words as it is used in the reading: *fringe* (para. 3), *altruism* (5), *egalitarian* (7), *disproportionate* (7), and *provocative* (9). Refer to your dictionary as needed.

Reacting to the Reading: Discussion and Journal Writing

1. Discuss whether you would sell a kidney for $10,000 if it could be safely removed in another country to avoid any legal problems in the United States.

2. In class or in your journal, explore your feelings about being an organ donor. Have you notified anyone of your intentions to donate (or not donate) an organ in the case of a catastrophic injury? If not, would you consider doing so? Explain your decision.

Applying Your Skills: Writing Assignments

1. **Paragraph Assignment.** Donating a kidney is a form of altruism — a regard for the welfare of others. Choose another form of altruism (such as donating blood or volunteering at a food bank), and write a paragraph arguing why it is valuable.

2. Brainstorm a list of health-related topics that affect you or someone you know personally. Possible topics include affordable health insurance or treatments that are not covered by health insurance. Choose one that you feel strongly about, and write an argument essay using your own experiences to support your position. Be sure to explain the issue and your claim clearly and to recognize opposing views.

3. Brainstorm a list of ways college students might help people who are in hospitals or nursing homes. Write an open letter to your school arguing for funding to start a program that would benefit patients and the confined. Then write a response letter as if you were someone refuting your original argument.

4. **Combining Patterns.** Write an essay about an experience with a hospital or doctor that changed your opinion of organized medicine for the better or worse. Define any unfamiliar terms, and use examples to illustrate your thesis. End with an argument calling for the medical community to change or continue their efforts in this area.

5. **Internet Research.** Research the rules governing who gets priority in receiving organs. Two places to start are the Web sites for TransWeb at www.transweb.org/index.htm and the Organ Procurement and Transplantation Network at www.optn.org/policiesandbylaws/policies.asp. If healthier patients are more likely

to survive transplantation, should they get precedence over sicker patients? Should young people be given priority over older people? Do smokers or alcoholics have equal rights to receiving organs? What about people suffering from AIDS? Choose a narrow topic; then, using research from the Internet, argue for a position related to establishing priority in receiving organ donations.

"Strip-Mining" the Dead: When Human Organs Are for Sale

Gilbert Meilaender

Gilbert Meilaender (b. 1946), an associate editor of the *Journal of Religious Ethics* and a professor of Christian ethics at Valparaiso University, specializes in questions of religious ethics and bioethics. His books include *Body, Soul, and Bioethics* (1995), *Faith and Faithfulness: Basic Themes in Christian Ethics* (1997), and *Bioethics: A Primer for Christians* (1997). Meilaender is a member of the President's Bioethics Council.

In this essay, which originally appeared in *The National Review* in October 1999, Meilaender argues that humans feel repulsed by the idea of selling organs — and often by the idea of donating organs after death — for deeply moral reasons. As you read, pay attention to the way he questions judgments that many people accept without thinking. Consider how his argument differs from Bruce Gottlieb's. What positions do the writers share, and on what issues do they differ?

Focus on Understanding   Read to discover in what way the term *strip-mining* applies to the issue of organ sales.

Focus on the Topic   In class or in your journal, write about what motivates people to donate organs, either their own or those of deceased relatives.

Eliminate suffering and expand the range of human choice. That sentence expresses the moral wisdom toward which our society is moving, and it is very minimal wisdom indeed. We can observe this minimalism at work especially well in the realm of bioethics, where we seem unable to find any guidance other than (1) relieve suffering and (2) promote self-determination. In accordance with such wisdom, we have forged ahead in the use of new technologies at the beginning of life and — with constantly increasing pressure for assisted suicide — at the end of it.

Less noticed — and perhaps not quite as significant — is the continuing pressure to increase the supply of organs for transplant. For the past quarter-century, transplantation technology has made rapid progress, though the "success rates" given for transplants may often conceal an enormous amount of suffering and frustration endured by those who accept a transplant as the price of possible survival. During this time, there has been continuing debate about what policies ought to govern the procurement of organs from the dead for transplant. Should we simply wait to see whether the dying person, or, after death, his family, decides to offer usable organs? Should we require, as some states now do, that medical caregivers request donation? Should we presume that organs for transplant may be salvaged from a corpse unless the deceased had explicitly rejected the possibility or the family rejects it later? Should we "buy" organs, using financial incentives to encourage people to sell what they had not thought or wanted to give? And if we did use financial inducements, could one also sell organs such as kidneys even before death?

What we think about such questions depends on why we think some people   3 might hesitate to give organs for transplant. If their refusal is a thoughtless act, perhaps we simply need greater public education and awareness to encourage more people to give. If their refusal is not just thoughtless but wrong, perhaps we should authorize medical professionals routinely to salvage cadaver organs for transplant. If their refusal is selfish or, at least, self-regarding, perhaps we should appeal to their self-regarding impulses with an offer of financial compensation.

Moreover, if it is, as we are so often told, a "tragedy" or a "catastrophe" that   4 many die while waiting for an organ transplant, perhaps we need to be more daring in our public policy. That is the view of many who are in the transplant business and many who ponder transplantation as a public-policy issue. While these issues have been debated over the last several decades, our society has steadfastly refused to consider any form of payment for organs. "Giving" rather than "selling" has been the moral category governing organ procurement. Indeed, the National Organ Transplant Act of 1984 forbids "any person to knowingly acquire, receive, or otherwise transfer any human organ for valuable consideration for use in human transplantation, if the transfer affects interstate commerce."

It's not hard to understand our national reluctance to permit the buying   5 and selling of human organs for transplant, for it expresses a repugnance that is deeply rooted in important moral sentiments. In part, the very idea of organ transplantation — which is, after all, in Leon Kass's striking phrase, "a noble form of cannibalism" — is unsettling. If we cannot always articulate clearly the reasons that it troubles us, the sentiment is nonetheless powerful. To view the body — even the newly or nearly dead body — as simply a useful collection of organs requires that we stifle within ourselves a fundamental human response. "We do not," C. S. Lewis once wrote, "look at trees either as Dryads° or as beautiful objects while we cut them into beams; the first man who did so may have felt the price keenly, and the bleeding trees in Virgil and Spenser° may be far-off echos of that primeval sense of impiety." Far more powerful impulses must be overcome if we are to view the human form simply as a natural object available for our use. Perhaps we are right to view it as such when transplantation is truly lifesaving, but doing so exacts a cost. By insisting that organs must be given freely rather than bought and sold, we have tried to find a way to live with the cost. The "donated" organ — even separated from the body, objectified, and used — remains, in a sense, connected with the one who freely gave it, whose person we continue to respect. By contrast, buying and selling — even if it would provide more organs needed for transplant — would make of the body simply a natural object, at our disposal if the price is right.

Dryads: spiritual beings from Greek mythology thought to reside in nature, especially in forests; **bleeding trees in Virgil and Spenser:** Virgil was a Latin author who wrote the epic poem *Aeneid*, and Edmund Spenser was a sixteenth-century British poet; both wrote about trees that bled when snapped or uprooted

Our repugnance is rooted also in the sense that some things are simply not for sale. As a medium of exchange, money makes possible advanced civilization, which depends on countless exchanges in which our interdependence is expressed. But if we allow ourselves to suppose that it is a universal medium of exchange, we are bound to lose our moral bearings. Although there is nothing degrading about buying and selling, since exchange binds us together and allows us to delight in the diversity of goods, commerce enhances human life only when that life itself is not also turned into a commodity. Hence, our society has over time had to make clear that certain things — ecclesiastical and public offices, criminal justice, human beings themselves — may not be bought and sold.

Discussing the limits to money as a medium of exchange, Michael Walzer recounts an instructive story from our own history. In 1863, during the Civil War, the Union enacted an Enrollment and Conscription Act, which was the first military draft at the national level in our history. But the act contained a provision that allowed any man whose name was drawn in the lottery to purchase an exemption by paying $300 for a substitute (which, in effect, also offered an incentive for others who wanted or needed $300, even at the risk of death). Anti-draft riots broke out in July 1863 after the first drawing of lots, and we have never since — at least in such overt, crass form — allowed citizens to buy their way out of military service. It is one of those things that should not be for sale, one instance in which money should not be allowed to serve as a medium of exchange, and so we block that exchange.

Similarly, we have decided to block exchanges for human organs, even though they do take place in some other countries. That decision has been under attack for some time. It has even been criticized by Thomas Peters, for example, as — behold here the degradation of our public moral discourse — "imposing" the value of altruistic donation on those who do not appreciate such a value or "coercing" families "to accept concepts foreign to them at a time of great personal loss." But the first real crack in the public-policy dike appeared in May of 1999, when the state of Pennsylvania announced its intention to begin paying relatives of organ donors $300 toward funeral expenses of their deceased relative. (Clearly, $300 doesn't buy as much as it did in 1863.)

Pennsylvania's decision has been characterized by Charles Krauthammer as "strip-mining" the dead — and this in an essay defending the decision. It would, Krauthammer asserts, violate human dignity to permit the living to sell organs, but the newly dead body may be treated as a commodity if doing so promises "to alleviate the catastrophic shortage of donated organs." (Note, again, the language of catastrophe. Just as many workers might not have known their labor was "alienated" until Marxists told them, so we might not have thought it "catastrophic" that we die rather than strip-mine the human body in order to stay alive until transplant technology began to tell us it was.) Indeed, Krauthammer quite reasonably claims that the Pennsylvania program is, if anything, far too timid. If the idea is to get more organs for transplant, he suggests that not $300 but $3000 — paid directly to relatives rather than to funeral homes — might be more the ticket.

To the degree that he persuades us, however, we might well judge that 10 Krauthammer himself has been too timid. Pennsylvania's plan for compensation continues to operate within the organ-donation system currently in place. It aims simply to provide a somewhat greater incentive for people to donate organs. What it will not affect is the reluctance — based in sound moral sentiment — of medical caregivers to ask dying people or their families to consider organ donation. If we really face a tragedy of catastrophic proportions, we might do better to allow organ-procurement firms seeking a profit to be the middleman. (After all, a human kidney was recently offered for sale on the Internet auction site eBay — and the bidding reached $5.7 million before the company stopped it.) With profit to be made, firms would find ways to overcome our natural reluctance to ask others to strip-mine the dead body. We could deal not only with our reluctance to give organs but also with our reluctance to ask for them by letting the market do what it does best. That Krauthammer does not suggest this — even for organs from the dead — suggests to me that he finds more "dignity" than he thinks not only in still-living human beings but also in the newly dead body.

Or, again, if it is a catastrophe that we face, we might simply abandon the 11 claim that it is always necessary to wait for death before procuring organs for transplant. For example, as Robert Arnold and Stuart Youngner have noted, a ventilator-dependent patient could request that life support be removed and that, eight or so hours before, he be taken to the operating room and anesthetized, to have his kidneys, liver, and pancreas taken out. Bleeding vessels could be tied off, and the patient's heart would stop only after the ventilator was removed later that day, well before the patient could die of renal, hepatic, or pancreatic failure. And, of course, if our moral wisdom is confined to relieving suffering and respecting autonomy, we may find ourselves very hard pressed to explain why this should not be done — especially in the face of a "catastrophic shortage" of organs.

One might ask, If my death is an evil, why not at least try to get some good 12 for others out of it? If my corpse is no longer my person, as it surely is not, why not treat it as a commodity if doing so helps the living? Ah, but that corpse is my mortal remains. There is no way to think of my person apart from it and no way to gaze upon it without thinking of my person — which person is a whole web of human relations, not a thing or a commodity. A corpse is uncanny precisely because we cannot, without doing violence to our humanity, divorce it fully from the person. To treat those mortal remains with respect, to refuse to see them as merely in service of other goods, is our last chance to honor the "extraterritoriality" of each human life and to affirm that the human person is not simply a "part" of a human community. Perhaps, if we do so honor even the corpse, I or some others will not live as long as we might, but we will have taken at least a small step toward preserving the kind of society in which anyone might wish to live.

More than a quarter century ago, writing about "Attitudes toward the newly 13 dead," William F. May called attention to one of the Grimm Brothers tales about a young man who is incapable of horror. He does not shrink back from a hanged man, and he attempts to play with a corpse. His behavior might seem childish, but it is in fact inhuman. And his father sends him away "to learn how to shudder" — that is, to become human. In our society — where we devote enormous energy and money to keeping human beings alive — perhaps we too, in the face of proposals to strip-mine the dead, should consider learning once again how to shudder.

Understanding the Reading

1. What are Meilaender's reasons for opposing human organ sales?
2. Explain the meaning of the quotation that transplantation is "a noble form of cannibalism" (para. 5).
3. Why does Meilaender oppose organ sales but seem to approve of organ donation?
4. What policy did the state of Pennsylvania enact in the spring of 1999? According to the author, what does this policy *not* affect?

Visualizing the Reading

Analyze the effectiveness of Meilaender's argument by completing the following chart.

Element	Questions	Answers
The claim	What is the author's claim? Is it stated or implied?	
The support	What facts, statistics, expert opinions, examples, and personal experiences are presented? Are appeals made to needs, values, or both?	
Purpose and audience	What is the author's purpose for writing? To whom do the reasons, evidence, and emotional appeals seem targeted?	
The writer's credibility	Is the author qualified and knowledgeable? Does he establish common ground with readers?	
The strength of the argument	Does the author supply several reasons with relevant evidence to back up the claim? Does he use fallacies or unfair emotional appeals?	

Element	Questions	Answers
Opposing view-points	Does the author acknowledge, accommodate, or refute opposing viewpoints with logic and relevant evidence?	

Examining the Characteristics of Argument Essays

1. How effectively is Meilaender's claim stated?

2. What line of reasoning does he use to present his argument: inductive or deductive? Does he include enough evidence to support his findings? Explain.

3. Explain the analogy between the Civil War draft exemption and organ donation. Is it effective? Why?

4. The last paragraph includes a reference to a Grimm Brothers tale. Is this reference effective in concluding the essay? Why or why not?

Building Your Word Power

1. What is the connotative meaning of the word *salvage* as it is used throughout the reading?

2. Why does the author put the words *tragedy* and *catastrophe* in quotation marks in paragraph 4?

3. Explain the meaning of each of the following words as it is used in the reading: *bioethics* (para. 1), *catastrophe* (4), *ecclesiastical* (6), *uncanny* (12), and *extraterritoriality* (12). Refer to your dictionary as needed.

For a definition of **connotative meaning,** *see the chart of commonly used language features on p. 21.*

Reacting to the Reading: Discussion and Journal Writing

1. Strip-mining usually involves the practice of stripping away soil and land to mine and sell products. Discuss whether organ sales can be fairly compared to strip-mining. What similarities or differences are there?

2. Discuss your feelings about whether a still-living human being and a newly dead body should be treated with the same degree of respect and dignity.

Applying Your Skills: Writing Assignments

1. **Paragraph Assignment.** Human dignity is an important part of Meilandaer's appeal. Based on a situation in which your own dignity was threatened and then either lost or preserved, write a paragraph that argues for the importance of dignity.

2. Brainstorm a list of other ways to eliminate human suffering. Choose one, and argue that students should be more involved in this cause, explaining both why and how. You may need to do some research to obtain supporting information such as statistics or eyewitness accounts. Conclude with a statement on the importance of service to others.

3. Meilaender suggests that part of being human is knowing how to shudder. Is "shuddering" universal to all animals, or is it a cultural phenomenon unique to humans? Write an argument essay that explains whether you think the ability to shudder is a distinct and necessary human characteristic. To support your claim, use examples from your own experience.

4. Combining Patterns. Watch some commercials on television or read some advertisements in a magazine, taking notes of any instances of emotional appeal. Describe the different types of appeals that you observed, including their effectiveness. In an essay, classify your findings and present an argument for why certain types of emotional appeals have the strongest effect.

5. Internet Research. Research a health issue that is the subject of an ethical debate, such as stem cell research. Possible topics can be found at the Center for the Study of Bioethics News Page from the Medical College of Wisconsin: www.mcw.edu/bioethics/news.html. After researching a topic, write an argument essay that explains the ethical issues involved, states a claim that clearly expresses your position, and recognizes and refutes opposing viewpoints.

Comparing the Arguments

These two essays present differing viewpoints on the issue of organ donation. To be well informed on an issue, it is often necessary to research and compare two or more viewpoints in order to develop your own position. This skill, called **synthesis**, involves drawing together two or more sets of ideas and identifying similarities and differences in order to develop new ideas or to discover new insights about them. You will need to synthesize a variety of sources to write research papers, articles and essays to prepare for class discussions, and even lecture notes and textbook readings to study for tests. Use the following questions to compare the two readings on organ donation.

Building Your Critical Thinking Skills: Synthesizing Sources

1. Compare how each writer introduces the issue. In what context does each writer frame the issue?

2. Evaluate the evidence each author offers in support of his claim. Which author presents more substantial evidence? Explain.

3. Which writer's argument do you find to be more convincing? Why?

4. How do you think Gottlieb might respond to Meilaender's claim?

5. What did you learn about this topic from the essays? Can you make conclusions about the issue of selling organs on the basis of these two sources? Explain.

The Effect of Media on Children:
Is Violent Media Harmful?

A cursory surfing through the seemingly endless cable channels on television, day or night, will expose you to a wealth of violent material — from new and disturbing shows to old westerns featuring shootouts and hangings. No one would argue that excessively violent R-rated movies and television shows like *CSI* that focus on solving horrific crimes are appropriate for young viewers. But what does one make of the sometimes violent material that the vast majority of parents deem appropriate for children? Children of all ages are being assaulted by images of violence from television, movies, radio, and video games. Even though the rate of exposure may be more graphic and constant today, certainly one could argue that familiar fairy tales like "Hansel and Gretel" and "Little Red Riding Hood" — or Disney films such as *Tarzan* and *Snow White* — are just as filled with violence, and few people question their appropriateness for children.

As all forms of media become saturated with violent images and content, the issue arises whether exposure to simulated violence affects children — and if so, how. One position holds that viewing violence encourages children to perform violent acts themselves. Another viewpoint maintains that because violence is a part of life, children should be exposed to it so they will be better equipped to deal with it. Still others argue that some violent content may even have positive effects on children. The essays that follow present two different viewpoints on the effects of media violence on children. As you read, follow each argument closely, evaluating the evidence offered in support of each position.

It's Important to Feel Something
When You Kill

Dave Grossman and Gloria DeGaetano

Dave Grossman retired from the U.S. Army as a lieutenant colonel and is now the director of the Killology Research Group, an organization devoted to examining the effect of killing and other violent behavior on culture and society. Grossman also writes, teaches, and speaks about the psychology of killing and violence. He coauthored the book *Stop Teaching Our Kids to Kill: A Call to Action against TV, Movie and Video Game Violence* (1999) with Gloria DeGaetano, a well-known educator and writer on children and the media. DeGaetano is the founder and CEO of the Parent Coaching Institute, an organization dedicated to supporting parents in successfully raising their children. In addition to lecturing and giving workshops on parenting, she has published articles in numerous periodicals, including *McCall's* magazine and the *Boston Globe*.

This selection is taken from a chapter in *Stop Teaching Our Kids to Kill*. As you read, notice how the authors use graphic details to illustrate their points. Also pay attention to their use of statistics and data; this information provides depth to their argument.

Focus on Understanding   As you read, identify the relationship the authors see between playing violent interactive video games and learning to kill.

Focus on the Topic   In class or in your journal, explore the reasons for the popularity of interactive video games.

During the last two decades interactive video games have emerged as one of the most popular forms of entertainment, particularly among teens. According to the nonprofit organization Mediascope, "Globally, annual video game revenues now exceed $18 billion. In the United States alone, video game revenues exceed $10 billion annually, nearly double the amount Americans spend going to the movies. On average, American children who have home video game systems play with them about ninety minutes a day."[1]

The kids are changing with the technology — how could they not be? They are riding the technology curve in a way we are not and never can. On many levels it's wonderful to have them exposed to this brave new cyberworld; the opportunities for them to learn, the resources at their fingertips, are tremendous and hard to fathom. The World Wide Web is like a vast, almost limitless encyclopedia, and unlike *Encyclopaedia Britannica*, kids can talk to it and it talks back. So it's especially disconcerting to see armies of these very kids wandering through cyberspace mutilating and killing everything in their path — and having a great time doing it. It's the dark side of heightened technology, but one to which we ought to be paying much closer attention.

More than any other aspect of these new video games, it's the accuracy of the simulations — the carnage, the blood, the guts — that is so advanced. Realism is the Holy Grail° of the video game industry. And the latest technology leaves little to the imagination — the simulations seem less fake, and therefore more effective. Compare it, if you will, to a well-made horror movie with a very believable plot, set in a town not unlike your own, with characters that could be right out of your neighborhood. The reality of it will undoubtedly affect you, more so certainly than watching a low-budget picture like *Godzilla*.

So, immersed as we are in technology in all facets of our lives, it's not hard to understand why children's games are more advanced and sophisticated — they're like everything else these days. But the fact that, in the last few years, video game manufacturers have chosen to amplify gruesome violence (note that 49 percent of young teens indicate a preference for violent games, while only 2 percent prefer educational ones),[2] to make it a mainstay in their products,

Holy Grail: a cup or plate that according to legend was used by Jesus at the Last Supper and has long been searched for

seems a direct result of where the television and movie industry have taken *their* content.

The relationship between viewing violent television and films and being at- 5 tracted to these elevated forms of interactive violent video games is well documented. We've talked a lot about the desensitizing effect on-screen violence has on kids, and how it fosters a need for more graphic, real-life displays of carnage and mayhem to keep kids interested. The entertainment industry knows this better than anyone, and the makers of these games are way past the curve. Graphically violent video games like Doom, Postal, Duke Nukem, and Mortal Kombat serve up just what the doctor did not order.

And you can see why. The real selling point with these games is that you get 6 to pull the trigger, you inflict the damage, rather than just watching someone else do it. As graphic as the violence is on TV and in movies, it can't quite compete with a medium where you, not an actor, can control the action. It's a whole new level of involvement — and it's terrifying.

Any teacher or coach of young people will tell you that hands-on experience 7 is what teaches best. Repetition of movements and the hand-eye connection are invaluable for learning most skills. And, especially with children, hands-on learning is usually a lot more fun and interesting than the alternatives. It's precisely this that makes interactive video games so potent a learning tool. As researcher Patricia Greenfield points out, "Video games are the first medium to combine visual dynamism with an active participatory role for the child."[3] Television, film, and video game violence may all be imaginary, but the latter lets you put your hands on it, aim, and fire. We don't think we have to tell you how deadly the combination can be of viewing ultraviolent images with the amusement park fun of shooting at things until they drop. . . .

The effects of violent video games on young adults' arousal levels, hostile 8 feelings, and aggressive thoughts have been measured. Results indicated that college students who had played a violent virtual reality game had a higher heart rate, reported more dizziness and nausea, and exhibited more aggressive thoughts in a posttest than those who had played a nonviolent game.[4]

Another study examined differences in cardiovascular reactions and hos- 9 tility following nonviolent play and violent video game play.[5] The subjects were thirty male college undergraduate students. Only male subjects were used because most video games are male oriented, males frequent video game arcades more often than do females, and the gender gap in video game play widens with age until the undergraduate years. Hostility and cardiovascular reactivity were examined after subjects played either a nonviolent game of billiards or a violent video game. The video game, Mortal Kombat, was presented in either a less violent (MK1) or a more violent (MK2) version. Results indicated that subjects who played the video game had higher heart rate reactivity than those who played billiards. Subjects who played the MK2 version showed greater systolic blood pressure reactivity than those who played the MK1 version or billiards. Subjects who played MK2 scored higher on the hostility measures than those who played MK1, who in turn scored higher than those who played billiards.

These two studies indicate that adults, with fully developed brains and central nervous systems, can be impacted negatively by violent video games. What about children and teens whose brains and response mechanisms are in the process of development? They are much more vulnerable to physiological arousal and conditioning effects. 10

A real — and the newest — concern we have with our children's exposure to violent video games is what the devices teach them physically. The mechanical, interactive quality of a "First Person Shooter" game like Doom or 007 Golden Eye makes it so much more dangerous to society than images on a television screen, however violent. "Why?" we are constantly asked. "It's a game. It may be violent and it's probably better our children weren't exposed to it, but . . ." Well, it's a lot more than that. Certain types of these "games" are actually killing simulators, and they teach our kids to kill, much the same way the astronauts on Apollo 11 learned how to fly to the moon without ever leaving the ground. Believe it or not, simulators can be that good. Sounds far-fetched, we know. But consider the following. 11

The military learned in World War II that there is a vast gulf, a leap, between being an ordinary citizen and being someone who can aim and fire a gun at another human being with intent to kill, even in war. They discovered that firing at bull's-eye targets in training did not properly prepare soldiers for combat. Bull's-eye targets are not humans; they are not even simulated humans. And shooting at a bull's-eye target may teach someone the mechanics of aiming a gun, pulling the trigger, and dealing with the recoil, but it doesn't teach what it takes to look at another human being in the eyes, lift up a weapon, and knowingly try to take their life. Soldiers in that war spent a lot of time firing their guns into the air or not at all. In fact, the firing rate was a mere 15 percent among riflemen, which, from a military perspective, is like a 15 percent literacy rate among librarians.[6] . . . 12

Today soldiers learn to fire at realistic, man-shaped silhouettes that pop up in their field of vision. This "simulated" human being is the conditioning stimulus. The trainee has only a split second to engage the target. The conditioned response is to shoot the target, and then it drops. Stimulus-response, stimulus-response, stimulus-response — soldiers and police officers experience hundreds of repetitions of this. Later, when they're out on the battlefield or walking a beat and somebody pops up with a gun, reflexively they will shoot, and shoot to kill. 13

These devices are used extensively, and the scientific data on their effectiveness is exhaustive. It began with flight simulators and tank crew simulators half a century ago. Their introduction is undeniably responsible for increasing the firing rate from 15 to 20 percent in World War II to 95 percent in Vietnam. In the Falklands war, the Argentine soldiers, trained to fire at bull's-eye targets, had a firing rate of approximately 10 to 15 percent. The British, trained to kill using modern methods, had well over a 90 percent firing rate. Thus we know that, all other factors being equal, 75 percent to 80 percent of the killing on the modern battlefield is a direct result of the simulators.[7] 14

Now these simulators are in our homes and arcades — in the form of violent video games! If you don't believe us, you should know that one of the most 15 effective and widely used simulators developed by the United States Army in recent years, MACS (Multipurpose Arcade Combat Simulator), is nothing more than a modified Super Nintendo game (in fact, it closely resembles the popular game Duck Hunt, except with a plastic M16 firing at typical military targets on a TV screen). It is an excellent, ubiquitous military marksmanship-training device. The FATS trainer (Fire Arms Training Simulator), used by most law enforcement agencies in this country, is more or less identical to the ultraviolent video arcade game Time Crisis. Both teach the user (or player) to hit a target, both help rehearse the act of killing, and both come complete with guns that have recoil — the slide slams back when the trigger is pulled. . . .

The military and law enforcement agencies across the country are none too 16 pleased that these devices are in the hands of civilians, especially kids. In a lawsuit against the video game manufacturers that has come out of the killings in Paducah, Kentucky, the heads of several major national and international law enforcement training organizations have offered to testify that these video games are identical to law enforcement firearms training devices, except with the safety catch turned off. That should say a lot. The video game industry boasts about the real quality of their products; the military and police are wondering why on earth such technology is on the street. What more proof do we need that these games are anything *but* games?

Across America we are reaping the bitter harvest of this "training" as ever 17 more kids shoot their girlfriends or their teachers or other individuals that they have grudges against. A horrific development in this is that rather than just stopping with their intended target, these kids keep firing — and a simple grudge turns into a mass murder. The point is, these games are indeed affecting our children and we can't hide behind the myriad other excuses when kids "go off." Because when they do, they do so in all the ways these games train them — to kill every living person in front of them until they run out of bullets or run out of targets. That results in a lot of dead bodies.

Michael Carneal, the fourteen-year-old boy who walked into a Paducah 18 school and opened fire on a prayer group meeting that was breaking up, never moved his feet during his rampage. He never fired far to the right or left, never far up or down. He simply fired once at everything that popped up on his "screen." It is not natural to fire once at each target. The normal, almost universal, response is to fire at a target until it drops and then move on to the next target. This is the defensive reaction that will save our lives, the human instinctual reaction — eliminate the threat quickly. Not to shoot once and then go on to another target before the first threat has been eliminated. But most video games teach you to fire at each target only once, hitting as many targets as you can as fast as you can in order to rack up a high score. And many video games give bonus effects . . . for head shots. It's awful to note that of Michael Carneal's eight shots he had eight hits, all head and upper torso, three dead and one paralyzed. And this from a kid who, prior to stealing that gun, had never shot a real handgun in his life! . . .

The incident that really brought the issue to the public's attention, though, 19 was the Columbine High School massacre, in Littleton, Colorado. It was well documented that Dylan Klebold and Eric Harris were literally obsessed with playing the video game Doom and other such games. And they were very good at it. These boys, like the other boys mentioned, practiced for hundreds and hundreds of hours, perfecting their craft. Therefore, it should not be altogether surprising that their killing spree resembled something out of the cyberworld of a typical Doom scenario. (In fact, Eric Harris reprogrammed his edition of Doom so that it looked like his neighborhood, complete with the houses of the people he hated.) They moved from room to room, stalking their prey and killing almost everyone in their path. And, not unlike most kids' response to video game mayhem, Dylan Klebold and Eric Harris laughed the killings off.

The realism of a game like Doom, played on the home computer, can be ex-   20
treme, especially with the multitude of "add-on" packages available to upgrade systems. For example, in the wake of the Columbine massacre, many in the game industry claimed that Doom, played only with a mouse or keyboard, can't possibly teach a player real combat skills. First, we have to understand that even when Doom is played with a mouse, it is still a good enough combat sim-ulator that the Marine Corps uses a modified version of it (called Marine Doom) to teach recruits how to kill. They use it as a tactical training device, as opposed to teaching motor skills — although when used with a pistol grip joystick it has some value there, too. Its primary value is in developing the will to kill by re-peatedly rehearsing the act until it feels natural.

It's safe to say that such technology is much more dangerous in the hands   21
of kids than among soldiers and cops — these above examples prove that, as does common sense. There often are no safeguards at home and in arcades, no supervision, nor anyone around to put this technology into perspective for a child. In the military and law enforcement worlds, the right option is often not to shoot, and recruits receive extensive training about this. Often, recruits are reprimanded, punished, or even "failed" and kicked out for making too many mistakes — that is, for shooting the wrong targets. But when a kid puts his quarter in a video machine, there is *always* the intention to shoot. There is never an incentive not to shoot. And there's always some stimulus to keep excitement high, heart rate up, thinking functions closed down. This process is extraordi-narily powerful and frightening. The result is ever more home-made pseudoso-ciopaths who kill reflexively, even when they don't intend to. . . .

So with all the evidence to suggest that these games are dangerous — that   22
they're modeled after military killing simulators, that they are super-violent and graphic, that the user is rewarded for killing, and that kids are playing with these games way too often and for too long — it is particularly egregious that they are being marketed to kids, and marketed in ways that highlight all that is bad for them. What kind of message does this send? Well, yet another on-line ad for Kingpin° gives us a pretty good indication: "The Creators of Redneck Rampage are about to bring you a new, urban drama that finally proves that crime pays."[8] As we ourselves tolerate these games and even label them fun, we are also telling our children that slower-paced, less emotionally arousing screen fare is boring. Arouse instead of awaken; excite instead of examine; splatter in-stead of study — this is what we're telling them. And they're listening.

Kingpin: video game that features a criminal world and extreme violence

Notes

1. Joel Federman, S. Carbone, Helen Chen, and William Munn, eds., *The Social Effects of Electronic Games: An Annotated Bibliography* (Studio City: Mediascope, 1996), i.
2. Jeanne B. Funk, "Reevaluating the Impact of Video Games," *Clinical Pediatrics*, vol. 32, no. 2, 1993, 86–90.
3. Eugene Provenzo, *Video Kids* (Cambridge: Harvard University Press, 1991), 47–48.
4. Sandra L. Calvert and Siu-Lan Tan, "Impact of Virtual Reality on Young Adults' Physiological Arousal and Aggressive Thoughts: Interaction versus Observation," *Journal of Applied Developmental Psychology*, vol. 5, no. 1, 125–139.
5. Mary E. Ballard and J. Rose Wiest, "Mortal Kombat: The Effects of Violent Video Technology on Males' Hostility and Cardiovascular Responding," March 8, 1995, paper presented at the sixty-first Biennial Meeting of the Society for Research in Child Development, Indianapolis, March 30–April 2, 1995.
6. S. L. A. Marshall, *Men against Fire*. Gloucester: Peter Smith, 1978, 51.
7. Ken Murray, Lt. Col. Dave Grossman, and R. W. Kentridge, "Behavioral Psychology," in *Encyclopedia of Violence, Peace and Conflict*. San Diego: Academic Press, 1999.
8. "Kingpin: Life of Crime," http://www.interplay.com/kingpin.

Understanding the Reading

1. According to the authors, what factors explain the popularity of interactive video games?

2. In what ways do violent video games alter players' attitudes toward killing? What physical effects do these games have on people while they are playing?

3. What do the military and the police teach trainees about shooting that video game players do not learn?

4. What happened at Paducah, and how do the authors use this incident to support their argument?

Visualizing the Reading

Study the boys shown in the photograph on the previous page. What emotions do they exhibit? Explain how their interaction with the video game does or does not support the authors' claim. If it does, suggest a place in the text where the authors could use this photograph to support their argument. If the authors had the opportunity to speak to the boys' parents, what do you imagine they would say? How might the boys themselves counter this argument?

Examining the Characteristics of Argument Essays

1. State the authors' claim in your own words.
2. Identify the main reasons the authors give to support their argument. Which ones do you find to be most compelling? Explain.
3. Evaluate the evidence that the authors offer in support of each reason. What types of evidence are included? Is this evidence convincing? Why or why not?
4. The authors acknowledge that advances in technology can be wonderful (para. 2), but they do not recognize or refute any other opposing viewpoints. Does this weaken their argument? Explain.
5. What other patterns of development besides argument do the authors use to support their claim?

Building Your Word Power

1. Explain the phrase "riding the technology curve" in paragraph 2.
2. Evaluate the use of the word *splatter* in the final paragraph. What does this vivid language contribute?
3. Explain the meaning of each of the following words as it is used in the reading: *disconcerting* (para. 2), *carnage* (3), *dynamism* (7), *ubiquitous* (15), and *myriad* (17). Refer to your dictionary as needed.

Reacting to the Reading: Discussion and Journal Writing

1. Discuss violence in schools. Evaluate its presence or absence in the secondary school you attended.
2. In class or in your journal, discuss your experiences with interactive video games. Do you enjoy playing them? What types of games do you prefer?

Applying Your Skills: Writing Assignments

1. **Paragraph Assignment.** Write a paragraph in which you explain to a young boy why he should not play violent video games.
2. The authors are critical of interactive video games and do not consider their possible benefits. Brainstorm a list of benefits of playing such video games. Develop an argument claiming that video games are a legitimate form of entertainment.
3. Brainstorm a list of situations in which violence is necessary and justifiable. Choose one, and write an argument essay that defends or refutes the use of vio-

lence in this case. Be sure to describe the type of situation where violence is justified, and include evidence and examples to support your claim.

4. Choose a form of entertainment (other than video games) — such as listening to a type of music, playing a sport, or watching movies — that some people consider unproductive or even harmful. Consider both the positive and negative effects of this pastime. Then write an argument essay supporting your position on whether this type of entertainment is primarily beneficial or detrimental.

5. **Combining Patterns.** Video games are one of many outgrowths of technology. Brainstorm a list of other types of technology (cell phones, PDAs, digital cameras, and the like). Choose one, and in an essay describe its function, explain the reasons for its popularity, and argue whether its overall impact has been positive or negative.

6. **Internet Research.** Youth violence is a social issue of great concern in our schools and communities. Research this issue in terms of how different groups are fighting against it. Information about one such organization, the Washington Physicians for Social Responsibility, can be found at www.wpsr.org/vprevention/default.htm. After researching some different approaches to this problem, choose one; in an essay, make a claim about the usefulness of the program based on your research.

Violent Media Is Good for Kids

Gerard Jones

Gerard Jones is the creator of a syndicated comic strip, the author of five books, and the writer of several graphic novels, including *Batman: Fortunate Son* (1999). He founded the organization Media Power for Children, and he serves as adviser to the Comparative Media Studies graduate program at the Massachusetts Institute of Technology.

The following essay originally appeared in *Mother Jones* magazine on June 28, 2000. Consider the evidence Jones brings forward to support an argument that runs counter to what most Americans believe. Notice, too, the audience that Jones seems to address, and consider why he may feel that this group in particular needs convincing.

Focus on Understanding   Read to discover what the author means by "creative violence" (para. 12).

Focus on the Topic   In class or in your journal, consider what effect violence in television, movies, novels, or music has had on you.

At 13 I was alone and afraid. Taught by my well-meaning, progressive, English-teacher parents that violence was wrong, that rage was something to be overcome and cooperation was always better than conflict, I suffocated my deepest fears and desires under a nice-boy persona. Placed in a small, experimental school that was wrong for me, afraid to join my peers in their bumptious rush into adolescent boyhood, I withdrew into passivity and loneliness. My parents, not trusting the violent world of the late 1960s, built a wall between me and the crudest elements of American pop culture.

Then the Incredible Hulk smashed through it.

One of my mother's students convinced her that Marvel Comics, despite their apparent juvenility and violence, were in fact devoted to lofty messages of pacifism and tolerance. My mother borrowed some, thinking they'd be good for me. And so they were. But not because they preached lofty messages of benevolence. They were good for me because they were juvenile. And violent.

The character who caught me, and freed me, was the Hulk: overgendered and undersocialized, half-naked and half-witted, raging against a frightened world that misunderstood and persecuted him. Suddenly I had a fantasy self to carry my stifled rage and buried desire for power. I had a fantasy self who was a self: unafraid of his desires and the world's disapproval, unhesitating and effective in action. "Puny boy follow Hulk!" roared my fantasy self, and I followed.

I followed him to new friends — other sensitive geeks chasing their own inner brutes — and I followed him to the arrogant, self-exposing, self-assertive, superheroic decision to become a writer. Eventually, I left him behind, followed more sophisticated heroes, and finally my own lead along a twisting path to a career and an identity. In my 30s, I found myself writing action movies and comic books. I wrote some Hulk stories, and met the geek-geniuses who created him. I saw my own creations turned into action figures, cartoons, and computer games. I talked to the kids who read my stories. Across generations, genders, and ethnicities I kept seeing the same story: people pulling themselves out of emotional traps by immersing themselves in violent stories. People integrating the scariest, most fervently denied fragments of their psyches into fuller senses of selfhood through fantasies of superhuman combat and destruction.

I have watched my son living the same story — transforming himself into a 6 bloodthirsty dinosaur to embolden himself for the plunge into preschool, a Power Ranger to muscle through a social competition in kindergarten. In the first grade, his friends started climbing a tree at school. But he was afraid: of falling, of the centipedes crawling on the trunk, of sharp branches, of his friends' derision. I took my cue from his own fantasies and read him old Tarzan comics, rich in combat and bright with flashing knives. For two weeks he lived in them. Then he put them aside. And he climbed the tree.

But all the while, especially in the wake of the recent burst of school shoot- 7 ings, I heard pop psychologists insisting that violent stories are harmful to kids, heard teachers begging parents to keep their kids away from "junk culture," heard a guilt-stricken friend with a son who loved Pokémon° lament, "I've turned into the bad mom who lets her kid eat sugary cereal and watch cartoons!"

That's when I started the research. 8

"Fear, greed, power-hunger, rage: these are aspects of our selves that we try 9 not to experience in our lives but often want, even need, to experience vicariously through stories of others," writes Melanie Moore, Ph.D., a psychologist who works with urban teens. "Children need violent entertainment in order to explore the inescapable feelings that they've been taught to deny, and to reintegrate those feelings into a more whole, more complex, more resilient selfhood."

Moore consults to public schools and local governments, and is also raising 10 a daughter. For the past three years she and I have been studying the ways in which children use violent stories to meet their emotional and developmental needs — and the ways in which adults can help them use those stories healthily. With her help I developed Power Play, a program for helping young people improve their self-knowledge and sense of potency through heroic, combative storytelling.

We've found that every aspect of even the trashiest pop-culture story can 11 have its own developmental function. Pretending to have superhuman powers helps children conquer the feelings of powerlessness that inevitably come with being so young and small. The dual-identity concept at the heart of many superhero stories helps kids negotiate the conflicts between the inner self and the public self as they work through the early stages of socialization. Identification with a rebellious, even destructive, hero helps children learn to push back against a modern culture that cultivates fear and teaches dependency.

At its most fundamental level, what we call "creative violence" — head- 12 bonking cartoons, bloody videogames, playground karate, toy guns — gives

Pokémon: popular Japanese cartoon

children a tool to master their rage. Children will feel rage. Even the sweetest and most civilized of them, even those whose parents read the better class of literary magazines, will feel rage. The world is uncontrollable and incomprehensible; mastering it is a terrifying, enraging task. Rage can be an energizing emotion, a shot of courage to push us to resist greater threats, take more control, than we ever thought we could. But rage is also the emotion our culture distrusts the most. Most of us are taught early on to fear our own. Through immersion in imaginary combat and identification with a violent protagonist, children engage the rage they've stifled, come to fear it less, and become more capable of utilizing it against life's challenges.

I knew one little girl who went around exploding with fantasies so violent   13
that other moms would draw her mother aside to whisper, "I think you should know something about Emily. . . ." Her parents were separating, and she was small, an only child, a tomboy at an age when her classmates were dividing sharply along gender lines. On the playground she acted out "Sailor Moon"°

Sailor Moon: Japanese anime series about a fourteen-year-old schoolgirl who fights evil

fights, and in the classroom she wrote stories about people being stabbed with knives. The more adults tried to control her stories, the more she acted out the roles of her angry heroes: breaking rules, testing limits, roaring threats.

Then her mother and I started helping her tell her stories. She wrote them,   14
performed them, drew them like comics: sometimes bloody, sometimes tender, always blending the images of pop culture with her own most private fantasies. She came out of it just as fiery and strong, but more self-controlled and socially competent: a leader among her peers, the one student in her class who could truly pull boys and girls together.

I worked with an older girl, a middle-class "nice girl," who held herself to-   15
gether through a chaotic family situation and a tumultuous adolescence with gangsta rap. In the mythologized street violence of Ice T, the rage and strutting of his music and lyrics, she found a theater of the mind in which she could be powerful, ruthless, invulnerable. She avoided the heavy drug use that sank many of her peers, and flowered in college as a writer and political activist.

I'm not going to argue that violent entertainment is harmless. I think it has   16
helped inspire some people to real-life violence. I am going to argue that it's

helped hundreds of people for every one it's hurt, and that it can help far more if we learn to use it well. I am going to argue that our fear of "youth violence" isn't well-founded on reality, and that the fear can do more harm than the reality. We act as though our highest priority is to prevent our children from growing up into murderous thugs — but modern kids are far more likely to grow up too passive, too distrustful of themselves, too easily manipulated.

We send the message to our children in a hundred ways that their craving 17 for imaginary gun battles and symbolic killings is wrong, or at least dangerous. Even when we don't call for censorship or forbid "Mortal Kombat,"° we moan to other parents within our kids' earshot about the "awful violence" in the entertainment they love. We tell our kids that it isn't nice to play-fight, or we steer them from some monstrous action figure to a pro-social doll. Even in the most progressive households, where we make such a point of letting children feel what they feel, we rush to substitute an enlightened discussion for the raw material of rageful fantasy. In the process, we risk confusing them about their natural aggression in the same way the Victorians confused their children about their sexuality. When we try to protect our children from their own feelings and fantasies, we shelter them not against violence but against power and selfhood.

Mortal Kombat:
violent video game

Understanding the Reading

1. Summarize the reasons Jones presents to convince readers that children need violent entertainment.
2. What effect did reading comic books have on the author and his son?
3. Why does the author feel that it is beneficial for children to be exposed to "creative violence"?
4. According to Jones, how can experiencing violent cartoons or video games help children get through various developmental stages?

Visualizing the Reading

Evaluate the types of evidence that Jones provides to support his claim by completing the following chart. For each type of evidence listed, provide at least one example from the reading. The first one has been done for you.

Type of Evidence	Example from the Essay
Personal experience	1. Reading comics as a boy helped the author gain confidence and eventually led to his becoming an action movie and comic book writer (para. 1–5).
Expert opinion	
Media examples	

Examining the Characteristics of Argument Essays

1. Locate the author's thesis, and state his claim in your own words. Is his presentation of the claim effective? Why or why not?

2. Which reasons in the argument do Jones's examples support? Is his evidence convincing? Explain.

3. To what needs and values does Jones appeal?

4. What opposing viewpoints does Jones recognize? Does he refute them? If so, how?

5. Jones uses a sentence fragment (a group of words that lacks either a complete subject or a verb) at the end of paragraph 3. Although college students should avoid using fragments in their writing, fragments do serve a purpose in less formal writing situations. For what purpose does Jones use this fragment?

Building Your Word Power

For a definition of **metaphor**, *see the chart of commonly used language features on p. 21.*

1. What does the author mean by the metaphor "then the Incredible Hulk smashed through it" used in paragraph 2?

2. Explain the meaning of each of the following words as it is used in the reading: *pacifism* (para. 3), *lament* (7), *protagonist* (12), *tumultuous* (15), and *invulnerable* (15). Refer to your dictionary as needed.

Reacting to the Reading: Discussion and Journal Writing

1. Do you agree that "creative violence" gives children a tool to master their rage? Explain your reasons.

2. Do you think that girls have the same need as boys to experience feelings vicariously through violent stories? Why or why not?

3. In class or in your journal, describe a movie, television, or literary character that you especially enjoyed or identified with as a child. What benefit did your exposure to this character provide for you?

Applying Your Skills: Writing Assignments

1. **Paragraph Assignment.** Is the violence portrayed in children's fairy tales similar to or different from the violence portrayed in comic books, on television, or in movies? Make a claim about this, including a few reasons to support it.

2. Take the opposing viewpoint: Write an article condemning violent media for children. Be sure to address the arguments that Jones presents, and include convincing evidence to support your claim.

3. Voluntary rating systems have been implemented to enable consumers to know the appropriateness of the content of video games, television shows, movies, and popular music. Do you think such systems have been successful? Why or why not? Write an essay arguing for or against the use of rating systems.

4. **Combining Patterns.** Should parents control older teenagers' access to offensive or violent video games, television shows, movies, Web pages, or types of music? Write an essay that presents an argument for or against allowing seventeen- or

eighteen-year-olds to view such material. Include your thoughts on the causes and effects of forbidding teenagers to see things that their parents deem "objectionable."

5. Internet Research. Visit the site for Marvel Entertainment at www.marvel .com/dotcomics/index.htm and research the different comic book characters featured or read some of the comic books available online. Identify some positive traits or healthy fantasies depicted in these comics. Then write an argument essay that describes how some comics could positively influence a young person. Use examples from your research to support your claim.

Comparing the Arguments

Most of your research in college will entail working with multiple sources. Sometimes these sources will present different views of a single issue. When you compare different sources, you are using **synthesis**, the process of comparing and putting ideas together to create new ideas or to discover new insights about them. Use the following questions to compare the two readings on the effect of violent media on children.

Building Your Critical Thinking Skills: Synthesizing Sources

1. Jones begins with a personal anecdote, whereas Grossman and DeGaetano begin with statistics. Which approach do you find more engaging? Which introduction is more effective in introducing the issue?

2. Compare the tones of the two essays. How do the tones differ? Is one of the tones more appropriate for the issue under discussion? If yes, why?

3. Evaluate the evidence offered in each essay to support the claim. Which essay presents more substantial and compelling evidence? Explain.

4. How do the essays differ in purpose?

5. Which argument do you find to be more convincing? Why?

Civil Liberties: Does the Patriot Act Go Too Far?

Passed just forty-five days after the 9/11 attacks, the USA Patriot Act enhances law enforcement efforts to monitor and arrest potential terrorists. The USA Patriot Act stands for "Uniting and Strengthening America by Providing Appropriate Tools Required to Intercept and Obstruct Terrorism." This legislation was passed by the House and Senate and then signed into law by President George Bush on October 26, 2001. The law gives law enforcement agencies new ways to find and stop terrorism by expanding the available tools in areas such as surveillance, conducting investigations, and obtaining court orders. The law also facilitates communication among various law enforcement agencies.

Despite its overwhelming support in both the House and the Senate at the time of signing, the Patriot Act remains controversial as Americans struggle with the question of just how much of their civil liberties they are willing to give up in the fight against terror. In both the House and the Senate, bills have been proposed that would limit the power of the Patriot Act. Further questions about the Act's power have been raised as news reports describe alleged abuses of the Act where it has been used to investigate nonterrorist crimes. Nevertheless, most Americans continue to support the bill and its efforts to combat terrorism. The two following readings present opposing viewpoints on this issue. As you read, identify what specific provisions of the Act they support or oppose and the reasons each author offers in support of his or her position.

Who's Reading over Your Shoulder?

Zara Gelsey

Zara Gelsey is a writer and director of communications for the Center for Cognitive Liberty and Ethics, a nonprofit law and policy center devoted to preserving freedom of thought and civil liberties. Gelsey's essay concerns one aspect of the USA Patriot Act: the right of the FBI to procure library records, including book circulation and Internet usage, without having to demonstrate probable cause.

This article first appeared in the September–October 2002 edition of *The Humanist*. As you read, notice how the author begins with an emotional appeal. This technique sets the tone for the article and hints at the viewpoint Gelsey is preparing to share.

Focus on Understanding   Read to discover what the author thinks about the FBI's ability to review an individual's library records.

Focus on the Topic   In class or in your journal, explain how you would feel if you knew someone was keeping track of the books and magazines you read. Would it influence your choices in reading matter? Explain.

I hate the feeling of someone reading over my shoulder. Not only is it superficially distracting, but it often affects how I respond to the text. Being conscious of being watched inhibits my thinking because I find myself reading through my watcher's eyes. It makes me suddenly self-conscious, wondering if the observer is making faulty suppositions about me based on the material I'm reading. The bored businessperson next to me on the train isn't a big deal, but the thought of the FBI peering over my shoulder in the public library definitely puts me on edge.

Ever since the U.S.A. PATRIOT Act was passed by Congress in October 2001, the FBI has been reading over our shoulders by visiting libraries across the country to demand library patrons' reading records and other files. Under the PATRIOT Act, the FBI doesn't have to demonstrate "probable cause" of criminal activity to request records; in fact, the so-called search warrant is issued by a secret court. Once granted, it entitles the FBI to procure any library records pertaining to book circulation, Internet use, or patron registration. Librarians can even be compelled to cooperate with the FBI in monitoring Internet usage.

This sort of secrecy is not only chilling, it is ripe for potential abuse. A similar Cold War version of library monitoring was called the Library Awareness Program, through which FBI agents specifically targeted Soviet and eastern European nationals. The American Library Association (ALA) effectively fought the LAP then and is now standing up to the PATRIOT Act searches. ALA policy on governmental intimidation, established in 1981, unequivocally opposes "the use of any governmental prerogative which leads to the intimidation of the individual or the citizenry from the exercise of free expression." The ALA sees the new FBI policy for what it is: blatant intimidation of patrons.

But beyond FBI intimidation tactics, the new library surveillance program is bound to backfire. What one reads does say something about one's interests — but it may say different things to different people. If one only sees a few details about someone else's life, their actions can easily be contorted to fit the observer's version of reality.

This is a classic sitcom plot line: an observer misconstrues a sequence of unrelated details and then has a skewed perception of the protagonist. Perhaps the observer reads a personal letter that is lying on a coffee table but doesn't realize it is part of a novel-in-progress. Based on this bit of information, the observer constructs conclusions, with a succession of trivial actions seemingly reinforcing the observer's misperceptions, all to the delight of the omniscient audience.

By seeking to discover what books certain people are reading, the FBI falls right into the role of the ill-informed observer in a similar plot line being played out in libraries across the country. Only it's not so delightful when the FBI concludes you're a terrorist because you're doing research at your local library for an article on suicide bombings and have amassed a circulation record it deems suspicious. A person who reads a book intending to make a bomb could be a suspect — as could anyone researching terrorist bombings in order to prevent them.

The same knowledge can be used for "good" or "evil." The fateful tree in the 7 Garden of Eden represented the knowledge of good and evil — opposing values intertwined on one tree. The FBI can't possibly know the intent of knowledge harvested from books, and affording the agency the opportunity to pretend it can is incredibly dangerous. Just as a person wearing rose-colored glasses° sees everything rosy, so the FBI is predisposed to find suspicious facts. If the FBI wants to scour libraries looking for "suspicious" reading records, it's going to find them — but its perception is inherently skewed by its intent.

wearing rose-colored glasses: seeing things optimistically

I view reading as access to information; the FBI views it as an indictment. 8 Government suddenly fears domestic suicide bombings, so reading lists are examined and suddenly an innocent researcher is a suspect. In the worst case scenario, details could be dragged from one's past which seemingly support such suspicions. In the best case scenario, the FBI has wasted a lot of time and tax dollars on tracking a nonexistent threat. Meanwhile, all of us feel the presence of Big Brother reading over our shoulders.

Yes, we want protection from terrorists and we want our government to 9 root out those who intend to harm us. But surveillance always spreads beyond its original purpose, justified each step of the way by manufactured fear and better-safe-than-sorry rationales.

We saw last winter how the War on Drugs was deftly tied to the tail of the 10 War on Terrorism. Today the FBI is looking for records of people who check out books on bomb-making; tomorrow it may question why you've checked out books about the Colombian drug war.

While the FBI may never visit your library — not that you'll know if they do, 11 as librarians are barred by law from disclosing the FBI's presence — this program of surveillance still has a chilling effect on cognitive liberty. The feeling of being monitored inhibits freedom of thought.

Take for instance Winston Smith in George Orwell's *1984*. When Winston 12 gets up the nerve to hide from the omnipresent telescreen to indulge in writing with pen and paper — an act not expressly forbidden but punishable nonetheless — he "seemed not merely to have lost the power of expressing himself, but even to have forgotten what it was he originally intended to say." Excessive surveillance trained him to self-censor, thereby stifling his creative and cognitive abilities. Likewise, the FBI's surveillance is bound to have a chilling effect on seekers of knowledge who rely on the public library system. It's implied that you'd better watch what you read because the FBI will be watching too. Intimidating readers in such a manner is, in effect, controlling what we read and how we think.

Freedom of thought and the freedom to read are intertwined. And while 13 monitoring library records isn't as direct as banning books, it is bound to cause self-censorship among readers — which may be the intended result anyway. The government may not be able to ban a book, so instead it will make it suspect to read that book. Thus, the FBI circumvents the First Amendment by threatening readers rather than prohibiting what they read.

We may not always like what people do with some of the information they 14 glean, but their right to do so is what ensures everybody's right of access to information. As Supreme Court Justice Anthony M. Kennedy recently observed in the majority opinion in *Ashcroft v. Free Speech Coalition:*°

> The mere tendency of speech to encourage unlawful acts is not sufficient reason for banning it. . . . First Amendment freedoms are most in danger when the government seeks to control thought or to justify its laws for that impermissible end. The right to think is the beginning of freedom, and speech must be protected from the government because speech is the beginning of thought.

Under the guise of protecting us from terrorism, these surveillance activi-15 ties intimidate library patrons by spying over their shoulders, collecting reading lists, and tracking Internet usage. The FBI is policing our minds by purporting to read them. Of course we want to kept safe — but not to the extent that we are patrolled and treated as suspect. Giving up privacy rights can't guarantee physical safety, but it will almost certainly inhibit intellectual freedom and limit cognitive liberty. We Americans who cherish our freedoms should seriously consider whether or not this is a compromise we are willing to make.

Ashcroft v. Free Speech Coalition: Supreme Court case (2002) that held that pornography is a danger to children only when it includes actual children, thereby providing First Amendment protection for any other pornography.

Understanding the Reading

1. According to the author, why are the freedom of thought and the freedom to read interrelated?
2. In what way does the author think the FBI is using the Patriot Act to evade the First Amendment?
3. Explain how the outcome of surveillance of what someone reads might be similar to a classic sitcom plot line.

Visualizing the Reading

Effective arguments include evidence to support each reason. The evidence may include facts, statistics, personal experience, or expert testimony. In the following table, list the evidence that Gelsey uses to support each reason in her argument. In the final column, rate the effectiveness of her evidence by explaining whether it is relevant, adequate, and convincing.

Reasons	Evidence (list)	Effectiveness (explain)
Secret monitoring of library records is "ripe for potential abuse" (para. 3).		
What one reads indicates different things to different people.		
"[S]urveillance always spreads beyond its original purpose" (para. 9).		
Surveillance will cause self-censorship.		

Examining the Characteristics of Argument Essays

1. What is Gelsey's claim? Highlight the sentence in which it is stated.
2. Gelsey makes use of a number of direct quotations. Is this type of evidence adequate and convincing? If not, what additional types of evidence would strengthen her argument?
3. What emotional appeals does Gelsey make? To what needs or values does she appeal?
4. Gelsey's audience is likely to include a combination of agreeing, neutral and wavering, and disagreeing readers. In light of this broad mix, how effectively does she acknowledge opposing viewpoints? Explain the effectiveness of her approach.

Building Your Word Power

For a definition of ***allusion****, see the chart of commonly used language features on p. 21.*

1. Explain the allusions to the Garden of Eden (para. 7) and the novel *1984* (para. 12).
2. Explain the meaning of each of the following words as it is used in the reading: *suppositions* (para. 1), *procure* (2), *unequivocally* (3), *misconstrues* (5), *protagonist* (5), *omniscient* (5), *cognitive* (11), *omnipresent* (12), and *circumvents* (13). Refer to your dictionary as needed.

Reacting to the Reading: Discussion and Journal Writing

1. Discuss the quotation by Supreme Court Justice Anthony M. Kennedy: "The right to think is the beginning of freedom, and speech must be protected from the government because speech is the beginning of thought" (para. 14). Explain why you agree or disagree with this statement.
2. In class or in your journal, explain what rights to privacy you are willing to give up in order to fight the war on terror.

Applying Your Skills: Writing Assignments

1. Paragraph Assignment. To what extent should librarians who feel that surveillance of reading materials is a violation of one's civil liberties be obliged to cooperate with the FBI under the Patriot Act? Write a paragraph taking a stand on the question, offering reasons to support your position.

2. Take the opposing viewpoint: Write an article supporting the search of patrons' library records. Be sure to address the arguments that Gelsey presents and to recognize opposing viewpoints.

3. Should books and Internet sites that describe how to make bombs or create poisons be allowed? Should potentially dangerous or "offensive" books, Web sites, or CDs be banned from public libraries? Write an essay supporting your position on censorship of this type of information.

4. If the FBI is interested in what people read, what other activities might reveal the potential to be a terrorist? Brainstorm a list of possible activities (movies viewed, friendships, religious affiliation, etc.), choose one, and explain how it may reveal a potential for terrorist activity. Develop an argument describing what level of monitoring, if any, is justifiable.

5. Combining Patterns. Make a list of books or magazines you've recently read, purchased, or checked out from the library. Describe the print materials, and write an essay explaining the conclusions a person might draw — either correctly or mistakenly — about you on the basis of your list. Conclude by stating a position about the danger or usefulness of drawing such conclusions.

6. Internet Research. Research the effect that the Patriot Act has had on college campuses. One source is the Web site for the American Library Association, (ALA): www.ala.org/ala/washoff/WOissues/civilliberties/theusapatriotact/campusissues .pdf. Choose one or more aspects of the Patriot Act that are of interest to students, such as turning over textbook orders to the FBI, and write an essay that takes a stand for or against this measure in light of the threat of terrorism.

Fears about the Patriot Act Are Misguided

Ramesh Ponnuru

Ramesh Ponnuru is a senior editor for *The National Review*. His articles have been published in numerous newspapers, including the *New York Times*, the *Washington Post*, and the *Wall Street Journal*. Ponnuru has also appeared on numerous television shows, such as CNN's *Inside Politics*, NBC's *The McLaughlin Group*, and Comedy Central's *Politically Correct*. This article first appeared in *The National Review* on June 2, 2003.

Notice how Ponnuru opens the article with background information about the Patriot Act and the debate about its effect on Americans' civil liberties. This technique familiarizes his readers with the Patriot Act and prepares them for the argument he will put forth. Also notice how the author begins with a question that is answered in the essay.

Focus on Understanding   As you read, learn what the author thinks of the public outcry against the USA Patriot Act.

Focus on the Topic   In class or in your journal, explain how your life or personal freedoms have changed since the terrorist attacks of 9/11.

ACLU: American Civil Liberties Union, founded to protect Americans' civil liberties

Nat Hentoff: author and renowned authority on the First Amendment and the Bill of Rights; **William Safire:** Pulitzer Prize–winning *New York Times* columnist; **John Conyers:** a U.S. congressman (D) from Michigan; **Dick Armey:** former House majority leader (R)

Has the war on terrorism become a war on Americans' civil liberties? A coalition of left- and right-wing groups fears so, and has been working hard to restrain the law-and-order impulses of the Bush administration. It's a coalition that includes the ACLU° and the American Conservative Union, Nat Hentoff and William Safire, John Conyers and Dick Armey.° 1

The coalition started to form in 1996, when Congress passed an anti-terrorism bill. But it really took off after September 11. Members of the coalition believe that Washington's legislative response — called, rather ludicrously, the "USA Patriot Act," an acronym for "Uniting and Strengthening America by Providing Appropriate Tools [Required] to Intercept and Obstruct Terrorism" — was a too-hastily conceived, excessive reaction to the atrocities. 2

Since then, the coalition has regularly found new cause for alarm. It has protested the administration's plans for military tribunals, the president's designation of "enemy combatants," and the Pentagon's attempts to consolidate data under a program called "Total Information Awareness." This spring, the civil libertarians of left and right worked together again to block Sen. Orrin Hatch's attempt to make permanent those provisions of the Patriot Act which are set to expire next year. They have organized, as well, against the possibility that the Justice Department will propose another dangerous anti-terror bill ("Patriot II"). 3

The civil libertarians have had some success. They forced modifications in   4
the Patriot Act before its enactment. They have inspired some cities to pass res-
olutions banning their employees from cooperating with federal authorities to
implement provisions of the act that violate the Constitution. (Officials in other
cities are, presumably, free to violate the Constitution at will.) They imposed
legislative restrictions on Total Information Awareness. They have inhibited the
administration from proposing anti-terror measures that would generate adverse publicity.

They themselves have gotten favorable publicity. It's an irresistible story for   5
the press: the lion and the lamb lying down together. The press has tended to
marvel at the mere existence of the coalition. They have not been quick to note
that there is a larger bipartisan coalition on the other side, which is why the
civil libertarians have been losing most of the battles. The Patriot Act passed
357–66 in the House and 98–1 in the Senate. In early May, the Senate voted
90–4 to approve another anti-terror provision — making it easier to investigate
"lone wolf" terrorists with no proven connection to larger organizations — that
the civil libertarians oppose.

More important, the press has not adequately scrutinized the civil libertar-   6
ians' claims. This has kept the debate mired in platitudes about liberty and security. It has also reduced the incentive for the civil libertarians to do their
homework, which has in turn made their case both weaker and more hysterical
than it might otherwise have been.

Take the attack on TIPS, the Terrorist Information and Prevention System.   7
This abortive plan would have encouraged truckers, deliverymen, and the like
to report suspicious behavior they observed in the course of their work. How effective this idea would have been is open to question. Most of the criticism,
however, echoed former Republican congressman Bob Barr, who said that TIPS
"smacks of the very type of fascist or communist government we fought so hard
to eradicate in other countries in decades past."

But of all the measures the administration has adopted, it's the Patriot Act   8
(along with the possible Patriot II) that has inspired the most overheated criti-
cisms. When it was passed, the Electronic Frontier Foundation wrote that "the
civil liberties of ordinary Americans have taken a tremendous blow with this
law." The ACLU says the law "gives the Executive Branch sweeping new powers
that undermine the Bill of Rights." But most of the concerns about Patriot are
misguided or based on premises that are just plain wrong.

Roving wiretaps. Thanks to the Patriot Act, terrorism investigations can   9
use roving wiretaps. Instead of having to get new judicial authorization for each
phone number tapped, investigators can tap any phone their target uses. This
is important when fighting terrorists whose MO° includes frequently switching
hotel rooms and cell phones. It's a commonsense measure. It's also nothing
new: Congress authorized roving wiretaps in ordinary criminal cases back in
1986. It's hard to see Patriot as a blow to civil liberties on this score.

Internet surveillance. Libertarians have been particularly exercised about   10
Patriot's green light for "spying on the Web browsers of people who are not even

MO: slang for a
person's method of
operation (modus
operandi)

criminal suspects" — to quote *Reason* editor Nick Gillespie. This is a misunderstanding of Patriot, as George Washington University law professor Orin Kerr has demonstrated in a law-review article. Before Patriot, it wasn't clear that any statute limited the government's, or even a private party's, ability to obtain basic information about electronic communications (e.g., to whom you're sending e-mails). Patriot required a court order to get that information, and made it a federal crime to get it without one.

Kerr believes that the bar for getting a court order should be raised. But he 11 notes that Patriot made the privacy protections for the Internet as strong as those for phone calls and stronger than for mail. Patriot's Internet provisions, he concludes, "updated the surveillance laws without substantially shifting the balance between privacy and security."

James Bovard traffics in another Patriot myth in a recent cover story for 12 *The American Conservative*: that it "empowers federal agents to cannibalize Americans' e-mail with Carnivore wiretaps." Carnivore is an Internet surveillance tool designed by the FBI. Don't be scared by the name. The FBI's previous tool was dubbed "Omnivore," and this new one was so named because it would be more selective in acquiring information, getting only what was covered by a court order and leaving other information private. But even if Carnivore is a menace, it's not the fault of Patriot. As Kerr points out, "The only provisions of the Patriot Act that directly address Carnivore are pro-privacy provisions that actually restrict the use of Carnivore."

Hacking. Also in *Reason*, Jesse Walker writes that Patriot "expands the def- 13 inition of terrorist to include such non-lethal acts as computer hacking." That's misleading. Pre-Patriot, an al-Qaeda member who hacked the electric company's computers to take out the grid could not be judged guilty of terrorism, even if he would be so judged if he accomplished the same result with a bomb. Hacking per se isn't terrorism, and Patriot doesn't treat it as such.

Speak and peek. The ACLU is running ads that say that Patriot lets the 14 government "secretly enter your home while you're away . . . rifle through your personal belongings . . . download your computer files . . . and seize any items at will." Worst of all, "you may never know what the government has done." Reality check: You will be notified if a sneak-and-peek search has been done, just after the fact — usually within a few days. The feds had the authority to conduct these searches before Patriot. A federal judge has to authorize such a search warrant, and the warrant has to specify what's to be seized.

Library records. Bovard is appalled that Patriot allows "federal agents to 15 commandeer library records," and the American Library Association shares his sentiment. Patriot doesn't mention libraries specifically, but does authorize terrorism investigators to collect tangible records generally. Law enforcement has, however, traditionally been able to obtain library records with a subpoena. Prof. Kerr suggests that because of Patriot, the privacy of library records may be better protected in terrorism investigations than it is in ordinary criminal ones.

The civil libertarians deserve some credit. Their objections helped to rid 16 Patriot of some provisions — such as a crackdown on Internet gambling — that didn't belong in an anti-terrorism bill. Armey added the Carnivore protections to the bill. The law, as finally enacted, places limits on how much officials may disclose of the information they gain from Internet and phone surveillance. Moreover, the civil libertarians make a reasonable demand when they ask that Patriot be subject to periodic re-authorizations, so that Congress can regularly consider making modifications.

The civil libertarians rarely acknowledge the costs of legal laxity: 17 Restrictions on intelligence gathering may well have impeded the investigation of Zacarias Moussaoui,° the "twentieth hijacker," before 9/11. David Cole, one of the movement's favorite law professors, goes so far as to lament that U.S. law makes "mere membership in a terrorist group grounds for exclusion and deportation."

> **Zacarias Moussaoui:** Moroccan man indicted in the United States in conjunction with the 9/11 terrorist attacks

And while civil libertarians may scant the value of Patriot, terrorists do not. 18 Jeffrey Battle, an accused member of a terrorist cell in Portland, complained about Patriot in a recorded phone call that was recently released in court. People were less willing to provide financial support, he said, now that they were more likely to be punished for it.

Speaking of the administration's civil-liberties record, Al Gore said last year 19 that President Bush has "taken the most fateful step in the direction of [a] Big Brother° nightmare that any president has ever allowed to occur." Dick Armey worries about "the lust for power that these people in the Department of Justice have." The civil-liberties debate could use a lot less rhetoric of this sort — and a lot more attention to detail.

> **Big Brother:** all-seeing dictator in George Orwell's novel *1984;* the term is commonly used to mean government surveillance

A calm look at the Patriot Act shows that it's less of a threat to civil liberties 20 than, say, campaign-finance reform. A lot of the controversy is the result of confusion. Opponents of the Patriot Act are fond of complaining that few people have bothered to read it. No kidding.

Understanding the Reading

1. Summarize Ponnuru's reasons for thinking that concerns about the U.S. Patriot Act are misguided.

2. According to the author, why has the coalition of left- and right-wing groups working against the Patriot Act received favorable publicity?

3. What example does Ponnuru cite to explain how terrorists regard the Patriot Act?

4. What is Ponnuru's explanation for the controversy surrounding the Patriot Act?

Visualizing the Reading

Ponnuru argues that some of the controversial provisions of the Patriot Act are in fact reasonable. To do this, he acknowledges and then refutes the opposing viewpoints relating to each provision. Evaluate Ponnuru's refutation by completing the following chart. The first one has been done for you.

Patriot Act Provision	Opposing Viewpoint	Refutation
Roving wiretaps (para. 9)	Violation of civil liberties	They have been used since 1986 and are not new.
Internet surveillance (para. 10–12)		
Computer hacking (para. 13)		
Sneak and peek (para. 14)		
Library records (para. 15)		

Examining the Characteristics of Argument Essays

1. What is Ponnuru's claim? Highlight the sentence in which it is expressed.
2. What types of evidence does Ponnuru use to support his argument? Is the evidence convincing? Why or why not?
3. How does Ponnuru organize his essay? Given the topic and the type of audience he is addressing, can you think of other effective ways to organize the essay? Explain your response.
4. In addition to refuting opposing viewpoints, Ponnuru accommodates some of the civil libertarians' objections to the Patriot Act. What accommodations does he make? In your opinion, does this information strengthen Ponnuru's argument? Explain.
5. Evaluate Ponnuru's conclusion. How does it support his argument?

Building Your Word Power

For a definition of **metaphor**, *see the chart of commonly used language features on p. 21.*

1. What does the metaphor "the lion and the lamb lying down together" mean (para. 5)?
2. Explain the meaning of each of the following words as it is used in the reading: *scrutinized* (para. 6), *platitudes* (6) *eradicate* (7), *cannibalize* (12), and *rhetoric* (19). Refer to your dictionary as needed.

Reacting to the Reading: Discussion and Journal Writing

1. Do you agree that the USA Patriot Act was "a too-hastily conceived, excessive reaction to the atrocities" (para. 2) of September 11? Why or why not?

2. In class or in your journal, describe the danger of complaining about a law, book, musical piece, or movie without actually reading, hearing, or seeing the material.

Applying Your Skills: Writing Assignments

1. **Paragraph Assignment.** Do you believe that individuals have the right to privacy protection on the Internet? Write a paragraph supporting your position with sound reasons and examples.

2. Take the opposing viewpoint: Write an article condemning the Patriot Act. Be sure to address Ponnuru's arguments and to recognize the opposing viewpoints that he mentions.

3. Ponnuru includes the argument that the Patriot Act may deter terrorism by discouraging people from providing financial support for terrorists. Do you think that threats of punishment deter people from acting? For example, do tough drug laws discourage people from using drugs? Does the death penalty discourage people from killing others? Write an argument essay expressing your position on this issue.

4. The author states, "Hacking per se isn't terrorism" (para. 13). Brainstorm a list of hypothetical situations that may result from computer hacking. Then write an essay agreeing or disagreeing with the author. Support your claim with hypothetical examples or with real ones that you find through research.

5. **Combining Patterns.** Assume a federal agency decided to "sneak and peek" into your home and that you were notified only after it had occurred. Write an essay narrating the event, describing your initial reactions and concerns and what searchers might have seen that could be misinterpreted. Include an argument explaining why you feel that sneak-and-peek searches are either justifiable or a violation of people's civil liberties.

6. **Internet Research.** Access the Patriot Act online at www.lifeandliberty.gov. Review its provisions, and choose one aspect you find to be especially controversial. Is this provision reasonable and necessary in the "war on terror"? Write an argument essay agreeing or disagreeing with the provision. To support your claim, include evidence from other online sources and from personal experiences.

Comparing the Arguments

Much of the work that you do in college involves **synthesis**, the process of identifying similarities and differences between sources in order to develop new ideas or to discover new insights about them. For example, you might be asked to read a number of articles that present differing views on movie rating systems and then recommend a system that you think might work best. Use the following questions to compare the two essays on the USA Patriot Act.

Building Your Critical Thinking Skills: Synthesizing Sources

1. Compare how each writer introduces the issue.

2. The Ponnuru's essay deals with numerous features of the Patriot Act, while Gelsey's essay addresses one provision — that of FBI access to library users' reading

records. How do the two approaches compare? Did you find the broader or narrower focus to be more effective? Explain.

3. Compare the evidence that each author uses to support his or her essay's thesis. How do the types of support vary? Is the evidence relevant, current, and credible?

4. Which essay appeals to your needs and values more directly? Are any unfair emotional appeals used?

5. Which argument do you find to be more convincing? Why?

Combining Patterns: Using Variety to Achieve Your Purposes

WRITING QUICK START

Carefully examine the photographs on this page, noting any details that would help someone who cannot see the images to understand the differences and similarities between the two types of dancing. How would you define each type of dancing? How would you describe each style? In what ways are they the same and different? Consider also the two couples. They are alike in their joy of dancing, but they differ significantly in age and appearance. How would you describe each couple? Working by yourself or with a classmate, write a paragraph discussing the two photographs. Be sure to describe each couple, compare their styles of dancing, and explain why they seem so exuberant.

573

What Is Combining Patterns?

In previous chapters of this book, you studied in depth the different rhetorical strategies that writers employ. Each chapter focused on a single rhetorical strategy, but in fact writers often use more than one strategy in a given piece of writing. While most essays reflect one primary pattern of development, individual sentences, paragraphs, and sections may incorporate other patterns. For example, in writing about the two photographs at the start of this chapter, you probably used comparison and contrast as your primary pattern of development — along with description to create a visual image of each couple, definition to identify the types of dancing, and cause and effect to explain why the couples seem so exuberant. When a writer uses more than one pattern, he or she is **combining patterns**. This approach is useful because it allows writers to be flexible, enabling them to develop and support their thesis with a variety of supporting evidence. You will find it necessary and helpful to combine patterns in much of the writing you do in college and in your career, as these examples demonstrate.

- Students in a *business law* class must attend a court trial and write a summary of the proceedings that describes the courtroom setting, narrates the events that occur, and explains the judicial process that is followed.
- As part of your responsibilities as *director of a day-care center*, you must write an accident report for a toddler who was injured in the outdoor playground. You must describe the situation, explain why it happened, and outline the process you followed in obtaining medical treatment.

In the following essay, Anna Quindlen uses a variety of patterns of development as she explains why September 11, 2001, should be made a national day of remembrance.

We Are Here for Andrea

Anna Quindlen

Anna Quindlen (b. 1952) wrote for the *New York Times* from 1981 to 1994, becoming only the third woman to write a regular column in that newspaper and winning a Pulitzer Prize for commentary in 1992. She left the *Times* to pursue writing novels and to spend more time with her family. Among her novels are *Object Lessons* (1991), *One True Thing* (1996), *Black and Blue* (1998), and *Blessings* (2002). Quindlen now writes a biweekly "Last Word" column for *Newsweek*, where this essay appeared in September 2003.

"We Are Here for Andrea" commemorates the second anniversary of the 2001 terrorist attacks on New York City and Washington, D.C. Quindlen fits the story of Andrea Haberman, a woman she never met, into the larger context of a memorial for all those lost on September 11. She draws inspiration and hope from the way firefighters, rescue workers, and ordinary Americans responded to the tragic events.

A motley collection of items have wound up on the bulletin board in the past year. There was a list of phone numbers for one kid's college, and now there is a list of phone numbers for another's. There are slips of paper with quotes from Margaret Mead and Hugo Black. There is the requisite fortune-cookie fortune: YOUR WORDS WILL HAVE A HYPNOTIC EFFECT ON OTHERS. There's a picture of the three kids together at Christmas and a postcard of a bulldog and an invitation to a book party I already attended and the instructions to the automatic outdoor light on the terrace and some business cards of people I will probably never call.

| 1 | Introduction: sensory details used to describe bulletin board |

And then there's Andrea Haberman. When I was a kid the nuns used to give us holy cards for special accomplishments, Saint Thérèse with her beauty-queen bunch of roses, Saint Andrew with his X-shaped cross. Andrea Haberman is my holy card now. Her face stares out into my office every day, a small laminated photograph that looks as if it was taken in a park, with sunshine gilding one edge of her long hair. She's smiling a little fixedly, the way most of us do in pictures unless we're taken by surprise. Above her face are the numbers 9-11-2001. Her father gave me two of these last year on the first anniversary of her death. One is in my wallet and one is on the bulletin board. I add things to the board all the time, but I never cover Andrea's face.

2 Introduces subject of extended example

Descriptive details personalize Andrea

I don't really know much about her except what her father told me on very short acquaintance. She was 25, working at the Chicago office of Carr Futures, came to New York on her first business trip and was on the 92d floor of the North Tower when it was hit. She was from Wisconsin. She was engaged.

3 Narrates how she died

But that's more than the hundreds of people who tried to rescue her knew. That's more than the thousands of people who tried to find her body knew. That's more than the millions of people who wept for her and all the others knew.

4 Suggests wider impact of her life and the loss of her life

The morning that Andrea Haberman died is enshrined now in public memory as the last innocent morning in American life, before its people knew how much they were hated in the world, knew that home turf was no advantage, knew that the most invincible symbols of greatness were so vulnerable that they could be laid low in less time than it takes to read a newspaper.

5

Contrasts the time before 9/11 to the time after

Everyone believed at the time that we would never forget that lesson. 6
Sometimes it seems it has already been forgotten.

But there was a more important lesson of that day, and it is infinitely 7
more important that it be remembered. That morning marked the tri-
umph of our best selves: the impatient martyrs of the fire companies who
hurried up the stairs, the grimy angels with blowtorches who cleared away
the steel, the heavenly chorus of people whose hearts seemed to lift from
their bodies to touch the suffering of others. People fell and people rose,
and the last is the lesson.

Uses descriptive details to illustrate why 9/11 marked the best of ourselves

The president proclaimed this second anniversary Patriot Day. That 8
isn't the point. This is not a story about America vanquishing its enemies;
sadly, the contrary was the case. But it is about good wrestling with evil
and refusing to cede the field. It is a story of love and memory, of a man
who hands you a photograph of his daughter and so hands you an opportunity, every day, to remember what matters just by looking up a little.

Compares Quindlen's view to the president's

Reference to Andrea

September 11 should be formally made a day of nationwide remem- 9
brance by Congress. But it should become a day unlike any other so recognized, not a holiday but a holy day. Not an excuse for white sales or
four-day weekends but a day of national service in the spirit of the spirit
that animated so many after this monumental national tragedy. It could
be a day on which millions of Americans give blood, or deliver canned
goods to soup kitchens, or bring new books to schools and libraries. It
could be a day of service on which every American asks and answers the
question that united so many on that first September 11: how can I help?

Thesis: makes a claim

Gives examples of how the day could be celebrated

There has been a lot of talk about moving on, now that two years have 10
passed. That talk is tragic. It is time for the United States to grow up and
learn that history is not served by turning your back on it, that there are
some things that cannot be smoothed over. Nor need they be. It is not an
either/or, memory and solace.

Refutes opposing viewpoint and argues in support of thesis

Andrea Haberman is wearing her engagement ring in the picture, I 11
think. Maybe she had just gotten it, and was still in that stage when you
unconsciously gesture with your left hand because you feel as if it's glowing. She is alive in the picture. WE ARE HERE FOR ANDREA HABERMAN, it says
at the top of my holy card, and it is like a haiku or a prayer. That's it, you
see — that's what was so extraordinary about that day. You didn't know
her, and neither did I, but in our own way we were there that day, with a
compassionate yearning. If emotion could transmit electrical impulses, all
of us together would have lit up the United States like a great lighthouse
for the rest of the world, like everything we wish we could be. We must
preserve that somehow. We cannot let it fade.

Conclusion: returns to extended example and argues to preserve what was special about that day

Figurative language

Characteristics of Essays That Combine Patterns

Effective essays that combine two or more patterns of development use a variety of rhetorical strategies to support the thesis. This approach has a number of advantages. First, it allows the writer maximum flexibility in choosing how to support his or her thesis. Second, it enables the writer to explore various facets of the topic. Finally, it lends variety, making the essay both interesting and engaging.

Essays That Combine Patterns Focus Predominantly on One Pattern

In most essays that combine two or more patterns, one pattern predominates. This strategy enables the reader to identify a clear structure around which the key points of the essay are organized. Other patterns of development — used where appropriate at the sentence or paragraph level, or within a broader section — can clarify, explain, or describe a particular point, advance the essay's purpose, or support the thesis. For example, in "We Are Here for Andrea," Quindlen uses argument predominantly to present her case for establishing a national day of remembrance. She also uses a number of different strategies, such as description and illustration, to clarify points, bring in additional information, and support her thesis.

Essays That Combine Patterns Express a Main Point

Essays that combine patterns express a single thesis. Depending on the purpose and patterns used, the thesis may be stated clearly or implied; however, all essays that combine patterns should make a clear point to the reader. In addition, the thesis statement in this kind of essay often suggests the primary pattern. In Quindlen's essay, for example, the primary pattern of development is argument. Accordingly, her thesis makes a clear claim: "September 11 should be formally made a day of nationwide remembrance by Congress" (para. 9).

Essays That Combine Patterns Use Details to Support a Thesis

The use of more than one pattern enables the writer to include a wide variety of details and examples to support his or her thesis in a meaningful and effective manner. Quindlen uses a number of different patterns to support her claim that September 11 should be a national day of remembrance. In fact, she uses these different patterns at specific points in the essay to lead up to her claim, effectively building a case that she then argues for in the rest of the essay. Consider the progression of Quindlen's patterns of development: Her opening descriptive details about Andrea's holy card and her life and engagement make the events of 9/11 personal and engaging. Quindlen then uses comparison and contrast to explain that the morning of 9/11 was "the last innocent morning in American life" (para. 5). She employs description again and cause and effect to explain why the day should be remembered (para. 7). Finally, just prior to making her claim in paragraph 9, Quindlen uses comparison and contrast again to differentiate between her own vision of what this anniversary should mean and what the president thinks it should mean.

When combining patterns, be sure that each rhetorical strategy you use has a clear purpose. For instance, an essay about AIDS as a world health problem might have cause and effect as its primary pattern of development. It might include definition to explain what AIDS is and classification to categorize the social, economic, and political effects of the disease. Illustration might even be used to describe individual cases of AIDS, making the essay poignant and personal. However, depending on the author's purpose, narration might not be a particularly useful pattern unless the reader had firsthand experience living or working in an AIDS-ravaged community. Be sure to use different patterns of development carefully; if a pattern doesn't contribute to your main point, don't use it.

Essays That Combine Patterns Create Variety and Interest

In addition to supporting the writer's main point, different patterns of development capture the reader's interest and make the essay lively and engaging. In the following paragraph from a memoir, notice how the writer uses several patterns to create interest and engage the reader.

> I began to cook most of the evening meals for the family. When Mama felt like doing the cooking, I would bake: cakes and corn pudding. I still remember the two Betty Crocker cookbooks she had. They were the same shade of green as the *Webster's Dictionary* that Daddy used for doing the crossword puzzles every day. I loved to cook *with* Mama, just to be near her, to be talking with her. But I was constantly frustrated that we never had all the ingredients a recipe would call for, so I couldn't ever get it exactly right. What is oregano? I'd ask my mother, unsure how to pronounce it. And what in the world was cumin? I'd spend hours searching for a recipe that called only for ingredients that Mama stocked. They were few and far between. Furthermore, Betty didn't season with bacon drippings or ham hocks, and she didn't cook the vegetables long enough to suit us.
>
> HENRY LOUIS GATES JR., *Colored People*

Although narration is the primary pattern, Gates uses comparison to explain what his mother's cookbook looked like and description to create a vivid image of his experience cooking with Mama.

Visualizing an Essay That Combines Patterns

Graphic organizers can be helpful in the content and organization of essays that combine patterns. Because such essays are unique and use different patterns in varying combinations, there is no single model for an applicable graphic organizer. However, the basic structure of the graphic organizer showing key elements to include (presented in Figure 1.2 on p. 14 in Chapter 1) can be used to display any essay's organization. The graphic organizer in Figure 14.1 uses this format to show the basic structure of "We Are Here for Andrea." An alternative approach would be to adapt the general format of any graphic organizer included in Chapters 5 to 13. For example, because the Quindlen essay uses argument predominantly, the basic structure of the graphic organizer for argument shown in Figure 13.1 (p. 501) could also have been adapted for use here.

Writing an Essay That Combines Patterns

To write an essay that combines patterns, use the following steps. For guidance in applying the primary pattern of development in your mixed modes essay, refer to the advice given for the specific patterns described in Chapters 5 to 13.

Planning an Essay That Combines Patterns

The first step is to choose a topic. When prewriting, use your knowledge of the various patterns of development to think about your topic in unique, creative, and diverse ways. Suppose you are writing a paper about organic foods. Using *narration*, you could relate the story of a person with allergies who adopts an organic foods diet and becomes healthier. Using *description*, you could explain the look, taste, or smell of organically grown foods. Using *illustration*, you could give examples of places to buy organic foods. Using *process*, you could explain how organic food is grown and what steps are taken to keep it uncontaminated. Using *comparison and contrast*, you could examine the long-term health benefits of nonorganic and organic foods. Using *classification*, you could identify types of organic farms or types of organic foods. Using *definition*, you could explain what does and does not constitute organic food. Using *cause and effect*, you could discuss why organic foods are becoming more popular. Using *argument*, you could urge your readers to eat more organic foods.

For more on prewriting strategies, see Chapter 2, p. 25.

Certainly you would not use all these approaches in a single essay, but two or more could be combined effectively to support a thesis about, for example, eating organically. For instance, you might decide to use argument as the primary method of development and then incorporate illustration, definition, and cause and effect to write an essay that explains what organic foods are (definition), urges readers to adopt an organic foods diet (argument), offers reasons for doing so (cause and effect), and gives examples of benefits associated with that type of diet (illustration).

The list of questions Using the Patterns of Development to Explore a Topic, in Chapter 2 on page 34, can help you consider how different patterns of development might be used in combination to approach your topic.

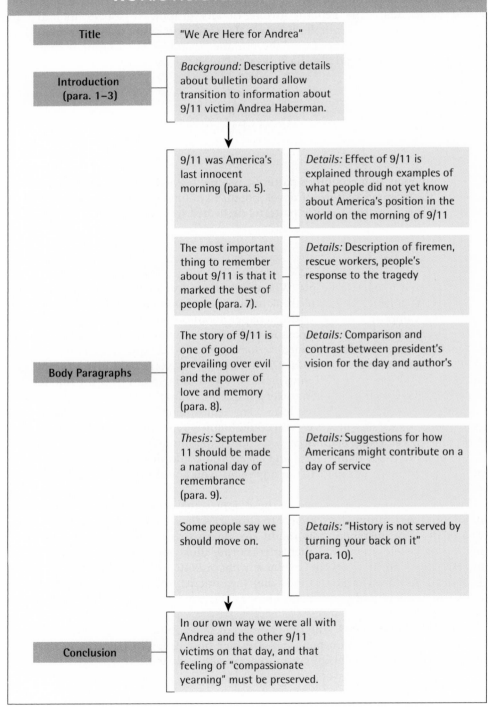

FIGURE 14.1 Graphic Organizer for "We Are Here for Andrea"

Title	"We Are Here for Andrea"
Introduction (para. 1–3)	*Background:* Descriptive details about bulletin board allow transition to information about 9/11 victim Andrea Haberman.

Body Paragraphs

9/11 was America's last innocent morning (para. 5).	*Details:* Effect of 9/11 is explained through examples of what people did not yet know about America's position in the world on the morning of 9/11
The most important thing to remember about 9/11 is that it marked the best of people (para. 7).	*Details:* Description of firemen, rescue workers, people's response to the tragedy
The story of 9/11 is one of good prevailing over evil and the power of love and memory (para. 8).	*Details:* Comparison and contrast between president's vision for the day and author's
Thesis: September 11 should be made a national day of remembrance (para. 9).	*Details:* Suggestions for how Americans might contribute on a day of service
Some people say we should move on.	*Details:* "History is not served by turning your back on it" (para. 10).

Conclusion	In our own way we were all with Andrea and the other 9/11 victims on that day, and that feeling of "compassionate yearning" must be preserved.

Developing Your Thesis

After deciding how to approach your topic, it is time to develop a thesis statement. The thesis should reveal your primary method of development. It may also suggest other patterns you will use in the essay, but the primary method should be clear to your readers, as this example shows.

> **Student services are divided into two main programs, Health and Counseling Services and Disability Services, each devoted to helping to improve the life of students on campus.**

This thesis makes it clear that classification is the predominant pattern of development; it also suggests that cause and effect will be used to explain how these services improve students' lives.

Generating Evidence to Support Your Thesis

An understanding of the different patterns of development can help you to generate relevant supporting evidence. For example, if you are writing an essay on homeopathic medicine, deciding to use comparison and contrast as the primary pattern might lead you to an explanation of the characteristics that make this kind of medicine unique and distinct from traditional medicine. Again, refer to the box Using the Patterns of Development to Explore a Topic (p. 34) for ideas on the wide variety of evidence you might use to support your thesis.

Drafting an Essay That Combines Patterns

After establishing a thesis and determining the most appropriate patterns of development for supporting it, you are ready to choose a method of organization. The organization will be determined by the primary pattern of development and any other patterns you plan to use in conjunction. For example, if you choose classification as a pattern of development for an essay on organic foods, you might organize the essay by category; if you choose illustration as a primary pattern, you might include numerous examples of people who benefited from an organic foods diet.

It may be useful to consult the guidelines for writing included in Chapters 5 to 13 for the primary pattern of development used in your essay. Also, keep the following three guidelines in mind.

Guidelines for Writing an Essay That Combines Patterns

1. **Choose patterns carefully.** Select only those that make an important contribution to the essay as a whole by supporting the thesis. The use of too many patterns can overwhelm the reader and make the essay difficult to follow.

2. **Use transitions between different patterns of development.** Transitions signal that you are moving from one pattern to another, enabling the reader to follow your train of thought easily.

(Continued)

(Continued)

3. **Make sure that your introduction and conclusion emphasize the primary pattern of development.** The introduction should provide necessary background, state the thesis, and suggest the primary pattern of development. The conclusion should draw the essay to a satisfying close while restating the main ideas, suggesting a new direction, or making a call to action — again, framed in language that echoes the primary pattern.

Analyzing and Revising

Analyzing and revising is the final step in the writing process, and one of the most essential. If possible, set your essay aside for a day or two before revising. In addition to consulting the revision flowcharts in Chapters 5 to 13 to analyze the primary pattern of development used in your essay, review the following tools from Chapter 4 to revise your paper.

- Guidelines for Revision (p. 70)
- Questions to Ask as You Revise (p. 71)
- Flowchart: Evaluating Your Thesis Statement, Topic Sentences, and Evidence (Figure 4.1, p. 73)
- Flowchart: Evaluating Your Paragraphs (Figure 4.2, p. 74)

Editing and Proofreading

For the primary pattern of development in your essay, and for other patterns that you relied on heavily, review the Editing Tips and Troublespots sections of Chapters 5 through 13. For general editing and proofreading suggestions, review the following tools from Chapter 4.

- Improving Your Sentences (p. 77)
- Improving Your Word Choice (p. 79)
- Common Errors to Avoid (p. 81)
- Guidelines for Proofreading (p. 85)

Students Write

Earlier in this book you were introduced to Robin Ferguson, an education major at a state university. In Chapter 3 you saw how she developed her thesis, created an informal outline, and drafted a few paragraphs. Here is the final version of her essay that combines patterns to support a thesis about her experience working as a literacy volunteer.

The Value of Volunteering

Robin Ferguson

I began working as a literacy volunteer as part of a community service course I was taking last semester. The course required a community service project, and without much thought, I chose the organization Literacy Volunteers of America simply as a means of fulfilling the course requirement. Much to my surprise, I found my experiences working as a volunteer to be life altering. Working as a literacy volunteer taught me about learning, teaching, and friendship -- and perhaps most important, opened my eyes to the good that comes from reaching out to help others.

When I first went through the training program to become a literacy volunteer, I learned about the process of learning -- that is, the way in which people learn new words most effectively. To illustrate this concept, the person in charge of training us wrote a brief list of simple words on the left side of a chalkboard and wrote phrases using the same words on the right side of the chalkboard. She instructed us to read the words and then asked which words we would be most likely to remember. We all said the words on the right because they made more sense in context. The trainer then showed us other examples of words in context so we could grasp how people learn new information by connecting it to what they already know.

The training I received, though excellent, was no substitute for working with a real student. When I began to discover how seriously peoples' lives are affected because they cannot read, I realized the true importance of reading. For example, when I had my first tutoring session with my client, Marie, a 44-year-old single mother of three, I found out she walked two miles to the nearest grocery store twice a week because she didn't know which bus to take. When I told her I would get her a bus schedule, she confided to me that it would not help because she could not read it, and therefore she wouldn't know which bus to take. She also said she had difficulty once she got to the grocery store because she couldn't always remember what she needed. Because she did not know words, she could not write out a grocery list. Also, she could only identify items by sight, so if the manufacturer changed a label, she would not recognize it as the product she wanted.

As we worked together, learning how to read built Marie's self-confidence, which gave her an incentive to continue in her studies. She began to make rapid progress and was even able to take the bus to the grocery store. After this successful trip, she reported how self-assured she felt. Eventually, she began helping her youngest son, Mark, a shy first grader, with his reading. She sat with him before he went to sleep, and

Margin annotations

1 — Background about how author began volunteering

Title suggests thesis

Thesis: suggests that narration and cause and effect will be used

2 — Topic sentence: narration

Extended example: process analysis is used to illustrate how trainees learned

3 — Cause and effect

Narration and illustration

4 — Topic sentence: suggests narration and cause and effect

Descriptive details
add interest

together they would read bedtime stories. When his eyes became wide with excitement as she read, her pride swelled, and she began to see how her own hard work in learning to read was paying off. As Marie described this experience, I swelled with pride as well. I found that helping Marie to build her self-confidence was more rewarding than anything I had ever done before.

Comparison and
contrast

As time went by, Marie and I developed a friendship that became permanent. Because we saw each other several times a week, we spent a lot of time getting to know each other, and we discovered we had certain things in common. For instance, I'm also a single parent. So we began to share our similar experiences with each other. In fact, we have even baby-sat for each other's children. I would drop my children off at her house while I taught an evening adult class, and in return I would watch her children while she worked on Saturday mornings.

5

Conclusion: restates
thesis and indicates
use of cause and
effect

Uses argument to
call for action

As a literacy volunteer, I learned a great deal about learning, teaching, and helping others. I also established what I hope will be a lifelong friendship with someone whom I otherwise would not have met. Working as a literacy volunteer was beneficial not only for Marie but also for me. It introduced me to a world of service and the good that comes from it in profound ways, and I encourage others to find the time to volunteer in order to make this world a better place for all of us.

6

Responding to "Students Write"

1. Evaluate Ferguson's introduction. How could she have made it more engaging?
2. Highlight the transitions that suggest narration — the primary pattern of development.
3. What does each pattern of development contribute to the essay?

Reading an Essay That Combines Patterns

Reading an essay that uses two or more patterns of development requires close attention. Because it is easy to focus on one pattern and overlook others, you should begin by previewing the reading to get an overview of its content and organization. Use the title, any headings, and the first and final paragraphs to predict what patterns will be used. Then read to confirm or revise your predictions. In general, when reading an essay that combines patterns, use these guidelines for reading actively and critically.

What to Look for, Highlight, and Annotate

Understanding the Reading

- Analyze the title and introduction. What do they suggest about the essay's content and organization?
- What different patterns does the writer use to develop the thesis?
- Does the conclusion restate the essay's thesis, present new information, urge action, or use a combination of these or other techniques?

Examining the Characteristics of Essays That Combine Patterns

- What is the thesis?
- Identify the predominant pattern. What other patterns are used?
- How do the patterns help the writer achieve his or her purpose?
- Annotate places in the text where different patterns are used to create variety and interest.
- Determine if — and where — details and evidence are added through the introduction of one or more additional patterns.
- Use a graphic organizer to analyze the effectiveness of the essay's organization and the support for the thesis.

How to Find Ideas to Write About

As you read, consider how the different patterns of development might be used to generate topics for writing. For instance, in the Ferguson essay cause and effect is used to explain how illiteracy affects Marie; this could lead you to write about the causes or effects (or both) of illiteracy. You might also write a longer essay about the process of training people to be literacy volunteers. Think also of issues that are similar or related to examples from your own experience. Perhaps you have done some volunteering; on that basis you could write an argument essay that advocates for national service, a narrative essay about your experiences, or a comparison and contrast essay that contrasts your experience with Ferguson's. The box Using the Patterns of Development to Explore a Topic, in Chapter 2 on page 34, can help generate ideas for writing that use different patterns of development based on your reading.

On Dumpster Diving

Lars Eighner

Lars Eighner was born in 1948 in Corpus Christi, Texas. After graduating from the University of Texas at Austin, he began writing essays and fiction for publications such as the *Threepenny Review*. When he lost his job as an attendant at a mental hospital, Eighner was no longer able to support himself on his writing alone, and he became homeless in 1988. It was the challenge of living on the street that led to the publication of *Travels with Lizbeth* (1993), a book about his homelessness experiences with his dog. Although the book received excellent reviews, Eighner returned to living as a homeless person for a time when his writing income alone could not support him. His other publications include the novels *Pawn to Queen Four* (1995) and *Whispered in the Dark* (1996) and a collection of essays, *Gay Cosmos* (1995). Eighner currently lives in Austin, Texas.

The following selection, which appeared in the *Utne Reader*, is an abridged version of an essay that was originally published in the *Threepenny Review*. Eighner's essay is written in the first person. Notice how this point of view gives added depth and intimacy to the topic. Also, pay attention to the author's tone and his attitude toward Dumpster diving.

Focus on Understanding   Read to discover what Dumpster diving is, who engages in it, and for what reasons.

Focus on the Topic   In class or in your journal, discuss homeless people that you have seen. How do you feel when you pass a homeless person on the street?

I began Dumpster diving about a year before I became homeless. 1

I prefer the term *scavenging*. I have heard people, evidently meaning to be polite, use the word *foraging*, but I prefer to reserve that word for gathering nuts and berries and such, which I also do, according to the season and opportunity. 2

I like the frankness of the word *scavenging*. I live from the refuse of others. I am a scavenger. I think it a sound and honorable niche, although if I could I would naturally prefer to live the comfortable consumer life, perhaps — and only perhaps — as a slightly less wasteful consumer owing to what I have learned as a scavenger. 3

Except for jeans, all my clothes come from Dumpsters. Boom boxes, candles, bedding, toilet paper, medicine, books, a typewriter, a virgin male love doll, coins sometimes amounting to many dollars: all came from Dumpsters. And, yes, I eat from Dumpsters, too. 4

There is a predictable series of stages that a person goes through in learning to scavenge. At first the new scavenger is filled with disgust and self-loathing. He is ashamed of being seen. 5

586

This stage passes with experience. The scavenger finds a pair of running [6] shoes that fit and look and smell brand-new. He finds a pocket calculator in perfect working order. He finds pristine ice cream, still frozen, more than he can eat or keep. He begins to understand: people do throw away perfectly good stuff, a lot of perfectly good stuff.

At this stage he may become lost and never recover. All the Dumpster divers [7] I have known come to the point of trying to acquire everything they touch. Why not take it, they reason, it is all free. This is, of course, hopeless, and most divers come to realize that they must restrict themselves to items of relatively immediate utility.

The finding of objects is becoming something of an urban art. Even [8] respectable, employed people will sometimes find something tempting sticking out of a Dumpster or standing beside one. Quite a number of people, not all of them of the bohemian type, are willing to brag that they found this or that piece in the trash.

But eating from Dumpsters is the thing that separates the dilettanti from [9] the professionals. Eating safely involves three principles: using the senses and common sense to evaluate the condition of the found materials; knowing the Dumpsters of a given area and checking them regularly; and seeking always to answer the question "Why was this discarded?"

Yet perfectly good food can be found in Dumpsters. Canned goods, for ex- [10] ample, turn up fairly often in the Dumpsters I frequent. I also have few qualms about dry foods such as crackers, cookies, cereal, chips, and pasta if they are free of visible contaminants and still dry and crisp. Raw fruits and vegetables with intact skins seem perfectly safe to me, excluding, of course, the obviously rotten. Many are discarded for minor imperfections that can be pared away.

A typical discard is a half jar of peanut butter — though nonorganic peanut [11] butter does not require refrigeration and is unlikely to spoil in any reasonable time. One of my favorite finds is yogurt — often discarded, still sealed, when the expiration date has passed — because it will keep for several days, even in warm weather.

No matter how careful I am I still get dysentery° at least once a month, of- [12] tener in warm weather. I do not want to paint too romantic a picture. Dumpster diving has serious drawbacks as a way of life.

I find from the experience of scavenging two rather deep lessons. The first [13] is to take what I can use and let the rest go. I have come to think that there is no value in the abstract. A thing I cannot use or make useful, perhaps by trading, has no value, however fine or rare it may be.

The second lesson is the transience of material being. I do not suppose that [14] ideas are immortal, but certainly they are longer-lived than material objects.

The things I find in Dumpsters, the love letters and rag dolls of so many [15] lives, remind me of this lesson. Now I hardly pick up a thing without envisioning the time I will cast it away. This, I think, is a healthy state of mind. Almost everything I have now has already been cast out at least once, proving that what I own is valueless to someone.

dysentery: an intestinal infection marked by abdominal pain, fever, and diarrhea

I find that my desire to grab for the gaudy bauble has been largely sated. I 16
think this is an attitude I share with the very wealthy — we both know there is
plenty more where whatever we have came from. Between us are the rat-race
millions who have confounded their selves with the objects they grasp and who
nightly scavenge the cable channels for they know not what.

I am sorry for them.   17

Understanding the Reading

1. According to the author, what stages do people go through before becoming "professional" Dumpster divers?
2. What risk associated with Dumpster diving does the author mention?
3. What lessons has Eighner learned from Dumpster diving?
4. What attitude does the author share with the wealthy?

Visualizing the Reading

The primary pattern of development in Eighner's essay is process analysis. To make the stages in the process of Dumpster diving clear to his readers, he enumerates, or lists, his main ideas. To analyze the effectiveness of this technique, complete the graphic organizer below.

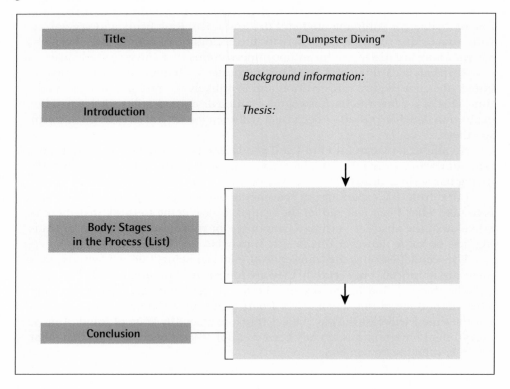

Examining the Characteristics of Essays That Combine Patterns

1. In addition to process analysis, what other patterns are used?
2. What kinds of sensory details does Eighner include? Highlight several particularly effective examples. What do these details contribute to the essay?
3. What distinguishing characteristics does Eighner present to define Dumpster diving?
4. What is the author's main point? What examples support this assertion?

Building Your Word Power

1. According to Eighner, what is the difference between *scavenging* and *foraging* (para. 2–3)?
2. Explain the phrase "gaudy bauble" as used in paragraph 16.
3. Explain the meaning of each of the following words as it is used in the reading: *niche* (para. 3), *pristine* (6), *bohemian* (8), *dilettanti* (9), and *transience* (14). Refer to your dictionary as needed.

Building Your Critical Thinking Skills: Bias

Bias is a person's own view or prejudice toward a topic. Because certain subjects arouse strong emotions in audience members even before they start reading, readers often interpret texts according to their own personal bias. *Reader bias* is the set of attitudes, beliefs, prejudices, and feelings that a reader can bring to an essay. For example, someone who is strongly opposed to gun control might bring this bias to his or her reading of an argument supporting gun control. When someone is biased toward a certain view or subject, he or she stands the chance of missing out on new ideas or losing the opportunity to better understand other perspectives. To avoid bringing bias to your own reading of texts, keep an open mind. Using your knowledge of bias, answer the following questions.

1. Explain how any preconceptions you had about the homeless may have affected your reading of Eighner's essay. Did this essay alter your opinion of the homeless? If yes, how?
2. What was your initial reaction to learning that Eighner eats out of Dumpsters? How do you feel about it now that you have read and studied the essay?

Reacting to the Reading: Discussion and Journal Writing

1. Discuss Eighner's attitude toward materialism, wealth, and personal possessions.
2. Does *scavenging* have a positive or negative connotation? Are shopping at garage sales and thrift stores forms of scavenging? Explain.
3. In class or in your journal, discuss the possible causes of homelessness.

Applying Your Skills: Writing Assignments

1. **Paragraph Assignment.** Personal possessions are of little importance to Eighner. As he acquires something, he considers throwing it out. Think of a personal

possession you could never imagine throwing away, and write a paragraph using at least two patterns of development to explain why the item is so important to you.

2. Eighner's essay reveals the degree to which America has become a wasteful, throwaway society. Write an essay using two or more patterns of development describing the problem and examining the effects of such wastefulness. Suggest ways in which wastefulness might be reduced or controlled.

3. Eighner comments on American values and the emphasis on acquiring and owning goods. Write an essay using two or more patterns of development that agrees or disagrees with Eighner's view of American values and materialism. Support your views with examples from your own experience.

4. Eighner describes the process through which he acquires what he needs for daily living. Consider what type of consumer you are: How do you shop? How do you decide what you need and what to buy? Are you an impulse buyer or a systematic shopper? After categorizing yourself as a particular type of consumer, write an essay using process analysis and any other patterns of development that seem useful to your purposes to explain how you make purchase decisions.

5. Internet Research. Many people are fascinated by what they find in the garbage or on the street. Explore the site for *Found* magazine at www.foundmagazine.com/ or research a lost and found service on the Internet. Then write a classification essay about what you see on the site. Describe the different types of found objects and the circumstances in which they are found. Choose some items from the site to describe in detail. Conclude with your thoughts on what such items evoke.

The Good-News Generation

John Leo

John Leo is a contributing editor at *U.S. News & World Report*, writing regularly about topics related to media and culture. His syndicated column currently appears in 140 newspapers every week. Prior to joining *U.S. News & World Report* in 1988, he contributed articles on social science and intellectual trends to publications such as *Time*, the *New York Times*, and the *Village Voice*. His most recent collection of essays is *Incorrect Thoughts: Notes on a Wayward Culture* (2000).

In this essay, which appeared in *U.S. News & World Report* in November 2003, Leo examines the broad characteristics attributed to various generations and focuses on "millennials," people born between 1977 and 1994. Note the sources that he cites in his generalizations about this group of people, and consider why — and to whom — information about the traits of the millennials might be important.

Focus on Understanding   As you read, identify what the "good-news generation" is.

Focus on the Topic   In class or in your journal, write about the different generations represented in your family.

Ours is a four-generation family. I am a "silent" or a "mature," born before 1946 ("duty, tradition, loyalty," are the watchwords to professional generation watchers, who like to find three nouns for each group). My esteemed spouse is a baby boomer ("individuality, tolerance, self-absorption"), our first two daughters are generation X-ers ("diversity, savvy, pragmatism") and our youngest daughter is a "millennial," a member of the cohort born between 1977 and 1994. One of the best researchers and generation-watchers, Ann Clurman of the Yankelovich Partners, suggests "authenticity, authorship, and autonomy" as the three nouns for the emerging millennials, also known as generation Y or the "echo boomers." 1

The comic overtones of dividing and labeling everyone this way are hard to miss, but there is some sense to it, too. The sharp break between the silents and the boomers, obvious to all, has fueled the search for clean dividing lines between the generations that came after. 2

Now the focus is almost entirely on millennials, 78 million strong and the largest birth cohort in American history. Speaking at the American Magazine Conference last week in the Palm Springs, Calif., area, Clurman described millennials this way: They are family oriented, viscerally pluralistic, deeply committed to authenticity and truth-telling, heavily stressed, and living in a no-boundaries world where they make short-term decisions and expect paradoxical outcomes. (The sense of paradox means that every choice results in some good consequences, some bad: Air bags save lives but kill people, too.) 3

591

By pluralistic, Clurman means that distinctions of race, ethnicity, and gen- 4
der are of little interest to millennials — they tend to overlook differences and
treat everyone the same. Part of the fallout is that opposition to gay marriage,
strong among older Americans, is low among millennials. Authenticity and integrity are prime values. Millennials want very much to succeed in life, says
Clurman, but "integrity trumps success." (Enron° should have hired millennial
executives.)

Enron: a large energy
corporation that was
forced to declare
bankruptcy in 2001 as
a result of a fraud
scandal

Yankelovich and other researchers have been picking up a renewed em- 5
phasis on family for years. The yearning for a good marriage is a dominant
value among millennials, Clurman says, and 30 percent of those surveyed say
they want three or more children. Indeed, one research company, Packaged
Facts and Silver Stork, recently predicted a 17 percent increase in the U.S.
birthrate over the next 10 years.

Clurman says that as a group, boomer parents are spending a lot of time 6
getting close to their millennial children. These are better relationships than the
gen X-ers had with boomer parents, or than boomers had with their own
mothers and fathers. According to Gallup,° more than 90 percent of teens say
they are very close to their parents. In 1974, over 40 percent of boomers said
they would be better off without their parents. J. Walker Smith, president of
Yankelovich, says the drive toward reconnection with family and community
was showing up in the data even before 9/11 and is exceptionally strong today.

Gallup: an opinion poll
that surveys public
opinion

Getting real. Brandchannel.com, an online marketing site run by 7
Interbrand, issued a gen Y report last week that echoes Yankelovich. Gen Y is
not turning out to be the edgy, cynical, ironic cohort many expected, the report
said. In addition to millennials' closeness to their parents, statistics on sexual
activity, violence, and suicide rates are down, and concern with religion and
community are up. Evidence on drinking and drugs is more mixed, but smoking, drinking, and drug use among eighth, 10th, and 12th graders fell simultaneously in 2002 for the first time. The millennial affection for the authentic over
the glitzy marketing product is marked by the rise of Avril Lavigne, "an ordinary
looking, midriff-free, nondancing singer hailed as the anti-Britney,"° reports
Brandchannel.com. Yankelovich makes the same point about Lavigne. Smith
says the millennials will watch over-the-top cultural products like reality TV
and the movie *Kill Bill*, but they stand apart from them and look around for
more genuine, less exploitative material.

anti-Britney: reference
to pop singer Britney
Spears

Millennials are apt to trust parents, teachers, and police. Apparently they are 8
likely to trust presidents, too. A Harvard poll released last week reported that
President Bush has a 61 percent favorability rate among American college students. This may not mean much. The millennials are not a very politically active
generation. But they are clearly able to resist programming by their professors,
90 percent of whom seem convinced that Bush is either Hitler or a moron. The
millennials are a very interesting generation. Now if they could just walk one
block without carrying a bottle of water and making four phone calls. . . .

Understanding the Reading

1. Identify the generations described in this article. What are the three nouns that Leo uses to describe the people in each generation?
2. Which generation represents the largest birth group in American history?
3. What does researcher Ann Clurman mean when she says millennials are "pluralistic" (para. 3–4)?
4. Which groups mentioned by Leo have close family relationships?

Visualizing the Reading

Look at the photo carefully. What is going on? Who is depicted? Using Leo's categories and some of your own, write a paragraph that explains to which generation each person in the photograph belongs. Include a definition for each category, based on Leo's definition or one of your own devising. Using Leo's essay as a model, explain each person's probable characteristics on the basis of the generation to which he or she belongs.

Examining the Characteristics of Essays That Combine Patterns

1. Identify Leo's thesis. How does he reveal the importance and relevance of the information he presents?
2. What is the primary pattern of development in Leo's article? What other patterns does he use?
3. For each pattern, explain whether it supports the thesis, adds details, adds variety and interest, or a combination of the three. In your view, is Leo effective in combining these patterns? Why or why not?
4. List the distinguishing characteristics of millennials, generation X-ers, baby boomers, and silent/matures.

Building Your Word Power

1. Explain what the author means by baby boomers having *self-absorption*, generation X-ers having *savvy*, and millennials having *authorship* (para. 1).

2. Explain the phrase "over-the-top cultural products" (para. 7). Does it have a positive or negative connotative meaning?

*For a definition of **connotative meaning**, see the chart of commonly used language features on p. 21.*

3. Explain the meaning of each of the following words as it is used in the article: *pragmatism* (para. 1), *autonomy* (1), *cohort* (3), *viscerally* (3), and *exploitative* (7). Refer to your dictionary as needed.

Building Your Critical Thinking Skills: Evaluating Sources

Authors frequently use information from other sources to support their main ideas. The types of evidence vary tremendously but may include research findings, expert opinions, and information from books and articles. Because not all sources are equally reliable, critical readers should evaluate all outside sources to make sure they are relevant and credible. In **evaluating sources**, consider credibility (as represented by well-known journals or nationally recognized Web sites, for example) and trustworthiness (as represented, for example, by people who are experts in their field and therefore are likely to provide reliable and accurate information). Finally, make sure that any sources used clearly support the thesis. Using your knowledge of evaluating sources, answer the following questions.

1. Highlight the sources that Leo uses to support his thesis. Are they credible? What does the author do to establish their credibility?

2. What further information would you need to assess the trustworthiness of Leo's sources?

Reacting to the Reading: Discussion and Journal Writing

1. According to one of the researchers cited in Leo's essay, "[t]he yearning for a good marriage" is important among millennials (para. 5). Discuss possible reasons for this.

2. Explore the challenges that arise from the differences between each set of generations. Why do you think millennials and baby boomers have closer relationships than other generations of children and parents?

Applying Your Skills: Writing Assignments

1. **Paragraph Assignment.** Do you belong to one of the generations described in this article? Write a paragraph using two or more patterns of development explaining why the description seems accurate or inaccurate.

2. Using the categories described in "The Good-News Generation," determine the generation to which each person in your own family belongs. For family members who do not fit within the categories described by Leo, create a new category for that age group. Using two or more patterns of development, write an essay that applies the descriptions in the article to your own family members, including

examples that either support or disprove what the researchers have reported about each generation.

3. Do some research into the origin of the phrase "baby boomer" or "generation X." Then write an essay that defines the term you have chosen, including its history and distinguishing characteristics. Illustrate your definition with descriptions of people — well-known figures, friends, or family members — who represent that generation.

4. Talk to one person from each of the generations described in the article. Ask each person to give you three nouns that they feel describe their generation, along with any explanations they care to give. In addition, ask them for three nouns that they would use to describe another generation, either younger or older. What conclusions can you draw about how the different generations perceive each other? Do any of the "watchwords" from your subjects appear in more than one generation? Using two or more patterns, write an essay about what you discover.

5. Internet Research. Visit the Web site for the Pew Research Center for the People and the Press at http://people-press.org. This organization studies Americans' attitudes toward the press, politics, and public policy. Identify an issue that interests you about a certain group of people, and read the available information. Then write an essay using two or more patterns of development that describes the issue and explains what the survey about it discovered. Comment on whether the survey results surprise you — and if so, why. Include details from the site as well as your own experiences to support a thesis about the issue.

Houseguest Hell

Chitra Divakaruni

Chitra Divakaruni (b. 1956) left Calcutta, India, for the United States in 1976, when she was nineteen years old. Working at a series of odd jobs — babysitting, slicing bread, washing laboratory glassware — to pay for her education, she earned advanced English degrees from Wright State University and the University of California at Berkeley. An award-winning author, Divakaruni has published pieces in dozens of magazines, including the *Atlantic Monthly* and the *New Yorker*. She is the author of *Mistress of Spices* (1997) and other novels, in addition to numerous essays, poems, and short stories.

"Houseguest Hell" first appeared in the anthology *The Bitch in the House* (2002). Divakaruni details the exasperations of feeling obligated to treat guests as a host in India would, but without the help of the household servants common in India — and with the additional burden of feeling guilty about resenting the guests' intrusion. As you read, note how the author uses anecdotes to make readers feel both empathy and amusement toward her predicament.

Focus on Understanding   Read to discover what the author means by "houseguest hell."

Focus on the Topic   In class or in your journal, describe about how you feel about houseguests — either being one or having them.

After months of rain and fog, I woke this morning to a brilliant cloudless 1
sky. Jays were chattering in the bushes, the Niles lilies were exploding in blues and whites all over my garden, and the Japanese maple had unfurled every one of its delicious green leaves, landing us squarely in the middle of spring. Anyone else would have been delighted. But I experienced a sinking sensation in the region of my heart. Because spring meant that the houseguests would soon be arriving.

Each year, sure as the swallows° of Capistrano, houseguests swoop down 2
on us in flockfuls. (Correction: on me. My husband, who escapes to the office each morning, has to deal with them only at the dinner table. I, who work full-time from home as a novelist and journalist, am a twenty-four-hour captive.) Houseguest season begins in late spring and can last, depending on my luck, until the end of summer, by which time I am a physical and emotional wreck. (I used to think that I was subjected to this particular torture because I live in the desirable San Francisco area, but my friend Surekha from Poughkeepsie° assures me that she suffers the same fate.) Since I am of Indian origin, so are

> **swallows of Capistrano:** reference to the annual springtime return of the Cliff Swallows to San Juan Capistrano, California, from their winter home in Argentina

> **Poughkeepsie:** a small city in New York state about 90 miles north of New York City

596

most of my guests. Many of them are also relatives. A deadly combination, this, houseguests who are relatives — especially if they are arriving directly from India. Because this means they require Maximum Maintenance.

Maintenance begins in the morning with tea. Not your instant drip-bag 3 kind, but brewed properly, Like-We-Do-at-Home. (Make note of this phrase; it will appear again.) Houseguest tea is boiled on the stove with milk, sugar, ginger, and cardamom. Yes, it does taste delicious, but have you ever tried cleaning out the pot afterward? My guests have not, because in India they have servants to do this — and here they have me.

Along with tea comes breakfast, cooked hot. (Like-We-Do-at-Home.) 4 Preferably something Indian, like idlis or pooris. The rice and lentil mix for idlis has to be soaked overnight, then ground and steamed. Poori dough has to be made ahead, rolled out, and fried. Both require accompaniments — a chutney or a curry — and leave you with a sinkful of dirty dishes. You're getting the idea.

After breakfast, we gird our loins for the real work: sight-seeing and shop- 5 ping. I love the beauties of the Bay Area, but circling the Golden Gate Bridge parking lot for the 563rd time as I search vainly for a spot is beginning to lose its charm. And here's another confession: I have a low threshold for shopping pain. Malls make me hyperventilate with anxiety. I have no clue as to where the brand names that roll so effortlessly off the tongues of my guests are to be found. ("You mean you don't know where the nearest Macy's outlet is?!" my guests exclaim incredulously. "How about Neiman Marcus? Surely you've been to Saks? Or at least to the Gap-Lane-Bryant-Fashion-Plaza-Men's-Wearhouse-Miller's Outlet?" They smile their compassion. "Don't worry. By the time we leave, you'll know it all.") We reach home at the end of the day, staggering under pyramids of boxes and bags. We kick off our shoes and collapse on the couch. Then someone says, "Ah, wouldn't it be nice to have a hot cup of tea."

Guess who gets up and makes it? And fixes a four-course dinner, with 6 dessert afterward. (Like-We-Do-at-Home.) And loads the dishes in the dishwasher. And mops the kitchen floor. And makes sure the bathroom is stocked with clean towels, soaps, shampoos, toothpastes, deodorizers, and Q-tips. And soaks the rice and lentils for tomorrow morning's idlis, so that they'll be ready in time for our trip to the Napa Valley.° All the while wondering how on earth she's going to find time to complete her *other* work, the creative, income-producing kind.

Guess who's spitting mad by the time she gets into bed, where her hus- 7 band's waiting with amorous inclinations. (Because he has entertained the guests with jokes over dinner and helped clear the table afterward, he thinks he's done his bit and is entitled to some fun and games.) Guess who's so furious she pulls the quilt over her head, because she knows that otherwise she'll start a quarrel, and maybe burst into tears, and then he'll say, "There you go again." He'll say, "It's your own fault. You don't have to do all this for them."

Napa Valley: an area famous for its wineries about 45 miles north of San Francisco

You're probably thinking the same thing.   8

Why is it that I feel impelled to behave this way? Why can't I just show my   9
guests where the Special K and Lipton's tea bags are? Why can't I point them to
the bus that would take them to the mall, or drop them at the BART station with
instructions to phone me when they get back from the city? Why can't I order
pizza for dinner and ice cream for dessert? Why can't I insist that my husband
take them sight-seeing over the weekend while I put up my feet and relax with
a good book?

I ask myself these questions over and over, trying to find a satisfactory   10
answer that will help me understand my unconscious needs. Perhaps it's because — despite the books I've published and the writing awards I've won —
I still feel that a big chunk of my identity as a woman is tied up in how well
I manage my home. Guests, when they come into my house, become part of
this responsibility. It's my job to be their caretaker. And in some paradoxical
way, even as I complain bitterly because my husband isn't participating, I
don't want him to encroach into my realm. I asked Alice, my Caucasian
friend, if she feels the same kind of obligation to her guests, or if this is an
Eastern thing. She says that whenever she has houseguests, she, too, has to
battle with the anxiety of having everything be perfect. ("Or what will they
say after they've left?") And unlike other aspects of her life that people may
comment on, criticism of her home and home habits tends to hit a particularly vulnerable, private spot. "We women still see ourselves as the Number
One Homemaker in the family," she comments. "Our sense of success hinges
upon it." Even when we have a nine-to-five job (or in the case of Alice, a senior executive at her company, a nine-to-nine job)? "Especially then," Alice
says. "We overcompensate out of some kind of genetically programmed
guilt." She thinks for a moment. "But I'm getting better. All last week, when
my second cousin and her family were visiting, we ate salads and takeout
dinners."

Hearing this, I'm filled with admiration and new resolve. Takeout dinners   11
it will be for me, too! But then I think of how my second cousin and her family
would react to such a menu. ("Rabbit fodder? Food in cardboard boxes? Is this
why we came, all the way to America? Why, at Home we'd never treat a guest
this way!") Perhaps part of the problem lies in my memories of my mother, a
genuinely hospitable person who has always enjoyed having our large extended
family — her side as well as my father's — come to visit. True, she did have a
maid to help with cooking and cleaning; also true, since my father supported
the family financially, it was understood that her job was to take care of the
house — and the guests who came into it. Still, the visits created a lot of extra
work for her. Any dish that required true skill she made herself, to be sure it
came out perfectly. I still remember how she would stay awake late at night,
after her household duties were done, shredding coconut and boiling it with
jaggery to make narus for the guests to snack on. Or in the afternoons, instead
of taking her usual nap, she'd be up on the terrace laying the quilts out in the

sun, so they'd smell good for the guests. But she was able to imbue these chores with a smiling sense of holiday that is somehow beyond my capacities. Unlike me, my mother was not distressed by the upsetting of her daily routine. I am not sure if this is because of her superior mental poise or because her routine was so different from mine, which bristles with imminent pub dates, demanding editors and agents, and hectic book tours — all a result, I realize, of my own ambition. Maybe my mother enjoyed getting away from the humdrum existence of husband-children-cooking-helping-with-homework to go for a jaunt to Victoria Memorial or a visit to the Kali temple. At night after dinner, she stayed up chatting for hours with the visiting women, listening to stories of faraway villages where scandals and disasters and miracles seemed to occur as a matter of routine.

Or perhaps the source of my mother's pleasure in guests and my discomfort 12
with them lies in a fundamental value difference between my birth culture and the one that I've adopted. For while Americans value privacy almost to the point of obsession, it is a concept that hardly even exists in India. Take, for example, our respective sleeping arrangements when guests come to stay. In my home, guests have their own bedroom (one that I have gone to great trouble and expense to decorate appropriately, with items that impress but can't easily be broken by their children). And when they enter it at the end of the day, I heave a great sigh of relief and go to my bedroom and shut my door. And lock it. And God help anyone who comes knocking on it before morning.

In India, however, we had no guest room. Most families didn't. When we 13
had guests, several big beds would be made on the floor. All the children slept on one, usually in a room where a grandparent could keep a benevolent eye on them. The men slept in the drawing room, and the women congregated on pallets in one of the bedrooms, talking and laughing late into the night. I remember how exciting it was when I finally was considered old enough to graduate from the children's room and join my mother in the whispery, moonlit half-dark filled with the smell of jasmine from the garlands the women wore in their hair. What a rite of passage! I have nothing similar to pass on to my children.

Here, then, is the real source of my frustration. I see the traditional Indian 14
way of hospitality in some ways as more gracious and mature and loving, where the guest is seen as "God come to visit." But I haven't figured out how to make this concept an appropriate and meaningful part of my own feminist lifestyle. I cannot replicate my mother's life. Even if I wanted to, it would never work. Our situations are very different, and our roles. I've spent much of my life battling the ideas of males-as-superiors and women-as-servers, which were realities she had to accept. Perhaps in the process my voice has grown strident. We all have to pay for the things we believe in. Her way was to give and give. Mine is not.

My mother was allowed no boundaries, no borders to separate what was 15
hers from what belonged to the family, the community, the society — and so

she never thought to do so, and thus could embrace her houseguests for the treat they were and for the delicacies they offered, without a hint of defensiveness. I, by contrast, have fought to gain my boundaries and borders — the ones I so need to create the space for my work — and now must fight to protect them. My mother was taught to acquiesce. I must learn how to say no without feeling that I'm betraying her. I must learn to refuse to give what people want from me when I feel it's unreasonable — but to do so with love.

I've started practicing already. I do it each morning in front of the bath-   16
room mirror, trying to get my smile just right. "No, Susheela auntie, I can't make another trip to the grocery tonight, even though we've run out of butter-milk. How about we drink some of this nice mango juice instead?" Or, "I remember how fond you are of chicken tandoori, Uncle Mohan. Well, tonight I'm taking you to Raja's Diner — it's their house specialty." From time to time, I take deep yogic breaths. From time to time, I employ what one of the *Don't Sweat the Small Stuff* books advises: I imagine the people I'm dealing with as infants, or as people who are 100 years old. I'm making great strides. Here's one of the latest additions to my repetoire: "This is the Grey Line Tours terminal, Janak and Uma. I've booked you on their Napa tour. I hear it's quite lovely. I'll be back at eight P.M. to pick you up." By the time next houseguest season arrives, I'm going to be a pro, ready to greet the spring and its accompanying barbarian hordes with firm charm — just that much more firm than We-Do-at-Home.

Understanding the Reading

1. Who comes to visit Divakaruni each summer? Why are these guests so much trouble?

2. What types of foods and entertainment do her guests expect? Why is it so hard for the author to meet these expectations?

3. How does Divakaruni's way of entertaining compare to her mother's? How are their experiences similar, and how are they different?

4. According to the author, how might she make the visits easier on herself? What steps does she plan to take in the future to alleviate her stress over having houseguests?

Visualizing the Reading

To review the content and organization of "Houseguest Hell," complete the following graphic organizer.

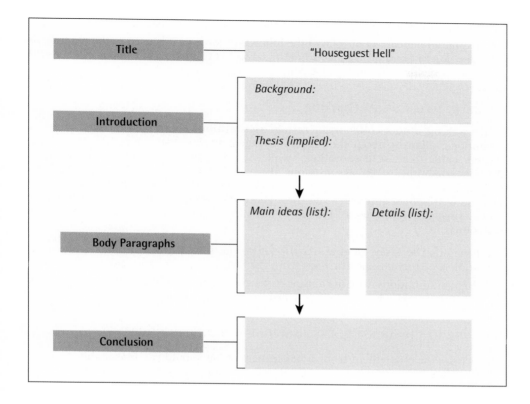

Examining the Characteristics of Essays That Combine Patterns

1. Narration is the primary pattern of development in Divakaruni's essay. How does she use conflict and tension to build toward a resolution? Does her use of dialogue contribute significantly to the narrative? Explain.

2. Examine the details about food. How do they contribute to the larger picture that the author paints about her houseguests?

3. What point of view does Divakaruni use? How do the questions to the reader contribute to this approach?

4. How does the author use comparison and contrast techniques to analyze her situation?

5. Evaluate the author's use of examples. Are there enough to support her thesis? Are the examples relevant and interesting? Explain.

Building Your Word Power

1. The author creates the phrase "Maximum Maintenance" in paragraph 2. Explain what this means.

For a definition of
connotative meaning,
see the chart of com-
monly used language
features on p. 21.

2. Explain the connotative meaning of the phrase "Like-We-Do-at-Home" (para. 3).

3. Explain the meaning of each of the following words as it is used in the reading: *incredulously* (para. 5), *paradoxical* (10), *resolve* (11), *imbue* (11), and *acquiesce* (15). Refer to your dictionary as needed.

Building Your Critical Thinking Skills: Identifying Assumptions

When writing, authors often make certain **assumptions** about their readers. These assumptions might be about the readers' background, interests, or beliefs. Sometimes writers cater to these assumptions, while at other times they try to dispel them. Authors sometimes make assumptions about their topic as well. For example, when writing about food preferences, a writer may assume that a food she enjoys, such as grits, is well known and well liked throughout the country, whereas in fact it is a regional specialty. Using your skills in identifying assumptions, answer the following questions.

1. Based on the essay, what assumptions do you think Divakaruni makes about her audience? Include specific lines from the text to support your answer.

2. What assumptions does the author make about her houseguests? How do these assumptions affect her behavior toward the guests?

Reacting to the Reading: Discussion and Journal Writing

1. Discuss the etiquette of being a houseguest. What should you reasonably expect of your host? What are the responsibilities of being a guest?

2. Divakaruni talks about her problem with her friend Alice. In class or in your journal, discuss the importance of sharing your troubles with someone you trust.

Applying Your Skills: Writing Assignments

1. **Paragraph Assignment.** Write a paragraph using two or more patterns of development to describe a situation in which you felt overburdened by someone else's demands. What effect did the situation have on you and your relationship to this person?

2. Brainstorm a list of times when you visited someone or people visited you. Pick two situations; then, in an essay using two or more patterns of development, compare and contrast the different experiences. Begin with background information about the visits. Establish clear points of comparison, and provide examples to support your thesis. Conclude with your thoughts on what you learned from these experiences.

3. The author describes her houseguests as being from "hell." In your experience, are there other individuals who deserve this label? Have you ever had a roommate from hell, a teacher from hell, or a date from hell? Write an essay that defines and describes this person, including an explanation of why he or she deserves the label.

4. Brainstorm a list of tourist attractions in your community. Then write an essay using two or more patterns of development that describes these attractions for potential visitors. Include an explanation of why these places are of interest. Consider

also ranking the sites in some way (most interesting, least expensive, strangest, etc.). Be sure to mention any significant experiences that you have had at any of these places.

5. Internet Research. Visitors to other countries must be careful to show sensitivity to and knowledge about other cultures. Online sources such as the Web site for the International Business Center at www.international-business-etiquette.com/ can provide useful information about the social and business climate in various countries. Research online the traditions and cultures of other countries. Then, in an essay using two or more patterns of development, discuss the potential for misunderstanding that might arise when traveling to a certain country or area of the world. Include your thoughts on how travelers can avoid these possible misunderstandings.

Naked Terror

Jeffrey Rosen

Jeffrey Rosen (b. 1964) has degrees from Harvard University, Oxford University, and the Yale University Law School. His writings have appeared in a broad range of publications, such as the *New York Times*, the *Atlantic Monthly*, and the *New Yorker*. He is currently the legal affairs editor at *The New Republic*. In addition to writing, Rosen teaches constitutional law and privacy law at the George Washington University Law School and is a frequent contributor to National Public Radio. His books include *The Unwanted Gaze: The Destruction of Privacy in America* (2001) and *The Naked Crowd: Reclaiming Security and Freedom in an Anxious Age* (2004).

This article, which is adapted from *The Naked Crowd*, first appeared in the *New York Times Magazine* on January 4, 2004. As you read, notice how Rosen uses an extended example about airport security to illustrate his thesis.

Focus on Understanding   Read to discover what relationship exists between the public's fears and some of the security measures that have been considered since the events of 9/11.

Focus on the Topic   In class or in your journal, write about your number one fear.

When the Bush administration raised America's antiterrorism alert status 1 from yellow to orange over the holidays, some travelers became anxious, while others took the warning in stride. If and when another attack on American soil occurs, however, everything we know about the psychology of fear suggests that it will lead to extreme public panic that may be disproportionate to the actual casualties. The public responds emotionally to remote but terrifying threats, and this leads us to make choices about security that are not always rational.

After the 9/11 attacks, for example, officials at Orlando International Airport 2 began testing a new security device. Let's call it the Naked Machine, for that's more or less what it is. A kind of electronic strip search, the Naked Machine bounces a low-energy X-ray beam off the human body. In addition to exposing any metal, ceramic or plastic objects that are concealed by clothing, the Naked Machine also produces an anatomically correct naked image of everyone it scrutinizes. The Naked Machine promises a high degree of security, but it demands a high sacrifice of privacy. With a simple programming shift, however, researchers at the Pacific Northwest National Laboratory in Richland, Wash., have built a prototype of a redesigned Naked Machine that extracts the images of concealed objects and projects them onto a sexless mannequin, turning the naked body into an unrecognizable and nondescript blob. This redesigned version of

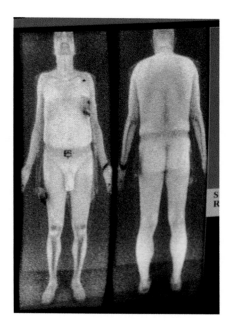

the Naked Machine — let's call it the Blob Machine — guarantees exactly the same amount of security while also protecting privacy.

The choice between the Blob Machine and the Naked Machine might seem   3
to be easy. But in presenting the choice hypothetically to groups of students and adults since 9/11, I've been struck by a surprising pattern; there are always some people who say they would prefer to go through the Naked Machine rather than the Blob Machine. Some say they are already searched so thoroughly at airports that they have abandoned all hope of privacy. Others say those who have nothing to hide should have nothing to fear. But in each group, there are some who say they are so anxious about the possibility of terrorism that they would do anything possible to make themselves feel better. They don't care, in other words, whether or not the Naked Machine makes them safer than the Blob Machine, because they are more concerned about *feeling* safe than being safe.

In their willingness to choose laws and technologies that threaten privacy   4
without bringing more security, the people who prefer the Naked Machine to the Blob Machine are representative of an important strain in public opinion as a whole. When presented with images of terrifying events, people tend to miscalculate their probability. A single memorable image — of the World Trade Center collapsing, for example — will crowd out less visually dramatic risks in the public mind. This explains why people overestimate the frequency of deaths from disasters like floods and fire and underestimate the frequency of deaths from more mundane threats like diabetes and strokes.

How can we protect ourselves from our psychological vulnerabilities? First, 5
we can turn off the TV. A study of psychological responses to 9/11 found that,
two months after the attacks, 17 percent of the American population outside
New York City reported symptoms of post-traumatic stress related to 9/11. High
levels of stress were especially notable in those who watched a lot of television.
This anxiety is only heightened by cable networks, which have converted themselves into 24-hour purveyors of alarm.

But cable TV isn't the only institution of democracy that has an incentive to 6
exaggerate risks. We've seen the temptations for politicians to pass along vague
and unconfirmed threats of future violence in order to protect themselves from
criticism in the event that another attack materializes. Ultimately, our success
in overcoming fear will depend on political leadership that challenges us to live
with our uncertainties rather than catering to them. After 9/11, for example,
Mayor Rudolph Giuliani understood that the greatest leaders of democracies in
earlier wars did not pander to public fears; instead, they challenged citizens to
transcend their self-involved anxieties, embracing ideals of liberty and justice
larger than themselves. It is hard to imagine Franklin D. Roosevelt° instituting
a color-coded system of terrorist alerts.

The vicious cycle at this point should be clear. The public fixates on low- 7
probability but vivid risks because of images we absorb from television and
from politicians. This cycle fuels the public's demand for draconian and poorly
designed laws and technologies to eliminate the risks that are, by their nature,
difficult to reduce. We have the ability to resist this dangerous cycle by choosing leaders who will insist on laws and technologies that strike a reasonable balance between freedom and security. What we need now is the will.

Franklin D. Roosevelt:
(1882–1945) 32nd
president of the United
States; in his four
terms he created the
New Deal programs
during the Depression,
led the United States
through World War II,
and helped found the
United Nations

Understanding the Reading

1. Does Rosen regard the public response to the threat of future terrorist attacks as
   rational? Why or why not?

2. What is the difference between the Naked Machine and the Blob Machine?
   According to the author, why do some people prefer the Naked Machine?

3. What two "institution[s] of democracy" (para. 6) affect Americans' psychological
   vulnerabilities?

4. According to Rosen, how can Americans break the cycle of exaggerated risks and
   the demand for poorly designed laws and technologies?

Visualizing the Reading

Rosen uses a variety of patterns to support his thesis. To analyze the effectiveness of
his essay, complete the following chart. The first one has been done for you.

Pattern	How It Supports the Thesis
Comparison and contrast	Compares the "Naked Machine" to the "Blob Machine" (para. 2–4). Illustrates the irrational choices that people make in response to remote threats.
Cause and effect	
Illustration	
Description	

Examining the Characteristics of Essays That Combine Patterns

1. What is Rosen's thesis statement? Do you think he provides adequate information to support it? Why or why not?
2. Evaluate the examples Rosen uses to support his thesis. Are they relevant, accurate, and representative? Explain.
3. What is the predominant pattern of development used in the essay?
4. Rosen cites a study of the psychological response in New York and elsewhere after the 9/11 attacks. For what purpose does he include this information?

Building Your Word Power

1. Explain the connotative meaning of the term "blob."
2. Explain the meaning of each of the following words as it is used in the reading: *prototype* (para. 2), *mundane* (4), *purveyors* (5), *pander* (6), and *draconian* (7). Refer to your dictionary as needed.

For a definition of **connotative meaning**, see the chart of commonly used language features on p. 21.

Building Your Critical Thinking Skills: Facts and Opinions

Authors use a mix of facts and opinions to support their ideas. **Facts** can be verified as true or false, whereas **opinions** are expressions of an author's beliefs or values, and as such they cannot be determined to be true or false. For example, a writer who states that drug addiction rates are declining because of an increase in funding for anti-drug programs in elementary schools is merely stating an opinion. However, if this claim were supported by facts from a reliable, validated study showing a direct correlation between the two phenomena, the statement would be a fact. Because the distinction between facts and opinions can be difficult to make, readers should carefully evaluate texts to determine whether or not a given statement offers enough evidence to be considered a verifiable fact or, instead, an opinion. Using your knowledge of fact and opinion, indicate whether the following statements from the text are Facts (F) or Opinions (O).

_____ 1. ". . . the Naked Machine bounces a low-energy X-ray beam off the human body." (para. 2)

_____ 2. "The Naked Machine promises a high degree of security, but it demands a high sacrifice of privacy." (para. 2)

_____ 3. ". . . 17 percent of the American population outside New York City reported symptoms of post-traumatic stress related to 9/11." (para. 5)

_____ 4. ". . . our success in overcoming fear will depend on political leadership that challenges us to live with our uncertainties rather than catering to them." (para. 6)

Reacting to the Reading: Discussion and Journal Writing

1. In class or in your journal, explain why you would or would not approve of intrusive security measures like the Naked Machine in a time of terrorist threats.

2. For what purposes might a politician "pass along vague and unconfirmed threats" (para. 6) to the public? Do you approve of the dissemination of such information? Why or why not?

3. Agree or disagree with the following statement: ". . . the greatest leaders of democracies in earlier wars did not pander to public fears; instead, they challenged citizens to transcend their self-involved anxieties, embracing ideals of liberty and justice larger than themselves" (para. 6). Explain your response.

Applying Your Skills: Writing Assignments

1. **Paragraph Assignment.** Imagine that you are required to go through a Naked Machine as a security precaution before entering a mall or your college campus. In a paragraph using two or more patterns, explain what your response would be. Feel free to be creative or even humorous, inventing characters and dialogue that reveal your reaction to this machine.

2. Brainstorm a list of actions or policies that would improve public safety. Choose one, and write a letter to your congressional representative that argues for its implementation. In your letter, describe the policy or action, give reasons why it would be effective, and recognize opposing views.

3. Using narration and other patterns of development, write an essay about your own experiences on 9/11. Describe how and when you learned of the attacks and what you did on that day as the events unfolded. Include a dominant impression about your reactions to this national tragedy.

4. Other than airport security, what common actions or policies routinely intrude on your rights to privacy? Consider, for example, surveillance cameras in stores or random highway roadblocks. In an essay using two or more patterns of development, consider whether such measures are useful or whether they unnecessarily intrude on your fundamental rights to privacy. Be sure to explain exactly how these security measures work, and include any personal experiences that you have had with them.

5. **Internet Research.** Rosen states that cable networks are "24-hour purveyors of alarm" (para. 5). Visit several online news sources such as www.cnn.com, www.Foxnews.com, and www.abcnews.com. Do you detect a pattern of programming that supports or disproves Rosen's assessment of cable networks? Write an essay using two or more patterns of development reporting your findings.

The Lottery

Shirley Jackson

Shirley Jackson (1919–1965) was born in San Francisco and moved to Rochester, New York, with her family at the age of fourteen. She attended the University of Rochester but dropped out after only one year because of depression, a condition that would afflict her sporadically throughout her whole life. In 1940 she graduated from Syracuse University. Throughout her life she wrote as much as she could, developing a daily writing regimen as an adult that continued even as she raised her four children.

This short story first appeared in the *New Yorker* in 1948. "The Lottery" is the most well known of Jackson's works; it has been frequently anthologized and dramatized on stage and for television. As you read, pay attention to how Jackson builds tension. Also notice how she uses dialogue effectively both to tell the story and to convey the shifting mood.

Focus on Understanding   Read to discover what the *lottery* referred to in the title is.

Focus on the Topic   In class or in your journal, write about a time when you were forced to participate in a ritual of some kind. How did your expectations compare to the actual experience?

The morning of June 27th was clear and sunny, with the fresh warmth of a full-summer day; the flowers were blossoming profusely and the grass was richly green. The people of the village began to gather in the square, between the post office and the bank, around ten o'clock; in some towns there were so many people that the lottery took two days and had to be started on June 26th, but in this village, where there were only about three hundred people, the whole lottery took less than two hours, so it could begin at ten o'clock in the morning and still be through in time to allow the villagers to get home for noon dinner.

The children assembled first, of course. School was recently over for the summer, and the feeling of liberty sat uneasily on most of them; they tended to gather together quietly for a while before they broke into boisterous play, and their talk was still of the classroom and teacher, of books and reprimands. Bobby Martin had already stuffed his pockets full of stones, and the other boys soon followed his example, selecting the smoothest and roundest stones; Bobby and Harry Jones and Dickie Delacroix — the villagers pronounced this name "Dellacroy" — eventually made a great pile of stones in one corner of the square and guarded it against the raids of the other boys. The girls stood aside, talking among themselves, looking over their shoulders at the boys, and the very small children rolled in the dust or clung to the hands of their older brothers or sisters.

Soon the men began to gather, surveying their own children, speaking of   3
planting and rain, tractors and taxes. They stood together, away from the pile
of stones in the corner, and their jokes were quiet and they smiled rather than
laughed. The women, wearing faded house dresses and sweaters, came shortly
after their menfolk. They greeted one another and exchanged bits of gossip as
they went to join their husbands. Soon the women, standing by their husbands,
began to call to their children, and the children came reluctantly, having to be
called four or five times. Bobby Martin ducked under his mother's grasping
hand and ran, laughing, back to the pile of stones. His father spoke up sharply,
and Bobby came quickly and took his place between his father and his oldest
brother.

The lottery was conducted — as were the square dances, the teen-age club,   4
the Halloween program — by Mr. Summers, who had time and energy to devote
to civic activities. He was a round-faced, jovial man and he ran the coal business, and people were sorry for him, because he had no children and his wife
was a scold. When he arrived in the square, carrying the black wooden box,
there was a murmur of conversation among the villagers, and he waved and
called, "Little late today, folks." The postmaster, Mr. Graves, followed him, carrying a three-legged stool, and the stool was put in the center of the square and
Mr. Summers set the black box down on it. The villagers kept their distance,
leaving a space between themselves and the stool, and when Mr. Summers said,
"Some of you fellows want to give me a hand?" there was a hesitation before
two men, Mr. Martin and his oldest son, Baxter, came forward to hold the box
steady on the stool while Mr. Summers stirred up the papers inside it.

The original paraphernalia for the lottery had been lost long ago, and the   5
black box now resting on the stool had been put into use even before Old Man
Warner, the oldest man in town, was born. Mr. Summers spoke frequently to the
villagers about making a new box, but no one liked to upset even as much tradition as was represented by the black box. There was a story that the present
box had been made with some pieces of the box that had preceded it, the one
that had been constructed when the first people settled down to make a village
here. Every year, after the lottery, Mr. Summers began talking again about a
new box, but every year the subject was allowed to fade off without anything's
being done. The black box grew shabbier each year; by now it was no longer
completely black but splintered badly along one side to show the original wood
color, and in some places faded or stained.

Mr. Martin and his oldest son, Baxter, held the black box securely on the   6
stool until Mr. Summers had stirred the papers thoroughly with his hand.
Because so much of the ritual had been forgotten or discarded, Mr. Summers
had been successful in having slips of paper substituted for the chips of wood
that had been used for generations. Chips of wood, Mr. Summers had argued,
had been all very well when the village was tiny, but now that the population
was more than three hundred and likely to keep on growing, it was necessary
to use something that would fit more easily into the black box. The night before
the lottery, Mr. Summers and Mr. Graves made up the slips of paper and put

them in the box, and it was then taken to the safe of Mr. Summers's coal company and locked up until Mr. Summers was ready to take it to the square next morning. The rest of the year, the box was put away, sometimes one place, sometimes another; it had spent one year in Mr. Graves's barn and another year underfoot in the post office, and sometimes it was set on a shelf in the Martin grocery and left there.

There was a great deal of fussing to be done before Mr. Summers declared 7 the lottery open. There were the lists to make up — of heads of families, heads of households in each family, members of each household in each family. There was the proper swearing-in of Mr. Summers by the postmaster, as the official of the lottery; at one time, some people remembered, there had been a recital of some sort, performed by the official of the lottery, a perfunctory, tuneless chant that had been rattled off duly each year; some people believed that the official of the lottery used to stand just so when he said or sang it, others believed that he was supposed to walk among the people, but years and years ago this part of the ritual had been allowed to lapse. There had been, also, a ritual salute, which the official of the lottery had had to use in addressing each person who came up to draw from the box, but this also had changed with time, until now it was felt necessary only for the official to speak to each person approaching. Mr. Summers was very good at all this; in his clean white shirt and blue jeans, with one hand resting carelessly on the black box, he seemed very proper and important as he talked interminably to Mr. Graves and the Martins.

Just as Mr. Summers finally left off talking and turned to the assembled vil- 8 lagers, Mrs. Hutchinson came hurriedly along the path to the square, her sweater thrown over her shoulders, and slid into place in the back of the crowd. "Clean forgot what day it was," she said to Mrs. Delacroix, who stood next to her, and they both laughed softly. "Thought my old man was out back stacking wood," Mrs. Hutchinson went on, "and then I looked out the window and the kids was gone, and then I remembered it was the twenty-seventh and came a-running." She dried her hands on her apron, and Mrs. Delacroix said, "You're in time, though. They're still talking away up there."

Mrs. Hutchinson craned her neck to see through the crowd and found her 9 husband and children standing near the front. She tapped Mrs. Delacroix on the arm as a farewell and began to make her way through the crowd. The people separated good-humoredly to let her through; two or three people said, in voices just loud enough to be heard across the crowd, "Here comes your Missus, Hutchinson," and "Bill, she made it after all." Mrs. Hutchinson reached her husband, and Mr. Summers, who had been waiting, said cheerfully, "Thought we were going to have to get on without you, Tessie." Mrs. Hutchinson said, grinning, "Wouldn't have me leave m'dishes in the sink, now, would you, Joe?" and soft laughter ran through the crowd as the people stirred back into position after Mrs. Hutchinson's arrival.

"Well, now," Mr. Summers said soberly, "guess we better get started, get this 10 over with, so's we can go back to work. Anybody ain't here?"

"Dunbar," several people said. "Dunbar, Dunbar." 11

Mr. Summers consulted his list. "Clyde Dunbar," he said. "That's right. He's   12
broke his leg, hasn't he? Who's drawing for him?"

"Me, I guess," a woman said, and Mr. Summers turned to look at her. "Wife   13
draws for her husband," Mr. Summers said. "Don't you have a grown boy to do
it for you, Janey?" Although Mr. Summers and everyone else in the village knew
the answer perfectly well, it was the business of the official of the lottery to ask
such questions formally. Mr. Summers waited with an expression of polite interest while Mrs. Dunbar answered.

"Horace's not but sixteen yet," Mrs. Dunbar said regretfully. "Guess I gotta   14
fill in for the old man this year."

"Right," Mr. Summers said. He made a note on the list he was holding.   15
Then he asked, "Watson boy drawing this year?"

A tall boy in the crowd raised his hand. "Here," he said. "I'm drawing for   16
m'mother and me." He blinked his eyes nervously and ducked his head as several voices in the crowd said things like "Good fellow, Jack," and "Glad to see
your mother's got a man to do it."

"Well," Mr. Summers said, "guess that's everyone. Old Man Warner make it?"   17

"Here," a voice said, and Mr. Summers nodded.   18

A sudden hush fell on the crowd as Mr. Summers cleared his throat and   19
looked at the list. "All ready?" he called. "Now, I'll read the names — heads of
families first — and the men come up and take a paper out of the box. Keep the
paper folded in your hand without looking at it until everyone has had a turn.
Everything clear?"

The people had done it so many times that they only half listened to the di-   20
rections; most of them were quiet, wetting their lips, not looking around. Then
Mr. Summers raised one hand high and said, "Adams." A man disengaged himself from the crowd and came forward. "Hi, Steve," Mr. Summers said, and Mr.
Adams said, "Hi, Joe." They grinned at one another humorlessly and nervously.
Then Mr. Adams reached into the black box and took out a folded paper. He
held it firmly by one corner as he turned and went hastily back to his place in
the crowd, where he stood a little apart from his family, not looking down at his
hand.

"Allen," Mr. Summers said, "Anderson. . . . Bentham."   21

"Seems like there's no time at all between lotteries any more," Mrs.   22
Delacroix said to Mrs. Graves in the back row. "Seems like we got through with
the last one only last week."

"Time sure goes fast," Mrs. Graves said.   23

"Clark. . . . Delacroix."   24

"There goes my old man," Mrs. Delacroix said. She held her breath while   25
her husband went forward.

"Dunbar," Mr. Summers said, and Mrs. Dunbar went steadily to the box   26
while one of the women said, "Go on, Janey," and another said, "There she goes."

"We're next," Mrs. Graves said. She watched while Mr. Graves came around   27
from the side of the box, greeted Mr. Summers gravely, and selected a slip of

paper from the box. By now, all through the crowd there were men holding the small folded papers in their large hands, turning them over and over nervously. Mrs. Dunbar and her two sons stood together, Mrs. Dunbar holding the slip of paper.

"Harbur. . . . Hutchinson."   28

"Get up there, Bill," Mrs. Hutchinson said, and the people near her laughed.   29

"Jones."   30

"They do say," Mr. Adams said to Old Man Warner, who stood next to him,   31
"that over in the north village they're talking of giving up the lottery."

Old Man Warner snorted. "Pack of crazy fools," he said. "Listening to the   32
young folks, nothing's good enough for *them*. Next thing you know, they'll be
wanting to go back to living in caves, nobody work any more, live *that* way for
a while. Used to be a saying about 'Lottery in June, corn be heavy soon.' First
thing you know, we'd all be eating stewed chickweed and acorns. There's *always*
been a lottery," he added petulantly. "Bad enough to see young Joe Summers up
there joking with everybody."

"Some places have already quit lotteries," Mrs. Adams said.   33

"Nothing but trouble in *that*," Old Man Warner said stoutly. "Pack of young   34
fools."

"Martin." And Bobby Martin watched his father go forward. "Over-   35
dyke. . . . Percy."

"I wish they'd hurry," Mrs. Dunbar said to her older son. "I wish they'd   36
hurry."

"They're almost through," her son said.   37

"You get ready to run tell Dad," Mrs. Dunbar said.   38

Mr. Summers called his own name and then stepped forward precisely and   39
selected a slip from the box. Then he called, "Warner."

"Seventy-seventh year I been in the lottery," Old Man Warner said as he   40
went through the crowd. "Seventy-seventh time."

"Watson." The tall boy came awkwardly through the crowd. Someone said.   41
"Don't be nervous, Jack," and Mr. Summers said, "Take your time, son."

"Zanini."   42

After that, there was a long pause, a breathless pause, until Mr. Summers,   43
holding his slip of paper in the air, said, "All right, fellows." For a minute, no
one moved, and then all the slips of paper were opened. Suddenly, all the
women began to speak at once, saying, "Who is it?" "Who's got it?" "Is it the
Dunbars?" "Is it the Watsons?" Then the voices began to say, "It's Hutchinson.
It's Bill," "Bill Hutchinson's got it."

"Go tell your father," Mrs. Dunbar said to her older son.   44

People began to look around to see the Hutchinsons. Bill Hutchinson was   45
standing quiet, staring down at the paper in his hand. Suddenly, Tessie
Hutchinson shouted to Mr. Summers, "You didn't give him time enough to take
any paper he wanted. I saw you. It wasn't fair!"

"Be a good sport, Tessie," Mrs. Delacroix called, and Mrs. Graves said, "All 46 of us took the same chance."

"Shut up, Tessie," Bill Hutchinson said. 47

"Well, everyone," Mr. Summers said, "that was done pretty fast, and now 48 we've got to be hurrying a little more to get done in time." He consulted his next list. "Bill," he said, "you draw for the Hutchinson family. You got any other households in the Hutchinsons?"

"There's Don and Eva," Mrs. Hutchinson yelled. "Make *them* take their 49 chance!"

"Daughters drew with their husbands' families, Tessie," Mr. Summers said 50 gently. "You know that as well as anyone else."

"It wasn't *fair*," Tessie said. 51

"I guess not, Joe," Bill Hutchinson said regretfully. "My daughter draws 52 with her husband's family, that's only fair. And I've got no other family except the kids."

"Then, as far as drawing for families is concerned, it's you," Mr. Summers 53 said in explanation, "and as far as drawing for households is concerned, that's you, too. Right?"

"Right," Bill Hutchinson said. 54

"How many kids, Bill?" Mr. Summers asked formally. 55

"Three," Bill Hutchinson said. "There's Bill, Jr., and Nancy, and little Dave. 56 And Tessie and me."

"All right, then," Mr. Summers said. "Harry, you got their tickets back?" 57

Mr. Graves nodded and held up the slips of paper. "Put them in the box, 58 then," Mr. Summers directed. "Take Bill's and put it in."

"I think we ought to start over," Mrs. Hutchinson said, as quietly as she 59 could. "I tell you it wasn't *fair*. You didn't give him time enough to choose. *Every*body saw that."

Mr. Graves had selected the five slips and put them in the box, and he 60 dropped all the papers but those onto the ground, where the breeze caught them and lifted them off.

"Listen, everybody," Mrs. Hutchinson was saying to the people around her. 61

"Ready, Bill?" Mr. Summers asked, and Bill Hutchinson, with one quick 62 glance around at his wife and children, nodded.

"Remember," Mr. Summers said, "take the slips and keep them folded until 63 each person has taken one. Harry, you help little Dave." Mr. Graves took the hand of the little boy, who came willingly with him up to the box. "Take a paper out of the box, Davy," Mr. Summers said. Davy put his hand into the box and laughed. "Take just *one* paper," Mr. Summers said. "Harry, you hold it for him." Mr. Graves took the child's hand and removed the folded paper from the tight fist and held it while little Dave stood next to him and looked up at him wonderingly.

"Nancy next," Mr. Summers said. Nancy was twelve, and her school friends 64 breathed heavily as she went forward, switching her skirt, and took a slip daintily from the box. "Bill, Jr.," Mr. Summers said, and Billy, his face red and his feet overlarge, nearly knocked the box over as he got a paper out. "Tessie," Mr. Summers said. She hesitated for a minute, looking around defiantly, and then set her lips and went up to the box. She snatched a paper out and held it behind her.

"Bill," Mr. Summers said, and Bill Hutchinson reached into the box and felt 65 around, bringing his hand out at last with the slip of paper in it.

The crowd was quiet. A girl whispered, "I hope it's not Nancy," and the 66 sound of the whisper reached the edges of the crowd.

"It's not the way it used to be," Old Man Warner said clearly. "People ain't 67 the way they used to be."

"All right," Mr. Summers said. "Open the papers. Harry, you open little 68 Dave's."

Mr. Graves opened the slip of paper and there was a general sigh through 69 the crowd as he held it up and everyone could see that it was blank. Nancy and Bill, Jr., opened theirs at the same time, and both beamed and laughed, turning around to the crowd and holding their slips of paper above their heads.

"Tessie," Mr. Summers said. There was a pause, and then Mr. Summers 70 looked at Bill Hutchinson, and Bill unfolded his paper and showed it. It was blank.

"It's Tessie," Mr. Summers said, and his voice was hushed. "Show us her 71 paper, Bill."

Bill Hutchinson went over to his wife and forced the slip of paper out of her 72 hand. It had a black spot on it, the black spot Mr. Summers had made the night before with the heavy pencil in the coal-company office. Bill Hutchinson held it up and there was a stir in the crowd.

"All right, folks," Mr. Summers said. "Let's finish quickly." 73

Although the villagers had forgotten the ritual and lost the original black 74 box, they still remembered to use stones. The pile of stones the boys had made earlier was ready; there were stones on the ground with the blowing scraps of paper that had come out of the box. Mrs. Delacroix selected a stone so large she had to pick it up with both hands and turned to Mrs. Dunbar. "Come on," she said. "Hurry up."

Mrs. Dunbar had small stones in both hands, and she said, gasping for 75 breath, "I can't run at all. You'll have to go ahead and I'll catch up with you."

The children had stones already, and someone gave little Davy Hutchinson 76 a few pebbles.

Tessie Hutchinson was in the center of a cleared space by now, and she held 77 her hands out desperately as the villagers moved in on her. "It isn't fair," she said. A stone hit her on the side of the head.

Old Man Warner was saying, "Come on, come on, everyone." Steve Adams 78 was in the front of the crowd of villagers, with Mrs. Graves beside him.

"It isn't fair, it isn't right," Mrs. Hutchinson screamed and then they were 79 upon her.

Understanding the Reading

1. What is the setting of this story? Where and when does it take place?
2. What is Old Man Warner's reaction to the news that the north village is considering giving up the lottery?
3. Why does Tessie Hutchinson want her married daughter and son-in-law to take part in the second drawing? What is inappropriate about her suggestion?
4. Who draws the paper with the black spot on it, and what happens to that person?

Visualizing the Reading

Details are especially important in "The Lottery" because it is through them that Jackson reveals her message. To analyze how each of the following details contributes to the meaning of the story, complete the chart.

Details	Importance
"They stood together, away from the pile of stones in the corner, and their jokes were quiet and they smiled rather than laughed." (para. 3)	Suggests a sense of foreboding and dread of what is to come
"The black box grew shabbier each year; by now it was no longer completely black but splintered badly along one side . . ." (5)	
"The people had done it so many times that they only half listened to the directions; most of them were quiet, wetting their lips, not looking around." (20)	
"'They do say . . . that over in the north village they're talking of giving up the lottery.'" (31)	
"It had a black spot on it, the black spot Mr. Summers had made the night before with the heavy pencil in the coal-company office." (72)	

Examining the Characteristics of Essays That Combine Patterns

1. The theme of a story is its central or dominant idea, the main point the author makes about the human experience. Identify several possible themes in "The Lottery." What evidence from the story supports your interpretation of the theme?

2. As with most short stories, the primary pattern of development in "The Lottery" is narration. What other patterns does Jackson use?

3. How do the details of the villagers' habits and mannerisms contribute to the mood of the story? Include examples from the text to support your answer.

4. What is the central conflict in "The Lottery"? How does Jackson build and sustain tension in the story?

5. What are the distinguishing qualities and characteristics of the main characters in "The Lottery"?

Building Your Word Power

1. What is the significance of the phrase "pack of crazy fools" as used by Old Man Warner in paragraph 32?

2. "[T]he feeling of liberty sat uneasily on most of the children" (para. 2). Explain the meaning of this phrase as used in the story.

3. Explain the meaning of each of the following words as it is used in the reading: *profusely* (para. 1), *boisterous* (2), *paraphernalia* (5), *perfunctory* (7), and *interminably* (7). Refer to your dictionary as needed.

Building Your Critical Thinking Skills: Symbolism

Authors of short stories often use **symbolism** to express their theme — that is, their comment on the human condition. A symbol is a thing, word, or idea that suggests a meaning beyond its literal one. For example, the color white is often associated with purity. As you read short stories, be sure to look beyond the plotline for possible symbols with deeper meanings and associations. It is helpful to underline key phrases and words that seem important or receive undue emphasis because these often suggest the use of symbolism. Be sure not only to analyze the obvious symbols in a reading, but also to consider the symbolic meanings of the events, people, and objects mentioned. Using your knowledge of symbolism, answer the following questions.

1. What might the black box symbolize? How is it described? Why might the color and condition of the box be important?

2. Evaluate the names of the following characters: Mr. Summers, Mr. Graves, Old Man Warner. What meaning does each name suggest?

3. What does the lottery itself stand for or represent?

Reacting to the Reading: Discussion and Journal Writing

1. Discuss family or religious traditions. Why do we keep them? Are there some that you feel we should discontinue?

2. This story was written in 1948 just after the end of World War II. Discuss how the events of that time might have influenced Jackson when writing her story.

3. In class or in your journal, discuss crowd mentality. Why do people do things with others that they might not otherwise do on their own?

Applying Your Skills: Writing Assignments

1. **Paragraph Assignment.** Write a paragraph about a violent or morally questionable activity in society that we seem to accept without question (for example, boxing matches, beauty pageants). Begin by describing this activity, and conclude with an argument for or against continuing it.

2. Brainstorm a list of public events that you have attended (concerts, rallies, etc.). After choosing one, write an essay using description and other patterns of development, to explore the role of ritual and conformity at public events. What rituals have you observed? To what activities or beliefs have you been expected to conform? Use sensory details and vivid language to paint a complete picture of the event.

3. Consider the ways that people act in groups. For instance, some people assume the role of leader, whereas others are followers. Using classification and other patterns of development, explain the characteristics of people in a group. You may find it helpful to compare and contrast differences between or within categories. For example, are there differences in the way men and women act? young people and old people? Support a generalization about these types with examples from your own observations.

4. Jackson presents tension between the old, traditional ways of doing things and the new, younger ways of thinking. Consider someone older in your life who has different views on the "right" way to do something. Using comparison and contrast and other patterns of development, write an essay that explains how this person's views differ from your own.

5. **Internet Research.** Jackson uses process to describe the ancient ritual of the "lottery." Using the Internet, research the history of a traditional event in our culture such as Valentine's Day, graduation, or Memorial Day. Based on your research, write a process essay that explains how and why traditions surrounding that event are carried out in a certain way. Use other patterns of development as appropriate to support a thesis about the process.

Part◆Three

Student Resource Guide

Finding and Using Sources

Depending on the assignment, you can use sources in a variety of ways. At times, you may plan a paper that is based primarily on your own experience but decide to add a few sources to provide additional support. At other times, you may start a paper by checking several sources to narrow your topic or to become more familiar with a topic before writing about it. Finally, you may be asked to write a research paper, which requires the most extensive use of sources.

When Should You Use Sources?

You should use sources whenever the topic requires more factual information than you can provide from your own personal knowledge and experience. Here are some warning signs that may suggest the need for sources.

- You feel as though you do not have enough to say.
- You do not feel comfortable with your topic.
- You have avoided certain aspects of your topic because you do not know enough about them.
- You have unanswered questions about your topic.
- Your essay is too short, but you do not know what to add.

When you plan and develop an essay using sources, you will follow the same process described in Chapters 2 to 4. Use the following guidelines to make your paper with sources successful.

Guidelines for Using Sources Successfully

1. **Start with your own ideas.** A multiple source essay should be based on your own ideas. Never start with the sources themselves; doing so will result in a summary, not an essay.

2. **Use sources to support your ideas.** Once you have identified the main points of your paper, decide what information is needed to support them. Incorporate sources that will make your ideas believable and acceptable to the reader.

3. **Focus on ideas, not facts.** To maintain a focus on ideas, ask yourself, "What do all these facts add up to?" For example, when writing about the issue of campaign finance reform, instead of concentrating on the amount of money corporations give to politicians, consider what impact the money has on the politicians' agendas.

4. **Avoid strings of facts and quotations.** Writing that strings together fact after fact or quotation after quotation is dull and does not convey ideas effectively. Try to refer to no more than one or two sources per paragraph.

How to Locate Sources

Sources of information range from books and videos to interviews and Web sites. Regardless of whether you use sources to add detail to an essay or to write a research paper, it is helpful to approach the process of locating, evaluating, and using sources in a systematic way (see Figure 15.1).

Locating Useful Library Sources

Your college library is one of the best and most immediate sources of reference materials. Learning to use the library will help you locate sources effectively, which is imperative for college success. To get the most out of your library, you need to know which of its research tools are best for your purposes. This section explains some of the resources available at your college library.

The Library Catalog

A library's catalog lists books owned by the library. It may also list available magazines, newspapers, government documents, and electronic sources. However, it does not list individual articles included in magazines and newspapers. Most libraries now have a computerized catalog, which enables you to search for sources electronically by title, author, or subject. Some libraries also allow access to their catalogs from outside computers, at home or in a computer lab on campus.

Figure 15.2 shows the results of a computerized search by subject for the topic *animal communication*. Computerized catalogs offer many conveniences. The

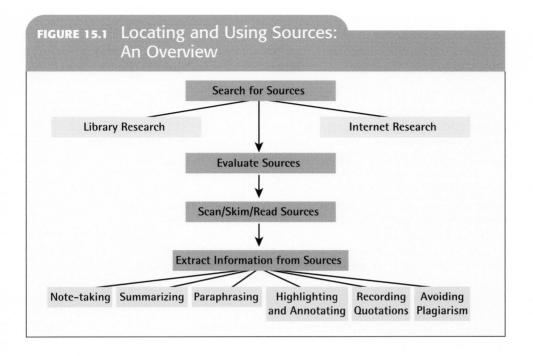

FIGURE 15.1 Locating and Using Sources: An Overview

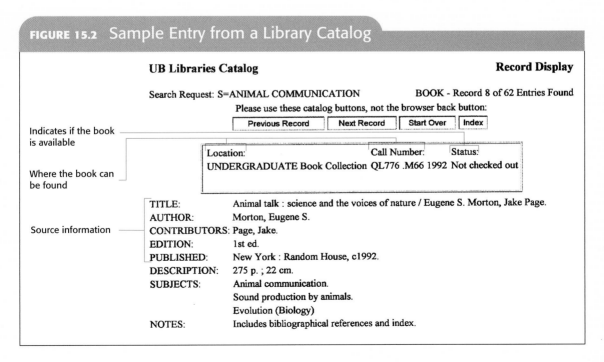

FIGURE 15.2 Sample Entry from a Library Catalog

screen often indicates whether the book is on the shelves or has been checked out and when it is due back. Some systems allow you to reserve the book by entering your request on the computer. Often, terminals are connected to printers that enable you to print the screen, providing an accurate record of each source and saving you from having to write down source information.

Some libraries still use traditional card catalogs consisting of 3-by-5-inch cards that index all the books in the library's holdings. The traditional catalog includes three types of cards: title, author, and subject. For works of fiction, only title and author cards are included. Arranged alphabetically, the three types of cards may be filed together, or there may be a separate catalog for the subject cards.

Both the computerized catalog and traditional card catalog provide call numbers that tell you where to locate books on the library's shelves. Use the library floor plan and the call-number guides posted on shelves to locate the particular section of the library indicated in the call number. Then scan the letters or numbers on the spines of books until you locate the book you need. Be sure to scan the surrounding books, which usually cover similar or related topics. By doing this, you may find other useful sources you overlooked in the card catalog.

Bibliographies

A bibliography lists sources on a particular subject, including books, articles, government publications, and other sources. Some bibliographies also provide brief summaries or descriptions of the sources they list.

To locate a bibliography on your subject online, just combine the word *bibliography* with a relevant keyword for your topic. For example, you can search your library's online catalog for *animal communication* and *bibliography*. (For more on using keywords, see p. 626.) Another option is to check the *Bibliographic Index*, a reference work that lists available bibliographies. A new volume is published each year, so be sure to check several recent volumes of the index.

Periodical Indexes

Periodicals include newspapers, popular magazines, and scholarly journals. Periodicals are differentiated by their content and frequency of publication. Popular magazines are written for the general public and include articles of general interest, easy-to-understand language, news items, interviews, and opinion pieces. Usually they do not include bibliographies, and any sources used are cited informally within the article. Some popular magazines are *Newsweek, Popular Science*, and *Psychology Today*. Scholarly journals are written for researchers, professionals, and students. Such journals typically include the results of research studies and experiments, statistics and analysis, in-depth evaluations of specialized topics, overviews of all the research on a given subject, bibliographies, and references. Examples include the *Journal of Bioethics, Film Quarterly*, and the *American Journal of Family Law*. For academic essays, it is best not to rely solely on information from popular magazines.

Because periodicals are published frequently (daily, weekly, or monthly), they often contain the most up-to-date information on a subject. Although magazines the library subscribes to are listed in the catalog, specific articles are not. To find them, you must use periodical indexes and abstracts. Indexes list articles by title, author, and subject. Abstracts list articles and also provide a brief summary of each one. Library catalogs list periodical indexes and abstracts held by the library.

Most indexes and abstracts are available as computer databases as well as in print form. These online indexes and abstracts may be accessed through the Internet, or they may be available on a campus network. Keep in mind that the name of the electronic version of an index or abstract may be different from that of the print version. Check with your librarian to see what databases are available and whether the library charges a fee for online services. Because online indexes are updated frequently, sometimes every week, you can use them to locate very current information. Most computerized indexes and abstracts cover only the most recent years, so you may need to consult print indexes if you need older material.

There are two types of periodical indexes — general and specialized. General indexes list articles on a wide range of subjects that have been published in popular magazines. Specialized indexes and abstracts reference scholarly or technical articles within a specific academic field of study.

Conducting Research on the Internet

The Internet is a major resource for all types of research. To use the Internet, your computer must be equipped with either a modem, which is connected to a phone or cable line, or a network card that hooks up to an Ethernet data line or a DSL (Digital Subscriber Line) port. Many colleges offer Internet access in dormitories, through campus computer centers, and in the library. The Internet offers a wide variety of sources — including listservs, newsgroups, and email — but you will most likely find the World Wide Web (WWW or the Web) to be the most helpful in both academic and workplace research because it offers you access to millions of diverse sources.

The World Wide Web

The World Wide Web is made up of a vast collection of Web sites — linked electronic documents that can include video and audio as well as text and graphics. Each Web site has a home page, which usually includes information about the site and a directory of links to other pages on the site. A Web site is accessed by way of a Web address, called a *uniform resource locator* (URL), and a Web browser, a computer program that enables you to view Web pages and navigate the Internet. Netscape Navigator and Microsoft Internet Explorer are the two most commonly used Web browsers. Most Web pages also include underlined topics called *hyperlinks*, which you click on to access related pages or sites

Every Web site has a unique URL that consists of three basic parts.

Protocol used to view Web page	Domain name	Path, or location of page

http://www.spu.edu/help/index.html

Beginning Research on the World Wide Web

The Web contains extraordinary amounts of information that span millions of Web sites, most of which are not organized. Therefore, you will need to use a subject directory or search engine to locate the information you need.

Subject Directory. A *subject directory* uses various categories and subcategories to classify Web resources. Some subject directories also include reviews or evaluations of sites. A subject directory can be especially helpful when you have decided on a general topic for an essay but still need to narrow it further. Some subject directories are part of a search engine, whereas others are stand-alone sites. Here are a few useful subject directories.

http://infomine.ucr.edu   www.lii.org

www.academicinfo.net   www.about.com

Search Engine. A *search engine* is an application that can help you find information on a particular topic. When you use a search engine, you begin by typing a keyword, phrase, or question into a search box. The search engine then looks for documents that contain the keyword or phrase you told it to search for. Here are some common search engines.

www.altavista.com   www.google.com

www.dogpile.com   www.yahoo.com

As you work with search engines, you will discover that a given search engine's usefulness often depends not only on your topic but also on how specific your keywords are. *Keywords* are words that describe your topic. If a keyword or phrase is too general, a search could turn up hundreds or perhaps thousands of sites, most of which will not be helpful. Your searches will be more productive if you use the following guidelines.

Guidelines for Using Search Engines Effectively

1. **Place quotation marks around a phrase to limit your search:** For example, "single motherhood" will give you topics related to single motherhood. Without quotation marks, the keyword search would provide all sources that use the word *single* as well as all the sources that use the word *motherhood*.

2. **Use AND or a plus (+) sign to join words that both must appear in a document:** *psychology* AND *history* would provide sources that mention both psychology and history.

3. **Use OR to indicate synonyms, when only one needs to appear in the document**. For example, *job* OR *career* would provide more options than just *job* or just *career*.

(Continued)

4. **Place NOT or a minus sign (−) before words that should not appear in the document.** For example, *camels* NOT *cigarettes* would provide sources on the animal only.

5. **Use parentheses to group one or more keywords together and combine them with another set of keywords:** For example, (*timepiece* OR *watch* OR *clock*) AND *production*.

6. **Use an asterisk (*) to indicate letters that may vary in spelling or words that may have variant endings:** "social psycholog*". The search will then find sources with the words *psychology*, *psychologist*, *psychologists*, and so forth.

Because different search engines usually generate different results, it is a good idea to use more than one search engine when researching a given topic. For a general search, you might start with a search engine such as Google. Once you've narrowed the topic, however, you might want to use a more specialized search engine, such as one that is geared to a particular discipline or specialty. For example, if your topic involves the Democratic Party, Google might point you to a site entitled Political Science Resources on the Web, which has its own search engine.

How to Choose and Evaluate Sources

Once you locate potential sources of information on a topic, you need to evaluate each one before reading and taking notes. Students often make the mistake of photocopying many articles, printing out dozens of Web pages, and lugging home numerous books only to find that the sources are not useful or several contain identical information. Save yourself time by taking a few minutes to identify which sources will be most relevant and reliable.

Choosing Relevant Sources

A relevant source contains information that helps to answer one or more of your research questions. Answering the following questions will help you determine whether a source is relevant.

- **Is the source too general or too specialized for your intended audience?** To decide if a source is too general or too technical, you should consider the audience for which it was written. For example, suppose you are researching the environmental effects of recycling cans and bottles. An article in *Reader's Digest* would be written for a general audience who would be more likely concerned with recycling efforts in the home but not the detailed environmental effects. Conversely, an article in *Environmental Science and Technology* would be written for scientists and may be too technical to be of use.

- **Is the source recent enough for your purposes?** Especially in rapidly changing fields of study, outdated sources are not useful, except when you need to give a historical perspective. For example, a five-year-old article on the use of air bags to improve car safety may not include recent information on the recently discovered dangers air bags pose to young children in the front passenger seat.

Choosing Reliable Sources

A reliable source is honest, accurate, and credible. Determine whether a source is reliable by using the following questions.

Questions for Evaluating Sources

1. **Is the source scholarly?** An article that appears in a scholarly journal or textbook has been reviewed by a panel of professionals in the field prior to publication. Therefore, scholarly sources tend to be trustworthy.

2. **Does the source have a solid reputation?** Some magazines, such as *Time* and *Newsweek*, are known for responsible reporting, whereas other periodicals have a reputation for sensationalism and should be avoided or approached skeptically.

3. **Is the author an expert in the field?** Check the author's credentials. Information about authors may be given in a headnote or at the end of an article, or on the title page or in the preface of a book. You might also check a reference book such as *Contemporary Authors* to verify credentials.

4. **Does the author approach the topic fairly and objectively?** A writer who overlooks opposing views, distorts facts, or ignores information that does not fit his or her opinion may present a biased and incomplete view of a topic. Although you can use a biased source to understand a particular viewpoint, you must also seek other sources that present the alternative views.

Evaluating Internet Sources

The Internet offers many excellent and reputable sources. It is important to remember, though, that not all sites are accurate and unbiased and that misinformation often appears on the Web. When using an Internet source, then, you should ask the following questions to evaluate its purpose, content, accuracy, and timeliness.

Questions for Evaluating Internet Sources

1. **Who sponsors or publishes the site?** Understanding the purpose of an Internet source will help you avoid its potential biases. To determine the purpose of a site, identify the sponsor — the organization or person who paid to place it on the Web. The extension information at the end of the URL often indicates whether a site is informational (*.edu* for school- and *.gov* for government-sponsored sites), commercial (*.com* for business-owned or profit-driven sites), or for advocacy purposes (*.org* for sites sponsored by a public service group or nonprofit organization). For example, the National Institutes of Health (www.nih.gov) site is government sponsored, so its information should be reliable and fairly objective. Remember that a site may be reliable but also advocate definite opinions, so be sure to present alternative views as well.

2. **Who wrote the information, and is it clearly presented and well written?** Often the writer's name and credentials are listed, and his or her email address may be provided. This kind of information can help you determine whether the Web page is a reliable resource. Regardless of who is the author of the site, the information should be well written and organized. If it is carelessly put together, you should be wary of it.

3. **Is the information presented verifiable and supported by credible evidence?** Because accuracy is especially important when you are researching an academic paper, ask yourself the following questions.

   • **Is a bibliography or a list of works cited provided?** If sources are not included, you should question the accuracy of the site.

   • **Can the accuracy of the information be checked elsewhere**? In most instances you should be able to verify Internet information by checking another source, preferably a print source.

   • **Is it clear that opinions are opinions?** It is not a good idea to trust writers who treat their own opinions as facts.

   • **Is the document in complete form?** If you're looking at a summary, use the site to try to find the original source. If you can't locate the original, be skeptical of the source that contains the summary. Original information generally has fewer errors and is often preferred in academic papers.

4. **Is the site current and up-to-date?** You can check the timeliness of a site by identifying when the site was established, the date of the last revision, and when the document you are looking at was posted, and by checking to see if the links are up-to-date.

Taking Notes and Avoiding Plagiarism

As you read sources, you will need to take notes to use later. The following section discusses note-taking, highlighting and annotating sources, and recording quotations. It also offers advice for avoiding plagiarism.

Extracting Information through Note-Taking

As you work with sources, be sure to record complete information for each one: author(s), title, beginning and ending pages, title, call number, publisher, place of publication, and copyright date. For journals, include the name of the journal along with the volume or issue number and the date of issue.

When taking research notes, you'll probably need to make summary notes, write paraphrases, annotate your sources, and copy quotations. As you take notes, think about the ideas in your source, how they fit with other ideas, and how they might work in your research paper.

For more on writing summaries, see Chapter 1, p. 13.

Writing Summary Notes

Much of your note-taking will be in the form of summary notes, which condense or reduce information from sources. It is a good idea to take summary notes when you want to record the gist of an author's ideas but do not need the exact wording or a paraphrase. Remember that everything you put in summary notes must be in your own words.

Writing Paraphrases

When paraphrasing, you restate the author's ideas in your own words. You use different sentence patterns and vocabulary but keep the author's intended meaning. In most cases, a paraphrase is approximately the same length as the original material. Compose a paraphrase when you want to record the author's ideas and details but do not want to use a direct quotation. You should never paraphrase an entire article; instead, paraphrase only the ideas or details you intend to use.

Read this excerpt from a source; then compare it to the sample paraphrase that follows.

EXCERPT FROM ORIGINAL

Learning some items may interfere with retrieving others, especially when the items are similar. If someone gives you a phone number to remember, you may be able to recall it later. But if two more people give you their numbers, each successive number will be more difficult to recall. Such proactive interference occurs when something you learned earlier disrupts recall of something you experienced later. As you collect more and more information, your mental attic never fills, but it certainly gets cluttered.

DAVID G. MYERS, *Psychology*

PARAPHRASE

When proactive interference happens, things you have already learned prevent you from remembering things you learn later. In other words, details you learn first may make it harder to recall closely related details you learn subsequently. You can think of your memory as an attic. You can always add more junk to it. However, it will become messy and disorganized. For example, you can remember one new phone number, but if you have two or more new numbers to remember the task becomes harder.

Use the following guidelines to write effective paraphrases.

Guidelines for Writing Paraphrases

1. **Read first; then write.** You may find it helpful to read material more than once before paraphrasing.
2. **If you must use any of the author's wording, enclose it in quotation marks.** If you do not use quotation marks, you may inadvertently use the same wording in your paper, which would result in plagiarism.
3. **Work sentence by sentence, restating each in your own words.** One easy way to avoid copying an author's words is to read a sentence, cover it up or look away, and then write. Check to be sure your version is accurate but not too similar to the original. No more than two or three consecutive words should be the same as in the original.
4. **Choose synonyms that do not change the author's meaning or intent.** Consult a dictionary, if necessary.
5. **Use your own sentence structure and sentence order.** Using an author's sentence structure can be considered plagiarism. Also rearrange the order of ideas within a sentence.
6. **Use two or more short sentences instead of a lengthy one.** If the original has a lengthy sentence, write your paraphrase in shorter sentences.
7. **Be sure to record the publication information (including page numbers) for all sources you paraphrase.** You will need this information to document the sources in your paper.

Highlighting and Annotating Sources

If you have a printout or photocopy from a source, highlighting and writing annotations (marginal notes) are effective ways to identify what is important and record your own responses. Highlight or underline key words and phrases and a writer's most important points, such as the thesis statement. Annotate by jotting down your ideas about what you are reading. Annotating is a way of "talking back" to the author — to question, challenge, agree, or disagree. By annotating, you can discover new approaches to your topic, critically evaluate the source, and come up with new ideas to write about. Whether you use highlighting or annotating, be selective about what you mark or comment on, keeping the purpose of your research in mind.

For more on highlighting and annotating, see Chapter 1, p. 10.

Recording Quotations

Sometimes it is advisable, and even necessary, to use a direct quotation — a writer's words exactly as they appear in the original source. Use quotations to record wording that is unusual or striking or to report the exact words of an expert on your topic. Such quotations, when used sparingly, can be particularly effective. Be sure to record a direct quotation, precisely as it appears in the source: The author's spelling, punctuation, and capitalization must be recorded exactly. Also write down the page number on which the material being quoted appears in the original source. Be sure to indicate that you are copying a direct quotation by including the term *direct quotation* and the page number in parentheses in your notes.

You may delete a phrase or sentence from a quotation as long as you do not change the meaning of the quotation. When deleting a phrase or sentence, use an ellipsis mark [. . .], three spaced periods, to indicate that you have made a deletion.

Avoiding Plagiarism

Plagiarism — the use of an author's ideas or words as if they were your own and neglecting to give the author credit — is a serious error. All quotations, summaries, and paraphrases must be documented. Most students do not plagiarize deliberately; they do not directly copy another writer's work and call it their own. Instead, plagiarism usually occurs as a result of careless note-taking or of the failure to acknowledge the ideas of others. The following box lists what does and does not require documentation.

What Does and Does Not Require Documentation

Documentation Required	Documentation Not Required
Summaries, paraphrases, and quotations	Common knowledge
Obscure or recently discovered facts	Everyday facts (presidential birth dates, names of Supreme Court Justices, and so forth)
Others' opinions	
Others' field research (results of opinion polls, case studies, statistics)	Standard definitions of academic terms
	Your own ideas or conclusions
Quotations or paraphrases from interviews you conduct	Your own field research (surveys or observations)

Especially when paraphrasing a source, check to be sure your wording is not too close to the original writer's. Compare the following original source quotation with its plagiarized paraphrase.

EXCERPT FROM ORIGINAL

Learning some items may interfere with retrieving others, especially when the items are similar. If someone gives you a phone number to remember, you may be able to recall it later. But if two more people give you their numbers, each successive number will be more difficult to recall. Such proactive interference occurs when something you learned earlier disrupts recall of something you experienced later. As you collect more and more information, your mental attic never fills, but it certainly gets cluttered.

DAVID G. MYERS, *Psychology*

EXAMPLE OF PLAGIARISM

When you learn some things, it may interfere with your ability to remember others. This happens when the things are similar. Suppose a person gives you a phone number to remember. You probably will be able to remember it later. Now, suppose two persons give you numbers. Each successive number will be harder to remember. Proactive interference happens when something you already learned prevents you from recalling something you experience later. As you learn more and more information your mental attic never gets full, but it will get cluttered.

Although this paraphrase does substitute some synonyms — *remembering* for *retrieving*, for example — it is still an example of plagiarism. The writer has changed neither the style nor the sentence order of the original.

Use the following tips to avoid plagiarizing sources in your writing.

Guidelines for Avoiding Plagiarism

1. **Place in quotation marks everything you copy directly from a source.**

2. **Make sure that a paraphrase does not mix the author's wording and your own.**

3. **Always acknowledge the unique ideas or opinions of others, even if you do not quote them directly and regardless of whether they are in print or another medium.** Movies, videos, documentaries, interviews, and computerized sources all require acknowledgment. Use an in-text citation to indicate that an idea or a point of view is not your own.

4. **While you do not need to acknowledge information that is common knowledge — such as well-known scientific facts and historical events — it is necessary to acknowledge any unique applications, opinions, or new research relating to well-known facts and events.**

Documenting Your Sources: MLA Style

The system described in this section is recommended by the Modern Language Association (MLA). If you are unsure of whether to use the MLA system, check with your instructor.

In the MLA system, both in-text citations used to identify sources within the text and a list of works cited are provided to document sources, as the models in this chapter show. For more information, consult the following source.

> Gibaldi, Joseph. *MLA Handbook for Writers of Research Papers*, 6th ed. New York: MLA, 2003.

The student paper that appears later in this chapter uses MLA style (see pp. 645–49), as do all student essays in Chapters 5–14.

In-Text Citations

When you paraphrase, summarize, or quote from a source in the text of your paper, you must credit the source of the borrowed material. You give credit by providing an in-text citation, a brief reference that lets readers know there is a complete description of the source in a list of works cited at the end of your paper. There are two basic ways to write an in-text citation.

Use an Attribution

The first time you mention a source, provide brief background information that provides a context and establishes the source as relevant or important. To introduce a quotation effectively, use an introductory phrase or clause: "As Markham points out" or "Bernstein observes that," for example. Introducing the source of a quotation provides a better flow of information to your readers and cuts down the length of the citation because only the page number need be included.

> Jo-Ellan Dimitius, a jury selection consultant whose book *Reading People* discusses methods of predicting behavior, observes that big spenders often suffer from low self-esteem (35).

Use the author's full name the first time you mention the author. After the first mention, give only the author's last name in subsequent citations to the same source.

In MLA style, lengthy quotations (more than three lines of poetry or more than four typed lines of prose) are indented in *block form*, ten spaces from the left margin.

Omit the quotation marks from and double-space a block quotation. Introduce a block quotation in the sentence that precedes it; a colon is often used at the end of the introduction. Note that for a block quotation, the parenthetical citation appears *after* the final sentence period. This is different from the style for short quotations within the text, in which the parenthetical citation precedes the period.

BLOCK QUOTATION, MLA STYLE

Although a business is a profit-making organization, it is also a social organization. As Hicks and Gwynne note:

> In Western society, businesses are essentially economic organizations, with both the organizations themselves and the individuals in them dedicated to making as much money as possible in the most efficient way. But businesses are also social organizations, each of which has its unique culture. Like all social groups, businesses are made up of people of both sexes and a wide range of ages, who play different roles, occupy different positions in the group, and behave in different ways while at work. (174)

Use a Parenthetical Citation

When citing a source parenthetically, include both the author's last name and the page number(s) in parentheses at the end of the sentence. Do not separate the name and page number with a comma.

"Countercultures reject the conventional wisdom and standards of the dominant culture and provide alternatives to mainstream culture" (Thompson and Hickey 76).

Many instructors prefer that you use attributions rather than parenthetical citations. For either type of citation, use the following rules.

- Do not use the word *page* or the abbreviation *p.* or *pp.*
- Place the sentence period after the closing parenthesis, unless the citation follows a block quotation. (See above.)
- If a quotation ends the sentence, insert the closing quotation marks before the parentheses.

The following section provides guidelines for formatting some common types of in-text citations in MLA style.

A single author.

According to Vance Packard . . . (58).
. . . (Packard 58).

Two or three authors. Include all authors' names, either in an attribution or in a parenthetical citation.

Marquez and Allison assert . . . (74).
. . . (Marquez and Allison 74).

Four or more authors. You may use either the first author's last name followed by *et al.* (in roman type, not italic) or all of the authors' last names. (The Latin *et al.* means "and others.") Whichever option you choose, apply it consistently within your paper.

Hong et al. maintain . . . (198).
. . . (Hong et al. 198).

Two or more works by the same author. When citing two or more sources by the same author or group of authors in your paper, include the full or abbreviated title in the citation to indicate the proper work.

Pendergrast describes . . . (*Coca-Cola* 96).
. . . (Pendergrast, *Coca-Cola* 96).

Corporate or organizational author. When the author of the source is only given as a corporation, organization, or government office, reference the organization's name as the author name. Use abbreviations such as *Natl.* and *Cong.* in parenthetical references of government authors.

According to the National Institute of Mental Health . . . (2).
. . . (Natl. Institute of Mental Health 2).

Unknown author. If the author is unknown, use the full title in an attribution or a shortened form in parentheses.

According to the article "Medical Mysteries and Surprises," . . . (79).
. . . ("Medical Mysteries" 79).

Work within an anthology or textbook. Name the author who wrote the work (not the editor of the anthology) and include the page number(s) from the anthology. The corresponding entry in the list of works cited begins with the author's last name; it also names the editor of the anthology.

IN-TEXT CITATION

According to Nora Crow . . . (226).
. . . (Crow 226).

WORKS CITED ENTRY

Crow, Nora F. "Swift and the Woman Scholar." *Pope, Swift, and Women Writers*. Ed. Donald C.
   Mell. Newark: U of Delaware P, 1996. 222-38.

Multivolume work. When citing two or more volumes of a multivolume work, indicate the volume number, followed by a colon and the page number.

Terman indicates . . . (2: 261).
. . . (Terman 2: 261).

Indirect sources. When quoting an indirect source (someone whose ideas came to you through another source, such as a magazine article or book), make this clear by adding, in parentheses the last name and page number of the source in which the quote or information appeared, preceded by the abbreviation *qtd. in.*

> According to Ephron (qtd. in Thomas 33), . . .

Literature and poetry. Include information that will help readers locate the material in any edition of the literary work. Include page numbers from the edition you use.

- *For novels*: Cite page and chapter numbers.
  (109; ch. 5)
- *For poems:* Cite line numbers instead of page numbers; use the word *line* or *lines* in the first reference only.
  FIRST REFERENCE: (lines 12-15)
  LATER REFERENCES: (16-18)
- *For plays*: Give the act, scene, and line numbers in Arabic numerals, separated by periods.
  (*Macbeth* 2.1.32-37)

Include complete publication information for the edition you use in the list of works cited.

Internet sources. In general, Internet sources are cited like their printed counterparts. Give enough information in the citation so that readers can locate the source in your list of works cited. If the electronic source provides page numbers, you should provide them too. If the source uses another ordering system, such as paragraphs (*par.* or *pars.*), sections (*sec.*), or screens (*screen*), provide the abbreviation with the appropriate number.

> Brian Beckman argues that "centrifugal force is a fiction" (par. 6).
> . . . (Beckman, par. 6).

If the source does not have paragraphs or page numbers, which is often the case, then cite the work by title or author.

> TITLE: According to the online art dictionary *ArtLex*, . . .
> AUTHOR: Teresa Schmidt discusses . . .
>   . . . (Schmidt).

Works Cited List

On a separate page at the end of your paper, you must include an alphabetical list of all the sources you cite. The list is headed *Works Cited*. Follow these general guidelines for preparing the list.

1. List only the sources you cite in your paper. If you consulted a source but did not cite it in your paper, do not include it in the list of works cited.

2. Put the list on a separate page at the end of your paper. The heading Works Cited should be centered an inch below the top margin of the page. Do not use quotation marks, underlining, or bold type for the heading.

3. Alphabetize the list by authors' last names. For works with multiple authors, invert only the first author's name.

> Kaplan, Justine, and Anne Bernays. *The Language of Names*. New York: Simon, 1997.

4. Capitalize the first word and all other words in a title except *a, an, the, to,* coordinating conjunctions, and prepositions.

5. Italicize or underline titles of books and names of journals. You can use italics if your instructor approves.

6. Indent the second and all subsequent lines of each entry five spaces. This is known as the *hanging indent* style.

7. Double-space the entire list.

The following sections describe how to format Works Cited entries for books, periodicals, electronic sources, and other sources.

Books

General guidelines and sample entries for books follow.

1. Begin with the author's last name, followed by the first name.

2. Provide the full title of the book, including the subtitle. It should be italicized or underlined and capitalized.

3. If applicable, include the original publication date, editor, translator, edition, and volumes used.

4. Give the place of publication. Do not abbreviate city names (use *Los Angeles*, not *LA*). Unless the city is not easily recognizable, it is not necessary to include an abbreviation for the state. When you do need to add a state abbreviation, use postal style (for example, *MT* instead of *Mont.*).

5. Use a shortened form of the publisher's name; usually one word is sufficient (*Houghton Mifflin* is listed as *Houghton*). For university presses, use the abbreviations *U* for *University* and *P* for *Press* with no periods.

6. Use the most recent publication date listed on the book's copyright page.

Book with one author.

> Rybczynski, Witold. *The Look of Architecture*. New York: Oxford UP, 2001.

Book with two or more authors. List the names in the order they appear on the title page of the book, and separate the names with commas. The second and subsequent authors' names are *not* reversed. For books with four or more authors, you can either list all names or list only the first author's name followed by *et al*.

TWO AUTHORS

> Postel, Sandra, and Brian Richter. *Rivers for Life: Managing Water for People and Nature*. Washington: Island, 2003.

FOUR OR MORE AUTHORS

Kelly, Rita Mae, et al. *Gender, Globalization, and Democratization*. Lanham: Rowman, 2001.

Book with no named author. Put the title first and alphabetize the entry by title. (Do not consider the words *A*, *An*, and *The* when alphabetizing.)

The Ticker Symbol Book. New York: McGraw, 1997.

Book by a corporation or organization. List the organization or corporation as the author.

American Medical Association. *American Medical Association Family Medical Guide*. Hoboken: Wiley, 2004.

Government publication. If there is no author, list the government followed by the department and agency of the government. Use abbreviations such as *Dept.* and *Natl.* if the meaning is clear.

United States. Dept. of Health and Human Services. Natl. Institute of Mental Health. *Helping Children and Adolescents Cope with Violence and Disasters*. Bethesda: NIMH, 2001.

Edited book or anthology. List the editor's name followed by a comma and the abbreviation *ed.* or *eds.*

Frazier, Ian, and Jason Wilson, eds. *The Best American Travel Writing 2003*. Boston: Houghton, 2003.

Work within an anthology. List the author and title of the work, followed by the title and editor of the anthology; city, publisher, and date; and the pages within the anthology where the work appears.

Tan, Amy. "Two Kinds." *The Story and Its Writer*. Ed. Ann Charters. Boston: Bedford, 2003. 1278-86.

Introduction, preface, foreword, or afterword.

Sacks, Oliver. Foreword. *Thinking in Pictures: And Other Reports from My Life with Autism*. By Temple Grandin. New York: Vintage, 1996.

Translated book. After the title include the abbreviation *Trans.*, followed by the first and last name of the translator.

Houellebecq, Michel. *The Elementary Particles*. Trans. Frank Wynne. New York: Knopf, 2000.

Two or more works by the same author(s). Use the author's name for only the first entry. For subsequent entries, use three hyphens followed by a period. List the entries in alphabetical order by title.

> Covey, Stephen R. *Principle-Centered Leadership*. New York: Simon, 1991.
>
> --- . *The Seven Habits of Highly Effective People: Restoring the Character Ethic*. New York: Simon, 1989.

Edition other than the first. Indicate the number of the edition following the title.

> Myers, David G. *Exploring Psychology*. 5th ed. New York: Worth, 2002.

Multivolume work. Give the number of volumes after the title.

> Kazdin, Alan E., ed. *Encyclopedia of Psychology*. 8 vols. Washington: American Psychological Association, 2000.

Encyclopedia or dictionary entry.

> "Triduum." *Merriam-Webster's Collegiate Dictionary*. 11th ed. 2003.

One volume of a multivolume work. Give the volume number after the title, and list the number of volumes in the complete work after the date, using the abbreviations *Vol.* and *vols*.

> Kazdin, Alan E., ed. *Encyclopedia of Psychology*. Vol. 3. Washington: American Psychological Association, 2000. 8 vols.

Article or chapter in an anthology. List the author and title of the article first and then the title of the anthology, the editor's name (introduced by the abbreviation *Ed.*), and the publication information.

> McGowan, Moray. "Multiple Masculinities in Turkish-German Men's Writing." *Conceptions of Postwar German Masculinity*. Ed. M. Kimmel. Albany: State U of New York P, 2001. 310-20.

Articles in Periodicals

General guidelines and sample entries for various types of periodical articles follow.

1. Use the same format for listing authors' names as for books (see p. 638). If no author is listed, begin the entry with the article title and alphabetize the entry by its title.
2. Italicize or underline the title of the periodical. Do not include the word *A, An,* or *The* at the beginning: *Journal of the American Medical Association, New York Times*.
3. Abbreviate the names of months except for *May, June,* and *July*.
4. List dates in the following order: day, month, year.
5. If an article begins in one place, such as pages 19 to 21, and is continued elsewhere, such as on pages 79 to 80, just write 19+ for the page numbers (do not write 19-80).

Article in a scholarly journal when each issue begins with page 1. After the journal title, include the volume number, a period, and the issue number, followed by the year in parentheses, a colon, and the inclusive page numbers.

> Schug, Mark C., and J. R. Clark. "Economics for the Heart and the Head." *International Journal of Social Education* 16.1 (2001): 45-54.

Article in a scholarly journal with issues paged continuously through each volume. Only the volume number precedes the year.

> Lawson, David M. "The Development of Abusive Personality: A Trauma Response." *Journal of Counseling and Development* 79 (2001): 505-09.

Article in a newspaper.

> Gay, Joel. "Glorious Wreck Rears Its Head." *Anchorage Daily News* 8 Sept. 2004, final ed.: A1+.

Article in a monthly magazine.

> Bethell, Tom. "Democracy: A Little Goes a Long Way." *American Spectator* Nov. 2003: 42-43.

Article in a weekly magazine.

> Henneberger, Melinda. "Tending to the Flock." *Newsweek* 13 Sept. 2004: 34-36.

Editorial or letter to the editor. Cite the article or letter beginning with the author's name, and add the word *Editorial* or *Letter* followed by a period after the title. An author's name or a title may be missing.

> "The Search for Livable Worlds." Editorial. *New York Times* 8 Sept. 2004: A22.
> Wolansky, Taras. Letter. *Wired* May 2004: 25.

Book or film review. List the reviewer's name and title of the review. After the title add the words *Rev. of* and give the title and author or director of the book or film reviewed. Include publication information for the review itself, not for the material reviewed.

> Gabler, Neal. "The Rise and Rise of Celebrity Journalism." Rev. of *The Untold Story: My Twenty Years Running the National Enquirer,* by Iain Calder, and *The Importance of Being Famous: Behind the Scenes of the Celebrity Industrial Complex,* by Maureen Orth. *Columbia Journalism Review* July/Aug. 2004: 48-51.

Internet Sources

Citations for Internet sources should include enough information to enable readers to locate the sources. Because electronic sources change frequently, it is often necessary to provide more information than you do for print sources. To help readers locate an online source easily, give its network address, or URL (uniform resource locator), at the end of your citation, enclosed in angle brackets (< >). If a URL is too long to fit on one line, divide it only following a slash.

General guidelines and sample entries for Internet sources follow.

1. Include authors' names when they are available.
2. Include the full title of the work. Enclose titles of articles in quotation marks; italicize or underline the titles of longer works.
3. Provide names of editors, compilers, or translators, if appropriate.
4. Tell where and when the material was originally published, if it was originally published in print. Include volume and issue numbers, names of periodicals, and so forth.
5. Include the date the document was published electronically as well as the date you accessed the document.
6. Provide page, paragraph, or section numbers, if available.

For some Internet sources it may not be possible to locate all of the required information; provide the information that is available.

World Wide Web site. Include the author's name (if it is not known, begin the entry with the title), title or site description (such as *Home page* if the site is untitled), date of publication, name of any sponsoring organization, date of access, and URL.

> *The Bulwer-Lytton Fiction Contest.* Ed. Scott Rice. 7 Sept. 1997. English Dept., San Jose State U. 8 Sept. 2004 <http://www.bulwer-lytton.com>.
>
> *The Huntington Archive of Buddhist and Related Art.* Ed. Andrew M. LaMoreaux. 15 Oct. 1995. College of the Arts, Ohio State U. 8 Sept. 2004 <http://kaladarshan.arts.ohio-state .edu/>.

Email. Provide the writer's name, the subject line (if available) in quotation marks, the words *E-mail to*, and the recipient's name. End with the date of the message.

> Morales, Anita. "Antique China." E-mail to Ruth E. Thompson. 11 Jan. 2002.

Article from an online journal.

> Kimball, Bobbi. "Health Care's Human Crisis: Rx for an Evolving Profession." *Online Journal of Issues in Nursing* 9.2 (2004). 8 Sept. 2004 <http://www.nursingworld.org/ojin/ topic24/tpc24_1.htm>.

Article from an online subscription service.

> Wood, Robert A. "School as a Risk Environment for Children Allergic to Cats and a Site of Transfer of Cat Allergen to Homes." *Pediatrics* 106.2 (Aug. 2000): 431. *Expanded Academic ASAP.* InfoTrac. Shoreline Lib., King County Lib. System, Shoreline, WA. 4 Oct. 2001 <http://infotrac.galegroup.com/itweb/kcls_remote>.

Posting to a listserv or newsgroup. Include the author's name, the title or subject line enclosed in quotation marks, the phrase *Online posting*, the date of posting, the name of the list, the date of access, and the list's URL or the moderator's or supervisor's email address. If possible, cite an archival version.

> McCarty, Willard. "Smart Medicines?" Online posting. 10 May 2004. Humanist Discussion
>   Group. 8 Sept. 2004 <http://lists.village.virginia.edu/lists_archive/Humanist/
>   v18/0002.html>.

Online book. Include the author's name; title (underlined); the name of any editor, translator, or compiler; original publication information (if available); date of access; and URL.

> Twain, Mark. *A Connecticut Yankee in King Arthur's Court*. New York: Harper, 1889. *Electronic*
>   *Text Center*. U of Virginia. 8 Sept. 2004 <http://etext.lib.virginia.edu/modeng/
>   modengT.browse.html>.

Other Sources

Publication on diskette, CD-ROM, or another electronic medium. These sources are cited much like a book. Include the author's name and title. If the work is available in print, include publication information.

> *The Time-Life Works of Shakespeare*. Videodisc. Chicago: Clearvue, 1995.

Material from a CD-ROM database. Give the title of the material (in quotation marks), the title of the database (underlined), and all other publication details. Place the date of electronic publication at the end of the reference.

> Hurley, Patrick J. "Writing Basic Arguments." *A Concise Introduction to Logic*. CD-ROM.
>   Australia: Wadsworth, 2000.

Personal interviews or personal communication. Indicate the name of the person, followed by the type of communication. For interviews you conducted, indicate the type of interview (telephone, personal, email, and so forth).

> Thompson, Alan. Telephone interview. 19 Jan. 2002.
> Chevez, Maria. Letter to the author. 14 July 2001.

See p. 642 for help with citing an email message.

Published interviews. List the person interviewed, and then list the title of the interview (if available) in quotation marks (underline the title if it is a complete published work). If the interview has no title, label it *Interview* and give the source. Include the date of the interview.

> Everett, Percival. Interview. *Bomb* Summer 2004: 46-51.

Published letters. If the letter was published, cite it as you would a selection in a book.

> Lewis, C. S. "To His Father (LPIII: 82)." 4 Sept. 1907. *The Collected Letters of C. S. Lewis,*
> *Vol. 1: Family Letters, 1905-1931.* Ed. Walter Hooper. San Francisco: Harper, 2004. 5.

Film, video, or DVD. List the title, director, and key performer(s). Include the name of the distributor and the year of distribution.

> *The Big Sleep.* Dir. Howard Hawks. Perf. Humphrey Bogart and Lauren Bacall. 1946. DVD.
> Warner Home Video, 2000.

Television or radio program. List the title of the program (underlined), then give key names (narrator, producer, director, actors) as necessary and the title of the series (neither underlined nor in quotation marks). Identify the network, local station and city, and broadcast date. When citing a particular episode or segment, include its title in quotation marks before the title of the program.

> "Beyond Vietnam." Narr. David Barsamian. *Alternative Radio.* Natl. Public Radio. KUOW,
> Seattle. 25 Aug. 2004.

Music recording. List the composer or performer, the title of the recording or composition, the names of the artists, the medium if not a CD (audiocassette, LP, audiotape), the production company, and the date. Titles of recordings should be underlined, but titles of compositions identified by form (for example, Symphony no. 5) should not.

> Lloyd-Webber, Andrew. *Phantom of the Opera.* Perf. Michael Crawford, Sarah Brightman, and
> Steve Barton. Polydor, 1987.

Students Write

The following research paper was written by Nicholas Destino for his first-year writing course at Niagara County Community College. Destino used the MLA style for formatting his paper and documenting sources. Notice his use of in-text citations and quotations to provide evidence in support of his thesis.

Destino 1

Nicholas Destino
Professor Thomas
English 101
10 November 2004

Do Animals Have Emotions?

Double-spaced

Centered title

   Somewhere in the savannas of Africa a mother elephant is dying in the company of many other pachyderms. Some of them are part of her family; some are fellow members of her herd. The dying elephant tips from side to side and seems to be balancing on a thin thread in order to sustain her life. Many of the other elephants surround her as she struggles to regain her balance. They also try to help by feeding and caressing her. After many attempts by the herd to save her life, they seem to realize that there is simply nothing more that can be done. She finally collapses to the ground in the presence of her companions. Most of the other elephants move away from the scene. There are, however, two elephants who remain behind with the dead elephant -- another mother and her calf. The mother turns her back to the body and taps it with one foot. Soon, the other elephants call for them to follow and eventually they do (Masson and McCarthy, *Elephants* 95). These movements, which are slow and ritualistic, suggest that elephants may be capable of interpreting and responding to the notion of death.

   The topic of animal emotions is one that, until recently, has rarely been discussed or studied by scientists. However, since the now famous comprehensive field studies of chimpanzees by the internationally renowned primatologist Jane Goodall, those who study animal behavior have begun to look more closely at the notion that animals feel emotions. As a result of their observations of various species of animals, a number of these researchers have come to the conclusion that animals do exhibit a wide range of emotions, such as grief, sympathy, and joy.

   One of the major reasons research into animal emotions has been avoided is that scientists fear being accused of *anthropomorphism* -- the act of attributing human qualities to animals. To do so is perceived as unscientific (Masson and McCarthy, "Hope and Joy" xviii). Frans de Waal, of the Yerkes Regional Primate Research Center in Atlanta, believes that if people are not open to the possibility of animals having emotions, they may be overlooking important information about both animals and humans. He explains his position in his article "Are We in Anthropodenial?" The term *anthropodenial,* which he coined, refers to "a blindness to the humanlike characteristics of other animals, or the animal-like characteristics of ourselves" (52). He proposes that because humans and

In-text citation of a work with two authors; short title given because two works by the authors are cited

Thesis statement

Attribution of quotation within text

Page number follows quotation

Destino 2

animals are so closely related, it would be impossible for one not to have some characteristics of the other. He contends, "If two closely related species act in the same
manner, their underlying mental processes are probably the same, too" (53). If de Waal
is correct, then humans can presume that animals do have emotions because of the
many similarities between human and animal behavior.

First main point

Grief has been observed in many different species. In many instances, their behaviors
(and presumably, therefore, their emotions) are uncannily similar to the behaviors of humans. Birds that mate for life have been observed showing obvious signs of grief when
their mates die. In *The Human Nature of Birds,* Theodore Barber includes a report from one
Dr. Franklin, who witnessed a male parrot caring for his mate by feeding her and trying to
help her raise herself when she was dying. Franklin observed the following scene:

Quotation longer than four lines indented ten spaces and not enclosed in quotation marks; period precedes citation for an indirect source

> Her unhappy spouse moved around her incessantly, his attention and tender
> cares redoubled. He even tried to open her beak to give her some nourish-
> ment. . . . At intervals, he uttered the most plaintive cries, then with his eyes
> fixed on her, kept a mournful silence. At length his companion breathed her
> last; from that moment he pined away, and died in the course of a few weeks.
> (qtd. in Barber 116)

First letter of a quotation changed to lowercase to fit into sentence; ellipsis mark used to indicate omitted material

Veterinarian Susan Wynn, discussing the physiological symptoms brought on by
emotional trauma in animals, notes that "[a]nimals definitely exhibit grief when they
lose an owner or another companion animal. . . . Signs of grief vary widely, including
lethargy, loss of appetite, hiding . . ." (5). This observation reinforces de Waal's position
that animals experience some of the same emotions as humans.

Perhaps the most extreme case of grief experienced by an animal is exemplified by
the true story of Flint, a chimp, when Flo, his mother, died. In her book, *Through a Window*, which elaborates on her thirty years of experience studying and living among the
chimps in Gombe, Tanzania, Jane Goodall gives the following account of Flint's experience with grief.

Source's credentials included within the text

> Flint became increasingly lethargic, refused most food and, with his immune sys-
> tem thus weakened, fell sick. The last time I saw him alive, he was hollow-eyed,
> gaunt and utterly depressed, huddled in the vegetation close to where Flo had
> died. [. . .] The last short journey he made, pausing to rest every few feet, was
> to the very place where Flo's body had lain. There he stayed for several hours,
> sometimes staring and staring into the water. He struggled on a little further,
> then curled up -- and never moved again. (196-97)

Destino 3

Of course, animal emotions are not limited to despair, sadness, and grief. Indeed, substantial evidence indicates that animals experience other, more uplifting emotions, such as sympathy, altruism, and joy.

Many scientists who study animal behavior have found that several species demonstrate sympathy to one another. In other words, they act as if they care about one another in much the same way as humans do. It is probably safe to assume that no animal is more sympathetic, or at least displays more behaviors associated with the emotion of sympathy, than chimpanzees. Those who have studied apes in the wild, including de Waal, have observed that animals who had been fighting make up with one another by kissing and hugging. Although other primates also engage in similar behaviors, chimps even go so far as to embrace, and attempt to console, the defeated animal ("Going Ape"). Another striking example of one animal showing sympathy for another is the account cited by Barber of a parrot comforting its sick mate. It is not, however, the only example of this type of behavior, especially among birds. Barber cites several other instances as well. According to Barber, documented records show that responsible observers have seen robins trying to keep each other alive. Also, terns have been known to lift another handicapped tern by its wing and transport it to safety. Likewise, a jay has been known to successfully seek human help when a newborn bird of a different species falls out of its nest. What makes this latter example particularly noteworthy is that the newborn wasn't a jay but an altogether different type of bird.

Had the jay been helping another jay, it would be easy to assume that the act of caring was the result of what scientists call *genetic altruism* -- the sociobiological theory that animals help each other in order to keep their own genes alive so they can reproduce and not become extinct. Simply put, scientists who believe in genetic altruism assume that when animals of the same species help each other out, they do so because there is something in it for them -- namely, the assurance that their species will continue. This theory certainly provides an adequate, unbiased scientific explanation for why animals such as birds might behave in a caring manner. However, if animals really help each other out only when doing so will perpetuate their species, then the jay would have had no genetic reason to help the newborn bird.

There is another popular explanation for why a bird of one species might help a bird of another species, however. Scientists who favor a related scientific theory called *mutual altruism* believe that animals will help each other because someday they themselves may need help, and then they will be able to count on reciprocal help (Hemelrijk

---

Transition to the second main point

Clear topic sentence

Information from a source paraphrased

Title used in citation since no author is given; no page number since the article occupies only one page

Information from a source summarized

Transitional sentence refers to incident reported in preceding paragraph.

Common knowledge that does not need to be documented

479-81). This theory is a plausible, nonanthropomorphic explanation for why animals show sympathy, regardless of whether they actually feel sympathy. This point is crucial because, after all, humans can't actually observe how an animal feels; we can only observe how it behaves. It is then up to the observer to draw some logical conclusion about why animals behave in the ways they do. The mutual altruism theory, however, also can be disputed. In many cases, animals have helped others even when the receiver of the help would probably never be in a position to return the favor. For example, there are many accounts of dolphins helping drowning or otherwise endangered swimmers. Phil Mercer, on the BBC Web site, reported that dolphins stopped a shark from attacking swimmers off the coast of New Zealand. The animals surrounded the swimmers for about 40 minutes while the great white shark circled. When the swimmers reached the shore, they remarked that they were sure that the dolphins acted deliberately to save them.

Not only do animals show sympathy, but they are also clearly able to express joy. For example, on many occasions primate experts have heard apes laugh while in the presence of other apes. These experts are sure that the noise they heard was laughter because of the clarity and tone of the sound. In their book, *Visions of Caliban*, Dale Peterson and Jane Goodall describe this laughter in detail.

> I'm not referring to a sort of pinched vocalization that might be roughly compared with human laughter, as in the "laughter" of a hyena. I'm referring to real laughter, fully recognizable laughter, the kind where you lie down on the ground and shake in a paroxysm of clear amusement and simple pleasure. (181)

According to Peterson and Goodall, only four species, in addition to humans, have the capacity to be amused and to show their amusement by laughing: chimpanzees, gorillas, bonobos, and orangutans.

Even the actions of animals who are not able to laugh uproariously indicate that they feel joy. Many animals engage in playful behavior that can only emanate from a sense of joy. In "Hope and Joy among the Animals," Masson and McCarthy tell an amusing, yet true, story about an elephant named Norma.

> A traveling circus once pitched its tents next to a schoolyard with a set of swings. The older elephants were chained, but Norma, a young elephant, was left loose. When Norma saw children swinging, she was greatly intrigued. Before long, she went over, waved the children away with her trunk, backed up to a swing, and attempted to sit on it. She was notably unsuccessful, even using her tail to hold the swing in place. (45)

Transition to the final main point

Entire title of article included because two works by Masson and McCarthy are cited.

Destino 5

Geese, according to experts, have an "emotional body language which can be read: goose posture, gestures, and sounds can indicate feelings such as uncertain, tense, glad, victorious, sad, alert, relaxed or threatening." Additionally, birds sometimes can be seen moving their wings back and forth while listening to sounds they find pleasant (McHugh).

In short, animals exhibit a large number of behaviors that indicate that they possess not only the capacity to feel but the capacity to express those feelings in some overt way, often through body language. If these are not proof enough that animals have emotions, people need look no further than their own beloved cat or dog. Pets are so frequently the cause of joy, humor, love, sympathy, empathy, and even grief that it is difficult to imagine animals could elicit such emotions in humans without actually having these emotions themselves. The question, then, is not "Do animals have emotions?" but rather, "Which emotions do animals have and to what degree do they feel them?"

Citation of Internet source consists of author's name only

Destino presents his own conclusion about animal emotions.

Works Cited

Barber, Theodore Xenophone. *The Human Nature of Birds*. New York: St. Martin's, 1993.

de Waal, Frans. "Are We in Anthropodenial?" *Discover* July 1997: 50-53.

"Going Ape." *Economist* 17 Feb. 1997: 78.

Goodall, Jane. *The Chimpanzees of Gombe: Patterns of Behavior*. Cambridge: Belknap Press, 1986.

---. *Through a Window*. Boston: Houghton, 1990.

Hemelrijk, Charlotte K. "Support for Being Groomed in Long-Tailed Macaques. Macaca Fascicularis." *Animal Behaviour* 48 (1994): 479-81.

Masson, Jeffrey Moussaleff, and Susan McCarthy. "Hope and Joy among the Animals." *Utne Reader* July-Aug. 1995: 44-46.

---. *When Elephants Weep: The Emotional Lives of Animals*. New York: Delacorte, 1995.

McHugh, Mary. "The Emotional Lives of Animals." *The Global Ideas Bank*. Ed. Nicholas Albery and Stephanie Wienrich. 1998. Institute for Social Inventions, London. 7 Dec. 2004 <http://www.globalideasbank.org/BI/BI-170.html>.

Mercer, Phil. "Dolphins Prevent NZ Shark Attack," *BBC News*. 23 Nov. 2004. BBC. 21 Jan. 2005. <http:bbc.co.uk/1/hi/world/asia-pacific/4034383.stm>.

Peterson, Dale, and Jane Goodall. *Visions of Caliban*. New York: Houghton, 1993.

Wynn, Susan G. "The Treatment of Trauma in Pet Animals: What Constitutes Trauma?" *Homeopathy Online* 5 (1998): 7 pp. 15 Dec. 2004 <http://www.lyghtforce.com/HomeopathyOnline/issue5/articles/wynn.html>.

Heading centered

Double-space between heading and first line, and between all subsequent lines

Entries are alphabetized by authors' last names

First line of each entry is flush with left margin; subsequent lines indent five spaces

Keys to Academic Success

Applying skills and organizing daily routines — these are the essential ingredients for academic success. Success begins with planning your time, using your course syllabus, and taking advantage of services available on campus. Success also requires new skills. You must project a positive academic image, participate in class, communicate with your instructors, and take effective notes and use them to study. Finally, college success requires managing your life by organizing a writing-study area, staying focused and studying smarter, and managing stress.

Developing Skills for Success

Only you are in charge of your own learning and reaching your goals. Success is not a matter of luck; it is a matter of skills. Specific skills, such as communicating effectively and presenting yourself as a successful student, will help you achieve success.

Plan Your Valuable Time

The biggest challenge for most college students is managing their time. The most successful students spend two hours outside of the classroom for every hour spent in the classroom (more for reading- or writing-intensive courses). Most of your time outside of classes is unstructured, and as a result many students never seem to get organized. Some are overwhelmed by the workload and the challenge of integrating college study into an already busy lifestyle; others tend to study nonstop, never relaxing and thus setting themselves up for burnout.

A key step in managing your time is establishing goals that are positive and realistic. Keep in mind a broader, long-term goal — like earning a bachelor's degree in four years — before setting short-term goals such as finishing an assigned paper by next Friday. If you let the days "just happen," you're not likely to get much accomplished. You need to plan your activities. Consider the following three types of plans — term, weekly, and daily — and choose the one that works best for you.

- **The term plan.** Establish a routine for study by blocking out four to six hours per week for each course. Study for each course during the same time period each week. For instance, you might reserve Monday, Wednesday, and Thursday evenings (8–10 P.M.) for your writing course.
- **The weekly plan.** Take ten minutes at the beginning of each week to figure out when you'll work on each course, taking into account upcoming assignments. For instance, for a Tuesday/Thursday writing class you might reserve the following time slots.

  Mon., 7–9 P.M.: Read and highlight chapter

  Tues., 7–8:30 P.M.: Start draft of paper

  Wed., 7–8 P.M.: Do assigned reading

  Thurs., 3–4 P.M.: Work on draft

  Sat., 12–1 P.M.: Revise paper

- **The daily plan.** Each evening, before you begin studying, assess what needs to be done and determine the order in which you will do these tasks.

Regardless of which plan you choose, it is essential to purchase (and use!) a student planner or pocket calendar for recording assignments, due dates for papers, upcoming exams, and study times. Keep this planner or calendar with you at all times, and check it daily. This simple tool will help you get and stay organized.

Use Your Course Syllabus

The syllabus is the most important document you will receive in your first week of class. A syllabus includes information on required texts, attendance policy, grading system, course objectives, weekly assignments or readings, due dates of papers, and dates of exams. Be sure to read it carefully at the beginning of the course and to check it regularly so that you are always prepared.

Pay particular attention to the course objectives section of the syllabus; the objectives state what the instructor expects you to learn in the course. They also provide clues about what the instructor feels is important and how he or she views the subject matter. If you have any questions about the course objectives, ask your instructor about his or her expectations for the course.

Discover College Services

Identifying and using your college's support services can make the difference between frustration and success. Here's how to increase your success by using these services.

- **Find out what is available.** Academic services include writing centers, computer labs, math labs, library tours, free workshops, academic skills centers, learning specialists, counseling services, and peer tutoring in specific courses. Don't hesitate to use these valuable services: They can give you an important academic advantage.

- **Visit your college's writing center, and learn what services it offers.** Writing centers offer individualized help with planning, organizing, drafting, and revising papers — usually for any college course, not just for writing class.

Present Yourself as a Successful Student

How you act and respond in classes determines what you get out of them. Don't underestimate the value of communicating daily — through your words and actions — that you are a hardworking student who takes the college experience seriously.

Use the following tips to establish and convey a positive academic image.

- Arrive to classes promptly.
- Sit near the front of the room.
- Look and act interested in the class.
- Make eye contact with your instructors.
- Complete reading assignments before class.
- Complete all assignments on time.
- Turn in neat, complete, well-organized papers and essays.
- Don't talk while your instructor is addressing the class.
- Say "hello" when you meet your instructors on campus.

Participate in Class

To be successful, it is not enough to project a good image; you must also actively participate in class at every opportunity. To do so, follow these guidelines.

- **Prepare to participate.** As you read an assignment, make notes and jot down questions to use as a starting point.
- **Organize your remarks.** Plan in advance what you will say or ask in class. Work on stating your ideas clearly.
- **Say something early in a discussion.** The longer you wait, the more difficult it will be to find something to say that has not already been said.
- **Keep your comments brief.** You will lose the attention of classmates if you ramble on.
- **Be sensitive to the feelings of others.** Make sure that what you say does not offend or embarrass other class members.

Participation in class involves more than just speaking out. It also involves making a serious effort to focus on the discussion and to record important ideas that others express. Be sure to take notes on class discussions, record whatever the instructor writes on the chalkboard, keep handouts from PowerPoint and similar presentations, and jot down ideas for future writing assignments.

Communicate with Your Instructors

You will find that your instructors are happy to help and are willing to serve as valuable sources of information on research, academic decisions, and careers in their respective fields. Most instructors post office hours — times during which they are available to talk and answer questions. Some instructors give out their email addresses so you can communicate by computer. Before meeting with your instructor, write out any questions that you have. If you need help with a paper, be sure to bring along all the work (drafts, outlines, research sources, etc.) you have done so far.

If you absolutely cannot attend class for a particular reason, be sure to notify your instructor in advance and explain. Unexcused absences generally lower your grade and send the signal that you are not taking your studies seriously. In addition, if personal problems begin to interfere with your school work, let your instructors know. They can refer you to the counseling services on campus and may consider granting an extension for work missed if the reason is valid.

Take Effective Class Notes and Use Them Well

To become a successful student, you need to take careful notes in each class and review them at least once a week. Following are two of the most popular and efficient methods of taking notes on class lectures, discussions, and readings.

The *columnar method* involves drawing a vertical line from top to bottom about a third of the way from the left-hand margin and recording notes in the columns on each side of the line. In the wider, right-hand column, you record ideas and facts as they are presented in lecture or discussion (or a reading). In the narrower, left-hand column, you note any questions as you think of them. When you go home and review your notes, you can summarize major concepts and sections in the left-hand column. This method allows you to quickly review an outline or overview of a lecture or discussion by reading the left-hand column, and to study specific information and examples in the right-hand column.

Columnar Note-Taking

Writing as Process	Prewriting: taking notes, writing ideas, drawing a cluster diagram, researching, writing questions, noting what you already know, outlining, etc.
	Writing: drafting
Revision	Rewriting: revision = "to see again"
	2 types: global = major rehaul (reconsidering, reorganizing)
	local = rewording, correcting grammar (editing for correctness & style)

In the *modified branch or outline method,* you use bullets for main ideas and indented slashes for more detailed information in that section. The more detailed the information gets, the farther to the right you indent.

Good note-taking is the hallmark of a successful student. It gets easier with practice, and developing your own symbols over time will make note-taking quicker for you. The important thing to remember is to take notes and review them regularly. Borrow notes from a good student when you cannot be in class. By taking good notes and using them well, you replace the inefficient and exhausting strategy of cramming for exams with a system of learning that allows deeper, longer-term retention of information.

Organizing and Managing Your Life

The final key to academic success is managing your tasks at home. To do so, you will need to organize a writing-study area, stay focused, and manage stress.

Organize a Writing-Study Area

Begin by designating an uncluttered writing-study area that you can work in daily. You don't need a lot of space; it merely needs to be relatively free of distractions, well lit, comfortable, and equipped with all the necessary tools you may need — pens, pencils, scratch pads, a clock, a computer, a calculator. Be sure to keep such reference tools as a dictionary and a thesaurus nearby as well.

If you live on campus, your dormitory room probably includes a desk or work area. If the dorm is noisy, though, consider studying in the library or another quiet place. Libraries offer free carrel space where you can work without distractions. Many also offer study rooms for group work or secluded areas with upholstered chairs if you do not need a desk.

If you live off campus, finding the right place may be more difficult but is well worth the extra effort. Your work area need not be a separate room, but it should be a place where you can spread out your materials and find them undisturbed when you return. If your commute to campus is lengthy, you should organize a place to work at home but also find a quiet place on campus where you can study between classes.

Stay Focused and "Study Smarter"

No matter how intelligent you are or what skills or talents you possess, your course work will be unnecessarily difficult if you cannot keep your mind focused. To "study smarter," not harder, do the following.

- **Work at peak periods of attention.** Study at the time of day when you are most efficient and least likely to lose concentration. Do not try to work when you are tired, hungry, or distracted by others.
- **Work on difficult assignments first.** It is usually best to work on the most challenging assignments first, when your concentration is at its peak.
- **Vary your activities.** Alternate assignments. For example, read, then write, then work on math problems, then read another assignment, and so on.
- **Use writing to keep yourself mentally and physically active.** Highlight and annotate as you read. These processes will keep you mentally alert.
- **Approach assignments critically.** Ask questions as you read. Make connections with what you have already learned and with what you already know about the subject.
- **Challenge yourself with deadlines.** Before beginning an assignment, estimate how long it should take and work toward completing the task within that time limit.
- **Reward yourself.** Use fun activities, such as emailing a friend or getting a snack, as a reward when you have completed an assignment.

Manage Stress

The pressures and obligations of school lead many students to feel overwhelmed. Here are some effective ways to reduce stress.

- **Establish priorities.** Decide what is most important and less important in your life. For example, if college is more important than your part-time job, don't worry about requesting a work schedule to accommodate your study schedule — because studying is your priority.
- **Be selfish and learn to say no.** Many people are stressed because they are trying to do too many things for too many people — family, friends, classmates, and co-workers. Allow your priorities to guide you in accepting new responsibilities.
- **Separate work, school, and social problems.** Create mental compartments for your worries. For instance, don't spend time in class thinking about a problem at work. Leave work problems at work. Deal with problems when it is appropriate.
- **Simplify your life by making fewer choices.** Avoid simple daily decisions that needlessly consume time and energy. For example, get up at the same time each weekday morning, set out your clothes before going to bed, and choose fixed study times and adhere to them without fail.
- **Focus on the positive.** Do not say, "I'll never be able to finish this assignment on time." Instead ask yourself, "What do I have to do to finish this assignment on time?"
- **Keep a personal journal.** Taking a few minutes to write down your worries and articulate emotions can go a long way toward relieving stress. Be sure to include your goals and how you plan to achieve them.

Glossary of Terms

Active reading   The practice of thinking about, questioning, and reacting to reading. Active readers preview the text before reading, annotate and highlight as they read, and review and evaluate what they have read. *See also* **previewing**, **annotating**, and **highlighting**.

Alliteration   The repetition of a sound, especially the initial sound, in a series of words. The repetition of the *g* and *ch* sounds in the title "Goin' Gangsta, Choosin' Cholita" is an example of alliteration.

Allusion   A brief and often indirect reference to a well-known person, place, or quotation from literature, popular culture, or history. For example, *The new list of house rules became their Magna Carta* makes an allusion to the 1215 English Charter that limited the power of the English kings, setting in motion a chain of events that eventually led to constitutional law.

Alternative viewpoints *See* **opposing viewpoints**.

Analogy   An extended comparison in which one subject is used to explain another. Analogies can make complicated ideas easier to understand, make unfamiliar objects easier to imagine, or show something in a new light. *The world's largest rodent, the capybara, is as roly-poly and water-loving as a hippopotamus, though not nearly as big* is an analogy that makes the unfamiliar capybara easier to imagine.

Annotating   An **active reading** strategy in which a reader records his or her ideas, impressions, reactions, and questions in the margins of a reading.

Argument   A **pattern of development** used by writers to make a logical, well-considered case for or against an issue. An effective argument supports a position, or **claim**, on an issue with reasons and **evidence**.

Assertion   A statement that takes a position or expresses a viewpoint. Also known as a **thesis**, effective assertions should state a clear position on a topic, not just present a **fact**. For example, *Global warming will disrupt millions of lives by triggering many more heat waves, droughts, and floods than the world currently endures*.

Assumptions   Conjectures that an author makes about the readers' backgrounds, interests, or beliefs. A writer can also make assumptions about the topic.

Audience   The readers of a particular piece of writing. A writer should always keep the audience in mind when planning and writing an essay.

Author's purpose *See* **purpose**.

Basis of comparison   The shared characteristics that an author focuses on in a comparison between two things. An author might compare Italian and Chinese cuisines on the basis of their healthfulness or their popularity, for example. *See also* **points of comparison**.

Bias   The set of attitudes, beliefs, prejudices, and feelings that a reader or writer brings to a topic. Writers show bias when they present an unbalanced view on a topic. Readers can avoid bringing their own bias to a piece of writing if they keep an open mind while reading.

Brainstorming   A **prewriting** technique for generating ideas that involves quickly jotting down a list of everything that comes to mind relating to a particular topic within an allotted time period.

Cause and effect   Also known as *causal analysis*, a **pattern of development** that analyzes why something happened (causes) and what happened because of something (effects). Cause and effect can be used to explain an event or phenomenon or to delve into motives or complex reasons. The *primary* cause or effect is the most important one; *secondary* causes or effects are less important. Be alert also to *hidden* causes or effects, which can be as important as — or even more important than — more obvious causes and effects.

Chronological order   The sequence in which events occur. Writers often use chronological order in narrative or process essays.

Claim   In **argument** essays, a statement that reveals the writer's position on an issue. The writer's claim usually appears as part of the **thesis** statement. *Claims of fact* can be proved or verified, *claims of value* focus on showing how one thing or idea is better than others, and *claims of policy* offer one or more solutions to a problem.

Classification and division   A **pattern of development** used to sort people, things, or ideas into categories (classification) or to break one thing down into parts (division).

Cliché   An overused expression that has lost its clarity and freshness. For example, *Every cloud has a silver lining.*

Climax   The point in a narrative at which **tension** is at its highest, just before the resolution of the **conflict**.

Clustering   *See* **mapping**.

Colloquial language   Slang, dialect, and other kinds of colorful or casual language used in conversation. Colloquial language is often used in narratives and fiction but is generally not appropriate for academic writing except when used as part of a quotation. Contractions (*wasn't, I'll*), slang expressions (*chill out, no way*), sentence fragments, and informal expressions are all colloquialisms.

Combining patterns   Using two or more **patterns of development** to develop an essay. This approach allows writers to be flexible, enabling them to develop and support their **thesis** with a variety of supporting **evidence**. *See also* **narration**, **description**, **illustration**, **process analysis**, **comparison and contrast**, **classification and division**, **definition**, **cause and effect**, and **argument**.

Common ground   A basis of trust and goodwill between an author and his or her **audience**. Establishing common ground — by mentioning mutual interests, concerns, or experiences — may make readers more open to considering an **argument** and is especially useful when writing for a disagreeing audience.

Comparison and contrast   A **pattern of development** used to show the similarities (comparison) and differences (contrast) between two things.

Conclusion   The final paragraph or paragraphs that draw an essay to a close. While conclusions vary, they often restate the **thesis**, suggest a new direction, or urge a call to action.

Conflict   A struggle, question, or problem that the characters in a narrative confront. The conflict can be between participants or between a participant and an outside force, such as the law, a moral or value, or an act of nature.

Connotative meaning   The set of feelings or associations that a word evokes in a reader. Some words have a positive or a negative connotation. Consider, for example, the expressions *golden hair* and *yellow hair*. The words *golden* and *yellow* have similar **denotative**, or literal, **meanings**, but the first expression has more positive connotations than the second.

Deductive reasoning   A type of reasoning that begins with a premise (an observation or statement that is widely accepted as true) and then uses this premise to draw a conclusion. For example, if it is accepted that the bus is usually late on snowy days, deductive reasoning could be used to predict that the bus will be late if it is snowing. *See also* **inductive reasoning**.

Definition   An explanation of a term; when used throughout an essay, a **pattern of development** that writers use to explain what something means. *See also* **standard definition** and **extended definition**.

Denotative meaning   A word's literal meaning, or dictionary definition, as opposed to its **connotative meaning**, which concerns the feelings and associations that a word evokes.

Description   A **pattern of development** that makes an event vivid to the reader by appealing to the five senses: sight, hearing, smell, taste, and touch. Effective descriptive writing aims to evoke feelings or create an overall impression.

Dialogue   Conversation among characters in a narrative. Dialogue can be used to advance the action, dramatize the **conflict**, give readers an impression of the speaker, or all of these.

Division *See* **Classification and division**.

Dominant impression The overall attitude, mood, or feeling about a subject that a piece of writing conveys to a reader.

Doublespeak Deliberately unclear or evasive language used intentionally (often by politicians, the government, and corporations) to hide or soften meanings. In the military, *collateral damage* is doublespeak for unintentional deaths. Doublespeak is a type of **euphemism**.

Emotional appeals Parts of an **argument** that draw on readers' feelings and beliefs rather than their ability to reason. Emotional appeals are directed toward readers' needs (food and drink, for example) or their values (honesty, for example).

Euphemism A polite or neutral word or phrase used in place of a disagreeable or potentially offensive term. For example, *passed away* is a commonly used euphemism for dying.

Evidence Facts and **opinions** — including examples, statistics, quotations, and research findings — used as support to convince the reader that the **thesis** is reasonable or correct.

Extended definition A lengthy, detailed definition that explores a term and all that it means; such a definition might require a long paragraph, a full essay, or an entire book. *See also* **definition**.

Facts Verifiable evidence drawn from a source that can be consulted or confirmed to be either true or false. Examples of facts are statistics, research findings, and personal experiences.

Fallacies Errors in reasoning and thinking. Fallacies can weaken an **argument** and call into question the believability of its supporting **evidence**. Fallacies include circular reasoning (or begging the question), hasty generalizations, sweeping generalizations, false analogies, non sequiturs, red herrings, post hoc fallacies, and *either-or* fallacies.

Figure of speech A comparison between two seemingly unlike objects or situations that makes sense creatively or imaginatively, but not literally. For example, *The traffic moved along like a herd of cows heading home*. **Hyperbole**, **metaphor**, **personification**, and **simile** are specific kinds of figures of speech.

Flashback A step backward in narrative time. Authors often explain a scene or event by using a flashback to return to past events.

Foreshadowing Moving forward in time to hint at events that will happen later in a narrative.

Formal outline An outline that uses a standard format with Roman numerals, Arabic numbers, and upper- and lowercase letters to designate the levels of importance in an essay. A *topic outline* uses key words and phrases. A *sentence outline* uses complete sentences. *See also* **outlining**.

Freewriting A **prewriting** technique that involves writing nonstop in sentence form whatever comes to mind about a topic for a specific period of time.

Generalization A broad statement about a topic, often one that makes an assertion about an entire group or category. The **thesis** of an **illustration** essay frequently contains a generalization.

Highlighting An **active reading** strategy in which a reader uses a highlighter or pen to selectively mark important elements, words, and phrases in a reading.

Hyperbole A **figure of speech** that makes a deliberate and obvious exaggeration. For example, *Stanley was so flexible that he could tie himself in a knot*.

Idioms Commonly used phrases that native speakers of a language readily understand but that do not translate directly into other languages. For example, *to badger* someone is to pester them; *to black out* is to lose consciousness.

Illustration A **pattern of development** that uses examples to support a **thesis** and make a topic easier to understand or imagine.

Implied thesis The main point or position in an essay when it is suggested rather than directly stated. Professional authors, particularly those who favor **narration** or **description**, sometimes use an implied thesis, but students and other academic writers should state their thesis directly. *See also* **thesis**.

Inductive reasoning A type of reasoning that starts with specific **evidence** and uses that evidence to make a generalization or conclusion. For example, if someone sneezes each time he visits a friend who has a cat, he can use his experiences to conclude that he is allergic to cats.

Inference   A reasoned guess about what is not known based on what is known.

Informal outline   A list of the main points and subpoints of an essay, written in key words and phrases. Also known as a *scratch outline. See also* **outlining**.

Introduction   An essay's opening sentences or paragraphs. In addition to establishing the **tone** of an essay, effective introductions identify the topic, provide background information about it, and often present the **thesis**.

Jargon   The specialized vocabulary used by a particular group or within a particular field of study. Because it is specific to certain groups, jargon often is not readily understood by the general public. For example, in lumberjack jargon, a *hayburner* is a horse; in baseball jargon, a *can of corn* is an easily caught fly ball.

Journal writing   A writing activity used to record daily impressions and reflections, to comment on experiences and observations, to explore relationships among ideas, and to respond to assignments and readings. In addition to offering practice for writing, journals can be used as a source of ideas for papers.

Least-to-most/most-to-least order   A method of organization in which supporting details are organized from least to most or most to least important, familiar, interesting, or persuasive.

Mapping   A **prewriting** strategy also known as *clustering* in which a writer creates a visual depiction of the relationships among ideas to respond to assignments and readings. Mapping offers a visual way to discover ideas and relationships about a topic.

Metaphor   A **figure of speech** that makes an implied comparison between two things without using the words *like* or *as*. For example, *The air-conditioned office was an oasis on the scorching July day*.

Most-to-least order   *See* **least-to-most order**.

Narration   A **pattern of development** used to relate a series of events, real or imaginary, in an organized sequence. Narratives are stories that make a point.

Negation   The method of defining a term by explaining what it is not. A writer may use negation to explain how a term is different from other terms in its class or to clarify a personal meaning about a term.

Opinions   Statements that reveal beliefs or feelings that are neither true nor false. Opinions include evaluations, viewpoints, and conclusions.

Opposing viewpoints   Sides of an **argument** that the writer does not support. A writer can strengthen an argument by *acknowledging* opposing viewpoints, *accommodating* them by building them into his or her own argument, or *refuting* them by pointing out problems or flaws in the opponent's reasoning or **evidence**.

Outlining   An organizational plan of the main points in an essay in the order the writer plans to discuss them. *See also* **formal** and **informal outlines**.

Pattern of development   One of the nine methods used to develop an essay: **narration, description, illustration, process analysis, comparison and contrast, classification and division, definition, cause and effect**, and **argument**. These patterns can be used alone or combined to develop an essay or used when prewriting to generate ideas about a topic. *See also* **combining patterns**.

Peer review   A process in which students read and comment on one other's essays.

Personification   A **figure of speech** in which an object is given human qualities or characteristics. For example, *The tender, reassuring rays of the rising sun caressed her cheeks as she awoke from a deep sleep*.

Plagiarism   Using an author's ideas or words as if they were one's own and neglecting to give the author credit. Plagiarism is a highly serious offense, so it is important to document all sources used in writing.

Point of view   The perspective from which an author writes. The point of view used most commonly in essays is first person (*I, we, mine, ours*) or third person (*he, she, they*). Less frequently, writers use second person (*you, your*).

Point-by-point organization   A method of organization used in **comparison and contrast** essays in which the author alternates things being compared, focusing on one characteristic at a time. *See also* **subject-by-subject organization**.

Points of comparison The **evidence** that a writer calls on to compare two subjects. In a comparison between two breeds of dog, the **basis of comparison** might be *attractiveness*, and the points of comparison might be *fur texture, expressiveness of eyes*, and *shape of face*.

Previewing An **active reading** strategy that provides a quick way to become familiar with an essay's content and organization. When previewing, read the title and author information, the **introduction**, any headings and the first sentence following them, **topic sentences**, the **conclusion**, and any prereading or end-of-assignment questions. Review also any photographs, tables, charts, or drawings that accompany the text.

Prewriting The stage in the writing process when the writer chooses a topic, narrows it down to a manageable scope, and develops a working **thesis**. To discover ideas, the following prewriting strategies can be used: **brainstorming**, **freewriting**, **questioning**, and **mapping**.

Process analysis A **pattern of development** used to explain in step-by-step fashion how something works, or is done, or is made.

Proofreading Reading through an essay to catch and correct surface errors — errors in grammar, punctuation, spelling, and mechanics — as well as keyboarding and typographical mistakes.

Purpose The reason an author writes a particular piece. Although there are many purposes for writing, the most common ones are *to express feelings, to inform*, and *to persuade*.

Questioning A **prewriting** strategy used to discover ideas about a topic. Questioning involves writing down every question that comes to mind about a topic.

Reader bias *See* **bias**.

Refutation A strategy used in **argument** essays in which the weakness of the opponent's argument is demonstrated.

Restrictive word meaning The meaning of a commonly used word that is unique to a particular

field or discipline. For example, in the military, a *strike* is an air attack.

Sarcasm A bitter type of humor used to make fun of someone or something.

Scratch outline *See* **informal outline**.

Sensory details Details that appeal to one or more of the five senses: sight, sound, smell, taste, and touch. Writers use sensory details to help the reader experience the object, sensation, event, or person being described.

Simile A **figure of speech** that makes a direct comparison using *like* or *as*. For example, *The dog was as black as coal*.

Spatial order A method of organization that presents details about a subject according to their position in space. An author using spatial order might describe a place or object from top to bottom, from inside to outside, or from near to far away.

Standard definition A brief **definition** that explains a term by identifying the *class* to which it belongs and the *characteristics* that distinguish it from other members of that class. For example, a *crop duster* (term) is an airplane (class) that sprays insecticide on planted fields (distinguishing characteristic).

Subject-by-subject organization A method of organization in **comparison and contrast** essays in which the author addresses all of the points about the first subject before addressing the same points about the second subject. *See also* **point-by-point organization**.

Summary The main ideas of an essay stated in the reader's own words. Because summaries concentrate on key ideas and points only, leaving out details, they are necessarily brief.

Symbolism The use of one thing, word, or idea to represent something other than the thing's, word's, or idea's literal meaning. For example, a white dress may symbolize virtue, an owl may symbolize mystery, or a vulture may symbolize death.

Synonyms Words that have similar meanings — for example, *courageous* and *brave*.

Synthesis The process of drawing together two or more sources on a given topic to discover similarities and differences and develop new ideas or insights about them.

Tension   The suspense created as the story in a narrative unfolds and the reader wonders how the **conflict** will be resolved.

Theme   The central or dominant idea or main point that the author makes about the human experience or condition in a piece of writing.

Thesis   Also known as a *thesis statement*, the main idea that the essay explains, explores, or supports. In academic and other formal types of writing, the thesis statement usually appears in the essay's **introduction**. Occasionally, an essay's thesis is suggested rather than stated directly. *See also* **implied thesis**.

Tone   An author's overall attitude toward the topic and the **audience** as revealed by his or her word choice, sentence arrangement, and formal or informal use of language. For example, an author might use a bitter tone in an essay about his or her negative high school experiences.

Topic sentence   The sentence that states the main point of a paragraph. The topic sentence is usually the first sentence of the paragraph.

Transitions   Words or phrases that link the relationships between ideas or events in an essay. Examples of transitions include *nevertheless, finally,* and *for example.* For a complete list of commonly used transitions, see page 60.

Unity   Coherence among all the sentences in a paragraph or all the elements of an essay. In a unified paragraph, for example, all the sentences directly support the **topic sentence**.

Vantage point   The position from which a description is written. With a *fixed vantage point*, a writer describes what he or she sees from a single position. With a *moving vantage point*, a writer describes the subject from a number of different positions.

Working outline   *See* **informal outline**.

Working thesis   *See* **thesis**.

Acknowledgments

Sherry Amatenstein. "Talking a Stranger through the Night." From *Newsweek*, November 18, 2002. Reprinted by permission of the author.

Maya Angelou. "Sister Flowers." Copyright © 1969 by Maya Angelou. Renewed 1997 by Maya Angelou, from *I Know Why the Caged Bird Sings* by Maya Angelou. Used by permission of Random House, Inc.

Deb Aronson. "How Nature Heals Us." From *Science and Spirit Magazine*, July–August 2003. Copyright © 2003 by Deb Aronson. Reprinted by permission of Science and Spirit Magazine.

Toni Cade Bambara. "The Lesson." From *Gorilla, My Love* by Toni Cade Bambara. Copyright © 1972 by Toni Cade Bambara. Used by permission of Random House, Inc.

Dave Barry. "We've Got the Dirt on Guy Brains." From *The Miami Herald*, Sunday, November 23, 2003. Copyright © 2003 by Dave Barry. Reprinted with permission of TMS Reprints.

Sharon Begley. "East vs. West: One Sees the Big Picture, the Other is Focused." From *The Wall Street Journal* (Eastern Edition), March 28, 2003, p. B1. Copyright © 2003 by Dow Jones. Reprinted with permission via Copyright Clearance Center. www.copyright.com.

Nell Bernstein. "Goin' Gangsta, Choosin' Cholita: Claiming Identity." Reprinted with the permission of the author.

David Bodanis. "A Brush with Reality: Surprises in the Tube." From *The Secret House* by David Bodanis. Copyright © 1986 by David Bodanis. Reprinted with permission of the Carol Mann Agency.

Shelly Branch. "One Term Says It All: 'Shut Up!'" From *The Wall Street Journal*, May 1, 2003. Copyright © 2003 by Shelly Branch. Reprinted with permission of Dow Jones via Copyright Clearance Center. www.copyright.com.

Mary Brave Bird. "The Sweat Bath Ritual." From *Lakota Woman* by Mary Crow Dog and Richard Erdoes. Copyright © 1990 by Mary Crow Dog and Richard Erdos. Used by permission of Grove/Atlantic, Inc.

William Broyles, Jr. "A War for Us, Fought by Them." From *The New York Times*, May 4, 2004, p. A29. Copyright © 2004 by The New York Times. Reprinted with permission.

Bill Bryson. "Snoopers at Work." From *I'm A Stranger Here Myself* by Bill Bryson. Copyright © 1999 by Bill Bryson. Used by permission of Broadway Books, a division of Random House, Inc. and Doubleday Canada.

Janice Castro, Dan Cook, Christina Garcia. "Spanglish." From *Time*, July 11, 1988. Copyright © 1988 by Time, Inc. Reprinted with permission.

Cindy Chupack. "Dater's Remorse." From *The Between Boyfriends Book* by Cindy Chupack. Copyright © 2003 by Cindy Chupack. Reprinted by permission of St. Martin's Press, LLC.

Cynthia Combs. "Profile of a Terrorist." From *Terrorism in the Twenty-First Century*, Third Edition, by Cynthia Combs. Copyright © 2003. Adapted by permission of Pearson Education, Inc., Upper Saddle River, NJ.

Frank Deford. "Athletics 101: A Change in Eligibility Rules is Long Overdue." Copyright © by Frank Deford. Reprinted by permission of Sterling Lord Literistic, Inc.

Rudy De La Torre. "Ethnic Definitions Hinder Society's Enlightenment." By Rudy De La Torre. From *The Daily Aztec*, August 27, 2003. Reprinted by permission of *The Daily Aztec*.

Chitra Divakaruni. "Houseguest Hell." From *The Bitch in the House* edited by Cathi Hanauer. Reprinted with the permission of the author. Chitradivakaruni@hotmail.com.

Lars Eighner. "On Dumpster Diving." From *Travels with Lizbeth* by Lars Eighner. Copyright © 1993 by Lars Eighner. Reprinted with permission of St. Martin's Press.

David Feige. "How to Defend Someone You Know Is Guilty." From *The New York Times*, April 8, 2001, Late Edition—Final, section 6, p. 59, column 4. Copyright © 2001 by The New York Times Company. Reprinted with permission.

Carol Bernstein Ferry. "A Good Death." From the September 17, 2001 issue of *The Nation*. Reprinted with permission. For subscription information, call 1-800-333-8536. Portions of each week's Nation magazine can be accessed at http://www.thenation.com.

Nathaniel Fick. "Don't Dumb Down the Military." From *The New York Times*, July 20, 2004, p. A19. Copyright © 2004 The New York Times Company. Reprinted by permission.

Zara Gelsey. "Who's Reading Over Your Shoulder?" From *The Humanist*, Sept.–Oct. 2002, volume 62, issue 5, p. 38 (2). Copyright © 2002. Reprinted with the permission of the author.

Matthew Gilbert. "You and Improved." From *The Boston Globe Magazine*, November 9, 2003. Copyright © 2003 by Globe Newspaper Co (MA). Reproduced with permission of Globe Newspaper Co (MA) in the format Textbook via Copyright Clearance Center. www.copyright.com.

Nikki Giovanni. "Campus Racism 101." From *Racism 101* by Nikki Giovanni. Copyright © 1994 by Nikki Giovanni. Reprinted by permission of HarperCollins Publishers, Inc.

Bruce Gottlieb. "How Much Is That Kidney in the Window?" From *The New Republic*, May 22, 2000. Copyright © 2000. Reprinted by permission of The New Republic.

Dave Grossman and Gloria DeGaetano. "It's Important to Feel Something When You Kill." From *Stop Teaching Our Kids to Kill* by Dave Grossman and Gloria DeGaetano. Copyright © 1999 by Dave Grossman and Gloria DeGaetano. Used by permission of Crown Publishers, a division of Random House, Inc.

Jeanne Wakatsuki Houston. "A Taste of Snow." From *Beyond Manzanar* by Jeanne Wakatsuki Houston. Copyright © 1985 by Jeanne Wakatsuki Houston. Reprinted by permission of the author.

Langston Hughes. "Salvation." From *The Big Sea* by Langston Hughes. Copyright © 1940. Copyright renewed 1968 by Arna Bontemps and George Houston Bass. Reprinted by permission of Hill and Wang, a division of Farrar, Straus and Giroux, LLC.

Shirley Jackson. "The Lottery." From *The Lottery and Other Stories* by Shirley Jackson. Copyright © 1948, 1949 by Shirley Jackson. Copyright renewed 1976, 1977 by Laurence Hyman, Barry Hyman, Mrs. Sarah Webster and Mrs. Joanne Schnurer. Reprinted by permission of Farrar, Straus and Giroux, LLC.

Gerard Jones. "Violent Media is Good for Kids." First appeared in *Mother Jones*, June 28, 2000. Copyright © 2000, Foundation for National Progress. Reprinted with permission.

Rita Kempley. "Abs and the Adolescent." From *The Washington Post*, October 22, 2003, p. C1. Copyright © 2003, The Washington Post. Reprinted with permission.

Martin Luther King, Jr. "The Ways of Meeting Oppression." From *Strive Toward Freedom* by Martin Luther King, Jr. Copyright © 1963 Martin Luther King, Jr. Copyright renewed 1991 Coretta Scott King. "I Have a Dream." Copyright © 1958 Martin Luther King, Jr. Copyright renewed 1986 Coretta Scott King. Reprinted by arrangement with the Estate of Martin Luther King Jr., c/o Writers House as agent for the proprietor New York, NY.

Gina Kolata. "Spinning." From *Ultimate Fitness: The Quest for Truth about Exercise and Health* by Gina Kolata. Copyright © 2003 by Gina Kolata. Reprinted by permission of Farrar, Straus & Giroux, LLC.

Geeta Kothari. "If You Are What You Eat, Then What Am I?" Reprinted by permission of the author.

Etta Kralovec. "No More Pep Rallies!" From *Forbes*, January 12, 2004. Copyright © 2004 Forbes, Inc. Reprinted by permission of *Forbes Magazine*.

Dorianne Laux. "What I Wouldn't Do." From *What We Carry* by Dorianne Laux. Copyright © 1994 by Dorianne Laux. Reprinted by permission of BOA Editions, Ltd. www.BOAEditions.org.

John Leo. "The Good-News Generation." From *U.S. News & World Report*, November 3, 2003, p. 60. Copyright © 2003 U.S. News & World Report, L.P. Reprinted with permission of publisher.

Eric Liu. "Po-Po in Chinatown." From *The Accidental Asian: Notes of a Native Speaker* by Eric Liu. Copyright © 1998 by Eric Liu. Used by permission of Random House, Inc.

Jeremy MacClancy. "Eating Chilli Peppers." From *Consuming Culture: Why You Eat What You Eat* by Jeremy MacClancy. © 1992 by Jeremy MacClancy. Reprinted by permission of the publisher.

Tom and Ray Magliozzi. "Inside the Engine." From *Car Talk* by Tom and Ray Magliozzi. Copyright © 1991 by Tom and Ray Magliozzi. Used by permission of Dell Publishing, a division of Random House, Inc.

Cherokee Paul McDonald. "A View from the Bridge." From the *Sun Sentinel*, February 12, 1989. Copyright © 1989. Reprinted with the permission of Knight Ridder/Tribune Information Services.

Gilbert Meilaender. "'Strip-Mining' the Dead: When Human Organs Are for Sale." From *National Review* 51, October 11, 1999, 42-44. Copyright © 1999 by Gilbert Meilaendar. Reprinted with permission of the author.

Gloria Naylor. "The Meanings of a Word." From *The New York Sunday Times*, February 20, 1986. Copyright © 1986 by Gloria Naylor. Reprinted by permission of SLL/Sterling Lord Literistic, Inc.

Mary Pipher. "Cultural Brokers." From *The Middle of Everywhere* by Mary Pipher. Copyright © 2002 by Mary Pipher. Reprinted by permission of Harcourt, Inc.

William Plasencia. "Web Logs Get Personal." From *Hispanic Magazine*, November 2003. Copyright © 2003. Reprinted with the permission of Hispanic Magazine.

Ramesh Ponnuru. "Fears about the Patriot Act Are Misguided." From *The National Review*, June 2, 2003. Copyright © 2003 by National Review, Inc., 215 Lexington Avenue, New York. Reprinted with permission of the publisher.

Anna Quindlen. "We Are Here for Andrea." Originally published in *Newsweek*, September 22, 2003. Copyright © 2003 Anna Quindlen. Reprinted by permission of International Creative Management, Inc.

Patricia Raybon. "A Case of 'Severe Bias.'" From *Newsweek*, October 1989. Copyright © 1989 by Patricia Raybon. Reprinted by permission of the author.

Wilbert Rideau. "Why Prisons Don't Work." From *Time*, March 21, 1994. Copyright © 1994 by Wilbert Rideau. Reprinted with the permission of the author. C/o The Permissions Company, P.O. Box 604, Mount Pocono, PA 18344. All rights reserved.

Jeffrey Rosen. "Naked Terror." From *The New York Times Magazine*, January 4, 2004, p. 5. Adapted from *The Naked Crowd: Reclaiming Security and Freedom in An Anxious Age* by Jeffrey Rosen. Copyright © 2004 Jeffrey Rosen. Reprinted with the permission of the author.

Tom Rosenberg. "Changing My Name after Sixty Years." Copyright © 2000 Tom Rosenberg. Used by permission. Tom Rosenberg, a San Fransicso writer, is the author of the forthcoming memoir, "Unaffiliated," based on this article which first appeared in *Newsweek*, July 17, 2000.

Ruth Russell. "The Wounds That Can't Be Stitched Up." From *Newsweek*, December 20, 1999. Copyright © 1999 by Ruth Russell. Reprinted by permission of the author.

Melissa Russell-Ausley and Tom Harris. "How the Oscars Work." Appeared at www.entertainment.howstuffworks.com. Reprinted by permission.

Scott Russell Sanders. "The Men We Carry in Our Minds." First appeared in *Milkweed Chronicle*. From *The Paradise of Bombs* by Scott Russell Sanders. Copyright © 1984 by Scott Russell Sanders. Reprinted by permission of the author and the author's agent, the Virginia Kidd Agency, Inc.

Richard Selzer. "The Discus Thrower." From *Confessions of a Knife* by Richard Selzer. Copyright © 1979 by David Goldman and Janet Selzer, Trustees. Reprinted by permission of Georges Borshardt, Inc., Literary Agency.

Joseph Sobran. "Patriotism or Nationalism?" Copyright © by Griffin Internet Syndicate. Reprinted with permission. Joe Sobran is an author, syndicated columnist, and editor of a monthly newsletter, SOBRAN'S, P.O. box 1383, Vienna, VA. 22183. 800-513-5053. Web site: www.sobran.com.

Gary Soto. "Piedra." From *The Effects of Knut Hamsin on a Fresno Boy: Recollections and Short Essays* by Gary Soto. Copyright © 1983, 1988, 2000 by Gary Soto. Reprinted by permission of Persea Books, Inc. (New York).

Brent Staples. "Just Walk On By: A Black Man Ponders His Power to Alter Public Space." From *Parallel Time* by Brent Staples. Copyright © 1994 by Brent Staples. Used by permission of Pantheon Books, a division of Random House, Inc.

Amy Tan. "Fish Cheeks." First appeared in *Seventeen Magazine*. Copyright © 1987 by Amy Tan. Reprinted by permission of the author and the Sandra Dijkstra Literary Agency.

Deborah Tannen. "Sex, Lies, and Conversation." From *The Washington Post*, June 24, 1990. This article is adapted in part from the author's book, *You Just Don't Understand* (Quill, 1990). Copyright © Deborah Tannen. Reprinted by permission.

Clive Thompson. "The Honesty Virus." From *The New York Times Magazine*, March 21, 2004, Late Edition — Final. Section 6, page 24, column 1. Copyright © 2004 David Wallis. Reprinted with the permission of the author.

Judith Viorst. "Friends, Good Friends — Such Good Friends." Copyright © 1977 by Judith Viorst. Originally appeared in *Redbook*. Reprinted by permission of Lescher & Lescher, Ltd. All rights reserved.

Susan Warren and Melanie Trottman. "When Plug Is Pulled on the Digital Age, the Basics Black Out." From *The Wall Street Journal*, Eastern Edition, August 18, 2003, p. A1. Copyright © 2003 Dow Jones. Reprinted with permission of The Wall Street Journal via Copyright Clearance Center.

Alton Fitzgerald White. "Ragtime My Time." Reprinted with permission from the October 11, 1999 issue of *The Nation*. For subscription information call 1-800-333-8536. Portions of each week's Nation magazine can be accessed at http://www.thenation.com.

Terry Tempest Williams. "The Clan of One-Breasted Women." From *Refugee: Unnatural History of Family and Place* by Terry Tempest Williams. Copyright © 1991 by Terry Tempest Williams. Pantheon Books. Reprinted by permission.

Elisabeth Wray. "The Seven Ages of Walking." From *Body & Soul Magazine*, November/December 2003, pp. 68–71. Copyright © 2003 by Elizabeth Wray. Reprinted with the permission of the author.

Pictures

3, © Mark Dadswell/Getty Images; **7,** © David Young Wolff/PhotoEdit, Inc.; **23,** © Bob Daemmrich/PhotoEdit, Inc.; **47,** © The New Yorker Collection 2000. John Caldwell from cartoonbank.com. All Rights Reserved; **66,** © PA/Topham/The Image Works; **69,** © Anne Ackerman/The Image Bank/Getty Images; **93,** © Bettmann/CORBIS; **113,** © Viviane Moos/CORBIS; **124,** © Kevin Maloney/AURORA; **143,** © Jeff Greenberg/PhotoEdit, Inc.; **171,** © Joanna B. Pinneo/AURORA; **182,** © Jose Azel/IPNStock.com; **192,** © Julio Etchart/Peter Arnold, Inc.; **220,** © Brad Wilson/Stone/Getty Images; **235,** © Digital Vision/Getty Images; **243,** © David Young-Wolff/PhotoEdit; **275,** © Patrik Giardino/CORBIS; **281,** © Digital Vision/SuperStock; **292,** © Mike Dobel/Masterfile; **317,** ©CORBIS; **329,** © Peter Hvizdak/The Image Works; **339,** © R. Ian Lloyd/Masterfile; **373,** © ThinkStock/Alamy; **382,** (top left) © Bettmann/CORBIS; **382,** (top right) © Bruno Barbey/Magnum Photos; **382,** (bottom), © CORBIS; **389,** © Reuters/CORBIS; **392,** © Topham/The Image Works; **413,** AP Photo/Danville Register & Bee, Trish Bunton; **436,** © Francisco Cruz/SuperStock; **439,** © Lowell Georgia/Photo Researchers, Inc.; **467,** © Dennis MacDonald/PhotoEdit, Inc.; **488,** © John Van Hassett/CORBIS SYGMA; **491,** Courtesy mediacampaign.org; **551,** © Andrew Lichtenstein/The Image Works; **556,** Courtesy of Universal Studios Licensing LLLP; **573** (top), © Ariel Skelley/CORBIS; **573** (bottom), © Jeffrey Greenberg/The Image Works; **593,** © Spencer Grant/Photo Researchers; **605,** © Reuters/CORBIS.

Index

Useful Lists, Boxes, and Figures

Editing Tips and Troublespots

Using Sources

Graphic Organizers

Revision Flowcharts

Instructor's Resource Manual

Seeing the Pattern

Readings for Successful Writing

Kathleen T. McWhorter

prepared by

Gail Hanlon

For information, write: Bedford/St. Martin's, 75 Arlington Street,
Boston, MA 02116   (617-399-4000)

ISBN: 0-312-41903-1

EAN: 978-0-312-41903-5

Preface

This manual is intended to assist both new and experienced instructors in using *Seeing the Pattern* more effectively and to save time in developing courses that use this text. Rather than suggest how to teach first-year composition, the manual offers a wide variety of tips, strategies, and approaches, allowing instructors to choose methodology that is compatible with their teaching style and philosophy.

Unit 1, "Resources for Teaching Composition with *Seeing the Pattern*" (p. 1), offers practical suggestions for developing a composition course using the text. The first section, "Teaching with *Seeing the Pattern*" (p. 3), introduces the textbook; includes organizational tips; discusses course goals, relationships with students, journal writing, and collaborative activities; and offers suggestions on how to use computers and software. To assist instructors further, "Developing Your Course Plan" (p. 17) presents sample course plans and a sample syllabus. Because so many students enrolled in first-year composition courses lack certain basic writing and reading skills, a section on teaching underprepared students has been included: "Helping Underprepared Students Improve Their Skills" (p. 23) describes both cognitive and affective characteristics of underprepared students and discusses instructional accommodations. It also offers suggestions for developing basic writing skills, building students' reading skills, and fostering critical reading and thinking. At the end of this section is a bibliography of books and articles for instructor reference.

Unit 2, "Teaching Tips and Suggested Answers for Individual Chapters in *Seeing the Pattern*" (p. 33), is designed to help instructors new to the book as well as those who are looking for new ways of teaching familiar readings. This section includes introductions to each chapter in the text. In addition, specific teaching suggestions are included for each reading in Chapters 5 through 10, along with suggested answers to the apparatus that accompanies each reading. These answers are not intended to be definitive; rather they are brief, sample responses designed to both aid instructors teaching a reading for the first time and stimulate discussion in the classroom while opening up a dialogue between instructors and students.

I wish to thank the authors who contributed sections to this manual. Michael Hricik of Westmoreland County Community College prepared "Teaching with *Seeing the Pattern*" and "Developing Your Course Plan." I am especially indebted to Gail Hanlon, who contributed to all aspects of the manual and prepared the teaching tips and suggested answers to the apparatus for all the readings in the book. At Bedford/St. Martin's, I thank Laura Arcari, Beth Ammerman, Laura King, and Harold Chester. Without their contributions, this manual would not have been possible.

Kathleen T. McWhorter

Contents

PART TWO: READINGS FOR WRITERS   41

Unit ◆ One

Resources for Teaching Composition with *Seeing the Pattern*

Teaching with *Seeing the Pattern*

Seeing the Pattern has been designed with instructors' needs in mind. To get the most out of this text, however, you'll need to organize in advance, keep up with your responsibilities for the course, preview chapter contents and assignments, and structure the course in a balanced way. If you make every effort to chart a plan as you begin, you will find that the end result of the course will be much more satisfying. This *Instructor's Resource Manual* will give you practical advice for using *Seeing the Pattern* and for maximizing the use of your time. It will also help you identify appropriate course activities to support your objectives.

Planning and Organizing Your Course

Before you even begin your semester or quarter, try to decide how you will meet the requirements specified by your department, division, or academic area. Typically, the department chair or an administrative assistant will be able to provide you with any departmental guidelines and syllabi from previous terms. This information will assist you in planning your syllabus, particularly if this is your first term with *Seeing the Pattern* or if this is your first term teaching this course. See pages 17–23 of this manual for sample course outlines and advice on writing a syllabus.

When you develop a course syllabus, it is usually a prudent strategy to make a weekly outline of assignments, with due dates for first and revised drafts of essays, as well as for other assignments or journals. (See the sample syllabus on p. 18 of this manual.) For yourself, try to make a more detailed outline in which you develop a fairly accurate class plan of how the activities for the term will be coordinated. For instance, you will want to determine if and when you will be scheduling student conferences, a library orientation, or visits to the writing center or the learning assistance center. If you are planning to visit any of your college's services, contact the appropriate person at the start of the term to get added to their calendar.

Finally, make sure that you connect your class activities throughout the term. For instance, as you make a detailed term plan, try to look back at the essays, in-class writings, discussions, and other activities to see if you can link them. You should attempt to move from lower-level rhetorical skills to higher-level skills by using a coordinated plan throughout the term. This plan will assist you in focusing on long-term goals and objectives. Likewise, if you have an especially busy week at a certain point in the term, you will find that you have a basic idea or outline of what should be done for the next week.

If at all possible, try to develop your notes for the first two weeks of the class even before the term begins. The first two weeks always seem to be overwhelming, so you are always better off having a plan already prepared. In addition, your level of confidence will be much higher going into the course if you have clear objectives and activities in mind. The impression that you give to your students in those initial weeks can be lasting.

Considering Your Primary Goals for the Course

When you are planning your course syllabus—and as you progress through the term—you should consider the four or five most critical skills that students should master. Consult the departmental course syllabus or course description to determine the most critical skills. If you're uncertain about this, ask a more experienced faculty member.

Focusing on Expressive and Informative Writing

If your course focuses primarily on expressive writing, you need to concentrate on writing that exhibits a clear and consistent main idea. You will typically assign a sequence of essays that exhibit logical progression, cohesiveness, and meaningful connection of ideas. The course will likely focus on basic editing, sentence construction, and paragraph-level writing. During the course you will help students develop a fuller awareness of the various rhetorical patterns of development as you assign progressively difficult readings. Strive to develop some higher-level thinking, reading, and writing skills as the term progresses. Keep in mind that you should see improvement in the students' writing and their organization of ideas. Writing involves thinking, and revision involves reseeing, so students will usually became more reflective and focused in their writing by the end of the term.

Many instructors begin a course based on expressive writing with either a narrative or a descriptive essay. Of course, if your department allows, you may choose another option. Whatever you do, try to avoid going beyond the initial limitations of your students. If you discover that your students are struggling with a particular essay, consider extending its due date. However, not all students will master every pattern of development, so you will need to move on. Keep in mind, though, that if you get too far off schedule, your whole term plan will start to unravel. Always strive to have your students meet the minimum number of essays or assignments established by your department.

Likewise, with informative writing, you will focus on essays such as comparison and contrast, classification or division, definition, and cause and effect. The focus here is to inform the reader more fully, with or without material from sources. These types of essays can work well without sources if students choose a narrowly defined topic at the start. The informative essays help students make the transition between personal writing and more involved research writing, such as argumentation. These essays help students develop skills in looking beyond their own experiences as they synthesize outside information to use in their essays.

Focusing on Informative and Research Writing

In a course that focuses on both informative and research-oriented writing, you will typically divide the course into two segments; be sure to allow more time for the research-oriented essays. For such a course, follow the main strategies mentioned in the previous section for the first part of the term, and then start to focus on developing the use of sources in writing. An excellent starting point is a less difficult research-oriented essay, such as a comparison and contrast or definition (with two or three sources). (See Chapters 9 and 11 in *Seeing the Pattern.*) Some instructors assign a definition paper by asking students to find several dictionary definitions of a particular word (for denotations) and then the same number of books or periodicals in which the word is used (for connotations) to show how the definitions differ. Other instructors assign an essay comparing and contrasting two authors who write in the same genre, with students using two or three reference books as sources.

Keep in mind that you should introduce more complex readings (both student and professional) with sources as you move through this section of the course. Try to place particular emphasis on analysis or interpretation of essays, synthesis of several essays, and evaluation of both sources and student essays. The writing in the second half of the course will help students develop a high degree of independent thought and will facilitate these levels of thinking as well. You want to help students feel comfortable in moving to a research paper and developing stronger reading skills for future academic success.

When you are working on papers with sources, you should allow more time for peer review, conferences, and revisions. It can be a good strategy to require a rough draft, a revised draft, and then an edited draft. If you do this, you will discover that students will have stronger final drafts and less tendency to procrastinate. The critical point with a course that includes research isn't just the writing but the level of thinking as the term progresses. You should require more detailed comments on the peer-edited essays and ask for more detailed responses to the professional essays and journal assignments.

Establishing a Good Relationship with Your Students

Developing a good relationship with your students is important. You will learn about your students through their writing and your discussions with them, so you need to develop a level of trust and understanding from the start.

Getting to Know Your Students

At the very beginning of the term, get acquainted with students by handing out 3¹/₂- by 5-inch index cards or an information form that elicits basic information from them such as contact information, writing courses they have taken so far, the types of reading they enjoy, and their strengths and weaknesses in writing. This activity will allow the students to see that you are personally interested in them. Also, you will get to know their names more quickly.

Clarifying Your Expectations

Many students who take a freshman-level course will be uncertain what is expected of them. It is helpful to focus on major and minor expectations in the first week. For instance, you may want the assignments for the class to have particular headings. If you have other specific expectations, go over these while reviewing your syllabus or during the first week of class. It's always a good idea to limit class rules to several points: be on time, work hard while in class, ask questions when something is unclear, and treat classmates and instructor with respect. Students often appreciate when you set limits because they know what you will allow and what you will not accept.

Discuss evaluation practices and their consistent application throughout the term. Do this at the start of the term so that the students understand your system of weighting grades and averaging the components with essays, peer reviewing, journals, portfolios, homework, class participation, quizzes, and so on. Try to be as specific as possible about how you will grade the essays and the prewriting, first draft, and revised draft. If you factor peer reviewing into the class participation grade or into some other category, be sure to mention that fact early in the course so that students will learn to give more specific comments from the start of the term. It helps to include this breakdown in the course syllabus, but you should also refer to it at several points during the term.

Most institutions have some type of attendance policy. However, you should allow some flexibility on this because exceptions or specific situations may occur for which you will have to allow a student some leeway. If your institution has a specific policy, try to follow it for consistency. Some institutions have no attendance policy, and you will have to develop some standards of your own. A very reasonable policy is to allow students to miss no more than 20 percent of the allowed classes; after that, you can impose a penalty on their in-class grade. Give consistently scheduled and unscheduled assignments and quizzes throughout the term. Missing one or two of these won't cause problems; missing more than that will impact a student's grade. If a student has not attended class for an extended period of time, it is advisable to contact that student directly or have a faculty-initiated withdrawal form sent to that student.

Setting Your Classroom Tone

When working with a new class, you should initially set the tone or atmosphere that you would like to maintain throughout the course. Don't be concerned with trying to emulate another instructor who is very successful with students. Be comfortable with your own style because it is a big part of your personal identity. If you develop a very informal and relaxed approach early on and then switch to a demanding style, you will encounter problems with students. The best approach is to start off with a more demanding style and then loosen up as you get to know the class.

Also make sure you inform your students how they should submit and organize essays and revisions. At the very least, it's a good idea to require students to put prewriting, peer reviews, and drafts of an essay into a manila folder for submission. This strategy forces students to be more organized, and it is easier for you to follow the flow of their work.

Anticipating Problems and Using Services at Your Institution

During each week of the term, you will typically encounter at least one type of academic, personal, or classroom-centered problem that you must deal with to keep a student or your class focused. In such cases, you should attempt to utilize the resources of your institution. Your school will likely have a writing center or an academic skills center. Don't personally try to tutor each student with writing-related problems. Refer students with writing difficulties to the writing center instead. Likewise, students who are having difficulties with study habits or organization can be referred to the academic skills center. If you have serious concerns about a particular student, you may want to take on a more personal role to ensure that he or she gets the needed help in a timely manner.

If a student approaches you to indicate a concern about a busy work schedule in relation to the course assignments, you may want to recommend that this individual consult with financial aid for a student loan. This is especially critical in the first three weeks of class because this is the time when a student may decide to withdraw from all classes rather than explore other options.

If you have a student with personal issues, especially those involving psychological concerns (such as depression or a total lack of focus), you should advise the student to make an appointment with a campus counselor or psychologist. As an English instructor, you can certainly be an empathetic listener, but you should always be cautious when offering advice. A student who demonstrates clear signs of depression or has other serious problems should be referred to counseling as quickly as possible.

Finally, you have several choices in dealing with class behavior problems. Some of the most common situations are these: arriving consistently late to class, talking excessively while you are talking, and attempting to dominate the class discussion. The best way to resolve these situations is to address them as quickly as possible with an oral comment. However, if they can't be addressed effectively in this manner, it's advisable to discuss the problem with the student after class. Be firm and direct, but initially try to ask a series of questions to determine the root of the problem. Talk about the possible consequences of continuing the behavior. After this initial meeting, give the student one other opportunity. Then, if the problem persists, consider taking administrative action as indicated in the faculty handbook of your institution.

Staying Organized as the Term Progresses

At the start of the term, you need to develop some basic strategies for staying organized. You should keep a copy of the course syllabus and your detailed course outline on the wall next to your desk and one taped to the inside cover of *Seeing the Pattern*. You can refer to both of these as the term progresses.

Keeping Consistent Records

It is always a good strategy to organize the overall content of the class. You won't be able to establish totally objective grades or criteria for all assignments because there is certainly a level of subjectivity in a writing course. However, you should track daily attendance, check off the submission of prewriting and multiple drafts, give points for major in-class assignments, and record all the grades for revised essays. Be sure to establish a clear policy on how many revisions you allow and what your essay grading policy is.

Whatever grading policies you establish, you should give students an accurate estimate of their class grade at several points during the term. This will help to reduce disagreements at the end of the term and allow you to catch any errors that you have made in recording grades. Many English instructors are now using spreadsheets for tracking grades. If you record grades the traditional way, you may want to photocopy your class grades at several times during the term in case you lose your grade book.

Finally, when you feel that you are struggling to keep up with the paper load, you should keep in mind that all essays, journals, or assignments don't need to be graded with equal thoroughness. For the graded essays, you might want to focus on several criteria in your own comments and then use peer reviewing to cover other areas. For the non-graded assignments, you can give a Credit or No Credit grade and focus on one or several areas for commentary.

Meeting Individually with Students

It can be beneficial to have at least two conferences with each student during the term. You can use these conferences to discuss a student's overall progress or to discuss the development of a particular essay. If you do use class time for conferences, it is time well spent. You can have the students do peer reviewing or collaborative small-group work while you are holding conferences, you can use this time for an out-of-class assignment in addition to the conferences, or you can choose to meet with students outside of class.

Using *Seeing the Pattern* Effectively

If you spend a limited amount of time early in the term—and as the term progresses—to explain the critical sections of *Seeing the Pattern*, you will find that your students will better understand key writing concepts. Be sure to inform your students that there is an introduction—"Using *Seeing the Pattern* to Improve Your Writing"—at the front of the textbook that includes information about the book and its features. Consider assigning this section or taking some time in the first day of class to go through the book's features, showing students what is in the book and explaining how to use it.

Beginning with Part 1

Because *Seeing the Pattern* is designed to be flexible, you can choose which chapters you would like to cover and in what order. You might want to use the writing process chapters first (Chapters 2–4), reserving Chapter 1 until you begin assigning the patterns of development in Part 2. You could spend two weeks with Chapter 2 ("Planning Your Essay") and one of the patterns of development, such as Chapter 5 ("Narration") or Chapter 6 ("Description"), so that you focus more strongly on prewriting with the initial essay. On the other hand, you may want to cover Chapters 1–4 by themselves or in conjunction with the first major writing assignment. In particular, you may want to use Chapter 4 at more than one point in the course. For specific suggestions on using the first four chapters, see pages 49-58 of this manual.

Using the Visual Features of *Seeing the Pattern*

You will notice that an excellent feature of *Seeing the Pattern* is the visual nature of the text. Illustrations and diagrams offer a visual approach to writing and engage today's more visual students. Each chapter in Parts 1 and 2 begins with a Writing Quick Start to give students a preview of the major objectives of the chapter and the pattern of writing. The initial exercises in each chapter act as a critical starting point for writing and discussion.

The graphic organizers in each chapter are especially valuable for spatial learners, but this feature of the book should be helpful to all students. Graphic organizers are diagrams that *visually* present the relationship among ideas within a piece of text. Many students, especially underprepared students, have difficulty recognizing the organization and overall structure of what they read. They fail to recognize hierarchical and coordinate relationships and consequently have difficulty remembering what they read. Graphic organizers offer a meaningful conceptual framework that enables students to understand relationships and make connections with their existing knowledge. According to cognitive psychologist David P. Ausubel, creating these kinds of graphic organizers — which he has termed *advance organizers* — builds bridges, or "ideational scaffolding," that enables readers and learners to construct and reconstruct meaning within text (148).

Graphic organizers work effectively because they encode information in memory in two ways — verbally and spatially. Thus, they provide two different layers of cueing, or two memory paths; if one fails, the other may work. Graphic organizers in *Seeing the Pattern* can be used as both reading and writing strategies. For each method of development, students are shown two graphic organizers. The first demonstrates the relationship among the unique elements of the particular type of essay and also functions as a model. The second applies the model organizer to a specific essay included in the chapter. Viewing a created graphic organizer and then creating their own graphic organizer facilitates students' comprehension and recall. Later in the chapter, students are also asked to complete a graphic organizer for one of the readings in the chapter. You may want to experiment with having students fill out graphic organizers or make their own organizers at various phases in their reading process.

In *Seeing the Pattern*, graphic organizers can also be used for the revision of writing. When a student draws a graphic organizer of an essay he or she has written, the structure and relationship of ideas or lack thereof becomes apparent. Lack of supporting ideas also becomes immediately obvious, as does misplaced or irrelevant information. Some students may find these tools more helpful than others and may like to work with organizers on a regular basis. Assign at least one organizer exercise online and then make them optional if only a few students prefer to use them. (Interactive versions of the graphic organizers are available online at www.bedfordstmartins.com /seeingthepattern.)

Revision flowcharts clearly indicate places where a student's draft might need to be revised. Presented in a visual format with directional arrows, a revision flowchart asks the student to identify and evaluate his or her own thesis and underline and evaluate topic sentences, among other revisions, moving slowly, section by section, through the paper. After using a few of these flowcharts, students will begin to recognize key areas and learn to apply questions such as "Does your thesis clearly state the generalization that your examples support?" to their own writing.

Annotated professional and student essays provide excellent models for students to evaluate because key sections and points (such as the thesis statement) are clearly highlighted. Modeling is a very effective method for helping students to improve their writing because they are more apt to critique a "student essay" than a professional one, at least until they become accustomed to the process and can move on to model professional essays. This kind of clearly marked text is also visually stimulating and easier to comprehend by students whose learning styles are visual in nature.

Throughout *Seeing the Pattern,* bulleted and numbered lists are elements that make the text visually accessible and aesthetically pleasing. See, for example, the What to Look for, Highlight, and Annotate sections where Understanding the Reading activities and Examining the Characteristics of [Narration] Essays summarize what to look for as the student reads a particular rhetorical mode. Each idea is clearly and simply stated. You might like to recommend that students highlight or flag any list they find themselves consulting frequently—there is a directory of lists on the inside back cover of the book.

Using the Reading Apparatus in Part 2

The reading apparatus in Part 2 will help you to motivate students to read assigned essays more carefully so that they will be prepared to discuss or write about the essays in greater detail in class. Once students become accustomed to working with these questions, either as take-home work or as in-class work, they will begin to read more actively, highlighting and annotating their text and looking up vocabulary words in anticipation of doing the assignments.

Understanding the Reading

These questions focus on the content rather than the form of each essay. If you find that students are not reading the assigned essays actively, remind them to read and reread closely, annotating and highlighting as they go along. If they are still not reading closely enough, assign these Understanding the Reading questions beforehand. You may also use Understanding the Reading to give quick pre-discussion quizzes. If you prefer not to give quizzes, you can ask students to read and answer these questions before class discussion; this allows them to formulate their ideas on paper before venturing into group discussion.

Visualizing the Reading

This section provides an excellent opportunity for students to evaluate what they have read, in a visual outline format, in a table, or in response to a visual image. Each one is designed to ask the questions that pertain to the unique characteristics of the chapter's rhetorical pattern. Visualizing the Reading can be used as a take-home assignment or as an in-class assignment when you feel that the discussion has been lagging or that students are not reading closely enough. Visualizing the Reading is also useful for work in pairs.

Examining the Characteristics of [Illustration] Essays

Each of the Examining the Characteristics sections is specifically tied in to the chapter's rhetorical mode. The questions will get students thinking about how, for example, illustration essays are strengthened by a series of striking examples, or how comparison and contrast essays must be organized point by point or subject by subject. It is useful to assign students to think about one of these questions as they read the essay so that they focus in on the particular characteristics of the rhetorical mode.

Building Your Word Power

This section ties in closely with active reading. You may find that students do not understand the connotations of words and figurative phrases, even after reading an essay closely. Assigning one or two questions from Building Your Word Power is an excellent way to make sure that students begin to slow down their reading pace enough to assess the meaning of figurative language and colloquial phrases in addition to unfamiliar vocabulary words. You may have to reiterate how important it is to look up unfamiliar words and phrases throughout the semester. Building Your Word Power can be used as quizzes before opening up a class discussion of the essay to ensure that all students become accustomed to looking up unfamiliar terms. These questions also stimulate good discussions about connotation, denotation, and tone.

Building Your Critical Thinking Skills

Each of these sections focuses on a different thinking skill—for instance, evaluating sources, making inferences. First there is a brief description of the thinking skill, and then a series of questions focuses in on the skill under consideration. Students then evaluate the reading based on the sources it provides, the inferences they can draw from it, and so on. You might find it useful to dovetail your lecture with the critical thinking skill that follows each reading—talking briefly, for example, about "evaluating sources" (being able to recognize incomplete or unreliable information) before the essay is discussed in class. When students write prior to engaging in class discussion, they are usually better prepared to articulate their ideas. It is best to have students spend ten minutes writing (or doing a focused freewrite) about the thinking skill before initiating class discussion.

Reacting to the Topic: Discussion and Journal Writing

These questions offer fodder for in-class discussion relating to the topic of the reading. You might use these topics for in-class writing opportunities or have students respond to them in their journals, either in class or at home.

Applying Your Skills: Writing Assignments

The six writing assignments included for each reading in the book offer a wide range of topics and modes, from brief personal essays to longer research assignments. The first assignment in each set is for paragraph-length writing, which offers a useful way to initiate students to writing in the mode in a short, accessible format. Because of their brief length, these assignments are ideally suited for in-class exercises. You will also find here at least one Combining Patterns assignment and an Internet Research assignment relating to a topic covered by the reading.

Assigning the Patterns of Development in Part 2

When you focus on Part 2 of the book, you will discover that, as with other parts of the text, these chapters are designed to be flexible. Some instructors cover fewer chapters, but in greater detail. This approach can be effective, helping students see the range of potential that exists within that particular pattern of development. Some instructors cover many of the patterns of development in less detail and assign a larger amount of short papers or assignments during the term.

Another excellent possibility is to pair together or cluster professional and student essays that are related thematically. For instance, an instructor could develop an assignment emphasizing synthesis, using a cluster of readings or a series of related themes throughout the term. If you are interested in organizing your course this way, refer to the thematic table of contents included in *Seeing the Pattern*.

When using Part 2 of the book, you may decide to focus on one or two patterns of development in conjunction with Chapters 1–4. If you are teaching expressive writing, you may want to start off with narration or description. Many instructors like to begin with illustration or classification and division as a way of getting students to organize their thoughts from the very start. You could also assign a limited number of chapters in Part 2 and discuss those in greater detail. It is especially critical early in the term to help students work through the section on writing an essay using the pattern of development. This section appears at the end of the introduction to the mode in Chapters 5–14. With the first one or two essays, you can work with students as a class or in small groups as they develop their essays. Typically, you would work on the prewriting stage in class as journal exercises. Drafting, revising, and editing can be done outside of class or in conjunction with peer review. Most instructors look at a first draft and a revised draft of an essay, but you can also have students do peer reviews of drafts in progress. During this process, you can act as a guide or adviser, but don't feel that you always have to be the authority on writing in the class. You will find that some of your best students are sharp and perceptive in their editing skills and in providing feedback. You can develop any additional questions or comments on the essays in progress that you like, but for consistency you may want to use the specific questions in the revision flow-charts, which are part of the introductions to the mode for each chapter in Part 2.

Using Part 3

Designed in part as a reference for students, you may find it helpful to refer or assign students all or part of this section of the book. If you include research writing in your course, Chapter 15 offers a brief guide to using and evaluating sources along with a comprehensive list of documentation models in MLA style. Chapter 16 provides a unique key to academic success.

If you are using sources in essays, consider scheduling a library orientation before getting started. Spend part of at least one class talking about evaluating sources for use in an academic essay. The sources that a student chooses can have a major impact on the overall quality of the finished essay, especially if only two or three sources are used.

You might want to refer students to Chapter 16, "Keys to Academic Success," in Part 3 early in the term. This chapter gives special attention to study skills, providing practical survival strategies for college work before class, in class, and while studying. It also reinforces necessary study, reading, and work habits that underprepared students need special help with.

Integrating Grammar Coverage into the Course

Consider giving mini-lessons on some major writing errors throughout the term. You may find it useful to review in class the Seven Common Errors to Avoid section in Chapter 4 at the beginning of the term. Also, each of the chapters in Part 2 includes an Editing and Proofreading section that alerts students to common grammatical errors associated with a particular pattern of development. By using these sections individually or in class, you can help strengthen your students' writing skills. A useful collaborative activity is to mark different-colored stars on the top of student essays based on the types of errors they contain, then pair students who have stars that are the same color. This technique allows students to see the same writing errors that they make themselves in another writer's paper. At times, the errors that students regularly overlook in their own writing will be easier to see in another student's paper.

Using Journals in the Course

You can use journals in several ways in conjunction with *Seeing the Pattern*. The Reacting to the Reading: Discussion and Journal Writing questions in Chapters 5–14 are designed to support journal writing. These questions can help you to integrate journal writing into the course in a consistent way. You can also use journal writing with the Focus on the Topic prereading activities in Chapters 5–14. To encourage prewriting, you might consider having students use their journals to develop their ideas for writing. Consider encouraging students to use a loose-leaf binder for a journal so that pages can be added.

Keep in mind that you don't always have to collect all of the journal assignments and preliminary essay work. To reduce the paper load, you can take ten minutes at the end of a class to walk around the room and scan student journals. Also, use peer review for journal entries in connection with student essays. If you do collect journals, you have several options. You can give a Credit/No Credit grade when you check journals every week or two, and a letter grade at two points during the course. If you count the journal as equivalent to an essay, as many instructors do, you might want to grade the journals at two points during the course and average the grades. You should grade the journals periodically so that students will put more effort into them. When they do, they will also realize your emphasis on the development of ideas in preparation for writing an essay. When grading journals, you should focus on students' quantity of entries and focus, but not so much on the quality of their thinking. Try to reward effort and consistency rather than just the detailed insights, which students will learn to develop further as your class proceeds.

Using Computers and Software

Links to Exercise Central are available at www.bedfordstmartins.com/seeingthepattern. This collection of online exercises is the largest available. It is thorough, simple to use, and convenient for you and your students. Exercise Central includes multiple exercise sets at a variety of levels, as well as an interactive reporting feature that guides students to appropriate exercise sets, thus ensuring that their practice time is well spent. Students receive customized, immediate feedback for all of their answers, including an explanation of why they are correct or incorrect — feedback that turns practice into learning experience.

Grammar diagnostic. This diagnostic quiz is provided as a self-study tool. Its purpose is to help students identify which areas of English grammar, usage, style, punctuation, and mechanics they have already mastered but need more practice with. Once students know which topics they need to focus on, they can use the exercise sets in Exercise Central to practice them.

Tracking. Exercise Central makes it simple for students to track their progress and for you to monitor your students' progress and activity. Whenever students sign in, they can check their customized lesson plan to see which topics they have mastered and which exercises they have completed.

Reporting. To simplify the task of course management, the reporting feature of Exercise Central allows you to monitor the progress of individual students or of the class as a whole; if you choose the latter option, you can see the results for a single exercise set or for all exercise sets at once. If you have several classes or sections, you can even set up customized reports that will display results for each class or section separately.

The first time you sign in to Exercise Central as an instructor, you will be asked to register by supplying some information about yourself, your class, and your institution. Once the registration process is complete, you will receive a password by email. When you sign in using this password, you will gain access to the instructor's area of Exercise Central. Complete instructions for using the standard reports and creating customized reports are available at Exercise Central, which you can access at www.bedfordstmartins.com/seeingthepattern. You may want to distribute to your students the following step-by-step instructions for accessing, logging on, and bookmarking the Exercise Central Web site.

A Student's Guide to Accessing Exercise Central in Ten Easy Steps

1. Enter **www.bedfordstmartins.com/seeingthepattern** into the address field of your browser.

2. Click on the **Exercise Central** link.

3. When the welcome screen opens for Exercise Central, click on the **Student** link.

4. Once the login screen opens, **Bookmark** the page.

   For Internet Explorer:
   - Click on **Favorites** on the top bar of the browser screen.
   - Click on **Add to Favorites** in the pull-down menu.
   - When the "Add Favorite" pop-up box appears, type *Exercise Central* in the **Name** field.
   - Click **OK**.

   For Netscape:
   - Click on **Bookmarks** at top of the browser screen, just below the address field.
   - Click on **Add Bookmark** in the pull-down menu.

5. In the first field of the login box, enter your **First Name**.

6. In the second field of the login box, enter your **Last Name**.

7. In the third field of the login box, enter your instructor's email address: _____.

8. In the fourth field of the login box, re-enter your instructor's email address: _____.

9. Click **Start**.

10. Click on **42-Item Diagnostic Quiz** or the appropriate exercise topic your instructor has assigned to begin.

Winding up the Course

As you move into the final weeks and days of your class, you will be slowing down the pace of assignments and essays, but don't allow students to become overly lax. Try to maintain the structured, organized class you started with at the beginning of the term. You will need to stress to students the importance of finishing off the term in a strong manner. Just as the first two weeks are critical for overall success, the last two weeks can definitely make a difference in a student's grade.

Be sure to complete the class evaluations given by your department, division, or academic area. You may also want to request a brief, anonymous evaluation of your own. Try to look for certain patterns or trends, either negative or positive, in determining your overall performance in the class.

If time allows, try to collect final essays before the last week of class. Alternatively, if you collect them on the last day of class, either meet on the assigned finals day or give students a time, date, and location where you will be available to return papers with their final grades. By doing this, you will reduce extra work for yourself during the next term if a student questions a final grade. When you return papers, also give each student an overall assessment of his or her progress in the course. Try to make this final conference a positive experience.

Developing Your Course Plan

When developing a course plan, you need to choose a structure that is appropriate for the level of your students' abilities and the guidelines of your department. You also need to consider the goals of the course. In addition, knowing the length of instruction (ten weeks or fifteen weeks) and the terms (one or two) will help you plan an appropriate course structure.

Writing a Course Syllabus

The syllabus is an important document in the classroom. It is the contract between the instructor and the students as to the topics, policies, and procedures of the course. The syllabus should contain all relevant information pertaining to the course, so that students will know exactly what is expected of them. Likewise, all course-related information such as the instructor's office hours, email address, and phone number should be included, so that students know how and when to get in contact with the instructor. Because the syllabus becomes the "policies and procedures" manual of the course, all pertinent material must be included. The following is a sample syllabus with a course plan for a fifteen-week semester course that includes research.

Sample Syllabus for a One-Semester Course That Includes Research

I. General Information

Course Title: English Composition I   *Course Number:* ENG 161
Prerequisite: English 070 or placement test   *Semester:* Fall
Instructor: John Gillam   *Phone:* (724) 555-7890
Email: gillam@indiana.edu   *Office Hours & Location:* MWF 3–5
                                                 English Department offices, Ryan Hall

II. Text

McWhorter, Kathleen T. *Seeing the Pattern.* New York: Bedford/St. Martin's, 2006.

III. Course Description

This course covers the fundamentals of college writing, including the paragraph, the expository essay, and the research essay. Emphasis is placed on developing a coherent thesis, writing concisely and clearly, and adapting one's writing to a particular audience. This course also emphasizes self-editing, mechanics, and grammar. (taken from college catalog)

IV. General Course Objectives

 1. The student will learn to write well-organized and well-researched papers.

 2. The student will learn to recognize her or his common grammatical mistakes.

 3. The student will become familiar with different patterns of expository writing.

 4. The student will be able to use several different writing patterns.

V. Specific Course Objectives

 1. The student will write papers using the following strategies: illustration, process analysis, classification and division, comparison and contrast, definition, cause and effect, and argumentation.

 2. The student will edit and proofread for errors in grammar, punctuation, mechanics, and spelling.

 3. The student will be tested on reading comprehension.

 4. The student will critically analyze readings that use specific writing strategies.

 5. The student will use the Internet as a tool for research.

 6. The student will write a research paper using appropriate documentation.

VI. Classroom Procedures

Absences: The student is responsible for attendance. Attendance affects performance, and all students are expected to take part in class discussions and peer-review editing sessions. Each student is expected to be present and is responsible for class notes and assignments. If absent, the student is responsible for arranging an appointment with the instructor to discuss the notes and assignments missed.

Format for papers: Papers must be typed double-spaced using a 12-point font. Be sure to keep a copy of each assignment for yourself.

VII. Disability Statement

If you need to have special arrangements made due to a physical or learning disability, please notify the instructor as soon as possible. (Disclosure of the type of disability is not required.)

VIII. Grading

All papers must be turned in on the due date. Late papers will be lowered one letter grade. No papers will be accepted after the last day of class. Please save all papers in a folder to be collected periodically.

IX. Tentative Schedule

Week of Sept. 5: Course Introduction
Ch. 1 ("A Guide to Active Reading," especially Using a Graphic Organizer)

Week of Sept. 12: Writing Assessments
Ch. 2 ("Planning Your Essay," especially Developing and Supporting your Thesis Statement) and Ch. 16 ("Keys to Academic Success")

Week of Sept. 19: Ch. 3 ("Drafting Your Essay")
Draft of Essay #1 due

Week of Sept. 26: Ch. 7 ("Illustration") and Ch. 15 ("Finding and Using Sources")
Draft of Essay #2 due

Week of Oct. 3: Ch. 8 ("Process Analysis")
Peer review of Essay #1 or #2
Revision of Essay #1 or #2 due

Week of Oct. 10: Ch. 8 ("Editing and Proofreading")
Final draft of Essay #1 or #2 due

Week of Oct. 17: Ch. 9 ("Comparison and Contrast")
Draft of Essay #3 due
Peer review of Essay #3

Week of Oct. 24:   Ch. 10 ("Classification and Division") and Ch. 15 (*continued,*
                    especially Evaluating Internet Sources)
                    Draft of Essay #4 due
                    Peer review of Essay #4
                    Final draft of Essay #3 due

Week of Oct. 31:   Ch. 11 ("Definition")
                    Draft of Essay #5 due
                    Peer review of Essay #5
                    Final draft of Essay #4 due

Week of Nov. 8:   Ch. 12 ("Cause and Effect")
                    Draft of Essay #6 due
                    Peer review of Essay #6
                    Final draft of Essay #5 due

Week of Nov. 15:   Ch. 13 ("Argumentation") and Ch. 15 (*continued,* especially
                    Avoiding Plagiarism)
                    Library Orientation
                    Final draft of Essay #6 due

Week of Nov. 22:   Ch. 13 (*continued*) and Part III "Student Resource Guide"
                    Working thesis and research questions due

Week of Nov. 29:   Ch. 13 (*continued*)
                    Summary and paraphrase due

Week of Dec. 6:   Ch. 14 ("Combining Patterns")
                    Research paper draft due

Week of Dec. 13:   Ch. 14 (*continued*)
                    Peer review of selections from research paper drafts

Week of Dec. 20:   Ch. 14 (*continued*)
                    Final research paper due

Single-Quarter Course Plan

This plan consists of a ten-week quarter including five written essays: one expressive, one informative, and three argumentative. Other essays or chapters can be substituted based on individual preferences.

Week 1   Ch. 1 ("A Guide to Active Reading") and Ch. 2 ("Planning Your Essay")

Week 2   Ch. 3 ("Drafting Your Essay") and Ch. 16 ("Keys to Academic Success")

Week 3   Ch. 5 ("Narration") or Ch. 6 ("Description") and Ch. 4 ("Revising and Editing Your Essay")

Week 4   Ch. 4 (*continued*) and Ch. 12 ("Cause and Effect")

Week 5   Ch. 12 (*continued*)

Week 6   Ch. 13 ("Argumentation")

Week 7   Ch. 13 (*continued*) and Ch. 15 ("Finding and Using Sources")

Week 8   Ch. 14 ("Combining Patterns") and Part III (Student Resource Guide)

Week 9   Ch. 14 (*continued*)

Week 10 Ch. 14 (*continued*)

A Course Plan Based on Expressive Writing

This plan is based on a fifteen-week semester that focuses on writing from personal experience. Students begin by narrating and describing past events. They then move on to writing about current topics and finally to problems and solutions based on field research.

Week 1   Ch. 1 ("A Guide to Active Reading")

Week 2   Ch. 2 ("Planning Your Essay," especially Prewriting to Start the Assignment)

Week 3   Ch. 3 ("Drafting Your Essay") and Ch. 4 ("Revising and Editing Your Essay")

Week 4   Ch. 4 (*continued*) and Ch. 5 ("Narration")

Week 5   Ch. 6 ("Description")

Week 6   Ch. 7 ("Illustration")

Week 7   Ch. 8 ("Process Analysis")

Week 8   Ch. 9 ("Comparison and Contrast")

Week 9   Ch. 9 (*continued*)

Week 10 Ch. 11 ("Definition")

Week 11 Ch. 12 ("Cause and Effect")

Week 12 Ch. 13 ("Argumentation")

Week 13 Ch. 13 (*continued*)

Week 14 Ch. 14 ("Combining Patterns")

Week 15 Ch. 14 (*continued*)

A Course Plan Based on a Thematic Approach

This plan follows the various patterns of writing, from narration to argumentation. Students will learn to follow the various patterns, while reading essays and doing guided assignments based on different writing patterns over a fifteen-week period.

Week 1   Ch. 1 ("A Guide to Active Reading")

Week 2   Ch. 2 ("Planning Your Essay," especially Prewriting to Start the Assignment), and Ch. 16 ("Keys to Academic Success")

Week 3   Ch. 3 ("Drafting Your Essay") and Ch. 4 ("Revising and Editing Your Essay")

Week 4   Ch. 4 (*continued*) and Ch. 1 (*continued,* especially How to Use a Graphic Organizer)

Week 5   Ch. 5 ("Narration")

Week 6   Ch. 6 ("Description")

Week 7   Ch. 7 ("Illustration")

Week 8   Ch. 8 ("Process Analysis")

Week 9   Ch. 9 ("Comparison and Contrast")

Week 10 Ch. 10 ("Classification and Division")

Week 11 Ch. 11 ("Definition")

Week 12 Ch. 12 ("Cause and Effect")

Week 13 Ch. 13 ("Argumentation")

Week 14 Ch. 14 ("Combining Patterns")

Week 15 Ch. 14 (*continued*)

A Course Plan Based on Research Writing

This plan concentrates on the steps involved in research writing. Students will do guided assignments based on different writing patterns while conducting research.

Week 1   Ch. 1 ("A Guide to Active Reading," especially Using a Graphic Organizer)

Week 2   Ch. 2 ("Planning Your Essay," especially Developing and Supporting Your Thesis Statement) and Ch. 16 ("Keys to Academic Success")

Week 3   Ch. 3 ("Drafting Your Essay")

Week 3   Ch. 4 ("Revising and Editing Your Essay")

Week 4   Ch. 7 ("Illustration") and Ch. 15 ("Finding and Using Sources")

Week 5   Ch. 8 ("Process Analysis")

Week 6   Ch. 9 ("Comparison and Contrast")

Week 7   Ch. 10 ("Classification and Division") and Ch. 15 (*continued*, especially Evaluating Internet Sources)

Week 8   Ch. 11 ("Definition")

Week 9   Ch. 12 ("Cause and Effect")

Week 10 Ch. 13 ("Argumentation") and Ch. 15 (*continued*, expecially Avoiding Plagiarism)

Week 11 Ch. 13 (*continued*) and Part III (Student Resource Guide)

Week 12 Ch. 13 (*continued*)

Week 13 Ch. 14 ("Combining Patterns")

Week 14 Ch. 14 (*continued*)

Week 15 Ch. 14 (*continued*)

Helping Underprepared Students Improve Their Skills

The first-year college classroom is continually evolving. Over the years, instructors have welcomed increasing numbers of adult students, ESL students, and minority students. Now instructors are finding growing numbers of underprepared students who lack many of the academic skills that traditional first-year college students possess. This section will describe underprepared students and offer teaching suggestions for helping these students become successful college writers. It will also discuss how to strengthen students' reading and critical thinking skills. Although the discussion must necessarily focus on the academic deficiencies of underprepared students, it is important to point out that these students have as many positive qualities as traditional students. Under-prepared students also make substantial and worthwhile contributions to a writing classroom — adding a variety of perspectives, new experiences, and diverse view-points.

Identifying the Characteristics of Underprepared Students

Underprepared students are challenging but rewarding. They often require special at-tention and may learn and think differently from other students. Instructors of under-prepared students not only must examine what and how to teach but also must dis-cover new ways to help these students learn.

The accommodations described in this section are not limited to underprepared students. You may find that these strategies will help capable students learn more eas-ily and develop a more positive attitude toward writing instruction.

Identifying Negative Academic Self-Image

Many underprepared students regard themselves as academic failures. Some think they lack the ability to learn and, specifically, the ability to learn to write. Many stu-dents think of themselves as unable to achieve or compete in an academic environ-ment. This attitude may be largely a result of numerous failures they have experienced in previous educational settings. Consistent, then, with their past history, they expect little of themselves and may seem negative, defeated, or disengaged even before the course begins.

Designing Instructional Accommodations. Refer students to Chapter 16, "Keys to Academic Success," in Part 3 for advice on improving academic self-image. Try to design assignments, especially initial ones in the term, so that the students experi-ence immediate success. The first opportunity to practice a newly learned skill should also demonstrate success. For example, the first assignment in learning to use descriptive language might involve asking students to write a list of words de-scribing but not naming an interesting object you bring to class. No matter what a student writes, it will be correct, and it will demonstrate to the student that he or she can use descriptive language.

Recognizing Lack of Self-Direction

Underprepared students often lack goals and direction in their pursuit of a college ed-ucation as well as in the management of their lives. They may have few or no long-term goals; their short-term goals are often unclear and changeable. As a result, these students tend to lack the discipline or focus to attend class, complete assignments, or work independently on long-term projects.

Designing Instructional Accommodations. Refer students to Chapter 16, "Keys to Academic Success," in Part 3 for advice on becoming self-motivated. Make assignments immediate and short-term. Establish clear due dates and supply regular feedback. Distribute a written course syllabus that details all requirements, your grading system, and as many due dates of assignments as possible. Check frequently to be sure that students complete assignments, do homework, and "stay with" the course. For graded essays, it may be helpful if you require students to submit their work at various stages of the writing process so that you can approve their thesis statement and then their first draft, for example.

Distinguishing a Passive Approach to Learning

Partly because of their lack of experience in and success with academic environments, underprepared students often exhibit a passive approach to learning. They seldom ask questions, initiate action, or pursue solutions to academic problems. Instead, they follow procedures as well as they are able to understand them, wait to be told what to do, and take whatever action seems expected. They seldom initiate study plans, seek help from instructors, or ask questions to clarify assignments.

Designing Instructional Accommodations. Refer students to Chapter 16, "Keys to Academic Success," in Part 3 for advice on becoming an active learner. Initiate class discussions and construct collaborative activities that require involvement and problem solving to encourage and shape more active learning. Often a forthright discussion of active versus passive learning characteristics is effective as well. To encourage students to ask questions and to improve their ability to do so, direct students at the beginning of class to write at least two or three questions they hope the course will answer or several statements of what they want to learn.

Coping with Negative Attitudes toward Instructors

Throughout their previous negative educational experiences, many underprepared students have come to associate instructors with unpleasant or uncomfortable learning environments. As a result, students are often closed, unresponsive, or evasive with their instructors.

Designing Instructional Accommodations. Refer students to Chapter 16, "Keys to Academic Success," in Part 3 for advice on communicating with instructors.

Establishing a framework of trust is difficult but necessary. Try to encourage openness, directness, honesty, and patience. Give careful, detailed explanations of course requirements, and listen willingly to students. Once you have established your authority and made sure that there are no behavior problems, you may find it helpful to present yourself as a person who experiences successes and failures just as students do.

Recognizing Lack of Familiarity with College Life and Academic Procedures

More than traditional students, underprepared students are confused and frustrated by the strangeness, formality, and seeming unfriendliness of the academic environment. Many underprepared students are the first in their families or among their friends to attend college; therefore, they lack the advantage of practical advice and support that many students receive from family and peers. They are unfamiliar with class schedules, college policies, and instructors' expectations.

Designing Instructional Accommodations. As a means of establishing trust as well as building familiarity with college life, offer as many practical "how-to-get-around" tips as possible. Also, as events occur on campus, take a few minutes to explain them. For example, when drop-and-add day begins, explain what is going on; when advance registration for the next term begins, alert the class and explain the procedures involved.

Identifying Lack of Time-Management Skills

Many underprepared students may lack the ability to plan and organize their time. Others may be working too many hours at part-time or even full-time jobs, and they may have numerous family responsibilities as well. Some underprepared students—especially those coming directly from high school, where their time is tightly structured—may have difficulty adapting to the relatively unstructured college environment. Underprepared students also tend to have high absentee rates. Their absenteeism is, of course, related to other characteristics such as lack of self-direction and poor time management skills. In addition, many underprepared students are overcommitted. They are working many hours at part- or full-time jobs and have not yet found a balance among family life, work, friends, and academic responsibility.

Designing Instructional Accommodations. Refer students to Chapter 16, "Keys to Academic Success," in Part 3 for advice on time management. You can help students by structuring your course consistently. For example, make essays always due on Fridays and in-chapter exercises always due on Mondays. Make deadlines and due dates clear, distributing them in writing and also announcing them in class. Establish also a clear, firm absence limit. You may have to make exceptions in obvious emergencies, but a firm absence policy is important. Do not accept late papers without penalty, and include a class participation component in your grading system.

Compensating for Lack of Experiential Background

Owing perhaps to inadequate preparation in high school or an immature approach to learning while in high school, underprepared students sometimes lack basic knowledge expected from college freshmen.

Designing Instructional Accommodations. Refer students to Chapter 16, "Keys to Academic Success," in Part 3 for advice on communicating with instructors. The immediate solution is, of course, to fill in gaps of knowledge as they arise by providing needed background information. Point out to the class that glosses added to the professional readings in the text supply information students may need to understand the reading.

Recognizing Avoidance of Reading

Many underprepared students choose not to read, because reading is not their primary method of obtaining information. Some find reading difficult, non-interactive, and time consuming; consequently, a few will try to "get by" without reading assigned essays.

Designing Instructional Accommodations. Refer students to Chapter 16, "Keys to Academic Success," in Part 3 for advice on using a syllabus. To encourage active reading, make sure that you accompany any given reading assignment with an activity that will engage the students and produce tangible results. In the headnote for most essays in the text, for example, students are directed to identify and highlight a particular feature of the essay. Use also the prereading questions before each reading to help focus students on something specific to read for in the essay.

Identifying Lack of Perseverance with Academic Tasks

Some underprepared students have difficulty persevering with lengthy or complicated academic tasks and multi-stage processes. Their goal is to complete a task as quickly as possible; as a result, they tend to jump immediately to the final step. These students, then, may skip prewriting, planning, and organizing their ideas and may begin by writing what they perceive to be a nearly final draft.

Designing Instructional Accommodations. Refer students to Chapter 16, "Keys to Academic Success," in Part 3 for advice on staying focused. Offer incentives for students to work through the writing process. Award a specific number of points for the submission of prewriting and so forth.

Developing Basic Writing Skills

Many underprepared students lack certain basic writing skills. They make errors in sentence structure (especially comma splices, fragments, and run-ons) and in grammar, punctuation, and mechanics. The reasons for these deficiencies are diverse. Some students never learned these basic skills in high school. Others have been out of school and have forgotten standard conventions. Still others are unaware that correctness is important and write carelessly, ignoring conventions.

Valuable instructor and classroom time need not be consumed addressing basic writing problems since students can learn to correct their own problems by using Exercise Central (p. 16).

Using the "Editing and Proofreading" Section in Chapter 4

This section of Chapter 4 includes writing instruction designed to explain basic rules and principles of grammar, punctuation, mechanics, and spelling in a straightforward, nontechnical manner. Numerous hand-edited examples are provided to assist students who learn better by studying examples than by reading rules. Exercises are also included to help students determine whether they understand and can apply each rule or principle.

Using Exercise Central

Exercise Central is an extensive bank of exercises on a variety of topics in grammar, punctuation, and mechanics. Students who need further practice on a given problem can access additional exercises at www.bedfordstmartins.com/seeingthepattern. A more detailed description of Exercise Central appears on page 16 of this manual.

Strengthening Students' Reading Skills

Many underprepared students do not read at the college level. As a result, they find assigned textbooks and essays challenging and sometimes frustrating. To assist such students, *Seeing the Pattern* contains numerous features to guide students through essays in the text, while providing them with skills and strategies for improving their reading skills. Numerous tables, flowcharts, bulleted lists, and diagrams both emphasize and condense important information.

Chapter 1 ("A Guide to Active Reading") provides a framework for improving students' reading skills. It dispels misconceptions students may hold about reading, presents a step-by-step guide to reading actively, and offers suggestions for understanding difficult text. This chapter can be taught in class, assigned for students to work through independently, or assigned selectively to students who demonstrate reading problems. Chapter 15 ("Finding and Using Sources") also provides useful information on reading critically.

Building Active Reading Strategies

Many students are passive readers; they do not interact with the ideas they read, and they fail to make connections between the ideas presented in the text and their own knowledge and experience on the topic. They accept ideas rather than question and evaluate them. Further, they do not monitor their comprehension or initiate strategies that will improve it. Unless directed to do so, many students do not preview before reading; highlight as they read; or review, synthesize, or summarize after they read. The section How to Read Actively in Chapter 1 offers students a step-by-step process for approaching a reading assignment. They learn to preview before reading, activate background knowledge, establish a purpose for reading, read with an intent, highlight and annotate, and review after reading. This guide can be applied to all essays in the text as well as to readings or textbook assignments in other academic courses. In fact, the process is a variation of the well-known SQ3R system, developed by Francis P. Robinson in 1961 and used ever since as a means of strengthening both reading and recall of expository text. Encourage students to use the five active reading strategies in all of their academic coursework.

The text contains several other features that promote active reading. Headnotes and prereading questions that accompany readings direct students to search for a particular element or apply specific skills. In each chapter, students are directed to draw a graphic organizer of at least one of the chapter readings, thereby encouraging the application of active reading strategies. Chapters 6–14 offer specific suggestions for reading essays based on each method of development, showing students how to adapt and apply the active reading strategies to specific types of reading materials. In these chapters, three of the seven types of questions (Understanding the Reading, Visualizing the Reading, and Examining the Characteristics of [Narration] Essays) that follow the readings enable students to evaluate their reading strategies and guide them in analyzing the essay.

Using Graphic Organizers

Many underprepared students have difficulty recognizing the organization and overall structure of what they read. They fail to see how ideas within the text connect and develop. Since material that is perceived as organized is easier to recall than that which is not, these students often have difficulty remembering what they read. Graphic organizers diagram these relationships *visually*, creating a meaningful conceptual framework that allows underprepared students to recognize patterns within the text. (For more on graphic organizers, see p. 9 of this manual.)

Strengthening Vocabulary Skills

Underprepared students often need to improve their vocabulary as well as their comprehension. The essays in *Seeing the Pattern* offer ample opportunity. Many of the essays contain words that may be vaguely familiar to students but are not part of their speech or writing. In many essays, glosses are provided for terms and references that are likely to be unfamiliar. Building Your Word Power questions following each reading have students analyze the use of language and require them to define vocabulary words from the reading, thus placing a continuing emphasis on vocabulary development. Here are a few suggestions for helping students improve their vocabulary.

1. Encourage students to develop a word awareness. You can do this by bringing to their attention a particularly well-chosen word, an apt phrase, or a high-impact word as you discuss professional essays in the text.

2. As you read student essays, mark a place or two where a more forceful or more descriptive word or phrase is needed.

3. Encourage students to keep a computer file or notebook of new words they want to begin to use in their own writing or speech.

4. Show students how to figure out the meanings of words from context clues. A few quick examples from one of the chapter essays is often sufficient to get them started.

5. Refer students with serious vocabulary problems to the college's academic skills center for further instruction.

Fostering Critical Reading and Thinking

Underprepared students often lack critical reading and thinking skills. They accept a writer's ideas at face value and fail to interpret, evaluate, and react to ideas. *Seeing the*

Pattern promotes critical thinking and reading in several ways. The readings in chapters 5–14 include Building Your Critical Thinking Skills questions that introduce students to important critical thinking concepts, such as tone, evaluating sources, and bias. Students must then apply this skill to the essay they have just read. The chapter apparatus also includes a Reacting to the Reading section that guides students in developing a critical response to each reading.

You can promote critical thinking in the classroom in the following ways.

1. Establish an open environment in which students are welcome to ask serious questions freely at appropriate times.

2. Serve as a role model. Ask critical questions often and encourage students to explore them with you.

3. Correct the misguided notion that critical thinking means only to find fault and that it emphasizes the negative.

4. Use a problem-solving paradigm to teach critical thinking. Use daily classroom problems, such as a fire drill that results in the class missing a scheduled in-class revision workshop, to guide students through the stages of (1) gathering information, (2) defining the problem, (3) identifying possible solutions, (4) evaluating solution paths, and (5) making a decision.

5. Require generalization. Give students practice in seeing how a specific writing skill can apply to a wide range of situations. Ask the class, for example, when a narrative might be useful in workplace settings, or in what college courses comparison and contrast might commonly be used.

Works Cited

Ausubel, David P. *Educational Psychology: A Cognitive View.* New York: Holt, 1968.
Robinson, Francis P. *Effective Study.* New York: Harper, 1961.

Unit ◆ Two

Teaching Tips and Suggested Answers for Individual Chapters in *Seeing the Pattern*

Part 1: Skills for Success in Reading and Writing

Part 1 is a guide to active reading and writing and provides a broad overview of the relationship between the two. Because this is a subject that students may initially consider unnecessary and simplistic, it may be challenging to help them to recognize how important it is to re-learn or refine their previous understanding of what it means to "read" an essay and to "write a good paper." Therefore, you will probably find it helpful to devote several class sessions at the start of the term to Part 1 of *Seeing the Pattern* in order to dissuade students from the idea that they can simply go on reading texts and writing papers exactly as they did in high school. Although you may at first encounter resistance to the idea that they need to re-learn how to read an essay and write and revise their papers, over time, as their writing improves, first-year students will begin to appreciate the writing and reading skills they develop in your introductory class.

CHAPTER 1   A Guide to Active Reading, p. 3

Chapter 1 is devoted to the idea of "active reading," also called close or critical reading. It is important to establish the connection between reading and writing critically early in the semester. If you take the time early on to reinforce the idea that analytical reading and writing are closely related, your students' ability to read, think, and write critically will develop more readily over the course of the semester. You may find it especially worthwhile to devote some class time to the concept of critical thinking, emphasizing that college-level writing depends upon the ability to analyze readings and to support opinions with evidence from a text (or texts). The section entitled Changing Some Misconceptions about Reading on page 4 is a good way to open up a discussion of critical thinking. This kind of discussion will help your students understand that they are being asked to engage in a new level of scholarly thinking.

Before giving the first reading assignment, you should review the Strategies for Reading (p. 5) with your students. This section outlines five active reading strategies that you may want to encourage your students to follow on a regular basis. You might, for example, want to go through the seven Guidelines for Previewing (p. 6) aloud with your students to show them how to "preview" the essays you assign in class. One way to make use of this feature would be to go down the list with them, asking them what kind of information a reader can glean from each of the previewing suggestions listed. To reinforce the usefulness of these techniques, you might also want to use the list in conjunction with the annotated essay by Etta Kralovec, "No More Pep Rallies!" (p. 7). Encourage your students to go through the previewing steps for every assigned reading throughout the semester.

Many first-year students simply do not understand why they should highlight key points (p. 10) and annotate their impressions (p. 10), or why they need to look up and remember the meaning of unfamiliar vocabulary words (p. 21). Remind them that college-level courses require a new kind of reading and that rereading or "reviewing" (p. 11) will foster a more sophisticated level of thinking. You might want to ask them to show you their copy of *Seeing the Pattern* at the beginning of the first few classes after you have discussed highlighting and annotating. Observe whether or not they are underscoring and writing in the margins. If you are still not seeing much annotation, remind them of what you would like to see. You might want to show them your own text, which is undoubtedly marked up, as an example of what you expect to see. Once they are highlighting and annotating their texts, ask them to share a word or idea they underscored (or questioned) with the class. Ask them to explain why they marked it and what they learned from doing so.

Another important concept that you may wish to introduce to your students is the idea that a text can be looked at visually, *before being read*, as if it were an object. Surprisingly enough, many students are completely unaware of the meaning of "key elements" (pp. 9–10) such as headings and type size or font differences. Point out that design and the textual formatting of titles, headnotes, headings, subheadings, and so on indicates various kinds or levels of headings. For example, "No More Pep Rallies!" (p. 7) uses highlighting and annotations to visually show the parts to look for when previewing a text. This essay can be used to show students how to apply the active reading strategies explained in the chapter. Let students know that you will be questioning them about or asking them to identify key elements, such as thesis statements, in every reading you assign during the semester.

Because all students will at some point encounter texts that are difficult to understand, it is a good idea to show them the table titled Difficult Readings: Specific Problems and Strategies for Solving Them (p. 12). Explain how they can use this table to identify the problem they are having (in the left-hand column) and then find strategies for reading and comprehension to address this difficulty (in the right-hand column).

You may want to go over the section Using a Graphic Organizer (p. 13) carefully, as these visual representations of an essay's content and structure are used throughout *Seeing the Pattern*. Many students find graphic organizers very helpful for identifying the flow of ideas in an essay. The graphic organizer is also a useful device for slowing down a student's pace as he or she reads a text. Identifying the thesis statement and other key aspects of the essay and seeing them arranged visually into sections may help students who have difficulty understanding how a text is organized. As they fill in the boxes, they can visualize the text in a new way, organized into parts: *introduction,* with background material and thesis; *body,* with topic sentences and key details; and *conclusion,* with restatement of thesis. By learning to slow down, reread, and pick apart a reading in order to fill out the graphic organizer, students will eventually find themselves able to structure and revise their own writing with greater ease.

Finally, if you plan to have your students work with the visuals included in *Seeing the Pattern* or in other texts, you may want to take a little time to discuss Reading Visuals (p. 18). Students are generally comfortable with and eager to discuss visuals but may have given little thought to how to think critically about them. As an in-class exercise, you may ask students to apply the Five Questions to Ask about Visuals to an image that appears with one of the readings in this text or elsewhere.

Chapter 2 Planning Your Essay, p. 23

Chapter 2 gives an overview of different prewriting strategies and then explains how to use these techniques in order to develop and support a thesis statement. Many students consider prewriting a pointless exercise, preferring instead to write a single draft in just one sitting—something that they often did in high school. In order to prevent this tendency to skip the preliminary phases of developing an essay, you may want to assign papers in a step-by-step fashion. Ask students to hand in their papers, phase by phase, over a period of weeks. For example, you might ask them to hand in their freewriting first, followed by any notes they jotted down, their narrowed topic, thesis statement, outline, first draft, and so on. Reiterating the advantages of using this technique throughout the semester will increase students' willingness to employ prewriting and will result in more carefully thought out and executed essays.

This chapter addresses many of the aspects of the first draft that cause students difficulty, including considering audience and tone. The two examples shown on page 27 of a student writing about an orientation session, first to a friend and then in the school newspaper, illustrate vividly how tone is transformed by the idea of audience. You may find it useful to assign Exercise 2.1 to help students discern the often subtle differences in tone and point of view, depending upon their audience. First-year students often have difficulty with the idea of "audience," asking what is meant by it since the only person who is going to see their writing is you, the instructor. You may need to review this topic over several class periods, explaining that it is necessary to assume that the audience needs some background even if they are familiar with the subject. It is often worthwhile to generate some discussion about this idea, experimenting with various audiences, from journal writing to freewriting that will be read aloud in class.

Learning to narrow down a topic is another skill that first-year students tend to have difficulty with. Exercises 2.4 (p. 32) and 2.5 (p. 33) can be used in class to give students practice in setting the parameters of paper topics. Once they've developed an understanding of how to successfully narrow and define a topic, they will be ready to move on to the thesis statement, one of the most difficult of all concepts to teach. Be prepared to show your students how to refine their thesis statements throughout the term. Tools on thesis development included in *Seeing the Pattern* that you may find especially useful include the list of Guidelines for Writing a Thesis Statement (pp. 38–39) and Exercise 2.8 (p. 39), which will help your students work toward a better understanding of what makes an effective thesis statement. Explain, too, that although many of the professional writers whose work appears in this text use "implied" thesis statements, it is best to begin by perfecting the explicit thesis statement (p. 39).

Chapter 3 Drafting Your Essay, p. 47

Chapter 3 explains how to outline and organize a first draft, beginning with a clear method of organization. As an introduction to this topic, you may want to refer students to the graphic organizer on The Structure of an Essay: Parts and Functions included at the start of the chapter (p. 49). Students may better grasp this subject if they work through a draft of their own using the Essay in Progress exercises included in this chapter. By applying the various stages of drafting an essay to writing of their own, students will better see how important an organizational plan is to the development of their essay.

By using the examples from the student essay discussed in this chapter, "The Value of Volunteering," your students can observe three different ways to develop their ideas: using an informal outline (p. 51), preparing a formal topic outline (p. 51), and creating a graphic organizer (p. 52). You may find it helpful to have the students create an outline or graphic organizer for all of the writing they do for the course. By requiring this step, you give students the opportunity to review and make changes to the organizational plan for their essay before they begin drafting it.

Once your students understand the importance of developing an organizational plan, they are ready to begin drafting their essay. Their writing will likely be strengthened if you spend some time in class working through the section on Writing Effective Paragraphs (p. 54). This section begins with a discussion on What Well-Focused Topic Sentences Must Do (p. 54). Mention to your students how closely the purpose of a topic sentence relates to that of a thesis statement. The list of Guidelines for Writing Topic Sentences on pages 55–56 can serve as a useful guide for students as they draft paragraphs for their essays, and the list of Guidelines for Writing Specific Paragraphs on page 58 will be of use in coaxing students to develop paragraphs that are more specific and interesting. Finally, in order to show students how to link their ideas within and between paragraphs, you should spend a little time discussing Connecting Supporting Details with Transitions and Repetition (p. 59). Commonly Used Transitional Expressions (p. 60) offers a handy list that will help your students' writing flow more clearly from topic to topic.

You will probably want to review the structure of an essay throughout the term, letting students work in pairs or small groups to evaluate their own writing on a regular basis. The Guidelines for writing effective introductions and conclusions (pp. 61–62 and 63–64) are especially useful tools; you will likely refer students to this material over the course of the term as needed. Knowing that other students will be reading their writing motivates students to write well, so you may want to devote some class time every week to peer review. Remember that what seems obvious to you, such as the function of a title (to "announce your subject" and "spark readers' interest"; pp. 64–65), often needs to be explicitly pointed out to first-year students. Even after you have done so, their titles may remain generic and vague (for instance, "Red States versus Blue States: A Comparison and Contrast Paper") for the first few weeks. Refer to the list of Five Tips for Writing Effective Titles (p. 000) over and over, and have students evaluate each other's titles in pairs, until you see results.

Chapter 4 Revising and Editing Your Essay, p. 70

Chapter 4 provides an overview of the revising and editing process. The revision process is one of the most difficult of all phases to explain to beginning students. Many of them simply do not understand what revision entails, no matter how many revision checklists you give them. Even if you assign first and second drafts, they will often only make whatever changes you explicitly marked on their copy. It is important, therefore, to stress early on the importance of revision. You may need to remind your students, over and over, what editing entails. Remind them that most professional writers edit their own work through countless drafts, even before submitting it to a professional editor, who then edits it yet again. As way of example, you might explain to the class the steps that you take to revise your own writing. It may be more real for students if they understand that all writers work through multiple drafts before finalizing a piece of writing.

Encourage students to visit you during office hours to discuss their drafts, or if time allows, set aside time in class to meet with students individually to discuss their drafts and how they might be improved. In addition, you might use peer review (p. 75). Go over the Peer Review Questions (p. 76) so that each student understands her or his responsibility as a critic and what elements to evaluate. Engaging students in an active discussion about their writing can open up their minds to a more critical evaluation of the strengths and weaknesses of their work, leading to stronger revisions.

You will probably find it helpful to have students apply the skills in this chapter to their own writing by using the Essay in Progress activities included throughout this chapter. You may also want to have students apply the Questions to Ask as You Revise (p. 71) to all of the writing that they do in the class. These questions will make the process of revision clearer and more enjoyable for them. Other useful tools include the revision flowcharts Evaluating Your Thesis Statement, Topic Sentences, and Evidence (pp. 73–74) and Evaluating Your Paragraphs (pp. 74–75). These visual features walk the students through the process of revision, step by step. It breaks the process of revision down to a series of parts and helps them to see, for example, that they can add in "transitional words" or "transitional sentences" (p. 118) if they forgot to insert them earlier.

This chapter also addresses the idea that revision means making one's sentences more concise, clear, and beautiful. Using the lists Improving Your Sentences (p. 77) and Improving Your Word Choice (p. 79), alone or in pairs, students can improve their work at the sentence level while creating interesting and lively writing. They can also begin to address common grammatical issues, comparing their work against the Common Errors to Avoid (p. 81). If particular issues need attention (for instance, confusing shifts), either on an individual level or by the entire class, you might want to assign other grammatical exercises in addition to those provided in this book. One resource for supplemental exercises is Exercise Central at www.bedfordstmartins.com/seeingthepattern. Gradually, as students grow accustomed to revising their work and studying lists like the Common Errors included here, they will begin to recognize their own mistakes. They will also begin to catch their errors more quickly in the revision process.

Part 2: Readings for Writers

Chapter 5 Narration: Recounting Events, p. 93

The narrative essay is usually familiar to most first-year college students because it involves storytelling of the kind they hear every day. You might want to begin with a definition of *narration*, that is, a story that makes a point. When presented as a story, the narrative essay becomes much more accessible to students who are apprehensive about expository writing. Another way to explain a narrative is to see it as an answer to the question, "What happened?" You will want to emphasize that creating a story is not just a matter of saying, "This happened, then that happened." Every narrative needs to be propelled by a strong narrative line. The narrator (or story teller) uses language to shape the narrative or tell the story in the most effective way. Pacing and point of view are important. The writer must leave out irrelevant details and organize the narrative to best effect (chronologically, spatially, or otherwise). Stress also that while a narrative is essentially a story, it is also a story that makes a point. This point is crucial because students will need to make a point in their own narratives through the use of a clear thesis statement.

This chapter includes a wide range of narratives. The annotated essay, "Right Place, Wrong Face" by Alton Fitzgerald White (p. 94) recounts events in a straightforward, chronological way—the tension mounts as readers see the author's belief in the justice system being dashed. Sherry Amatenstein's narrative, "Talking a Stranger through the Night" (p. 112), sets up tension through the use of foreshadowing when she prays not to get a suicide caller as she mans a crisis hotline in New York City. When the call comes in, she then finds herself absorbed in making sure that the caller wants to live. Although the phone call takes hours, the author selects only those lines of dialogue that are crucial to the reader's sense of the progress being made. The tension is based on the question in the reader's mind, "Will the suicide caller stay on the line or hang up and kill herself?"

Amy Tan's "Fish Cheeks" (p. 118), Langston Hughes's "Salvation" (p. 122), and Cherokee Paul McDonald's "A View from the Bridge" (p. 127) are all tightly woven sketches that employ key moments and key lines of dialogue to further the action and heighten the tension. Each piece is written in straightforward chronology (alternating summation and action), and each uses vivid sensory details to make the story come alive. Toni Cade Bambara's "The Lesson" (p. 133) is a short story that relies heavily upon colloquial language to reveal character, contrast races and classes, suggest emotion, and further the action. All of these readings offer models of narration that students can emulate in their own writing.

Alton Fitzgerald White, "Right Place, Wrong Face," p. 94

Alton Fitzgerald White, a young, successful black actor who lives in Harlem, is arrested as a suspect when the police respond to a call describing "young Hispanics with guns" (para. 6). Ironically, at the time of the story White is playing the part of Coalhouse Walker Jr.—a black man who is similarly abused—in the Broadway play *Ragtime,* yet the event takes White by surprise and causes him to lose faith in the justice system. He had naively expected to be treated with "consideration" (2) by the police.

In opening up a discussion about this essay, you might ask students about their knowledge of New York City, especially Harlem and mid-town Manhattan where White works. For background, be sure to point out that although Harlem has a reputation for being dangerous, it has many safe neighborhoods for black middle-class professionals, such as the neighborhood White lives in. You might want to initiate a discussion about situations in which black men are wrongly considered suspects by police officers. This scenario is one that is documented and well known in the black community; most black men are warned early that such a thing might happen in their lifetime. You might want to discuss the reasons that White identifies himself not as black but simply as an actor from Cleveland, Ohio, who was raised to be a "gentleman" (1) and to have "manners" (2).

As you work through the section on Characteristics of Narrative Essays (p. 97), you might return again to the White essay. The annotations clearly mark the points of conflict, tension, and climax and other narrative techniques used by White. You might have students add additional annotations of their own to mark notable passages of dialogue and physical description as well as events that build suspense and further the narrative.

Aphonetip Vasavong, "You Can Count on Miracles," p. 108

This student essay tells the story of a crucial moment in Aphonetip Vasavong's life. The dramatic story of her family's escape from political persecution in Laos has all the elements of a good narrative. Because her family must leave secretly, at night, without telling their neighbors where they are going, the conflict is dramatic. When eight-year-old Vasavong gets lost in the woods but cannot risk calling out for help, a rabbit appears suddenly to "lead" (para. 6) her to her family. The rabbit's mysterious assistance lends Vasavong's story an almost mythological quality. Students will no doubt enjoy analyzing this narrative since it is a real-life story that could, perhaps, have been told with even greater skill. It might be useful to assign students to break into small groups to rewrite the story so that it has maximum impact. Tell them that they can fictionalize, adding in details such as active verbs, dialogue, and sensory details (especially sounds). Instruct them to try to maintain Vasavong's voice and basic story line. Have them rewrite the ending so that it has greater impact.

Responding to "Students Write," p. 108

1. Students are likely to have different views on the effectiveness of Vasavong's thesis. While overall Vasavong's essay presents a strong narrative, her thesis is not very effective, sounding almost like a cliché. Encourage students to revise this thesis into a more meaningful statement that makes a clearer point about the events of the essay.

2. The author doesn't really elaborate on the idea of "coincidences that are so unusual and meaningful that they could not have happened by chance alone" put forth in the first sentence. Given the prominence of this point at the start of the essay, students may note that idea could be expanded upon. Because most students are likely to be unfamiliar with the situation in Cambodia during the 1980s, more historical and background details about Laos and the Communist regime would have been helpful. Still other students might ask why an eight-year-old girl would be left at the end of the line. Wouldn't an adult or older child be put there to make sure that everyone was safe?

3. Most students are likely to say that Vasavong very effectively establishes conflict and creates tension. To move beyond this, have students identify how she creates tension and encourage them to identify any points in the essay where points of tension and conflict could be improved.

4. Vasavong uses foreshadowing with the mention of the rabbit in the first paragraph. Because this use of foreshadowing is related to the essay's thesis, you might want to link this discussion to that of question 1.

5. To encourage critical analysis of the title, introduction, and conclusion, refer students to the relevant sections of Chapter 3 that explain the Do's and Don'ts of writing effective titles, introductions, and conclusions. While answers will vary, most students will probably agree that the title is satisfactory because it conveys the author's belief that the rabbit guiding her way was a kind of miracle. Likewise, students are likely to agree that the introduction is good because it foreshadows the rabbit's part in the story. The conclusion, however, is somewhat weak because Vasavong does not adequately explore the meaning of the rabbit leading her to safety not being "attributed to chance alone" (para. 6). In analyzing the conclusion, encourage students to reflect again on the essay's thesis and how the thesis and conclusion might have been strengthened by a more clearly stated point about Vasavong experiences.

Sherry Amatenstein, "Talking a Stranger through the Night," p. 112

Amatenstein's narrative vividly establishes how the events of a single night spent staffing a crisis hotline changed her view of the world. The first two nights quickly diminish the author's idealism as she deals with problem callers, one after another. Then, on the third night, a dreaded suicide call comes in, after only a brief training session on how to handle such emergencies. Several hours later, Amatenstein has successfully calmed the caller's fears and possibly averted a suicide. After she hangs up, Amatenstein realizes how the process of helping the suicide caller made her feel more connected to the human community, a moment of true epiphany for her.

In discussing this essay, you might want to provide some background information about the issue of suicide and how it is prevented or addressed by psychologists and others. A discussion about volunteering or helping those less fortunate, and where such altruism fits into our culture, might also be useful. Ask students to share their experiences volunteering and how their expectations were met or foiled. In particular, ask if any of them want to share an experience in which helping someone else helped them as well.

Understanding the Reading, p. 114

1. Amatenstein reveals that she is the child of Holocaust survivors and has always wanted to "ease other people's pain," especially after 9/11 (para. 1).

2. She receives calls from "men who wanted to masturbate," "repeats" who called over and over again to relate their "horrific childhoods," and callers who "railed" or were "abusive" if she wouldn't give them advice (3). These early conversations made Amatenstein less idealistic about her work at the crisis hotline and less sympathetic toward the people calling.

3. Examples of how the author was helpful to Sandy, the suicide caller, include: the caller was able to think of "an interest in books on spirituality" (8), which gave her pleasure; she kept talking for two hours even though her throat hurt from crying (8–10); after hearing Amatenstein read a prayer, Sandy said she thought she'd be all right for the night (10); and she asked about when the narrator would be staffing again (11).

4. Amatenstein learned that because she herself had been feeling lonely "[d]espite having people in my life" (13), the experience with Sandy meant just as much to her as it did to Sandy. Through this experience the author learned that connecting with "another troubled soul in New York City" (13) was of greater value than the material comforts of her own life.

Visualizing the Reading, p. 115

Possible answers include:

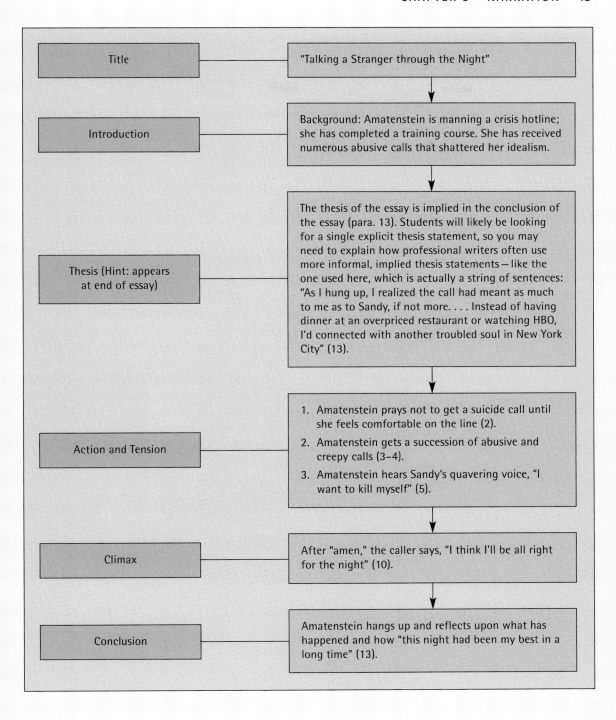

| Title | "Talking a Stranger through the Night" |

Introduction — Background: Amatenstein is manning a crisis hotline; she has completed a training course. She has received numerous abusive calls that shattered her idealism.

Thesis (Hint: appears at end of essay) — The thesis of the essay is implied in the conclusion of the essay (para. 13). Students will likely be looking for a single explicit thesis statement, so you may need to explain how professional writers often use more informal, implied thesis statements—like the one used here, which is actually a string of sentences: "As I hung up, I realized the call had meant as much to me as to Sandy, if not more. . . . Instead of having dinner at an overpriced restaurant or watching HBO, I'd connected with another troubled soul in New York City" (13).

Action and Tension
1. Amatenstein prays not to get a suicide call until she feels comfortable on the line (2).
2. Amatenstein gets a succession of abusive and creepy calls (3–4).
3. Amatenstein hears Sandy's quavering voice, "I want to kill myself" (5).

Climax — After "amen," the caller says, "I think I'll be all right for the night" (10).

Conclusion — Amatenstein hangs up and reflects upon what has happened and how "this night had been my best in a long time" (13).

Examining the Characteristics of Narrative Essays, p. 114

1. Amatenstein's dialogue is crucial to the narrative, a point that will likely be clear to most students. She uses it sparingly for effect. The first line of dialogue is the suicide caller's voice, and thereafter every statement is selectively chosen to heighten tension. The next few lines are either the suicide caller or the narrator trying to draw her out, trying to help her remember reasons why she might want to live. The resulting effect is one of tension that draws readers in as they read on to discover the fate of the suicide caller.

2. Amatenstin includes sensory details: the taste of peanuts, the sight and sound of the "Oprah" show, the smell of leaves (para. 10). The author likely chose to include these because they are familiar details that most readers can relate to, that remind them of the simple joys of life. The details contribute to the narrative because they personalize Sandy while showing how the narrator reaches out toward her over the course of their conversation.

3. The main narrative technique that the author uses to make readers care about the suicide caller is the use of key lines of dialogue. Amatenstein also recounts the tragic events in Sandy's life: her parents disowned her, she had a bone-crushing fall and then was hit by a cab, and her boyfriend died of cancer (5–6). And the author includes physical description such as: "Sandy's . . . quavering voice" (5), "Since she was handicapped, she couldn't even walk to her window to jump out" (5), and "Now she was in constant pain" (6). Students are likely to cite the narrative techniques of dialogue, recounting events, and first-person point of view as tools that Amatenstein uses to draw readers into the story about Sandy. The author also builds and creates tension through the use of foreshadowing. At the start of the essay, she notes: "I prayed I wouldn't get [a suicide call]" (2). Through this technique, she establishes a conflict: the threat of suicide. The tension is sustained by the question of whether the suicide caller will stay on the phone long enough to change her mind.

4. The implied thesis is effective because it makes a clear point about what the experience of aiding Sandy meant to the author. The use of an implied thesis statement at the end is more satisfying because it is less predictable than an explicit thesis placed early in the essay.

5. Students are likely to find the conclusion satisfying because it has an element of surprise. While Amatenstein had hinted earlier in the essay about her own loneliness, the clear connection that she draws in the conclusion between her own troubles and that of a stranger make for a moving and satisfying conclusion.

Building Your Word Power, p. 115

1. The picture created by the simile "I tossed life-affirming statements at her like paint on a canvas" (para. 7) is that of a splattered abstract expressionist painting.

To help students who are having trouble with this simile, you might want to show them a picture of a painting done by an abstract expressionist like Jackson Pollack.

2. To "fan the spark" (7) means to blow on a coal or ember to make a fire burn brighter.

Building Your Critical Thinking Skills: Inferences, p. 116

1. The events of September 11 might have made the author appreciate all the help New Yorkers gave each other in the wake of the disaster. Being a New Yorker herself, September 11 might also have made Amatenstein think more about how community is strengthened when people help one another in an emergency.

2. One can infer that the author's parents experienced a lot of emotional suffering that she witnessed but was unable to alleviate as a child.

3. The author, a journalist, has a network of friends, family, and colleagues in the city but still finds New York "isolating" (para. 4) and "lonely" (13). A possible inference that students might make regarding Amatenstein's comment in paragraph 13 about eating in an "overpriced restaurant" is that the narrator finds her life in New York to be superficial.

Amy Tan, "Fish Cheeks," p. 118

Amy Tan is best known for *The Joy Luck Club* (1989), a novel about four Chinese American mother-daughter relationships. In "Fish Cheeks," she sketches a brief autobiographical scenario full of conflict. As a teenager, Tan is apprehensive about her family's Chinese customs and ethnic foods when her mother invites to dinner a white boy Tan has a crush on. Tan's shame prevents her from recognizing that her mother has served Tan's favorite foods, including fish cheeks, at what her mother no doubt sees as a special occasion for her daughter.

You may find it useful to break the class into small groups to discuss American cultural norms and how notions of the "melting pot" and ethnic differences fit into the American ideal. Have each group report back to the class about their findings. You might also have students freewrite about their own family's unique customs. Be sure to emphasize the need to respect other cultures and to recognize that even though some cultural groups are more assimilated than others, every ethnic group in America (including those descended from the pilgrims) has its own unique practices and traditions.

Understanding the Reading, p. 119

1. Tan is upset because she is worried about what Robert will think of "our shabby Chinese Christmas" (para. 2). She thinks that he will see her in an exoticized

Chinese context, in which her relatives will seem "noisy" (2) and ill mannered by American standards and the food will seem disappointingly un-American.

2. Students are likely to have different notions about why Tan's mother chose to serve a traditional Chinese menu. One possibility suggested by the text is that she wanted to teach her daughter a lesson about not being ashamed of her Chinese heritage. In paragraph 7, Tan's mother states this clearly when she says, "You want to be the same as American girls on the outside. . . . But inside you must always be Chinese. You must be proud you are different." The other possibility suggested in paragraph 8 is that her mother chose a Chinese menu full of Tan's "favorite foods" in order to make Tan happy while treating their guests to an authentic Chinese meal.

3. In paragraphs 5 and 6, the minister and his family respond in the ways that Tan predicted in terms of not understanding the different Chinese customs associated with food (such as helping oneself to communal dishes while using one's own chopsticks rather than waiting for food to be passed, in accordance with American etiquette [5]). The son, Robert, grimaces when he sees a whole fish replete with eyes (5); Robert is embarrassed when Tan's father burps in order to be polite and explains about the "Chinese custom to show you are satisfied" (6); and Robert's father, the minister, then manages "to muster up a quiet burp" (6).

4. The author comes to realize years later that she was so ashamed of being Chinese that she did not even recognize that the dishes on the table that night were her "favorite foods" (8). She had so desired to be identified with American customs and values that she overlooked the importance of her Chinese heritage. In maturity, Tan is able to appreciate her mother's "lesson" (8) and how important it is to be proud of being different.

Visualizing the Reading, p. 120

Possible answers include:

Narrative Characteristic	Examples
Makes a point or thesis	Implied: Tan learned to be proud of her Chinese heritage.
Uses dialogue	1. "Amy, your favorite" (para. 5) 2. "It's a polite Chinese custom to show you are satisfied" (6). 3. "You want to be the same as American girls on the outside. . . . But inside you must always be Chinese" (7).

Includes sensory details	"slim new American nose" (1); "shabby Chinese Christmas" (2); "noisy Chinese relatives" (2); "pulling black veins out of the backs of fleshy prawns" (3); "[a] slimy rock cod with bulging eyes" (3); "licked the ends of their chopsticks" (5); "belched loudly" (6)
Recounts action	1. Mother preparing the meal (3) 2. The arrival of the minister's family (4) 3. The dinner, ending with the shameful burping episode (5–6) 4. Tan's gift from her mother along with her lesson (7)
Builds tension	Tension builds over the course of the essay as Tan's shame and embarrassment intensify. Examples from the text include: "What would Robert think of our shabby Chinese Christmas?" (2); "I saw that my mother had outdone herself in creating a strange menu" (3); "Dinner threw me deeper into despair" (5); "offering me the tender fish cheek. I wanted to disappear" (5); the burping incident stuns Tan "into silence for the rest of the night" (6).
Presents a sequence of events	Every paragraph in the essay has forward momentum, introducing a new sequence in the linear story line. For example, paragraph 1 identifies that the story takes place "the winter I turned fourteen"; paragraph 2 presents the next sequence, opening with: "When I found out that my parents had invited the minister's family over for Christmas eve dinner, I cried"; and so on.

Examining the Characteristics of Narrative Essays, p. 119

1. Tan's purpose may be to help other "outsiders"—that is, new immigrants or others whose cultural or ethnic backgrounds are not considered mainstream—to develop pride in their own cultures.

2. The questions create tension as the readers anticipate Tan's embarrassment. This serves to heighten the readers' surprise at the end of the essay when they realize that their sympathies with Tan's predicament have been falsely aligned and that Tan came to realize how wrong she was to feel such shame over her Chinese heritage.

3. Dialogue, because it is used so sparingly, represents crucial moments in the text. The first two lines of dialogue—both of them remarks that Tan's father makes at the table (para. 5, 6)—represent the most shameful moments for the narrator. The final lines of dialogue come from Tan's mother (7) and convey a lesson to the young Tan about being proud of being Chinese. All the lines of dialogue in the essay reveal that the author's parents were most likely aware of her shame throughout the dinner and acted in such a way as to teach their daughter to appreciate her "otherness" and to not shy away from her Chinese heritage.

4. The mother's advice in paragraph 7 about being proud of being different and her statement to Tan that "Your only shame is to have shame" makes for an implied thesis. It is more effective here than a traditional thesis statement because it more subtly acknowledges the narrator's inner conflict. It also reveals her parents' recognition of her desires and conflict even as they combat it by refusing to be more "American" for their daughter.

Building Your Word Power, p. 120

1. The allusion is to the Virgin Mary, Christianity, and the Christmas holiday — associations that are not traditionally associated with Chinese culture. The color white links Robert with the Caucasian race and with the concept of purity. Given that this essay is written years after the events of the story took place, this description could be read as an expression of Tan's "virginal" love for him at the time, or alternately, as a slightly sarcastic description of a boy whom she perhaps grew to disdain later in life.

2. The use of hyperbole in paragraph 3 illustrates Tan's distorted perspective of the dinner created by her fear and shame.

Building Your Critical Thinking Skills: Point of View, p. 120

1–3. Tan's use of first person is effective because the fourteen-year-old perspective is full of self-consciousness and exaggerated emotion and drama. Examples from the text include her wish for a "new American nose" (para. 1) and, when she ignores Robert, writing, "I pretended he was not worthy of existence" (4). This kind of self-consciousness and embarrassment about one's parents is a common experience for teenagers, and students are likely to understand and relate to it. Certainly, it is conceivable that Tan chose to use the first person precisely for this reason; it works to "dupe" the reader into siding with Tan's fourteen-year-old self, only to present an alternative, more mature understanding of the events of the story at the end of the essay. If the third person had been used, readers might have learned more about the parents' knowledge of Tan's embarrassment. Readers might also have learned whether or not Robert liked Tan and what he thought of her family.

Langston Hughes, "Salvation," p. 122

In this short essay, Hughes creates a vivid picture of himself as a child, suffering the social and religious pressure to convert and "see Jesus" at a revival. Having taken the phrase literally, Hughes waits expectantly for Jesus to appear to him in the flesh. But, after a long time, the oppressive heat and the pressure of his aunt, the minister, and the congregation all praying and pleading with him to be saved finally forces him to lie about seeing Jesus.

Because of Hughes's expert use of tension to create drama and suspense, this essay might usefully be studied with a graphic organizer. The class might break into small groups to analyze it, step by step, noting where the conflict occurs, how tension is heightened, and how Hughes uses dialogue and other narrative techniques to heighten tension. Remember when discussing this essay that your students are likely to have different reactions to it depending on their own religious beliefs. Encourage students to express their personal views and reactions, but make sure that the discussion remains respectful of these different views and beliefs.

Understanding the Reading, p. 124

1. The special meeting for children was designed to bring them into the church, to be "brought to Christ" (para. 1) in order to save their souls.

2. Westley is different from Hughes because he doesn't suffer the same sense of moral conflict in deciding to lie about seeing Jesus. Because Westley's father is an immoral person (a "rounder" [6]), one might infer that Westley doesn't see anything wrong with lying.

3. The aunt thinks Hughes is overcome by his experience of having been saved, but actually he is crying because he has lost his faith in Jesus since Jesus didn't come and because he lied to his aunt and the congregation.

4. Hughes learns that he is capable of being pressured to lie. The events of the story also force him to reevaluate his own religious beliefs, leading him to no longer believe in Jesus.

Visualizing the Reading, p. 124

For students unfamiliar with revival meetings, this picture serves to capture some of the religious fervor that many parishioners experience at such events. As Hughes describes, revivals are full of "much preaching, singing, praying, and shouting" (para. 1), and this picture certainly matches the author's description of a revival. Additional details from the picture that could add meaning to Hughes's essay include a raising up of the arms to the heavens, closing one's eyes to feel the spirit of God, and the collective emotion and rejoicing of a revival.

Examining the Characteristics of Narrative Essays, p. 124

1. Hughes's narration reveals the feeling of social pressure to conform and his belief that Jesus will appear to him in visible form.

2. You may find it useful when discussing this question to create a list on the chalkboard as students suggest details from the text. Students might note: "a wonderful rhythmical sermon, all moans and shouts and lonely cries and dire pictures of hell" (para. 3); "And the little girls cried" (3); "old women with jet-black faces and

braided hair, old men with work-gnarled hands" (4); "And the whole building rocked with prayer and song" (4). Note that students may have slightly different images of the revival meeting and the people there, depending on their own religious experiences and beliefs.

3. The conflict for Hughes is that he can't "see" (7) Jesus. He feels ashamed that he isn't saved but doesn't want to lie about it like Westley does. The narrative technique that Hughes uses to great effect to build and sustain tension is the use of dialogue. Examples include: the preacher calling out "Won't you come? Won't you come to Jesus?" (3); Westley giving up and saying "I'm tired o' sitting here. Let's get up and be saved" (6); and Hughes's aunt sobbing "Langston" (9). Hughes also uses transitional words to great effect to illustrate the excruciating passage of time: "Still I kept waiting to *see* Jesus" (5); "Finally all the young people had gone to the altar and were saved" (6). Students will likely see how the action of the story creates tension: the fact that everyone had gone up to be saved but Hughes and Westley; and then after Westley gives up, how Hughes was alone with the "mighty wail of moans and voices" (7).

4. Auntie Reed's dialogue reveals her highly emotional and very religious perspective. The preacher's words reflect the high-minded, persuasive, and stylized language of an evangelical revival preacher. Westley's utterance of the blasphemous "God damn!" (6) reveals his casual, colloquial language and nonreligious attitude.

5. Hughes's thesis is implied: that he lost whatever faith he had in Jesus in the process of pretending to be "saved." It is effective because it reveals a child's perspective and literal understanding of the world, a child's expectation and misunderstanding that cannot be fully explained to an adult.

Building Your Word Power, p. 125

1. The idiom "by leaps and bounds" (para. 1) means rapidly.

2. The metaphors "sea of shouting" and "waves of rejoicing" (13) mean that the congregation is moving or acting as a single, unified mass like the ocean, rather than as individuals. They are swept up in the enthusiasm of the moment.

Building Your Critical Thinking Skills: Connotative Meaning, p. 125

1. In the context of the story, *saved* has a negative connotation because it is only about the appearance of being saved. Hughes, who is so clearly truthful and sincere, cannot be saved, while Westley, who is a nonbelieving liar and a sinner, is believed to be saved. To "save further trouble" (para. 11), Hughes finally lies and is then falsely believed to be saved. Ironically, he is not a sinner at the beginning of the story but becomes one (a liar) in order to be recognized as saved.

2. Hughes thinks Jesus will appear visibly before him, whereas his aunt means that he will experience Jesus in his soul and "see the light," or finally understand and believe in Jesus's teachings.

Cherokee Paul McDonald, "A View from the Bridge," p. 127

Cherokee Paul McDonald recounts an ordinary day that is made extraordinary by an encounter with a blind boy. As the narrator is jogging along the water, a young boy with a fishing rod asks for his help. Pausing reluctantly, the jogger soon becomes engaged as he watches and ends up coaching the boy as he reels in a large silver tarpon. The jogger doesn't realize that the boy is blind until late in the story when the boy asks him to describe the fish he has reeled in. As he describes the fish, the jogger finds himself fully engaged in the process, straining to describe it fully. In the process, he finds himself "seeing" in a new way.

Students will benefit from a close reading of this well-crafted essay. You might consider asking them to reread it, searching for clues to the boy's blindness as if it were a mystery story. Ask them to also seek out points in the essay where they can identify a shift in the author's attitude toward the boy (especially changes in tone). They might also want to look for narrative transitions that signal a change in focus. By now, this narrative arc in which the narrator has an "epiphany" of some sort has probably become familiar to your students. Ask them to evaluate the effectiveness of this particular epiphany. You might then havwe them freewrite about a similar moment in their own lives.

Because of the relationship between seeing in "Salvation" (p. 122) and seeing in this essay, you may find it useful to discuss these two essays in conjunction. In addition to the narrative techniques used by the two authors, you might discuss the larger points that each author makes about "seeing" and how the two endings — one optimistic and one pessimistic — contrast to one another.

Understanding the Reading, p. 129

1. The jogger is initially annoyed to be interrupted by the boy. His attitude toward the boy changes as he becomes interested in watching and advising the boy while he reels in the catch. When the jogger realizes that the boy is blind, he is amazed at how good a fisherman the boy is, forcing him to reconsider how one "sees" the world around him.

2. Clues to the boy's blindness are his odd "wrap-around sunglasses" (para. 3); his "fumbling" with the rod (4); his inability to see the shrimp by his foot (8); his failure to realize that the fish is still hooked (20); his failure to reply when the jogger exclaims "Whooee, is that a nice fish or what?" (25); and most telling, his remark "Hey, mister, tell me what it looks like" (29).

3. Because the boy is such a good fisherman and is able to do so many things without seeing, the jogger can't tell initially that the boy is blind.

4. The jogger means that by having to describe the fish to the boy he became more aware of both the fish's beauty and that of the world around him, making him realize his own good fortune in being able to see.

Visualizing the Reading, p. 129

Possible answers include:

Narrative Characteristic	The Boy	The Jogger (narrator)	The Fish
Physical description	1. "He was a lumpy little guy with baggy shorts" (para. 2) 2. "stupid-looking '50s-style wrap-around sunglasses" (3)	1. "I puffed on by, glancing down into the empty bucket as I passed" (4). 2. "hands on my hips and the sweat dripping from my nose" (7)	1. "the silver is . . . made up of *all* the colors" (33) 2. "He has all these big scales, like armor" (35)
Dialogue	1. "Could you tell me what he looks like, mister?" (32) 2. "I don't want to kill him" (37).	1. "What do you want, kid?" (7) 2. "Whooee, is that a nice fish or what?" (25)	n/a
Events	1. The kid "dropped the baited hook" (13). 2. "The kid cranked like mad, and a beautiful grin spread across his face" (22).	1. The narrator climbs down the seawall (27). 2. The narrator takes the fish off the hook (37–38).	1. The tarpon jumps "almost six feet out of the water" (14). 2. The tarpon swims slowly off (38).

Examining the Characteristics of Narrative Essays, p. 130

1. The title implies that only the jogger can see the literal view from the bridge. But on a figurative level, his view is transformed by understanding the blind boy's perspective (or vantage point).

2. The first impression readers get of the boy is of a somewhat sloppy kid, odd and unstylish. The words the narrator uses to describe him and his clothes in paragraphs 2 and 3 include: "lumpy," "baggy," "faded," "falling down," "shaggy," and

"stupid-looking . . . sunglasses." Later, as his view of the boy shifts, he presents the boy as skilled and competent: "The kid played it perfectly" (24); "the kid kept the rod tip up and the line tight" (24).

3. As the narrator begins to use more descriptive language (33–36), readers sense that he is more compassionate and kinder than he seemed at first. The tone changes from one of impatient questioning to one of encouraging, coaching, listening, and helping. Events also slow down as the narrator becomes more contemplative.

4. The implied thesis is that the boy teaches the narrator to see. Students will have many different possible explicit theses, but one common explicit thesis would be something like: "I thought I knew what was important in life, but my experience with the blind boy taught me to really see the beauty in this world and to appreciate everything around me."

5. Your students are likely to have different perspectives on the effectiveness of the author's conclusion. Some will find it moving and satisfying, while others might find the author's expression of faith in the boy's optimism to be somewhat clichéd. A different, feasible conclusion might be to end at paragraph 47 with the boy's words, without the narrator's response.

Building Your Word Power, p. 130

1. Some of the fishing terms McDonald uses are: *rod and reel* (para. 4), *bait bucket* (4), *baited hook* (13), *tarpon* (14), *line* (16), *reel* (16), *crank* (16), *drag setting* (16), *rod tip* (17), and *slack* (21). You might want to ask if any students in the class fish; if yes, perhaps they could explain to the rest of the class what some of this jargon means.

2. Both figures of speech use militaristic language: "silver missile" creates a picture of a rocket shooting upward; "scales like armor" implies a suit of mail that is tough but flexible.

Building Your Critical Thinking Skills: Symbolism, p. 131

1. The bridge creates a vista or view, enhancing the narrator's ability to see, yet the child can't see. Also, the language that the jogger uses to describe the fish to the child creates a bridge of communication between them.

2. Most students will probably agree that the boy represents innocence. Examples from the text to support this view include: the boy trusts the jogger even though he is a stranger (para. 5); the boy doesn't want to kill the fish (37); and the boy believes he will become a sports fisherman (47). While initially his blindness suggests vulnerability, as the story proceeds his disability suggests the classic idea of blindness representing greater insight.

3. You are likely to get a broad range of answers from students to this question. One possible answer is that the fish symbolizes the goals people pursue in life, the things that make life worth living.

Toni Cade Bambara, "The Lesson," p. 133

Toni Cade Bambara's short story is told from the perspective of a young black girl, Sylvia, who goes on a day trip to F.A.O. Schwarz toy store with an educated neighbor, Miss Moore, and other neighborhood children. During the cab ride to the Upper East Side, Sylvia silently mocks and criticizes Miss Moore for her educated language and her constant attempts to teach the children about arithmetic and economic rights, among other things. But seeing the price tag on a sailboat that reads "one thousand one hundred ninety-five dollars" (para. 25) stuns Sylvia into realizing that there is a great deal about economic disparity that she does not know. She is still reluctant to accept Miss Moore as a mentor but goes off alone to think over what she has seen.

The tone of this essay is so clearly driven by Sylvia's tone of voice, colloquial language, and dialogue that it might be worthwhile to begin a discussion about the effect created by a narrator such as Sylvia. You might want to ask students, for example, about her use of the word *hate* when she talks about Miss Moore and how Sylvia's humor and frank observations contribute to the reader's impression of her. You could ask students to break into groups that "liked" or "didn't like" Sylvia as a character. Ask them to report back as a panel to the group about why they did or didn't like her, using examples from the text. The same exercise could be done for the character of Miss Moore.

Understanding the Reading, p. 139

1. As the story progresses, readers learn that Sylvia is street smart and clever but doesn't like school or respect education. She is disdainful of people like Miss Moore who ask her to think too much and who are, in her view, condescending. She lives a sheltered life in Harlem and although she wants money, she doesn't understand that she has to earn it (para. 3). The young age of the narrator is evidenced by her desire for fun and excitement ("I'd much rather go to the pool or to the show" [2]). While she defensively mocks anything she doesn't understand, her character is redeemable and capable of learning and contemplation, as readers learn at the end when she goes off alone to contemplate what she has learned during her trip to F.A.O. Schwarz (58).

2. Sylvia seems to resent being asked to think by Miss Moore. It is implied that she and the other children may feel that Miss Moore and her educated ways are condescending toward them.

3. The outing makes the children recognize the profound social and economic differences between them and the wealthy white people who frequent a store like F.A.O. Schwarz.

4. The lessons taught are about social, economic, and racial inequality.

Visualizing the Reading, p. 139

Possible answers include:

Event, Action, Dialogue, or Description	Significance
1. Miss Moore is the only woman on the block with no first name. (para. 1)	This suggests formality and distance; it also suggests respect.
2. "I'm really hating this nappy-head bitch and her goddamn college degree." (para. 2)	Sylvia hates what Miss Moore represents: education and civility.
3. Sylvia decides she needs the cab driver's tip more than he does. (para. 3)	Sylvia doesn't understand what it means to earn money.
4. "I feel funny, shame." (para. 40)	Sylvia realizes that she is different from the wealthy people who can afford to buy such expensive toys, and this realization makes her feel embarrassed to be there.
5. "'You sound angry, Sylvia. Are you mad about something?'" (para. 43)	Sylvia doesn't want to acknowledge how her inequality makes her feel. She would rather make fun of Miss Moore and remain seemingly unaware of her status as a poor, black girl from Harlem.
6. "Where we are is who we are, Miss Moore always pointin out." (para. 44)	This suggests that being in the "ghetto" limits one's social status.
7. "Imagine for a minute what kind of society it is in which some people can spend on a toy what it would cost to feed a family of six or seven." (para. 49)	This comment is about values and social inequities. It is a reason to be angry and determined, not ashamed. Miss Moore suggests here that one needs to be educated in order to be empowered.

Examining the Characteristics of Narrative Essays, p. 140

1. Given that this may be the first short story that students encounter in your class, it may be worthwhile to explain the difference between thesis statements and themes. The broad theme in Bambara's story is that social injustice is harmful

and that some people don't have a fair chance—whether because of lack of education, lack of money, or the color of their skin—to get ahead economically.

2. The slang, dialect, and swearing create a vivid characterization of a young girl who is at odds with society and her elders. Students are likely to have different reactions to this style of writing—some may be offended and critical of the protagonist, others may be sympathetic to her immaturity and obvious disadvantages associated with her status as a poor, uneducated, African American girl.

3. The conflict of the story is the protagonist not wanting to learn the lesson and to remain ignorant. The tension is sustained through Sylvia's resentment of Miss Moore. The climax occurs when Sylvia goes off alone to think about what she has learned (para. 58).

4. Had a third-person perspective been used, readers could have seen how Miss Moore felt about Sylvia's attitude. Readers also would have had more insight into Miss Moore's motives for taking the children to F.A.O. Schwarz and how she hoped to educate and influence them.

5. Place is important in "The Lesson" not only because the action of the story occurs as the characters move from Harlem to the Upper East Side (Fifth Avenue), but also because the two neighborhoods offer a concrete example of the social inequalities between the residents of these two New York City neighborhoods. Readers know Harlem by Bambara's details about "the junk man" and "the winos who cluttered up our parks" (1). These details are contrasted by the descriptions of "everybody dressed up in stockings" and "One lady in a fur coat, hot as it is" (3) used to convey the atmosphere on Fifth Avenue.

Building Your Word Power, p. 141

1. The connotation of "real money" as used in paragraph 2 by Miss Moore is the real value of money—how money is used and how far it goes, or doesn't go, toward buying things.

2. This metaphor paints a vivid picture of Miss Moore working as one would in a factory or a mine with her hands, using them much as worker would as she tries to teach with her gestures.

Building Your Critical Thinking Skills: Colloquial Language, p. 141

1. The period may be the 1950s because the prices are so low for everyday items like a taxi ride (para. 3), a model sailboat (27), or bunk beds (44). Other elements of the story that date the piece include references to pinafores (2), paperweights (13), and a blotter and letter-opener (18).

2. Miss Moore has a college education; as a result, her language is more formal and standard than that used by the children who are uneducated and live in a ghetto. The stark differences between the language used by Miss Moore and that used by the children set up a profound difference between them, a difference that Sylvia keenly feels and rebels against.

3. Students are likely to sense how crucial the use of colloquial language is to the story because of the way it describes and defines the different characters. Most students will find Sylvia humorous because she is witty, has a sharp eye and a foul mouth, and makes amusing observations. She is particularly good at sizing up other people's characters in a sarcastic manner. For example, she says: "You got some ole dumb shit foolishness you want somebody to go for, you send for Aunt Gretchen" (1).

Chapter 6 Description: Portraying People, Places, and Things, p. 144

The descriptive essay is enjoyable for most first-year college students because it involves vivid, sensory details and can be written in the first person. You might want to begin with a definition of *description*, that is, writing that appeals to the senses through the use of vivid detail. You might also want to briefly discuss how narration and description overlap, because they are most often presented together. Give students lots of examples of what you mean by "vivid" and "precise" details, using the examples in this chapter to help them recognize when a description is dull and vague. You will also want to emphasize the idea of "significant detail," the concept that not every single detail is as important as another. Explain how tiresome it would be if a writer told a story in which every single detail he saw or heard or tasted was thrown in. Remind students that they are already familiar with the use of descriptive language through the stories they hear or tell on a daily basis to their friends or families. You might ask them to think, for example, of someone they know who is a particularly good storyteller. How does this individual use details to create a vivid impression?

Just as you did when you talked about narration, you may want to explain that the storyteller shapes the narrative in a descriptive essay artfully by arranging the storyline in the most effective way possible. The author accomplishes this by choosing only those details that create a single dominant impression and point of view. A storyteller or writer must organize the story or narrative to best effect (chronologically, spatially, or from least-to-most or most-to-least importance).

The revision flowchart included in this chapter (pp. 156–158) will help students understand what revising or editing a descriptive essay entails. As mentioned in Part 1, revision is often a difficult concept for first-year students to grasp, so using the revision flowchart throughout the semester will increase their understanding of the editing process. Because students often work harder to polish a descriptive passage when they know that they will be sharing it with the other students in the class, you might want to have them read each other's work on a regular basis. Using the flowchart to evaluate each other's work in pairs may also increase their interest in the process.

In this chapter, Jeremy MacClancy's essay, "Eating Chilli Peppers" (p. 144), assembles an array of sensory details, using similes to describe the stimulating sensations hot peppers create. In "The Discus Thrower" (p. 163), Richard Selzer also uses many similes, comparing his amputee patient to a bonsai tree, a log, and a sailor on deck. Eric Liu, in "Po-Po in Chinatown" (p. 174), uses similes and vivid details to compare his grandmother's voice to Yoda's and her talkativeness to a tidal wave, among other things. The readings in this chapter also offer a range of perspectives from which to discuss point of view. MacClancy uses the third person to lend his informational piece about the use of hot chillis a formal but conversational tone. Mary Brave Bird's "The Sweat Bath Ritual" (p. 169) also has an educational purpose, but it is written in the first person. Eric Liu, Gary Soto in "Piedra" (p. 180), and Maya Angelou in "Sister Flowers" (p. 185) all use the first person to describe powerful experiences from childhood and young adulthood. Liu's and Angelou's pieces are detailed portraits of individual people who had a great influence on them; Selzer also focuses on a single person, a patient who affected his life as a doctor.

Jeremy MacClancy, "Eating Chilli Peppers," p. 144

As the graphic organizer on page 151 shows, Jeremy MacClancy's essay moves from a description of hot peppers as painful and thrillingly stimulating to an argument that they are beneficial. He uses lots of active verbs to convey the taste of the peppers and the exciting physical and psychological sensations they cause. Because he is an anthropologist and because this essay was written as an informative piece, he uses the third person to educate the reader about crosscultural eating habits and motivations for eating chillis, comparing the pleasurable side effects to a drug high. He also outlines the more productive crosscultural use of hot peppers in folk medicine.

MacClancy's essay can be used to illustrate how even informative or academic essays can be made more lively and compelling through the use of active verbs, varied sentences (p. 148), and figurative language (p. 149). Remind students that they will be doing similar work when they begin to write comparison and contrast and other more analytical essays.

Danielle Cruz, "I Survived the Blackout of 2003," p. 159

Danielle Cruz's essay provides an example of unpolished student work. It is useful for students to see such work, in addition to the professional essays that make up the bulk of this anthology, because students often hesitate to find fault with the work of professional writers. Essays like Cruz's give them an opportunity to read critically, looking for "flaws," just as they will when they do peer revision. The marginal annotations and highlighting included for this essay help students to recognize structural transitions, the thesis statement, and other key elements of the piece.

Responding to "Students Write," p. 161

1. Cruz's dominant impression is positive. It is stated implicitly in the first sentence of the essay when she describes how her outlook on the world has been shifted by her experiences during the blackout of 2003 that affected New York City and much of the Northeast.

2. Some effective sensory descriptions in Cruz's essay include: "the comforting rumble of the AC" (para. 1); "a bag of half-frozen okra for a pillow" (6); and "the sweet smell of lavender [candles]" (6). As a class or in small groups, have students improve upon less effective details, such as the description of a neighbor as a "familiar-looking woman" (2).

3. Comparisons include the blackout of 2003 with the events of 9/11 (2) and "dog-walkers pushing through the crowd like salmon headed to spawn" (3).

4. Questions that Cruz does not address include: What caused the blackout? What was Cruz doing in New York? It would also be helpful to know more about her occupation and where she came from.

5. The title is satisfactory but not very original. In the introduction, it might be useful to include more about where Cruz came from and what she was doing in New York City. The conclusion is good—it conveys her positive impression of the spontaneous sense of community created in the aftermath of the blackout.

Richard Selzer, "The Discus Thrower," p. 163

Selzer's essay describes a few brief, fairly unproductive encounters between a doctor (the narrator) and his dying amputee patient. As his doctor, Selzer is curious about the patient but remains detached. Selzer knows that the patient is dying alone and angry—alienating the nurses by repeatedly throwing his plate at the wall—yet he doesn't communicate with him. Instead, Selzer "spies" on or observes him for clues about his background and his behavior. Sparse dialogue conveys the lack of communication between them.

Encourage students to read this piece several times, looking carefully at Selzer's tone, which may be difficult for many students to comprehend. You might want to talk briefly about the issue of patient care in the United States and what is expected or not expected of doctors and other medical professionals. You might also ask students to consider a doctor's mandate to "cure," and how that might be thwarted when he or she knows that a patient is terminal. You might have students break into small groups to discuss the role of empathy in the doctor/patient relationship—has it been shown, for example, to enhance healing? Students could share an experience of feeling cared for (or not cared for) and how it influenced their progress.

Understanding the Reading, p. 165

1. According to Selzer, the patient is blind and legless, and something "vile" is making his skin turn brown (para. 2). Over the course of the essay, readers never learn what caused his amputations or his blindness and, ultimately, his death.

2. The head nurse is upset because the patient won't eat, throws his plate, and in a word, is "Nasty" (27). She wants the doctor to do something about the situation, but Selzer only stalls her, saying, "We'll see" (30).

3. The patient exhibits delight, laughing when he throws his plate (34).

4. Selzer learns of the patient's death from the head nurse, who feels that his death is a "blessing" (49). Selzer reacts to the man's death much as he has throughout the essay: unemotionally. He returns to the man's room "a spy looking for secrets" to view his body, lying there "grave, dignified" (50) in bed.

Visualizing the Reading, page 165

Possible answers include:

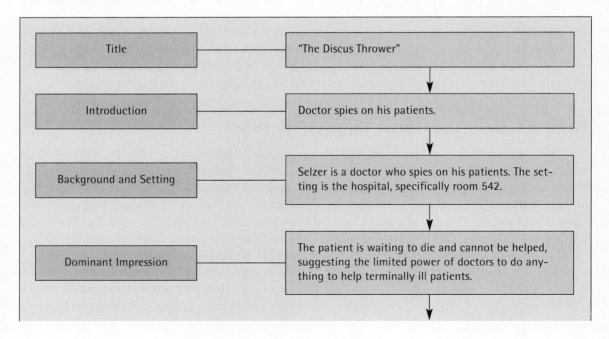

Title	"The Discus Thrower"
Introduction	Doctor spies on his patients.
Background and Setting	Selzer is a doctor who spies on his patients. The setting is the hospital, specifically room 542.
Dominant Impression	The patient is waiting to die and cannot be helped, suggesting the limited power of doctors to do anything to help terminally ill patients.

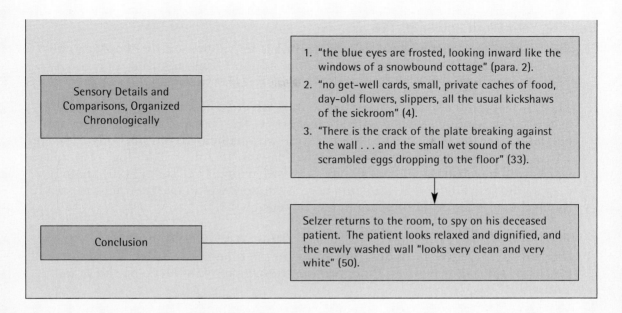

Examining the Characteristics of Descriptive Essays, p. 166

1. The dominant impression is that the patient in the bed is unhappy (except when he throws his plate) and waiting to die. Selzer's purpose for writing might be to describe his own sense of helplessness as a doctor when he cannot do anything to save a patient.

2. Encourage students to reread the essay, highlighter in hand, to mark all the places where Selzer uses effective sensory details. Examples include: a body like a "bonsai" (para. 2), and dreaming of a time "when his body was not a rotting log" (19). Selzer also uses sound to effectively describe key events: the patient's laughter "could cure cancer" (34); "the crack of the plate breaking against the wall" (33).

3. The author's vantage point as a doctor is somewhat effective because Selzer knows that the patient is in the "last stage" of his illness (2). However, despite what most people would consider an insider's vantage point, the reader receives only hints about the disease but doesn't know what caused the amputations or the blindness or why the patient has no visitors.

4. After the patient's death, Selzer notices that the wall where the patient had thrown his plate every day is very clean. Earlier, the hospital room was described as empty of personal effects (4); after the patient's death, it is described as "very white" (50). The overall sense is one of peace and tranquility, contrasting with the earlier descriptions of a very ill man who is detached and angry at his predicament.

Building Your Word Power, p. 166

1. The connotation of *spy* (verb) in paragraph 1 is to watch secretly in order to obtain information. In paragraph 50, the connotation of *spy* (noun) is a person who seeks to obtain secret information through close observation.

2. The "snow-bound cottage" image (para. 2) is effective because the patient's blind eyes are like windows glazed with ice and snow. The "bonsai" (2) analogy is only partially accurate because the patient's limbs are truncated; but his body is not really in miniature, it is more like a tree that has lost its limbs. The "log" (19) image works well because the patient's body is mostly trunk. The "sailor" (20) analogy may sound less effective to students because sailors would use their legs to steady themselves on deck and the patient has no legs.

Building Your Critical Thinking Skills: Tone, p. 167

1. Students are likely to have different views on the tone of the essay. Selzer's overall tone is distanced or neutral, though some students may find it to be sad or pessimistic.

2. The dialogue, used sparingly by Selzer, is also neutral, not very emotional or expressive, except for the nurse's and aide's remarks (para. 27, 36, 41), which exhibit frustration, bewilderment, and anger.

3. Expect different responses to this essay, depending on how students react to the perceived tone. Because the author's tone is generally unemotional and distant, many readers may feel somewhat unsympathetic to the patient. But some readers may also feel a little curious about the patient, perhaps even slightly sympathetic to him, because he is alone, is unable to connect with the staff, and does not complain. The tone will also affect how students perceive the doctor, who remains a mysterious figure throughout. Some will likely be offended by his somewhat "cold" actions, while others will find his behaviors and quiet contemplation to be caring and understanding in a quiet and respectful way.

Reacting to the Topic: Discussion and Journal Writing, p. 167

You might want to have students break into two large groups to discuss their feelings about the doctor's attitude toward and efforts to help the patient. They could then form panels (pro and con) to defend or criticize the doctor's bedside manner.

Mary Brave Bird, "The Sweat Bath Ritual," p. 169

Mary Brave Bird is best known for her autobiographical book *Lakota Woman* (1990). In "The Sweat Bath Ritual," she gives a first-person, informative description of her experience of the sweat lodge ritual. Her aim is to inform others about the ritual in a literal way and also to convey some of its psychological and spiritual benefits.

Although she is Native American, the story begins at a time when she did not know much about traditional ways. Because the story is presented in chronological order, sometimes summarizing a series of events, the reader learns along with the author what the ritual feels like, what it entails, and what it means.

You might want to have the class freewrite for a few minutes and then break into small groups to discuss how they would feel about engaging in a ritual like this one. Would they, for example, enjoy being a cultural anthropologist or a travel writer, traveling around the world to participate in and learn about ceremonies such as this one? Why or why not? Have them report back to the class about their feelings. They could also freewrite about a similar experience when they were first exposed to an unfamiliar cultural practice, such as the time they attended their first bar mitzvah or a formal dinner where they had to negotiate several kinds of forks and plates.

Understanding the Reading, p. 171

1. Mary Brave Bird goes to a sweat lodge because she had not yet participated in this ancient ceremony. By experiencing this ceremony, which "precedes all sacred ceremonies" (para. 3), she hopes to have a better understanding of both this and the other Native rituals of her tribe.

2. The interior of the sweat lodge is dark. The dome is formed of willow sticks that are tied with red strips of cloth. There is a circular fire pit in the center (4).

3. The white limestone rocks that are placed in the lodge are covered with a "spidery network of green moss," which is supposed to "represent secret spirit writing" (5).

4. At first the author felt that she wouldn't be able to withstand the heat because it "hurt" (10), but afterwards she felt elated and connected to the Indian community and to the spirit world. Through her experience, Mary Brave Bird learns about the transformative power of ritual (10).

Visualizing the Reading, p. 171

The physical description of the lodge as written by Brave Bird is actually clearer than what one can see in this image. This may come as a revelation to some students, given the power that most undergraduates likely ascribe to visuals over text. However, the physical experience of being in a sweat lodge is vividly shown in this photograph. Students are likely to comment on the reddish glow of the fire, the sweat glistening, and the almost religious experience this man is undergoing. You may wish to contrast the emotion shown here with that shown in the picture of a revival meeting that accompanies "Salvation" on page 122.

Examining the Characteristics of Descriptive Essays, p. 172

1. You may find it helpful to create lists of details that appeal to the senses of smell, taste, touch, sound, and sight. Examples include: smell—"Green cedar . . . filling

the air with its aromatic odor" (7); taste—"catch the sacred smoke with their hands, inhaling it" (8); touch—"My body tingled" (10); sound—"we can hear the river's voice" (3); and sight—"spidery network of green moss" (5).

2. This essay is organized chronologically in terms of the author's first sweat. Brave Bird presents herself as a newcomer, presumably like most readers, because even though she is Native American, she has never experienced the sweat ritual. This perspective makes her essay a highly descriptive and informative account. The chronological method of organization is effective because it enables the reader to participate in Brave Bird's experience as she does, from her fear that she won't be able to handle the heat, to her sense of relief and elation once the ceremony has ended (para. 10).

3. Some comparisons that Brave Bird uses include: comparing the lodge to an "igloo-shaped hut" (7), an effective comparison in terms of shape if not in terms of temperature; the simile "like inhaling liquid fire" (10), a vivid description of the extreme heat within the lodge; and the analogy "newly born" (10), a slightly clichéd but apt explanation of the transformative power of the experience. These and other comparisons help the reader to see that although the ceremony entails some discomfort, it is ultimately rewarding and transformative.

4. The author's background contributes the idea that even a Native American can be skeptical about the value and power of traditional Native ritual. In writing this essay, Brave Bird may have intended to foster respect for Native spirituality among both Native and non-Native people.

Building Your Word Power, p. 172

1. Seeing with the "eye in one's heart" refers to experiencing the world with a loving, nonjudgmental attitude.

2. "Liquid fire" would pour down one's throat, into one's belly, causing the severe discomfort that Brave Bird is describing.

Building Your Critical Thinking Skills: Evaluating Authors, p. 172

1. You might want to use this section to underscore the importance of scanning (or previewing) a writer's biographical information before reading an essay. Have students consider how the information included in the headnote shaped their reading of the piece. Ask also how this essay would be read differently, for example, if the headnote described Brave Bird as a white anthropologist.

2. The first three paragraphs of Brave Bird's essay explain why she is eminently qualified to write about this experience: she is a Native American, she has experienced other traditional rituals, and she wishes to experience the sweat lodge ritual for the first time in her "family's sweat lodge" (para. 3).

Eric Liu, "Po-Po in Chinatown," p. 174

Eric Liu describes a series of visits to see his grandmother in Chinatown in New York City. He does not say where he himself lives, but it is clear that his visits to her in Chinatown are somewhat of a pilgrimage to an unfamiliar and exotic territory. Although there is an element of familial obligation to Liu's visits, he also appears to enjoy seeing this woman who represents his family's origins. Her attachment to the past and to all things Chinese, from language and politics to food, makes his visit feel like a voyage to another century.

The vividness of the portrait Liu creates is a result of his close attention to sensory details. You might want to begin a discussion of this essay by having students freewrite about the sensory impressions they retained after reading the essay. Then have them freewrite again, but about the main ideas that underlie the essay. Ask them to think about Liu's main purpose in writing. This may develop into a discussion of the intellectual or rhetorical purpose that often underlies a descriptive essay such as this.

Understanding the Reading, p. 176

1. Liu's relationship to his grandmother is a mixture of obligation and fondness. The distance between them is reflected in the languages they use (she speaks the Sichuan dialect of Chinese), their age difference, religion (she is a devout Christian), and geographic distance (she doesn't visit his house). Despite these differences, their closeness is evidenced throughout the essay. Examples include their shared laughter as they do exercises together (para. 7) and the way Liu holds her close at the end of the visit (9).

2. Po-Po seems very fond of Liu. She wants to share her ideas with him, especially her knowledge about China (5). There is a clear affection shown by Po-Po toward Liu, as illustrated through the way she always entertains him with stories (5), feeds him a huge lunch, and gives him money when they part (9).

3. Po-Po appears to live very modestly, though whether this is through a frugal nature or by necessity, Liu does not say. Examples from the text to support this include the fact that she lives in public housing (1), wears old glasses, uses a lawn chair for furniture, and has a frayed toothbrush (3). Her life revolves around the Chinese American community, and her primary interests have to do with China and her Christian faith.

4. Students are likely to have different responses to this question. One possible view is that the author is commenting on the value of the Chinese tradition of respect for one's elders. Another possibility is that Liu is commenting on assimilation and the varying degrees to which Chinese Americans adapt to, embrace, or reject American life.

Visualizing the Reading, p. 177

Possible answers include:

Characteristic	Examples
Active verbs	1. "*shuffled* to the kitchen" (para. 2) 2. "*scurrying* with excitement" (2) 3. "I *gorged* myself" (4)
Sensory details (sound, smell, touch, sight, taste)	Sound: "she chattered excitedly" (5) Smell: "broiled fish" (4) Touch: "stroke her knotted back" (9) Sight: "the filmy, clouded mirror" (3) Taste: "stir-fried shrimp still in their salty shells" (4)
Varied sentences	"With an impish smile, she proclaimed my American name in her Yoda-like voice: *Areek.* She got a kick out of that" (2).
Comparisons	"Yoda-like voice" (2); "like a performer" (5); "like a child" (5)
Connotative language	"to attack this meal" (4); "torrent of opinions" (5); "tidal momentum" (5)

Examining the Characteristics of Descriptive Essays, p. 177

1. The implied dominant impression that Liu creates is one of a garrulous, expressive, and lively elderly woman. Her talkativeness is revealed in the following quotes: Po-Po "chattered excitedly" (para. 5); "she would take a sip of 7 UP and swerve back to something in the news" (5); her words created a "tidal momentum, relentless" (5); and "If there was a lull" (7).

2. Occasional Chinese words and phrases are used throughout such as when Liu and his grandmother meet (2), when Po-Po invites him to eat (3), and when Liu describes the food she prepares (4). The understanding of the Chinese words used will be clear to students from the context. In some cases the actual meaning is defined ("*Lai chi ha*, Po-Po would say, inviting me to eat" in para. 3), while in other cases it is implied by the context of the situation (for instance, when Po-Po greets her grandson in para. 2). The use of Chinese is effective because it becomes another descriptive element, adding detail to our impression of the elderly Chinese women.

3. The method of organization is chronological. The details range from his arrival at Po-Po's door to a physical description of her and her apartment to what they eat for lunch and talk about afterwards. The essay concludes with a description of their parting hug and words.

4. The descriptive details used for Po-Po convey the sense of an energetic, happy, and expressive woman. Examples include: "scurrying with excitement" (2); "She offered a giggle" (2); and "she would chuckle" (8). She is also very generous, feeding her grandson a "banquet's worth" of food (4) and giving him "a little red envelope of money" at their parting (9). She is also, as previously mentioned, talkative ("she chattered excitedly" [5]), strong willed ("If I interjected, she'd cut me off" [6]), religious ("she revealed to me her own way of prayer" [9]), and loving (*"How I wish I had wings so I could see where you live"* [9]).

Building Your Word Power, p. 177

1. *Attack* and *gorged* (para. 4) suggest that Liu considers it his duty to show his appreciation by making a valiant effort to eat the enormous amount of food that Po-Po prepares. Po-Po's expression of disappointment is likely intended to goad him into eating even more.

2. Answers will vary. It may be fun to have students try to act out Po-Po's mannerisms as described by Liu.

Building Your Critical Thinking Skills: Selective Omissions, p. 178

1–2. You might want to have students break into pairs to discuss questions 1 and 2. Then have each pair report their ideas to the class.

3. To enhance student understanding of the essay and the Chinese culture that it explores, you might consider asking students to do some Internet research in advance. Have each student choose a subject touched on in the essay (for instance, Chinatown in New York City, manners, food, Aung San Suu Kyi, or the latest developments in Taiwan), and ask them to write a paragraph and deliver a short presentation about that aspect of Chinese culture to the class.

Reacting to the Topic: Discussion and Journal Writing, p. 178

1–2. You might want to prepare a short talk to accompany this essay by researching traditional Chinese American attitudes toward elderly relatives. You might also want to ask students to do some research into the attitude toward elders in another, less industrialized culture than that of the United States. Then initiate a discussion about what it means to honor the elderly. How might contemporary U.S. culture as a whole be judged according to Chinese or other standards? You could combine this discussion with Assignment 4 under Applying Your Skills, page 178.

Gary Soto, "Piedra," p. 180

Gary Soto creates a vivid vignette of a summer day spent by the Piedra River in California with his family. This particular day is significant to Soto because it is when he realized that he would one day leave his family's world to experience another kind of life. The essay, full of details about the natural setting, alternates between summary and moment-to-moment depiction of the day's events. Because of this, it is an excellent resource for teaching both narration and description. To capitalize on the features of "Piedra," you might want to have students analyze how narration and description overlap in this essay. Have students break into pairs or small groups and then identify the points at which Soto uses key elements—such as transitional words, summary, sensory details, and dialogue—to craft his piece and create a dominant impression about this ordinary yet momentous day.

"Piedra" is rich with sensory details that make Soto's experience of this day come to life for the reader. To explore this descriptive technique further, you might have students break into pairs to interview each other (for five minutes or so) about all of the sensory details they can recall as they describe scenes from the essay. You might then have them jointly write a paragraph based on the list they created together and share their writing with the class.

Understanding the Reading, p. 181

1. Soto visits the banks of the Piedra River with his family. Through the course of the essay, readers learn that the Sotos are Mexican (para. 2), that Soto's mother wants her children to study hard so that they can go to college (2), that Soto has a stepfather (4), that Soto's parents look tired (5), and that Soto plays fairly well with his sister and brother (5).

2. The children play both physically active and imaginative games as they explore the natural setting together, whereas the parents remain physically inactive, not really exploring the landscape or even interacting with each other (5).

3. Soto dreams about the lives of rich people like the Griffins (2), especially romantic daydreams about the Griffin daughters (3). He also dreams on the mountain that he will have a chance to live a better life (7). Details such as his romantic interest in the Griffin girls suggest that Soto is entering puberty.

4. Soto spent the afternoon venturing off alone to climb a mountain beyond a No Trespassing sign. The essay does not state definitively why climbing the mountain was important to Soto, so students are likely to have different answers to this question. One possible answer is that through this time alone he acquired some perspective on his own life and the possibilities that exist beyond "the badness" in his life so far (7).

Visualizing the Reading, p. 182

The person in the photograph interacts with the river actively by rowing out on the flat, smooth water. The image creates a feeling of serenity. Soto's interaction with the

Piedra River differs in that he experiences it from the shore only. He hears it roar noisily and crash over rocks (para. 1), then can no longer hear it from the top of the mountain where it looks "thin as a wrist" (7). Despite this difference, the relationship to the bodies of water that both Soto and the rower in the picture have is fundamentally the same: the proximity to water is soothing and beneficial.

Examining the Characteristics of Descriptive Writing, p. 182

1. The sound of the Piedra River is conveyed by "the roar of water" (para. 4), "the river loud at our side" (5), and how the "gushing water spilled noiselessly" as Soto climbs further and further away from it (7). Other senses appealed to include taste (of coffee and cigarettes [5]; "hot dogs and barbeque chips and soda" [6]); touch (lizards that "ran along our fingers" [5], "hugging my knees" [7]); smell ("mowed pasture" [2]); and sight ("gray-cold current" [1], "glittery sand and soggy leaves" [5]).

2. The details Soto uses for the river are vivid, sensual, and active, indicating how the river appealed to his senses. Words like *splayed, leaped,* and *feed* (1) all indicate these qualities. These details contribute to a dominant impression of Piedra as a place of peace and happiness.

3. Soto's vantage point is moving—first in the car, then next to the river, then from the mountain top. It is effective because it allows him to illustrate that just as he moves physically through the events of the essay, he is moving beyond his current situation metaphysically, growing up and away from his family in various ways.

4. Students are likely to find the ending with its solo hike to be effective because it is a bit unexpected and it presents a moment of adolescence when one strikes off on one's own that they can relate to. The conclusion describes a moment in time when Soto is able to take his dreams of escape to another level. "I will have my chance" may mean different things to different students. One possibility is that Soto will have an opportunity to be happier than his parents (for instance, to become better educated, to have a better job, to meet people from other socioeconomic groups, and so on).

Building Your Word Power, p. 182

1. The phrase *"those* people" (para. 2) has a negative connotation. It means that Soto's mother does not want to associate with or be associated with Mexican migrant workers.

2. The phrase "itching with rust" (2) creates an image of a red skin rash.

Building Your Critical Thinking Skills: Point of View, p. 183

1–2. Soto uses first-person point of view. This point of view reflects more than the boy's experience because it incorporates his mother's comments about the need to get good grades (para. 2), the view presented in romance novels he has read (3), the fishermen "shushing" the children (5), and his brother and sister calling him names (6).

3. By using a first-person point of view, Soto tells nothing about what his family members were thinking during that day at the river or about their family background.

Maya Angelou, "Sister Flowers," p. 185

In this passage from a memoir, Maya Angelou creates a portrait of an older, educated black woman who changed her life, indirectly helping her become a writer. "Sister Flowers" describes a difficult period of Angelou's life following a childhood rape and how her association with Mrs. Bertha Flowers helps her emerge from this dark time. Angelou describes her admiration for the gracious, well-educated Mrs. Flowers; the shame she felt because her mother was not as educated or polite; and her delight when Mrs. Flowers gave her personal attention and encouragement. This selection is an excellent one to have students dissect, reading it several times to hone their understanding of how this master memoirist constructs and artfully shapes the past so that it follows logically, delivers a sense of immediacy, and conveys a dominant impression about the role of Mrs. Flowers in her life.

Understanding the Reading, p. 189

1. Marguerite feels ashamed of her mother's interactions with Mrs. Flowers because her mother is informal and does not use proper grammar (paras. 7–10).

2. Mrs. Flowers appeals to Marguerite because she is gracious and aristocratic (2), educated, and "as refined as whitefolks" and "more beautiful" (12).

3. Mrs. Flowers wants Marguerite to open up and express herself because "[w]ords mean more than what is set down on paper" (24). She tries to instill this in Marguerite by reading aloud to her (37).

4. Through her lessons with Mrs. Flowers, Marguerite learns about the beauty of language (42) and the power of feeling liked and respected for being herself (44).

Visualizing the Reading, p. 189

Possible answers include:

Sense	Examples
Sight	1. "Her skin was a rich black that would have peeled like a plum if snagged" (para. 3) 2. "flat round wafers, slightly browned on the edges and butter-yellow in the center" (34)
Taste	1. "The sweet vanilla flavor" (39) 2. "Southern bitter wormwood" (42)
Touch	1. "snag her skin" (3) 2. "the rough crumbs scratched the insides of my jaws" (34)
Smell	1. "The odors in the house surprised me" (28) 2. "The sweet scent of vanilla" (29)
Sound	1. "soft yet carrying voice" (6) 2. "She was nearly singing" (37)

Examining the Characteristics of Descriptive Essays, p. 190

1. Angelou is communicating the idea that Sister Flowers represented another way of life because she was educated and refined. It also shows that Sister Flowers's kindness and interest in Angelou allowed her to blossom as a person and begin to heal from the effects of the rape.

2. Angelou describes Mrs. Flowers's appearance (2), her voice (6), her gait (8), and her house (32). She uses a least-to-most-important organization of the details.

3. Angelou's dominant impression of Sister Flowers is one of refinement. Details include: "printed voile dresses and flowered hats" (para. 2), "gloves" (3), a soft voice (6), "Like women in English novels" (11), "beautiful" (12), and "spoke each word with . . . clarity" (22).

4. Angelou describes her mother in terms of her poor grammar (10) and the activities of the aristocratic white women in novels who "walked the moors . . . sat in front of roaring fireplaces, drinking tea" (11). This is in contrast to her more reverent description of Sister Flowers.

Building Your Word Power, p. 190

1. "I sopped around" suggests that Angelou sulked around. "[L]ike an old biscuit, dirty and inedible" implies that Angelou felt both unattractive and no longer desirable because of the taint of the rape.

2. The phrase "mother wit" means folk wisdom.

Building Your Critical Thinking Skills: Details, p. 190

1–3. Answers will vary. You may want to invite students to share their answers with the class.

Chapter 7 Illustration: Explaining with Examples, p. 192

The main aspect of the illustrative essay—giving a series of examples to support an idea—should be familiar to most first-year college students because it is something that they likely do themselves in the course of everyday conversation. You might want to begin with a definition of *illustration*, that is, backing up one's thesis with examples. Illustration is an essential skill for your students because they will be required to provide examples, or evidence, whenever they write a paper in college. Good writing is characterized by generalizations that are well supported by specific examples. Explain to the class that examples are the evidence, anecdotes, facts, quotations, and statistics that back up a thesis. Just as in narration and description essays, the examples in an illustration essay must be organized in a meaningful way.

The graphic organizer on page 200 will help students visually see how to organize the examples in an illustration essay. The revision flowchart on pages 205–206 will help them revise their drafts to make sure that the examples used are relevant, representative, and of interest to readers. In this chapter, the Editing and Proofreading section (p. 204) emphasizes the need to make verbs consistent in tense and to use first, second, or third person consistently as well. This section also describes and illustrates sentence fragments, a common problem for first-year students. The student essay, "Internet Hoaxes" (p. 207), has each topic sentence highlighted so that students learn where a topic sentence can be located. This will help them see that each topic sentence is a generalization followed up by examples. The chapter also covers the idea of introducing *alternative viewpoints* (p. 237) in order to provide a more balanced presentation of a given issue.

Each essay in this chapter uses a series of illustrations or examples to lend credibility to its thesis. For example, Bill Bryson's "Snoopers at Work" (p. 193), declares that Americans are being spied upon and that this violation of privacy is considered legal. He then delivers a series of examples of legal violations—taking place everywhere from changing rooms to office cubicles—backing up his thesis with examples that prove his case. In "Just Walk On By: A Black Man Ponders His Power to Alter Public Space," Brent Staples (p. 211) gives a series of vivid examples to show how he, and other black men, experience social discomfort and discrimination because white people stereotype and fear them. To build her argument that teenage boys increasingly are becoming concerned about their physical appearance, Rita Kempley (p. 217) uses a series of quotes from "experts" of various sorts. Quotations from psychologists, sociologists, authors, and others, as well as from teenage boys themselves, serve to develop her thesis. Nell Bernstein (p. 230) interviews a number of California teenagers to discover why they feel that they can "claim" any identity that they like. She asks them about "gangsta," "cholita," white, mixed-race, and other identities in order to provide examples of this new diverse community. Geeta Kothari (p. 223) uses a short autobiographical sketch to explore her national and cultural identity. She outlines a series of examples that illustrate how betwixt and between she feels as a South Asian American. From not having tuna fish salad sandwiches like her childhood classmates to not knowing how to cook Indian dishes as an adult, Kothari reveals that she felt less than American as a child and less than South Asian as an adult.

Bill Bryson, "Snoopers at Work," p. 193

Bill Bryson declares that American citizens' right to privacy does not extend to changing rooms, office email, or even the local bar after work because secret surveillance has been upheld by the courts. Although his thesis is shocking, Bryson backs it up with a rich assortment of valid and striking examples that provide convincing support. Point out to your students how Bryson uses helpful transitions to keep the reader apprised of his thesis and where he is headed (for instance, "I know this because . . ." (para. 2); "But it gets even more sinister than that . . ." [11]).

You might want to do some research on the issue of privacy and how it is defined by law so that you can preface this essay with a short talk. For discussion or debate, you might ask students to consider how much privacy they think people should be willing to forgo and under what circumstances. You might ask them to freewrite on the meaning of the phrase "innocent until proven guilty" or break into small groups to discuss "the right to privacy."

The graphic organizer for Bryson's essay (p. 200) provides students with the thesis at the heart of the essay and also identifies the examples he provides, one by one. It might be helpful to go over this graphic organizer with the class slowly and carefully. Review each of Bryson's examples to evaluate their effectiveness; this will prepare your students to analyze other essays that are less clearly outlined. You could initiate a discussion about the pattern in which examples are presented—does it progressively illuminate the importance of the issue of privacy? Does the pattern gradually introduce examples that might persuade a skeptical reader that there is something seriously wrong with this erosion of American privacy?

Melissa Parker, "Internet Hoaxes: A Multiplying Problem," p. 207

In this student essay, Parker compiles extensive evidence for her thesis that Internet hoaxes are damaging in numerous, often overlooked ways. You might initiate an interesting discussion about the kinds of appeals made by other types of hoaxsters—from greed to altruism. Ask students to brainstorm examples of hoaxes they have heard of and to analyze the underlying appeal. Have them write a short piece about the list of hoaxes they compile, organizing them into a pattern, such as from least to most damaging.

Responding to "Students Write"

1. Parker's thesis statement is sound and reflects the same organizational format used in her essay.

2. Answers will vary. The introduction provides useful background information, but it could be more interesting with the addition of an example in which someone was duped.

3. To assess the quantity and quality of examples used, have students create a list of each example. Next to each one, student's should rate its effectiveness in terms of supporting Parker's thesis. This exercise should lead into a larger discussion about the types of examples used and their appropriateness.

4. Students will likely find these statistics thought-provoking. This example could have been even more effective had Parker added in the "average hourly wage."

5. The conclusion reemphasizes the key points by reiterating the essay's main idea that hoaxes are more than just a nuisance.

Brent Staples, "Just Walk On By: A Black Man Ponders His Power to Alter Public Space," p. 211

Staples eloquently illustrates the irony that he, an educated journalist and so-called "softy" (para. 2), should be constantly mistaken for a criminal, as many black men are. He opens his essay with the startling phrase "My first victim was . . .," and then he proceeds to give examples of all of the times he has been mistaken for a mugger or rapist since that first experience of being mislabeled as a threat at the age of twenty-two. His willingness to consider the issue of racial profiling with an open mind, to probe the possibility that his first experience might have been caused by his clothing, or the late hour, or something else; his eloquent writing style; and his genuine concern for women (who have real reason to fear men on the street at night)—all add to the strength of his examples. From Chicago to Soho, he has experienced white people's fear and suspicion and has smothered his rage and shame to develop a series of effective personal remedies. In order to reduce the fear he creates in white people, he now employs various calming strategies, from keeping his distance to whistling classical music whenever he walks down the street at night.

Understanding the Reading, p. 213

1. Staples has the power to alter public space because he is a black man and black men are often feared by the general public as potential rapists, muggers, and other criminals. This ability makes his life at times awkward and humiliating. Such power can even be dangerous because if he does something as simple as run into a building, he is likely to be perceived as a criminal, and if the police are called, his life could be in danger.

2. Staples managed to escape the violence of Chester, Pennsylvania — the "angry industrial town" where he grew up — by becoming one of the "good boys" (para. 6).

3. Staples attributes his survival to his timidity and his ability to stay out of the way and not get involved in fights or criminal activity (7).

4. To make his presence less threatening to others, Staples has learned to "take precautions" (11): he walks around people on subway platforms, walks past lobbies if the people inside look afraid, is "congenial" (11) to the police, and whistles classical music (12).

Visualizing the Reading, p. 214

Possible answers include:

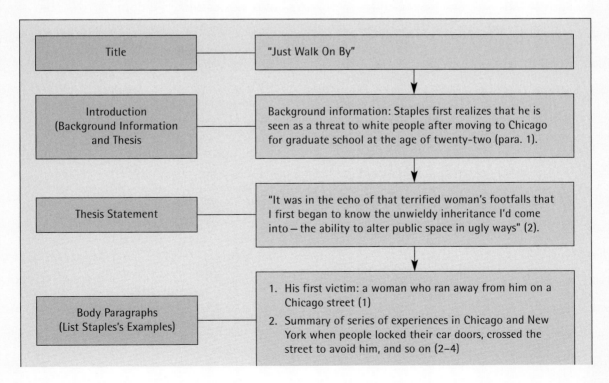

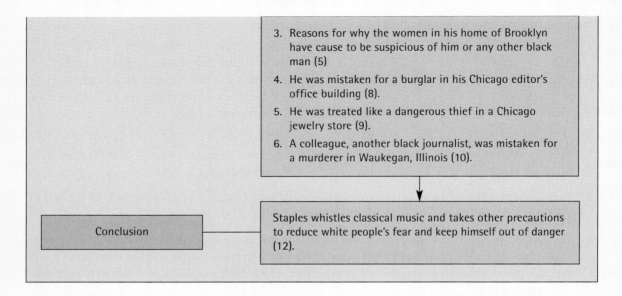

3. Reasons for why the women in his home of Brooklyn have cause to be suspicious of him or any other black man (5)

4. He was mistaken for a burglar in his Chicago editor's office building (8).

5. He was treated like a dangerous thief in a Chicago jewelry store (9).

6. A colleague, another black journalist, was mistaken for a murderer in Waukegan, Illinois (10).

Conclusion — Staples whistles classical music and takes other precautions to reduce white people's fear and keep himself out of danger (12).

Examining the Characteristics of Illustration Essays, p. 214

1. Staples's thesis appears in paragraph 2: "It was in the echo of that terrified woman's footfalls that I first began to know the unwieldy inheritance I'd come into—the ability to alter public space in ugly ways." His thesis is adequately supported by the series of examples—both his own experiences and those of friends—presented throughout the essay.

2. Staples is presumably writing for a white audience, since most people of color probably already know about this phenomenon. His purpose is to let people know what it is like to be a black man whose motives are constantly questioned by strangers. The examples that support his thesis are chosen to educate rather than to condemn. This is evident in the way Staples respectfully acknowledges other possible reasons—such as the justifiable fear of women who encounter strange men at night—for why people might be afraid of him late at night.

3. Answers will vary. One particularly striking example is the episode when he was mistaken for a mugger in his editor's building; this event must have been deeply humiliating to him as a professional (para. 8).

4. Examples of descriptive language used by Staples: "with a beard and billowing hair" (1), "the *thunk, thunk, thunk, thunk* of the driver . . . hammering down the door locks" (3); "as though bracing themselves against being tackled" (5). Such vivid descriptions enable the reader to experience Staple's sensory perception of white people's fear.

5. Answers will vary. For example, the topic sentence in paragraph 7 ("As a boy, I saw countless tough guys locked away; I have since buried several too") is followed by examples from his life of guys he knew who died ("a teenage cousin, a brother of twenty-two, a childhood friend").

Building Your Word Power, p. 214

1. "Warrenlike streets" has a connotation of a dark, narrow maze.

2. "Unwieldy inheritance" suggests the heavy burden of being perceived as a criminal that comes with being a black man in America.

Building Your Critical Thinking Skills: Cause and Effect Relationships, p. 215

1. According to the author, his appearance and proximity made the white woman run in fear: a tall, young black man with a beard, billowing hair, and a military jacket who seemed to be walking dangerously close behind her (para. 1).

2. The author's experience growing up in the tough city of Chester taught him to be careful and to avoid trouble. Through these experiences, he chose "to remain a shadow" (7).

Rita Kempley, "Abs and the Adolescent," p. 217

In this short piece on how pre-teen and adolescent boys are being affected by media images of beautiful, muscular teenage boys, Kempley uses a series of quotes from "experts" of various sorts, including psychologists, sociologists, authors, personal trainers, and athletic directors, as well as from boys themselves. The quotations give readers some quick insight into the attitudes of young boys, information about the status of teen culture, and anecdotal evidence that supports or contradicts it.

You might want to begin discussing this essay by taking a poll of what your students think about Kempley's theory. How did they feel about media images of teenage boys when they were in middle school or high school? Is it true, for example, that young boys formerly didn't care about their physiques? Didn't their fathers or grandfathers, for example, wish for larger muscles? Students could make a list of examples from their own experience, both pro and con, that would support or contradict Kempley's thesis. You could then have the class break into two panels to debate the issue pro and con, citing their own anecdotal evidence to support their view of the essay's thesis. As an alternative (or in addition) to this activity, you could ask students to list the pros and cons of weightlifting for aesthetic beauty and strength rather than playing other sports to maintain fitness. Encourage students to think critically about Kempley's article since its thesis is somewhat speculative, without many significant long-range statistics to support it.

Understanding the Reading, p. 219

1. According to the essay, men as a group have become very body conscious, especially teenagers and boys as young as age ten (para. 3).

2. The essay argues that media and advertising images are creating a new aesthetic ideal for boys that includes looking "ripped" (1), or toning their muscles (3).

3. The young men cited by Kempley try to achieve physical perfection through weightlifting and steroid use (23).

4. The phrase "negative treadmill" (22) refers to the ways in which the beauty culture (advertising and the media, especially girls' and women's magazines) has made many women dissatisfied with their looks and unhappy with their physical appearance. Many women spend time and money (and sometimes become anorexic/bulimic or psychologically depressed) trying to reach an ideal that they cannot attain. The negative aspects Kempley mentions specifically are buying "more products" (22) and thinking that their bodies are "flawed" (21).

Visualizing the Reading, p. 220

Students will have different views about the boy's concerns. Specific points in Kempley's essay that this image might illustrate include paragraphs 21, 22, and 23. You might also have students freewrite in response to this image in the voice of the teenage boy looking into the mirror. Then have them write in the voice of a teenage girl. Ask a few students to read their two versions aloud. How are they different? How are they alike?

Examining the Characteristics of Illustration Essays, p. 220

1. Kempley supports the generalization that boys—through media pressure and other outside influences—are becoming more interested in their physical appearance to the detriment of their health and well-being.

2. Most of Kempley's examples are quotations from "experts" of various kinds, including psychologists, sociologists, authors, personal trainers, and athletic directors, as well as teenagers and middle-school boys themselves. Because students are often accustomed to accepting any evidence offered by a professional writer as fact, you may need to prod your students to critically weigh all of the examples Kempley gives. Some are more representative than others, but some of her evidence seems weak. For example, one psychiatrist says that she is seeing more "steroids" being used by boys, but she does not give an exact percentage or even an estimate to support her statement (para. 23).

3. Answers will vary. An example of information that might have strengthened Kempley's thesis would be the inclusion of data from a long-term study showing the extent to which media imagery has changed the body image of men and boys over time.

4. While some students may like the fact that the final quote adds some levity to an otherwise serious piece, others will wish that Kempley had taken the opportunity to conclude with a more formal ending that summarized her findings and re- stated her thesis.

Building Your Word Power, p. 220

1. The metaphor "I'm just a piece of meat" means being objectified and evaluated only in terms of physical characteristics.

2. "Jocks' refuge" means a place where athletes feel comfortable.

Building Your Critical Thinking Skills: Evaluating Sources, p. 221

1. Because many of Kempley's sources are journalistic rather than academic, this question might be a good one to spend time on in class. You might want to go through the names of her sources aloud in class, one by one, evaluating each per- son's qualifications and engaging students in a discussion of how reliable his or her information is. This activity might lead into a discussion of academic sources and how they differ from journalistic ones.

2. Depending on your students' research experience, they may need some help in identifying where one would turn to best verify information that appears in a journalistic essay.

Geeta Kothari, "If You Are What You Eat, Then What Am I?" p. 223

South Asian American writer Geeta Kothari explores the sometimes tenuous links be- tween food and cultural identity. Beginning with a vivid scene in which she and her mother puzzle over a can of tuna, Kothari explores her sense of being neither South Asian nor American when it comes to food. Because stylistically this essay differs from those the students have already encountered in this chapter, you may find it useful to have students reread the essay together, breaking it down into a list of examples used by Kothari in order to assess the effectiveness of her thesis and support.

With this essay as a point of departure, you might want to initiate a discussion of cultural differences in America and use food to focus in on these differences. You might discuss, for example, what group most closely represents the "American" in American food. Students could break into small groups to come up with a list of com- mon American foods (for instance, hot dogs, hamburgers, pizza) and then develop a theory about the different cultures these typical foods came from. In the process, such an activity might challenge students to think about how certain types of Chinese food are considered American, whereas the "fish cheeks" discussed in Amy Tan's essay (p. 000) are definitely not.

Understanding the Reading, p. 226

1. Kothari's family eats lentils, rice, bread, vegetables, lamb, and other things (para. 21), but they don't eat processed foods like hot dogs, hamburgers, or pork. As a child, Kothari wanted to eat the foods that other schoolchildren eat like tuna salad and bologna (1), foods that her family finds "repugnant" (1).

2. During the hot season in India, her family is very careful not to eat certain foods like "ice cream" and "salad" and they boil their water because of the prevalence of diseases like dysentery (11).

3. The tuna fish episode indicates that although Kothari's mother did not have a lot of time or interest to explore American customs with her daughter, she wanted her daughter to be happy as she tried to "satisfy" her "longing for American food" (1).

4. The author does not want to eat red meat, which her husband likes. He accommodates her food preferences by cooking only poultry at home and eating red meat only in restaurants or at other people's houses (26).

Visualizing the Reading, p. 227

Possible answers include:

Example	What It Illustrates
Tuna story (para. 1–10)	Illustrates the difference between American and Indian foods, and reveals the mother's inability to grasp American ways.
Visiting relatives in India (para. 11–13)	Reveals her parents' cultural background and why they are cautious about certain American foods; also shows that they feel at home in India because they understand the customs.
Visit to uncle's diner in New Delhi (para.14–16)	Shows that the author dislikes her parents' restrictions about food.
Visit to Indian restaurant in New York (para. 17–19)	Reveals that Indian cuisine is finally entering mainstream, American culture, opening a bridge between the author's world and that of her friends.
Boyfriend's food preferences (para. 22–26)	Depicts the cultural differences in food preferences between the author and her boyfriend (now husband) and how they bridged them.
Author's attempts to cook Indian food (para. 27–32)	Illustrates that the author wants to get in touch with her ancestral roots by learning more about Indian food.

Examining the Characteristics of Illustration Essays, p. 227

1. The main point is that in terms of her food preferences, Kothari lies culturally in between Indian and American culture. She makes generalizations about what it means to be stuck between the two cultures through statements such as wanting to "eat what the kids at school eat" (para. 1) and "Indians eat lentils" (30).

2. Kothari uses examples from her personal experiences to support her main point. Students' answers will vary, but one example that is likely to make an impression on them is Kothari's dislike of her husband's "musky" smell after he eats red meat (26).

3. To help the reader understand difficult or abstract concepts, such as the unfamiliar food items mentioned in the essay, Kothari often explains what exactly they are, such as her descriptions of "dosa" (19) and "methi roti" (27). While this technique will be helpful for students, some may wish that Kothari had explained the differences between Punjabi and South Indian cooking a bit more (21).

4. Kothari organizes her examples chronologically.

5. Other methods of development that Kothari uses include description ("crushed bone and hair glued together by chemicals and fat" [1]); comparison and contrast (the description of the canned tuna fish not looking like tuna salad [1–5]); narration ("One time my mother makes . . . [21]); and cause and effect (how the orange soda makes her sick in India [14–15]).

Building Your Word Power, p. 227

1. The similes "like an internal organ" and "like a half-blind bird" in paragraph 3 allow the reader to understand how peculiar and alien the tuna fish must have seemed to Kothari and her mother.

2. The connotation of the word *home* for the author's mother is India, a place where she knows the rules, knows how to take care of and guide her daughter, and feels safe (para. 12). For Kothari, *home* is where she feels comfortable because no one asks why she eats certain foods or who she is (32).

Building Your Critical Thinking Skills: Drawing Conclusions, p. 228

1. As a child, Kothari concludes that her mother is a disappointment because she knows so little about American culture (para. 8–10). This observation adds poignancy to the story because her parents cannot help her navigate life in America in the ways she wishes they could.

2. Kothari concludes that her inability to cook Indian food suggests that she is not really her parents' daughter and, therefore, not really Indian (33). This leads her to further conclude that because she "cannot bear the touch and smell of raw

meat" (33) she is not an American either, putting her in a position somewhere between the two cultures.

Nell Bernstein, "Goin' Gangsta, Choosin' Cholita: Claiming Identity," p. 230

Nell Bernstein uses interviews with California teenagers to explore how cultural ideas about self-definition and identity in America are changing. To many of these teenagers, racial, ethnic, and other identities are flexible, able to be chosen rather than assigned. This essay should prove to be of great interest to first-year students since it contains many references to popular culture and involves their approximate age cohort. Because many of Bernstein's examples contradict or challenge other examples within the essay, her thesis is somewhat complex and nuanced; you may need to help students work through the essay's thesis and examples when evaluating the effectiveness of Bernstein's illustrative techniques.

In class discussion, students might adopt the various stances represented here in order to sift through the logic of Bernstein's thesis that a new generation is "claiming" or "choosing" identities of all kinds. Students might enjoy debating which identities are fixed and which are somewhat malleable (from racial to neighborhood identification). You might also want to use the "Focus on the Topic" activity to guide the discussion toward forms of cultural "claiming" that your students are familiar with, either personally or from pop culture.

Understanding the Reading, p. 235

1. To April Miller, racial or ethnic identity means that a person is whatever he or she chooses to be. According to Bernstein, Miller defines herself by how she dresses, her music, her words, and whatever she pledges "allegiance" to (para. 9).

2. Bernstein proposes the following reasons for why teenagers have developed such attitudes about their racial and ethnic identity: the increasingly diverse population in California (7), media images of pop culture (9), the hybridization of America (10), California's diverse public schools (11), the glamour of gangsta lifestyles (41), a backlash against whites in the state of California (43), the prevalence of interracial marriages in California (45).

3. According to the author and the people interviewed for this essay, rap music plays a role in the formation of cultural identity by making white suburban kids think that ghetto life is glamorous (29–30) and by popularizing urban, inner-city clothing styles.

4. The young people profiled in the essay change their attitudes toward identity as they grow older. As Will Mosley and Adolfo Garcia's remarks show, they gradually

dispense with the "blatant mimicry" of the images shown in rap videos (30), but they maintain a belief that they can "live in a suburban tract house . . . and still call themselves 'city' people on the basis of musical tastes" (30).

Visualizing the Reading, p. 236
Possible answers include:

Teenager(s)	What the Example Illustrates
April Miller (para. 1–9, 53)	She is Anglo but "claims" a Mexican identity; feels that the choice of ethnic identification is hers.
Nicole Huffstutler, Heather, and Jennifer Vargas (para. 15–24)	Nicole (who has Indian blood) and Heather claim a white identity because of "pride" in what they are. Jennifer claims a "mostly Mexican" identity. Nicole and Heather take Jennifer's "claim" of racial identity—despite the fact she is part Caucasian—to be a concession to their community's belief that "white is a bad race."
Will Mosley, Adolfo Garcia, and Matt Jenkins (para. 25–34)	Will and Matt, who are white, and Adolfo, who is Latino, identify with gangsta and ghetto culture. Although they have "outgrown trying to be something they're not," they still identify themselves as "city people" even though they live in a suburb.
Jesse Martinez, Oso Martinez, and Alex (para. 36–40)	Jesse and Oso, who are Latino, and Alex, who is Asian, are in a gang that claims a white gang as its "older generation." They prefer suburban to city culture, "longing for a Beaver Cleaver past" that is a thing of the past.
Andrea Jones (para. 41–44, 52)	Andrea is African American and comes from the suburbs; she believes that appreciating aspects of different cultures is "beautiful" but that using "pop culture stereotypes just to blend" is sad.
Roland Krevocheza (para. 45–49)	Roland is half Mexican and half Eastern European but embraces his white heritage because it is more unusual in the mostly Mexican neighborhood where he lives.

Examining the Characteristics of Illustration Essays, p. 236

1. Bernstein makes the generalization that a new generation believes that people can be whatever they "claim" to be. She supports it with quotations from California teenagers of different races from different areas and different walks of life.

2. Bernstein makes the term *identity* real and understandable by describing how the teenagers in the essay identify themselves through dress ("Her lipstick is dark, the

lip liner even darker" [para. 1]); language ("'nigga' as a term of endearment" [13]); and they way they describe themselves ("city people" [28]).

3. Using the Visualizing the Reading activity, have students rate each example according to how relevant, representative, and striking and dramatic it is. Then encourage students to assess whether the author provides enough examples to support her thesis, and if not, what additional examples they would have liked to see.

4. Answers will vary. Opening and concluding with the example of April Miller is a useful technique to both draw the reader in and bring the essay to a conclusion.

Building Your Word Power, p. 236

1. The figurative expression "sooner or later we'll all get nailed" reveals that April's father believes there is a backlash against white people in California and that NAFTA is taking jobs away from white people.

2. *Claiming* as it is used in the essay means adopting whatever neighborhood, ethnicity, or cultural identity one chooses. The author uses it in various contexts to illustrate its various meanings, such as in paragraph 14, when she explains its meaning through the series of examples.

Building Your Critical Thinking Skills: Alternative Viewpoints, p. 237

1. Will Mosley and Adolfo Garcia offer an alternative to April's views because they no longer "claim" an ethnicity based on clothing, considering their earlier wearing of gangsta clothes to be "blatant mimicry" (para. 30).

2. Andrea Jones views white teenagers' imitation of black culture as "shallow mimicry" (41) and believes that people should be proud of their own culture. Her view contributes to the essay because she does not identify with "city" or ghetto culture, although she is proud of being black (43).

3. Some students may note that because the essay offers only examples from interviews with young people from Califorina, it doesn't offer a true understanding of whether this phenomenon is confined primarily to California or reflects young people all across this country.

Reacting to the Reading: Discussion and Journal Writing, p. 237

You might want to preface class discussion with some remarks about racial tolerance and showing consideration for fellow students, since this issue can be inflammatory.

Dorianne Laux, "What I Wouldn't Do," p. 239

In this poem, Laux uses active verbs and vivid adjectives to conjure up the series of unskilled jobs she held before becoming a poet who teaches writing at the university level. The poem's subject, unskilled and low-paying jobs, should appeal to college students since it may mirror some of their experiences as employees. Combining vivid details with examples, it is a perfect centerpiece for freewriting and discussions on work.

Students might like to write about work experiences from their own point of view, as Laux does from a poet's perspective. Ask students to think about how they might identify themselves—from dancer or musician to video gamer or athlete—and then write about their work experiences with that identity in mind. Invite students to share their work with the class or in pairs.

Understanding the Reading, p. 240

1. The author has held a series of low-paying jobs, such as working in a fast-food restaurant, cleaning houses, making donuts, and cooking in a sanatorium. In addition to paying low wages, all of these jobs require few or no skills.

2. Laux's favorite job was making donuts. She liked it because she worked alone at night "surrounded by sugar and squat mounds of dough" (lines 29–34). She didn't like the *TV Guide* solicitation job because of the disappointment in people's voices when they realized that she was only calling to sell them something (1–3, 35–45).

3. Answers will vary. The author seems somewhat satisfied with her various jobs but not very enthusiastic. Evidence from the poem that suggests this includes low-key statements like "Cleaning houses was fine" (12) and the fact that she "drifted" (18) from job to job.

Visualizing the Reading, p. 240

Possible answers include:

Feature	"What I Wouldn't Do"
Narrator (Who is speaking in the poem?)	The author, Dorianne Laux
Audience (To whom is the poem addressed?)	Laux is not clear on this, though presumably the poem is addressed to anyone who has ever done menial or unskilled labor or to those who share her reluctance to "sell" things to people who haven't asked to be solicited.
Subject (What is the subject of the poem?)	The subject of the poem is working for a living and having to reject certain kinds of work if they interfere with one's values.
Tone (What feelings does the narrator express about her subject?)	The narrator's feelings are somewhat neutral, except in the title and the last few lines. Students may find the overall tone of the poem to be one of melancholy.

Thesis (What main point does the narrator express about her subject?)	The main point is that while the narrator could happily do many kinds of work, she couldn't solicit or disappoint people, even if she needed the money.
Examples (What examples support the thesis?)	1. Telemarketer (selling *TV Guide*) 2. Fast-food worker 3. Working at a laundromat 4. Housecleaner 5. Sanatorium cook 6. Gas station attendant 7. Working in a donut shop

Examining the Characteristics of Illustration Essays, p. 241

1. Laux's theme about the human experience is that even though everyone has to work for a living, there are some jobs that one has to say no to because the work goes against one's sense of what is right. Her unstated generalization about work is that it is possible to find moments of satisfaction and even beauty in most jobs, no matter how menial. Possible alternative interpretations: only work that doesn't exploit others is tolerable (lines 42–45); most work has some element of sensory joy ("all the onion rings I could eat" [lines 4–5] or the "A-minor ping" of the bell in line 18); or Laux will do "*almost* anything for money" (as suggested in the title).

2. Laux uses a series of six examples of menial, low-level jobs that she has held to explain why she couldn't do the phone solicitation job. Because these types of jobs are probably familiar to younger students, they will likely find Laux's examples to be relevant and representative.

3. Laux appeals to the senses of taste ("all the onion rings I could eat" [4–5]), sound ("A-minor ping" [18]), touch ("plucking bright coins from a palm" [9]), smell ("deep fried burritos" [6]), and sight ("flesh-colored plastic plates" [22–23]).

4. Laux indicates transitions within her poem through phrases such as "Before that" (4); "And at the laundromat" (8); "I drifted," (18); "I liked the donut shop best" (29); and "It wasn't that I hated calling them" (35). The transitions are chronological, but they shift from past to present tense. They are also somewhat obscure, presented without the clear, logical markers that are usually required in an essay.

Building Your Word Power, p. 241

1. The connotative meanings of the word *job* include an occupation and a task, or something that has to be done.

2. The figure of speech "hungry hands" in line 7 implies, literally, the hands of some-one who is hungry, and figuratively, hands like those of starving people or beggars who reach out with their palms cupped in desperation.

Building Your Critical Thinking Skills: Analyzing Poetry, p. 241

1. Laux uses lots of active verbs—such as "grabbing" (line 8), "plucking" (9), and "scooped" (21)—to convey a picture of activity or work. Some of the words in the poem have various shades of meaning. For example, "lazily" (16) describes the bell's clapper but could also apply to Laux as a dreamy, unproductive house-cleaner. Through the use of words like "bright" (9), and "jewelled" (16), Laux's use of descriptive language contributes to her message by illustrating the ways in which she found satisfaction and beauty in her work, no matter how menial the job. Her use of active verbs (see above) also conveys the occasional strenuousness of the work.

2. Students are likely to have different emotional responses to this poem, depending perhaps on their own experiences working. The title conveys an emotional atmos-phere or mood of slight foreboding, but much of the description of Laux's jobs in-dicates relative satisfaction or contentment with the work.

Chapter 8 Process Analysis: Explaining How Something Works or Is Done, p. 243

Process analysis is a simple, direct way of explaining how something is done, step by step. Recipes and directions are good examples of how process analysis is used in or-dinary life. Students enjoy writing these kinds of essays when they are presented as a challenge. You might, for example, want to ask them to explain something as routine as making a peanut butter sandwich in the simplest way possible so that even someone who has never seen or eaten one can make it. Remind students that as in description and narration essays, it is essential to use sensory details and figures of speech to make their writing more compelling, especially if the essay includes technical jargon or outlines a complicated process.

Although it can stand alone, the process analysis pattern is sometimes inserted into the midst of another kind of essay. Writers often incorporate it into essays that are principally defined by another pattern, such as comparison and contrast. When a writer does this, he or she should clearly introduce the transition into process analysis and then transition back into the primary pattern of development.

To begin, you might want to go over all of the characteristics of the process analy-sis essay as outlined in the chapter. Note in particular that such essays usually include an explicit thesis statement. Most of the pieces in this chapter have an explicit thesis statement, so you will have ample opportunity to model for students how to develop explicit thesis statements of their own. The annotated essay, "How the Oscars Work" (p. 244), presents a clear example of process analysis. The graphic organizer on page 252 shows the organizational structure of the essay and presents a model for how students might outline their own process analysis essay. When they begin writing, encourage them to make use of the flowchart on p. 251; it will help them identify and number the steps in their process to make sure that their essay is clear and organized in chronological or logical order.

The process analysis essay should present clearly outlined steps, usually in chronological order. For example, Melissa Russell-Ausley and Tom Harris describe the Academy Award process in chronological order. They simplify the complex processes of nominating and voting and tallying by breaking them into separate steps. David Feige also does this as he describes the legal process of defending a client in "How to Defend Someone You Know Is Guilty" (p. 278). Tom and Ray Magliozzi in "Inside the Engine" (p. 284) use logical order to explain how an engine works—for example, how the oil circulates. In "You and Improved" (p. 262), reporter Matthew Gilbert satirizes the steps involved in TV makeover shows to provide a critique of them.

Process analysis should define key terms, the way Tom and Ray Magliozzi define *crankshaft* and other words that may be unfamiliar to their readers. Process analysis should also provide necessary background information, the way "How the Oscars Work" includes information on the forms, ballots, and equipment involved in Oscar nominations and awards. Public defender Feige also provides background information by describing what he does when he first meets a client, what information he collects, how he decides what defense to use, and so on.

Tom and Ray Magliozzi supply adequate detail, and because theirs is a how-to essay, they anticipate and offer help with potential problems. They instruct the reader to avoid problems by paying attention to warning lights and taking certain actions such as not driving the car once the oil light goes on. Overall, their primary advice is to change the oil and filter every 3,000 miles. Cindy Chupack also advises her readers *buyers beware*, in "Dater's Remorse" (p. 273), humorously outlining problems that women might encounter if they do not shop wisely for a husband.

Analogies are another important component in process analysis. In "Campus Racism 101" (p. 267), Nikki Giovanni compares college with prison in order to emphasize her point that a college education provides an opportunity for more freedom and choice. Chupack uses an extended analogy between selecting men to date and shopping for clothes or furniture. Tom and Ray Magliozzi make humorous comparisons between men checking to see that their zippers are up and car owners double-checking to see if their warning lights work.

Melissa Russell-Ausley and Tom Harris, "How the Oscars Work," p. 244

Melissa Russell-Ausley and Tom Harris (editors of HowStuffWorks.com) make the process of the Oscars accessible and interesting by analyzing the awards' features in a step-by-step fashion. Like most process analysis essays, it provides an explicit thesis statement: "Let's take a look at the organization behind the Oscars, see what the 'Academy' actually is, and learn how Oscars are awarded" (para. 2). The authors explain the process chronologically and provide background information about how the Academy Awards became known as the Oscars.

Kyle Mares, "Creating Your Own Web Site," p. 258

This student essay compiles and illustrates a list of steps for creating a Web site. To emphasize the importance of the process he is going to describe, Mares opens his essay with the idea that posting one's résumé online is a useful tool for both job hunting and connecting with like-minded people online. Mares then outlines a five-step process to create a Web site. Over the course of his essay he defines key terms like *fee-based* and *dedicated*, producing a satisfying, informative essay that students can analyze in terms of their own needs.

Responding to "Students Write," p. 260

1. The writer's thesis statement and introduction explain why making a Web site might be useful and important to readers. Mares's introduction explains that having a Web site and résumé online can lead to jobs and connect someone to others with similar interests, and his thesis suggests that one can "reap . . . benefits" (para. 1) from having a Web site.

2. Potential trouble spots include the drawbacks posed by the unwanted ads and limited storage space of free Web publishing, the "cost" of "fee-based" services, and the very high cost of having one's own Web server (2). Mares also mentions problems such as complaints if the site is poorly designed (5) and the task of keeping it updated (6).

3. While Mares's essay offers an introduction to the process of creating a Web site, the level of detail is probably not great enough to create a Web site using Mares's instructions. Additional detail about how to use HTML or "authoring programs," for example, would be helpful (3). It might be useful to poll Web-savvy students who have created sites before to see if they found Mares's essay useful, and if not, in what areas it is lacking.

4. Mares's conclusion is satisfying because it emphasizes that the process of creating the site is in itself rewarding, and it emphasizes the rewards (9).

Matthew Gilbert, "You and Improved," p. 262

Reporter Matthew Gilbert mocks the TV makeover trend, from homes to bodies and clothes. He questions that "expert" advice can make someone happy, suggesting that all that these programs do is encourage people to criticize themselves. He uses questions that mimic those heard on shows like *Queer Eye for the Straight Guy*, such as "Are you actually going out in public in such infantile baseball caps?" (para. 6) and "Is there a way out of this disgrace?" (7) to mock their style. In a more serious vein, he theorizes that the drive for self-improvement is part of an American tradition.

Because it involves contemporary popular culture, this essay should spark a great deal of interest among your students. You might begin with a discussion of whether it is true that Americans as a group "hunger for transformation" (12). Have students consider also whether makeover shows that use plastic surgery, like *Extreme Makeover*, go too far. Students may wish to write about the idea of self-worth and how it relates to an individual's social image.

Understanding the Reading, p. 264

1. The five steps in the tongue-in-cheek makeover process are (1) scrutinize your home; (2) criticize your appearance; (3) criticize your wardrobe; (4) pause to revise, to rethink, to renovate; and (5) accessorize.

2. According to Gilbert, people like makeover shows because they "suit the traditional American hunger for transformation and self-realization" (12). In the author's view, such shows appeal to people who dream of improving their lives.

3. In Gilbert's opinion, people are especially likely to feel that they need a makeover if they are "dreamers and yearners" (12) and when they have "insecurities" (14) that lead them to want to radically change their lives.

4. Gilbert's purpose for writing is to critique these shows. He thinks that while there is nothing wrong with making something over, people watching such shows lose "perspective" in the transformative power of change, falsely believing that change alone will make them happy (13). Furthermore, according to Gilbert, such shows lead people to compare themselves to "a standard of beauty and behavior that isn't right for you," resulting in "idealized and unreal" visions of how they should look, act, and live (15).

Visualizing the Reading, p. 264

Possible answers include:

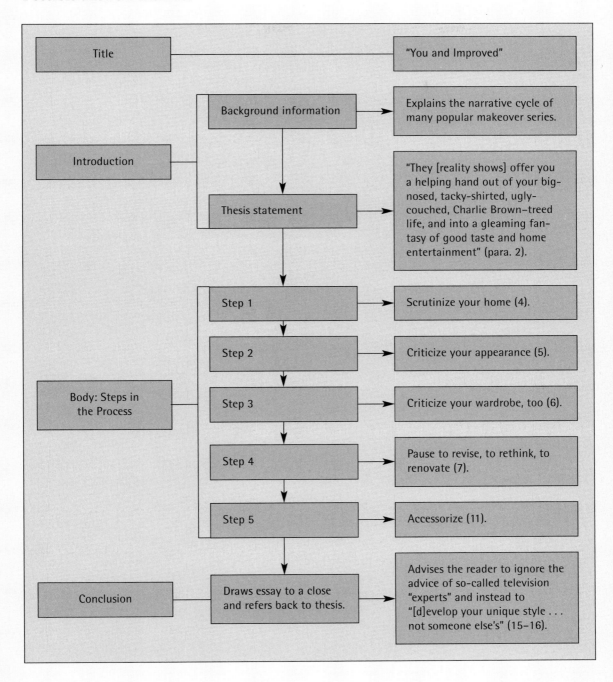

Title		"You and Improved"
Introduction	Background information	Explains the narrative cycle of many popular makeover series.
	Thesis statement	"They [reality shows] offer you a helping hand out of your big-nosed, tacky-shirted, ugly-couched, Charlie Brown–treed life, and into a gleaming fantasy of good taste and home entertainment" (para. 2).
Body: Steps in the Process	Step 1	Scrutinize your home (4).
	Step 2	Criticize your appearance (5).
	Step 3	Criticize your wardrobe, too (6).
	Step 4	Pause to revise, to rethink, to renovate (7).
	Step 5	Accessorize (11).
Conclusion	Draws essay to a close and refers back to thesis.	Advises the reader to ignore the advice of so-called television "experts" and instead to "[d]evelop your unique style . . . not someone else's" (15–16).

Examining the Characteristics of Process Analysis Essays, p. 264

1. For the author's thesis, see the graphic organizer above. This is a how-it-works essay because it explains how a reality show draws people in, inviting them to "scrutinize" (para. 4) and "criticize" (5) themselves.

2. As background information Gilbert presents the narrative cycle of many makeover series, explaining how popular shows such as *Trading Spaces* and *Queer Eye for the Straight Guy* promise to "eliminate the embarrassing 'before' in favor of the tasteful happily ever 'after'" (2).

3. The organizational technique Gilbert uses is chronological, from "before" to "after" (2). He most likely chose this technique in order to mirror the path used by most makeover shows.

4. The author uses colorful details to humorously describe the "before" person: "your big-nosed, tacky-shirted, ugly-couched, Charlie Brown–treed life" (2). For sensory details, he uses images like "flawlessly glazed turkey" (13) and "fraying Khakis" (6). Figures of speech incorporate gentle humor, as in macaroni and cheese being the "poor man's protein fix" (4).

Building Your Word Power, p. 265

1. *Vintage* as used in paragraph 6 refers to a certain kind of old or second-hand-store clothes that are considered fashionable, unlike other old clothes.

2. The phrase "We are steeped in the tyranny of the glossy magazine spreads" means that the glut of visual images of ideal bodies and homes featured in magazines and advertising has made people aspire to something they cannot ever realistically achieve.

Building Your Critical Thinking Skills: Humor, p. 265

1. Answers may vary. Most students will probably find Gilbert's tone to be somewhat lighter than sarcasm. He uses humor to encourage readers to challenge and reject media definitions of beauty.

2. Gilbert combines humor with process analysis by mimicking the tone and agenda of reality shows. For example, step 4 in his process—"Pause to revise, to rethink, to renovate. Is there a way out of this disgrace?" (para. 7)—would never be spoken as such on a show, but similar subtexts are evident in the tone used by shows' experts. Gilbert also mocks the falsely high-toned language of programs like *Queer Eye for the Straight Guy* when he writes, "Are you ready to select a pocket square, more commonly known as a handkerchief . . .?" (11).

Reacting to the Reading: Discussion and Journal Writing, p. 265

2. The media's role in how people form opinions of themselves is a topic that should lead to some interesting discussion. Forming a critique of the media may be difficult for first-year students, but these kinds of discussions are useful if you guide students by asking questions.

Nikki Giovanni, "Campus Racism 101," p. 267

Giovanni, a professor of English at Virginia Tech, titles her essay as if it were an introductory college course for black students on how to survive racism at a primarily white college, like the one where she teaches. Her process consists of a list of guidelines or rules for how to survive and thrive at a white college. She follows it with a question-and-answer format to effectively illustrate the kind of insensitive questions black students may encounter. Giovanni's tone is one of mildly scolding impatience with the idea that it is better to drop out rather than face racism. But it is clear that Giovanni has high expectations for black students. To better prepare your students, you might want to provide some background material on the history of black education at the college level in the United States before getting into a discussion of Giovanni's tone and guidelines.

Understanding the Reading, p. 270

1. Giovanni thinks her presence is important at Virginia Tech because there are some black students at the school. She also thinks it is important for white students to interact with black people in authoritative positions while in college (para. 2).

2. Some of the challenges that black students may face at predominantly white colleges include being insulted (for instance, being called "nigger" [4]); racist or sexist professors who don't like them (10); and insensitive questions or remarks from white students (13). Giovanni notes that these are all challenges that black students will experience outside of college as well.

3. Giovanni thinks it is important for students to meet and cultivate relationships with their professors because it will indicate that the students are serious about doing well (6).

4. According to the author, a black student's most important job in college is "to obtain an education" (34).

Visualizing the Reading, p. 270

Possible answers include:

Question	Potential Trouble Spot
"What's it like to grow up in a ghetto?" (para. 14)	Racial stereotyping; some students assume all black people lived in a ghetto.
"Can you give us the Black perspective on Toni Morrison, Huck Finn, . . ."(para. 16)	Assumes that a single black student can speak for "all" black people.
"Why do all the Black people sit together in the dining hall?" (para. 18)	Assumes is that a group of white people sitting together is not exclusive, whereas a black group is.
"Why should there be an African-American studies course?" (para. 20)	Fails to acknowledge the important contributions of Africans and African Americans.
"Why are there so many scholarships for 'minority' students?" (para. 22)	Assumes that minorities are unfairly being given easy access through affirmative action quotas and scholarships.
"How can whites understand Black history, culture, literature, and so forth?" (para. 24)	Fails to recognize that black people have historically had to learn white history, culture, and so on.
"Should whites take African-American studies courses?" (para. 26)	Fails to recognize that many courses focus only on the work of white people but are not called "white studies."

Examining the Characteristics of Process Analysis Essays, p. 271

1. The essay title suggests that the author's purpose is to explain the fundamentals of dealing with racism on campus.

2. The essay's thesis statement is implicitly stated in paragraph 4: "There are discomforts attached to attending predominantly white colleges, though no more so than living in a racist world." This thesis identifies the process to be discussed (how to cope with the "discomforts") and suggests Giovanni's attitude toward it (the process is no more difficult than the obstacles that blacks face in everyday life).

3. Giovanni makes readers understand the importance of the process she recommends by comparing college to prison and then explaining how a college education differs because it gives students "a passport to greater opportunities" (para. 4).

4. The background information establishes the author's qualifications for writing about racism by indicating that Giovanni is black and a tenured professor. It also helps readers understand the process that she explains by letting them know that

she cares about her students, even if she is strict in tone. For example, when she says, "We need to quit it," she identifies herself with other black people who have criticized their own race (1).

5. Students' responses may vary. Giovanni's tone is one of impatience with students who are too sensitive to deal with racist comments. She thinks they should have the strength and courage to get an education, no matter what difficulties they face.

Building Your Word Power, p. 271

1. Answers may vary.

2. The different connotative meanings of *discriminate* are: to be selective about something, and to form a bias against someone (for instance, racial discrimination). The former meaning is used by Giovanni in paragraph 10.

Building Your Critical Thinking Skills: Point of View, p. 272

1. Giovanni uses the first person. This perspective reinforces her message to students because it indicates that she is black like them and therefore has an intimate understanding of their difficulties.

2. Answers will vary.

Reacting to the Reading: Discussion and Journal Writing, p. 272

1–2. Be sure to preface any discussion with a few remarks about creating community in the classroom and the need to exhibit tolerance and understanding for everyone's point of view. Questions like number 1 often raise difficult issues, such as what constitutes "preferential treatment" and so on, so it is best to provide some historical background on civil rights and the issue of legal redress. It might also be a good idea to begin with question 2 since it will provide some common ground from which to consider racial differences.

Cindy Chupack, "Dater's Remorse," p. 273

Cindy Chupack creates a humorous analogy between shopping and dating men. Adopting the stance of the experienced and somewhat jaded dater who has made many poor consumer choices, Chupack cautions other women against the types she has encountered, become enamored of, and escaped from. The essay strains its analogies at times as it tries to bring certain ideas together for the sake of humor. To encourage a critical reading of what is likely to be a highly entertaining essay for your students, you might want to assign them to identify and discuss the weakest similes in the piece. After discussing this essay, consider having students try to create a similarly humorous essay about an issue of their choice (for example, traveling with friends or choosing someone to dance with at a party).

Understanding the Reading, p. 275

1. The author's relationship with long distance phone companies relates to the topic of dating because it serves as the basis for an analogy between the choices she has as a long distance phone consumer and the choices she makes in her dating life.

2. According to Chupack, dating someone who is "the human equivalent of a fashion fad" may end up becoming more of an "emotional investment" than expected (para. 4).

3. Chupack uses the analogy between dating and buying furniture to explain how, just like a couch that doesn't go with anything else in the house is an impractical purchase, men who are very different from oneself and one's lifestyle may "mean changing your entire life" (6). Likewise, Chupack advises women to stay away from "fixer-uppers" because they "are more likely to stay forever flawed, no matter what we do" (5).

4. The author assumes that readers are looking for a husband (8).

Visualizing the Reading, p. 275

Possible answers include:

Step	Shopping Analogy	Dating Advice
1	"Go with a classic, not a trend" (para. 4).	Avoid men who are radically different from the types you usually date.
2	"Beware of the phrase 'Some assembly required'" (para. 5).	Avoid men that you have to fix up — they tend to remain flawed.
3	"Make sure your purchase goes with the other things you own" (para. 6).	Don't date someone whose lifestyle is so unlike yours that your entire life will be changed.
4	"Check with previous owners" (para. 7).	If he is older than twenty-five, find out why his other relationships ended so that you don't end up with a lemon.
5	"Caveat emptor" (para. 8).	Be a wise shopper to reduce the number of times it doesn't work out.

Examining the Characteristics of Process Analysis Essays, p. 276

1. Chupack's thesis appears at the beginning of paragraph 3: "The unfortunate truth is that while most of us are savvy shoppers, we're not sufficiently selective when looking for relationships, and that's why we often suffer from dater's remorse."

2. Chupack's essay is not ordered chronologically. While her steps are essentially interchangeable, she does move from advice geared toward women dating men more casually ("Go with a classic, not a trend") to factors that are likely to have long-term implications for women who enter into serious relationships or marriages with the types described ("Check with previous owners").

3. While the author does not offer a lot of detail for the steps in her process, the examples are vivid and compelling, so some students will likely (depending on their own dating experiences) find Chupack's advice useful.

4. Befitting the humorous tone of her essay, Chupack's conclusion ends lightly yet convincingly as she cautions readers, "Caveat emptor" (para. 8).

Building Your Word Power, 276

1. In paragraph 7, *lot*, as in "used car lot," is used figuratively to mean still dating or available, not married.

2. The connotation of *secondhand* and *used merchandise* in paragraph 7 is men who have been in other serious relationships.

Building Your Critical Thinking Skills: Analogies, p. 276

1. Chupack develops her analogy between shopping and dating through the steps in her process. To encourage students to evaluate Chupack's analogies critically, have them go through each step listed above in Visualizing the Reading, examining the details in the text to assess whether all aspects of the analogy are logical and useful.

2. Have students brainstorm in class to discover ways in which shopping and dating differ. Chupack addresses these differences only by saying that "looking for a husband is a bit more complicated than choosing a major appliance" (para. 8).

David Feige, "How to Defend Someone You Know Is Guilty," p. 278

David Feige offers a glimpse into a public defender's emotional response to his clients, even the guilty ones. Feige draws the reader in at the start of his essay with an anecdote about a seemingly unlikable crack addict named Kevin, saying "I loved Kevin" (para. 1). Feige writes like a trial lawyer who uses shock tactics and hyperbole to draw the reader in with statements such as "I rarely bother with 'the facts'" (3). His step-by-step outline of what he does and doesn't do to defend a client becomes even more intriguing when he contends that it is emotion that keeps him committed to his work. Students may find it especially surprising to read that he considers building "trust" (4) with his clients his main task.

In class, it might be useful to note that Feige uses transitional phrases to keep his narrative chronologically consistent, even as the focus shifts between his defense of this individual client and legal procedures in general. Students may like to discuss the idea of a public defender—how the role came about and what it means for the American system of justice. You might initiate discussion by asking questions such as: What would it mean for society if the right to a fair trial and "representation" did not exist? You might also ask students to come up with a scenario—using freewriting—in which they are mistakenly considered a criminal suspect. What if all the "facts" fell into place against them? Would they want Feige to represent them?

Understanding the Reading, p. 280

1. Readers learn that the author will "happily" defend any client, "guilty or innocent" (7). They learn that he defends the guilty for several reasons, including the fact that once he gets to know them he likes them. He also has empathy for them because no one else is rooting for them (9) and because they are "hated" and "desperately need my protection" (11).

2. The author doesn't think too much about the victims of the crimes in which his clients are involved because he is focused on defending his clients. The victims remain "abstract" for the simple reason that the perpetrator is "very human and very real" (9) to him. Just as the prosecutors seek to dehumanize his clients, he too dehumanizes the victims. He can do this because he understands that the victims are being cared for by other lawyers, their families, the police, and so on.

3. Kevin is being tried for buying cocaine from an undercover policeman and then attacking him with a screwdriver. Kevin denies this version of events, saying that he had bought some crack and then "out of nowhere" was shot (7). Feige planned to defend him by saying that the police fabricated the sale of cocaine to cover up the shooting of Kevin (7).

Visualizing the Reading, p. 280

Answers will vary. The primary characteristics in a lawyer that would be of value to the man depicted in this image—according to Feige's essay—would be a willingness to take the time to get to know and understand the man as a person, and an interest in protecting his client no matter what the circumstances of the crime.

Examining the Characteristics of Process Analysis Essays, p. 281

1. Feige uses an implied thesis about why he feels the compelling need to protect and defend suspected criminals. The main process he describes is that of defending a potentially guilty client. Other processes described in this article are Feige's defense of Kevin, the procedures a lawyer and client follow, and how other public defenders describe their reasons for defending guilty clients.

2. The details about Kevin that the author provides are: he has a lengthy rap sheet and a crack addiction, he was shot by the police after supposedly attacking an un-

dercover policeman, and he has a family he loves but is too embarrassed to visit. The rap sheet and gunshot wound are important because they indicate the probability that Kevin was involved in the crime. The details about his family are important because they humanize Kevin. These kinds of details make Feige "really like" his clients (para. 10).

3. The author organizes the steps in his essay chronologically.

4. One potential trouble spot that Feige identifies is how to address the issue of whether his client is telling "the truth" (4). Because Feige knows that the truth "is often the only thing my clients have left," he understands that they will not "part with" it easily (4). His solution to this problem is to accept whatever version of the crime his client gives him, using that as a defense (5). He takes "the defenses as I take my clients—as they are" (5).

5. Answers will vary. Note: Feige does include a brief explanation of the outcome of Kevin's trial in parentheses in paragraph 7.

Building Your Word Power, p. 281

1. "Putting him in a suit would look like a lie" (para. 6) means that a judge and jury will not believe that a homeless crack addict ever wears a suit and that this "lie" won't help persuade them that he is innocent.

2. The author's use of legal jargon, such as "robbery in the second degree" (2) and "plausible defense" (7), contributes to the essay by reminding the reader that most suspects would be lost without the help of a lawyer.

Building Your Critical Thinking Skills: Facts and Opinions, p. 281

1. Fact

2. Opinion

3. Fact

4. Opinion

5. Opinion

Reacting to the Reading: Discussion and Journal Writing, p. 282

1. You might want to consider the issues of race and class as they pertain to *justice*. You might also want to preface the discussion by giving students a little background on how the legal system in the United States has changed over time. Also, some discussion of how the legal rights of women, slaves, and others have been altered over time might be useful.

Tom and Ray Magliozzi, "Inside the Engine," p. 284

The Magliozzi brothers (well known as *Car Talk*'s Tappet Brothers) begin with a brief anecdote about what happens when people don't pay attention to warning lights or gauges in their car. The authors then explain some of the basic features of an engine, such as how the oil circulates. After that, they deliver pointers on the most important signs to pay attention to, the necessity of maintaining and heeding warning lights, and fundamental maintenance procedures to invest in at regular intervals. As they proceed, they explain complex terms and automotive jargon in order to make their how-it-works essay easy to understand, using analogies to familiar things to help their readers understand clearly how certain processes work.

Students will enjoy this essay because it provides essential information made palatable through humor. They may also appreciate its clear and simple presentation and use of simile. The article may spark an interest in writing and sharing some short process analysis essays in class. Ask students to brainstorm a subject about which they know quite a bit and think they could explain step by step (for example, diving or throwing a football). Challenge them to share it and evaluate its effectiveness in pairs before presenting it aloud to the class.

Understanding the Reading, p. 288

1. The customer's car broke down because it had run out of oil. The lesson the authors teach through this example is that the cost of neglecting some basic features of car care may be very high.

2. Oil is very important because it lubricates the car's engine and keeps the metal parts cool (para. 5). A car's oil warning light comes on when the engine has lost pressure, meaning that it is very low on oil and/or the oil pump is not working (14).

3. The problem the authors associate with gauges is that people may take their eyes off the road while they are driving to look at the gauges (10).

4. The authors say the best way to protect a car is to change the timing belt (24) and the oil every 3,000 miles (28).

Visualizing the Reading, p. 289

Paragraph	How-to Advice
13	Shut the engine off if the oil warning light comes on.
16	Make sure that your warning lights work.

17	Don't overfill your oil.
26	Change rubber timing belts every 60,000 miles.
27	Change the water pump when you change the rubber timing belt.
28	Change the oil and oil filter every 3,000 miles.

Examining the Characteristics of Process Analysis Essays, p. 289

1. The Magliozzis' thesis is: "The oil is critical to keeping things running since it not only acts as a lubricant, but it also helps to keep the engine cool" (para. 5). This thesis doesn't state clearly why the process is important to readers, but it implies that if there is no oil, the engine will overheat.

2. The level of detail on the subject of what oil does (5–8) is fairly elaborate, but this seems appropriate because most readers won't have an understanding of this process and will therefore need the sort of detailed explanation that the Magliozzis give.

3. The authors use humor (for instance, the cookies and milk story [3]) and analogies to more familiar things (for instance, checking one's zipper and then one's oil pressure [30]) to make the topic interesting and understandable. The level of knowledge and mechanical savvy the authors assume their readers possess is rudimentary.

4. Potential areas of confusion the authors identify are: paying too much attention to the gauges if one doesn't have warning lights (10); not knowing enough to stop the car if the warning light comes on (13); not making sure that the warning lights work (16); overfilling the oil (17); not knowing that the timing belt should be changed when recommended (25); not remembering to change the water pump when recommended (27); and not remembering to change to the oil and filter every 3,000 miles (28). Answers may vary.

5. The authors use analogy (for instance, the oil pump is like a heart and the oil acts like a cushion to the metal [7]) to make technical terms understandable to readers who lack mechanical knowledge.

Building Your Word Power, p. 289

1. The oil is described as "coursing through the veins of the engine" (para. 7). This use of personification enhances the story by making the mechanism seem more vivid and alive, analogous to a human heart.

2. Answers will vary.

Building Your Critical Thinking Skills: Evaluating Authors, p. 290

1. The authors of "Inside the Engine" are qualified to give professional car advice because they are trained auto mechanics who have owned a garage for many years. In addition, they were both educated at MIT, one of the nation's top institutions for engineering and science, making them both highly qualified to explain complicated processes.

2. The authors generally stick to advice that falls within their realm of expertise. When they do discuss other topics (for instance, radios in cars), the advice is given humorously and is not intended to be taken seriously.

Chapter 9 Comparison and Contrast: Showing Similarities and Differences, p. 292

This chapter should be of great interest to students because *comparison and contrast* is one of the most useful of all essay forms. Students who master this rhetorical mode will have mastered a skill that they can readily utilize in future college papers and on essay exams. You will probably want to devote several sessions to comparison and contrast, explaining that these essays must be organized carefully, point by point or subject by subject. To illustrate the organizational structure of comparison and contrast, it might be helpful to show students the graphic organizers on pages 299 and 300 for subject-by-subject and point-by-point arrangements. As explained on page 298, careful planning and outlining are essential preliminary steps for this mode. It is very important to reiterate that the points of comparison must be significant and similar enough to warrant comparison. Analogies, although useful, must also be accurate in order to be used effectively. Refer students to the Use analogies guideline on page 304 for more on this. To create better-flowing comparison and contrast essays, you will want to emphasize the need for clear transitional words (phrases such as *similarly*, *in contrast*, and *on the one hand*) as signals or markers for the reader. Have students do revision exercises in order to perfect their ability to guide the reader through the series of points.

The essays included in this chapter present a wide range of examples of the mode for students to analyze, evaluate, and model. Joseph Sobran's essay, "Patriotism or Nationalism?" (p. 293), uses a point-by-point organization very effectively, making this essay a good illustration of how an author compares only "key characteristics." The graphic organizer for Sobran's essay (p. 301) is also very useful for reducing a complex essay to three or four essential points. In "We've Got the Dirt on Guy Brains" (p. 311), Dave Barry humorously argues that differences between men and women are genetically determined. Barry's essay might be compared thematically with "East vs. West" (p. 321), in which Sharon Begley shows how Western and Eastern psychological perspectives of the world differ. Using the point-by-point method, she illustrates that although human thought varies from culture to culture, it can be modified by exposure to new cultures. Jeanne Wakatsuki Houston uses a subject-by-subject organization in "A Taste of Snow" (p. 316), an essay comparing two very different winters from her childhood. Both winters carry symbolic overtones in a subtle way. She begins with her first taste of snow, a happy memory of wonder that took place during an unhappy period when her family was placed in an internment camp during World War II. Then she transitions back to her earlier memories of happiness in winters spent on the California coast, where it never snows. "A Case of 'Severe Bias'" (p. 326), by Patricia Raybon, uses a point-by-point arrangement to support her thesis that media images of black people are inaccurate and damaging. She provides a series of stereotypes, beginning with her own personal experience, and then cites statistical evidence, such as the fact that there are more poor white women on welfare than black women, to counteract the stereotypes of African Americans perpetuated by the media. In "Sex, Lies, and Conversation" (p. 331), Deborah Tannen also uses a point-by-point organization to argue, like Begley, that although differences exist in how men and women perceive communication, they can be modified by learning.

Joseph Sobran, "Patriotism or Nationalism?" p. 293

Joseph Sobran uses a point-by-point arrangement to caution readers against "the seductions of nationalism" (para. 12). He concentrates initially on defining and establishing differences between patriotism and nationalism and then selects key points of comparison, as shown in the graphic organizer (p. 301). Students will benefit from analyzing the way the essay opens with a definition of *nationalism* before proceeding with its persuasive argument against the dangers of nationalism. This topic works well for a discussion of the political climate that followed the events of 9/11. You might like to encourage students to evaluate issues such as the intersection of domestic security and civil rights or the idea of the melting pot in the post-9/11 period. The theme of nationalism in the United States might also be explored historically. Students could, for example, compare and contrast the internment of Japanese Americans during World War II (described in Houston's essay, "A Taste of Snow," which appears later in this chapter on p. 316) with the treatment of Arab Americans after 9/11.

Heather Gianakos, "Border Bites," p. 307

In this student essay, Heather Gianakos skillfully compares Mexican and Southwestern cuisines in a point-by-point style using key points such as uses of corn, chicken, beef, and pork. You might like to assign students to write in-class essays of their own about a particular cuisine, following this essay as a model. You might also review Gianakos's "Works Cited" in class in order to familiarize students with the more extensive research they will do later in the term. Have them discuss which quotes most impress them and how they would evaluate the sources she cites.

Responding to "Students Write," p. 309

1. Gianakos's purpose in writing is to compare and contrast Mexican and South-western cooking. She supports her thesis effectively by detailing the "subtle, fla-vorful differences between the foods featured in Mexican and Southwestern cui-sine" (para. 1) through a comparison of the origins of ingredient use, and the uses of corn, chicken, beef, and pork.

2. Gianakos organizes her essay chronologically. She explains the origins of ingredi-ent use and then provides the historical background of each ingredient — the key points of comparison and contrast in her essay.

3. Generally, the author effectively presents details to support each point of compar-ison. For example, she effectively details how Southwestern cooking often grew out of difficult conditions such as having to pack foods for travel and cook them over open fires on the range (2), whereas Mexican cuisine developed in an envi-ronment where there were plenty of fresh ingredients. To describe the differences in cooking styles and tastes, Gianakos relies heavily on sensory details of sight, smell, and taste: "Fried chicken rolled in flour and dunked into sizzling oil or fat" (4); "the richly seasoned, corn- and tomato-heavy style of Mexican food" (7).

4. Gianakos's use of sources contributes to her essay by giving it more authority.

Dave Barry, "We've Got the Dirt on Guy Brains," p. 311

In this essay reprinted from his well-known weekly humor column, humorist Dave Barry lays claim to a scientific breakthrough called "Male Genetic Dirt Blindness" (para. 4). Using pseudo-scientific jargon to compare and contrast male and female perceptions of dirt, he playfully contends that men's reluctance to do housework or communicate with their partners at home may be genetic rather than learned. You might like to use this essay to initiate a discussion of humor and how it works in this instance. Another discussion topic could be generalizations or stereotypes, especially age-old gender stereotypes such as the one Barry treats. You might invite students to provide counter-examples from their own store of anecdotal evidence to the contrary, or to explore the idea that Barry's thesis is dated, not applicable to younger genera-tions now in college. Students might also write an in-class essay that provides a simi-larly humorous pseudo-theory, but one that takes the woman's point of view.

Understanding the Reading, p. 313

1. The author describes himself as a "modest person" (para. 1), a "journalist" (5), and a husband (7).

2. Barry's original claim regarding men's ability to do housework was that "Male Genetic Dirt Blindness" made them unqualified to do housework because they were genetically unable to perceive dirt. The new proof he offers to back up this claim is a book, *What Could He Be Thinking? How a Man's Mind Really Works*, which states that because men supposedly take in less sensory detail than women, they don't perceive dirt and disorder in the same way (5).

3. The key piece of information cited from the book Barry mentions is that a man's brain "'takes in less sensory detail than a woman's, so he doesn't see or even feel the dust and household mess in the same way'" (5). Another difference involves the "cingulate gyrus," though Barry does not know exactly what this is, leading him to create a hilarious hypothesis of his own to explain this part of the brain. The only other sources quoted in Barry's essay are his own observations about male-female relationships.

4. Two examples of the types of situations in which Barry feels men and women differ in their thinking are: a man would rather lie on the sofa and watch TV than communicate with his mate (8), and a man will think the bathroom is clean when a woman doesn't (3).

Visualizing the Reading, p. 313

Possible answers include:

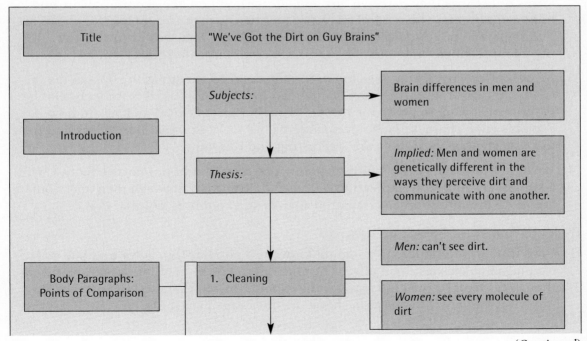

(Continued)

(Continued)

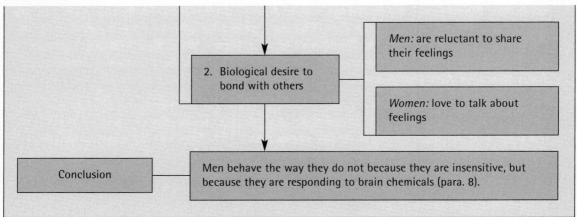

Examining the Characteristics of Comparison and Contrast Essays, p. 314

1. Barry's purpose in writing is to playfully propose that men and women are different because of innate, biological differences rather than cultural influences. His basis of comparison involves the ways men and women perceive dirt (para. 2–5) and communicate with one another (6–8).

2. Barry uses an implied thesis that women and men are genetically different in terms of the way they perceive dirt and clutter and how they communicate and bond with others. The sex-linked characteristics he uses to support this thesis are that men tend not to notice dirt while women do (2) and that women enjoy talking about feelings while men do not like to communicate about feelings (7–8).

3. Answers will vary. Barry does not use many detailed examples to support his thesis, though given that the essay is intended to be humorous, it is unlikely that he is seriously trying to prove his thesis. To encourage a critical analysis of how he explains each characteristic, have students list every example Barry uses and then discuss whether the details are interesting and relevant.

4. Barry organizes his essay point by point. The essay might not be as effective with a subject-by-subject organization because the contrasts between men and women are more humorous when compared side by side, point by point.

Building Your Word Power, p. 314

1. Brad Pitt, as your students no doubt know, is a popular film actor and one of *People* magazine's sexiest men alive. The allusion to Pitt in the first paragraph means that Barry likes to imagine many things about himself that are not true, thereby implying that anything he says should be questioned critically.

2. These images are effective and humorous in the context of the essay because they mimic scientific jargon and the tendency to use fruit metaphors to describe medical conditions (for instance, a grapefruit-size tumor).

Building Your Critical Thinking Skills: Humor, p. 314

1. Barry uses humor in this essay to poke fun at differences between men and women that people often laugh about socially but that are generally treated respectfully and scientifically in our serious, liberal, "p.c." culture.

2. Without humor, the essay would not be as effective because many men and women who are concerned about changing gender roles would not take lightly the idea that genetics determine some men's dislike of housework or difficulties with communication in intimate relationships.

3. Answers will vary.

Reacting to the Reading: Discussion and Journal Writing, p. 314

Issues such as gender roles can lead to heated discussions if they are not properly prefaced with remarks about political tolerance. You might set the tone by discussing the history of gender relations and how they have changed over time. Question 3 might be a good place to start in order to show that many women are messy and many men are neat. Be aware that some younger students may not even understand or subscribe to Barry's humor. They may welcome an opportunity to challenge his humor in view of historical and sociological changes brought about by three decades of feminism.

Jeanne Wakatsuki Houston, "A Taste of Snow," p. 316

Jeanne Wakatsuki Houston compares two very different winters from her childhood. She arranges the essay in a simple subject-by-subject fashion. She opens with a recounting of the first time she tasted snow. This otherwise happy memory occurred in the midst of a stark period in her life, when her Japanese American family was sent to an internment camp in California. Houston then describes her lush, earlier memories of a happy "American" childhood on the California coast, where it never snows. Students might find Houston's use of symbolism (particularly of snow, Christmas and other holidays, and nature) of interest. You might suggest that they read the essay closely at least two times in order to analyze Houston's nuanced use of symbolism. This essay has some thematic overlap with the issue of patriotism and nationalism addressed in Sobran's essay (p. 293). Approaching the two essays in conjunction might generate an interesting discussion and a possible comparison and contrast essay.

Understanding the Reading, p. 318

1. Houston was living in Owens Valley because after the bombing of Pearl Harbor the U.S. government forced many Japanese Americans to relocate to internment camps for the rest of World War II.

2. Houston was interested in the snow because she had never seen it before, having lived previously in Ocean Park, on the California coast where it never snows.

3. Before Houston went to Manzanar, her life was like that of any other California child. She played on the promenades (para. 4), celebrated traditional American holidays (5), and considered her family an American family just like any other.

Visualizing the Reading, p. 318

Possible answers include:

Points of Comparison	Manzanar	Ocean Park
Location	The high desert of Owens Valley, California	Dudley Avenue, a block from the beach
Temperature/weather	cold and snowy	warm and sunny
Impression of landscape	mountains and desert; a "stark landscape of white on white" (para. 3)	ocean and sand
Christmas	An improvised Christmas tree of "a bare manzanita limb embellished with origami cranes" (6)	"a lush, brilliantly lit fir tree" (6)

Examining the Characteristics of Comparison and Contrast Essays, p. 318

1. Answers will likely vary because Houston's intent in writing is not stated overtly. Her purpose in writing this essay may have been to inform others about the existence of Japanese internment camps in World War II, or it may have been simply to express her memories of these very different periods and places in her life.

2. The author uses an implied thesis that she cannot summon memories of her childhood in California without recalling her time at Manzanar (para. 6). Students may have difficulty identifying Houston's thesis. To help them, have them read the essay's conclusion, looking for clues about the significance of the two places that the author contrasts.

3. Answers will vary. The subject-by-subject organization is effective because it creates a child's-eye view of her experience at Manazar that contrasts sharply with her former, sun-filled childhood experience on the California coast.

4. Using the graphic organizer above, have students evaluate the effectiveness of each point of comparison addressed by Houston. She uses highly descriptive language, full of rich sensory details that appeal to taste ("cotton candy, wispy and delicate" [1]); touch ("uncomfortable wetness when the snow melted upon contact" [2]); sight ("orange-flowered dress and white high-topped shoes" [5]); and sound ("the 'kata-kata' clatter of wooden clogs scraping across sand and gravel" [3]).

5. Other patterns of development used by Houston include narration and description. These contribute to her comparison and contrast by providing the rich details that constitute the basis of her contrast between the two places from her childhood.

Building Your Word Power, p. 319

1. Answers may vary. By "beauty had its price to be paid" in paragraph 2, the author may be suggesting that she was already learning that enjoyment in her life would inevitably be followed by pain.

2. When Houston states that the two Christmases exist "like . . . a memory within a memory" (para. 6), she means that the two are so emotionally intertwined that she cannot think of one without the other.

Building Your Critical Thinking Skills: Symbolism, p. 319

1. Christmas symbolizes Houston's memories of these two places. In her memories, the holiday represents a wondrous time of abundance and beauty, whether it comes from nature's splendor during her time of deprivation at Manazar or in the more conventional sense during her time in Ocean Park.

2. Snow appears to symbolize the beauty of nature and its transformative nature, both to alter the world physically and to soften and soothe an otherwise painful time in the author's life. It also suggests the pain of cold, the "price to be paid" for beauty (para. 2).

3. Owens Valley may symbolize a cold, dry (unfertile or sterile) place of exile; it is cut off by mountains and devoid of sunshine. Ocean Park may symbolize the sunny playground of her childhood before she was initiated into the pain of exile. Water represents fertility, so the "ocean" in Ocean Park may also symbolize a place of creativity and abundance.

Reacting to the Reading: Discussion and Journal Writing, p. 319

1–2. These questions provide an opportunity to discuss the idea of community and how celebrations such as the Fourth of July foster a sense of interconnectedness.

A sense of place is often connected to a sense of community. These subjects provide excellent opportunities to have students combine what they have learned thus far about narration, description, and comparison and contrast. Sharing some writing about their home towns or families can also foster a sense of community among your students.

Sharon Begley, "East vs. West: One Sees the Big Picture, the Other Is Focused," p. 321

Science writer Sharon Begley summarizes recent research about how learned crosscultural differences may affect thinking. Using a wide range of sources, from cognitive psychologists to people who have lived in various cultures, she provides support for her thesis that cultural conditioning influences cognition. Careful to note that these differences are not genetic or fixed, Begley provides examples of people who have learned to bridge cultures. She advocates crosscultural study as a means to attain a new kind of global knowledge and understanding.

This essay provides an excellent transition into argumentation or the research paper. Students will enjoy evaluating the accuracy and reliability of the various sources used in the essay. You might like to initiate a discussion of the use of sources, delineating the difference between anecdotal evidence and serious academic sources. One possible discussion topic is the nature versus nurture debate about genetic versus learned behavior, possibly linked thematically with Barry's pseudo-scientific thesis about male-female differences (p. 311). Another possible topic is the idea of universal as opposed to culturally specific thought. You might make further thematic links in discussing this topic with Houston's essay on Japanese Americans during World War II (p. 316).

Understanding the Reading, p. 323

1. Modern cognitive psychologists assume that the nature of human thought is universal (para. 3), that people think, reason, and perceive their surroundings the same everywhere.

2. The aquarium experiment showed that Asians tend to pay more attention than Westerners to backgrounds and to the relationships between things (7–9).

3. Eastern and Western ways of thinking differ in that Westerners see categories whereas Asians see relationships (6). As illustrated by the aquarium experiment, Westerners' "basic sensory perception" is also different. Westerners pay attention to the "focal object" while Asians attend to the overall background and relationships within it (9). Westerners also attribute causality more to "actors" than to "context" (10). Finally, Westerners and Asians draw inferences differently (12). Westerners "prefer abstract universal principles" while Asians "seek rules appropriate to a situation" (13).

4. According to the author, the thinking patterns of people who live away from their native cultures for some time begin to shift, adapting native thinking patterns and incorporating them into their existing ways of thinking (14). Begley contends that by incorporating cultural diversity and, hence, different ways of viewing issues, businesses may be more likely to "see problems clearly and solve them" (14).

Visualizing the Reading, p. 323

Possible answers include:

Point of Comparison	Supporting Evidence
1. **Sensory perception:** Japanese remember more background elements than do Americans.	Study conducted in Michigan in which students were shown photos of aquariums
2. **Remembering objects:**	Taka Masuda's aquarium study in Michigan; psychologist Richard E. Nisbett's book, *The Geography of Thought*
3. **Business dealings:**	Example of an Australian–Japanese sugar deal that went bad in the 1970s
4. **Drawing inferences:**	Research study in which Ann Arbor and Beijing college students predicted economic growth rates
5. **Abstract principles vs. situational rules:**	Research study in the Netherlands in which Easterners and Westerners had to indicate what to do about an employee whose work was suddenly subpar after an otherwise distinguished career

Examining the Characteristics of Comparison and Contrast Essays, p. 323

1. Begley wants to demonstrate that Eastern and Western thought are different but that they are not "hard-wired" (para. 14). She also contends that continued exposure to cultural diversity would create more crosscultural understanding. Her purpose in writing is made clear in her conclusion when she says that these differences can be bridged, leading to deeper cultural understanding (14).

2. Begley's thesis is presented in paragraph 4 through the form of a quotation from a psychologist: "'Human cognition is not everywhere the same. . . . [T]he characteristic thought processes of Asians and Westerners differ greatly.'"

3. The main ideas that make up the basis of Begley's comparison are that new studies prove there are differences in the way Westerners and Asians think and that while these divergences in thinking have led to conflicts in business and politics,

they are not genetic, or hard-wired, so cultural differences can be bridged through cultural diversity and understanding. The details of the various studies add to her comparison by illustrating concretely how different the world views of Asians and Westerners really are, how they can look at exactly the same image and see very different things.

4. For background information about human thought, the author mentions Hume and Locke (seventeenth- and eighteenth-century philosophers) and makes a quick reference to the modern assumptions of "cognitive psychologists" (3). While the references to Hume and Locke are likely to be lost on most students, the explanation by the Harvard University psychologist in paragraph 3, about how cognitive scientists have typically viewed thinking around the world, is clear and easy to understand, so most students will probably agree that Begley provides enough background information.

5. Begley's essay is organized point by point. Answers will vary, but given the complexity of her discussion and the number of points of comparison that she covers, a subject-by-subject organization may not have been as effective.

Building Your Word Power, p. 324

1. The phrase "parse it so finely," as used in paragraph 1, means to explain something by breaking it down into component parts.

2. The idiom "hard-wired" as used in paragraph 14 means genetically determined.

Building Your Critical Thinking Skills: Evaluating Sources, p. 324

1. Using the Visualizing the Reading exercise that lists each source cited by Begley, encourage students to consider each source critically, noting whether the author includes enough information for a reader to track down the original source. Presumably many of these research studies are cited in *The Geography of Thought*, the Nisbett book on which Begley's essay is based, so to find out further information about any of these sources, one would probably want to start with this text.

2. Most of Begley's sources are psychological studies with crosscultural applications. She also uses some examples from business and politics. These examples lend credibility and a serious tone to the author's position.

Patricia Raybon, "A Case of 'Severe Bias,'" p. 326

Raybon begins her essay with a series of media images of black women as welfare recipients, drug addicts, and prostitutes, and then she challenges the validity of these images by describing her own life (as an award-winning writer) and the lives of other "ordinary, hard-working" (para. 13) black people she knows. By illustrating the ways in which popular media images contrast with the reality of most black Americans' lives, the author makes the case for more positive and accurate media imagery of African Americans.

Because Raybon relies on her own research in this personal comparison and contrast essay, it might be useful for students to identify the kinds of examples she uses, evaluating their impact and effectiveness. You might assign students to write a similar kind of essay, using a parallel series of sources, on a topic they are personally familiar with and feel qualified to support with their own observations.

Understanding the Reading, p. 328

1. Readers learn that the author lives in the inner city in Denver (para. 12), is forty years old (1), is not a drug addict or a prostitute (1), and does not fit other stereotypical media images of black women who live in the inner city (1).

2. The media outlets Raybon accuses of being biased are "television . . . newspapers and magazines" (6).

3. Examples of the bias that Raybon describes are: programs about crack, homelessness, and other issues in which all the images are of black people (4); television shows on neutral or positive issues like nutrition in which almost all the images are of white people (4); and film reviews of Spike Lee's film *Do the Right Thing* that contended that a ghetto must have "addicts and drug pushers" for authenticity (11).

4. According to Raybon, negative images of black people are damaging to black people because they must face the "image and perception" created by the media on a daily basis (9). As a consequence, white people regard high-functioning black people as unusual or "different" (10), and "ordinary, hard-working" black people never see themselves reflected in the media (13).

Visualizing the Reading, p. 328

Possible answers include:

> Features typical of most black Americans: loving family, middle-class lifestyle, leisure time devoted to the family, suburban lifestyle, enjoying the outdoors, tailgating

Raybon could have used this photo as a contrast to the stereotyped images of black people perpetuated by the media: images of crack addicts, gang members, welfare mothers, and so on. This image of a black family enjoying a picnic outdoors illustrates clearly the author's call for media images of "ordinary, hard-working, law-abiding, tax-paying [black] Americans" (13).

Examining the Characteristics of Comparison and Contrast Essays, p. 328

1. Raybon's thesis is presented in paragraph 3: "Indeed, media coverage of black America is so one-sided, so imbalanced that the most victimized and hurting segment of the black community—a small segment, at best—is presented not as the exception but as the norm." The author is writing to *persuade.* She wants readers to understand that the media portrayal of black people is inaccurate, insidious, and hurtful.

2. The author introduces the subjects of her comparison and contrast essay by listing the things that she—an educated, black, female journalist—is not. She compares herself to the media stereotype of black women as addicts, prostitutes, welfare mothers, and so on (para. 1). The background information she provides by way of contrast is that she is black, forty years old, is married to a man who doesn't abuse her, has children who are not in gangs, and doesn't live in a "tenement" (1).

3. Because students are likely to be very aware of the media portrayal of blacks, most will likely agree that Raybon's technique for contrasting her subject is very effective.

4. The author uses point-by-point comparison. As to its effectiveness, answers will vary.

5. The points of comparison Raybon offers to support her thesis include: imbalanced media images of black people as "poor, criminal, addicted, and dysfunctional" (3); media images of white people as being overwhelmingly healthy, happy, and economically secure; and the way these media images result in ordinary, hard-working blacks being perceived as "different" (10). Raybon concentrates on both differences and similarities. For example, she contrasts the differences between herself as an educated journalist and the image of black women as crack addicts and welfare mothers (1). Raybon concentrates on the similarities between most whites and blacks in describing the neighborhoods where most blacks live: there are "children playing and couples walking their dogs" (12).

Building Your Word Power, p. 329

1. The different connotations of "black America" in the first three paragraphs represent the differences between the media's view of black America (as poor and criminal) and the black community's view of itself (as having working-class and middle-class components).

2. In using the phrase "free press" in paragraph 7, the author refers to the press as being independent of government interference. It is able to "[hold] the mirror on American reality" by reinforcing false images of the black community over and over until they are considered normative.

Building Your Critical Thinking Skills: Cause and Effect Relationships, p. 329

1. According to Raybon, the effect of the "severe bias" in the media is to distort perceptions about the black community.

2. The last paragraph reveals Raybon's hope that her essay will enable readers to see the truth of the black community clearly — "strong people, surviving people, capable people" — rather than through the biased lens of the media.

Deborah Tannen, "Sex, Lies, and Conversation," p. 331

Linguist Deborah Tannen offers a series of examples to illustrate her thesis that gender differences in communication are learned but can also be transformed. Threading throughout the essay an anecdote about a talkative man who describes his wife as the "talker in our family" (para. 1, 22), Tanner deploys extensive evidence from experts and her own research to illustrate that women's and men's expectations about communication differ. She concludes her essay optimistically, arguing that these different expectations and patterns can be transformed using the model of crosscultural understanding.

Thematically, this essay can be linked with Begley's piece (p. 000) on crosscultural differences in Eastern and Western cognition, also learned and also able to be transformed. You might assign students to write a comparison and contrast essay that utilizes the theories about learned versus innate cognition put forth by both Tannen and Begley. Class discussion about learned versus genetic differences might also prove interesting; students could form two panels to support one or the other side of the nature versus nurture debate, using anecdotal or statistical evidence to support their positions.

Understanding the Reading, p. 335

1. The opening anecdote about the man at a women's group illustrates the irony that although men talk more in public, they often talk less at home (para. 2).

2. Observable communication differences between young girls and boys are: girls use communication to "create and maintain friendships," whereas boys' friendships are based more on doing things together and less on talking (9–10); when they do talk, girls face each other and look into each other's faces, whereas boys tend to sit side by side and look elsewhere, except for occasional glances at one another (12); and girls talk at length about a single subject, whereas boys change topics often (13).

3. In conversing, men tend to not face the person they are addressing, while women look into each other's faces directly. Women often perceive this difference in body language as a sign that men are not interested or are not listening.

4. To overcome the communication problems described by Tannen, women and men need to learn to recognize their different communication patterns, coming to a "cross-cultural understanding" and then working to voluntarily alter these patterns to avoid miscommunication (26).

Visualizing the Reading, p. 335

Possible answers include:

Evidence	Purpose
Reference to political scientist Andrew Hacker (para. 3)	Gives legitimacy to the thesis and demonstrates that the thesis is not a new idea
Sociologist Catherine Kohler Riessman's observations from her book *Divorce Talk* (para. 3)	Illustrates the importance of the issue of communication between the sexes, and indicates that women identify "communication" as crucial to intimacy
The author's own research (para. 4)	Illustrates the different expectations about "conversation" that men and women have
American Psychologist article by Stanford University's Eleanor Maccoby (para. 7)	Identifies how children's development is shaped by differences in "peer interaction" in single-sex groups
Psychologist Bruce Dorval's videotapes (para. 12)	Show that physical alignment (face to face or at angles) is different at every age
The author's own research (para. 13–16)	Shows how girls stay on one topic, whereas boys switch topics frequently
Linguist Lynette Hirschman's research (para. 17)	Indicates that women make more "listener noise," whereas men give silent attention
Reference to *Fighting for Life* by Walter Ong (para. 20)	Points out that men use "warlike, oppositional formats to do almost anything"

Examining the Characteristics of Comparison and Contrast Essays, p. 336

1. Tannen's thesis about gender communication is that "although American men tend to talk more than women in public situations, they often talk less at home. And this pattern is wreaking havoc with marriage" (para. 2).

2. Tannen uses a point-by-point organization. A subject-by-subject organization might have been used to good effect, but the types of examples used (for instance,

more anecdotes) would probably need to be altered somewhat to support this type of organization.

3. The points of comparison that Tannen uses to support her thesis include: children's development and peer interactions (7), body language (14), and conversational habits (15–20). The author focuses mostly on differences but does identify a few similarities. Students will likely agree that Tannen treats her subjects fairly and objectively.

4. Tannen's exploration of the causes of these communication differences strengthens the essay because it both serves to illustrate the differences and illuminate her point that because such differences arise through learned behavior, they can be changed.

Building Your Word Power, p. 336

1. The phrase "wreaking havoc" (para. 2) brings to mind the idea of creating chaos.

2. Some examples of linguistic jargon used by Tannen: "peer interactions" (7); "cross-cultural communication" (8); "topical alignment" (13); "listener-noise" (17); and "participatory listenership" (18).

Building Your Critical Thinking Skills: Original Sources, p. 337

This section provides an excellent opportunity to give first-year students some preliminary information about bibliographic research. Explain the importance of learning how to find sources online and in the library. Emphasize its usefulness throughout their academic career. You might want to have students write a short essay in class comparing and contrasting the effectiveness of Barry's and Tannen's use of sources.

Chapter 10 Classification and Division: Explaining Categories and Parts, p. 339

You can easily explain classification and division to students if you define *classification* as grouping things into categories and *division* (closely related to process analysis, Chapter 8) as breaking a single item into parts. Both modes describe types or parts. Each uses only one principle of classification or division, with parts that include all of the members of the group. Judith Viorst's essay on friendship, "Friends, Good Friends—Such Good Friends" (p. 340), provides a familiar subject with which to introduce your students to this rhetorical mode. Since such patterns are sometimes difficult to recognize when they are imbedded in a personal essay like this one, you might like to go through the graphic organizer on page 348 line by line and detail by detail in order to explain the pattern of organization underlying this essay. Likewise, Ryan Porter's annotated student essay, "Motor Heads" (p. 356), will illustrate clearly to students how to craft a thesis statement that includes a "principle of classification" and use concrete examples to aid the reader's understanding.

David Bodanis's "A Brush with Reality: Surprises in the Tube" (p. 360) is a division essay that breaks down an ordinary, everyday commodity—toothpaste—into its various ingredients, describing each in great detail in order to convince readers that toothpaste is not all that it is cracked up to be. Elizabeth Wray's "The Seven Ages of Walking" (p. 366) classifies kinds of walking. She demarcates the life stages at which she thinks a person's experience of walking changes. Scott Russell Sanders, in "The Men We Carry in Our Minds" (p. 372), uses the principle of classification to group men into four categories—laborers, soldiers, bosses, and educated men—in order to explain his sense of alliance with women across class lines. Thematically, you might consider linking Sanders's essay to Tannen's essay (p. 331) on communication between women and men. Also in this chapter, Martin Luther King Jr.'s classic essay "The Ways of Meeting Oppression" (p. 379) uses the principle of classification to identify three responses to oppression. Finally, Cindy Combs's "Profile of a Terrorist" (p. 385) will be of interest to students in the post-9/11 era. In it, Combs classifies terrorists into three groups.

Judith Viorst, "Friends, Good Friends—Such Good Friends," p. 340

Judith Viorst, best known perhaps to students for her children's book *Alexander and the Terrible, Horrible, No Good, Very Bad Day* (1972), here evaluates her friendships according to their degree of intimacy. She uses the principle of classification to distinguish among the various "kinds" of friendship she shares with the people in her life. Viorst's sources are mostly personal observations about a few friends, which makes her piece a personal rather than an academic essay. Students may usefully evaluate whether this essay might be strengthened with evidence such as Deborah Tannen provides in "Sex, Lies, and Conversation" (p. 331). You might also link this essay thematically with Tannen's essay for a discussion about the psychology of women's expectations for intimacy in relationships.

Ryan Porter, "Motor Heads," p. 356

Ryan Porter's student essay is clearly annotated for its thesis statement, details, topic sentences, helpful examples, and other features. In this classification piece, Porter creates somewhat exaggerated "types" of car lovers, dubbing them with titles like "aficionado" and "gear head," but the essay shows how classification can be used to great effect. Students might like to evaluate the effectiveness of Porter's use of vivid details like "glittering external exhaust pipes" (para. 2).

Responding to "Students Write," p. 358

1. Porter establishes the importance of his classification by suggesting that ours is a "car culture" and that everyone cares about cars (para. 1).

2. Other patterns of development Porter used to develop the essay are: description ("dual-cowl phaeton" [2]), narration ("Five weeks later you're stranded on the side of the road" [4]); and illustration ("such as the fabled Duesenberg, Hispano-Suiza, or Bentley" [3]).

3. Answers may vary.

4. Porter's tone is humorous and at times somewhat sarcastic. His audience is primarily those who drive cars and may even love them but generally are not obsessive about them. It is possible that he writes also for the actual "car nuts" he describes, as he notes in paragraph 8 that his reader "may be one yourself." If his audience consisted of serious car aficionados only, his humor would be less effective because "car nuts" might feel mocked by his descriptions of their behavior.

David Bodanis, "A Brush with Reality: Surprises in the Tube," p. 360

David Bodanis scrutinizes the ingredients that go into toothpaste. He uses vivid details and some exaggeration to make his point that toothpaste is neither especially healthy nor worth the price. The section Applying Your Skills: Writing Assignments (p. 364) will be especially helpful to students because it provides writing assignments related to marketing techniques and their effect on consumers. Some discussion about an industry that does not take the health of consumers into account might prove interesting. Students might research or provide more anecdotal evidence about food products such as fast food and how they are regulated by the U.S.D.A.

Understanding the Reading, p. 362

1. The ingredients in toothpaste are: water, chalk, titanium dioxide, glycerine glycol, seaweed, paraffin oil, detergent, peppermint oil, formaldehyde, and fluoride.

2. The author includes information about the origins of chalk ("the crushed remains of long-dead ocean creatures"; para. 3) because it highlights how revolting this ingredient truly is.

3. The ingredient that inhibits the growth of bacteria is formaldehyde (11).

4. As a final thought on the subject, the author offers the idea that "plain water will often do as good a job" (12). The implication is that the author thinks that toothpaste is unnecessary.

Visualizing the Reading, p. 362

Possible answers include:

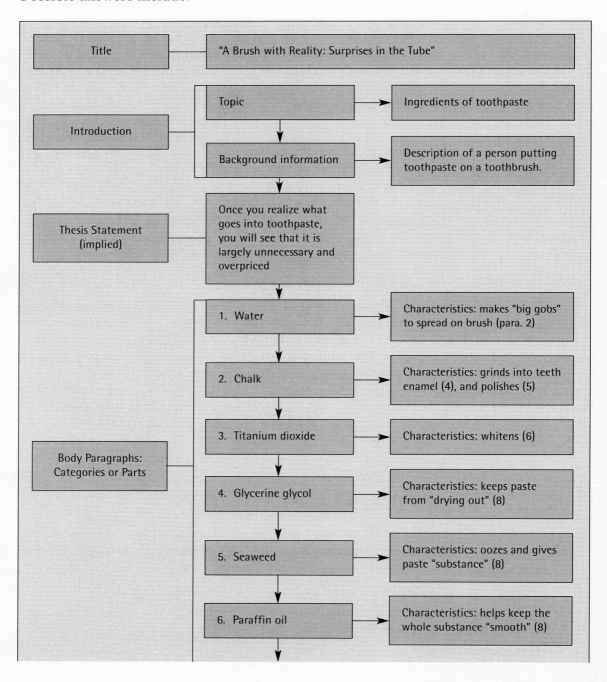

Title	"A Brush with Reality: Surprises in the Tube"

Introduction

Topic	→	Ingredients of toothpaste

Background information	→	Description of a person putting toothpaste on a toothbrush.

Thesis Statement (implied) — Once you realize what goes into toothpaste, you will see that it is largely unnecessary and overpriced

Body Paragraphs: Categories or Parts

1. Water	→	Characteristics: makes "big gobs" to spread on brush (para. 2)
2. Chalk	→	Characteristics: grinds into teeth enamel (4), and polishes (5)
3. Titanium dioxide	→	Characteristics: whitens (6)
4. Glycerine glycol	→	Characteristics: keeps paste from "drying out" (8)
5. Seaweed	→	Characteristics: oozes and gives paste "substance" (8)
6. Paraffin oil	→	Characteristics: helps keep the whole substance "smooth" (8)

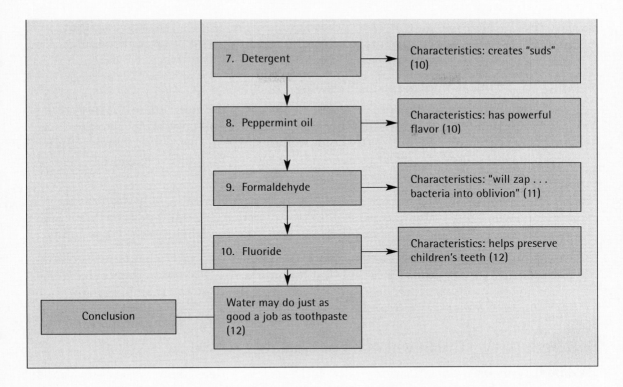

Examining the Characteristics of Classification and Division Essays, p. 362

1. Students may or may not find the author's purpose clear initially, but it should be fairly obvious by the conclusion when the author says water often does as good a job (12).

2. The categories should be seen as fairly complete. Bodanis's categories are clearly defined, and none overlap.

3. Answers will vary. Students will likely choose details that explain the more surprising ingredients, such as titanium dioxide, "the stuff bobbing around in white wall paint to make it come out white" (6) or glycerin glycol, "related to the most common car antifreeze ingredient" (8).

4. Answers will vary. Because the conclusion neatly ties up the essay and clarifies the author's intent in writing, most students will probably find it satisfying.

Building Your Word Power, p. 364

1. The phrase "reassuring white" in paragraph 6 suggests that titanium dioxide serves no other purpose than to make one's teeth white in order to give the appearance of cleanliness.

2. By "finicky distaste" and "host of other goodies" (7), the author suggests that manufacturers engineer an image of toothpaste in contrast to a reality that it is neither appetizing nor healthy.

Building Your Critical Thinking Skills: Drawing Conclusions, p. 364

1. The conclusion the author draws about water being the most plentiful ingredient in toothpaste is that it is lucrative because it doesn't cost anything, allowing large profits on each tube of toothpaste sold. Bodanis also draws the conclusion that because water often does just as good a job on one's teeth, people should save money and just use water to brush their teeth.

2. Bodanis's conclusion about consumers of toothpaste (para. 6, 7, 10) is that they are concerned more about appearances (for instance, the whiteness of their teeth and the taste of their toothpaste) than knowing the facts behind the ingredients.

3. Based on his use of details such as toothpaste being sold for "a neat and accountant-pleasing $2 per pound" (2) and that it contains inedible ingredients like glycerine glycol and formaldehyde, Bodanis seems to be drawing the conclusion that toothpaste is a marketing scam.

Elizabeth Wray, "The Seven Ages of Walking," p. 366

Elizabeth Wray uses classification to develop a series of ideas about walking as a mode of movement whose purpose changes over time. Her stages are based on observations of her extended family and are illustrated with anecdotes and examples. Students may like to critique the comprehensiveness and exclusiveness of her age groups, taking into consideration women who work long hours or don't have children or people who cannot walk because of a disability.

Understanding the Reading, p. 369

1. It will be easy for students to identify the stages of walking because of the headings in Wray's essay. The stages include toddlerhood, childhood, teens and twenties, thirties, forties and fifties, sixties, and old age.

2. Walking in early life is important, according to Wray, because it offers a way to "reach for" and "discover" the world (para. 4). In later life, walking becomes a way to feel alive and still connected to the world (18).

3. The author reveals a great many details about her personal life and the people who are dear to her: she lives with her extended family in a Victorian in San Francisco (1 and 16), she was a toddler in the 1950s (2), she is now in middle age (3), her mother grew up in Alabama (7), she has a son named Kit (8), she worked as an editor in New York City while yearning for a career in theater (10), she has a daughter named Anava who is in college (10), and her mother died of cancer (17–18).

4. According to Wray, walking is useful because it "gives us a way to be in the world" (4), provides "wonder" (4), makes us "feel good" (6), provides an opportunity for "contemplation" (10), promotes "exercise and meditation" (13), and is "fun" (14).

Visualizing the Reading, p. 369

Possible answers include:

Life Stage	Function(s)
Toddlerhood	To explore the world
Childhood	To move just for the sake of moving (6)
Teens and twenties	To make a social statement by saying "who they are" (9) or to be alone to think (10)
Thirties	To have "contemplative time" (12)
Forties and fifties	To exercise or practice meditation (13) or to walk for a cause (15)
Sixties	To help the very young or very old (16)
Old age	To walk without a goal, just experiencing nature in order to feel alive (17–18)

Examining the Characteristics of Classification and Division Essays, p. 370

1. Wray's thesis is that "[w]alking, like life, has its stages and repetitive patterns" (para. 3). Her principle of classification is age. This principle relates to the author's own life because she has experienced most of the stages herself, either personally or through close observation of family members in those age groups.

2. Students may challenge Wray's categories, citing people they know who are anomalous—for example, physically challenged people who cannot walk.

3. The categories are organized in broad age segments.

4. Other patterns of development used by Wray include: narration (the story of her 84-year-old father getting lost [1]); description ("catalpa leaves patterning the light on the front porch" [4]); process analysis ("a whole repertoire of movement through space: hop, skip, twirl, slide, gallop" [6]); and illustration.

5. The personal details illustrate each of the categories. While some students will find this technique effective, others will feel that Wray's thesis could have been strengthened through the use of more objective examples and details.

Building Your Word Power, p. 370

1. The allusion to the "human condition" in paragraph 5 means that everyone ages and dies.

2. The word *recess* (para. 9) has become childish to the author's son because it suggests play, which he feels is a childish activity.

Building Your Critical Thinking Skills: Analogies, p. 370

1. Wray uses the analogy to the seven ages of man from *As You Like It* as a means of organizing her essay into the progression through the ages as people are "walking through life" (para. 3). The analogy is appropriate because it serves both to explain the organization that the author will follow and to illuminate a familiar phrase of Shakespeare's.

2. Wray's analogy between her mother and an "usher" will probably be reasonably clear to students because the image of a theater usher showing someone the way is familiar and believable.

Scott Russell Sanders, "The Men We Carry in Our Minds," p. 372

Scott Russell Sanders vividly and compassionately describes the different types of men he saw as a boy and how these groups offered glimpses into the different possibilities he might have when he grew up. Along with his close identification with such men came an envy of women because they seemed to enjoy more leisure and to age more slowly. When he attended an Ivy League college on a scholarship, Sanders began to see that the divide between laborers and bosses (para. 1) or men who "ran the world" (10) placed him in alliance with women who sought to gain such power. You might like to provide some background on the women's movement and the class structure in the United States during the 1960s, the time this essay takes place, before initiating a discussion about the laborer and boss divide and how it does or does not play out along gender lines in contemporary society.

Understanding the Reading, p. 375

1. The types of men the author describes are: laborers (para. 1-3); soldiers (4); the men on television (5); and the educated men who "ran the world" (10).

2. Sanders envied women when he was a boy because their lives seemed more "expansive" and freer, and because they seemed to "enjoy a sense of ease and grace" (8). His view of women changed in college because the feminists he met helped him to understand that the "grievances of women" were similar to his own (8).

3. The author was different from many other students at Brown University because he was a scholarship student from a working-class family.

4. As a child, Sanders expected to be a laborer or a soldier when he grew up.

Visualizing the Reading, p. 375
Possible answers include:

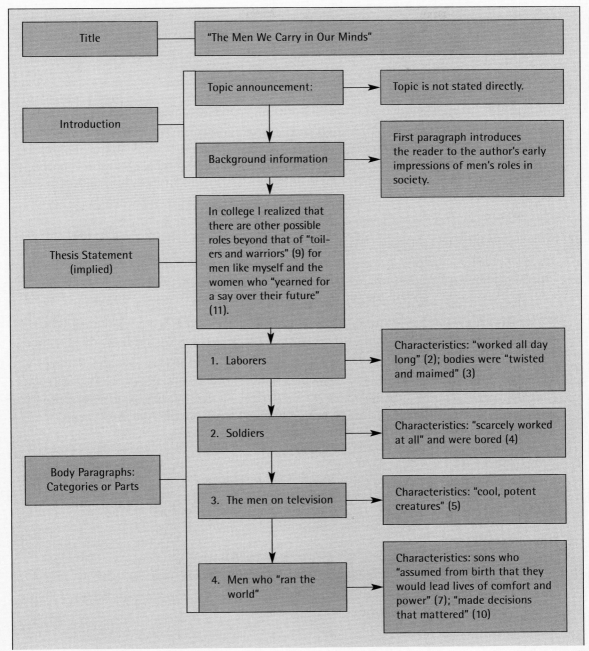

| Title | "The Men We Carry in Our Minds" |

Introduction
- Topic announcement: → Topic is not stated directly.
- Background information → First paragraph introduces the reader to the author's early impressions of men's roles in society.

Thesis Statement (implied): In college I realized that there are other possible roles beyond that of "toilers and warriors" (9) for men like myself and the women who "yearned for a say over their future" (11).

Body Paragraphs: Categories or Parts
1. Laborers → Characteristics: "worked all day long" (2); bodies were "twisted and maimed" (3)
2. Soldiers → Characteristics: "scarcely worked at all" and were bored (4)
3. The men on television → Characteristics: "cool, potent creatures" (5)
4. Men who "ran the world" → Characteristics: sons who "assumed from birth that they would lead lives of comfort and power" (7); "made decisions that mattered" (10)

(Continued)

(*Continued*)

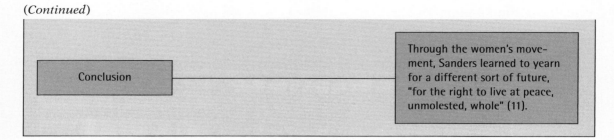

Examining the Characteristics of Classification and Division Essays, p. 376

1. Sanders's implied thesis is included in the graphic organizer above. Sanders's categories are based on the kind of work men do, how it affects them physically, and how much power they wield. He organizes the categories chronologically, reflecting the progression of his awareness of the different possible roles for men as he grows and matures. Answers about the effectiveness of Sanders's choices will vary.

2. Answers will vary.

3. Answers will vary. Some students may find overlap between "the men on television" category and the final category of men who rule the world.

4. Sanders uses other patterns of development in his essay, including: narration ("The first men . . . I remember seeing" [1]); description ("dingy grey-and-black zebra suits" [1]); comparison and contrast (a comparison of the lives of men and women [8]); and illustration (different types of laborers [2]).

5. Because Sanders uses an implied thesis, the conclusion clarifies it more so than reaffirming it. The insight Sanders offers is that he discovers a new-found alliance with women and others who have not "assumed from birth that they would lead lives of comfort and power" (7).

Building Your Word Power, p. 376

1. Some of the descriptive words Sanders uses in paragraph 3 include: *twisted, maimed, ached,* and *creased*. These words emphasize the physical difficulty and danger of factory work and other types of hard labor.

2. Answers will vary.

Building Your Critical Thinking Skills: Evaluating Titles, p. 377

1. The title suggests the different types of men that one encounters in life and how these types are embedded in one's mind.

2. Answers will vary.

Martin Luther King Jr., "The Ways of Meeting Oppression," p. 379

The Reverend Martin Luther King Jr., well known for his civil rights leadership during the 1960s, here argues eloquently for the efficacy of nonviolent resistance to racial injustice in America. Strongly influenced by Ghandi and faced with the growing Black Power movement, King wields the classification mode with great skill, redefining and reinterpreting responses to oppression, using biblical and philosophical truths to support his scholarly and forceful argument. Students may benefit from a discussion of social movements that are characterized by either peaceful protest or the threat of violence, citing as many historical examples as they can.

Understanding the Reading, p. 381

1. According to King, some people prefer to remain oppressed because they have "become conditioned to it" (para. 1).

2. King considers "acquiescence" to be cowardly.

3. Violence is an impractical method for achieving racial justice because it does not bring "permanent peace" and it creates even more social problems (4). According to King, it is also immoral because "it seeks to humiliate the opponent rather than win his understanding," thriving on "hatred rather than love" (5).

4. The "truth" of acquiescence is that "one should not be physically aggressive toward his opponent" (7), and the "truth" of violence is that "evil should be resisted" (7). The principle of nonviolent resistance reconciles these truths by ensuring that "no individual or group need submit to any wrong, nor need anyone resort to violence" (7).

Visualizing the Reading, p. 382

Using King's categories, one would classify the photos as follows: (1) Martin Luther King Jr. at the civil rights march: nonviolent resistance; (2) Black Panthers: violence; (3) Man drinking at a segregated water fountain: acquiescence. An alternative way to classify the pictures would be to group (1) and (2) together as examples of resistance but to put (3) in a category of nonresistance because the individual as shown is not visibly striving to alter his situation.

Examining the Characteristics of Classification and Division Essays, p. 381

1. The thesis statement appears in the very first sentence of the speech: "Oppressed people deal with their oppression in three characteristic ways." Unstated are the three ways—acquiescence, violence, and nonviolent resistance—that King goes on to detail in length in his essay. His thesis does not reveal why the classification is relevant or important; he presents this information later in the essay when he describes "acquiescence" and "violence" as "inferior methods" as he makes his case for nonviolent resistance (para. 8).

2. King most likely presents acquiescence, violence, and nonviolent resistance in that order because it parallels the history of black slavery, the rise of the black power movement, and the civil rights movement.

3. The categories in the essay are exclusive and comprehensive; they do not overlap significantly with one another. King provides a similar amount and kind of detail for each category, making his argument for nonviolence compelling.

4. King uses the following clear transitions to help readers stay on track as they move from one category to another: "One way is acquiescence" (1), "A second way" (4), and "The third way" (7).

5. Other patterns of development used by King include: narration ("Almost 2800 years ago Moses set out" [1]); description ("A voice echoes through time" [5]); and cause and effect ("It creates bitterness" [5]).

Building Your Word Power, p. 383

1. The allusion to everyone being "his brother's keeper" (para. 3) means that one has a moral obligation to care for those in need. "An eye for an eye" (5) means exacting revenge. King uses familiar biblical allusions like these to remind his readers of the ethics involved in the civil rights movement. He relies on biblical allusions because he is a preacher as well as a political leader.

Building Your Critical Thinking Skills: Figures of Speech, p. 383

Answers will vary.

Cindy C. Combs, "Profile of a Terrorist," p. 385

Author of *Terrorism in the Twenty-First Century* (2003) and coauthor of the *Encyclopedia of Terrorism* (2002), Cindy Combs distinguishes kinds of terrorists and their motivations, comparing and contrasting as well as categorizing. Students should find this topic compelling and may want to form small groups to evaluate her categories. The Focus on the Topic exercise on page 385 that asks students to explore their thoughts about terrorism prior to September 11, 2001, will provide a crucial lead-in to a discussion of the essay. Most students before the events of September 11 probably did not perceive terrorism as a threat inside the United States, so their concerns may have changed significantly in the years following that attack.

Understanding the Reading, p. 389

1. According to the author, the differences among "crazy," "criminal," and "crusader" terrorists include (1) their motivations: criminals have personal gain or profit as a motive, crazies' motives are clear only to them, and crusaders are motivated by a "higher cause"; (2) their willingness to negotiate: criminals are more

likely to negotiate for personal gain, whereas crazies may not understand that they may die, and crusaders usually refuse to betray their cause and don't fear death; and (3) their expectation of survival: crazies and criminals have a strong expectation that they will live, whereas crusaders rarely negotiate because they do not care if they die (table, p. 387).

2. The typical outcome for crazies is that negotiation can work successfully if the negotiator can figure out the goal of the perpetrator and if the perpetrator can understand that he or she faces death upon refusing to negotiate (16). The typical outcome for criminals is good because they "will negotiate," "their demands are generally logical," and they have a strong will to live (17). The typical outcome for crusaders is not good because they rarely negotiate and do not fear death (15).

3. The author uses the example of the plane that crashed in Pennsylvania to illustrate how the way the pilots responded to the hijacking, based on a terrorist profile that was different from what they faced, was a "contributing factor to the sequence of events on that day" (para. 20).

4. The author wants law enforcement agencies to know more about terrorists so that they will be able to develop more accurate profiles and respond to terrorist situations more effectively.

Visualizing the Reading, p. 389

Students will have little difficulty identifying Osama Bin Laden as a "crusader."

Examining the Characteristics of Classification and Division Essays, p. 390

1. The author's thesis is that "[u]nderstanding the individual who commits terrorism is vital, not only for humanitarian reasons, but also to decide how best to deal with those individuals *while they are engaged in terrorist acts*" (6). Her thesis does not state the principle of classification used in the essay.

2. Combs names the categories used in her classification in paragraph 7. She provides clear examples and details to explain the "criminal" and "crusader" categories, but gives less attention to and information on "crazies." There is some overlap between crazies and criminals with crusaders, because the acts they commit are all criminal and their motives are often "crazy"; but the author clarifies this by reminding readers that only crusaders are "well trained, well prepared, and well disciplined" (14).

3. Frederick Hacker's table (p. 389) and other references to his work aid in understanding Combs's classification by defining the single figure of the terrorist according to his or her psychological motives, willingness to negotiate, and expectation of survival. The resulting profile of the terrorist's ability and willingness to

negotiate then determines the kinds of strategies that might usefully be employed against him or her.

4. Students may have struggled to identify the author's thesis earlier in the essay but will likely find the conclusion's restatement of the thesis to be more effective. In addition to suggesting why the classification is relevant and important, this restatement more effectively reveals the principle used to classify the topic.

Building Your Word Power, p. 390

1. "Mixed bag" as used in paragraph 9 means confused or jumbled philosophies.

2. "Blind obedience" creates the image of someone following directions as they walk with a blindfold on, unconcerned that they cannot see.

Building Your Critical Thinking Skills: Author's Purpose, p. 390

1. This essay is excerpted from a textbook on terrorism, so presumably the intended audience is college students enrolled in a political science or criminal justice course. The level and tone of this essay are appropriate for this audience.

2. The author attempts to convince readers that this kind of profiling is accurate and important and that negotiating with "crusaders" is probably futile.

3. Combs does not present more than one view on the issue of classifying terrorists. Encourage students to consider whether this one-sided approach weakens her argument.

Chapter 11 Definition: Explaining What You Mean, p. 392

The basic characteristic of a *definition* will be relatively easy for students to grasp. Just as a dictionary explains a term, so does a definition essay explain something, albeit in a longer, extended form. Often, in personal essays or academic papers, a standard dictionary-style definition will serve as a preliminary step or lead-in to a longer exposition on a particular topic. These kinds of expositions are called "extended definitions." For example, in the first essay (p. 393), Mary Pipher, a clinical psychologist, describes *cultural brokers* as having "information on everything," explaining that this occupational niche involves helping immigrants make a smooth transition into a new culture. Student writer Geneva Lamberth, in "Eating Disorders: Serious and Legitimate Illnesses" (p. 407), opens her essay with a standard definition of eating disorders before launching into extended definitions of two of the most common forms of eating disorders: bulimia and anorexia nervosa. By working through the annotations included for these two essays, you can highlight for students visually the key characteristics of definition essays.

The readings in this chapter will expose students to a wide variety of styles and illustrate the effectiveness of definition in writing. In "Spanglish" (p. 411), Janice Castro, Dan Cook, and Christina Garcia define this blend of Spanish and English, giving examples of how it has become widespread in the United States. You may find it helpful to make use of the "Building Your Critical Thinking Skills" apparatus that accompanies this reading in class: It discusses tone (p. 415), something that first-year students often have difficulty understanding. Practice in this area helps them to more quickly and ably discern the nuanced meanings of any essay they read in their courses.

Many of the readings in this section are likely to have strong appeal to today's students. In "One Term Says It All: 'Shut Up!'" (p. 417), Shelly Branch explores the new non-rude definition of "Shut up!" as it transmogrifies into the equivalent of "No kidding?! Are you serious?!" William Plasencia, in "Web Logs Get Personal" (p. 422), uses an extended definition to explain *blogging*, the practice of posting certain kinds of journals or diaries online, and then analyzes the growth of this phenomenon. In "Spinning" (p. 432), Gina Kolata uses an extended definition to explain a form of exercise that has recently grown in popularity.

Explain to students that an extended definition may depart from a standard, dictionary definition. It can also be used to correct popular misconceptions. Gloria Naylor's "The Meaning of a Word" (p. 426), for example, describes the pain she felt when she was called "nigger" as a child and compares that usage with the more contemporary, often positive tone of the word as used by and among black people. She theorizes that words become powerful by "consensus," analyzing how the connotations of the terms shift, depending upon the speaker and the context.

Geneva Lamberth, "Eating Disorders: Serious and Legitimate Illnesses," p. 407

In both her title and her text, student writer Geneva Lamberth defines eating disorders as "legitimate medical illnesses" (para. 1). She first defines the term, then the causes, then the three options for treating eating disorders. Since this is a topic of interest to many students, who may know someone who suffers from an eating disorder (or even suffer from one themselves), they may find it quite interesting to read or write about it in class but be reluctant to openly discuss it. As a more neutral way to address the issue, you may want to initiate a discussion of how media images of beauty contribute to these disorders.

Responding to "Students Write," p. 409

1. Answers may vary. Most students are likely to agree that examples of individuals suffering from eating disorders would have personalized the essay and made the importance of the topic stand out more clearly.

2. Because the different types of treatment are very complex, this section is the weakest part of Lamberth's essay. Terms such as *pharmacological, cognitive-behavioral,* and *psychodynamic* will be unfamiliar to most readers. At the very least, clear definitions of these and other terms used in this section are needed to make the material understandable.

3. Answers may vary. You may want to have students brainstorm aloud in class to develop a more compelling and interesting title for this essay.

4. Answers may vary.

Janice Castro, Dan Cook, and Christina Garcia, "Spanglish," p. 411

Media scholar Janice Castro, along with *Time* writers Dan Cook and Christina Garcia, define "Spanglish," a new blend of English and Spanish, illustrating the many ways that this language hybrid is entering mainstream U.S. culture. You might begin by taking a close look at this essay's organization, analyzing how it moves back and forth among definitions, generalizations, and examples.

Another fruitful way to approach "Spanglish" might be to ask students to describe at least three ways in which this new hybrid language is used, and then compare the essay with "Goin' Gangsta, Choosin' Cholita" (p. 230). Do the two essays provide evidence for the idea that U.S. culture is changing, especially for younger generations such as theirs? Within the context of your discussion about this essay, you might also invite students to form small groups and create a list of other foreign words and phrases that have been incorporated into the English language over their lifetime (for instance, *jihad*). How do immigration and culture influence and shape the English language?

Understanding the Reading, p. 413

1. The addition of Spanish words to the English language has caught on more than that of other languages from Asia or Europe because there are more Latin American immigrants now living in the United States and more Americans take Spanish in high school and college than any other language (para. 6).

2. An example from the reading of an English word that is easier to use than its Spanish equivalent is *income tax* (5). Using English words like this is a benefit to Spanish speakers in America because it saves time (9).

3. Advertisers have used Spanglish to tap into the buying power of Spanish-speaking Americans by "sprinkling" it into their ads. This tactic has created some embarrassing gaffes, such as telling airline passengers that they could fly "without clothes" (when the advertisers meant in "leather" seats) (10), when words are not translated properly or spelled accurately.

4. According to the authors, Latinos react to the misuse of Spanglish with amusement. They might express this in Spanglish as *no problema* (10).

Visualizing the Reading, p. 414

Possible answers include:

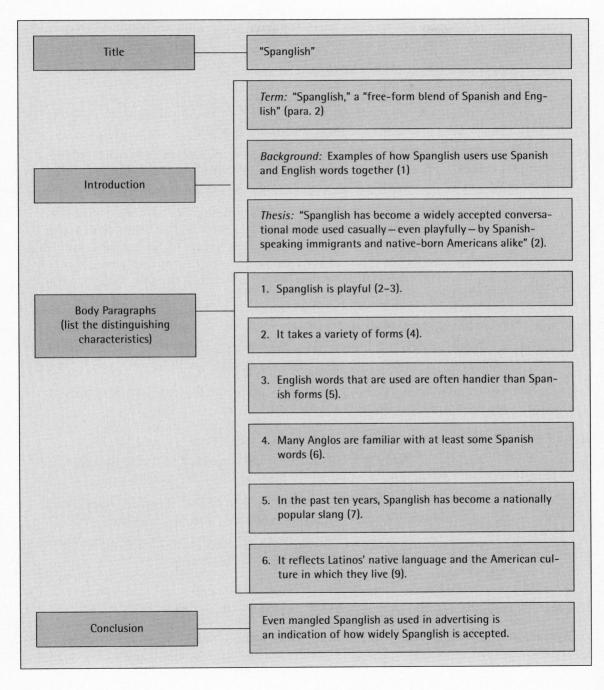

Title	"Spanglish"
Introduction	*Term:* "Spanglish," a "free-form blend of Spanish and English" (para. 2)
	Background: Examples of how Spanglish users use Spanish and English words together (1)
	Thesis: "Spanglish has become a widely accepted conversational mode used casually — even playfully — by Spanish-speaking immigrants and native-born Americans alike" (2).
Body Paragraphs (list the distinguishing characteristics)	1. Spanglish is playful (2–3).
	2. It takes a variety of forms (4).
	3. English words that are used are often handier than Spanish forms (5).
	4. Many Anglos are familiar with at least some Spanish words (6).
	5. In the past ten years, Spanglish has become a nationally popular slang (7).
	6. It reflects Latinos' native language and the American culture in which they live (9).
Conclusion	Even mangled Spanglish as used in advertising is an indication of how widely Spanglish is accepted.

Examining the Characteristics of Definition Essays, p. 414

1. The standard definition of *Spanglish* appears in paragraph 2. The authors identify the class to which the term belongs (a language) and the characteristics that distinguish it as "common linguistic currency wherever concentrations of Hispanic Americans are found" (2).

2. The main point the authors make about Spanglish is that it is here to stay and consequently worth reading about.

3. The authors expand the definition of Spanglish beyond the second paragraph by identifying the various forms it takes. Answers may vary.

4. Spanglish takes a variety of forms, such as a handy shorthand (5) or "a sort of code for Latinos" (9). These and other details contribute to the extended definition as a whole by illustrating why this language is growing and how it is used.

5. Patterns of development used by the authors include: cause and effect (that the popularity of Spanish is due to the "explosive increase" in the number of Latin American immigrants); classification (the different forms of Spanglish); and illustration (the many examples cited in the essay). These different patterns of development help to clarify the term for readers by illustrating the use and growth of this language hybrid.

Building Your Word Power, p. 415

1. *siéntate*: sit down; *quiero un*: I want a; *cerveza*: beer; *uno dos tres*: one two three; *parquean*: park; *carros*: cars; *ir al*: go to the; *almuerzo*: lunch; *bronco*: rough, coarse.

2. *Explosive* and *collided* as used in paragraph 7 indicate that the introduction of Spanish phrases was somewhat sudden, even jarring.

Building Your Critical Thinking Skills: Tone, p. 415

1. The overall tone of the essay is informative. This tone makes the reader feel that Spanglish is interesting and a worthwhile addition to U.S. culture.

2. The first and last paragraphs contribute to the tone of the essay by suggesting that Spanglish crosses geographical regions, classes, and types of media.

3. Answers may vary. Another kind of tone in the essay is casual — for instance, "Spanglish is as much a part of daily life as sunglasses" (para. 2).

Shelly Branch, "One Term Says It All: 'Shut Up!'" p. 417

Journalist Shelly Branch explores the new definition of "Shut up!" as it becomes a new equivalent of "Are you serious?!" As Branch defines this usage, "Shut up!" now expresses "amazement or disbelief" (para. 4). Branch illustrates the new usage through a series of citations, including the opinions of editors, linguists, and writers. This evidence indicates that through "linguistic . . . amelioration" (5) the phrase is losing its negative associations.

Students should find this essay quite interesting since it deals with a contemporary linguistic phenomenon. You might like to initiate a discussion of how the meanings of words have changed over time, and ask students to think of other words whose meanings have changed in their own lifetime. They might break into small groups to select a word and then trace its evolution for the class. You might also want to have students break into small groups to choose a word that has nuances or associations, depending upon context or intonation, such as *okay, dude, right,* or *sure.* Have them consider why it is different in various contexts—is it the intonation? the context? the speaker? Then have them write about the various meanings of the word, making first a generalization about the term and then providing supporting examples.

Understanding the Reading, p. 419

1. The new use of "Shut up!" is to express "disbelief, shock and joy" (para. 2). Some examples of its different use are a "chief of staff" who uses it with his colleagues (1), an Elantra ad (3), and a character in *The Princess Diaries* (12).

2. The writers for the Elantra ad decided to use "Shut up!" because the more they used it the funnier it seemed. They were initially concerned that it would offend older Hyundai dealers (in their fifties), but when the dealers saw the TV spot they found it very funny (8).

3. The author cites an episode of *Seinfeld* as an example of the use of "Shut up!" on television (13).

4. The history of the phrase "Shut up!" reaches back to sixteenth-century England, where it was figuratively used to mean withholding money or kindness (11). Branch cites the *Oxford English Dictionary* (11) as a source for the evolution of this phrase.

Visualizing the Reading, p. 419

Possible answers include:

Method of Development	Example
Process	Explains how to pronounce the phrase (para. 9–10).
Narration	Provides anecdote about the chief of staff who uses this phrase as an "exclamation point" with his colleagues (1).

Description	Describes of an episode of *Seinfeld* in which Jerry vividly describes how a man "splashed Gatorade on his head, got pneumonia, and dropped dead" (13).
Illustration	Cites other words that have undergone transformation, such as *nice* and *stupid* (5).
Comparison and contrast	Contrasts those who think the phrase is legitimate (for instance, the *New Oxford American Dictionary* editor [4]) with those who find it "rude" (Drew Barrymore [15]).

Examining the Characteristics of Definition Essays, p. 420

1. Branch does not use a standard thesis statement, instead relying on a series of sentences in paragraph 2 to explain both the definition ("People use it as much to express disbelief, shock and joy as to demand silence") and why it is worth reading about ("the term has made its way from schoolgirl chatter to adult repartee and into movies and advertising"). While this is not a formal thesis statement in the style that is expected from your students, Branch does clearly convey both the basic definition of the term and why this new meaning is of interest.

2. Branch's explanation of how to pronounce "Shut up!" (para. 9–10) is important to a full understanding of the current use of the term because how it is pronounced differentiates it from the "rude" meaning.

3. Some of the other ways that Branch defines the term are by giving examples of how people use it, such as in the Hyundai ad (3), and by listing phrases that it replaces, such as "Oh my God!"(2).

4. Answers may vary.

5. Students may find the essay's introduction to be vague because there is no context for how the phrase is used; it is not clear why exactly Hartnagel uses the phrase with his colleagues. Students also may find the conclusion to be vague because the author's choice to quote Drew Barrymore seems arbitrary and may not represent a strong "source" with readers. An editor or writer, or even an actor known for her or his precision with words, might have been a better source for those who "don't like the phrase."

Building Your Word Power, p. 420

1. "Schoolgirl chatter" suggests informal, excitable gossip, and "adult repartee" suggests witty retorts used in informal settings such as parties.

2. Parents are thanking author Meg Cabot "sarcastically" (para. 12) because her use of the phrase in *The Princess Diaries* has caused their children to see it incessantly and because to some ears, despite the new meaning, it still has a negative connotation.

Building Your Critical Thinking Skills: Inferences, p. 420

1. One can infer that Hartnagel's relationship with the California assemblyman he works for is one of younger employee to older boss (para.1). Hartnagel probably refrains from saying "Shut up!" when the assemblyman is around because members of older generations don't use it and would consider it too informal and offensive if they misunderstood it.

2. More than two hundred actresses had to be auditioned for the Elantra spot because they did not understand how to enunciate the phrase correctly so that it was humorous (9).

William Plasencia, "Web Logs Get Personal," p. 422

Plasencia describes blogging, the growing practice of posting the equivalent of journals or diaries online. In his extended definition he provides examples of how people use blogs, from purely personal expression to political discussion, and also praises blogging's potential to finally realize the dream that the Internet would equalize access to information and be free.

First-year students may know quite a bit about blogs and be eager to discuss why people would want to post their personal feelings on the Internet where "anyone" could read them. You might ask them to evaluate what an unwelcome "anyone" might mean, including someone's former friend, girlfriend or boyfriend, parents, and so on. You might initiate a discussion of the difference between this kind of private but public diary and its relationship to other cultural phenomena such as reality TV. If you plan on having students write research papers at some point in the term, you might also assign them to begin by reading and reporting on blogs related to subjects that interest them. They might, for example, present a brief oral presentation on the current material they were able to find about their potential topic.

Understanding the Reading, p. 423

1. According to Plasencia, people create and maintain Web logs in order to express themselves and to receive "responses" from others (para. 2) "without the fear of criticism" (6); to have "a voice" (5); and to find community (6). All kinds of people read them, including homemakers, business executives, and artists (3).

2. Two ways that people use Web logs are: to "vent" (2), and to update "friends and family" (4).

3. The computer requirements necessary to have a Web log are: to use a "hosted service" that provides access to one's Web log, or to set up one's own Web site through a free software program, such as MovableType (3).

4. According to the reading, blogs may allow the Internet to become the "great equalizing medium" it was intended to be (5).

Visualizing the Reading, p. 423

Possible answers include:

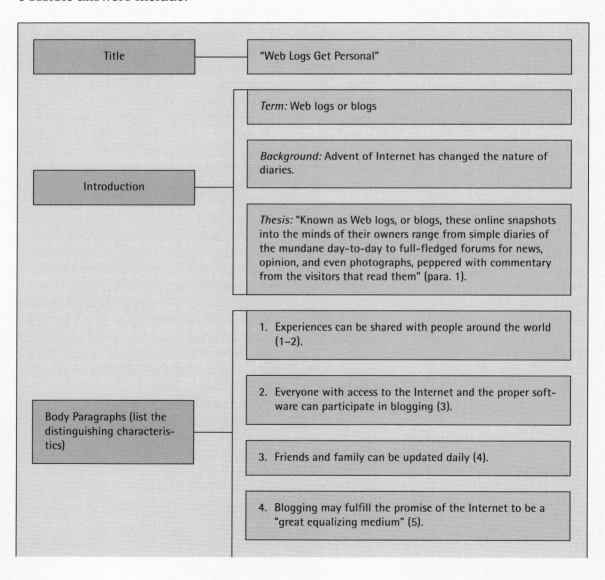

Title	"Web Logs Get Personal"

Introduction	*Term:* Web logs or blogs
	Background: Advent of Internet has changed the nature of diaries.
	Thesis: "Known as Web logs, or blogs, these online snapshots into the minds of their owners range from simple diaries of the mundane day-to-day to full-fledged forums for news, opinion, and even photographs, peppered with commentary from the visitors that read them" (para. 1).

Body Paragraphs (list the distinguishing characteristics)	1. Experiences can be shared with people around the world (1–2).
	2. Everyone with access to the Internet and the proper software can participate in blogging (3).
	3. Friends and family can be updated daily (4).
	4. Blogging may fulfill the promise of the Internet to be a "great equalizing medium" (5).

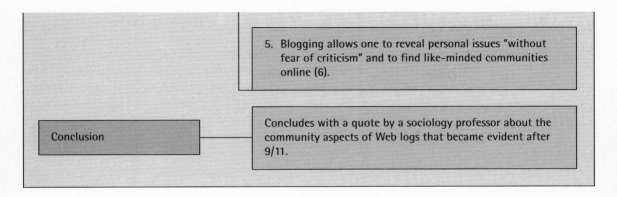

5. Blogging allows one to reveal personal issues "without fear of criticism" and to find like-minded communities online (6).

Conclusion — Concludes with a quote by a sociology professor about the community aspects of Web logs that became evident after 9/11.

Examining the Characteristics of Definition Essays, p. 423

1. See the thesis in the Visualizing the Reading activity above. The author's thesis does not explicitly suggest the importance or usefulness of Web logs. Plasencia instead chooses to address these issues over the course of his essay through the distinguishing characteristics of the term.

2. The author uses a least-to-most-important organizational framework to present the distinguishing characteristics of the term, from the use of the blog for personal expression to its use for political discussion and community building. Answers may vary.

3. Because so much of Plasencia's essay relies on outside sources, it is very important that details about his sources are included.

4. Other patterns of development used by the author include: description ("photographs, peppered with commentary from the visitors that read them" [para. 1]); narration ("Lorena Haldeman . . . updates her Web log every day" [4]); and cause and effect (the effects on blogging after 9/11 [7–8]). These different modes contribute to the essay by clarifying the author's thesis and purpose in writing.

5. The author ends with a reference to 9/11 because the events triggered important community-building via Web logs.

Building Your Word Power, p. 424

1. *Blog* means Web log; *blogging* means the act of writing and posting to a blog; and a *blogger* is someone who writes his or her own blog.

2. *Peppered* means sprinkled here and there.

Building Your Critical Thinking Skills: Evaluating Sources, 424

Students may enjoy the challenge of forming two panels to debate the usefulness and legitimacy of Plasencia's supporting evidence and sources.

Gloria Naylor, "The Meanings of a Word," p. 426

Novelist Gloria Naylor, well known for her novel *The Women of Brewster Place* (1982), here discusses and defines the word *nigger* as she experienced it growing up among her relatives. She contrasts that use of the word with the first time she heard it as an insult from a white boy. This essay is an excellent one to use if you have a mixed-race class. You might talk about the history of insults that have been used against nearly every ethnic group in America at one time or another. You might assign students to classify or divide one of the terms they have heard, much the way Naylor has done with this insult. You might also like to have a group discussion of how words like *queer* or *cripple* can be transformed by a group who uses the term positively. This might also be a good time to initiate a discussion of the meaning of the term *American*, without qualifiers like *black* or *Native*.

Understanding the Reading, p. 428

1. The author thinks written language is "inferior" to the spoken word because words gain power through the senses of sight, sound, smell, and touch.

2. The little boy was prompted to use the word *nigger* because Naylor said something to him about his math grade being lower than hers. While the young Naylor didn't know what the word meant, she was humiliated by its use because she sensed that it was an insult (para. 3).

3. During the author's childhood, weekends were spent in Harlem with a close-knit network of relatives (4).

4. According to Naylor, black people use the word *nigger* to "signify the varied and complex human beings they [know] themselves to be," whereas white people understand it solely to mean degradation or worthlessness (14).

Visualizing the Reading, p. 429

Possible answers include:

Method of Development	Example
Narration	Naylor tells the story of her experience in third grade (para. 3).
Description	Naylor describes the checkers games, babies crying, and grownups gossiping in her grandparents' house in Harlem (4–5).
Illustration	Naylor gives an example of how the word *girl* is pronounced to express praise (11).

| Cause and effect | Naylor explains that the way the white boy said the word *nigger* caused her to recognize it as an insult and to ask her mother what it meant (3). |
| Classification | Naylor classifies the two meanings of the word *nigger* in the black community (6–10). |

Examining the Characteristics of Definition Essays, p. 429

1. The author states her thesis at the end of paragraph 2: "Words themselves are innocuous; it is the consensus that gives them true power." Naylor does not include a definition of the term itself in her thesis; however, the thesis relates to the extended definition that follows because the essay explains how the term *nigger* derives negative power from white racist consensus and is rendered impotent through black consensus.

2. Some of the distinguishing characteristics that Naylor uses to explain her extended definition are: the context and tone of how the word is used, and how the sex and number of the person(s) it is applied to influence the word's meaning. So, for example, "that nigger pulled in $6,000 of overtime" (para. 8) is positive because it expresses praise and applies to a single individual male. Naylor includes the detailed descriptions of her own family gatherings to let readers know about the atmosphere in which she first heard this word.

3. Naylor also includes a definition of the term *girl* because it is used similarly to *nigger* when applied to an individual woman (11).

4. Naylor uses her extended definition to dispel the idea that *nigger* can never have a positive connotation. She defines how black people can use the word for praise in the singular (6) or for disapproval in the plural (10), signifying the "varied and complex human beings" that the members of the black community know themselves to be (14).

5. Answers may vary. The last sentence is deeply moving because it acknowledges the racism that all African Americans in America must endure.

Building Your Word Power, p. 429

1. The allusion to the "chicken and egg" dispute refers to the question of whether language shapes human perception of the world or whether everyone sees the world exactly the same way, regardless of language—a question that thus far has not been answerable.

2. The connotation of *bad* as used by Naylor in paragraph 3 is naughty or offensive. The connotation of *hear* (15) in this context is that until that moment Naylor had not really recognized the word as an insult.

Building Your Critical Thinking Skills: Comparison and Contrast, p. 430

1. The author contrasts written language unfavorably with spoken language because the former cannot capture the "richness" and sensuality of life (para. 1).

2. The author's family and friends compared and contrasted hardworking black people with "trifling niggers" (10) who refused to look for work and lacked "self-respect."

3. The black use of *nigger* can mean either praise or disapproval, whereas the white use is only insulting. The black use is characterized by either pride or disappointment, and the white use by hatred.

Gina Kolata, "Spinning," p. 432

New York Times science writer Gina Kolata gives an extended definition of the sport of "spinning," a form of group aerobic exercise using special stationary bicycles. Kolata uses a number of rhetorical modes, including narration, cause and effect, division and classification, and comparison and contrast, to illustrate how she and her husband became intrigued by and eventually addicted to spinning. Students might like to try using a number of techniques to describe their own favorite hobby, beginning with definition. Sharing informative, personal essays with the class may foster a sense of understanding and camaraderie among the students.

Understanding the Reading, p. 436

1. The author's husband, Bill, prefers road biking to other kinds of exercise (para. 3).

2. Bill attributes his annual depression to his inability to ride outdoors when it gets dark too early or the weather gets too cold and icy (3).

3. Kolata describes the bicycles that are used for Spinning as set in metal frames, with only one flywheel, with adjustable seats and a resistance knob (6). A bike should fit so that the seat is high enough for the rider to extend her or his leg with a foot on the pedal and the handlebars only one or two inches above or below the seat. When extended, arms should not be locked at the elbows (7).

4. One increases or decreases the resistance on a Spinning bike in order to get a less strenuous or harder workout.

Visualizing the Reading, p. 436

Answers may vary. While some of the riders in the photo appear to be working very hard, others look relaxed, as if they are listening to the instructor, like the people described in paragraph 10 who just pedal along at "a low resistance."

Examining the Characteristics of Definition Essays, p. 437

1. Answers may vary. One possible thesis is that this sport allows people to get an excellent workout but they have to put the effort into challenging and exerting themselves to test their limits.

2. The distinguishing characteristics of Spinning are that it is conducted indoors, on stationary bikes; workouts are done to music with an instructor in a darkened room; and friction created by resistance knobs maximizes or minimizes the workout. Answers may vary.

3. Kolata uses an extended definition to explain heart-rate monitors (para. 14). Answers may vary.

4. Other patterns of development include: narration ("the cold evening in November of 2000 when I first stepped into a Spinning room" [1]); cause and effect (how effort increases heart rate [17]); and description ("in a darkened room, on stationary bikes that look remotely like road bikes" [4]). The author distinguishes Spinning from exercising on stationary bikes like LifeCycles by first describing how boring they are and how they "do not look or feel like a real road bike" (3). She then explains how, in a Spinning class, participants "do more than simply sit back and pedal their bikes" (4).

Building Your Word Power, p. 437

1. The word *funk* as used in paragraph 3 means depression. Words like *downcast*, *discouraged*, *glum*, and *grey moods* provide clues to its meaning.

2. Answers may vary.

Building Your Critical Thinking Skills: Author's Purpose, p. 437

1. Kolata's book title, *Ultimate Fitness: The Quest for Truth about Exercise and Health*, suggests that the author's purpose in writing may be to dispel misinformation about exercise and health. The use of the word *quest* implies that the book is likely to be personal in nature.

2. Answers may vary.

Chapter 12 Cause and Effect: Using Reasons and Results to Explain, p. 439

Because *cause and effect* (also known as causal analysis) is fairly straightforward and logical to explain, you should be able to cover the material with ease. It is especially helpful to explain how cause and effect works by reviewing the graphic organizers included in this chapter. Be sure to caution students to clearly identify the difference between causes (reasons that something happens) and effects (results of the things that happen) in order to keep the chain of events clear. Note too that the cause and effect essay is usually informative or persuasive (rather than expressive). The three types of cause and effect essays are outlined in the chapter in both print and visual formats (through graphic organizers): causes and effects, a chain of causes and effects, and multiple causes and effects.

You will likely find it useful to begin discussion by analyzing the annotated essay "How Nature Heals Us" by Deb Aronson (p. 440). It uses a "most to least" order that starts with familiar and obvious kinds of contact with nature and moves toward less obvious kinds of contact. Aronson seeks to inform readers about the healing effects of nature and to dispel assumptions about what relieves stress. The graphic organizers on pages 446–448 will be useful tools in showing exactly how a cause and effect essay is constructed. Nathan Nguyen's "Gambling on Our Future" (p. 456), is clearly marked and highlighted to guide students through his argument. He speculates that a chain of events has led to an increase in problem gambling, citing statistics and providing expert opinions to support his views.

The remaining essays in this chapter offer a wide range of types, from personal pieces to journalistic accounts to research writing. You might want to initiate a discussion of Clive Thompson's "The Honesty Virus" (p. 460) by exploring its thematic relationship to "Web Logs Get Personal" in Chapter 11 (p. 422). In his essay, Thompson discusses how online communication differs from oral communication in that people are less likely to lie online than in person. "When the Plug Is Pulled on the Digital Age, the Basics Black Out" (p. 466) offers more insight into the effects of technology in modern life as the authors explore the effects of the massive power outage that much of the northeastern United States experienced in August 2003. Ruth Russell's deeply moving essay, "The Wounds That Can't Be Stitched Up" (p. 472), about the effects of a drunk driving accident that severely injured Russell's family members, illustrates how an essay can be both persuasive and personal. Another personal essay included here is "Changing My Name after Sixty Years" by Tom Rosenberg (p. 477): The author explores the journey he took to change his name, explaining both the causes behind his decision to change his name legally and the effects of his decision on his friends and family. The final reading in the chapter, "The Clan of One-Breasted Women" by Terry Tempest Williams (p. 482), offers an account that is both personal and scientific, as it traces the long-lasting effects of the atomic bomb testing that was conducted in the author's home state of Utah in the 1950s.

Nathan Nguyen, "Gambling on Our Future," p. 456

Nathan Nguyen's research paper theorizes that a series of events has led to an increase in problem and addictive gambling in the United States. This paper on a current social problem provides an excellent model to explain not only cause and effect but also the use of research to support ideas with academic opinions and impressive statistics.

Responding to "Students Write," p. 458

1. Answers may vary.

2. Answers may vary. Alternative ways to introduce the topic might involve including a question that cites a statistic about gambling's increase over the past few years or an anecdote illustrating the effects of addiction on someone of interest.

3. Answers may vary.

4. Nguyen might have ended by offering a story about a program that is helping people to stop gambling or by offering some solutions to the problem.

Clive Thompson, "The Honesty Virus," p. 460

Writer Clive Thompson explores the recent claim by a Cornell University professor that people lie less frequently online than in person. Thompson uses a series of examples to contend that rather than being deceptive online because of a sense of anonymity, as predicted in the early days of the Internet, people are actually more forthcoming, expressive, and truthful online. You can use this reading to start a class discussion about why people might feel more comfortable sharing their feelings and being honest with total strangers than with those they meet face to face. What social and psychological factors, for example, might lead to such behavior?

Understanding the Reading, p. 463

1. The results of Jeffrey Hancock's study of his students' online behavior indicated that his students were more honest online than in person or on the phone (para. 1).

2. According to Thompson, the "digital age is tough on its liars" because email records are never erased and can be brought back to "haunt" liars (5).

3. Thompson speculates that what causes people to be honest when they are online is that they fear they might be caught (4) or that they are "disinhibited" (9).

4. Online communication differs from offline communication in that it does not entail "face-to-face" contact (9), it is recorded in email memory (6), and it can be anonymous and geographically distant (9). People communicate differently on the Internet because nothing is forgotten (6) and they feel geographically distant and almost invisible (9).

Visualizing the Reading, p. 463

Possible answers include:

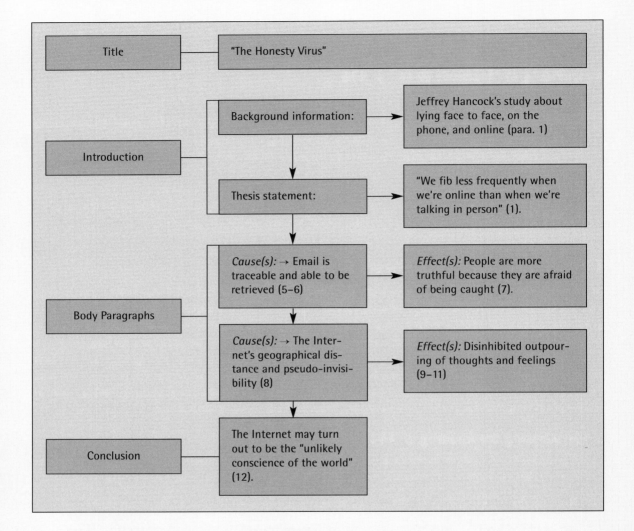

Examining the Characteristics of Cause and Effect Essays, p. 464

1. The author's purpose in writing is both informative and persuasive. He gives background information about early expectations that the Internet would allow for rampant deception and then argues (using evidence gathered by scholars and others) that anonymity and distance are causing the opposite of what was expected.

2. Thompson's thesis statement is expressed through the statements: "We fib less frequently when we're online than when we're talking in person" (para. 1) and that we are more truthful online because "We're worried about being busted" (para. 4).

3. The types of evidence the author uses to support his thesis are: academic studies (1); examples ("Even Microsoft was tripped up by old e-mail messages" [5]); and quotations from experts ("50 percent of those who write in via e-mail express suicidal feelings, compared with only 20 percent of those who call in" [9]).

4. The popular assumption about the Internet that Thompson is seeking to dispel is that it encourages lying. Depending on students' personal experiences online, they may or may not find Thompson's case effective.

5. Other patterns of development used by Thompson include: definition (explanation of *disinhibited* [9]); narration ("Remember when George W. Bush first met Vladimir Putin . . .? [11]); and illustration (examples of how technology records and saves information [6]).

Building Your Word Power, p. 464

1. The prefix *pseudo* means false. By *pseudo-invisibility* as used in paragraph 8, the author means that they people online are seemingly invisible in the sense that no one can see them face to face but they are in fact traceable and able to be found.

2. Three synonyms for *lying* in the essay are "fib[bing]" (para. 1), "mishandled the truth" (1), and "prevarications" (11).

Building Your Critical Thinking Skills: Tone, p. 464

1. Answers may vary, but some words or phrases that contribute to the overall tone of the essay are "fib" (para. 1), "scary zone" (3), "busted" (4), "unless you're talking to Linda Tripp" (4), "although he told me that on the phone, so who knows?" (5), "gotcha politics" (6), and "punk" (7). The essay's tone might be described as casual and slangy.

2. Answers may vary.

3. The author's tone toward conservative politicians is irreverent and skeptical. It may reveal that his political opinions are fairly progressive.

Susan Warren and Melanie Trottman, "When the Plug Is Pulled on the Digital Age, the Basics Black Out," p. 466

Journalists Susan Warren and Melanie Trottman describe the effects of the August 2003 massive power outage on much of the northeastern United States. The effect of the blackout, which many of your students may recall or personally experienced, was great because of our culture's dependency on electricity to run everything from cash registers to hotel card keys. Such dependency has deepened over the past ten years, which the authors are careful to point out, suggesting that events like this one must not be forgotten. Students may like to write about and discuss the increasing reliance on technology that they have observed in their own lifetimes.

Understanding the Reading, p. 469

1. This power outage differed from the widespread outages of the past because the Electronic Age had made people more reliant on electricity (para. 2).

2. Some of the more difficult aspects of the blackout for the shopkeepers were that electronic cash registers (2), electric hair trimmers (11), and credit cards (16) didn't work.

3. Cell phones worked but couldn't be recharged, and many networks were jammed (12). Cordless phones also didn't work, leaving the only working phones those that were plugged directly into a wall (18).

4. In addition to candles, employees at one hotel used glow-sticks to guide people down the halls (14).

Visualizing the Reading, p. 469

Possible answers include:

Cause →	Effects Become Causes →	Effects
Northeast Blackout of 2003	1. Company cash registers wouldn't work.	1. Employees had to make do with paper and pencils.
	2. Electronic keycards and locks wouldn't work (para. 2).	2. Hotel staff had to discharge guests or use master keys to unlock hotel rooms
	3. Stoves with an electric ignition didn't work (10).	3. People had to eat cold food.
	4. Electric hair trimmers didn't work (11).	4. People had to leave the barbershop with hair half trimmed.
	5. Cell phones worked but couldn't be recharged (12).	5. People couldn't make phone calls or had to find a phone plugged into the wall.
	6. Cordless phones didn't work (12, 18).	6. People drove in cars to recharge phones, but then needed gas and couldn't get it because gas pumps weren't working.

Examining the Characteristics of Cause and Effect Essays, p. 469

1. The authors' purpose in writing is not overtly stated, but given the number of examples, one can assume that their purpose is to warn readers about Americans' overreliance on electricity.

2. The essay's thesis appears as a series of sentences in paragraph 1: "For the better part of a decade, the digital dream has been a wireless, cashless, instantly connected society. But . . . [w]hen you're unplugged, even very simple tasks bec[o]me impossible."

3. To explain the causes and effects of the blackout, the authors use vivid examples of ordinary people trying to make do without electricity. The examples support the thesis by illustrating how helpless people were rendered by the loss of electricity.

4. The other pattern of development is narration. This technique contributes to the essay by making the story of the effects of the blackout vivid and immediate.

5. Answers may vary. Students might say that a final sentence such as "Next time, we'll be prepared" would make the ending feel more conclusive.

Building Your Word Power, p. 469

1. The phrase "digital dream" means a "wireless, cashless, instantly connected society" (para. 1).

2. The phrase "plain-Jane model" means a basic, old-fashioned, plug-into-the-wall phone (18).

Building Your Critical Thinking Skills: Identifying Assumptions, p. 470

1. The *Wall Street Journal* targets the business community, so the authors might have assumed that their readers would be most interested in the potential financial losses that businesses can experience as a result of widespread electrical outages.

2. Examples targeted toward business people include: companies with electronic cash registers (para 2); electronic keys and lights in hotels (2, 14); electronic tools used extensively in restaurants (3); electronic scales in grocery stores (7); and electric trimmers in hair salons (11).

3. Students might enjoy having a discussion of the "digital dream" of a wireless and connected society and what it means in terms of the environment. Have them break into groups first to come up with three points each.

Ruth Russell,"The Wounds That Can't Be Stitched Up," p. 472

Ruth Russell narrates the story of the drunk driver who hit her family's car when she was young and then spent very little time in jail. Years later, she saw him again driving drunk and was motivated to write this story. She wonders why he wasn't blamed by local people and tells the reader how the town's attitude in excusing the drunk driver and "blaming the victim" (her family who didn't have seat belts on) affected her life. Students may like to analyze the underlying feelings that the writer does not address directly. Do they agree, for example, that she has made a strong case by presenting her family as further victimized by their town?

Understanding the Reading, p. 474

1. Her mother's car was hit head-on by a drunk driver who was in the wrong lane with no headlights on (para. 7). Her mother lost several teeth and her face was severely cut up, her sister almost died with a "fractured skull" requiring surgery that left a permanent scar (6), and her youngest brother was traumatized with a black eye.

2. The man who hit the author's family was jailed for the weekend and lost his license for thirty days (10). The local people in Russell's town like the drunk driver and excused his behavior because he is a "war hero" who had a hard family life (12).

3. The man who hit Russell's family ended up living in her apartment building (13). Russell meets him when he is drunkenly speeding past and then reversing into the apartment building's parking lot (14).

4. The title refers figuratively to the author's memories, which cannot be erased.

Visualizing the Reading, p. 474

Possible answers include:

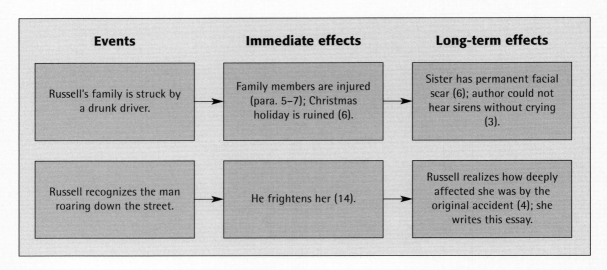

Events	Immediate effects	Long-term effects
Russell's family is struck by a drunk driver.	Family members are injured (para. 5–7); Christmas holiday is ruined (6).	Sister has permanent facial scar (6); author could not hear sirens without crying (3).
Russell recognizes the man roaring down the street.	He frightens her (14).	Russell realizes how deeply affected she was by the original accident (4); she writes this essay.

Examining the Characteristics of Cause and Effect Essays, p. 474

1. The author's thesis appears in paragraph 4: "Twenty-three years have passed, but only recently have I realized how deeply affected I was by events caused by a drunk driver so long ago." Her essay focuses on effects such as physical scarring and long-term fears.

2. Russell organizes her essay according to chronology, from the original devastating accident to the time she sees the drunk driver years later.

3. To fully explain the effects of the accident, the author uses details such as the effect of the sirens on her for years afterwards (para. 3) and her sister's scars (6).

4. The pattern of development used to organize the events in this essay is narration. This pattern contributes tension to the essay and illustrates how the accident eroded the author's sense of safety in the world.

Building Your Word Power, p. 475

1. The "power" that the author refers to in paragraph 3 is the force of the memory that caused her to feel sorrow for years afterwards.

Building Your Critical Thinking Skills: Author's Purpose, p. 475

1. Although twenty-three years have passed since the accident, the author seems to still be bothered by the fact that the drunk's behavior was excused in the community because he was a well-liked war hero (para. 12), and that he was not "accused" the way her family were for not wearing seat belts (11). The trigger for writing is the event when she runs into him years later, after he swerves drunkenly into her apartment parking lot.

2. The transition, "Sometimes when I tell this story" (11), indicates that the author's purpose in writing is to explore why the drunk driver was forgiven by locals. In the same paragraph she defends her family, perhaps because she feels that they have been blamed more (for not wearing seat belts) than the drunk driver was for hitting them.

3. Russell's treatment of the drunk driver suggests that she still doesn't think he has paid for his crime. She seems justifiably incredulous that he is still allowed to drive.

Tom Rosenberg, "Changing My Name after Sixty Years," p. 477

Tom Rosenberg speculates about the reasons his family Anglicized their name after leaving Germany and its effect upon his life, trying to deny or hide his Jewishness. He also explores his decision years later to take back his Jewish surname out of pride and in response to political repression in the wake of 9/11. Students might find it useful to first freewrite about what it would mean to have to hide the origins of one's name out of fear. They could then form small groups to discuss how Americans of various ethnic groups have sought to Anglicize their names and what that decision means in terms of America's ideal of the melting pot.

Understanding the Reading, p. 479

1. The author's parents may have been motivated to change their name by "fear, a desire to assimilate or a combination of both" (para. 2). Other immigrants' names were often changed by "an immigration bureaucrat" upon arrival at Ellis Island (2).

2. The author has been associated with "Theta Chi" (5), a Christian fraternity, and has attended a Unitarian church and a Jewish temple (7). The religious affiliations contributed to the way he raised his children by allowing him to express "tolerance" (7) and to acknowledge his Jewish background to a greater extent than he had in the past.

3. The author decided to change his name because he felt that he was still denying his background and he wanted to express "pride" in his Jewishness (15).

4. The rabbi proposed that the author take a Hebrew first name as well (10). The author was initially shocked because he thought it would mean becoming more religious (11), but he now sees it as a way to express "pride" (15).

Visualizing the Reading, p. 479

Possible answers include:

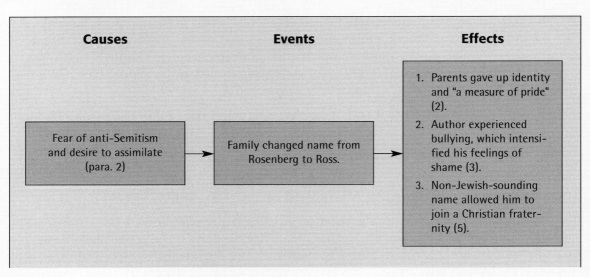

Causes	Events	Effects
Fear of anti-Semitism and desire to assimilate (para. 2)	Family changed name from Rosenberg to Ross.	1. Parents gave up identity and "a measure of pride" (2). 2. Author experienced bullying, which intensified his feelings of shame (3). 3. Non-Jewish-sounding name allowed him to join a Christian fraternity (5).

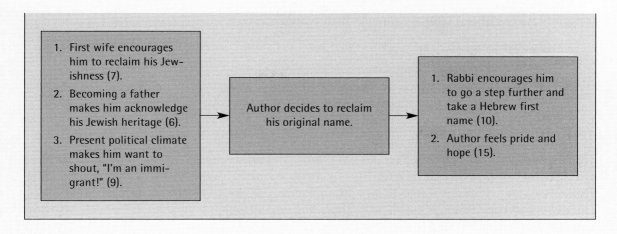

Examining the Characteristics of Cause and Effect Essays, p. 479

1. Rosenberg's essay is expressive, informative, and persuasive. He wants to express his "shame" and denial (para. 4), to inform people about the history and effects of anti-Semitism (1), and to persuade people that it is best to embrace one's heritage (15).

2. His implied thesis is that it is best to embrace one's heritage rather than hide it or try to deny it.

3. The inclusion of different causes and effects relates to Rosenberg's thesis and purpose in writing by indicating the serious reasons behind his decision to change his name. The author includes personal details about his marriages and religious practices because having a Christian wife in his first marriage was a positive experience that helped him to reconnect with his Jewish heritage. Having children made him reflect upon how damaging his parents' hiding was and inspired him to embrace Jewish culture and spirituality.

4. Answers may vary.

5. Rosenberg uses narrative dialogue for his conclusion. Answers may vary.

Building Your Word Power, p. 480

1. The connotation of the word *baggage* as used in paragraph 1 is guilt.

2. The expression "continued to dog me" as used in paragraph 10 means that the author's memories continued to bother him.

Building Your Critical Thinking Skills: Inferences, p. 480

_____ 1. Rosenberg joined a predominately Christian fraternity because Jewish fraternities would not accept him.

___✓___ 2. Rosenberg would approve if his children wanted to change their names.

___✓___ 3. Rosenberg's relationship with his first wife contributed to his decision to change his name.

___✓___ 4. Rosenberg is an active member of his temple.

Terry Tempest Williams, "The Clan of One-Breasted Women," p. 482

In this personal essay Terry Tempest Williams describes her childhood in Utah, seeing generations of women in her family die from or have surgery for breast cancer. She writes this essay in response to her uncovering the possible cause, nuclear testing in the desert in the 1950s, which radicalizes her and drives her to develop a new attitude toward authority of all kinds. The issues in this essay about personal authority and challenging unjust authority are central ones for college students. The essay should provide interesting discussion combined with freewrites and personal essays about your students' own experiences with issues that galvanized them to action.

Understanding the Reading, p. 488

1. The recurring dream cited by Williams at the start of the essay is of a flash of light in the sky. Her father tells her that it was a nuclear test that she actually watched as a young girl.

2. According to Williams, the cancer in her family was caused by exposure to the fallout from nuclear testing.

3. The factors that made it easy for the government to conduct nuclear tests in Utah in the 1950s and 1960s were a conservative political climate in which opposition to nuclear testing was unacceptable and an attitude that "[p]ublic health was secondary to national security" (para. 20–21). The government responded to the rise in cancer rates years later by denying that there was any "basis" to believe there was a cause and effect relationship between the two (22).

4. The dream at the end of the essay is of powerful women joining together to protest the violation of the earth (42). In real life, Tempest Williams and other protesters trespass on military property to protest the Nevada test site (49).

Visualizing the Reading, p. 488

Answers may vary. Encourage students to consider the "visible" effects of the nuclear fallout shown here with the more "invisible" effects of military tactics, which indicate a similar attitude toward civilians. Just as policymakers decided to drop the atomic bomb on innocent civilians in Hiroshima, so too does the U.S. government ignore and deny responsibility for harming innocent civilians during the nuclear bomb tests of the 1950s.

Examining the Characteristics of Cause and Effect Essays, p. 489

1. The author makes her main point toward the middle of the essay in paragraph 37: "Tolerating blind obedience in the name of patriotism or religion ultimately takes our lives." Her purpose in writing is to emphasize that it is important to challenge authority when that authority is unjust.

2. The causes and effects discussed in Williams's essay are nuclear fallout and cancer. Williams suggests that the nuclear testing caused breast cancer in her family but acknowledges that she can't prove it (35). The fact that the court case *Irene Allen v. The United States of America* was initially won (though later overturned) suggests that there is ample evidence to suggest a direct connection but that it may fall short of a direct causal relationship.

3. Williams's use of descriptive language and sensory details provides vivid images of the landscape she grew up in, the nuclear test she witnessed as a girl, and the effects of cancer in her family. Examples from the essay include: "the sandstoned landscape, bare-boned and beautiful" (para. 12); "this golden-stemmed cloud, the mushroom" (16); "as they vomited green-black bile" (32).

4. Other patterns of development include: description ("the way she held herself in a purple velvet robe" [9]); narration ("They were taken to a white, square building on the other side of Mercury" [46]); and illustration ("Mrs. Allen's case was the first on an alphabetical list of twenty-four cases" [23]). These patterns enhance the causal analysis by showing how the author's individual family experience was also part of a larger historical event.

5. Williams's conclusion reinforces her main assertion through the example of how she and women like her decided to no longer tolerate "blind obedience" and instead challenged the government. Answers may vary.

Building Your Word Power, p. 489

1. Doublespeak such as "low-use segments of the population" (para. 20) and "virtually uninhabited desert terrain" (38) mean that although people reside in that area, the government considers them insignificant.

2. The meaning of the metaphor "becoming a midwife to the rebirth of their souls" (32) means that she helped them to die.

Building Your Critical Thinking Skills: Facts and Opinions, p. 489

Facts (F) or Opinions (O).

___F___ 1. "Most statistics tell us breast cancer is genetic." (para. 4)

___O___ 2. ". . .living in Utah may be the greatest hazard of all." (4)

   F   3. "Within a few minutes, a light ash was raining on the car." (16)

   F   4. "Irene Allen lived in Hurricane, Utah." (24)

   O   5. "Tolerating blind obedience in the name of patriotism or religion ulti-mately takes our lives." (37)

   F   6. " Ours was an act of civil disobedience." (52)

Reacting to the Reading: Discussion and Journal Writing, p. 490

2. The notion of blind obedience put forth by Williams is likely to generate interesting class discussion. Have students form two panels, pro and con, and then have them present their material to the class as a whole to stimulate discussion and questions.

Chapter 13 Argumentation: Supporting a Claim, p. 491

Many college students are eager to enter into political and social arenas, to vote and debate issues and have a voice in their broader community. Learning how to write and think critically and to formulate arguments is critical to that transition. As shown here, *argument* has three basic parts: an issue, a claim, and support. This chapter clearly defines each aspect of argumentation, and students should quickly grasp the basic stance required for it. At some point in their papers, students should also acknowledge and refute opposing viewpoints. The list of Guidelines for Refuting Evidence (pp. 505–506) will assist students in acknowledging and refuting their opposition in a step-by-step fashion. You will note that the graphic organizer for argumentation is more flexible than those for other modes because it does not designate the order in which an argument is presented and it leaves space to begin with a claim or evidence or even opposing views. Because the form of an argument can be so variable—drawing as well on other modes of development—you will need to stress the importance of the thesis and clearly supported claims.

   A number of contemporary controversial issues are covered in this chapter. Wilbert Rideau, in the annotated essay "Why Prisons Don't Work" (p. 493), makes the claim that prisons don't make society safe, using induction to dismiss the various arguments in their favor. Studying Rideau's essay in conjunction with the annotated student essay, "Ethnic Definitions Hinder Society's Enlightenment" by Rudy De La Torre (p. 511) will show students visually how successful arguments are structured. Euthanasia is movingly discussed in Carol Bernstein Ferry's "A Good Death" (p. 515), a letter by the author in support of her own right to a "painless death" with emotional appeals about the pain that her prolonged suffering would cause her family. Frank DeFord's "Athletics 101: A Change in Eligibility Rules Is Long Overdue" (p. 520) deals with the amateur rules governing eligibility to play college and professional sports. This topic is likely to be of interest to many students, particularly at institutions where sports play a large role in campus culture. Martin Luther King Jr.'s "I Have a Dream" (p. 524) offers students a chance to analyze a classic speech, breaking it down to appreciate how King effectively uses language and argument to argue for civil rights.

This chapter also provides pairs of arguments for and against organ donation, with Bruce Gottlieb's "How Much Is That Kidney in the Window?" (p. 531) in favor and Gilbert Meilaender's "'Strip-Mining' the Dead" (p. 538) against; violent video games, with Dave Grossman and Gloria DeGaetano's "It's Important to Feel Something When You Kill" (p. 545) against and Gerard Jones's "Violent Media Is Good for Kids" (p. 554) in favor; and the Patriot Act, with Zara Gelsey's "Who's Reading over Your Shoulder?" (p. 560) against the library surveillance provision and Ramesh Ponnuru's "Fears about the Patriot Act Are Misguided" (p. 566) in favor. These pairs of essays will provide students with an opportunity to use what they have learned about synthesizing and evaluating arguments.

Rudy De La Torre, "Ethnic Definitions Hinder Society's Enlightenment," p. 511

Student Rudy De La Torre's essay questions why people need to ask about a person of color's ethnicity when they first meet that person. De la Torre speculates what would happen if someone said, "What difference would it make?" He argues that people should be evaluated on the basis of their actions, by what they have contributed to society rather than by their ethnic heritage. This essay may lead students into a discussion of the meaning of ethnicity in America.

Responding to "Students Write," p. 512

1. Have your students brainstorm a list of title ideas and then vote on which one best conveys Torre's thesis in a catchy and interesting way.

2. Even though Torre's historical responses to "What are you?" provide food for thought, depending on one's understanding of world history they may or may not be clear to the reader.

3. Answers may vary.

4. Many students are likely to find this conclusion to be fitting because it encapsulates Torre's claim that racial classification is reductive and limited.

Carol Bernstein Ferry, "A Good Death," p. 515

Carol Bernstein Ferry, a wealthy benefactor and advocate for euthanasia, here defends the right to die "a good death," as she calls it in her title. She wrote this article after she was diagnosed with cancer, and she committed suicide three months after it was published. Arguing that euthanasia is the right of any sane adult, she deftly anticipates and acknowledges her opponents. Issues such as euthanasia are important ones for students to consider. They may like to express their personal feelings in journals before engaging in more logical debate. Students may enjoy debating the pros and cons of euthanasia, using religious, medical, and humanitarian arguments. You might ask them to do some preliminary research on the subject and then have them present their findings to the class. In discussing this essay, remind students that it is important to try to remain somewhat neutral in order not to become swept up in one's feelings during debate.

Understanding the Reading, p. 517

1. Ferry plans to commit suicide because she is terminally ill with emphysema and advanced in age, at seventy-six years of age.

2. No one will be assisting Ferry in her death because they could be legally implicated in her death (para. 3).

3. Ferry is happy about the life she has lived. She views the time she has left as a "gift" (3).

4. According to Ferry, the barriers to dying in peace are the legal restrictions on assisted suicide that say that she has to do it alone. She could be more "certain" that she would die peacefully if she could have the help of a second person (3). Ultimately, through her letter, Ferry hopes to change the attitude in the United States that cannot accept each person's life as his or her own (5).

Visualizing the Reading, p. 517

Possible answers include:

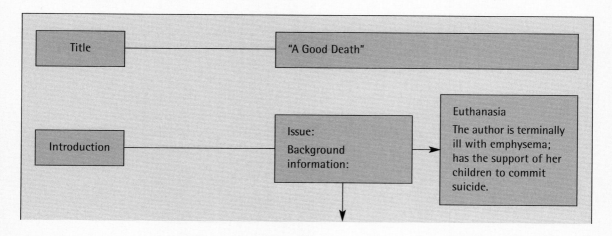

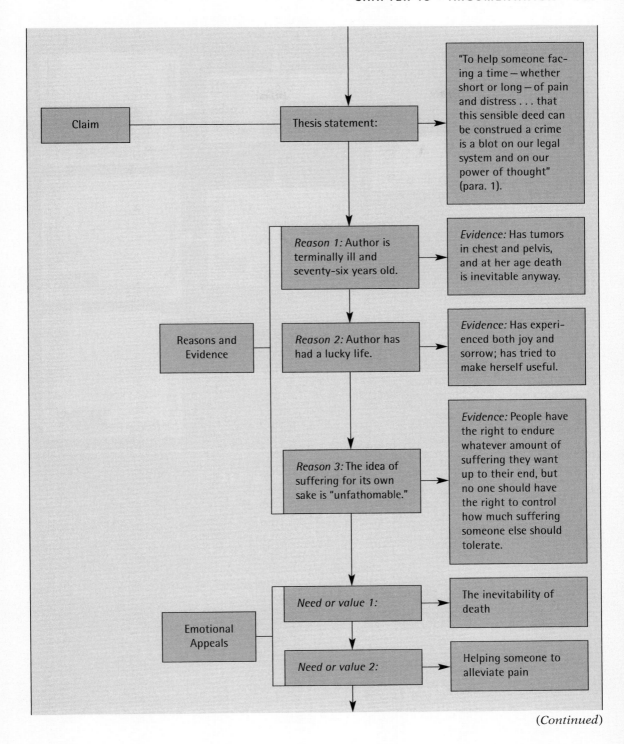

(Continued)

(*Continued*)

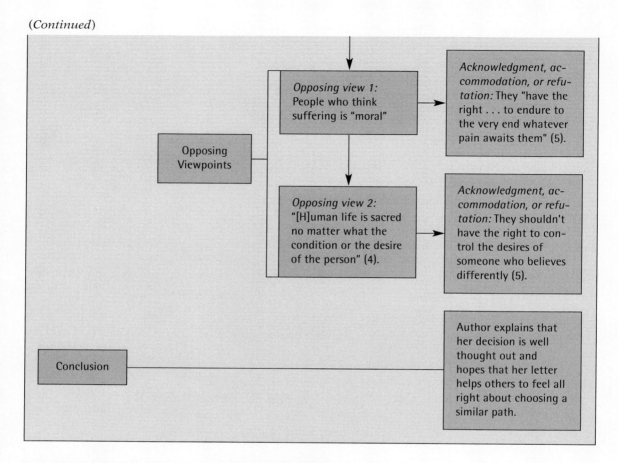

Examining the Characteristics of Argument Essays, p. 517

1. The type of audience Ferry is writing for is probably neutral or wavering because her letter was submitted to a newspaper that reaches a broad audience. However, elements of her letter seem to be directed toward a smaller group of disagreeing people, the religious and political leaders she views as her primary opponents.

2. Answers may vary. Ferry qualifies her support of assisted suicide by explaining how medical help for the terminally ill is useless and how much sorrow and anxiety the family and friends of someone who is dying must undergo.

3. The reasons that Ferry uses to support her claim are: she has the support of family, she is going to die soon anyway, and she has lived a long and good life.

4. Ferry addresses opposing viewpoints by questioning the religious view that sees a moral beauty in "suffering for its own sake." She refutes the notion that "human life is sacred no matter the condition or the desire of the person" by explaining

that people who feel that way can do what they will with their own life, but they have no right to decide for others who feel differently. Answers may vary.

5. Ferry uses inductive reasoning to order her argument by working from the facts of her own situation toward the overarching idea of euthanasia. Her method of organization is logical in that it moves from her personal situation to public views.

Building Your Word Power, p. 517

1. The connotative meaning of the word *death* as used by Ferry is suicide because that is what she means by "painless death."

2. The idiom "put up roadblocks" as used in paragraph 5 means to oppose or place obstacles in the way of someone's progress.

Building Your Critical Thinking Skills: Evaluating Letters, p. 517

1. Some of the opinions Ferry expresses are that "each person's life is his own" (para. 5) and that politicians and religious leaders should not interfere with an individual's right to die peacefully. In support of her view, she presents her own case for taking her life.

2. The bias she reveals is that she is in fact terminally ill and suffering and that she plans to end her life.

3. The letter is addressed to a general audience. Answers may vary.

Frank Deford, "Athletics 101: A Change in Eligibility Rules Is Long Overdue," p. 520

Frank Deford, a staff writer for *Sports Illustrated* and a TV and radio commentator, defines the "antiquated amateur rules" as outdated and something that should be discontinued, especially since they unfairly advantage the privileged. He compiles a list of examples to support his views, including the idea that in many other fields interns are encouraged to gain professional experience and earn money if they can. Students may enjoy debating this issue since they would be going to school with "professional athletes" if this rule changed. Have them break into groups to discuss the issues involved. Then have them form panels in favor of the amateur rules and against them.

Understanding the Reading, p. 521

1. According to the author, educators, the NFL, and the NBA care more about the eligibility of basketball and football players than the eligibility of golfers and tennis players because basketball and football are the only sports that attract "big-ticket crowds and rich television contracts for the universities" (para. 2).

2. In support of changing eligibility rules, Deford offers the following reasons: they are antiquated, and they unfairly disadvantage college athletes.

3. The author compares students who serve as radio station interns to college athletes in order to show that many interns can make money in their profession—and are even encouraged to do so—and still remain amateurs, whereas athletes cannot (5).

4. According to Deford, the eligibility rules were originally established to protect upper-class athletes from having to come into contact with "young working men" (8).

Visualizing the Reading, p. 522

Possible answers include:

Example	What It Contributes to the Argument
Tiger Woods	Shows that the golf community is not concerned about the issue of amateur rules.
Pete Sampras, Andre Agassi, and Venus and Serena Williams	All dropped out of college to play professionally but no one cared, showing that people are only concerned about athletes for college sports that draw big-ticket crowds and television contracts.
Baseball prospects abandoning school for the minor leagues	Shows that no one cares about athletes leaving school to turn pro unless it is for a college sport that generates a lot of money.
Radio internship	Shows that amateurs in other fields are able to make money.
College singer making money in a dance band	Shows that amateurs in other fields are allowed and even encouraged to make money in their field.
Chris Young of Princeton	Shows the irrationality of a system that punishes an amateur for being good enough to play professionally.

Examining the Characteristics of Argument Essays, p. 522

1. People who are interested in sports of all kinds read *Sports Illustrated*. DeFord urges the readers of the magazine—presumably fans of college basketball and football—to take action to rid the schools of this policy by using examples to show how irrational and nonsensical amateur eligibility rules are.

2. Deford's claim in stated in paragraph 3: "Throw out all the antiquated amateur rules." While his position on the issue is clear and specific, his thesis is not very effective because it doesn't explain why this would be a good thing to do.

3. Deford cites examples both from other sports where amateur rules don't generate much fuss and from non-sports-related instances involving university students who are praised for earning money relating to their field of study. Through these examples, DeFord exposes the hypocrisy of the current system.

4. DeFord appeals to the value and need for fairness as he exposes the hypocrisy in eligibility rules.

5. Deford refutes the view that athletes who are paid bonus money will "goof off and do nothing but play their sport" by explaining that wealthy students with "huge trust funds" do this all the time but no one cares about them (para. 7).

Building Your Word Power, p. 522

1. By "cries of academic anguish" in paragraph 2 the author means that universities hypocritically pretend to be concerned about the athletes' education when their motives are actually about profit.

2. The idiom "big-ticket crowds" means that people will pay a lot to see these athletes play, and "box-office appeal" means that the athletes' names are well known enough to draw a crowd (para. 2).

Building Your Critical Thinking Skills: Tone, p. 523

1. Deford describes the eligibility rules in college athletics as *antiquated, nutty,* and *idiotic.* These informal words contribute emotional suasion to the tone of his argument.

2. Deford uses sarcasm to discredit the people who support eligibility rules in the essay's opening sentence: "As the NBA draft approaches, there is, anew, a great deal of weeping and wailing and gnashing of teeth about the poor basketball players who will be deprived of more higher education." He also uses sarcasm through the words he italicizes in paragraphs 4 and 5.

3. Answers may vary.

Martin Luther King Jr., "I Have a Dream," p. 524

Martin Luther King Jr. gave this powerful civil rights speech at the 1963 March on Washington for Jobs and Freedom. Although it contains many of the rhetorical devices commonly used in speeches, it also holds up well as a piece of writing. You may like to provide some background on the civil rights era, let students listen to the speech on a tape recorder if possible, and have them examine it closely for persuasive elements. Some historical background on the Emancipation Proclamation (and the fact that the speech was delivered at the base of the Lincoln Monument) and the Declaration of Independence (which some of the students may like to provide historical information about) would also be useful as a preface.

Understanding the Reading, p. 527

1. According to King, one hundred years after the signing of the Emancipation Proclamation African Americans still face many types of discrimination and therefore are still not free.

2. Using the analogy of a bad check, King contends that America has defaulted on a check, a promissory note "that all men would be guaranteed the unalienable rights of life, liberty, and the pursuit of happiness" (para. 3).

3. King urges his followers to return to Mississippi, Alabama, and other communities to agitate for social change.

4. In order for America "to be a great nation" (21), all people must have freedom. King's dream is that America will make good on its promise to give black people equal opportunity.

Visualizing the Reading, p. 527

Possible answers include:

Figurative Expression	Meaning
". . . we have come to our nation's Capitol to cash a check." (para.3)	Implies an obligation between the words of the Constitution and the Declaration of Independence and the rights of the Negro. Use of this analogy gives the cause a sense of importance and legitimacy.
"*Now* is the time to lift our nation from the quicksands of racial injustice to the solid rock of brotherhood." (para. 4)	Through the analogy of racial injustice as quicksand, King suggests the urgency of the cause and the ultimate solidity of the goal.
"The whirlwinds of revolt will continue to shake the foundations of our nation until the bright day of justice emerges." (para. 5)	Suggests that civil rights agitation will not end until equality has been achieved; strengthens his argument because it shows how determined they are in their struggle for civil rights.
"Let us not seek to satisfy our thirst for freedom by drinking from the cup of bitterness and hatred." (para. 6)	Cautions black people not to hate white people because of the injustices they have suffered. This figurative expression warns of the wrong path toward freedom.
"You have been the veterans of creative suffering." (para. 8)	Suggests that the history of inequality is a long one and that black people have endured many kinds of suffering.
"With this faith we will be able to transform the jangling discords of our nation into a beautiful symphony of brotherhood." (para. 19)	King is describing a nation with potential; like a symphony that can overcome bad notes to make beautiful music, so too can racial intolerance be overcome to create a better world. Lends his cause hope of peaceful coexistence and racial harmony.

Examining the Characteristics of Argument Essays, p. 528

1. Because King's audience that day was overwhelmingly in agreement with him, he did not to have to address dissenting opinions at great length. He acknowledges his opponents but concentrates on the shared dream of his audience members: equality for black people in America.

2. King's claim is that America still owes black people true equality (para. 3). He presents it by citing the promises made in the Constitution and the Declaration of Independence (3) and the Emancipation Proclamation (1).

3. His reasons and evidence are: that the founding fathers intended true equality for all as stated in the Constitution and the Declaration of Independence (3); that black people are still living in poverty, as "an exile in his own land" (2); that "[t]here will be neither rest nor tranquility in America" until blacks are truly free (5); and that blacks will not be satisfied as long as they are subjected to police brutality, cannot gain lodging in motels and hotels, and cannot live where they like (7). Answers may vary.

4. The values that King appeals to in his speech are fairness and human decency. Answers may vary.

5. To acknowledge opposing viewpoints King mentions the state of Georgia, where he hopes that "the sons of former slaves and . . . of former slaveowners will be able to sit down together at the table of brotherhood" (12), and he alludes to Alabama, where the governor's "lips are presently dripping with the words of interposition and nullification" (16). He counters these opposing viewpoints by presenting a positive view of a future where the opposition will no longer hold sway over the lives of blacks.

Building Your Word Power, p. 528

1. The "symbolic shadow" (para. 1) refers to Lincoln, whose monument the crowd is standing beneath and who signed the Emancipation Proclamation. The Proclamation liberated the slaves in states that had seceded, giving the "light of hope" (1) to black people. The "long night" refers to slavery, and "daybreak" to that moment when the slaves were freed (1).

Building Your Critical Thinking Skills: Evaluating Speeches, p. 529

1. King captures the attention of his audience by opening with an echo of the Emancipation Proclamation (para. 1), repeating various words such as *now* (4), and using vivid imagery such as "lonely island of poverty" (2).

2. Repeated words and catch-phrases are "now" (4), "I have a dream" (10–18), and "let freedom ring" (21–27). In addition to engaging the listener, this device helps build King's argument as he moves from the situation that black Americans have had to endure to a vision of the future for both blacks and the United States that he is arguing for.

3. The conclusion appeals to both the American political idea of "freedom" and the religious ideal of freedom. It projects into the future by talking about speeding up "that day when all God's children" will be free and urges listeners to take action by letting "freedom ring."

ORGAN DONATION: SHOULD PEOPLE BE ALLOWED TO SELL THEIR ORGANS?

Bruce Gottlieb, "How Much Is That Kidney in the Window?" p. 531

Lawyer and freelance writer Bruce Gottlieb outlines and dismisses a series of arguments against legalizing the sales of kidneys for transplants, using various persuasive techniques, including emotional appeals. This article is worth reviewing closely with students to evaluate the effectiveness of the author's tone, examples, statistics, and so on. As an argumentative essay, it must meet a certain standard of proof in order to be effective; students will enjoy critiquing it and the next article about organ donation, based on what they have learned.

Understanding the Reading, p. 534

1. Gottlieb favors organ sales because it offers a solution to a situation in which people are dying.

2. The author thinks that kidney sales should be the only type of organ sales to be legalized because they are unique in that "somebody with just one can live an almost entirely normal life" (para. 8).

3. Black and Hispanic populations (who represent, respectively, 35 and 12 percent of the people on the waiting lists) would be most affected if there were an increase in available kidneys (7).

4. The doctors mentioned in the article changed their minds about kidney sales because the shortage "became more acute" (9).

Visualizing the Reading, p. 534

Possible answers include:

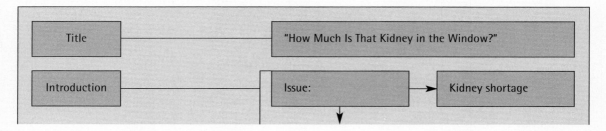

| Title | "How Much Is That Kidney in the Window?" |

| Introduction | Issue: | → | Kidney shortage |

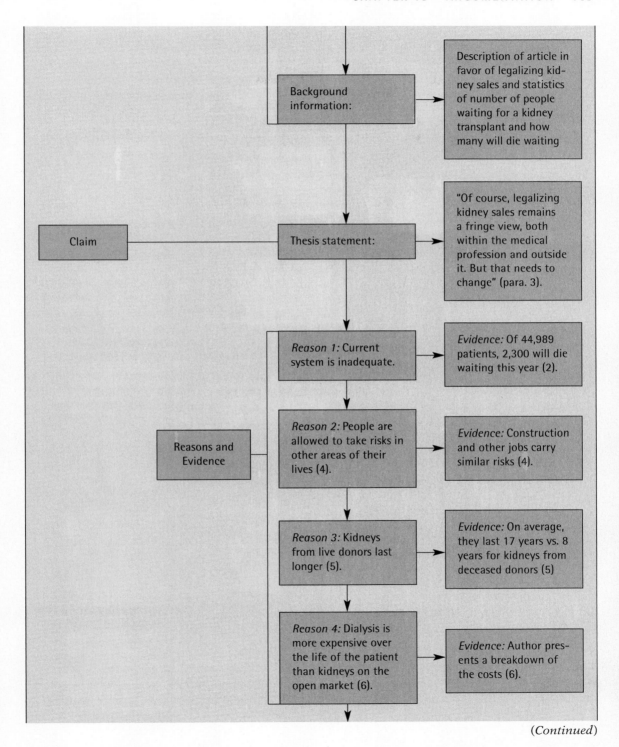

Background information: → Description of article in favor of legalizing kidney sales and statistics of number of people waiting for a kidney transplant and how many will die waiting

Claim — Thesis statement: → "Of course, legalizing kidney sales remains a fringe view, both within the medical profession and outside it. But that needs to change" (para. 3).

Reason 1: Current system is inadequate. → *Evidence:* Of 44,989 patients, 2,300 will die waiting this year (2).

Reasons and Evidence — *Reason 2:* People are allowed to take risks in other areas of their lives (4). → *Evidence:* Construction and other jobs carry similar risks (4).

Reason 3: Kidneys from live donors last longer (5). → *Evidence:* On average, they last 17 years vs. 8 years for kidneys from deceased donors (5)

Reason 4: Dialysis is more expensive over the life of the patient than kidneys on the open market (6). → *Evidence:* Author presents a breakdown of the costs (6).

(*Continued*)

(*Continued*)

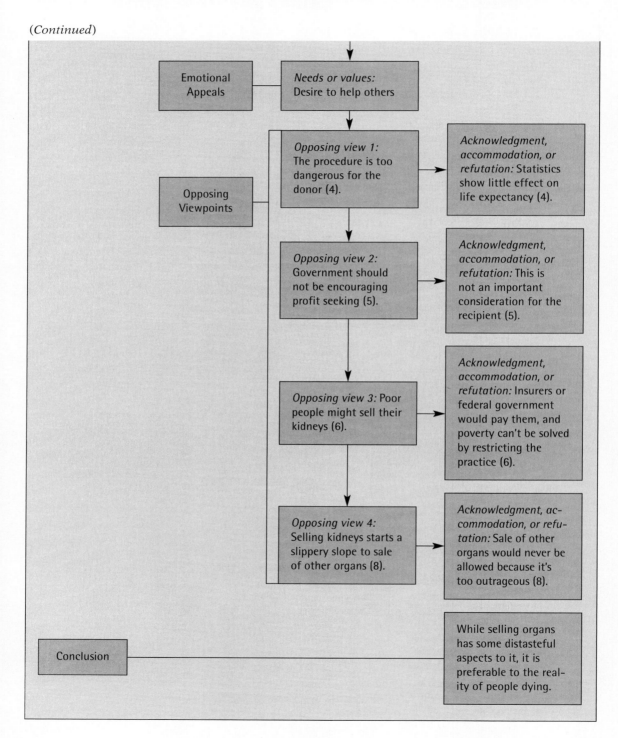

Examining the Characteristics of Argument Essays, p. 534

1. Answers may vary.

2. The author's claim is one of value because he says that saving the lives of those awaiting kidneys is more important than the problems that may arise if poor people sell their kidneys for money.

3. Gottlieb arranges opposing viewpoints in order of importance from least to most serious objection. Answers may vary. Gottlieb refutes opposing viewpoints with clear logic and evidence.

4. The author's uses of statistics—such as the number of years that a kidney from a live as opposed to a dead donor lasts (para. 5), and how little donation affects the life span of the donor (4)—offers compelling evidence that may affect the reader's acceptance of his argument. The mention of a controversial figure like Jack Kevorkian is a curious beginning to what is otherwise a clear and effective argument. The inclusion of this anecdote may hinder Gottlieb's arguments because Kevorkian is known as "Dr. Death" and is currently serving a prison sentence.

5. Answers may vary. More emotional appeals might have been more effective.

Building Your Word Power, p. 536

1. The idiom "slippery slope" means that if one thing is allowed to happen, related things will follow inevitably. One's "gut reaction" is one's instinctive reaction to something.

Gilbert Meilaender, "'Strip-Mining' the Dead: When Human Organs Are for Sale," p. 538

Gilbert Meilaender, an editor and member of the President's Bioethics Council, contends that people's objections to the sale of human organs are instinctive and profoundly moral. Moving through the arguments that have been used to encourage or "pressure" people into reconsidering the idea of selling organs, he questions the use of the hyperbolic words *tragedy* and *catastrophe* (para. 4). This issue provides lively student debate, pro and con, taking first one side and then the other. Have your students freewrite first, then break into small groups to strategize their arguments, and then present their ideas as a panel.

Understanding the Reading, p. 542

1. Meilaender's reasons for opposing human organ sales are: it is morally repugnant (para. 5); the body should be respected (12); certain things are not to be bought and sold (6); and placing organs on the market would undercut human society (10).

2. Describing transplantation as "a noble form of cannibalism" means that even though the goals for organ transplantation may be ultimately noble, the act itself is as morally unacceptable as cannibalism.

3. Meilaender seems to approve of organ donation because it is still "connected with the one who freely gave it, whose person we continue to respect" (5).

4. The policy the state of Pennsylvania enacted in the spring of 1999 was to "[pay] relatives of organ donors $300 toward funeral expenses" (8). According to the author, this policy does not affect "the organ-donation system currently in place" (10).

Visualizing the Reading, p. 542

Possible answers include:

Element	Questions	Answers
The claim	What is the author's claim? Is it stated or implied?	Stated: "It's not hard to understand our national reluctance to permit the buying and selling of human organs for transplant, for it expresses a repugnance that is deeply rooted in important moral sentiments" (para. 5).
The support	What facts, statistics, expert opinions, examples, and personal experiences are presented? Are appeals made to needs, values, or both?	Examples include: Leon Kass quote, "a noble form of cannibalism" (5); C. S. Lewis on trees (5); Michael Walzer on buying replacements in Civil War (7); eBay already had bidding on kidney (10).
		Appeals are made to the basic needs of fear (of having one's body "salvaged" [2] after death) and the repulsion toward organ selling and to the value of knowing that "certain things . . . may not be bought and sold" (6).
Purpose and audience	What is the author's purpose for writing? To whom do the reasons, evidence, and emotional appeals seem targeted?	The author is writing to a general audience to convince them that the sale of organs is immoral.
The writer's credibility	Is the author qualified and knowledgeable? Does he establish common ground with readers?	The author seems to be qualified only to write on the subject from the religious and moral perspective. He establishes common ground by listing the difficult questions facing society (2–3).

The strength of the argument	Does the author supply several reasons with relevant evidence to back up the claim? Does he use fallacies or unfair emotional appeals?	Answers may vary. Depending on one's religious views, the section on the corpse as "mortal remains" might be construed as an unfair emotional appeal (12).
Opposing viewpoints	Does the author acknowledge, accommodate, or refute opposing viewpoints with logic and relevant evidence?	Answers may vary.

Examining the Characteristics of Argument Essays, p. 543

1. Answers may vary.

2. Meilander uses deductive reasoning to dispel the idea that the kidney shortage is a "catastrophe." Answers may vary.

3. The analogy between the Civil War draft exemption and organ donation is that wealthy people can buy themselves "life," in effect, by offering money in exchange for what could be the potential of physical harm, or even death, to the "seller."

4. The reference to the Grimm Brothers tale about the ability "to shudder" is effective because it appeals to shared human instincts, emotions, and values.

Building Your Word Power, p. 543

1. The connotative meaning of the word *salvage* as used throughout the reading is to pick over or save from the scrap heap.

2. The author puts the words *tragedy* and *catastrophe* in quotation marks in paragraph 4 because he feels that they are used hyperbolically.

Analyzing the Arguments

Building Your Critical Thinking Skills: Synthesizing Sources, p. 544. Class discussions of this section should prove very useful. Have students write comparison and contrast essays about the two articles before entering into class discussion or breaking into panels to support one or the other article.

THE EFFECT OF MEDIA ON CHILDREN: IS VIOLENT MEDIA HARMFUL?

Dave Grossman and Gloria DeGaetano, "It's Important to Feel Something When You Kill," p. 545

In this well-researched argument, Dave Grossman, the director of an organization that studies the effect of killing and violent behavior on society, and Gloria DeGaetano, a writer on children and the media, argue against violent video games using as support data from a series of compelling studies that illustrate just how directly video games impact the real-life ability and desire to kill. The authors' most important evidence may be that the military uses similar video games to teach soldiers to kill. This issue is one that students will probably find very engaging because they have grown up with interactive video games, may play them frequently, and are familiar with stories of Columbine and other school killings.

Understanding the Reading, p. 551

1. According to the authors, the popularity of interactive video games may be traced to their realism; that the user can control the action; and stimuli that keep players' "excitement high" (para. 21).

2. Violent video games alter players' attitudes toward killing by fostering more aggressive thoughts (8) and teaching players to look someone in the eye as they kill (12). The physical effects of violent video games include raised heart rate, dizziness and nausea, and manifestation of "more aggressive thoughts" (8).

3. The military and the police teach trainees that sometimes the best strategy is not to shoot (20–21).

4. The authors use the incident of a fourteen-year-old boy killing five fellow students at his school as support in their argument because the boy shot the students much as one would shoot a target in a video game: He didn't move his feet or body, fired only once per target, aimed for the head (awarded extra points in video games), shot everything in sight, and had excellent aim even though he had never before used a real handgun (18).

Visualizing the Reading, p. 551

Answers may vary. The boys have a detached, cold expression. Their interaction with the video game supports the authors' claims that video games offer "an active participatory role for the child" (para. 7); that due to their physical nature, certain "'games' are actually killing simulators" (11); and that when kids play video games, "[t]here is never an incentive not to shoot" (21). Possible places in the essay where this image might be used to effect include the paragraphs cited above. For the final segment of this activity, you may wish to have students break into two groups, parents and the boys, and then have them role-play their responses for and against playing violent video games.

Examining the Characteristics of Argument Essays, p. 552

1. The authors' claim is that because interactive video games very effectively teach and encourage killing, they are dangerous and should not be used by children.

2. The main reasons the authors give to support their argument are: military uses games like Doom to teach soldiers how to kill (para. 20); these games provide hands-on simulation of killing (11); and children's "brains and response mechanisms" are not fully developed and are therefore more impressionable (10). Answers may vary.

3. The authors cite many psychological studies (9–12) and analyses of individual cases like the one at Paducah (16–18). Answers may vary.

4. This is likely to be construed as a weak spot in an otherwise well-supported essay, particularly as some students are likely to be gamers, or know gamers well, and they will have likely seen or experienced little increased propensity for violence.

5. Other patterns of development include: narration ("Hostility and cardiovascular reactivity were examined after subjects played" [9]); description ("pistol grip joystick" [20]; cause and effect ("developing the will to kill by repeatedly rehearsing the act until it feels natural" [20]); and illustration (Paducah and Columbine).

Building Your Word Power, p. 552

1. The phrase "riding the technology curve" means that children are adapting to and changing more quickly in response to the rapid shifts in technological advances.

2. *Splatter* as used in the final paragraph suggests killing and blood.

Gerard Jones, "Violent Media Is Good for Kids," p. 554

Comic strip writer Gerard Jones founded the organization Media Power for Children and serves as adviser to the Comparative Media Studies graduate program at the Massachusetts Institute of Technology. In this essay, he goes against the popular view that media violence has a bad effect on children, describing it instead as cathartic and even psychologically beneficial. This issue is one that students may be familiar with and may enjoy debating. Have them freewrite about violent programs that they have watched, especially any that they think may have helped them to deal with or even overcome emotional or personal problems. Then have them debate the Jones and Grossman/DeGaetano articles, pro and con, analyzing the effectiveness of each one's use of evidence.

Understanding the Reading, p. 557

1. The reasons Jones presents in support of his claim that children need violent entertainment are: it helps them to integrate their public and private psyches (para. 5); through violent stories, they learn to be human (9); through violent entertainment, they learn to accept parts of their selves (9); violent entertainment fosters

developmental functions (11); and violent games and stories can provide a tool for mastering rage (12).

2. Reading comic books like the Hulk allowed the author to find a "fantasy self" (4) and to deal with his feelings of rage. He read his son Tarzan comics to overcome the boy's fear of climbing trees (6).

3. The author feels that it is beneficial for children to be exposed to "creative violence" because it helps them to "engage the rage they've stifled" (12).

4. According to the author, experiencing violent cartoons or video games helps children through developmental stages by allowing them a "dual identity" with which to negotiate the conflicts between their public and private selves (11).

Visualizing the Reading, p. 557

Possible answers include:

Type of Evidence	Example from the Essay
Personal experience	1. Reading comics as a boy helped the author gain confidence and eventually led him to become an action movie and comic book writer (para. 1–5).
Expert opinion	Stories are how we learn what it is to be human (clinical psychologist, 9).
Media examples	The author's love of the Incredible Hulk as a young boy (2–5); Ice T's "mythologized street violence" helped a girl to become well adjusted (15).

Examining the Characteristics of Argument Essays, p. 558

1. The author's claim is that violent stories offer tools for children to master their rage. Answers may vary.

2. The story of Jones's son imagining himself as a dinosaur supports his idea that stories can help children to integrate aspects of their psyche (para. 6). The story of the girl who acted out violent fantasies shows that they helped her to become "socially competent" (14). The final example is of a girl who used gangsta rap as a means to escape a difficult family situation (15). Answers may vary.

3. Jones appeals to the needs of adolescence: fear, anger, desire for power, and rage. The author also addresses the value holding violence to be bad, but here he suggests that we as a society are sending confusing and mixed messages about this value to children because of the natural aggression that we all harbor.

4. Jones recognizes the opposing viewpoints of "pop psychologists" who say violent stories are "junk culture" (7). He refutes them by quoting "clinical psychologists" who say such stories are valuable.

5. Jones uses a sentence fragment to isolate and emphasize the idea of violence because it is so central to his thesis.

Building Your Word Power, p. 558

1. The metaphor "then the Incredible Hulk smashed through it" means that the author had been sheltered from pop culture and its violence until he was introduced to the Hulk.

Analyzing the Arguments

Building Your Critical Thinking Skills: Synthesizing Sources, p. 559. Class discussions of this section should be lively and interesting. To increase their skills in synthesizing sources, you might have students write comparison and contrast essays about the two articles before entering into class discussion or breaking into panels to support one or the other article. Based on the readings, have students break into two groups and then debate each other using the two readings as sources for their position, pro or con.

CIVIL LIBERTIES: DOES THE PATRIOT ACT GO TOO FAR?

Zara Gelsey, "Who's Reading over Your Shoulder?" p. 560

Writer Zara Gelsey evaluates the legitimacy of the FBI's policy of monitoring library records without "probable cause" under the Patriot Act. Gelsey argues that the right to privacy is being violated in unprecedented ways. This issue is a very important one for students to inform themselves about and debate. You might like to assign them to research and report on the changes in civil liberties brought about by the Patriot Act. Initiate a debate about when, if ever, these changes are likely to be reversed, given that the War on Terrorism appears to have no deadline. Students could debate the value of the Patriot Act, pro and con, after breaking into small groups.

Understanding the Reading, p. 563

1. According to the author, the freedom of thought and the freedom to read are interrelated because if one feels intimidated or inhibited one is likely to censor oneself (para. 13).

2. The author thinks that the FBI is using the Patriot Act to evade the First Amendment by "threatening readers rather than prohibiting what they read" (13).

3. The outcome of surveillance of what someone reads might be similar to a classic sitcom plot line in that a series of "unrelated details" are pieced together to "construct conclusions" that are untrue (5).

Visualizing the Reading, p. 563

Possible answers include:

Reasons	Evidence (list)	Effectiveness (explain)
Secret monitoring of library records is "ripe for potential abuse" (para. 3).	It intimidates patrons (3).	Details about a case in which a researcher was mistaken for a terrorist would strengthen this idea.
What one reads indicates different things to different people.	Analogies to a classic sitcom plot line (5); hypothetical example of the FBI concluding you're a terrorist because you are doing research on suicide bombings (6); makes the FBI "predisposed to find suspicious facts" (7).	Fairly effective, though an actual case of "mistaken identity" would have made for more compelling evidence.
"[S]urveillance always spreads beyond its original purpose" (para. 9)	War on Drugs was tied to the War on Terrorism (10).	Weak because the single example is not well explained.
Surveillance will cause self-censorship.	Reference to George Orwell's *1984* (12); circumvents the First Amendment (13).	Again, could be made stronger with a concrete example.

Examining the Characteristics of Argument Essays, p. 564

1. Gelsey's claim appears toward the end of her essay: "Thus, the FBI circumvents the First Amendment by threatening readers rather than prohibiting what they read" (para. 13).

2. Answers may vary. Using examples from fiction like the novel *1984* (12) does not seem as effective as an example of a real researcher taken for a "suspect" would be.

3. One of the emotional appeals Gelsey makes is evident in her description of the FBI as "peering over my shoulder" (1). She appeals to the need for privacy and the value of freedom of thought.

4. Gelsey acknowledges the broader need for protection from terrorists in paragraph 9, but she doesn't address any opposing viewpoints relating specifically to library surveillance.

Building Your Word Power, p. 564

1. The allusion to the Garden of Eden means that knowledge can be used for good or evil. The allusion to George Orwell's *1984* refers to a novel in which the government became dictatorial, violating its citizens' rights.

Ramesh Ponnuru, "Fears about the Patriot Act Are Misguided," p. 566

National Review editor Ramesh Ponnuru expresses skepticism that the Patriot Act poses a threat to American civil liberties, citing legal precedents prior to 9/11, dismissing fears expressed by those on both the right and the left, and arguing that the end justifies the means. He acknowledges that without such outcry the Patriot Act might have violated many more civil liberties, but he still dismisses the idea that such gradual infringements of civil liberties might lead to a less democratic society. This is an important issue for students to consider. Ask them to do some research in advance of class discussion in order to be prepared to defend their position. Have students adopt positions pro and con on the introduction of the Patriot Act, and ask them to consider when and if it should expire.

Understanding the Reading, p. 569

1. According to Ponnuru, concerns about the Patriot Act are misguided because: there were already legal precedents for the use of roving wiretaps (para. 9); Internet surveillance requires a court order (10); the Act hasn't shifted the balance between privacy and security (11); and the feds already had the right to break into someone's house for a "sneak and peek" before the Act was established (14). On balance, the author believes that "legal laxity" would be worse (17).

2. According to the author, the coalition of left- and right-wing groups working against the Patriot Act has received favorable publicity because the press finds this oddly bipartisan coalition "irresistible" (5).

3. The example Ponnuru cites to explain how terrorists regard the Patriot Act is Jeffrey Battle, who complained that it had reduced the "financial support" terrorists had received from individuals because of their fear of reprisal (18).

4. Ponnuru explains the controversy surrounding the Patriot Act by suggesting that the opposition has not read it and is merely hysterical over misunderstood and imagined infringements (20).

Visualizing the Reading, p. 569

Possible answers include:

Patriot Act Provision	Opposing Viewpoint	Refutation
Roving wiretaps (para. 9)	Violation of civil liberties	They have been used since 1986 and are not new.
Internet surveillance (para. 10–12)	Allows for "spying on the Web browsers of people who are not even criminal suspects" (10).	Patriot Act requires a court order and has privacy provisions as strong as those for phone calls, stronger than for mail.
Computer hacking (para. 13)	The definition of terrorist activity includes non-lethal acts like computer hacking.	Such a definition is misleading because only specific kinds of hacking, like taking out a power grid, would be considered terrorism.
Sneak and peek (para. 14)	ACLU says that the government can secretly enter your home and search it.	This can be done, but only with a search warrant and you must be notified that it happened after the fact.
Library records (para. 15)	Federal agents can "commandeer library records" (15).	Traditionally, such records could be accessed by law with a subpoena.

Examining the Characteristics of Argument Essays, p. 570

1. Ponnuru's claim that some of the provisions of the Patriot Act are reasonable occurs in paragraph 8 when he says that "most of the concerns about the Patriot Act are misguided or based on premises that are just plain wrong."

2. The types of evidence Ponnuru uses to support his argument are: quotations from legal experts (para. 10); quotations from the coalition against the Patriot Act (12); and an example of how terrorists have responded to the Act (18). Answers may vary.

3. Ponnuru organizes his essay by least to most important, culminating in the response of a terrorist to the Act. Answers may vary.

4. Ponnuru accommodates some of the civil libertarians' objections to the Patriot Act, such as the idea that "Internet gambling" should be excluded and acknowl-

edging that they did manage to insert some necessary restrictions on the Act (16). Answers may vary.

5. Ponnuru's conclusion suggests that the opposition is hysterical and has not read the Act closely. It supports his argument by suggesting that a calm look at the facts will prove that people are reacting irrationally to legislation that doesn't infringe on civil liberties any more than they were before and in the end does much good in the nation's War on Terrorism.

Building Your Word Power, p. 570

1. The metaphor "the lion and the lamb lying down together" in paragraph 5 means that political enemies are on the same side against the Act.

Analyzing the Arguments

Building Your Critical Thinking Skills: Synthesizing Sources, p. 571. The Patriot Act topic is controversial and certain to generate a heated discussion. Because much of the controversy circles around hearsay for the simple fact (as Ponnuru points out) that few people have taken the time to read the Act, it would be useful to assign groups of students to read the parts of the Act mentioned by these two authors and then report their findings to the class. If possible, have the same groups look into some of the claims made by Ponnuru to see if his information about certain tenets of the Act being in place before the Act was enacted are indeed true. Armed with this additional information, are students still swayed by one or the other argument, or do they find themselves changing positions based on their own research? Once students have tried to winnow out the truth in these two essays for themselves, you might want to open up the discussion to the larger issues associated with argument and the possibility of abuse of spreading misinformation through writing.

Chapter 14 Combining Patterns: Using Variety to Achieve Your Purposes, p. 573

This chapter represents the culmination of the semester's work, when students can combine the patterns they most enjoy using to create a varied, skillful piece of writing with various kinds of arguments and evidence. In general, one rhetorical pattern should predominate, but other modes can be used to supplement and enliven the piece as needed. Because the formats of essays that combine modes are so variable, a general graphic organizer for this type of essay is not included. Encourage students who find this organizational tool helpful to create their own, modifying its structure according to the patterns used. You might find it helpful to refer students back to the basic structure of the graphic organizer showing the key elements to include on page 000 of Chapter 1.

The essays in this chapter represent a wide variety of styles and approaches; analyzing the different modes used by these authors will illustrate for students the wide range of writing choices they have now that they have mastered each of the individual modes discussed in this book. Anna Quindlen primarily uses argumentation in her 9/11 story, "We Are Here for Andrea" (p. 574), but supplements it with other modes. Her essay is annotated to show the different modes and is represented visually with a graphic organizer (p. 580) that can be used to take students through the essay point by point. Student writer Robin Ferguson uses narration to tell her story, "The Value of Volunteering" (p. 583), but also uses process analysis, cause and effect, and other modes. Her story too is annotated for students who need some assistance identifying these patterns. Lars Eighner, in "On Dumpster Diving" (p. 586), uses primarily process analysis to explain eloquently how someone becomes a professional scavenger; and John Leo, in "The Good-News Generation" (p. 591), uses predominantly definition to distinguish among the various generations. Chitra Divakaruni, in "Houseguest Hell" (p. 596), uses narration to tell her story about inconsiderate guests who descend upon her San Francisco home year after year. In "Naked Terror" (p. 604), Jeffrey Rosen uses an extended example to support his thesis that airport security in the wake of 9/11 is largely designed to give the "appearance" of security. And Shirley Jackson's short story "The Lottery" (p. 609) is a much-anthologized piece that uses narrative as well as process analysis to describe a cruel rite practiced in a little New England village.

Robin Ferguson, "The Value of Volunteering," p. 583

In this section, students can review and evaluate the final version of student writer Robin Ferguson's essay about her experience working as a literary volunteer. Students were introduced to Ferguson in Chapter 3, and they may find it interesting to refer back to the earlier prewriting that she did before turning in this final, more polished version. Told as a personal narrative, Ferguson's essay also combines cause and effect, description, illustration, and other modes to explain the positive impact of volunteering on her life. Her experience helping Marie, a single mother, to read proved more rewarding than she had anticipated. Students will enjoy comparing Ferguson's experience to their own experiences as volunteers. Sharing what they write will also serve as a way to get to know each other even better.

Responding to "Students Write," p. 584

1. Answers may vary. Ferguson could have made her introduction more engaging by creating some suspense—for example, by opening with a phrase such as "Little did I know."

2. The transitions that suggest narration are: "I began working" (para. 1); "When I first" (2); "As we worked together" (4); and "As time went by" (5).

3. The use of narration contributes the feeling of a story to the essay (for instance, the plot of how Ferguson came to appreciate what she was learning, the character of Marie, her hard-working single-mother student). The use of cause and effect explains the reason why volunteering was meaningful to Ferguson. Process analysis explains how Ferguson acquired learning strategies in her volunteer training. Illustration explains the effects of illiteracy on her student. Description makes the story more vivid, drawing the reader in and personalizing Ferguson's experience. The use of comparison and contrast contributes to a sense of what the teacher and student had in common, such as being single parents. Finally, Ferguson concludes her essay with argument, calling for action to help illiterate people to reclaim full lives.

Lars Eighner, "On Dumpster Diving," p. 586

Lars Eighner, a sometimes homeless fiction and essay writer, describes in exquisite detail the stages of becoming a scavenger, breaking down the process of scavenging vividly as if he needed to teach his readers how to do it themselves. Using first-person narration and an informative tone, Eighner quickly makes his intelligence and radical worldview clear, but his reasons for remaining homeless, are mysterious. Students may find it difficult to understand why someone so obviously talented and educated would be homeless, but they will be fascinated by the world he shows. You might like to preface the class discussion with some information about homelessness, in particular contributing factors such as the "deinstitutionalization" of the mentally ill in the United States.

Understanding the Reading, p. 588

1. According to the author, the stages people go through before becoming "professional" dumpster divers are: feeling shame and self-loathing (para. 5); coming to the realization that people throw away "a lot of perfectly good stuff" (6); trying to acquire everything one comes across (7); and restricting oneself to acquiring only those things with immediate utility (7).

2. The principal risk associated with dumpster diving is "dysentery" (para. 12).

3. Eighner has learned two lessons from dumpster diving: to take only what he can use and leave the rest; and to acknowledge "the transience of material being" — that is, ideas are longer lived than material objects.

4. The attitude the author shares with the wealthy is that there is always plenty more where something comes from, so it's unnecessary to collect "gaudy bauble[s]" (16).

Visualizing the Reading, p. 588

Possible answers include:

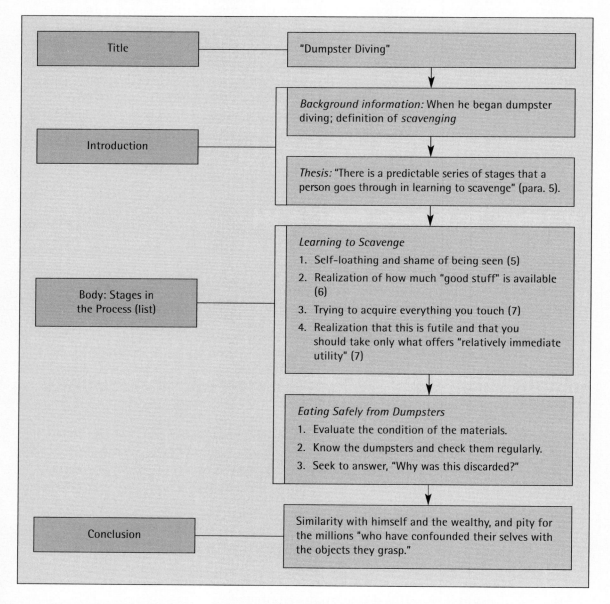

Title	"Dumpster Diving"
Introduction	*Background information:* When he began dumpster diving; definition of *scavenging*
	Thesis: "There is a predictable series of stages that a person goes through in learning to scavenge" (para. 5).
Body: Stages in the Process (list)	*Learning to Scavenge* 1. Self-loathing and shame of being seen (5) 2. Realization of how much "good stuff" is available (6) 3. Trying to acquire everything you touch (7) 4. Realization that this is futile and that you should take only what offers "relatively immediate utility" (7)
	Eating Safely from Dumpsters 1. Evaluate the condition of the materials. 2. Know the dumpsters and check them regularly. 3. Seek to answer, "Why was this discarded?"
Conclusion	Similarity with himself and the wealthy, and pity for the millions "who have confounded their selves with the objects they grasp."

Examining the Characteristics of Essays That Combine Patterns, p. 589

1. In addition to process analysis, other patterns used in this essay include: narration ("I began dumpster diving about a year before I became homeless" [para. 1]); defi-

nition (dumpster diving); comparison and contrast (scavenging vs. foraging [2–3]; relationship between himself and the wealthy [16]); description ("pristine ice cream, still frozen" [6]); division (types of food to be found in dumpsters [10–11]); and cause and effect (getting dysentery [12] and lessons learned [13–14]).

2. Eighner includes sensory details relating to sight, touch, and taste, including "running shoes that fit and look and smell brand-new" (6); "[r]aw fruits and vegetables with intact skins" (10); and "desire to grab for the gaudy bauble" (16).

3. Distinguishing characteristics Eighner presents to define dumpster diving are: living from the refuse of others (3); eating from dumpsters (9); and risking illness (12).

4. The author's main point is that dumpster diving has some drawbacks but is a valid way of life that has taught him larger lessons about life. He supports this point through examples of the "perfectly good stuff" he uses that would otherwise go to waste, and the ultimately "valueless" nature of material possessions (such as love letters and rag dolls).

Building Your Word Power, p. 589

1. According to Eighner, the difference between *scavenging* and *foraging* is that scavenging involves picking over other people's refuse whereas foraging is specifically a matter of gathering things like nuts and berries.

2. The phrase "gaudy bauble" means anything that is shiny and desirable but ultimately worthless.

Building Your Critical Thinking Skills: Bias, p. 589

1. Answers may vary.

2. Answers may vary.

John Leo, "The Good-News Generation," p. 591

John Leo, a writer for *U.S. News & World Report,* discusses the new generation known as "millennials," born between 1977 and 1994. Although he gently mocks the new science of generations, he acknowledges that he is encouraged by the generalizations about millenials, also known as generation Y. Students should find this subject interesting and may like to contribute their own observations about each of the generations they are familiar with. Encourage them to systematically evaluate the categories, adding new elements in accordance with their own thesis. You might have them create new categories within categories—dividing, for example, gen Y into two or three kinds of gen Y-ers. They might also like to compare and contrast gen X and gen Y, or speculate about what gen Z might be like.

Understanding the Reading, p. 593

1. The generations described in this article are: silents ("duty, tradition, loyalty"); baby boomers ("individuality, tolerance, self-absorption"); gen X-ers ("diversity, savvy, pragmatism"); and millenials ("authenticity, authorship, autonomy") (para. 1).

2. The millenials represent the largest birth group in American history.

3. When Clurman says millennials are "pluralistic" (para. 3–4), she means that they overlook differences such as race, ethnicity, and gender (4).

4. The groups that have close family relationships are millenials and their boomer parents (7).

Visualizing the Reading, p. 593

Answers will vary.

Examining the Characteristics of Essays That Combine Patterns, p. 593

1. Leo's thesis appears in paragraph 2: "The comic overtones of dividing and labeling everyone this way are hard to miss, but there is some sense to it, too." He reveals the importance and relevance of this topic through his details about each generation.

2. The primary pattern of development in Leo's article is classification. He also uses definition (of each group); comparison and contrast (with other generations); illustration (the distinguishing characteristics for each category); and description ("an ordinary looking, midriff-free, nondancing singer" [7]).

3. Classification: supports the thesis; comparison and contrast: supports the thesis and adds details; illustration: adds details; description: adds variety and interest.

4. The distinguishing characteristics of millennials are that they are "family oriented, viscerally pluralistic, deeply committed to authenticity and truth-telling, heavily stressed, and living in a no-boundaries world" (3). Generation X-ers are characterized by "diversity, savvy, pragmatism" (1). Silents are characterized by a sense of "duty, tradition, loyalty" (1). And baby boomers are characterized by "individuality, tolerance, self-absorption" (1) and are developing close bonds with their millennial children (7).

Building Your Word Power, p. 594

1. Baby boomers being characterized by *self-absorption* means that they devote time primarily to their own mental and physical well-being; generation X-ers having *savvy* means that they are worldly-wise and sophisticated; and millennials having *authorship* means that they like to take individual responsibility for their work.

2. The phrase "over-the-top cultural products" means products that are elaborately and dramatically conceived, reproduced, and advertised. It has a somewhat negative connotation.

Building Your Critical Thinking Skills: Evaluating Sources, p. 594

1. Answers may vary. Ann Clurman is described as a "generation-watcher" (1) and Leo reinforces her reputation by adding that she is "one of the best," but he does use a disproportionate amount of information from her company, Yankelovich Partners, including quotations from the president of that same company. A Gallup poll is reputable (6), as is a Harvard poll if it is formally connected with the university, although this one is not identified as such (8).

2. Answers may vary.

Chitra Divakaruni, "Houseguest Hell," p. 596

Award-winning novelist and essayist Chitra Divakaruni has published numerous essays, poems, and short stories in the *Atlantic Monthly* and other magazines. In this personal essay, Divakaruni complains about her frequent houseguests from India, speculating about why she can't seem to say No to her guests' demands. Her yearly dilemma will likely amuse students and introduce them to a culture that they may not be familiar with.

Students should enjoy finding the various, underlying reasons that Divakaruni uncovers for not being able to say No to her guests. To identify her reasons, have them outline the essay using a graphic organizer. You might like to lead a discussion about Divakaruni's complex motivations as a busy writer with American needs for privacy and scheduling and feminist expectations about freedom from excessive hosting. Evaluate these other influences in her life in light of her close ties to India and her memories of how her mother delighted in entertaining guests.

Understanding the Reading, p. 600

1. Indian relatives come to visit Divakaruni each late spring until the end of summer. They are a lot of trouble because they expect Divakaruni to entertain them and take care of them. As she so aptly puts it, "they require Maximum Maintenance" (para. 2).

2. The guests expect her to cook Indian foods like rice and lentils (4) and to prepare hot tea. Her guests also expect her to entertain them by personally accompanying them on shopping and sight-seeing trips. It is hard for Divakaruni to meet these expectations because she has a busy schedule as a writer and because she does not have the servants she would have had in India to do all of the cleaning and housework.

3. Divakaruni's way of entertaining is different from her mother's because her mother found visits from relatives and friends to be a delightful experience that she anticipated with a "smiling sense of holiday" (11). Their experiences are similar in that they both feel an obligation as women to entertain and to be a "caretaker" (10) to their guests. But the experiences are different because Divakaruni is a writer and a feminist who lives in America and has worked hard not to have to cater to people's needs, whereas her mother was a traditional wife in India who had the help of servants. Her mother didn't mind having her "daily routine" interrupted, whereas Divakaruni does (11).

4. The author might make the visits easier on herself by ordering take-out food, taking guests to restaurants, and serving them "Special K and Lipton's tea bags" (9) instead of cooking traditional foods. She could also send her guests off on the subway or buses instead of driving them or having her husband take them "sightseeing over the weekend" (9). She plans to suggest these things in the future with "firm charm" (16).

Visualizing the Reading, p. 600

Possible answers include:

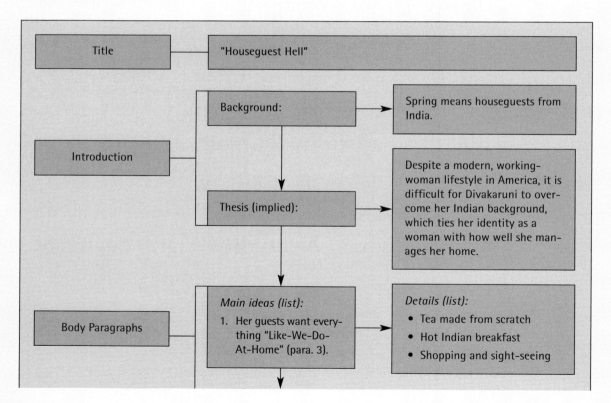

same

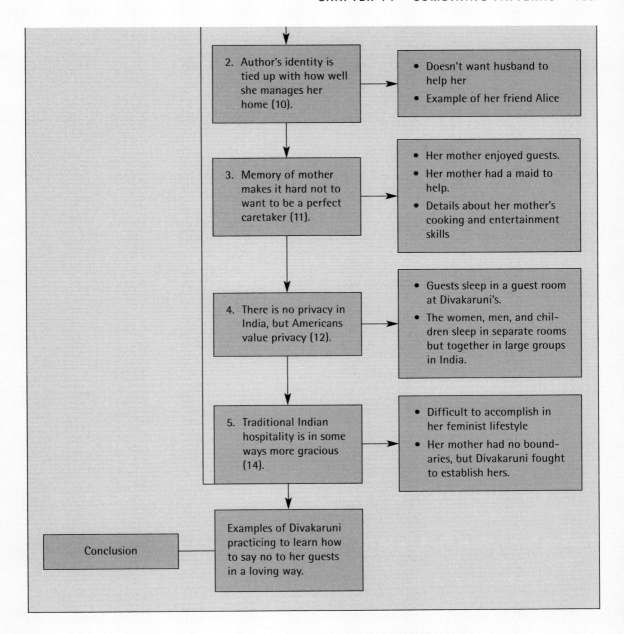

Examining the Characteristics of Essays That Combine Patterns, p. 601

1. Divakaruni uses conflict and tension to build toward a resolution by mysteriously referring to the arrival of her dreaded guests as something she cannot prevent and by describing herself as a "twenty-four-hour captive" (para. 2). Her use of dialogue, especially the disembodied questions that relatives ask repeatedly, contributes

significantly to her narrative by giving the reader some sense of the entitled attitude of her guests. For example, "Surely you've been to Saks?" (5) and "Ah, wouldn't it be nice to have a hot cup of tea" (5).

2. Divakruni's details about Indian food contribute to the larger picture of her houseguests by showing that traditional foods like tea take a long time to prepare and require a lot of clean-up, which her guests do not offer to help with. The same preparation occurs in India, but in the world where she grew up the servants did all the clean-up and prep work.

3. Divakaruni uses first-person point of view. The questions to the reader contribute to this approach by revealing the author's emotional reaction to being a host, for example, "Guess who's spitting mad by the time she gets into bed . . .?" (7).

4. The author uses comparison and contrast techniques most importantly to analyze her situation as compared to her mother's (11). She also uses comparison and contrast when discussing her friend Surekha (2) and Alice, her "senior executive" friend (10).

5. Answers may vary.

Building Your Word Power, p. 601

1. "Maximum Maintenance" means that the author's guests require a lot of personal attention, entertainment, and caretaking because they do not offer to help out with chores or cooking or anything else.

2. The connotation of "Like-We-Do-at-Home" is that the guests expect Divakaruni to entertain them in the style they are accustomed to in India, where a guest is considered "God come to visit" (para. 14). In India, however, many women do not work outside the home, and in upper caste families the servants help with cooking, cleaning, and so on.

Building Your Critical Thinking Skills: Identifying Assumptions, p. 602

1. Based on details in the essay, presumably Divakaruni assumes that her audience does not know a great deal about India. She explains, for example, that "rice and lentil mix for idlis has to be soaked overnight" (4). She also seems to assume that the reader can understand and appreciate the dilemmas she faces as a feminist American working woman with a very traditional heritage.

2. The author assumes that her houseguests will not help themselves if she does not wait on them and that they expect to be treated exactly as they are in India. When they say, for example, "Ah, wouldn't it be nice to have a hot cup of tea," she gets up to make it (5).

Jeffrey Rosen, "Naked Terror," p. 604

Jeffrey Rosen teaches law, is a radio commentator, is the legal affairs editor at *The New Republic,* and has written articles about law for the *New York Times,* the *Atlantic Monthly,* and the *New Yorker.* He argues that irrational demands for airport security have led to an invasion of privacy in the post-9/11 era. He contends that fear creates a vicious cycle in which citizens demand solutions to problems that cannot readily be fixed. Instead, people are given solutions that only "appear" to solve the problem and in fact can serve as an invasion of privacy. Students could usefully discuss how media images post-9/11 frightened them and how they now feel about solutions to the threat of terror.

Understanding the Reading, p. 606

1. Rosen regards the public response to the threat of future terrorist attacks as irrational because it is emotional, leading people to "miscalculate" the probability of threat (para. 4).

2. The difference between the Naked Machine and the Blob Machine is that one shows the outline of the naked body and the other distorts and disguises it (3). According to the author, some people prefer the Naked Machine because they have "abandoned all hope of privacy," or they "have nothing to hide," or they are more concerned about "*feeling* safe than being safe" (3).

3. According to Rosen, the two "institution[s] of democracy" that affect Americans' psychological vulnerabilities are TV and politicians (6).

4. Americans can break the cycle of exaggerated risks and the demand for poorly designed laws and technologies by finding better leaders (7).

Visualizing the Reading, p. 606

Possible answers include:

Pattern	How It Supports the Thesis.
Comparison and contrast	Compares the "Naked Machine" to the "Blob Machine" (para. 2–4). Illustrates the irrational choices that people make in response to remote threats.
Cause and effect	Watching images of 9/11 caused post-traumatic stress in viewers outside New York City (5). Supports his argument for turning off the TV.
Illustration	The World Trade Center images crowd out "less visually dramatic risks in the public mind" (4). Supports his point that people are prone to disproportionate panic instead of understanding that mundane threats like strokes are far more likely to cause harm.

Description	Used to describe the Blob and Naked Machines, providing interest and clarifying his comparison and contrast of these two devices (2–4).

Examining the Characteristics of Essays That Combine Patterns, p. 607

1. Rosen's thesis statement is: "The public responds emotionally to remote but terrifying threats, and this leads us to make choices about security that are not always rational" (para. 1). Rosen provides clear support for his thesis.

2. Answers may vary.

3. The predominant pattern of development used in the essay is cause and effect.

4. Rosen cites a study of the psychological response in New York and elsewhere after the 9/11 attacks to illustrate the impact of TV in creating "psychological vulnerabilities" (5).

Building Your Word Power, p. 607

1. The allusion to Rudolph Giuliani is a reference to the former New York mayor who encouraged the citizens of New York to overcome their fears in the wake of 9/11.

Building Your Critical Thinking Skills: Facts and Opinions, p. 607

__F__ 1. ". . . the Naked Machine bounces a low-energy X-ray beam off the human body." (para. 2)

__O__ 2. "The Naked Machine promises a high degree of security, but it demands a high sacrifice of privacy." (para. 2)

__F__ 3. ". . . 17 percent of the American population outside New York City reported symptoms of post-traumatic stress related to 9/11." (para. 5)

__O__ 4. ". . . our success in overcoming fear will depend on political leadership that challenges us to live with our uncertainties rather than catering to them." (para. 6)

Shirley Jackson, "The Lottery," p. 609

Writer Shirley Jackson is best known for this chilling short story about a New England village. In her fable, the villagers kill one person every summer because it has long been a tradition, although the origins of the tradition have been forgotten. Students may enjoy speculating about the meaning of this story, especially if it is conjoined with some discussion of group psychology, historical mass movements, and peer pressure.

Understanding the Reading, p. 616

1. The setting of this story is in a rural village square in June.

2. Old Man Warner's scoffs at the news that the north village is considering giving up the lottery, suggesting that it is a foolish decision (para. 32).

3. Tessie Hutchinson wants her married daughter and son-in-law to take part in the drawing to maximize the chance that she herself will not select the wrong slip of paper. It is an inappropriate suggestion because as a mother she should want to protect her daughter.

4. Tessie draws the paper with the black spot on it, and the vollagers stone her to death (79).

Visualizing the Reading, p. 616

Possible answers include:

Details	Importance
"They stood together, away from the pile of stones in the corner, and their jokes were quiet and they smiled rather than laughed." (para. 3)	Suggests a sense of foreboding and dread of what is to come.
"The black box grew shabbier each year; by now it was no longer completely black but splintered badly along one side . . ." (5)	Suggests that the ritual is very old.
"The people had done it so many times that they only half listened to the directions; most of them were quiet, wetting their lips, not looking around." (20)	Suggests that people are familiar with this annual ritual and, although compliant, are nervous and anxious about it.
"They do say . . . that over in the north village they're talking of giving up the lottery." (31)	Suggests that they could discontinue the ritual, that some people don't believe the lottery is necessary anymore.
"It had a black spot on it, the black spot Mr. Summers had made the night before with the heavy pencil in the coal-company office." (72)	The black spot signifies death.

Examining the Characteristics of Essays That Combine Patterns, p. 616

1. The main theme in "The Lottery" is the idea that many traditional societies require human sacrifices or scapegoats (in this case, to ensure a good harvest). This idea is supported by the way that no one protests having to stone Tessie in the

end. Another possible interpretation is that if overpopulation ever became a problem, people might have to "thin the herd" just like farmers do. This is suggested by Mr. Warner's comment that if it weren't for the lottery, they'd "all be eating stewed chickweed and acorns" (para. 32).

2. Other patterns used in the story include process analysis (how the lottery works [4–79]) and description (the "faded or stained" black box [5]).

3. Answers may vary. For example, the way that people laugh nervously indicates that they are anxious about the lottery, setting an ominous and foreboding tone.

4. The central conflict in "The Lottery" is who will pick the black-spotted slip. Jackson builds and sustains tension by drawing out the lottery process through dialogue and by the fact that although indications from the story suggest that the lottery is not a happy affair, readers do not truly know what the black dot represents until the first stone is cast at the end of the story.

5. The distinguishing qualities and characteristics of the main characters are that Mrs. Hutchinson fights the process up until her end, complaining that it isn't "fair" (45), Mr. Hutchinson is compliant and uncomplaining even in the light of the impending doom within his family, and Mr. Summers is conservative and formal and insists upon following the traditional ways.

Building Your Word Power, p. 617

1. The significance of the phrase "pack of crazy fools" as used by Old Man Warner is that the force of tradition is what is important with the lottery, and those who don't believe in the tradition are therefore foolish.

2. The connotation of this phrase in the context of the story is that the lottery is a fair system, anonymous and rule-bound, and that Mrs. Hutchinson is a poor sport since she is the only one to complain that it isn't fair.

Building Your Critical Thinking Skills: Symbolism, p. 617

1. The black box might symbolize death because it is coffin-like and black. An alternate interpretation would be that it symbolizes Pandora's Box. The color and condition of the box might be important because they show how old the tradition is.

3. The name "Mr. Summers" may suggest the summer harvest which is what the townspeople are sacrificing someone for; "Mr. Graves" suggests death; "Old Man Warner" suggests a town crier or cautioner.

4. The lottery itself may stand for or represent the desire for a social scapegoat.

Useful Lists, Boxes, and Figures